ACCESS®
BOSTON

Orientation	4
Beacon Hill	12
Government Center/Faneuil Hall	30
North End	44
Waterfront/Fort Point Channel	60
Financial District/Downtown	72
Chinatown/Theater District	96
Back Bay	108
Kenmore Square/Fenway	140
South End	154
Charles River Basin	164
Cambridge	172
Other Neighborhoods	194
Day Trips	202
History	211
Index	214

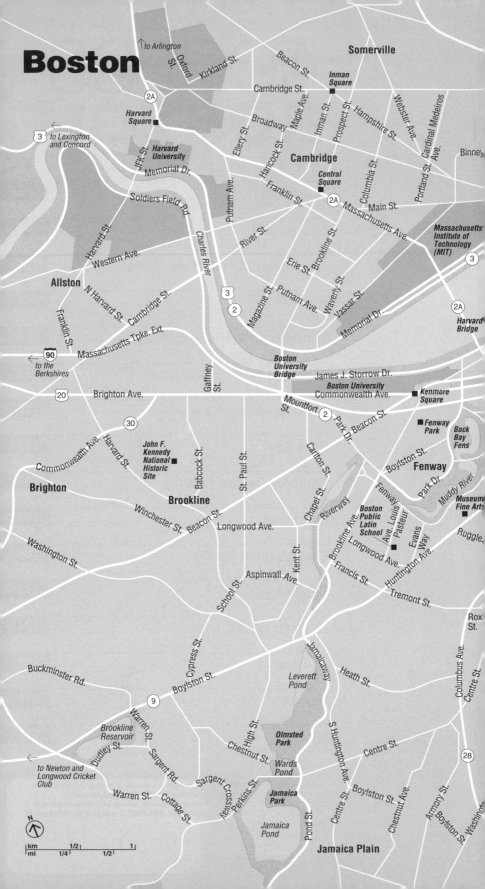

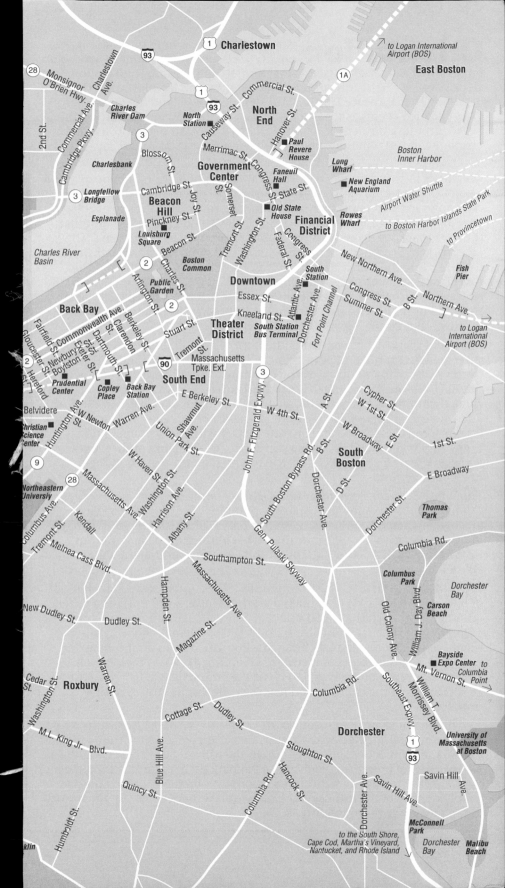

Orientation

Although Boston is only the 20th-largest city in the country, its grandeur—based on more than 350 years of history—is genuinely impressive. The **Freedom Trail** alone connects 16 historical sites from colonial and Revolutionary days, including the **Old State House**, **Paul Revere House**, and the **Old North Church**. Such events as the Boston Massacre, the Boston Tea Party, Paul Revere's midnight ride, and Samuel Adams's impassioned protests against taxation without representation have all left their mark on the city and its residents.

Despite its historic ambience, Boston's student population—about 250,000 a year flock to the city and nearby **Cambridge**—keeps the spirit young and constantly in flux. Many are tempted to stay on, and do. "It's so livable," they marvel, meaning walkable and packed with odd pleasures—not that the shortest distance between two points is ever a straight line here. The older parts of Boston, particularly **Beacon Hill** ("the Hill"), with its Brahmin residents, and the **North End**, as well as Cambridge (across the **Charles River**), were laid out helter-skelter along cow paths, Native American trails, and the ghosts of long-gone shorelines (from the very start, the city has stretched its limits with infusions of landfill). Logic is useless in assailing the maze, but getting "lost" is half the fun.

You could spend a day wandering the narrow and sometimes cobblestoned streets of Beacon Hill and never run out of charming 18th- and 19th-century town houses with interior lives you can only guess at. Furnish your own dream abode out of the grab bag of **Charles Street** antiques stores in Beacon Hill, or while away a lazy afternoon sampling the market wares in the North End—here a nibble of fresh mozzarella, there a briny olive, and virtually everywhere a cappuccino and biscotti topped with lively conversation. Eventually you'll gravitate, as the natives do, to the banks of the Charles River, where runners, walkers, bicyclists, and skaters whip by on their invigorating rounds.

Though the climate is trying at times (the seaborne weather can be quite capricious), it's certainly never boring. Summer's lush abandon cedes gradually to bracing autumns and bitter-cold Februaries, but greenery and sanity reemerge in May with the magnolias abloom along magnificent **Commonwealth Avenue** and the willows weeping around the **Public Garden** lagoon.

After a day on your feet, you'll be anxious to dive into a seafood feast (one of Boston's trademarks) or perhaps a gourmet meal. As recently as a dozen years ago, you might have had trouble coming up with more than a handful of interesting restaurants in Boston; now the problem is choosing among them—a number of talented chefs have flourished in an atmosphere of camaraderie rather than competition. Literature likewise provides rich repasts. **Harvard Square** is said to boast the largest per-capita concentration of bookstores in the country, and readings often draw crowds in the hundreds.

And finally there are the Boston sports teams: the **Celtics**, the **Bruins**, and the ever-maddening **Red Sox**. As frustrated as they may get with the players, **Red Sox** fans are inevitably caught up in the romance of tiny **Fenway Park**, a classic dating from the golden age of ballpark design. But this should come as no surprise to anyone who knows a born-and-bred Bostonian. They are a people who savor the intimacy, the authenticity, and, above all, the history of their lovely city—and rightly so.

How To Read This Guide

ACCESS® BOSTON is arranged by neighborhood so you can see at a glance where you are and what is around you. The numbers next to the entries in the following chapters correspond to the numbers on the maps. The type is color-coded according to the kind of place described:

Restaurants/Clubs: Red   **Hotels:** Blue

Shops/ ⊤ **Outdoors:** Green   **Sights/Culture:** Black

♿ **Wheelchair accessible**

Wheelchair Accessibility

An establishment (except a restaurant) is considered wheelchair accessible when a person in a wheelchair can easily enter a building (i.e., no steps, a ramp, a wide-enough door) without assistance. Restaurants are deemed wheelchair accessible *only* if the above applies *and* if the rest rooms are on the same floor as the dining area and accommodate a wheelchair.

Rating the Restaurants and Hotels

The restaurant ratings take into account the quality, service, atmosphere, and uniqueness of the restaurant. An expensive restaurant doesn't necessarily ensure an enjoyable evening; however, a small, relatively unknown spot could have good food, professional service, and a lovely atmosphere. Therefore, on a purely subjective basis, stars are used to judge the overall dining value (see the star ratings at right). Keep in mind that chefs and owners often change, which sometimes drastically affects the quality of a restaurant. The ratings in this guidebook are based on information available at press time.

The price ratings, as categorized at right, apply to restaurants and hotels. These figures describe general price-range relationships among other restaurants and hotels in the area. The restaurant price ratings are based on the average cost of an entrée for one person, excluding tax and tip. Hotel price ratings reflect the base price of a standard room for two people for one night during the peak season.

Restaurants

★	Good
★★	Very Good
★★★	Excellent
★★★★	An Extraordinary Experience
$	The Price Is Right (less than $10)
$$	Reasonable ($10-$15)
$$$	Expensive ($15-$20)
$$$$	Big Bucks ($20 and up)

Hotels

$	The Price Is Right (less than $100)
$$	Reasonable ($100-$1750)
$$$	Expensive ($175-$250)
$$$$	Big Bucks ($250 and up)

Map Key

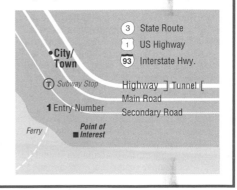

Area code 617 unless otherwise noted.

Getting to Boston

Airport

Located two miles east of downtown Boston on a peninsula across the harbor from the city, **Logan International Airport (BOS)** services more than 50 domestic and international airlines in its five terminals. The airport is fully accessible to people with disabilities.

The **Logan Airport Hilton and Towers,** a new, 600-room property located right at the center of the airport, was slated to open as this book went to press. The 10-story hotel will offer views of the Boston skyline, a health club with an indoor pool, a business center, and shops and restaurants. For information call 800/HILTONS.

Airport Services

Airport Emergencies	567.2233
Currency Exchange	567.2313

Customs and Immigration	561.5745
Ground Transportation Hotline	800/235.6426
Information	561.1800
Lost and Found	561.1714
Medical Clinic	569.8652
Paging	
Terminal A:	561.1940
Terminal C:	561.1806
Terminal E:	561.1804
Parking	561.1670
Police	561.1700
Traveler's Aid	542.7286

Airlines

Air Canada	800/776.3000
Alitalia	267.4600, 800/223.5730
America West	800/235.9292
American/American Eagle	800/433.7300

British Airways 800/247.9297

Cape Air...800/352.0714

Colgan Air...800/272.5488

Continental 569.8400, 800/525.0280

Delta 567.4100, 800/221.1212

Delta Connection/Business Express....800/345.3400

Lufthansa 800/645.3880

Midway..800/446.4392

Midwest Express 800/452.2022

Nations Air..770/984.9440

Northwest...800/225.2525

Spirit 800/772.7117

Swissair...800/221.4750

TWA 800/221.2000

United..800/241.6522

US Airways 800/428.4322

Virgin Atlantic 800/862.8621

Getting to and from
Logan International Airport

By Boat The **Airport Water Shuttle** (330.8680, 800/23.LOGAN) travels across **Boston Harbor** between the **Logan Boat Dock** and **Rowes Wharf** at **Atlantic Avenue** on the edge of downtown Boston. A free shuttle bus runs between the airline terminals. The water shuttle is a favorite way to and from the airport for several good reasons: It's fast (a seven-minute trip, including the bus); the one-way fare is only $10 for adults; it's scenic; and it avoids traffic entirely.

By Car It's best to plan not to arrive at or leave from Boston's busy air terminal between 4PM and 6PM on a weekday—especially a Friday. Legendary traffic snarls can make the trip via the **Callahan Tunnel** (to **Logan**) or the **Sumner Tunnel** (out of the airport) as long as 30 minutes, sometimes even more. The **Ted Williams Tunnel,** which has connected South Boston to East Boston and the airport since late 1995, is reserved for commercial traffic most of the time. It's open to passenger cars weekends, overnight during the week, and occasionally at other times to relieve severe traffic congestion.

To get to Boston from Logan, bear left on the first ramp coming out of the airport, and follow the signs to Sumner Tunnel (there's a toll). At the end of the

tunnel is the North End. Look for signs for the Central Artery. Take the Central Artery North exit for Back Bay and points west; for downtown, head in the direction of Central Artery South.

To get to the airport from downtown, follow the Central Artery ramp signposted "Airport" to the Callahan Tunnel (there's no toll in this direction). A large horseshoe-shaped road takes you past all five terminals. There is long-term parking in the middle of the horseshoe and short-term parking at each terminal.

Rental Cars Free shuttle buses will transport you from outside the terminals' baggage-claim areas to car-rental counters (they are all open 24 hours).

Avis 800/331.1212

Budget..800/858.5377

Hertz..800/654.3131

National 800/227.7368

Thrifty..800/367.2277

By Limousine A luxurious transportation alternative, limousine service between **Logan International Airport** and downtown Boston can cost between $40 and $60 (including tip and toll). Contact one of the following companies for further information:

A&A Limousine/Carey of Boston...............623.8700

Boston Coach 387.7676

Custom Transportation 848.6803

By Subway The **Massachusetts Bay Transportation Authority** (**MBTA;** 722.3200, 800/392.6100) is the least expensive way to travel to and from the airport, and one of the quickest. Take the *Blue Line* to the **Airport** station (a 10-minute ride from the **Aquarium** or **Government Center** stops in downtown) and connect with free **Massport** shuttle buses that make stops throughout the airport (look for a sign on each bus indicating which terminal). Travel time to the airport from the **MBTA** station is about 10 minutes.

By Taxi Cab stands are located at all airport terminals; the common practice is to share a ride with others headed your way, as traffic congestion can easily run up the cost of the trip. Fares can skyrocket during peak travel times and can be almost as high as the cost of a limousine.

Getting Around Boston

A crucial element of your stay is mastering Boston's transportation services and routes. The major ways of getting around are bus, foot, subway (the **T**), and taxi. Of these, walking is highly recommended, because of Boston's compact size. The **T** works well if the stations are convenient to your destination.

Bicycles Bikers have several scenic options in Boston. Two particularly appealing paths are the **Greenbelt Bikeway** and the **Dr. Paul Dudley White**

Bikeway. The Greenbelt outlines the entire perimeter of Boston's famous **Emerald Necklace,** an eight-mile chain of parkland extending from **Boston Common** to **Franklin Park.** The Dudley starts along the Charles River, then traverses several sections of town. You can rent mountain bikes and "hybrids" (a cross between a touring and a mountain bike) at **Community Bike Shop** (496 Tremont St, at E Berkeley St, 542.8623) or **Back Bay Bicycles & Boards** (333 Newbury St, between Hereford St and

Massachusetts Ave, 247.2336). Maps of local trails are available at the bike shops or from **Hosteling International** (12 Hemenway St, between Haviland and Boylston Sts, 536.9455). Also see "Boston By Bike: Plum Paths for Pedal Pushers" on page 94.

Buses The **MBTA** (722.3200, 800/392.6100) operates the city's buses, subways, streetcar lines, commuter trains and boats, and vans for riders with special needs. Crosstown and local buses travel throughout greater Boston and Cambridge. Tokens (which are available at any subway station), exact fare, or **MBTA** passes (see "Subways" below) are required.

The **South Station Bus Terminal** (700 Atlantic Ave, between Kneeland and Summer Sts) is part of the **South Station Transportation Center.** Bus lines that service Boston include:

Bonanza......................800/556.3815 (northeast US)

Concord Trailways............................800/636.3317
....(New Hampshire)

Greyhound....................800/231.2222 (nationwide)

Peter Pan Bus Lines...........................800/237.8747
..............(central Massachusetts, New York City)

Plymouth and Brockton....508/746.0378 (Cape Cod)

Driving If you have a choice, don't drive. Boston is a pedestrian city, with confusing street patterns in many neighborhoods. Even if you have the derring-do to "compete" with Boston's notoriously brazen drivers, be forewarned that the signage here is generally poor and that there are lots of one-way streets.

On highways, the speed limit is 55 miles per hour. Right turns on a red light are permitted in Massachusetts except where prohibited by posted signs. Tolls are charged for the **Massachusetts Turnpike (Interstate 90),** various bridges, and tunnels to/from **Logan International Airport.**

For information on weather and traffic conditions on the Massachusetts Turnpike, call 508/248.4581; for information on traffic conditions in greater Boston, call 617/374.1234.

Parking Street parking is limited and highly regulated, so read signs carefully. Many neighborhoods, particularly Beacon Hill, have almost no parking for nonresidents. It's very common to be ticketed and/or towed away to Boston's hinterlands. If your car is towed, retrieving it will be costly and time-consuming.

There are numerous parking garages in town, and various open lots, some of which are listed below. Prices vary widely for hourly and day rates, with the most expensive in the **Financial District/Downtown** and Back Bay areas.

In Boston

Auditorium Garage 50 Dalton St (at Scotia St). 247.8006

Back Bay Garage Clarendon St (between St. James Ave and Boylston St) and St. James Ave (between Berkeley and Clarendon Sts). 266.7006

Boston Common Garage Charles St (between Boylston and Beacon Sts). 954.2096

Boston Harbor Garage 70 East India Row (at Milk St). 723.1731

Copley Place Parking 100 Huntington Ave (between Garrison and Stuart Sts). 375.4488

Government Center Garage 50 Sudbury St (between Congress and Cambridge Sts). 227.0385

Post Office Square Parking Garage Post Office Sq (entrances on Pearl and Congress Sts). 423.1430

Prudential Center Garage 800 Boylston St (between Exeter and Dalton Sts). 267.2965

In Cambridge

Charles Square Garage 5 Bennett St (between Eliot St and University Rd). 491.0298

Harvard Square Parking Garage Eliot St (between John F. Kennedy and Winthrop Sts). 354.4168

Subways Run by the **MBTA,** Boston's subway system—known locally as the "T"—is the nation's oldest. Four lines—*Red, Blue, Orange,* and *Green*—radiate from downtown. The symbol **T** outside the entrance indicates stops. Inbound trains go to central downtown stations: **Park Street, Downtown Crossing, State,** and **Government Center;** outbound trains head away from these stops. Tokens (available for purchase at stations), exact fare, or passes (see below) must be used.

The **T** has minor eccentricities, best learned from experience. For example, on the *Green Line,* many of the street-level stations do not have ticket booths, so you must have exact change ready (tokens are also accepted, supplemented by change). Drivers do not make change, although helpful passengers often will. Note: Certain inbound lines charge higher fares from outlying stations; always ask. And going outbound on the *Green Line,* no fare is charged if you board at an aboveground station. Smoking is not allowed in stations or on trains.

MBTA subway trains operate Monday through Saturday from 5AM to 12:45AM, and Sunday and holidays from 6AM to 12:45AM. Discount passes for senior citizens are available at the **Downtown Crossing Concourse;** student passes are sold at schools (children 5 to 11 pay half fare, children under 5 ride free). The Boston Passport, a visitor pass good for one, three, or seven days is sold at the **Boston Common Visitor Information Center** (open daily from 9AM to 5PM), or at the **Airport** station (open daily between 9AM and 4:30PM). At press time they cost $5, $9, and $18.

For daily recorded service conditions, call 722.5050. (A **Telecommunications Device for the Deaf** can be reached at 722.5146.) Those with special traveling needs should call 722.5123, 800/533.6282, or TDD 722.5415. Monthly passes (722.5219) are available at various rates and give passengers the option of combining subway and bus travel.

Taxis There are usually plenty around town, except between 3 and 7PM (especially on Friday) and in the worst weather. They're easiest to find near major hotels, on **Newbury Street**, and at **Downtown Crossing** and **Faneuil Hall Marketplace.** Available cruising taxis have a lighted sign on the roof. Some local companies are:

In Boston

Boston Cab	262.2227
Checker Taxi	536.7000
Red and White Cab	242.8000
Red Cab	734.5000
Town Taxi	536.5000

In Cambridge

Ambassador Brattle	492.1100
Cambridge Yellow Cab	625.5000
Checker Cab of Cambridge	497.9000

Tours Tours in Boston focus on the city's charm and rich historic legacy. There are, naturally, walking tours, as well as harbor and Charles River excursions. Trolley tours make a circuit past some of the city's—and the country's—most historic landmarks, and have reboarding stops convenient to most **Freedom Trail** sites and in Back Bay. Here's a sampling of some leading tours:

The **Freedom Trail** is Boston's most famous and popular walking tour. Although it is designed as a self-guided tour (pick up a map and brochure at the **Boston Common Visitor Information Center**), several guided walks are also available. **Boston's Beginning: A Freedom Trail Starter** (635.7412) is conducted by the Boston Park Rangers and covers the beginning sites of the **Freedom Trail,** from pleasure grounds **(The Common)** to burial grounds **(Granary** and **King's Chapel). Boston By Little Feet** (367.3766) offers a child's-eye view of the **Freedom Trail,** including an introduction to architecture and history. The **Freedom Trail Tour** (242.5642) touches on such sites as **Old South Meeting House, Old State House, Faneuil Hall, Paul Revere House,** and **Old North Church.**

Other walking tours cover specific neighborhoods. The **Beacon Hill Stroll** (426.1885) guides visitors past the buildings of the north and south slopes, the flats, and **Louisburg Square,** highlighting architecture and past and present residents. **North End Tours** (367.3766) explores Boston's oldest neighborhood, its narrow streets, and Old World markets and exposes visitors to the sights and sounds of this predominately Italian community.

Since the 17th century, the Boston Harbor islands have served as sites for public facilities (quarantine hospitals, pauper colonies, immigration stations, almshouses, reform schools, and prisons)—and, occasionally, for illegal businesses. In the 19th century one island was the site of a factory where local girls produced cigars that Bostonians were led to believe were made in Spain and for which they were charged premium prices.

Bus and trolley tours are another popular way of seeing the city. **Old Town Trolley** (269.7010) offers many tours through the Boston area; its **Cambridge** tour covers Harvard Square, **MIT, Tory Row,** and **Longfellow House.** The **Brew Pub City Trolley Tour** (269.7150) offers an introduction to Boston's brewing history and includes visits to three pubs, each serving food. **JFK's Boston** (482.3275) trolley tours stop at places the nation's 35th president spent his formative years, including his **Brookline** birthplace and **Harvard University;** the tour also includes a visit to the **John F. Kennedy Library and Museum.**

You can enjoy the Boston skyline from the deck of one of the city's many harbor cruises. **Bay State Cruises** (723.7800) specializes in great views and fascinating history; excursions include a stop at **Georges Island,** site of a restored Civil War–era fort. Free water taxis that make a circuit to several other harbor islands leave from Georges Island. The **New England Aquarium** (973.5281) offers thrilling whale-watching adventures narrated by naturalists aboard private charters complete with full galley (April through November). For an amusing excursion encompassing both land and sea, take a **Duck Tour** (723.3825), a one-hour trip that includes a drive around the city—and into **Boston Harbor**—in a quacking amphibious vehicle.

One of the largest sight-seeing operators that cover areas beyond the city limits is offered by **Gray Line** (236.2148), with motorcoach excursions to **Cape Cod, Concord, Gloucester, Lexington, Plymouth,** and **Salem.**

Trains MBTA (722.3200, 800/392.6100) commuter trains leave from **North Station** (Causeway St, between Beverly St and Lomasney Way) for destinations north and west of the city. This is where droves of Bostonians catch the *Rockport Line* to the **North Shore** and its beaches. Nicknamed "the beach train," it fills up fast on hot summer days. The **MBTA** *Green* and *Orange Lines* also stop here.

Amtrak (800/872.7245) trains depart from **South Station** (Atlantic Ave and Summer St) and stop at **Back Bay Station** (145 Dartmouth St, between Columbus Ave and Stuart St), and at **Route 128 Station** in **Westwood,** 15 minutes west of Boston.

Commuter trains also leave from **South Station** for points south of the city. The *Red Line* stops at **South Station** and the *Orange Line* stops at **Back Bay/South End Station** (which also serves as **Amtrak**'s **Back Bay Station**).

Walking The entire city could be walked briskly in a day, so a lot of your sight-seeing is best done on foot. Half the fun is wandering along the twisting, nonsensical streets. If you would prefer a more premeditated route, you can always follow the **Freedom Trail** (see "Tours" above). In Boston, you are never much more than a few blocks from parkland, thanks to Frederick Law Olmsted's **Emerald Necklace,** or water, thanks to Boston's harborfront and the **Charles River Esplanade.**

FYI

Accommodations In addition to the hotels listed in each chapter, there are a variety of guest houses and bed-and-breakfasts in Boston and Cambridge. **Beacon Guest Houses** (248 Newbury St, between Fairfield and Gloucester Sts, M-F, 262.1771; evenings, weekends, holidays 266.7142) attracts many tourists and foreign visitors to their inexpensive pension-style accommodations. The office screens guests and provides single and double efficiencies (twin beds only) for brief or long-term stays in converted town houses. The rooms have no telephone, TV, or maid or room service, but each has a private bath and kitchenette with some utensils, linens, and towels.

There are also many bed-and breakfast referral organizations serving a number of neighborhoods and towns. Some of these include:

A Cambridge House Bed-and-Breakfast Inn
.....................................491.6300, 800/232.9989

Bed & Breakfast Agency of Boston
.....................................720.3450, 800/248.9262

Bed & Breakfast Associates
.....................................720.0522, 800/347.5088

Bed and Breakfast Cambridge and Greater Boston
....720.1492

New England Bed & Breakfast Inc. 244.2112

Climate Boston's weather can be capricious: Summer can be very hot and humid, although sea breezes provide some relief; winter is usually cold and either damp with snow and ice or brisk and sunny. The most comfortable times are spring and fall, but each season has its charms.

Months	Average Temperature (°F)
December-February	30
March-May	46
June-August	71
September-November	53

Drinking You must be 21 years old to purchase liquor. Laws vary in Cambridge and Boston, and also depending on the establishment's license, but in general, no liquor is sold in bars after 2AM or before noon on Sunday. In stores, no liquor is sold after 11PM Monday through Saturday, and none is sold on Sunday except near the New Hampshire border.

Hours Opening and closing times for shops, attractions, coffeehouses, etc. are listed by day(s) only if normal hours apply (opening between 8 and 11AM and closing between 4 and 7PM). In unusual cases, specific hours are given.

Money Boston banks do not commonly exchange foreign currency, so be sure to handle any such transactions at **Bay Bank Foreign Money Exchange** at **Logan International Airport (Terminal E,** 567.2313). You can buy foreign currency at **Thomas Cook Foreign Exchange** (160 Franklin St, at Congress St, 426.0016), and **Bank of Boston** (100

Federal St, between Matthews and Franklin Sts, 434.2200). Banks, many stores, and restaurants accept traveler's checks, generally requiring a photo ID. You can purchase them at **American Express** (1 Court St, at State St, 723.8400), **Thomas Cook** (160 Franklin St, at Congress St, 426.0016), and at most major banks. Banks are generally open Monday through Friday from 9AM to 4PM.

Personal Safety Always keep an eye on the traffic, as Boston drivers—and cyclists—are aggressive and often run red lights. Use common sense; be careful if you venture off well-worn paths in the city.

The subways are safe within Boston, Cambridge, and Brookline, but keep your wits about you. After dark, avoid the parks, the **Combat Zone** (the red-light district along Washington Street near **Chinatown**), alleys, and dimly lit side streets.

Publications Local newspapers and periodicals include: the *Boston Globe* (daily), *Boston Herald* (daily), *Christian Science Monitor* (Monday through Friday), *Boston Phoenix* (weekly, published on Friday), *Boston Magazine* (monthly), and the *Tab* (weekly, with different editions for specific neighborhoods). Especially helpful for events information are the *Phoenix*, the *Herald*'s Friday "Scene" section, and the *Globe*'s Thursday "Calendar" section.

Radio Stations

AM:		
680	WRKO	Talk Radio
850	WEEI	Sports
1300	WBZ	News
FM:		
89.3	WTBU	Pop/Rock
92.5	WXRV	Easy Listening
93.7	WEGQ	Pop
94.5	WJMN	Rap/Hip Hop
98.5	WBMX	Pop
100.7	WZLX	Classic Rock
101.7	WFNX	Rock
102.5	WCRB	Classical
104.1	WBCN	Rock/Alternative
107.9	WXKS	Rock/PopChart

Restaurants Reservations are essential at most trendy or expensive restaurants, and it's best to book far in advance at such dining spots as **Biba, L'Espalier,** and the **Rialto.** If you want to avoid crowds, ask about late seatings. In general, jackets and ties are not required except at posh places, and most establishments accept credit cards.

Shopping Boutiques and galleries bedeck Back Bay's upscale **Newbury Street.** A longer—and not quite so elite—shopping thoroughfare is lower **Boylston Street,** also in Back Bay. For the latest in clothing fashions catering to college students, you can't beat

Cambridge, which is also the place to track down hard-to-find books. Nirvana for bargain hunters is the original **Filene's Basement** (426 Washington St, at Summer St, 542.2011) in the Financial District. There are also numerous shopping complexes throughout Boston, including **Faneuil Hall Marketplace** (bounded by Commercial St and Faneuil Hall Sq, and Chatham and Clinton Sts), **Copley Place** (100 Huntington Ave, between Garrison and Dartmouth Sts), and the **Prudential Center** (800 Boylston St, between Exeter and Dalton Sts); in Cambridge visit **The Shops at Charles Square** (Bennett St, between Eliot St and University Rd) and the **Cambridgeside Galleria** (First St and Cambridgeside Pl).

Smoking There's a strong antismoking sentiment in Boston and Cambridge, with some restaurants banning it entirely and most offering nonsmoking sections. Many public places forbid smoking.

Street Plan Logic won't help you figure out the maze of Boston's thoroughfares. It's best to get a good detailed map of the city; even longtime residents have to haul one out when planning to stray from familiar paths.

Taxes In Massachusetts, a five-percent sales tax is charged on all purchases except services, food bought in stores (not restaurants), and clothing under $175. A five-percent meal tax is added to all restaurant bills. There's a 12-percent hotel tax.

Telephone The area code for Boston, Cambridge, Brookline, and other Greater Boston communities is 617. Massachusetts has four other area codes. They are 508 (for Cape Cod and other parts of eastern Massachusetts), 781 (for some North Shore and South Shore suburbs that previously had the 617 area code), 978 (for some northeastern and central Massachusetts communities that previously had the 508 area code), and 413 (for the western part of the

state). At press time, additional area codes were scheduled to be introduced; recorded messages will inform callers of the new codes when they go into effect.

Tickets **Ticketmaster** (931.2000) is a computerized ticket service for Boston-area sports, theater, concerts, and other events. The **Hub Ticket Agency** (240 Tremont St, at Stuart St, 426.8340) also handles sports and theater happenings. **Concertix** (876.7777) sells tickets for the **Regattabar** jazz performances. If you prefer paper to plastic, ask for cash-only outlet locations or stop at one of three **BosTix** outlets (482.BTIX)—for half-price tickets—at **Faneuil Hall, Copley Square** (Dartmouth and Boylston Sts), and **Holyoke Center** in Harvard Square.

Time Zone Boston is located in the eastern time zone, the same as New York. Daylight saving time is observed from the first Sunday in April to the last Saturday in October.

Tipping Leave a 15- to 20-percent gratuity in restaurants and for personal services. Taxi drivers expect a 15-percent tip.

Visitors' Information Offices The main visitors' information center is the **Greater Boston Convention and Visitors Bureau** at **Prudential Center** (800 Boylston St, between Exeter and Dalton Sts, 536.4100, 888/SEE.BOSTON). It is open Monday through Friday from 9AM to 5PM. There is also a branch on **Boston Common** (Tremont St, no phone), which is open every day except Christmas. Other sources of local information include the **Cambridge Visitor Information Booth** (Harvard Sq, Cambridge, 497.1630), the **Charlestown Navy Yard Visitor's Center** (Charlestown Navy Yard, Bldg 5, Charlestown, 242.5601), and the **National Park Service Visitor Center** (15 State St, at Devonshire St, 242.5642). All are open daily from 9AM to 5PM.

Phone Book

Emergencies

Ambulance/Fire/Police 911
AAA Emergency Service 800/222.4357
Dental 636.6828
Hospitals
    Beth Israel/Deaconess Medical Center
    ....632.7000
    Brigham and Women's Hospital...........732.5500
    Massachusetts General Hospital 726.2000
Pharmacies
    CVS (Beacon Hill) 523.1028
    ....(daily until midnight)
    CVS (Cambridge).......876.4032 (open 24 hours)
    Walgreen's (Back Bay).......................236.1692
    Walgreen's (Dorchester)....................282.5246
    ....(open 24 hours)
Poison Control...232.2120
Rape Crisis Hotline 492.7273

Visitors' Information

American Youth Hostels (AYH) 731.5430
Amtrak..800/872.7245
Bay State Cruise Company (ferry service). ...723.7800
Better Business Bureau.............................426.9000
Disabled Visitors' Information 800/462.5015
Greyhound Bus..526.1810
Mass Bay Lines (ferry service) 542.8000
Massachusetts Bay Transportation
    Authority (MBTA) 722.3200,
    daily conditions 222.5050; 800/392.6100
National Park Service................................242.5642
Road Conditions 374.1234
State Forests and Parks 727.3180
Time 637.1111
US Customs 565.6133
US Postal Service 451.9922
Weather...936.1111

Main Events

January

Ice-skating at the Frog
Pond on Boston Common
and at the Public Garden Lagoon;
Chinese New Year (which is sometimes celebrated
in February), Chinatown; **Old Sturbridge Village
Yankee Winter Weekends**, Sturbridge. January also
kicks off a three-month series of food and wine
festivals called **Boston Overnight**.

February

Harvard's Hasty Pudding Club Awards, Cambridge;
Inventor's Weekend, Museum of Science; **Kid's
Computer Fair**, The Computer Museum; **New
England Boat Show**, Bayside Expo Center;
Valentine's Festival, various hotels.

March

Evacuation Day (17 March), commemorating the
British army's retreat from Boston in 1776; **St.
Patrick's Day Parade** (17 March), South Boston;
New England Spring Flower Show, Bayside Expo
Center.

April

Annual Lantern Hanging (17 April), Old North
Church; **Boston Marathon** (third Monday in April);
Patriot's Day (third Monday in April), commemor-
ating battles of the American Revolution with
Reenactment of the Battle of Lexington, Paul
Revere's/William Dawes's rides, parade, and other
events; **Swan Boats** return to the Public Garden
Lagoon (mid-April, **Patriot's Day** weekend); **Earth
Day**, Charles River Esplanade; **baseball
season** begins, Fenway Park; **whale-watching**
cruises begin; **Arts Festival**, Harvard University,
Cambridge; **American Indian Day**, The Children's
Museum; **Artists' Ball**, the Cyclorama in the South
End; **The Big Apple Circus**, Fan Pier.

May

All Walks of Life (AIDS walk); **Art Newbury Street**
(open galleries); **Beacon Hill Hidden Garden Tour;
tulips bloom** in the Public Garden; **Boston Pops**
season begins, Symphony Hall (through June);
Brimfield Outdoor Antiques Show, Hamilton; **Lilac
Sunday**, Arnold Arboretum; **Boston Kite Festival**,
Franklin Park; **Polo Matches** at Myopia Hunt Club,
Hamilton (on Sunday through October); **Walk for
Hunger**.

June

Blessing of the Fleet, Provincetown and Gloucester;
Boston Globe Jazz Festival, Hatch Shell and other
locations; **Bunker Hill Day**, Charlestown (17 June);
Dairy Festival, Boston Common; **Gay Pride March**.

July

USS *Constitution* Turnaround (4 July); **Boston
Harborfest** (4 July weekend); **Chowderfest**, City Hall
Plaza (4 July weekend); **Boston Pops Esplanade**

Orchestra Concerts,
Charles River Esplanade
(3-5 July). **Tanglewood
Music Festival**, Boston
Symphony Orchestra in the
Berkshires (through August);
**Bastille Day, Marlborough
Street** in Back Bay (14 July);
**Brimfield Outdoor Antiques
Show**, Hamilton; **Lowell Folk
Festival**, Lowell; **North End
Italian Feste** (most weekends
through August); **US Pro Tennis
Championships** at the Longwood
Cricket Club, Brookline.

August

Salem Heritage Days, Salem.

September

**Boston Film Festival/Cambridge
River Festival**, Charles River
bank, Cambridge; **The Big "E"
Eastern States Exposition**,
Springfield; **King Richard's
Renaissance Fair**, South Carver.

October

Topsfield Fair, Topsfield;
Haunted Happenings,
Salem; **Head-of-the-
Charles Regatta** (next to
last Sunday of month);
Cranberry Festival,
Cranberry World,
South Carver.

November

Thanksgiving Day Celebration, Plymouth; **Boston
Ballet's Nutcracker**, The Wang Center; **Boston Globe
Book Festival**, Hynes Center; **Boston Ski and Travel
Show**.

December

Christmas Tree Lighting, Prudential Center;
**Boston Common Tree Lighting; Boston Tea Party
Reenactment; First Night** (31 December until
midnight).

Beacon Hill

In one of North America's most European cities, Beacon Hill is the most continental of neighborhoods. This redbrick quarter of handsome houses crowded along crazy-quilt streets is a walker's dream (and a driver's nightmare). It offers intriguing architecture, interesting historical sites, and exquisite squares in abundance as well as unusual shops and a handful of fine eateries.

A stroll across **Boston Common**, an enormous grassy blanket that Bostonians have used since the city's birth, is the perfect prelude to a morning or afternoon spent poking about the nooks and crannies of historic Beacon Hill. The neighborhood's slopes are easiest to navigate in good weather, but it's well worth a bit of slipping and sliding to enjoy serene winter stillness here. (Along **Mount Vernon Street**, iron handrails fastened to buildings assist those making the steep climb.)

In colonial times, what is now a fashionable enclave was infant Boston's undesirable outskirts—crisscrossed with cow paths and covered with brambles, berries, and scrub. The Puritans called it "Trimountain" because of its three-peaked silhouette. But the land was whittled away by early developers to create new lots and landfill, and only one hill remains today. The completion in 1798 of the majestic **State House**, designed by **Charles Bulfinch**, drew attention to the area's potential. Affluent Brahmins and a number of cultural

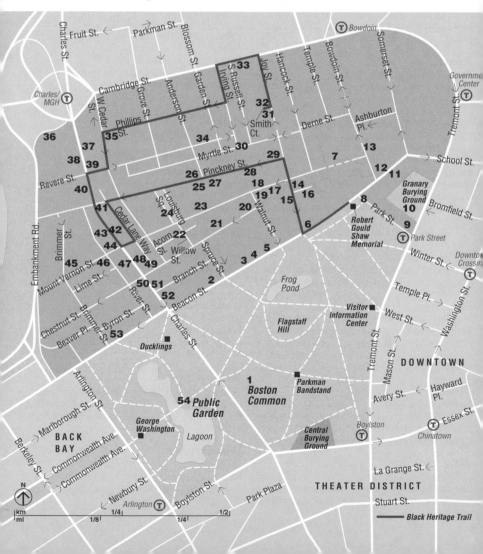

luminaries were drawn here as Beacon Hill blossomed in the first half of the 19th century and the city's intellectual and artistic renaissance unfolded. Beacon Hill is composed of approximately three districts. The flats, the newer, more orderly section, runs down to the **Charles River** from **Charles Street**. Up from Charles Street is the sunny south slope, extending from **Beacon Street** to **Pinckney Street**, and the shady north slope, descending from Pinckney to **Cambridge Street**. While the south slope's mansions and row houses exude Brahmin privilege, the north slope's smaller houses and former tenement walk-ups reflect a history of ethnic diversity and the struggle of many groups—especially African-Americans—to make their way here. Coursing through Beacon Hill, infusing it with vitality, is Charles Street, an eclectic, surprisingly friendly thoroughfare where most of the area's shops, services, and businesses are located.

In older cities, the chicken-or-the-egg question is: Which came first, the streets or the dwellings? It's clear that the houses came first on the hodgepodge "Hill," and that the streets have simply made do. As you wend your way over bumpy brick sidewalks, you'll probably agree that Beacon Hill wouldn't be so appealing without the jigs and jogs of the streets, the surprise of **Louisburg Square**, and the glistening river glimpsed below. In this intimate, people-scaled place, small details reveal the layers of lives that have enriched this large heap of brick and granite. Gardens enliven the rooflines; ornate door knockers, boot scrapers, and wrought-iron embellishments dress up some of the most modest facades; and tunnels lead to concealed courtyards and hidden houses.

Most of the homes are Greek Revival or Federal in style, but refreshing upstarts have sneaked in here and there. Master carpenters, called "housewrights," built most of the structures when the trained American architect was a brand-new breed. Notice the many graceful bowfronts—a local innovation.

Officially declared a historic district in 1955, today the neighborhood and its precious repository of buildings is zealously watched over by the Beacon Hill Civic Association, which even dictates exterior color choices. Come back in 30 years, and the structures will look the same. But, as buildings change hands there's less single ownership, and more condos and luxury apartments belong to young professionals instead of "Proper Bostonians." Today this area is home to Jewish and Italian immigrants and their descendants, bohemian artists, and college students as well as Boston's famous "First Families"—the Cabots, Lodges, Codmans, and Lowells, to name a few—who have held sway over Beacon Hill for generations.

After thoroughly immersing yourself in Beacon Hill's tranquil charm, watch the world go by over an espresso at **Caffè Bella Vita**, find that slip of a street called **Acorn**, then come down from the heights and take an afternoon promenade in the **Public Garden**.

---

1 Boston Common The oldest public park in the country extends 50 sprawling acres. Now the city's heart, it was once Boston's hinterland. In the early 1600s the grounds were part of the farm belonging to Reverend William Blaxton, the first English squatter on the Shawmut Peninsula. A reclusive bachelor in the style of Thoreau, Blaxton shattered his own blissful solitude by generously inviting the city's Puritan founders to settle on his peninsula and share its fresh water. Then, finding his neighbors too close for comfort, Blaxton sold them the land in 1634 and retreated to Beacon Hill. There the city's first—but not last—eccentric tended to his beloved orchard, reputedly riding about on his Brahma bull for recreation. But when the busybody Puritans tried to convince Blaxton to join their church, he fled south to Rhode Island.

The park has belonged to Bostonians ever since. Cattle grazed its grass until the practice was outlawed in 1830. Justice—of a sort—was meted out here with whipping posts, stocks, and pillories. Indians, pirates, and persecuted

Quakers were hanged here, as was Rachell Whall in the late 1700s, for the crime of highway robbery (she stole a 75¢ bonnet). This is where Redcoats camped during the Revolution and Civil War troops once mustered. Until 6 July 1836, African-Americans couldn't pass freely through the land. General Lafayette returned to the US in 1824 and shot off a ceremonial cannon here, and the Prince of Wales, future King Edward VII, reviewed the troops on these very same grassy lawns in 1860.

Long the site of great public outdoor theater—sermons, duels, puppet shows, balloon ascensions, hopscotch championships, fire-engine and flying-machine demonstrations, horse races, antislavery meetings, fireworks, hoop rolling, and ox roasting—the **Common** still offers some of Boston's best people-watching. Arrive before nine on a sunny morning, and relish your leisure while working folk push on to their jobs, leaving you to saunter among the magicians, musicians, mounted police, artists, babies in strollers, religious proselytizers, in-line skaters, soapbox orators, pigeons, and pushcart vendors along the park's walkways. Return some summer evening to watch a softball game in one corner, while in another corner an unofficial dog-walking group meets after work to chat while their quadrupedal pals romp. One cautionary note: As is true in most urban areas, the park is not a safe place to be after dark. ♦ Bounded by Tremont, Park, Charles, Boylston, and Beacon Sts

Within Boston Common:

Park Street Station Designed by **Wheelwright and Haven,** the first subway system in the US opened here to incredible fanfare on 1 September 1897. "First Car Off the Earth!" trumpeted the *Boston Globe.* (The subway line originally ran only as far as today's **Boylston Station,** just one stop across Boston Common.) Before you hurry aboveground to escape the dank air, the popcorn and doughnut smells, and the throngs on the platforms, look for the mosaic mural by the turnstiles. It depicts the first subway car—actually a streetcar which became an underground railway here—entering the tunnel, with a woman rider holding aloft that day's *Globe.* Aboveground, the two copper-roofed, granite-faced kiosks are National Historic Landmarks. ♦ Park and Tremont Sts

Visitor Information Center Head a short distance down Tremont Street to this freestanding center, where information is available on museum exhibitions, helicopter rides, and whale watches. This is also the place to pick up a map of Boston's renowned **Freedom Trail.** ♦ Daily

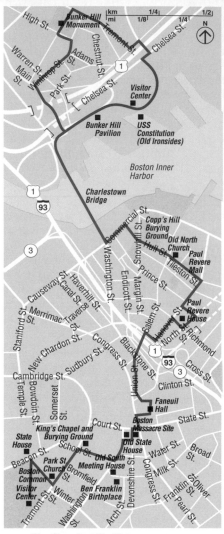

The Freedom Trail Begin the famous self-guided tourist pilgrimage at the **Visitor Information Center** and track an elusive red line connecting 16 historical sites from colonial and Revolutionary times, including **Paul Revere's House** and the **Old North Church** (see the map above). For further information on the trail, see "A New Revolution On the Freedom Trail" on page 23.

Boston Common Ranger Station Situated behind the **Visitor Information Center,** this is the place to obtain details about the many walks and tours led by park rangers. Offerings include historic tours of the **Common** and the **Granary Burying Ground;** a "What's in Bloom?" walk and a "Family Stroll" in the **Public Garden;** the "Make Way for Ducklings" tour, which includes a reading of the famous children's storybook (the walk starts at the **Garden**'s bronze ducklings); and the "Horse of Course" program, which traces a day in the

Restaurants/Clubs: Red   **Hotels:** Blue
Shops/♦ Outdoors: Green   **Sights/Culture:** Black

life of a park ranger's trusty steed. ◆ Free. Daily. 635.7383, 635.7412

Parkman Plaza This plaza's bronze figures enshrine Puritan values. The path to the left of *Industry* is called Railroad Mall because in 1835 it led to the terminal of one of Boston's first railroads. A brief, lovely stroll down Railroad Mall leads to the recently renovated Neo-Classical **Parkman Bandstand,** the site of **Shakespeare in the Park** performances during the summer (call 800/SEEBOSTON for information).

Central Burying Ground Follow Railroad Mall to find history etched on 18th-century tombstones. Legend has it that American soldiers who died at the Battle of Bunker Hill and British soldiers who succumbed to illness during the Siege of Boston lie here. At least a dozen Boston Tea Party guests are also buried in this graveyard, as is portrait artist Gilbert Stuart, who painted Martha and George Washington. Stuart died in poverty, having been eclipsed by less talented but more socially skilled painters. The inscriptions that mention "strangers" refer to Irish Catholic immigrants buried here. In early colonial graveyards like this one, headstones often face east—from whence would come the Day of Judgment trumpet call—and are paired with footstones, creating a cozy bed for the occupant's eternal rest.

Flagstaff Hill Climb the **Common**'s highest point, atop which the *Soldiers and Sailors Monument* commemorates Civil War combatants. Gunpowder was stored here long ago.

Frog Pond True, it's a frogless, sometimes-empty concrete hollow instead of the marshy amphibian abode it once was (Edgar Allan Poe derisively called Bostonians "Frogpondians"), but it has become a popular winter ice skating spot and in steamy weather the pond is filled with children cavorting under its fountain. (Even the cynical Poe called the **Common** "no common thing.")

Beacon Street Mall In the shadow of the **State House,** this wide, dappled promenade along the **Common**'s north side is where Ralph Waldo Emerson and Walt Whitman once paced back and forth, arguing about whether or not to take the sex out of Whitman's *Leaves of Grass*. Though Emerson was utterly convincing, Whitman concluded: "I could never hear the points better put—and then I felt down in my soul the clear and unmistakable conviction to disobey all, and pursue my own way." Despite their disagreement, the friends went off together to partake of "a bully dinner."

Robert Gould Shaw Memorial Across from the main entrance to the **State House,** sculptor Augustus Saint-Gaudens's monument honors the 54th Massachusetts Regiment, the nation's first black regiment, which enlisted in Boston. The troops fought in the Civil War under the command of 26-year-old Shaw, son of a venerable Boston family. For two years, until a shamefaced Congress relented, members of the 54th refused their pay because they received only $10 a month instead of the $13 paid to white soldiers. Shaw and half his men died in a valiant assault on Fort Wagner, South Carolina, in 1863.

Saint-Gaudens took 13 years to complete this beautifully wrought bas-relief, which Shaw's abolitionist family insisted must honor the black infantrymen as well as their son. Erected in 1897, the monument today seems somewhat patronizing for its portrayal of the white Shaw as a heroic figure on horseback, towering above the black troops, but it was, in fact, remarkably liberal in its day. Draw near to study the portraitlike treatment of the men's expressive faces. The angel of death hovers above. The story of Shaw and his brave regiment is recounted in the 1989 film, *Glory.* **Charles McKim,** of the architectural firm **McKim, Mead & White,** designed the memorial's classical frame. It sits on a small plaza whose granite balustrade overlooks the park.

Black Heritage Trail A guided 1.6-mile walking tour that traces the history of Boston's 19th-century black community begins at the **Robert Gould Shaw Memorial.** Call the **Boston African American National Historic Site** (742.5415) for information.

2 William Hickling Prescott House Built in 1808, this graceful pair of brick bowfronts, now joined, is adorned with many of the delicate Greek architectural details favored by architect **Asher Benjamin.** The left-hand house, now a National Historic Landmark and headquarters for the National Society of the Colonial Dames of America, inspired the setting for *The Virginians* by British author William Makepeace Thackery (houseguest of a former owner). During Wednesday guided tours, visitors can peruse the colonial and Victorian artifacts collected and preserved by the Dames. ◆ Admission. W; tours by reservation. 54-55 Beacon St (between Spruce and Charles Sts). 742.3190

3 Harrison Gray Otis House This is the last (circa 1805) and largest of the three imposing residences designed by **Charles Bulfinch** for the larger-than-life grandee Harrison Gray Otis—a Boston mayor, a US senator, and one of the city's first big-time developers. Otis, a man who believed in living the good life, added a fourth repast to his regular meals, breakfasted daily on pâté de foie gras, and—surprise, surprise—suffered with gout for 40 years. Otis feted all of fashionable Boston in his magnificent rooms. Each afternoon the politicians and society guests who gathered in the drawing room consumed 10 gallons of spiked punch. Amazingly, Harry's house didn't have plumbing. (Bathwater was considered a health menace because it supposedly attracted cockroaches, so tubs weren't allowed until the 1840s.) The American Meteorological Society is the current resident of the house; visitors are welcome to walk through the interior, but there are no exhibits. ♦ Free. ♦ M-F. 45 Beacon St (between Walnut and Spruce Sts)

4 Somerset Club Painter John Singleton Copley lived in a house that once stood on this site, until he went to England in 1744 and never returned. Now an ultra-exclusive private club, the Greek Revival granite bow-front that replaced Copley's house aggressively protrudes beyond its neighbors' facades. **David Sears** erected the right-hand half in 1819, adding the left half in 1831—doubling **Alexander Parris**'s original design and spoiling it in the process. Look for the baronial iron-studded portal with its lion's-head knockers—a very showy touch for Beacon Hill. Closed to the public. ♦ 42 Beacon St (between Walnut and Spruce Sts)

5 Appleton-Parker Houses Built in the early 1800s by **Alexander Parris,** these two Greek Revival bowfronts were the abodes of Boston's merchant prince Nathan Appleton, of the textile-manufacturing family, and his former partner, Daniel Parker. Henry Wadsworth Longfellow courted and married Fanny Appleton in her family's front parlor in 1843. And at one Appleton soiree, sardonic Edgar Allan Poe, characteristically misbehaving before the ladies, was given the heave-ho. Both houses are National Historic Landmarks, but are closed to the public. ♦ 39-40 Beacon St (between Walnut and Spruce Sts)

On the Appleton-Parker Houses:

Purple Windowpanes A number of homes along this stretch of Beacon Street boast unusual lavender-hued windowpanes. The famed "purple panes" of Beacon Hill are prized historical artifacts and the proud possession of only a handful of houses on the Hill. Actually, the treasured tint was a fluke—in shipments of glass sent from Hamburg to Boston between 1818 and 1824, manganese oxide reacted with the sun to create the color. Although numerous copies exist, very few authentic panes have survived. (They can also be seen at 29A Chestnut Street and 63 Beacon Street.)

6 Little, Brown and Company Established in 1837, this venerable Boston publishing house has on its backlist Louisa May Alcott, John Bartlett (of that household tome *Bartlett's Familiar Quotations*), J.D. Salinger, Evelyn Waugh, Fanny Farmer (of cookbook fame), Margaret Atwood, and Berke Breathed, creator of the retired *Bloom County* cartoon strip. The firm moved its headquarters here in 1909, and although the Adult Trade division decamped to New York several years ago, certain imprints remain. ♦ 34 Beacon St (at Joy St)

6 George Parkman House In one of the most sensational murders of the century, Dr. George Parkman was murdered in 1849, allegedly by Harvard professor John Webster, a fellow Boston socialite who had borrowed money from him. Lemuel Shaw, the judge handling the case, was related to the victim, and sent Webster to his hanging. After the furor, Parkman's son, George Francis Parkman, retreated from public scrutiny with his mother and sister, remaining a recluse in this house until his death in 1908. Built in 1825 by **Cornelius Coolidge,** the house overlooks **Boston Common.** Parkman must have found solace in this unchanging landscape because he left $5.5 million in his will for the **Common**'s maintenance. For generations, Boston mayors lived in this house, which belongs to the city; it is now used only for civic functions. ♦ 33 Beacon St (between Bowdoin and Joy Sts)

7 The State House The 23-karat gilded dome of the **Massachusetts State House** (pictured on page 17) glitters above the soft, dull hues of Beacon Hill, luring the eye. In fact, it was the capitol building (always called "the State House," never the "Capitol") that first drew wealthy Bostonians away from the crowded waterfront to settle in this more salubrious neighborhood, which was still considered "country" at the start of the 18th century.

Charles Bulfinch spun out his remarkable designs at a breathtaking rate, leaps and bounds ahead of city officials in his brilliant urban-planning maneuvers. Completed in 1798, the **State House** is his finest surviving gift to Boston. When construction began, Governor Samuel Adams, the popular Revolutionary War patriot, laid the cornerstone with Paul Revere's help.

Facing the **Common,** the imposing south facade is dominated by a commanding portico with 12 Corinthian columns, surmounting an arcade of brick arches. Topping the lantern—which is illuminated on evenings when the state legislature is in session—above the dome is a gilded pinecone, a symbol of the vast timberlands of northern Massachusetts, which became the state of Maine in 1820.

This striking Neo-Classical edifice cut a much less flashy figure in Bulfinch's time. The two marble wings were added more than a century later by **Chapman, Sturgis, and Andrews.** The dome was originally made of whitewashed wood shingles, replaced in 1802 with gray-painted copper sheeting installed by Paul

The State House

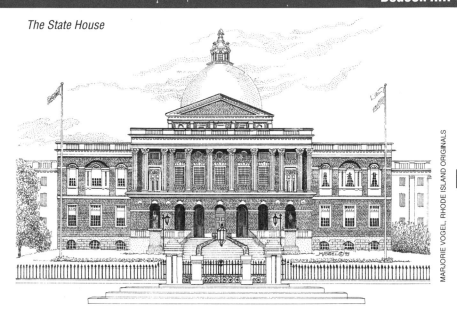

Revere and Sons; gilding wasn't applied until 1874. The dome was briefly blackened during World War II to hide it from moonlight during blackouts, so it wouldn't offer a target to the Axis bombers.

In 1825 the redbrick walls were painted white (a common practice when granite or marble was too costly); in 1845 they were repainted yellow; and in 1917 they were painted white again to match the new marble wings. Not until 1928 was the redbrick exposed once more. Around the back, safely out of sight from Beacon Street, is the monstrous yellow-brick heap of an extension, six times the size of the original building.

Statues of the spellbinding orator and US senator Daniel Webster, educator Horace Mann, and Civil War general Thomas Hooker on his charger stand beneath the central colonnade. On the lawns below are more pensive images. There's Anne Hutchinson (below the left wing), who was banished from Boston in 1645 by the Puritan community for her freethinking religious views. (Not until 1945 did the Great and General Court of Massachusetts revoke the edict of banishment.) And there's Quaker Mary Dyer (below the right wing), who was hanged on the **Common** for protesting Anne's banishment. Note also the statue of a serious, striding John F. Kennedy.

Climb the steps and enter by a door to the far right. This leads to **Bulfinch**'s **Doric Hall** (named for its 10 colossal columns) on the second floor under the dome. The hall's main doors only open when a US president visits or a Massachusetts governor leaves the building for the very last time.

Visitors may see the rest of the building on guided tours. On the third floor is the resplendent **House of Representatives** gallery. Here hangs the *Sacred Cod* carved in pine, presented to the legislature in 1784 by Boston merchant Jonathan Rowe as a reminder of the fishing industry's importance to the state economy. This wooden fish effigy garnered such ridiculous reverence that in 1895, when the House of Representatives was relocated within the **State House,** the fish was wrapped in an American flag and carried to the new seat of government by four messengers, escorted by a committee of 15 House members. And on 26 April 1933, when the fish was "codnapped" by *Harvard Lampoon* as a prank, all business in the House was suspended for several days, the members fuming over their missing fish. The thieves relented, and phoned to tell the House that their mascot was concealed in a closet beneath their chamber.

In the barrel-vaulted **Senate Reception Room,** the original **Senate Chamber,** each of four original Ionic columns by **Bulfinch** was carved from a single pine tree. Directly beneath the gold dome is the sunburst-ceilinged **Senate Chamber,** where Angelina Grimké became the first woman to address a US legislative body when she gave an anti-slavery speech in 1838. ◆ Free. M-F; tours by reservation. Beacon St (between Bowdoin and Joy Sts). 727.3676 &

Charles Street began as a seawall. Before Back Bay was filled in, this street marked Beacon Hill's western shoreline, where tides rose and fell nearly 15 feet.

8 Park Street Called Sentry Lane in the 17th century, this was the pathway the sentry took to the top of Beacon Hill, where a bucket of tar mounted on a post in 1634 was ever-ready for emergency lighting (until it blew down in 1789). An almshouse, a house of correction, an insane asylum, and a "bridewell" (a lovely name for a jail) stood along this street when it was part of Boston's outskirts; now Park Street is home to a number of decidedly reputable institutions. In 1804 architect **Charles Bulfinch** straightened out the lane and designed nine residences facing the **Common** that became known as **Bulfinch Row.** Only the **Amory-Ticknor House** at the corner of Beacon Street survives, although it's disastrously altered. ◆ Between Tremont and Beacon Sts

On Park Street:

The Union Club Formerly separate 19th-century mansions owned by two of Boston's most illustrious families, the Lowells and Lawrences, this is now a private club, whose members meet to converse over lunch. The right wing was demolished in 1896 and later replaced. ◆ No. 8 (at Park St Pl)

9 Brimstone Corner The intersection of Park and Tremont Streets was supposedly given this name because of the fire-and-brimstone oratory of the **Park Street Church**'s Congregational preachers—including abolitionist William Lloyd Garrison, who gave his first antislavery address here in 1829. But a more banal explanation is that brimstone, used to make gunpowder, was stored in the church's crypt during the War of 1812. ◆ Park and Tremont Sts

Park Street Church

At Brimstone Corner:

Park Street Church People heading northeast along the **Common** can't help but look at this majestic 1809 Congregational church, looming opposite the subway station. Henry James heaped praise on the elegant late-Georgian edifice, pronouncing it "perfectly felicitous" and "the most interesting mass of brick and mortar in America." Influenced by his much more illustrious English compatriot **Christopher Wren,** architect **Peter Banner** capped the crowning glory of his career with a stalwart 217-foot-tall telescoping white steeple that points to the sky like an orator's emphatic forefinger. Locals have always relied on its easy-to-read clock for time and a rendezvous point. The illustrious **Handel & Haydn Society,** formed here in 1815, drew many of its voices from the church choir over the years. And here the anthem "America" was first sung on 4 July 1831; 24-year-old Samuel Francis Smith reputedly dashed off its lyrics a half-hour before schoolchildren sang it on the church steps. The church once stood next to a workhouse, the Puritan answer to home-lessness and poverty. ◆ Tu-Sa July-Aug; by appointment only Sept-June. Services Su 9AM, 10:45AM. 1 Park St. 523.3383 ᕈ

10 Granary Burying Ground Nestled next to the **Park Street Church,** this graveyard was named for the 1738 granary that the church replaced. Created in 1660, it is the third-oldest graveyard in the city. In this shady haven lie the remains of many Revolutionary heroes—among them Samuel Adams, John Hancock, James Otis, Robert Treat Paine, and Paul Revere—although the headstones have been moved so often you can't really be sure who's where. The five victims of the Boston Massacre (including black patriot Crispus Attucks), philanthropist Peter Faneuil (for whom **Faneuil Hall** is named), Benjamin Franklin's parents (he's in Philadelphia), and "Mother Goose" are also here. Judge Samuel Sewell likewise rests easy here, having cleared his conscience as the only judge to ever admit publicly that he was wrong to condemn the Salem witches.

The best reason to visit this two-acre necropolis is to examine the tombstones' extraordinary carvings (rubbings are forbidden here) of astonishing skeletons, urns, winged skulls, and

©VOGEL

contemplative angels. In this haunting place, you will be transported back to the 17th century, from which the earliest tombstones date. The winged hourglasses carved into the Egyptian-style granite gateway (designed in 1830 by **Solomon Willard**) were added later in the 19th century. ◆ Free. Daily. Tremont St (between Park and Beacon Sts)

11 The Boston Athenaeum

Although **Edward Clark Cabot** modeled the 1849 building after **Palladio's** Palazzo da Porta Festa in Vicenza, Italy, the **Athenaeum** is a Boston institution to its bones. Enlarged and rebuilt in the early 1900s by **Henry Forbes Bigelow,** the structure is now a National Historic Landmark. Only 1,049 ownership shares exist to this independent research library, founded in 1807, and all can be traced to their original owners. Non-members are invited to tour the building and look at—but not touch—books on the first and second floors, and to visit the **Athenaeum Gallery,** which offers ongoing exhibitions. Two groups frowned upon in most public places—dogs and smokers—are welcome here. Take a tour and visit Boston's most pleasant place for musing, the high-ceilinged, airy **Reading Room** on the fifth floor, with its sunny alcoves. As poet David McCord wrote, the room "combines the best elements of the Bodleian, Monticello, the frigate *Constitution,* a greenhouse, and an old New England sitting room." Also be sure to step out onto the fifth-floor terrace, with its gorgeous plantings and fine view of the **Granary Burying Ground.** The superb collections here include George Washington's private library and Confederate imprints, as well as history, biography, and English, American, and Gypsy literature. There's a notable mystery collection too.

Members and visitors who've gained special dispensation can handle many of the books, but may receive a lesson in the proper way to remove a volume from its shelf (work your fingers around its sides, *don't* pull it out from the top!). Take a ride in the charmingly hand-painted elevator, a former employee's handiwork, with its framed bookplate display. Part of the library's appeal is the way Oriental carpets and art treasures are strewn about. Keep an eye out for the wonderful statue of *Little Nell* on the first floor next to the stairs. ◆ Free. M-Sa. Tours by reservation. Open only to members and qualified researchers, but special exhibits and receptions—many open to the public—are mounted September through June. 10½ Beacon St (between Tremont and Park Sts). 227.0270 ዼ

BLACK GOOSE

12 Black Goose ★★$$ Crowds gather regularly for the Coliseum-size Caesar salads and abundant plates of pasta with pesto served in the midst of majestic Corinthian columns. In good weather, find a sun-warmed table out front for lunch, and watch scholars and book-browsers coming and going beneath the **Boston Athenaeum's** dignified sandstone facade across the way. ◆ Italian ◆ M-F lunch and dinner; Sa dinner. Reservations recommended. 21 Beacon St (between Somerset and Bowdoin Sts). 720.4500 ዼ

12 Lodge's Pushcart A compact showcase of North End Italian treats, this grocery store/deli counter serves overstuffed calzone and deep-dish *pizza grande,* along with specialty coffees and *pizzelle* (waffle cookies). ◆ M-F; Sa until 3PM. No credit cards accepted. 23 Beacon St (at Bowdoin St). 723.5353

13 The Fill-A-Buster $ Gracious Vaios Grigas's friendly crew serves hearty fare with Greek highlights—egg-lemon soup, spinach-cheese pie, and kabobs—for a clientele of pols and media types. The breakfast specials are bountiful, and you can smell Grigas's famous homemade muffins a block away. Once you're a regular here, they'll have your coffee poured and waiting before you've crossed the threshold. ◆ Greek/American/Takeout ◆ M-F breakfast and lunch. 142 Bowdoin St (between Beacon St and Ashburton Pl). 523.8164

14 Lyman Paine House This understated house's distinctive character comes from its intriguing asymmetrical windows and refined Greek Revival ornamentation. ◆ 6 Joy St (at Mount Vernon St)

15 Appalachian Mountain Club Founded in Boston in 1876, the **AMC** can provide plenty of information on outdoor recreation in Boston and New England. ◆ M-F. 5 Joy St (between Beacon and Mount Vernon Sts). 523.0636

The Eliot & Pickett Houses

Bed & Breakfast

16 The Eliot & Pickett Houses $ Conveniently located at the top of Beacon Hill, these two adjoining 1830s brick town houses feature 20 comfortably appointed guest rooms, most with private baths. There's a fully stocked kitchen for guests who prefer to eat in. In season, guests have access to the roof deck with its grand views of the city and the nearby gold-domed **State House.** ♦ 6 Mount Vernon Pl (just east of Joy St). 248.8707; fax 742.1364 ♿

17 32 Mount Vernon Street Julia Ward Howe and Dr. Samuel Gridley Howe took up house-keeping here in the 1870s. Dr. Samuel is best known for founding the Perkins Institute for the Blind, but he also organized the Committee of Vigilance to protect runaway slaves, helping hundreds of fugitives and pulling off an occasional daring rescue when word arrived that slaves were aboard the ships pulling into Boston Harbor. Julia composed "The Battle Hymn of the Republic" as well as many volumes of poetry. A suffragist and social reformer, she wrote and lectured on the rights of women and African-Americans. General Ulysses S. Grant and writer Bret Harte were among the couple's notable houseguests. It's still a private residence and closed to the public. ♦ Between Joy and Walnut Sts

18 Nichols House Museum Remarkable Miss Rose Standish Nichols, niece of sculptor Augustus Saint-Gaudens, spent most of her genteel life in this house, built in 1804 by **Charles Bulfinch.** A gardening author, world traveler, peace advocate, and pioneer woman landscape architect who earned her own living, Nichols also founded the International Society of Pen Pals in her front parlor. Stop in to see

Acorn Street

MARJORIE VOGEL, RHODE ISLAND ORIGINALS

the furnishings, memorabilia, and ancestors' portraits—collected by her family over centuries—which Nichols bequeathed to the public along with her home. The witty curator, William Pear, takes visitors on an entertaining tour of the only Beacon Hill home open to the public. ♦ Admission. Feb-Dec (call for days and hours). 55 Mount Vernon St (between Joy St and Louisburg Sq). 227.6993 ♿

Within the Nichols House Museum:

The Beacon Hill Garden Club The club's annual spring Hidden Gardens Tour is the public's one chance to roam through greenery that otherwise can only be glimpsed tantalizingly beyond brick walls. ♦ 227.4392

19 John Callender House One of the first houses on the street, Callender's small abode cost $2,155 for the lot and $5,000 to $7,000 for construction when it was built in 1802. A new roof was affixed to the Federal-style brick house and the entrance moved slightly, but it's still standing. A lavish garden blooms in the back. A private residence, it's closed to the public. ♦ 14 Walnut St (at Mount Vernon St)

20 13, 15 and 17 Chestnut Street Charles **Bulfinch** was kept busy building for patrons' daughters, and, in fact, this most famous trio of row houses was dubbed the "Daughter Houses." In 1805, while her husband, Colonel James Swan, cooled his heels in a French debtors' prison, Boston heiress Hepsibah Swan had these houses built as wedding gifts for her daughters. **No. 13** is a National Historic Landmark. All are private homes and closed to the public. ♦ Between Walnut and Willow Sts

21 29A Chestnut Street In 1865 tragedian Edwin Booth was enjoying a successful run in *The Iron Chest,* a drama about a murderer haunted by his crime, and was staying here at the home of the theater manager. But on the eve of Edwin's last performance, brother John Wilkes Booth murdered President Abraham Lincoln. Edwin's last performance was canceled, and he left secretly for New York, not appearing before an audience again for nearly a year. The house is still a private residence and closed to the public. ♦ Between Walnut and Willow Sts

22 Acorn Street Stand at the crown of this street, one of Boston's skinniest, and watch cars shimmy and shake as they climb its cobbled length. On one side, look up at the trees waving from hidden gardens backing Mount Vernon Street; opposite are diminutive houses that belonged to coachmen serving families in mansions on Chestnut and Mount Vernon Streets. Study the entrances to **Nos. 1, 3,** and **5** and notice the ornamental acorns that correspond in number with each address. The original homeowners would be pleased to know that their humble houses now hobnob with the best on the real-estate market. ◆ Between Willow and W Cedar Sts

23 Harrison Gray Otis House (1802) Ever an onward-and-upward kind of fellow, Otis abandoned a spanking-new manse on Cambridge Street, also designed by **Charles Bulfinch,** to take up residence in this fashionable neighborhood of his own making. One of the only houses in the area with ample elbow room, this towering struc ture was intended to set a Jones's standard of freestanding mansions on generous land-scaped grounds, but Boston's population boom soon made this impossible. It is now on the National Register of Historic Places, but is not open to the public. ◆ 85 Mount Vernon St (between Joy St and Louisburg Sq)

24 Louisburg Square Suddenly, the houses open wide and strollers find themselves at the edge of one of Boston's most serenely patrician spots. (Be sure to pronounce that "s"; you'll horrify locals if you say "Louie-burg"!) The redbrick row houses (built 1835-47) and the oval park they overlook aren't extraordinary in themselves; it's the square's timeless aura that has always appealed to Bostonians. Deteriorating statues of *Aristides the Just* and *Columbus* coolly survey all comers. Many famous people have crossed the thresholds of houses on this street. After becoming a literary success, Louisa May Alcott brought her perennially penniless family to **No. 10,** where mercury poisoning (she got it while a Civil War nurse) slowly crippled her. **No. 20** is a happier address: Here soprano Jenny Lind ("The Swedish Nightingale"), who skyrocketed to fame with the help of P.T. Barnum, was married in 1852 to her accompanist. Samuel Gray Ward, a representative of Lind's London bankers, also lived at **No. 20;** among his banking coups was arranging America's purchase of Alaska from Russia for $7.2 million. ◆ Between Mount Vernon and Pinckney Sts

25 Pinckney Street Begin at its base, and with luck you'll arrive at the summit just as the late-afternoon sunlight turns golden, and the trees become sparkling lanterns stretching down toward the Charles River. Called the "Cinderella Street" of Beacon Hill by one author, it was once the dividing line between those who were and those who were not. There are both handsome and humble buildings here, and all are utterly delightful. ◆ Between Joy St and Embankment Rd

25 62 Pinckney Street Built in 1846 and owned by George S. Hilliard, this residence was a stop on the underground railroad that ran through Boston in the 1850s. Whether Hilliard knew fugitive slaves were harbored in his home is debatable, but his staunchly abolitionist wife, Susan Tracy Hilliard, certainly did. Workmen discovered the secret attic chamber in the 1920s. The house is still a

private residence and closed to the public. ◆ Between Joy St and Louisburg Sq

26 Boston English High School The first interracial public school in Boston (boys only) opened in this austere cruciform edifice—now divided into condominium units—in 1844. ◆ 65 Anderson St (at Pinckney St)

27 Pie-Shaped House The interior reveals what the exterior conceals: Squeezed between its neighbors, this house comes to a point like a piece of pie. Look at the roofline for a clue. ◆ 56 Pinckney St (between Joy St and Louisburg Sq)

28 House of Odd Windows When Ralph Waldo Emerson's nephew renovated this former carriage house in 1884, he turned the facade into a montage of windows—each singular and superbly positioned—in an inexplicable burst of artistry. Notice the quirky eyebrow dormer at the top. ◆ 24 Pinckney St (between Joy St and Louisburg Sq)

28 20 Pinckney Street Bronson Alcott—mystic, educator, "other-worldly philosopher," and notoriously bad provider—brought his wife and four daughters to live here from 1852 to 1855. The close-knit family and their struggle with poverty inspired daughter Louisa's heartstring-tugger *Little Women.* ◆ Between Joy St and Louisburg Sq

29 9½ Pinckney Street The Hill's hodgepodge evolution created labyrinthine patterns of streets and housing that led to hidden gardens and even hidden houses (**No. 74½ Pinckney Street** is the famous "Hidden House," left to your imagination). The iron gate here opens onto a tunnel that passes through the house and into a courtyard skirted by three hidden houses. Crouch down for a glimpse. ◆ Between Joy and Anderson Sts

29 Middleton-Glapion House George Middleton, an African-American jockey, horse-breaker, and Revolutionary War veteran, and hairdresser Louis Glapion collaborated in the late 1700s on this minute clapboard house, so untouched by time that the pair might have strolled out the front door this morning. ◆ 5 Pinckney St (between Joy and Anderson Sts)

On 1 October 1979 Boston Common was the site of a public Mass given by Pope John Paul II, his first Mass offered in the US, on the occasion of his first pastoral visit to America. During the Mass, celebrated in the rain with tens of thousands in attendance, the pope said: "May God's peace descend on this city of Boston, and joy to every conscience and heart."

American novelist Henry James, who lived much of his adult life in Europe, characterized Beacon Hill's Mount Vernon Street as "the most civilized street in America."

30 Myrtle Street When Brahmin elegance begins to stultify, seek out this narrow, down-to-earth street. Tenements and Greek Revival row houses commune along this stretch with laundries, markets, shoe repair shops, a playground, a pizza parlor, and other unfashionable establishments that make it the neighborhood's most for-real street. Look at the rooflines and spot the funky gardens that aren't found on any "Hidden Gardens of Beacon Hill" tour. Perched here in the heights, you can see the lazy Charles River and **Massachusetts Institute of Technology** over in Cambridge.
♦ Between Hancock and Revere Sts

31 Museum of Afro American History The **Abiel Smith School,** the first grammar and primary school for black children in Boston, opened here in 1834, replacing the school that had met in the **African Meeting House** basement (see below). It was named for a white businessman who bequeathed the funds for its construction. The school closed 20 years later when the state upheld the demand for integrated schools, ending the practice of taxing blacks to support schools that excluded their children. Visitors may tour the building, although there aren't many artifacts on display. Exhibits of photographs by African-American photographers or with African-American themes are mounted here as well.
♦ Free. M-F; daily in summer. 46 Joy St (at Smith Ct). 739.1200

COURTESY OF THE MUSEUM OF AFRO AMERICAN HISTORY

31 African Meeting House Free African-American artisans built this meeting house (pictured above) in 1806, and **Asher Benjamin**'s architecture influenced its townhouse style. A National Historic Landmark, it's the oldest black church still standing in the US. Nicknamed "Black Faneuil Hall" during the abolitionist era, this is where William Lloyd Garrison founded the New England Anti-Slavery Society on 6 January 1832. Late last century, the African-American residents of the neighborhood began migrating to the South End and Roxbury; by the 1920s, Irish and Jewish immigrants had moved in. The meeting house was sold to a Jewish congregation and remained a synagogue until it became part of the **Museum of Afro American History** (see above) in the 1970s. ♦ Free. Daily. 8 Smith Ct (just west of Joy St). 739.1200

32 William C. Nell House America's first published African-American historian and a member of William Lloyd Garrison's circle, Nell boarded in this farmhouse from 1851 to 1856. He led the crusade for integrated public schools in the city, and his Equal School Association organized the boycott of the neighboring **Abiel Smith School** until the state legislature abolished restrictions on black children's access to public schools. African-American clothing-dealer James Scott, who purchased Nell's house and ran it as a rooming house starting in 1865, sheltered fugitive slaves here. It is now a National Historic Landmark, but it is closed to the public. ♦ 3 Smith Ct (just west of Joy St)

33 Venice Ristorante ★$ This is the kind of place you can walk by a hundred times without noticing, but stop in once and try the food and you're sure to become a regular. Crisp-crusted pizzas topped with ultrafresh ingredients even come in a "personal" size for one. Or choose from an enormous selection of salads, pastas, subs, and daily specials. There's free delivery. ♦ Pizza/Takeout ♦ Daily lunch and dinner. 204 Cambridge St (at S Russell St). 227.2094 &

34 Rollins Place Countless passersby have glanced down this cul-de-sac off Revere Street and been charmed by the little white house tucked snugly at its end. But the inviting Southern-style facade is really a false front. The architectural trompe l'oeil masks a cliff that runs between Revere Street and the lower Phillips Street. Continue down the same side of Revere Street and slip into Goodwin, Sentry Hill, and Bellingham Places, all charming dead-end streets that also disguise the cliff, but without such fanciful deceit. ♦ 27 Revere St (between Garden and Anderson Sts)

COURTESY OF THE BOSTONIAN SOCIETY/OLD STATE HOUSE

35 Lewis Hayden House Fugitive slaves themselves, Lewis (pictured above) and Harriet Hayden became noted abolitionists, and their 1833 home was a station on the underground railroad. William and Ellen Craft, a famous couple who escaped by masquerading as master and slave, stayed here. And in 1853 Harriet Beecher Stowe, who had already published *Uncle Tom's Cabin,* visited the Haydens and was introduced to 13

A New Revolution On the Freedom Trail

Boston's **Freedom Trail** is a pilgrimage along some of America's most historic streets to 16 sites dating from the city's colonial and early republic years. In particular, the trail connects public buildings, homes, churches, burying grounds, and battlefields where the early events of the American Revolution unfolded. Nowhere else in America is such a dramatic story told in such an authentic historic setting.

The **Freedom Trail**, a 3-mile-long walking tour that links the 16 sites, had its beginning in 1951. William Schofield, an editor and daily columnist at the old *Herald Traveler*, and Bob Winn of the **Old North Church**, observing that tourists were unable to locate the key sites of the American Revolution, started putting up plywood signs in **Downtown** Boston and the **North End**. In 1958, a brick and red-paint sidewalk path joined the sites, creating the "connect-the-dots" walking route that has been a unique tourist attraction for travelers to Boston ever since. In 1974, in anticipation of America's Bicentennial, the **Boston National Historical Park** was created as part of the National Park Service to oversee some of the **Freedom Trail** sites. More recently, $45 million in federal funds has paid for extensive renovations of three treasured sites on the historic trail: **Faneuil Hall**, the **Old South Meeting House,** and the **Old State House.** Most **Freedom Trail** sites, however, remain managed by independent nonprofit organizations, an arrangement that helps preserve their authenticity. But while each site tells a tale of freedom and independence, their stories have been isolated, rather than woven into a broader narrative. This is changing.

In 1995 a public government/private industry committee was assembled to provide recommendations to revitalize the trail. While the sites will continue to be independent entities, plans are being implemented to link them in intriguing new ways so that their historic story comes more vividly alive. Some changes have been completed—a new brick and granite path now connects all the sites, and there's new signage at each. Other improvements in the works include medallions mounted outside each site that will highlight its significance, and audio "wands," triggered by remote sensors located along the trail that will enable visitors to take a wide range of self-guided tours. In addition, there will be new transportation options, such as the **Freedom Trail Trolley,** and a water connection from the North End across to **Charlestown. The National Park Service Visitor Center** (15 State St, at Devonshire St, 242.5642) continues to be the best source for current information on the **Freedom Trail** and the departure point for free ranger-guided tours.

The **Freedom Trail** is being reintroduced, not just as a line in the pavement but as a story line of the people of Boston who launched a revolution.

Chapter 1: Revolution of Minds and Hearts

This section of the trail covers the following sites: **Boston Common** (1634); the **State House** (1795), built on land bought from John Hancock's family, and designed by **Charles Bulfinch; Park Street Church** (1809) and **King's Chapel** (1668); both **Granary Burying Ground** (1660) and **King's Chapel Burying Ground** (1630); the site of **Boston Latin School** (1635), which launched Boston's reputation as a center for education, and a statue of Benjamin Franklin, a former student at the school; the **Old Corner Bookstore** (1718); and **Old South Meeting House** (1729), the place from which the Boston Tea Party departed, and where an award-winning exhibit lets visitors hear the fiery debates that led to the decision to dump 340 chests of tea into **Boston Harbor.**

Chapter 2: The People Revolt

Emphasizing the ferment and turbulence of ideas and the actions that led to revolt, the trail leads from the **Old South Meeting House**—where ordinary citizens' protests to aspects of English rule led General Gage to say, "I fear we will never gain control of the colonists"—to the **Old State House** (1713), Boston's oldest public building, from which the English governors ruled Boston, to the **Boston Massacre Site** and **Faneuil Hall** (1742), with its second-floor meeting hall that was called by the Marquis de Lafayette "the Cradle of American Liberty" for the debates held there.

Chapter 3: Neighborhood of Revolution

Here the story line moves to the North End, Boston's oldest neighborhood, focusing on the dramatic risks and individual acts that launched the revolution. There's the **Paul Revere House** (1680), where, if he were alive today, Revere undoubtedly would acknowledge that he was not the lone rider of lore, but one of many individuals whose acts of courage and conscience led to American freedom. In the steeple of **Old North Church** (1723), Boston's oldest surviving church, the two lanterns were hung on the night of 18 April 1775, to signal that "the British are coming!"

Chapter 4: Boston Goes to War in Defense of Freedom

Here the trail picks up at **Copp's Hill Burying Ground** (1659) from which the British fired on Charlestown toward **Bunker Hill.** In Charlestown, the **Bunker Hill Monument** commemorates the first major battle of the American Revolution (17 June 1775), and marks the location of the redoubt from which the colonists repelled the repeated waves of British attack. Nearby is the USS *Constitution* (1797), the oldest commissioned warship afloat in the world and the last stop on the Freedom Trail.

newly escaped slaves—the first she'd ever met. The house is still a private home and closed to the public. ♦ 66 Phillips St (between Grove and W Cedar Sts)

The John Jeffries House

36 The John Jeffries House $ A former residence for nurses, this gracious hotel at the foot of Beacon Hill has been completely renovated into a European-inspired inn decorated in turn-of-the-century Federal style. The 46 units range from cozy single rooms to spacious deluxe suites boasting country French fabrics and featuring kitchenettes, private baths, color TV, and telephones. Nonsmoking floors are available. Guests enjoy a complimentary continental breakfast served in the parlor. The inn is convenient to public transportation and within walking distance of many of Boston's major attractions. ♦ 14 Embankment Rd (between Revere and Charles Sts). 367.1866; fax 742.0313 &

37 The King & I ★$$ What started out as a fling with Thai restaurants in the 1980s has turned into a passionate, some say obsessive, affair with that cuisine in Boston. The offspring of this affair are scattered throughout the city, and it's often hard to tell them apart. This bright, courteous restaurant has always stood out, however, for its entrancing, delicate versions of dishes like Paradise beef. For an after-dinner treat of a different sort, cross Charles Street and enter the passage to the left of the Charles Street Animal Clinic. You'll see an arch framing trees, the river, and passing cars. Enter here and admire the curved charm of West Hill Place, another of the neighborhood's quaint and narrow streets. ♦ Thai ♦ M-Sa lunch and dinner; Su dinner. Reservations recommended for dinner. 145 Charles St (between Revere St and George Washington Cir). 227.3320

38 Danish Country Antique Furniture Here brightly colored rugs, tableware, crafts, and folk art can be found in, on, and among handsome blond furniture dating from the mid-18th century onward. So often antique furniture cringes from returning to active service, but owner James Kilroy's Danish desks, armoires, tables, chests, and chairs sturdily welcome the prospect. His shop is cheery when compared with many other dark and dour Hill establishments. ♦ Daily. 138

Charles St (between Revere St and Embankment Rd). 227.1804

38 Marika's You'll need to navigate very carefully through this crowded collection of glassware, furniture, paintings, tapestries, and treasures from all around the world. Owner Matthew Raisz's grandmother, Marika, emigrated from Budapest and founded this shop in 1944. It's prized particularly for its extraordinary jewelry. ♦ Tu-Sa. 130 Charles St (between Revere St and Embankment Rd). 523.4520

38 George Gravert Antiques The pleasant proprietor of this shop has been in the antiques business for more than 30 years, specializing in European furniture and accessories that are clearly chosen by an expert eye. Something timeless and trustworthy about the place will make you want to linger even after you've ogled everything twice. Although he caters to wholesalers, Gravert won't mind if casual shoppers come in and browse. ♦ M-F. 122 Charles St (between Revere St and Embankment Rd). 227.1593 &

39 Period Furniture Hardware Company This almost-80-year-old shop is aglow with gleaming surfaces to stroke. Many antiquers have abandoned their wearisome Holy Grail quest for such-and-such genuine wall sconce from such-and-such period for the almost-as-satisfying pleasures of these reproductions of hardware from the 18th century onward. If only the price tags weren't the real thing. ♦ M-F; Sa until 2PM. 123 Charles St (between Revere St and George Washington Cir). 227.0758

39 Boston Antique Coop I & II These two cooperatives in one building set out a tempting smorgasbord of American, Asian, and European antiques. The place has all the ambience of a garage sale, but it's great fun and local antiques dealers snoop about here, too. Downstairs at **Coop I,** four dealers display sterling, porcelain, paintings, jewelry, bottles, vintage photography, bric-a-brac, and more. Upstairs at **Coop II,** eight dealers specialize in decorative items, vintage clothing, and textiles. ♦ Daily. 119 Charles St (between Revere St and George Washington Cir). Coop I 227.9810, Coop II 227.9811

40 Helen's Leather Care to prance about in python or buckle on some buffalo? You can even opt for ostrich at this leather emporium, which boasts an exotic collection of handmade boots. In case you didn't know, the mammoth wooden boot out front tells you you've arrived at New England's biggest Western boot dealer. Also for sale are popular brands of shoes, clothing, briefcases, backpacks, and other leather whatnots. ♦ Daily. 110 Charles St (between Pinckney and Revere Sts). 742.2077

41 Starbucks ★$ This former **Coffee Connection** still carries that establishment's unsurpassable coffee, as well as its own well-known Seattle-based brews. Walk in and inhale the potent, sultry aroma of the beans, then sit at one of the tiny window tables and nurse your choice. ♦ Cafe/Takeout ♦ M-F 6AM-7PM; Sa-Su 7AM-7PM. 97 Charles St (at Pinckney St). 227.3812 ♿ Also at numerous locations throughout Boston and Cambridge

42 The Sevens ★★$ No wonder this is the neighborhood's favorite pub. Often crowded, with free-for-all conversations bouncing between the bar and the booths, it's a gregarious place meant for sitting back and sipping a draft when the rest of the world seems a little lonely. Try the pub lunch—a generous, satisfying sandwich and bargain-priced mug of draft beer. ♦ American ♦ Daily until 1AM. No credit cards accepted. 77 Charles St (between Mount Vernon and Pinckney Sts). 523.9074

42 The Hungry i ★★$$$$ If you're at all claustrophobic, think twice before stepping down into this extremely intimate restaurant—one of the city's most romantic choices. For Sunday brunch, you can also dine alfresco in a diminutive courtyard. Fish and game star in the brief, but inventive, menu. ♦ American ♦ M-F dinner; Sa and Su brunch and dinner. Reservations recommended. 71½ Charles St (between Mount Vernon and Pinckney Sts). 227.3524

43 James Billings Antiques & Interiors James Billings concentrates on 18th-century English furniture and decorative arts. Lise Davis, his wife and partner, is an interior decorator who specializes in the ever-more-popular English country house look. The couple—who belong to the British Antique Dealers Association and have been in business in Essex, England, since 1961, and in Boston since 1982—blend their talents in this opulently appointed shop. ♦ M-Sa. 88 Charles St (between Mount Vernon and Pinckney Sts). 367.9533

43 Eugene Galleries It's easy to lose all track of time in this enthralling emporium, which specializes in Boston views and maps—old prints, sketches, postcards, and photographs. Stop here after touring the city—it's the ideal place to see how your favorite sights have been captured through the centuries. You'll also find oddments of every sort—a Victorian dustpan, sheet music, paperweights, fire-and-brimstone sermons, and a *History of the Great Fire of Boston,* to name a few. ♦ M-Sa. 76 Charles St (between Mount Vernon and Pinckney Sts). 227.3062

COURTESY OF JOHN SHARRATT ASSOCIATES

44 Charles Street Meeting House It's a shame they stuck a food shop in the front of this forthright structure completed in 1807 (pictured above)—even if it is a popular outpost of the inimitable **Rebecca's** cafe (see page 27). An octagonal belfry crowns the rectangular central tower, a handsome ensemble by **Asher Benjamin,** the architect who designed **Faneuil Hall** and inherited **Bulfinch**'s unofficial role of architect laureate of Boston. The meeting house's first congregation was the Baptist Society, who found the nearby Charles River convenient for baptisms. Later, although abolitionists—including William Lloyd Garrison, Frederick Douglass, Harriet Tubman, and Sojourner Truth—often orated from the pulpit, church seating was segregated. Timothy Gilbert, a member of the congregation, challenged the tradition and was expelled for inviting several African-American friends to sit in a white pew. (Gilbert then founded the **Tremont Temple** in 1842, Boston's first integrated place of worship.) The African Methodist Episcopal Church met here from 1867 until the 1930s, and the Unitarian Universalists moved in after the Depression. Later, when the **Afro-American Culture Center** was located here, poet Langston Hughes gave readings. Renovated in 1982 by **John Sharratt Associates** and put on the National Register of Historic Places, shops and private offices have since replaced the church and community activities that once took place here. ♦ 121 Mount Vernon St (at Charles St)

The gold-domed State House, designed by Charles Bulfinch and dating from 1795, spawned Boston's nickname, "The Hub." Oliver Wendell Holmes (the author and doctor, not his son, the justice) remarked in "The Autocrat of the Breakfast Table" (1858) that the "Boston State House is the hub of the solar system."

45 The Church of the Advent The story goes that flamboyant parishioner Isabella Stewart Gardner, founder of the museum in the Fenway, scrubbed this Episcopal church's steps during Lent as penance. The tale also goes that proper Bostonians sniffed and wondered why Isabella wasn't required to scour the entire edifice. The Gothic Revival structure (completed in 1888 by **Sturgis and Brigham** and pictured above) distributes its great girth on an awkward site through a chain of conical-roofed chapels, accommodating nearby domestic architecture as a good Beacon Hill neighbor should. The interiors are also ingeniously arranged and splendidly embellished. The church boasts one of the finest carillons in the country. There's also a lovely garden in the rear. ♦ M-F (enter through church office); Su 7:30AM-1PM. 30 Brimmer St (at Mount Vernon St). 523.2377

Known in the 17th century as "The Way to the Poorhouse" because of the almshouse at the corner of Park Street, Beacon Street began as an undeveloped area on the edge of Boston. Formally laid out in 1708, the street began to acquire its present sedate and stately character in the first half of the 19th century, when its brick row houses, most in early Federal style, were built. This bright thoroughfare bordering the Common became known as "the sunny street that holds the sifted few."

Visitors wanting to slip into the Boston routine unnoticed should be sure to note that the names Boston Common and the Public Garden are both singular. Nothing marks an out-of-towner more quickly than mention of Boston Commons or the Public Gardens.

46 Sunflower Castle Remodeled in 1878 by **Clarence Luce,** this amusing Queen Anne cottage began life in 1840 as an anonymous little plain Jane of a building; now it takes its name from the enormous, gaudy sunflower ornament pressed on its brow. Maybe boredom with Beacon Hill's de rigueur palette and mincing details inspired **Luce** to paint the stuccoed first floor brilliant yellow and sheath the second story in China-red tile. His whimsy unleashed, he added exuberantly carved brackets and posts, and a griffin. It's still a private home and closed to the public. ♦ 130 Mount Vernon St (at River St)

47 Charles Street Supply A really good hardware store is always an alluring place. Even if you've never gone to war with weeds or handled a two-by-four, you'll itch to tackle some project, *any* project, at the sight of all those home-improvement aids spilling onto this overstuffed store's sidewalks. Sure, the prices are high, but owner Richard Gurnon and his staff offer plenty of how-tos along with the tools. ♦ Daily. 54-56 Charles St (between Chestnut and Mount Vernon Sts). 367.9046

Blackstone's of Beacon Hill

47 Blackstone's of Beacon Hill Owner Richard Dowd provides reproductions to historical societies all across the US, so this is the place to come for brass and mahogany trivets, candlesnuffers, and door knockers. Also available are porcelain and enamel renditions of the **Public Garden**'s famous **Swan Boats,** designed for the shop by Limoges and Crummles, and handmade stained-glass picture frames. ♦ Daily. 46 Charles St (between Chestnut and Mount Vernon Sts). 227.4646

47 Paramount Steak House ★$ This is a Greek diner squeezed into a Charles Street shoe box. A gathering spot for locals, it offers typical greasy-spoon breakfasts (self-serve and very cheap) that one is expected to consume with dispatch during busy hours. (You'll know if you're too slow.) Its appeal is illusive to the casual observer, but so many are dedicated to the place that there's surely something here. Nothing on the menu is small—try the Greek salad, moussaka, or souvlaki. ♦ Greek/American/Takeout ♦ Daily breakfast, lunch, and dinner. 44 Charles St (between Chestnut and Mount Vernon Sts). 523.8832 ঙ

47 Figs ★★$$ There are just a dozen tables at this cozy cousin to the popular **Olives** in Charlestown, but it's certainly worth the wait.

Fig and prosciutto pizza with rosemary crust; semolina dumplings baked in spaghetti squash, ham, sage, and parmesan; and fresh Maine lobster with leek risotto and cream sauce are some of the favorites at this popular brick-walled eatery. ◆ Italian ◆ M-F dinner; Sa-Su lunch and dinner. 42 Charles St (between Chestnut and Mount Vernon Sts). 742.FIGS. Also at: 10 City Sq (at Park and Main Sts), Charlestown. 242.1999 &

48 French Bouquet One of Boston's most inspired florists, Susan Bates uses locally grown flowers and Holland imports, as well as dried and silk varieties. Her bouquets are simply beautiful. Attentive staff willingly provide street-side service. ◆ M-Sa. 53A Charles St (between Chestnut and Mount Vernon Sts). 367.6648

48 Ristorante Toscano ★★★$$ Conscientiously patrolled by its ultracivilized owners, this brisk, friendly Florentine trattoria offers a diverting lineup of daily specials, headlining such luscious stars as carpaccio, smoked-salmon pasta, and rack of lamb. And this is one of the only places in town you're likely to encounter *bollito misto* (boiled meats). Sophisticated and self-assured, this restaurant is one of Boston's favorites. There's valet parking evenings. ◆ Italian ◆ M-Sa lunch and dinner; Su dinner. Reservations recommended. 41-47 Charles St (between Chestnut and Mount Vernon Sts). 723.4090

49 Cedar Lane Way When evening has nearly crept over the Hill, enter this skinny lane from Chestnut Street. Say hello to the cats in the windows of the tiny dwellings and try to sidestep the residents' trash cans and potted plants while you look up and admire their gardens spilling over brick retaining walls. The lane turns to cobblestones after crossing Pinckney Street and ends beneath a lantern's intimate glow. ◆ North of Chestnut St

50 Caffè Bella Vita ★$ We'll tell you up front that the service is inexplicably harried and harebrained, and the pastries and cappuccino only so-so in this redbrick storefront cafe. But take a look around, and you'll know right away why you came. Long after the last drop of espresso is a memory, people linger here gazing out at the Charles Street parade. Every table is near a plate-glass window, making this a good place to write a long letter on a winter afternoon. Plus, the *biscotti di Prato* (say "almond cookies," or you'll get a blank look) are great dunkers. ◆ Cafe ◆ Daily 9AM-midnight. No credit cards accepted. 30 Charles St (at Chestnut St). 720.4505 &

51 Rebecca's ★★★$$ Yes, it's trendy, and you won't want your heart to know how much butter the succulent monkfish is swimming in. But silence those qualms and enjoy owner Rebecca Caras's consistently sure touch with seasonal bounty, which has made this cheerful bistro such a success that she's launched little take-out satellites all over the city. Watch the chefs in the open kitchen assemble excellent omelettes, salads, and pasta concoctions, or ogle the chorus line of desserts, which always includes sky-high pies. To avoid the crush, come early for dinner while the loyal clientele are still at their health clubs. There's valet parking evenings. ◆ American/Takeout ◆ Daily lunch and dinner. Reservations recommended. 21 Charles St (between Branch and Chestnut Sts). 742.9747 &

52 Beacon Hill Thrift Shop Don't be hoity-toity about stopping in here; Boston's resourceful Brahmins would surely look askance at anyone silly enough to snub a bargain. One of Boston's oldest thrift shops, it's pleasingly cramped and cluttered with knickknacks and doodads, plus some truly fabulous finds. Manager Elizabeth Moore is always ready to make a deal, ably assisted by a loyal corps of women volunteers from the Hill. All proceeds benefit the New England Baptist Hospital League Nursing Scholarships. ◆ M-W, F-Sa. 15 Charles St (at Branch St). 742.2323

52 De Luca's Market This grocery store carries all sorts of gourmet fixings for a sumptuous picnic on the esplanade or supper by a fire. There's a little bit of everything here, and if you can't find your favorite treat, they'll order it. Of course, quality commands a high price. In business since 1905, the market wangled a wine-and-liquor license (a major feat on the Hill) some years back and purveys an extensive selection. ◆ Daily 7AM-10PM. 11 Charles St (between Beacon and Branch Sts). 523.4343. Also at: 239 Newbury St (at Fairfield St). 262.5990

53 The Hampshire House Built by **Ogden Codman** in 1909, this town house borrows from Greek and Georgian Revival and Federal styles, and is best known for housing two of Boston's most popular restaurants. ◆ 84 Beacon St (at Brimmer St)

Within The Hampshire House:

Library Grill ★★★$$$ The silver-spoon spirit still thrives in this upstairs restaurant, with the polished paneling, leather chairs, and moose heads creating a men's-club ambience. The Sunday brunch is the meal to try: The manly decor becomes more and more pleasant when the splendid eggs Benedict and crisp corned-beef hash arrive. Have a second impeccable Bloody Mary, listen to the piano music, and let the morning slip away. Return some evening with your favorite person to gaze at the **Public Garden** and gorge on exceptional European-inspired American cuisine. The menu changes seasonally, but specialties include Narragansett Bay scallop and shrimp stew, and beef tenderloin with Gulf shrimp and peppercorn sauce. There's ballroom dancing to live music on Friday and Saturday evenings. ♦ American ♦ M-Sa dinner; Su brunch and dinner. Reservations recommended for dinner. Validated parking after 4PM on weekends. 227.9600

Bull & Finch ★$ This is the basement bar that inspired the long-running TV sitcom "Cheers." All the brouhaha has eclipsed a lot of the pub's authentic charm, but if you time it right, you can sidestep the boisterous throngs of tourists and

college students. Slip in at a quiet hour for a beer and some pub-style fare (the burgers are great). One of Boston's nicest bartenders, Eddie Doyle, works here days. A DJ plays pop hits for dancing on Friday and Saturday nights. ♦ American ♦ Daily lunch and dinner. Bar: daily 11AM-1AM. 227.9605 &

54 Public Garden You can't lounge as freely on the grass here as on the **Common,** but this park is an idyllic, lush retreat that always seems larger than it truly is. Artists love the garden's manicured look, and the advertising and film communities stage photo shoots all over. Several out-of-the-way bowers offer havens from urban tumult, and there's no better place for a springtime romance to bloom.

One of the oldest botanical gardens in America, the property began as desolate, soggy salt-marsh flats located along a great bay of the Charles River estuary. Ropewalks spanned the area, and Bostonians clammed and fished when the tides allowed. In April 1775 the British soldiers embarked by boat for Lexington and Concord from a spot near the garden's **Charles Street Gate.**

There's also a remarkable history of outspoken citizen involvement enshrined in this spot. Throughout the early 1800s, real-estate developers hankered after its 24 acres, only to be thwarted again and again by vigilant citizens dreaming of a magnificent botanical park. Bostonians finally ratified a bill in 1859 that deemed the garden forever public. That same year, **George Meacham,** a local novice architect, won $100 for his English-inspired vision of a public garden dominated by a sinuous pond and ribboned with paths. His grandiloquent scheme was modestly altered in the final form. Today the garden is watched

over and beautified by "garden" angels: The Friends of the Public Garden, formed in the 1970s. Plantings change seasonally, beginning with hearty pansies and tulips that triumph over Boston's uncertain spring weather. ♦ Bounded by Charles and Arlington Sts, and Boylston and Beacon Sts

Within the Public Garden:

Footbridge Enter the garden by taking the ceremonial Haffenreffer Walk off Charles Street and step onto the spunky, whimsical footbridge, designed in 1867 by **William G. Preston.** It's an appealing exaggeration of the engineering marvel of its day—the suspension bridge. Repaired and reinforced, the bridge's spiderweb cables are only decorative now. Lean back against the baby bridge and gaze across the garden toward Beacon Street, ignoring the ugly downtown stretch in the distance along Tremont Street. From bridge-side, watch Boston's entire socioeconomic spectrum pass by on the surrounding walkways.

Swan Boats and Lagoon One of Boston's most famous sights, the **Swan Boats** cruise serenely by while dozens of chatty ducks wait for handouts on the four-foot-deep, four-acre lagoon. A pair of real swans, ceremoniously escorted to the lagoon every spring, also sail snootily about. Rowboats, canoes, and a little side-wheeler named the *Dolly Varden* once plied these waters, but the **Swan Boats** have reigned alone now for more than a century. Their creator, Robert Paget, an English immigrant and shipbuilder, was inspired by Richard Wagner's opera *Lohengrin,* in which the hero crosses a river in a boat drawn by a swan.

Paget's descendants still own the quaint fleet he launched in 1877. The 6 existing boats now carry up to 20 passengers per boat instead of the original 4, and weigh 2 tons. The oldest, *Big Bertha,* dates from 1918. Only children are thrilled by the 15-minute figure-eight voyage pedal-powered at 2 miles per hour—but if you're tired, it's a fine way to rest your feet. In the winter, the lagoon becomes a picturesque ice-skating pond. ♦ Nominal fee. Daily from mid-Apr–late Sept. Swan Boats 522.1966, skate rentals 482.7400

Plants and Trees Amble amid the colorful legacy of William Doogue, the garden's controversial superintendent from 1878 to 1906, who instituted its famous Victorian floral displays that are rotated seasonally. Some Bostonians griped about Doogue's extravagant use of showy hothouse plants, including palms, cacti, and yucca. In 1888, some 90,000 plants were laid out in 150 beds. But most people were thrilled, and Doogue's style has endured, though on a more modest scale. Nearly 600 trees of more than 100 varieties grow in the garden, most labeled with their Latin and common names, a practice inspired by the 19th-century passion for learning. The garden's weeping willows offer splendid shade for reading.

Statues Sure, some of the garden's sculpture is mediocre, but all in all it's an oddly appealing lot. The most striking statue is Charlestown native Thomas Ball's gallant *George Washington* on horseback (erected in 1869), facing Commonwealth Avenue (near the Arlington Street gate). Anecdotes tell how Ball was obsessed with accurately depicting the triumphant patriot's steed; he frequented local stables and employed a famous local charger, Black Prince, as his model. To George's right (facing Commonwealth Avenue) is the granite and red-and-white marble *Ether Fountain,* the garden's oldest monument, donated in 1867 to commemorate the first use of anesthesia, 21 years before, at Massachusetts General Hospital.

Some other statues to seek out: Facing Boylston Street are abolitionist senator *Charles Sumner* (sculpted by Thomas Ball); antislavery spokesman *Wendell Phillips* (created by Daniel Chester French in 1914; Henry Bacon designed the base); and Polish independence leader *Tadeusz Kosciuszko* (sculpted in 1927 by Theo Alice Ruggles Kitson). By the Charles Street gate is philanthropist *Edward Everett Hale* (completed in 1912 by Bela Lyon Pratt), patriot Nathan Hale's nephew. Flamboyant Unitarian preacher and transcendentalist *William Ellery Channing* (sculpted in 1903 by

Herbert Adams) faces Arlington Street. Channing's writing influenced many young authors of his day, including Ralph Waldo Emerson. Three fountain statues portray images of childhood: Near Arlington Street is sculptor Mary E. Moore's *Small Child* (erected in 1929), and near Charles Street are Anna Coleman Ladd's *Triton Babies* (erected in 1924), and *Bagheera* (erected in 1986) by Lilian Swann Saarinen, wife of architect **Eero Saarinen,** which illustrates the scene from Rudyard Kipling's *Jungle Book* in which the black panther Bagheera tries to trap an owl.

Ducklings The best-loved garden sculptures (unveiled in 1987) are Boston artist Nancy Schön's larger-than-life bronzes of Mrs. Mallard and her eight ducklings, the heroes of Robert McCloskey's illustrated children's tale *Make Way for Ducklings* (published in 1941). As the story goes, after stopping all traffic on Beacon Street, the canard clan marches off to rendezvous at the lagoon with Mr. Mallard. It's easy to spot the ducks along the path between the lagoon and the gateway at Charles and Beacon Streets—look for children sitting on them, embracing and patting them, or waddling nearby quacking. When one of the ducklings was stolen in 1989, a pair of bartenders—Eddie Doyle of the nearby **Bull & Finch** (aka "Cheers") pub and Tommy Leonard of Kenmore Square's **Eliot Lounge** started the "Bring Back Mack" fund-raising campaign. Now Mack is back with his pack.

Public Garden

Government Center/ Faneuil Hall

This part of town is not so much a neighborhood as it is a collection of interesting sights sprinkled among impersonal office towers and heavily trafficked, characterless streets. More or less bound by **State, Court,** and **Cambridge Streets** to the south, the tangle of highways at the edge of the **Charles River** to the west and north, and the **Central Artery** to the east, the main attractions here are **Faneuil Hall Marketplace,** with its blend of history and contemporary consumer delights; **Blackstone Block,** a tiny remnant of "Old Boston"; and the **FleetCenter,** home of the **Celtics** basketball team and the **Bruins** hockey team.

Established communities that once existed here were swept away during the 1960s, when the city tried to rejuvenate itself through drastic and painful urban renewal, forcing thousands of city residents to move. Architect **I.M. Pei**'s master urban design plan imposed monumental order on 56 acres: 22 streets were replaced with six; slots for big, bold new buildings were carefully plotted; and a vast plaza was created and crowned with an iconoclastic city hall symbolizing "New Boston."

The name **West End,** nearly forgotten now, at one time referred to the 48 acres stretching from the base of **Beacon Hill** to **North Station.** The West End's fashionable days ended in the 19th century, and by the 20th century many considered the area a slum. Yet more than 10,000 people—mostly Russian, Greek, Albanian, Irish, Italian, Polish, Jewish, and Lithuanian immigrants—inhabited brick row houses on the lively, intimate streets. Older Bostonians recall when Government Center was the raucous and irrepressible **Scollay Square,** where Boston's racier nightlife crowd caroused in saloons, burlesque shows, shooting galleries, adult theaters, pawnshops, tattoo parlors, and cheap hotels. Many still regret that this historic, freewheeling square was obliterated to make way for businesses and federal, state, and city offices—attracting somewhat more reputable, but much less colorful, residents.

Incredibly altered and dislocated from its past, this area now seems oddly situated. Abutting the history-drenched Waterfront, North End, and Beacon Hill, Government Center is more a passageway to other destinations than a place to linger. Only vestiges of the past remain, like **Old West Church,** the **Harrison Gray Otis House,** the **Bulfinch Pavilion** and **Ether Dome** at **Massachusetts General Hospital,** and the famous **Steaming Kettle**

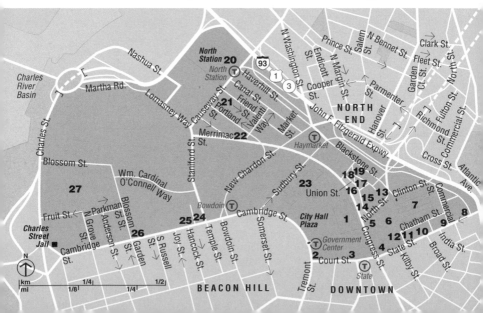

landmark. Most of the contemporary architecture has a 1960s' look, often alienating and aloof. The newest buildings still can't decide what they're doing here. The old, authentic languages, layers, color, and complexity are gone. Some say the West End's demise was necessary to let a new city image live. While it's true that much of what's gone doesn't merit mourning, it's also true that most of the new is nothing much to brag about.

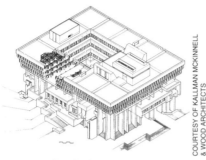

1 Boston City Hall Dramatically towering over a windswept brick plain, **Kallmann McKinnell & Wood Architects**'s massive structure (pictured above) looks precisely like what it is—a factory where Boston governmental operations crank along. **Gerhard Kallmann** and **Michael McKinnell**, also architects for the **Hynes Auditorium** in Back Bay and the **Boston Five Cents Savings Bank** on School Street, won a national competition for this project, the eye-catching centerpiece of New Boston.

Like an old warehouse, the 1968 building's exterior frankly communicates the functions and hierarchies of what's happening inside. Its sprawling, open lower levels house departments that directly serve the public, while more aloof bureaucracy is relegated to the upper floors, and the publicly account able mayor and city council offices are suspended between. Summertime concerts, public celebrations, and political events spill onto **City Hall Plaza**. Although its interior is somewhat dim and neglected looking, this municipal building remains an edifice of heroic intentions, its massing and shadows always eloquent. ◆ City Hall Plaza, Court and Cambridge Sts. 635.4000

2 Sears Crescent Building A holdover from old Scollay Square, this gracefully curving 1816 building—renovated in 1969 by **Don Stull Associates**—moderates **City Hall**'s aggressive stance and softens nine-acre **City Hall Plaza**'s impersonality. The building recalls the days when Boston streets sprouted every which way and the city didn't care that the shortest distance between two points is a straight line. Built by **David Sears**, whose Beacon Hill mansion is now the **Somerset Club**, this block was once Boston's publishing center, where Emerson, Hawthorne, and other literary types gathered.

Cozying up to this structure is the little **Sears Block** building (completed in 1848), where Boston's homey landmark, the gilded

Steaming Kettle, puffs around-the-clock. The city's oldest animated trade sign, the kettle was cast in 1873 by coppersmiths Hicks and Badger, and commissioned by the Oriental Tea Company. Fed steam by a pipe from the company's boiler room, the kettle was an instant curiosity when it was hung in Scollay Square. Its big day came when Oriental Tea held a contest to guess its mascot's capacity. Weeks of fervent speculation ended on 1 January 1875, when more than 10,000 people gathered to watch William F. Reed, City Sealer of Weights and Measures, decree the official measure of 227 gallons, two quarts, one pint, and three gills—now engraved on the kettle's side. Eight winners shared the prize: a chest of premium tea. Reporting on the event, the *Boston Sunday Times* referred to the famous Boston Tea Party and bragged, "The tea-kettle excitement has run nearly as high as the tea excitement of old, and is almost a historical incident in the career of our noble city." Once Scollay Square was razed, the kettle was relocated in 1967 to the **Sears Block**. Now a landmark, it graces a **Starbucks** coffee shop (formerly the **Steaming Kettle Coffee Shop**). ◆ 63-65 Court St (at Cambridge St)

3 Ames Building Fourteen stories high, this proud and distinctive structure—now on the National Register of Historic Places—was once the tallest office building on the Eastern seaboard. Abounding with arches, modulating from the weighty ones at the base to the delicate chain under the cornice, the vigorous building was designed in 1889 by **Henry Hobson Richardson**'s successor firm, **Shepley, Rutan, and Coolidge.** Although the great architect had died a few years earlier, his influence clearly was not forgotten, especially in the Romanesque architectural details and lacy carvings.

One of Boston's first skyscrapers, the sturdy building is supported by nine-foot-thick masonry walls, not the light-steel frame that became popular soon afterward. It's the second-tallest structure built this way in the world. The building only briefly dominated the city's skyline and is now dwarfed by 20th-century behemoths, but it exerts an enduring presence. ◆ 1 Court St (at State St)

There's only one Faneuil Hall—the brick building with the grasshopper on top—but the entire marketplace is collectively called Faneuil Hall, too. To add to the confusion, it's also known as Quincy Market (the name of the main historic market building).

THE BAY TOWER ROOM

4 Bay Tower Room ★★$$$ It's a private club by day, but come evening, this restaurant offers stunning views, festive atmosphere, and costly but good food selected "to celebrate the seasons." Located on the 33rd floor of the **Sheraton World Headquarters Building,** the dramatic dining room is an assemblage of alcoves and tiers where every table claims a view: miniaturized **Faneuil Hall Marketplace** crowds, the **Custom House Tower** with its lighted clock face nearly close enough to touch, boats crossing **Boston Harbor,** and planes circling **Logan International Airport.** (Try to arrive before sunset.) The cuisine is sometimes uneven and other times just fine, with successes including lobster ravioli, oysters, chateaubriand, grilled seafood, rack of lamb, roasted venison tenderloin, and an extraordinary fruit shortcake. There's live music nightly Monday through Saturday. Free validated parking is available under the building after 5PM; enter from Merchant's Row. ♦ American ♦ M-Sa dinner. Reservations recommended; jacket required in dining room; no jeans allowed. 60 State St (at Congress St), 33rd floor. 723.1666

4 Houlihan's $$ One in a national chain of more than 50 restaurants, this watering hole has predictable, passable food and is usually packed. It attracts a big business-lunch crowd and a major after-work singles scene. A DJ entertains nightly, Monday through Friday from 5PM to 2AM and Saturday and Sunday from 4PM to 2AM. ♦ American ♦ Daily lunch and dinner. Reservations recommended; no tank tops after 7PM. 60 State St (at Congress St). 367.6377

5 Dock Square The open area between Congress Street and **Faneuil Hall** earned its name in colonial times when it was young Boston's landing place and an important threshold to the New World. People and goods constantly passed across the square as they traveled to and from the boats docked near its edge. The town dock was eventually extended into Town Cove and later the cove was filled in to create more land. On the way to **Faneuil Hall,** look for Anne Whitney's 1880 bronze of *Samuel Adams.*
♦ Congress and North Sts

6 Faneuil Hall From the heights of the steps behind **City Hall,** look for the most familiar and beloved of Boston's many curious objects of affection: Spinning in harbor-sent breezes and glinting in the sun atop **Faneuil Hall** (pictured below) is master tinsmith Deacon Shem Drowne's gold-plated grasshopper, a weather vane modeled in 1742 after a similar one topping London's Royal Exchange. Grasshoppers symbolize good luck; and in a city where many a fine old building has been lost to fire or progress, this critter has certainly done right by **Faneuil Hall.** In 1740, when wealthy French Huguenot and English merchant Peter Faneuil offered to erect a market building for the town at his own expense, citizens voted on his proposal. It barely passed, 367 to 360, a lukewarm welcome for a landmark that has been a historic center of Boston life ever since.

Painter John Smibert designed the original structure. Built in 1742, it housed open-market stalls, a meeting hall, and offices. All were gutted by fire in 1761, but an identical building was soon rebuilt. Peddlers and politicians have always peacefully coexisted here, inspiring local poet Francis W. Hatch to write: "Here orators in ages past have mounted their attack/Undaunted by proximity of sausage on the rack." As the Revolution approached, the impassioned oratory of patriots such as Samuel Adams and James Otis fired up the populace, drawing huge crowds and earning **Faneuil Hall** the nickname "Cradle of Liberty." At a 1772 town meeting here, Adams proposed that Boston establish the Committee of Correspondence and invite the other colonies to join, thus establishing the clandestine information network that promoted united action against British repression. The hall's nickname was

Faneuil Hall

further cemented when Boston's famous antislavery orator Wendell Phillips presented his first address here in 1837. William Lloyd Garrison and Massachusetts senator Charles Sumner joined the battle for the abolitionist cause from the same rostrum.

In 1806, when the crowds just couldn't squeeze in anymore, **Charles Bulfinch** handsomely remodeled and enlarged the cramped hall.

He preserved its stalwart simplicity but doubled its width, added a floor, and created a marvelous second-floor galleried assembly room that citizen's groups use to this day. Among the room's dozens of portraits of famous Americans, look for George P.A. Healy's *Liberty and Union, Now and Forever* depicting Massachusetts senator Daniel Webster on the floor of the US Senate defending the Union in 1830 against a southern senator's contention that states could veto federal laws. Gilbert Stuart's well-known portrait of George Washington taking Dorchester Heights from the Redcoats is also here. On the third floor are the headquarters and museum of the Ancient and Honorable Artillery Company of Massachusetts (227.1638), a ceremonial organization with a proud past as the oldest military organization in the Western Hemisphere; it was chartered in 1638 by Massachusetts's first governor, John Winthrop. On display is the company's vast collection of arms, uniforms, documents, and memorabilia. The museum is open weekdays; there's no admission charge.

Back at ground level, make a quick tour of the souvenir shops and food counters that have replaced the more down-to-earth produce and feed stalls that once occupied this space. Times have changed, but the adaptable hall thrives on. Its political pulse also beats strong; during election years, contenders debate here. ♦ Daily. Faneuil Hall Sq, North St (between Clinton and Congress Sts)

Next to Faneuil Hall:

1 Faneuil Hall Square Representative of New Boston's sometimes cavalier attitude toward the city's history, this building by **Graham Gund Associates**, built in 1988, strives to relate to the other marketplace structures. But as hard as it tries, it comes off as a new kid on the block with too much style and not enough substance. Inside are branches of three national chain stores: **Abercrombie & Fitch,** featuring casual clothing for outdoorsy types; **Express,** a sportswear shop for women and men; and **Bath & Bodyworks,** an emporium selling soaps, lotions, and bath accessories. ♦ Daily. 742.6838

BosTix Stop by this outdoor kiosk to purchase tickets to many of Boston's arts and entertainment events. The tickets are half-price on the day of performance, full-price in advance. The in-person, cash-only service sells tickets for visiting Broadway shows and dozens

of local theater, dance, and music performances, plus comedy clubs, sports events, jazz concerts, campgrounds, nightclubs, dinner theaters, tourist attractions, and summer festivals. ♦ Tu-Su. Also at: Copley Sq, Dartmouth St (between St. James Ave and Boylston St); Holyoke Center, 1350 Massachusetts Ave (between Holyoke and Dunster Sts), Cambridge. 482.BTIX

7 Faneuil Hall Marketplace/Quincy Market Beyond **Faneuil Hall** stands a long, low trio of buildings (pictured on page 34) bursting with international and specialty food stalls, restaurants, cafes, boutiques, bars, and an army of pushcarts peddling wares to tempt the impulsive buyer. Officially named **Faneuil Hall Marketplace** but often called **Quincy Market** (the name of its main building), the complex offers everything from junk food to gourmet meals, kitsch to haute couture. The whole extravaganza attracts more than 14 million visitors a year, inviting comparisons to Disney World. But touristy and slick as it is, the marketplace possesses the authentic patina of history. It has lived a long, useful life, having served as a meat and produce market for more than a century and a half before its current incarnation.

The marketplace's 535-foot-long granite centerpiece, a National Historic Landmark, is **Quincy Market.** It is named for Josiah Quincy, the Boston mayor who revitalized the decrepit waterfront by ordering major landfills, six new streets, and the construction of a market house to supplement overcrowded **Faneuil Hall.** Architect **Alexander Parris** crowned the 1826 Greek Revival central building with a copper dome and planted majestic Doric colonnades at either end. The building projected a noble face seaward, for it was right at the harbor's edge in those days. Two granite-faced brick warehouses, today called the **North** and **South Markets,** later rose on either side according to **Parris's** plans. For 150 years the ensemble was the dignified venue for meat and produce wholesale distribution and storage.

By the 1970s, however, the marketplace was decaying and in danger of demolition. **Benjamin** and **Jane Thompson** of **Benjamin Thompson & Associates** convinced the city and developers that the complex could become Boston's gathering place again if it were recycled to suit contemporary urban life. The firm restored most of the marketplace in 1978, adding such innovations as festive signage and glass canopies, and transforming vegetable and meat stalls into fast-food outlets and cafes, bars and boutiques. Boston lost its waterside meat-and-potatoes–style market to colorful abundance of another sort.

The main **Quincy Market** building is now a runway of fast foods from around the world. As you stroll down the "Colonnade" (center aisle) of the alley-like building, you'll pass

33

*Faneuil Hall
Marketplace*

COURTESY OF CARLOS DINIZ ASSOCIATES

concessions selling baklava, barbecue, chowder, fudge, gourmet brownies, pizzas, salads, sausage on a stick, raw oysters, Indian pudding, french fries, ice cream—the whole gastronomic gamut. Visitors make their purchases at the individual counters and then search (often in vain) for a table in the building's large central rotunda. On the sides of **Quincy Market** are two glassed-in walk-ways filled with cafes, take-out eateries, and pushcart vendors. There's even a popular piano bar that draws a large after-work crowd that's quick to start an impromptu sing-along.

The two rows of buildings flanking **Quincy Market,** the **North** and **South Markets,** also were upgraded considerably from their original state as warehouses. The shops they now house are a mix of highbrow and informal, traditional and bizarre.

When Boston winter finally gives up, sidewalk cafes dot the cobbled pedestrian streets between the three buildings. An outdoor flower market near the north side of **Faneuil Hall** blankets the cobblestones with greenery, bringing colors and smells of each season to this corner of the city: autumn pumpkins, Christmas trees and poinsettias, spring

bunches of welcome daffodils, and summer bouquets. And crowds often gather round the cobblestoned square between **Faneuil Hall** and **Quincy Market**'s West Portico, the prime spot for musicians, jugglers, and other entertainers.

In short, the scheme to gently breathe life back into the old buildings has proven to be a fantastic success, a model for renewal projects across the country and around the world. While many people are turned off by the throngs and the "buy, buy, buy" mood of this shop-and-snack mecca, it definitely deserves a visit—if only to see the worthy old buildings and enjoy the outdoor spectacle of pedestrians and street performers. An information desk is located under the **South Canopy.** It isn't easy to spot among the pushcarts, and the staff is often indifferent, but pick up the extremely helpful printed directory. ♦ Daily. Bounded by Commercial St and Faneuil Hall Sq, and Chatham and Clinton Sts. 338.2323

Within Quincy Market:

The Comedy Connection This club attracts the under-30 crowd, especially college students, with established stand-up comedians as well as new talent. Drinks and bar food are served throughout the shows.

◆ Admission. Nightly. Credit cards accepted for advance reservations Th-Sa; cash only at the door. Second floor. 248.9700 &

Waterstone's Booksellers Located on the second floor of **Quincy Market,** this bookstore features best-sellers, periodicals, and a section devoted to Boston/New England travel. There's also a children's area, which will entertain youngsters while their parents browse. ◆ Daily. Second floor. 589.0930 & Also at: Exeter Street Theatre Building, 26 Exeter St (at Newbury St). 859.7300

Boston & Maine Fish Company Live lobster, up to a whopping 25 pounds, and other super-fresh seafood are packed for travel or shipped anywhere in the US from this retail market. The prices are high, but sometimes worth it to satisfy a hankering for fruits of the Atlantic. You can get all the fixings for an authentic New England clambake, minus the seaside pit: lobsters, steamer clams, chowder, and utensils. If you just want some steamers to take home for supper, they'll steam them while you wait. ◆ Daily. Colonnade. 723.3474, 800/626.7866

The Salty Dog Seafood Bar and Grille ★★$$ Get some of the best oysters in town, good chowder and fried clams, and other fresh and undisguised seafood in this noisy little hut of a place. There's no pastry cart here, and they don't take reservations, but you can dine alfresco from April through November. A lot of regulars stay away during the summer to avoid the inevitable throngs. ◆ Seafood/American ◆ M-Sa lunch and dinner; Su brunch and dinner. Lower level. 742.2094

Boston Chipyard The award-winning best chocolate chip cookies in town are always fresh and always delicious. Choose the traditional favorite or variations with peanut butter, extra chocolate, nuts, oatmeal, or raisins. A California mom opened the shop here more than 20 years ago, using her own recipe, a favorite of her son and his friends. Come for a late-night fix of milk and cookies. They're available by mail order, too. ◆ Daily. North Canopy. 742.9537

Within North Market:

Marketplace Cafe ★$$ Dine outdoors in the summer and in a greenhouse setting in the winter on a variety of appetizers, salads, sandwiches, and simple entrées. Light, bright, and casual, this bistro is especially festive and welcoming on warm evenings. ◆ American ◆ M-F lunch and dinner; Sa-Su brunch and dinner. Street level. 227.9660

The Marketplace Grill and Oar Bar ★★★$$ A cut above other culinary choices here, this spacious brick-walled room—

sparsely decorated with a pair of impossibly long and skinny sculls hung overhead—overlooks the marketplace hubbub and serves exemplary American cuisine at very reasonable prices. Chef Jamie Mohn presents artfully composed plates, such as a meal-unto-itself goat-cheese salad, and his improvised pastas of the day—for example, al dente fettuccine topped with grilled salmon, sun-dried tomatoes, and cool slivers of avocado—are nothing less than inspired. It's worth withstanding the allure of the market's clamoring food stands to have a studied, civilized meal in this second-story hideaway—a real find. ◆ American ◆ M-Sa lunch and dinner; Su jazz brunch. Reservations recommended. Second level. 227.1272

Durgin-Park ★★$$ Come to this restaurant for true Yankee cooking and a taste of Boston's bygone days. Don't listen to detractors who say this place is overrated; give it a try and enjoy a fast-paced, filling meal. Founded in 1827 (the same year their logo—pictured above—was drawn), this cranky, creaky, but well-loved institution dates from the marketplace's old days, when produce held the spotlight instead of today's gourmet melee. Notice the ancient plank floors and tin ceilings. Waitresses legendary for their brisk "gotta-job-to-do" manner serve raw clams and oysters, phone-book–size prime rib, starchless fish chowder, Boston scrod (with baked beans, of course), chops, steaks, fresh seafood, chicken potpie, and more solid old favorites. Just be sure to save room for the scrumptious fresh strawberry shortcake, made on the premises, or the rich Indian pudding. Everybody dines family style at tables set for 16 and decked out in red-checkered cloths. Ask about validated parking. ◆ American ◆ Daily lunch and dinner. No credit cards accepted. Second floor. 227.2038

Downstairs at Durgin-Park:

The Oyster Bar at Durgin-Park ★★$ Serving appetizers and sandwiches only, this is a great alternative to the noisy place upstairs if you want a light repast and a little calm. Try the soothing clam chowder and briny steamers. There are no tables; just the bar and counters. Dessert is not on the menu, but just ask and someone will bring it down from the restaurant. ◆ American ◆ Daily lunch and dinner. 227.2038

The Women's Heritage Trail

The achievements and contributions of women have enriched the city of Boston for almost four centuries, yet the significance of women and their stories has often been overlooked. The Boston **Women's Heritage Trail,** established in 1990, is an attempt to remedy that situation. In a city known for its walking tours, the development of a women's trail seemed a natural way to trace women's rightful place in the history of Boston. Seven walks have been established, each one focusing on a particular neighborhood: **Downtown,** the **North End, South Cove/Chinatown, Beacon Hill,** the **South End, Jamaica Plain,** and **Roxbury.** The trails are described in a self-guided tour booklet, which includes maps of the sites and details about the women associated with each; the booklet available at some bookstores and at the shop of the **National Park Service Center** (15 State St, at Devonshire St, 242.5642). A description of the four trails located in central areas of Boston follows:

Downtown: The Search For Equal Rights

Boston's early–17th-century struggles over religious freedom are examined in this walk through the stories of Anne Hutchinson and Mary Dyer. Statues of the two women—to date, the only public statues of women anywhere in Boston—stand in front of the **Massachusetts State House** on Beacon Hill. Plaques affixed to the statues briefly outline the women's lives. Anne Hutchinson (1591-1643) and her husband, William, arrived in Boston on 18 September 1634. They built a home on the site of the original **Old Corner Bookstore.** Anne Hutchinson became popular, prominent, and powerful, and respected as a midwife—she herself had 15 children. She was a brilliant thinker and a leader of the controversial Antinomian sect, which took issue with prevailing Puritan thought. Hutchinson believed that men and women could receive grace only from God, and accused the ministers of preaching that "good works" signified holiness. She was taken to court for her beliefs and in 1637 was banished for heresy. Like most religious refugees of the era, she and her family fled to Rhode Island.

Like her friend Anne Hutchinson, Mary Dyer, a mother of five, disagreed with the all-male Puritan ministry. She was twice banished to Rhode Island. The third time she returned to Boston (in 1660), she was hanged.

Also covered in the Downtown walk is Phillis Wheatley (1753-84), the first published African-American woman poet. Soon after arriving in Boston in 1761 on the slave ship *Philli,* the young girl was purchased at auction by the Wheatley family. Her mistress, Suzannah Wheatley, became her mentor, and by 1771 the former slave had become a member of the **Old South Meeting House.** In 1773 Phillis gained international fame when her book of poems was published. In 1784, at about the age of 30, she died destitute. The museum at the **Old South Meeting House** has an exhibit about her life and a copy of her book of poems.

North End: A Diversity of Cultures

This walk spans Boston history from Revolutionary times to the influx of immigrants during the 19th and early 20th centuries. It focuses on the lives of women from the variety of ethnic groups that populated the North End during that period. Beginning with Yankee women active in support of the Revolutionary War (such as Rachel Walker Revere, the resourceful spouse of patriot Paul Revere), it continues with the activities of the Irish (including Rose Fitzgerald Kennedy who was born here), Jewish, and Italian women who made the North End their first home in Boston.

South Cove/Chinatown: Action For Economic and Social Justice

The lives of the three Peabody sisters are the focus of this tour. Elizabeth who introduced kindergartens to Boston, ran a bookshop at 15 West Street (today, **West Street Grill**). Her younger sisters were each married in the family parlor behind the store: Sophia, an artist, became the wife of author Nathaniel Hawthorne, and Mary, an educator, became the wife and associate of educator Horace Mann.

Beacon Hill: Writers, Artists, and Activists

This journey traces the ways in which women writers and artists living on Beacon Hill used their talents to further social causes—from the abolition of slavery to peace movements. Also covered here are the stories of African-American women who were abolitionists, among them Edmonia Lewis, a well-known sculptor, and Harriet Hayden, a survivor and then activist in the "underground railroad." Hayden and her husband, also an escaped slave, owned a house on Beacon Hill at 66 Phillips Street. When she died in 1893, Harriet bequeathed a scholarship for "needy and worthy colored students" to **Harvard Medical School.**

Although not based on the **Women's Heritage Trail** specifically, two free guided walking tours that also focus on women are available. Park rangers (242.5642) give tours of sites on **Boston Common** and adjacent streets that have connections with Louisa May Alcott, Julia Ward Howe, Lucy Stone, Elizabeth Peabody, Margaret Fuller, Mary Dyer, Anne Hutchinson, "Mother" Elizabeth Goose, and Phillis Wheatley. In addition, **Boston National Historical Park** rangers (242.5688) offer a tour called "Remembering the Women," which features women during the American Revolution period, in particular Abigail Adams and Rachel Revere.

Geoclassics Featuring an unusually broad array of fossils, minerals, and gemstones, this shop offers simple and tasteful necklaces and rings as well as semiprecious stones set in silver or gold. Though owner Claudio Kraus prices some children's offerings at $1 or $2, other pieces can run $1,000 and up. There are also some unusual paperweights and more run-of-the-mill sundries. ♦ Daily. Street level. 523.6112

Zuma's Tex-Mex Cafe ★$$ Subdued it's not—the very first sight that greets visitors as they enter this basement cafe is a sandpit artfully sporting an O'Keeffe-style cattle skull. The small, packed space is abuzz with neon accents and scattered video monitors broadcasting surfer tapes. Owner Steve Immel's mission—to serve "foods of the sun"—is carried out in a menu that offers everything from sizzling fajitas and quesadillas zapped with hot, hot, hot sauce to Italian pasta and Japanese teriyaki. Try one of the fresh-fruit "neon" margaritas. ♦ Tex-Mex/International ♦ Daily lunch and dinner. Basement. 367.9114

Within South Market:

Whippoorwill A standout among the independent stores that have found a home in the market, this subterranean crafts shop tends to specialize in the whimsical. Mixed in among the kaleidoscopes, chimes, woven clothes, and other staples are such oddities as Josh and Michael Cohen's heart-bedecked ceramic condom boxes—"the perfect gift for the safety-conscious 1990s." This is a good place to look for such one-of-a-kind tokens of affection. ♦ Daily. Basement. 523.5149

8 Marketplace Center This gauche gate-crashing building—erected in 1985 by the **WZMH Group**—tries to look as if it belongs on this important historic site, even mimicking its venerable neighbors somewhat in materials and style. While it could have been worse, the building is awkward, especially its graceless atrium gateway with makeup-mirror–style fixtures. Although the opening preserves the pedestrian walk-to-the-sea leading to Boston

Harbor at **Waterfront Park,** the too-tall, too-wide building creates a barrier where none existed before. The marketplace's stockpile of shops includes many chain stores like **Brookstone, Banana Republic, Mrs. Fields' Cookies, Williams-Sonoma, The Gap,** and more. ♦ 200 State St (between Atlantic Ave and Commercial St). 478.2030

Within Marketplace Center:

Doubleday Book Shop Spacious and bright, with a friendly staff, this link in the nationwide chain carries books for the general public, with strong sections in fiction, cooking, and local information. It's convenient, too, since bookstores in this neighborhood are scarce. Pick up some reading material to accompany a take-out lunch from **Quincy Market.** ♦ Daily. Street level. 439.0196. Also at: Prudential Center, 800 Boylston St (between Exeter and Dalton Sts), Street level. 536.2606

Chocolate Dipper Watch thick streams of fragrant, gooey chocolate blending away here while the staff readies luscious fresh fruit and truffles for dipping. Try strawberries, raspberries, cherries, grapes, banana, pineapple, or orange slices enrobed in dark, milk, or white chocolate. The extra-rich truffles come in more than a half-dozen flavors, and a wide variety of other chocolates are also made on the premises. ♦ Daily. Street level. 439.0190. Also at: Washington and School Sts. 227.0309

9 The Black Rose ★$ Its name is the English translation of *Roisin Dubh,* a Gaelic allegorical name for Ireland that symbolizes the repression of Irish Catholics by the British. Famous Irish faces and mementos line the walls, and Irish music accompanies bargain-priced homestyle meals such as meat loaf, lamb stew, fish-and-chips, Yankee pot roast, and boiled lobster (don't look for gourmet here). The big, hospitable bar offers numerous Irish beers and stout on tap and there's live Irish music nightly. It's a great place to meet friends after work, sing along with some folk musicians, watch a **Celtics** game on the big-screen TV, or linger over a pint of Guinness or an Irish coffee. ♦ Irish-American ♦ Daily lunch and dinner. 160 State St (at Commercial St). 742.2286

10 Cunard Building The boldly inscribed name on this Classical Revival building built in 1901 by **Peabody and Stearns** recalls another bright moment in Boston's past. The building was once the headquarters for the famous Cunard Steamship Line, which pioneered transatlantic steamship routes. Boston was proud to beat out New York City as the first American city to enjoy the innovative service. Nautical motifs aplenty—crowned Poseidon heads, anchor-and-dolphin lighting stanchions, a wavelike ornamental band—add an adventurous air to an otherwise sober structure. ♦ 126 State St (between Chatham and Merchants Rows)

Clarke's

11 Clarke's $$ On one side, there's a big neighborly saloon where crowds flock to watch sports events on TV, eye prospective dates, or wind down after work; on the other, a comfortable, no-frills restaurant and bar where you can order straightforward New England dishes like broiled scrod, or big sandwiches and burgers with a side of great fries. A shuttle bus takes patrons to **FleetCenter** events. Co-owner Dave DeBusschere, formerly of the **New York Knicks,** sometimes drops by to watch the **Celtics** play. ♦ American ♦ Daily lunch and dinner. Reservations recommended for large parties. 21 Merchants Row (at Chatham St). 227.7800

12 Bertucci's ★★$ Another spacious outpost of the very popular local pizza and pasta chain, this branch hops in tune with nearby **Faneuil Hall Marketplace.** Count on tasty fresh pizzas, calzones, and salads. Look for the fun mural, depicting pizza-making, above the bar. ♦ Pizza/Italian/Takeout ♦ Daily lunch and dinner. 22 Merchants Row (north of State St). 227.7889. Also at: 21 Brattle St (between Palmer and Church Sts), Cambridge. 864.4748

13 Blackstone Block A charming snippet of Old Boston, this tiny neighborhood is laced with winding lanes and alleys whose names— Salt Lane, Marsh Lane, and Creek Square— recall an era when water still flowed here. The block's history dates to colonial times; its architecture spans the 18th, 19th, and 20th centuries. People, chickens, geese, hogs, garbage, and carts laden with goods from nearby ships once commingled on the block's dirt streets. This area was once on the narrow neck of land—frequently under water—that led from Shawmut Peninsula to the North End. Meat markets flourished here throughout the city's history, and still do along Blackstone Street, named for Boston's first settler William Blaxton (his name was spelled both ways). ♦ Bounded by Blackstone and Union Sts, and North and Hanover Sts

13 Regal Bostonian Hotel $$$ Intimate and gracious, this hostelry is one of the most pleasant places to stay in Boston. Much of the charm comes from its residential scale and the way it blends with 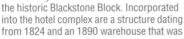 the historic Blackstone Block. Incorporated into the hotel complex are a structure dating from 1824 and an 1890 warehouse that was built by **Peabody and Stearns** (architects for the **Custom House Tower**). Many of the 152 rooms have French doors opening onto private balconies that overlook **Faneuil Hall Marketplace.** Six honeymoon suites have Jacuzzis and working fireplaces, and two of the rooms have canopy beds. The lobby is appealingly low-key, with historic displays on permanent loan from the Bostonian Society. There's a first-rate restaurant on the premises (see below), and the airy **Atrium** cocktail lounge is a comfortable place to snack on appetizers and listen to live jazz (no jeans or sneakers allowed). Amenities include baby-sitting and complimentary overnight shoe shines. Nonsmoking floors are available, as are rooms equipped for people with hearing impairments. At press time the hotel owner, Regal Hotels International, was renovating 109 existing guest rooms and an adjacent building that will house 47 new guest rooms and meeting space. ♦ North and Blackstone Sts. 523.3600, 800/343.0922; fax 523.2454 &

Within the Regal Bostonian Hotel:

Seasons ★★★★$$$$ The swank, glass-enclosed dining room atop the hotel offers generous cityscapes and marvelous views of **Quincy Market**'s gold dome, the famous **Faneuil Hall** weather vane, and the **Custom House Tower**'s glowing clock; newcomers to Boston are sure to be dazzled. This dining spot is famous as a training ground for Boston's top chefs (Lydia Shire, Jasper White, Gordon Hamersley, et al). An avatar of the new wave of "healthy gourmet" cuisine, current chef Peter McCarthy uses flavor-infused oils and vinegars in lieu of heavy sauces, and the results scintillate. As befits its name, **Seasons'** menu changes quarterly but has featured such New England and international treats as duckling with ginger and scallions, roasted rack of lamb and pumpkin couscous, baked swordfish with olive compote, and wild mushroom tartlet. Service is gracious. The award-winning, all-American wine list is impressive, and the staff ably recommends. The billowy ceiling balloon shades add a romantic touch, and piano music filters up from the **Atrium** lounge. Politicos and businesspeople come here for power breakfasts. There's valet parking. ♦ American ♦ Daily breakfast, lunch, and dinner. Reservations recommended; no jeans or sneakers at dinner. 523.9970

14 Statues of Mayor Curley Follow North Street to an amiable little park tucked between Union and Congress Streets, which features two statues of Boston's controversial but beloved mayor James Michael Curley (1874-1958) by Lloyd Lillie. In one, Curley is seated on a bench in a very approachable pose; many a photo has been taken over the years of the mayor "chatting" with whomever plops down next to him. The other statue portrays an upright Curley as the man of action and orator. Four times mayor, four times congressman, and former Massachusetts governor, Curley was born in Boston's South End. Truly a self-made man, this flamboyant politician gave Bostonians plenty to admire, gossip about, and remember him by. Curley smoothly ran Boston's infamous and powerful Irish political machine, inspiring poet Francis W. Hatch to quip, "Vote often and early for Curley." Edwin O'Connor had Curley in mind when he wrote *The Last Hurrah.* But Curley was also known as the "Mayor of the Poor," and his civic contributions included establishing **Boston City Hospital.** ♦ Union Park, North St (between Union and Congress Sts)

15 Marshall House ★★$$ When the **Union Oyster House** (see below) is too crowded or too much for your wallet, come to this popular spot. You may still have a wait, but it won't be as long. This place actually opened in 1982, yet manages to look as if it had been here a century, with plenty of brass and wood. Eat informally at the bar or bar tables, or in the snug rear dining room. Start off with selections from the raw bar—oysters, steamers, cherrystones, littlenecks—and proceed with fresh seafood entrées prepared in the open kitchen in the middle of the restaurant. There are two lobster specials every day, a wide choice of beers, and big burgers and sandwiches. You can't make a reservation, so leave your name and take a stroll around **Faneuil Hall Marketplace;** you won't be bored. ♦ Seafood/American ♦ Daily lunch and dinner. 15 Union St (between North St and Salt La). 523.9396

16 New England Holocaust Memorial Dedicated in 1995, the 50th anniversary year of the end of World War II, the memorial is a result of a group effort by Nazi concentration camp survivors who now reside in the Boston area. The memorial features six five-story glass towers, each representing the gas chambers of the major Nazi death camps in Europe. The stark memorial is the work of San Francisco architect **Stanley Saitowitz.** Etched on green-tinted glass panels are the numbers one to six million to represent the number of Jews killed in the Holocaust. Also etched on the panels are quotations and stories from Holocaust survivors. Saitowitz sought to create a memorial that was ambiguous, open-ended, and hopeful—like freedom itself. ♦ Union Park, Congress St (between North and Hanover Sts) ♿

A Boston Tradition

17 Union Oyster House ★★$$$ Dine in one of the few spots in Boston where time simply refuses to move forward. The city's oldest restaurant (founded circa 1715) and the oldest in continuous operation in the US, this eatery has served seafood at this spot since 1826.

When the restaurant's original owners opened their oyster-and-clam bar, they installed the current half-circle mahogany bar that supposedly became Daniel Webster's favorite haunt. Webster reputedly downed each half-dozen oysters with a tumbler of brandy and water, and usually consumed six platefuls at a sitting.

Today this is truly a one-of-a-kind place, best on a cold winter's day when you can follow chilled oysters with steaming chowder or oyster stew and your choice of a wide range of fresh seafood entrées. The first-floor booths are the original ones, with a plaque adorning the booth where JFK liked to dine. Even if you don't stop to eat, look in the window and watch the oyster-shucking at the bar. ♦ Seafood/American ♦ Daily lunch and dinner. Reservations recommended. 41 Union St (at Marshall St). 227.2750 ♿ (first floor only)

18 Bell in Hand Tavern $ Operating since 1795, though not always at this site, this is the oldest tavern in the US. Its moniker is illustrated by the curious old sign on its plain facade, much like pubs in Great Britain. It was named by original proprietor Jim Wilson, Boston's town crier until 1794, who rang a bell as he progressed through town announcing the news. Benjamin Franklin's childhood home once stood on this site. On a cold afternoon, duck in for a draft beer and an appetizer, burger, or sandwich. (Kitchen hours vary, so food isn't always available.) ♦ American ♦ Daily. 45 Union St (between Marshall and Hanover Sts). 227.2098

The Boston Stone, set in the foundation of a shop on Marshall Street, is a millstone brought from England during the 1600s. Originally used to grind colored powders into paint, it became to Boston what its counterpoint, the London Stone, was to that city—the official point from which all distances from Boston were measured.

Pronunciations of "Faneuil" abound, with little agreement about which is correct. Is it Fan-yool, Fannel, Fan-*you*-ill, Fan-*yul,* or Fan-*ee*-yul? Who knows? But the first two are by far the most common.

Boston's Tea Parties

Few would disagree that as tea parties go, Boston's is the best known. The only contender might be the Mad Hatter's in Lewis Carroll's *Alice in Wonderland*. But that was fantasy—unlike the Boston Tea Party during which 340 chests of fine tea shipped from England were dumped into **Boston Harbor,** forever linking the city with tea.

Once the war was over, Bostonians once again sought the pleasurable ritual of afternoon tea practiced for centuries by their British ancestors. Today there are still a number of spots in Boston where visitors can indulge in their own "tea parties."

The Boston Harbor Hotel Not far from the site of the original Boston Tea Party, this hotel serves tea in the **Harborview Lounge** overlooking the waterfront. Be sure to choose one of the pie-crust–shaped tables by the windows, which offer a view of the harborfront cruise ships and water shuttles tied up outside. The low-ceilinged room is large and furniture is on the grand scale; classical music plays in the background. The complete tea includes warm scones, clotted Devonshire cream, and fruit preserves. ♦ M-F 2:30-4:30PM. Rowes Wharf, Atlantic Ave (between Northern Ave and East India Row), No. 70. 439.7000

The Boston Park Plaza Hotel Afternoon tea is offered in **Swan's Court,** located at the far end of the handsome lobby. Finger sandwiches, tea cake, scones, and fresh sliced strawberries with whipped cream accompany your choice of tea. ♦ Daily 3-5PM. 64 Arlington St (between Columbus Ave and Park Plaza). 426.2000

The Four Seasons Hotel Traditional afternoon tea is served in the spacious **Bristol Lounge.** The setting is refined yet relaxed, the service gracious. Finger sandwiches, Viennese pastries, scones, and English tea breads are served separately, after a choice has been made from the broad choice of regular, herbal, and decaffeinated teas. Tea here (rather than drinks after work) has become a favorite meeting option among the local business community. For leisurely lingerers, live piano music begins at 5PM. ♦ Daily 3-5:30PM. 200 Boylston St (between Charles St S and Hadassah Way). 338.4400

The Ritz-Carlton Hotel This hotel has been offering formal afternoon tea since it opened in 1927. Tea is taken on the second floor in **The Lounge,** an interior room with the intimate atmosphere of a comfortable drawing room. The lime, pink, and cream decor has appealing sconce and lamplighting, and the walls are hung with 19th-century oil paintings. A harpist provides a backdrop to the hushed conversations appropriate to the occasion. The ingredients for a full tea come to the table attractively arranged on a multitiered compote. Service begins with a selection of open-face sandwiches —miniature works of art that are tasty as well as pretty—followed by tea breads, pastries, and scones with clotted cream and strawberry preserves. ♦ Daily 3-5:30PM. 15 Arlington St (between Newbury St and Commonwealth Ave). 536.5700

18 Green Dragon Tavern ★$ First opened in 1657, this place was once deemed "the headquarters of the Revolution" by Sam Adams, Daniel Webster, and Paul Revere. Occupying British soldiers kept a close watch on the tavern, but the Sons of Liberty were nevertheless able to plan the Boston Tea Party here. Today, the old place is authentically Irish in ambience, complete with wood-plank floors and lace-curtained windows. Popular menu specials include Irish beef stew, beer-batter fish-and-chips, Irish bangers and mash, and a superb Irish grill. There are 13 varieties of beer on draft. ♦ Irish/American ♦ Daily lunch and dinner until 2AM. 11 Marshall St (between Union and Hanover Sts). 367.0055

19 Ebenezer Hancock House This three-story redbrick house (one of Boston's rare surviving late–18th-century downtown residences), was probably completed in 1767 by John Hancock's uncle, Thomas, from whom John later inherited it. Here John's younger brother, Ebenezer, lived and maintained his office as deputy paymaster of the Continental Army. His biggest duty came in 1778, when Admiral D'Estaing's fleet conducted two million silver coins from King Louis XVI of France to pay local troops, salvaging their morale. Restored, the house is now lawyers' offices and not open to the public. ♦ 10 Marshall St (at Creek Sq)

19 The Haymarket On Friday and Saturday a fleet of pushcart vendors selling fruit, vegetables, and fish sets up for open-air business along Blackstone Street. The narrow sidewalk is clogged with veteran shoppers making their rounds and bewildered novices trying to learn the ropes. Saturday is busiest. Come for bargains, especially at the end of the day, but be forewarned that the vendors, many of them North Enders, will treat you brusquely if you pick over their merchandise selectively. *They* fill the bags; you just pay, European style. So what if a tomato or two is worse for the wear? It's satisfying to avoid the supermarkets' boring sterility. When the market finally winds down for the day, squashed produce and scattered cartons make passage here challenging, but the place is soon restored for the next day's deluge. Along this stretch of Blackstone Street are old establishments like the **Puritan Deef Company** and **Pilgrim Market,** which purvey meats and cheeses that complement the **Haymarket**'s offerings. There's also a great greasy stand-and-eat pizza place. ♦ F-Sa dawn–mid-afternoon. Blackstone St (between Creek Sq and Hanover St)

20 North Station Trains operating from here transport eager sports fans and daily flocks of commuters from the North Shore. In the summertime, the station rings with voices, as cheerful crowds await the beach train (the route stopping at Beverly, Manchester, Gloucester, Rockport, and other towns with spacious public beaches). Across from the station's main entrance is **MBTA**'s *Green Line,* which carries riders in and out of central Boston. ♦ Causeway St (between Beverly St and Lomasney Way). 723.3200

At North Station:

FleetCenter This $160 million state-of-the-art home to the **Boston Celtics** and **Boston Bruins** opened in the 1995–96 season. The spectacular 755,000–square-foot arena and entertainment complex rests above the new **MBTA** parking garage. Like its beloved predecessor, the **Boston Garden,** the arena hosts such family events as the circus and the **Ice Capades** as well as concerts year-round. Unlike the **Garden,** however, the arena offers air-conditioning and access by both elevator and escalator. The **Garden**'s famous parquet floor—built during World War II when only short wood was available—was moved to the arena, along with a rafterful of championship banners (and retired numbers of legendary **Celtics** Bill Russell, Bob Cousy, John Havlicek, and Larry Bird, and **Bruins** Bobby Orr, Johnny Bucyk, and Phil Esposito). The center, highly visible from both north and south, features grand-scaled windows looking out over the city's inner harbor. After the game, head over to the **Commonwealth Brewing Company** (see below); or just follow die-hard fans to nearby bars. ♦ Recorded information 624.1000 ♿

21 Hilton's Tent City The name is no empty boast. What began as a modest army surplus store in 1947 has ballooned into the biggest and best source of tents, with five floors holding the largest tent display in the country and complete accessories for camping and backpacking. It also sells men's and women's clothing for skiing, mountaineering, and backpacking, as well as hiking, work, and sporty boots and shoes (no running shoes or sneakers). Remember the old hardware store in your hometown? This is that kind of funky, dusty place packed with indispensable bargains—it guarantees the lowest prices around on all its stock. ♦ Daily. 272 Friend St (between Valenti Way and Causeway St). 227.9242

22 101 Merrimac Street Boston's first faux-historic building, a 10-story office complex that looks like a conglomeration of rehabbed warehouses, was, in fact, designed from scratch by **The Architects Collaborative** in 1991. Duck inside to catch New York muralist Richard Haas's trompe l'oeil palm court, a domed winter garden eked out of two dimensions. The ubiquitous **au bon pain** (248.9441) has a small cafe here, should you wish to rest and nosh a while. ♦ At Lancaster St

22 Commonwealth Brewing Company ★$ "Let no man thirst for the lack of real ale" is the motto here. This working brewery and restaurant produces 10 or so kinds of English ale on the premises, including the acclaimed Boston's Best Burton Bitter, all dispensed on tap at the appropriate 52 degrees. The cavernous main level glows with copper fixtures, pipes, and tables (polished nightly), and huge tanks of beer. In the downstairs tap room, redolent with fermenting yeast, you can watch the brewing process through glass walls. Light meals, ribs, and snacks are available, but the main attraction is definitely the ale. A lot of people come here before and after games at **FleetCenter,** and needless to say, it gets pretty noisy. There's live music Saturday nights. ♦ American ♦ Daily lunch and dinner. 138 Portland St (between Valenti Way and Causeway St). 523.8383 ♿

Old West Church, now a church again, served as a branch of the Boston Public Library as recently as 1960. It was the polling place where John F. Kennedy, himself a candidate, voted in the presidential election that year.

While a prisoner at Charles Street Jail in 1904, legendary Boston mayor James Michael Curley ran for the city's board of aldermen and won. Curley was serving time for taking a postal exam for a friend.

23 John F. Kennedy Federal Office Building
Indifferent and impersonal in appearance, this one-million-square-foot building designed in 1967 by **The Architects Collaborative** (**Walter Gropius**'s firm) and **Samuel Glaser Associates**, is a perfectly appropriate home for the Internal Revenue Service, the Federal Bureau of Investigation, and many of the other federal agencies one doesn't want to tangle with. A Robert Motherwell mural marks the spot where the 26-story tower is connected to its long, low-rise mate. ♦ Sudbury St (between Congress and Cambridge Sts)

24 Old West Church
A 1737 wood-framed church stood on this site until the British razed it in 1775, suspicious that Revolutionary sympathizers were using the steeple to signal the Continental troops in Cambridge. The decorous redbrick Federal replacement, a National Historic Landmark designed by **Asher Benjamin** in 1806, is kin to **Charles Bulfinch**'s **Massachusetts State House** and **St. Stephen's Church,** and Benjamin's **Charles Street Meeting House**—all flat-surfaced and delicately ornamented with classical motifs. Formerly Unitarian and now Methodist, the church exudes quiet composure along Cambridge Street's physical and architectural chaos. Inquire about concerts featuring the fine Charles Fisk pipe organ. ♦ Daily; Su service 11AM. 131 Cambridge St (at Lynde St). 227.5088

Boston, an elision of St. Botolph's Town, was named after the English Lincolnshire town, which in turn was named for the patron saint of fishing, whose name was derived from *bot* (boat) and *ulph* (help).

The first regularly issued American newspaper, *The Boston News-Letter,* was published in 1704.

MARJORIE VOGEL, RHODE ISLAND ORIGINALS

25 Harrison Gray Otis House
This 1796 house—a trial run for Otis and his architect-of-choice—was the first in a series of three increasingly lavish residences that **Charles Bulfinch** designed for his friend (who had a taste for flamboyant living and fine architecture). Otis lived here for just four years before moving his family to grander quarters on Mount Vernon Street, followed by another move to Beacon Street. When he lived in house number one, Harry Otis was a prestigious lawyer and freshman member of Congress. He ultimately became Boston's third mayor and a major land speculator who transformed rustic Beacon Hill into a wealthy enclave, again with **Bulfinch**'s help. Set in what was briefly fashionable Bowdoin Square, this Federalist mansion is austerely handsome, much more opulent inside than out. By the end of the 19th century, Bowdoin Square's elegance had frayed away, and Otis's former home endured a spotty career as a women's Turkish bath, then a patent medicine shop, and finally a boarding house defaced with storefronts.

In 1916 the **Society for the Preservation of New England Antiquities (SPNEA)** acquired the house—now one of 34 New England properties the group runs—and meticulously restored its former splendor. The society is now headquartered here, and the building houses the **SPNEA**'s fabulous architectural and photographic archives. Tours of the interior are available. The house's decor dates from 1790 to 1820 and includes some Otis family belongings. With its next-door neighbor, the **Old West Church,** the **Otis House** is a reminder of the early years of the Republic; the two are lonely survivors who refuse to be overwhelmed by their high-rise surroundings. ♦ Admission. Tu-Sa. Guided 40-minute tours on the hour; groups limited to 15, by reservation only. 141 Cambridge St (at Lynde St). 227.3956

26 Holiday Inn–Government Center $$
Adjacent to **Massachusetts General Hospital,** this 15-story hotel has 300 rooms, with the nicest on the **Executive Level.** There's an outdoor pool, and rooms for nonsmokers and people with disabilities are available. **Foster's Bar and Grill,** located across from the hotel lobby, offers a complete breakfast, lunch, and

dinner menu. The location is convenient for sightseers, who can easily walk to **Faneuil Hall Marketplace** or cross Cambridge Street and meander over to Beacon Hill. Discounted parking is also available. ♦ 5 Blossom St (at Cambridge St). 742.7630, 800/465.4329; fax 742.7804 &

27 Massachusetts General Hospital
Although a hospital is rarely a voluntary destination, this medical center—widely considered to be the nation's best general hospital —is worth a look.

The main hospital building, the **George R. White Memorial Building** on Fruit Street, was built in 1939 by **Coolidge, Shepley, Bulfinch, and Abbott.** The late–Art Deco structure is now a city landmark. The most noteworthy edifice in the medical complex, however, is the **Bulfinch Pavilion.** To find this National Historic Landmark amid the "**Mass General**" maze, enter from North Grove Street off Cambridge Street, or ask directions in the main hospital building.

In 1817 Boston's trailblazing architect **Charles Bulfinch** won the commission to create this edifice of Chelmsford granite, quarried by inmates of the state prison. Questions persist about Bulfinch's actual role in the pavilion commission, since it was his last project before he was called to Washington, DC, by the president to design the Capitol rotunda. His assistant, **Alexander Parris**—who later gained fame in his own right, particularly for designing **Quincy Market**—prepared the working drawings and supervised construction, probably influencing the pavilion's final form much more than its name suggests. Delayed by the War of 1812, the cornerstone was laid in 1818 and the first patient was admitted in 1821. Today the building is still used for patient care, offices, and research.

Progressive for its day and gracefully proportioned, the Greek Revival building's enduring fame derives from the medical achievements that took place in the amphitheater beneath the skylit dome. It was in this theater, the hospital's operating room from 1821 to 1867 (now called the **Ether Dome**), that the first public demonstration of the use of ether in a surgical procedure took place. On 16 October 1846, Dr. John C. Warren, cofounder of the hospital and its first surgeon, operated on a patient suffering from a tumor in his jaw. A dentist named Thomas Green Morton administered the ether with his own apparatus, after supposedly almost missing the operation because he was having last-minute adjustments made to the inhaler device. When the procedure was finally finished, the patient awoke and said he had felt no pain. Dr. Warren proudly announced to his colleagues, "Gentlemen, this is no humbug." Within a year, ether was in use worldwide to prevent surgical pain. Not only does the amphitheater house memories of medical success, it's also home to *Padihershef,* a mummy brought here from Thebes, Egypt, in 1823. It was the first Egyptian mummy in the US. The hospital's original fund-raiser, *Padihershef* is also the only remaining witness to the **Ether Dome**'s finest moments. To visit the **Ether Dome**, call ahead to be sure it's not in use. ♦ 55 Fruit St (between N Grove and Charles Sts). 726.2000

Bests

Susan Park
President, Boston Harborfest

Trinity Church (Back Bay): organ concerts on Friday in the winter.

Commonwealth Avenue (Back Bay): walking up the avenue in the spring with the magnolias in bloom.

The Cyclorama (South End): attending the flea markets and finding a treasure.

Symphony Hall (Fenway): attending a concert.

Maison Robert (Downtown): a leisurely summer lunch in the outdoor cafe.

Ed Gordon
Executive Director, Gibson House Museum/President, Victorian Society in America, New England Chapter

Chatting with friends in the courtyard at a **Gibson House Museum** "Twilight Talks" reception.

Admiring "painted ladies" in Boston neighborhoods during **Victorian Society** walking tours.

Visiting art galleries on **Newbury Street.**

Antiquing on **Charles Street.**

Browsing and buying collectibles at the **Cyclorama Flea Market** in the **South End.**

Lining up at the **Commonwealth Pier** on a hot summer morning for the ferry to **Provincetown.**

Watching the sun stream through the aquamarine opalescent stained glass of **Trinity Church**'s Ascension window.

Watching the world go by while enjoying a Sam Adams beer at **Milano's Italian Kitchen** on Newbury Street.

Buying fresh flowers and homemade desserts at the fall **Copley Square Farmers Market.**

Drinking Irish beer and dining at the authentic 1880s **Doyle's Cafe** in **Jamaica Plain.**

Visiting artist lofts during the annual **Fort Point Channel,** South End, and **Cambridgeport** open studios tours.

Strolling through the grounds of **Mount Auburn Cemetery** in the spring and fall.

The Vietnamese restaurants and stores of the **Harvard Avenue** area in **Allston.**

North End

You'll know you've wandered into the North End when you hear the plangent strains of a tenor solo wafting over the virtually untrafficked streets. North Enders know that if they ever *move* their cars in this most densely populated section of Boston, their precious parking spots will be lost; hence the curbside stasis. However, the sidewalks—in what today is possibly America's most Italian neighborhood, even with gentrification—are abuzz with impassioned food shoppers and venerated elders who, in summer, haul their lawn chairs down to the sidewalks to create an alfresco living room. Gala window displays brighten up the endless rows of redbrick facades, monotonous except at street level, and alluring aromas from *pasticcerie, trattorie, ristoranti, mercati,* and *caffè* escape into the tangled streets. The happy banter of children, who effortlessly switch between English and Italian depending on whether they're talking to school friends or family, can be heard throughout. And within this insular, fiercely proud Italian enclave winds the red ribbon of the **Freedom Trail**, directing tourists to the **Paul Revere House**, the **Old North Church**, and other vestiges of colonial Boston.

This is the spirited, colorful, bursting-at-the-seams North End. Don't even attempt to come here by car. It's best reached on foot by a somewhat ignominious route: From the **Haymarket** subway stop (on the *Green* or *Orange Lines*), a short pedestrian tunnel sneaks under the elevated **Fitzgerald Expressway**, commonly called the **Central Artery**. Your path may be gritty and noisy, but you'll be cheered on by children's mosaics in the tunnel walls, and outdoor murals that greet visitors at **Cross Street** on the North End side of the expressway.

The heart of this vivacious, voluble district is Mediterranean, but Italians have held sway here only since 1920 or so. This is Boston's original neighborhood,

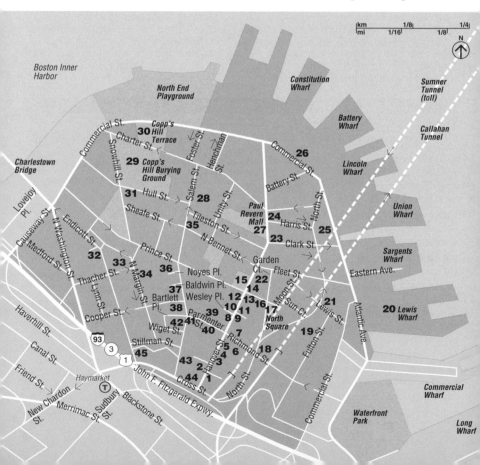

where the city's early Puritan residents settled during the 17th century, their eyes on the sea. As piers, wharves, and markets sprang up along the **Waterfront**, the North End was the wealthiest, most populous, and in every way the most important part of town. It has undergone many changes since then. The glory days ended following the Revolution, when the area's aristocratic Tory population fled to England, and elite Bostonians moved to Beacon Hill and Bay Village. The black community gradually migrated to the Hill as well. In the 19th century, waves of immigrants—first Irish, then Eastern European Jews, then Portuguese, then Italians—poured into the North End, which had deteriorated into a slum. Over some 70 years, Italian-Americans have industriously restored the neighborhood. Their traditions, rituals, and festivals—focused around the family, the church, and the cafes—have become the North End's bulwark.

Most of the neighborhood's streets follow a jumbled 17th-century pattern. When infant Boston still fit onto the Shawmut Peninsula, the North End was a second peninsula—almost an island—divided from the first by **Mill Creek**. Today the Central Artery follows the old creek's track, cleaving the North End from downtown. At press time, a massive project was underway which will include dismantling the elevated highway by the year 2004.

Changes are already afoot, so spend some time here while the fascinating cultural layers remain in place. The people you pass on the streets are still the children and grandchildren of *paesani* from villages in Sicily, Abruzzi, and Calabria. On **Hanover Street**, the main commercial thoroughfare, cafe jukeboxes play Italian pop music. Parallel and to the left is **Salem Street**, where meat and provisions shops do a brisk business. A block to the right brings you to quaint **North Square** and **North Street**, which originally followed the shoreline (it is now blocks away from the water, thanks to subsequent landfill projects).

Notice the loaded laundry lines (you won't see *those* on Beacon Hill), minimal building ornamentation (except for a bit of wrought iron here and there), and dearth of green space (aside from some well-used parks and rooftop gardens). Glance up—more than one elderly North Ender is leaning out a window to check on who's coming, who's going, and who's doing what they shouldn't be doing. This is a close-knit place, after all, where people watch out for one another and strangers get the once-over more than once. But don't let that intimidate you.

Be sure to visit the North End in July and August when each weekend there's a festival dedicated to a different patron saint. Join the throngs for one of these *feste*, when North Enders commandeer the streets for morning-till-night processions, dancing, and eating.

---

1 Hanover Street The straightest and widest street in the labyrinthine North End runs through the heart of the district and boasts the greatest concentration of restaurants, bakeries, cafes, banks, services, and shops selling everything from religious articles to Italian leather goods. Two famous department stores began here in 1851. At **No. 168,** Eben Jordan started a dry-goods store that eventually became the **Jordan Marsh Company;** Rowland H. Macy opened a similar operation nearby that grew into the **R.H. Macy Company** of New York City. (Interestingly, in 1996, **Macy's** bought the **Jordan Marsh** chain). Block after block, four- and five-story buildings crowd in so closely that the Waterfront's nearness stays a secret until you reach the bend by **Charles Bulfinch's St. Stephen's Church.** Tourists stream along the narrow sidewalks as they follow the **Freedom Trail** to the **Old North Church** (see page 55) or seek out popular dining spots such as the **Daily Catch** (see page 49). But most of the street scene belongs to the people who live here. Even on a sleepy Sunday afternoon, this thoroughfare pulses with the vigor of Italian-American culture. ♦ Between Cross and Commercial Sts

(see page 55) (see page 49).

Restaurants/Clubs: Red	Hotels: Blue
Shops/🍴 Outdoors: Green	Sights/Culture: Black

1 Il Fornaio $ Best known for its fresh breads, this popular neighborhood cafe is where locals sit back and take in the world (even if it's just reading the daily newspaper). The favorite brew here is the Italian roast espresso, a rich, smooth blend that's just on the edge of bitterness. Also available is a good selection of hot and cold Italian fare including oversized sandwiches and imported cheeses. ♦ Cafe/Takeout ♦ Daily 8AM-8PM. 221 Hanover St (at Mechanic St). 742.3394

2 Trio's Using recipes from Abruzzi and Sicily, some of which go back 300 years, the Trio family (Tony, Genevieve, and their son Louis) whips up an awesome array of homemade pastas and sauces. Take home gnocchi, tortellini, *tortelloni, agnolotti, cavatelli,* ravioli, red-pepper linguine, or lemon fettuccine along with your choice of ginger-vermouth, gorgonzola, anchovy-nut, white-clam, piquant marinara, or pesto sauce. Everything is made fresh—if you look into the kitchen you'll see the pasta machines churning out that day's supply. The Trios also prepare lasagna and other entrées. It's primarily a take-out operation, but there are a handful of stools if you can't wait to dig in. ♦ M-Sa; Su 9AM-1PM. No credit cards accepted. 222 Hanover St (between Cross St and N Hanover Ct). 523.9636

Vadopazzo

3 Vadopazzo ★★$$$ Not your standard Italian restaurant, this nicely decorated spot, with a contemporary, marble-and-mahogany decor, serves up excellent risottos: saffron, wild mushroom, black truffle, and seafood to name but a few. Also on the extensive menu are pizzas, pastas, carpaccios, and a variety of entrées, including veal chop with porcini mushrooms, baked stuffed lobster, grilled salmon, and boneless duck. The triple-chocolate cake or the strawberries-and-cream cake will end the evening on a sweet note. ♦ Italian ♦ Daily dinner. Reservations recommended. 241 Hanover St (between Mechanic and Richmond Sts). 248.6800

4 Caffé Paradiso Espresso Bar ★$ There are cheerier places to be on a bright summer day, but this is (by Boston standards) a night-owl spot, with the only 2AM liquor license on the street. Stop here on the night of a *festa* or other celebration—the whole neighborhood shows up and has a great time. The lively crowd keeps the jukebox cranking. There's a full line of Italian bitter aperitifs; pastries, homemade gelati, spumoni, and *sorbetti;* plus an enormous array of desserts that you won't see in any of the local bakeries. There are outdoor tables in the warm-weather months. ♦ Cafe ♦ Daily 6:30AM-2AM. 255 Hanover St (between Mechanic and Richmond Sts). 742.1768. Also at: 1 Eliot St (at Eliot Sq), Cambridge. 868.3240; 3 Water St (between Devonshire and Washington Sts). 742.8689

Upstairs at the Caffé Paradiso Espresso Bar:

Trattoria a Scalinatella ★★★$$$ This small (only 10 tables) brick-walled walk-up is one of an increasing number of gourmet restaurants in the North End. Wood beams and a fireplace help create the feeling of a private sanctuary. Owner Paolo Diecidue is happy to acquaint guests with the menu of seasonal local fare and fresh produce from his own farm. Try the *casarecci mara bosco* (pasta with arugula, porcini mushrooms, and farm-raised clams), crab cakes, or rack of wild boar. Be sure to leave room for Sicilian *bomba* (sponge cake made with ricotta, rum, marzipan, and chocolate chips). ♦ Italian ♦ Daily dinner. Reservations recommended. 742.8240

4 Modern Pastry Giovanni Picariellos Senior and Junior are renowned for their diabolically delicious homemade *torrone,* a nougat-and-almond confection drenched in chocolate. This ever-popular, more-than-60-year-old *pasticceria* also offers great *sfogliatelli* (pastry shells filled with vanilla cream and egg), *pizzelle* (a light waffle), and cannoli. There are several tables for those who can't wait to sample their sweets. ♦ Daily. 257 Hanover St (between Mechanic and Richmond Sts). 523.3783

5 La Piccola Venezia ★★$ Forget decor, forget romance, forget trendy angel-hair pasta concoctions—there are other reasons to frequent this no-frills spot. First, there's the hearty Italian home cooking, which runs the gamut from familiar favorites—lasagna, spaghetti with meat sauce, sausage cacciatore—to such hard-to-find, traditional Italian fare as gnocchi, polenta, tripe, *baccala* (salt cod), and scungilli. Second, everything's inexpensive, and third, portions are enormous. When your wallet is light but your appetite is immense, this place is perfect. ♦ Italian ♦ Daily lunch and dinner. No credit cards accepted. 263 Hanover St (between Mechanic and Richmond Sts). 523.3888

6 Villa-Francesca ★$$ This restaurant claims its share of star diners, including a slew of **Red Sox** baseball players. The food is nothing special—large portions spruced up with lots of lemon and white wine—but an Italian singer Monday through Friday has a big following and provides the finishing touch to the overblown, Old World ambience. When you want a little schmaltz with your romance, try this place. Just be sure your date has a sense of humor. ♦ Italian ♦ M-Sa dinner; Su lunch and dinner. 150 Richmond St (between North and Hanover Sts). 367.2948

7 Salumeria Italiana It's definitely worth a stop at this Italian deli to pick up some *prosciutto di Parma*, an import that wasn't available for years. The store also sells a good variety of cheeses, breads, salamis, olive oils, and espresso coffees. Come at lunchtime and proprietor Erminio Martignetti will make what celebrity chef Jasper White calls "probably the greatest cold-cut sandwich in the world." ♦ M-Sa. 151 Richmond St (between North and Hanover Sts). 523.8743

8 Salumeria Toscana It's a pleasure just to step inside this upmarket Italian foodstuffs store—everything looks and smells so good. Just the place to buy the makings for a terrific picnic, it's chockfull of pastas, meats, cheeses, and pastries, all imported from Italy or homemade locally. ♦ Daily 10AM-10PM. 272 Hanover St (between Parmenter St and Wesley Pl). 720.4243

9 Caffé Graffiti ★$ Depending on the time of day, stop in for a glass of wine, a generous calzone, or one of Boston's best cappuccinos and a tasty, award-winning homemade pastry. ♦ Cafe ♦ Daily 7:30AM-midnight. 307 Hanover St (at Lothrop Pl). 367.3016

10 Ristorante Saraceno ★$$ Neapolitan recipes are featured at this family-owned and -operated restaurant. In addition to the usual antipasti and entrée lineup, specialties include good veal saltimbocca, *shrimp* and *lobster fra diavolo*, and linguine with seafood. The scrolled menus add a note of pretension to an otherwise straightforward and pleasant place, which is recommended by many North Enders. Ask for a table in the small upstairs room; downstairs, with its gaudy murals of Capri, the Bay of Naples, and Amalfi, is rather confining. ♦ Italian ♦ Daily lunch and dinner. Reservations recommended. 286 Hanover St (at Wesley Pl). 227.5888 ċ

10 Caffé Vittoria ★$ This place is almost too much, with its faux marble tables and ornamentation, *un cortile* that isn't *really* a courtyard, *un grotto* that isn't *really* a grotto, and more-lurid-than-life murals of Venice and the Bay of Sorrento in the back. But a little braggadocio isn't all bad, and this more-than-60-year-old Italian cafe—Boston's first, they claim—exerts a full-bodied charm all its own. The antique coffee grinders are absolutely authentic, as are the black-and-white photos of North Enders on the walls, and the opera-singing espresso makers (people, not machines) by the windows. Venture beyond cappuccino; try an anisette, grappa, Italian soda, or maybe a gelato. Come during the day when your companions will be older men lingering over newspapers and chatting in Italian; you'll quickly get a sense of how deeply rooted Italian culture is in this neighborhood. At night it's a totally different place—festive and boisterous. ♦ Cafe ♦ Daily 8AM-midnight. No credit cards accepted. 296 Hanover St (between Wesley Pl and Prince St). 227.7606 ċ

Boston is full of public squares that are named after someone, but the North End has an especially large supply, including Joseph S. Giambarresi Square, Arthur A. Sirignano Square, and Gus P. Napoli Square. Most honor Italian-American public figures, war heroes, and the like.

The first subway in the New World opened in Boston on 1 September 1897. Some 200 workers dug out by hand 67,000 cubic yards of dirt under Boston Common along Tremont Street. In the process, workers unearthed nearly 1,100 skeletons of people who had been buried in the Central Burying Ground on the Common. Only about 75 could be identified by headstones. The remains were reinterred elsewhere in the cemetery. The newly opened subway had two stations, Park Street and Boylston Street. The two stations remain stops on Boston's present subway system, and the original station kiosks at Park Street are national historic landmarks.

Art Alfresco

Boston and Cambridge boast a wealth of outdoor sculptures that add to the charm and character of this history-rich area.

Each of the nine blocks of the **Commonwealth Mall** features a memorial sculpture. Among them are historian *Samuel Eliot Morison* by Penelope Jencks (between Exeter and Fairfield Sts) and explorer *Leif Erickson* by Anne Whitney (between Massachusetts Ave and Charlesgate E). The Viking sculpture was donated in 1887 by philanthropist Even N. Horsefod, who believed that Erickson had landed in Cambridge in the year 1000, making him the true European discoverer of America.

Although female sculptures are few in number, animal subjects abound. The most famous is the *Make Way for Ducklings* family in the **Public Garden.** The figures, sculpted by Nancy Schön, are representations of the drawings from the children's book by Robert McCloskey. Schön also created the *Tortoise and the Hare* in **Copley Square.** Other animal sculptures in town include the 112-pound bronze *Bear* on the sidewalk outside **FAO Schwarz** (Berkeley and Boylston Sts); *Bugs Bunny* outside the **Warner Bros. Store** at **Faneuil Hall Marketplace;** and *Paint & Henry,* a pair of abstract horses sculpted from welded sheet copper at **Copley Place.**

The huge bronze equestrian sculpture of *George Washington* in the **Public Garden** facing Commonwealth Mall was dedicated in the 1860s. Sculptor Thomas Ball, who had studied sculpture in Florence, prided himself on the detail of the steed upon which the general sits. Two other beloved equestrian sculptures in Boston, both by sculptor Cyrus Edwin Dallin, are *Paul Revere* (Paul Revere Mall, between Hanover and Unity Sts) in the **North End,** and *Appeal to the Great White Spirit,* the moving work of a Native American on horseback, in front of the **Museum of Fine Arts** (Huntington Ave, between Forsyth Way and Museum Rd).

Widely acknowledged as Boston's most outstanding piece of public art is the *Robert Gould Shaw/54th Regiment Memorial,* sculpted by Augustus Saint-Gaudens. The work, which stands in **Boston Common** across from the **State House,** honors Shaw, a Boston native and colonel of the first free black regiment in the Union Army (whose story is told in the 1989 film *Glory*). The compelling bas-relief piece, which took 14 years to complete and was dedicated in 1897, depicts Shaw and 23 members of his volunteer company, many of whom were killed in their 1863 attack on Fort Wagner, South Carolina.

Quest Eternal is the name of the sculpture of the heroic-size mythological Everyman by Donald DeLue that stands in front of the **Prudential Tower** (Boylston St, between Exeter and Dalton Sts). Reaching heavenward with his left hand, the muscular, five-ton bronze male is an impressive sight, especially when the sun makes him shimmer.

Boston Celtics owner Red Auerbach and the powerful and charismatic Mayor James Michael Curley may also fall under the heroic (or at least the legendary) heading. Auerbach's intimate portrait in bronze is at **Faneuil Hall Marketplace.** Curley, the notorious mayor who ruled the city three times between 1914 and 1949, has two bronze memorials: one sitting on a park bench, and one standing, in **Union Park** (just north of **Faneuil Hall**). A bust of another local hero, Arthur Fiedler, the legendary conductor of the **Boston Pops,** can be found on the **Charles River Esplanade.** Located across from the **Arthur Fiedler Footbridge** (Beacon St and Embankment Rd), this depiction of the maestro is six cubic feet in size, mounted on a pedestal. The sculptor, Helmick, used 80-inch–thick sheets of metal that were designed by computer. When seen from too close a range, the image is fuzzy; viewers need to step back before the remarkable likeness resolves itself. Helmick's intent was to show Fiedler as he was: A person who didn't choose to get close to people.

The *Free at Last* sculpture, dedicated to the memory of Martin Luther King Jr. (1929-68), stands in front of **Boston University's Marsh Chapel.** Dedicated to the "Distinguished Alumnus and Nobel Laureate for Peace" and sculpted by Sergio Castillo, the work features 50 abstract doves—one for each state—rising in formation.

An easy walk or ride across the **Charles River** from Boston is the **Massachusetts Institute of Technology** campus, which offers many outdoor artistic expressions. Situated among the buildings that abut **Memorial Drive** fronting the river is Alexander Calder's *The Great Sail.* The campus boasts two Henry Moore pieces—*Three-Piece Reclining Figure—Draped* and *Working Model for Lincoln Center.* Louise Nevelson's *Transparent Horizon* and Picasso's *Figure Decoupee* can also be found, as can several works by Jacques Lipchitz and one by Beverly Pepper. The free brochure *Art and Architecture at MIT—A Walking Tour* is available at **MIT's Albert and Vera List Visual Arts Center** (Weisner Bldg, 20 Ames St, between Amherst and Main Sts, First floor, 253.4680).

Robert Gould Shaw/54th Regiment Memorial

10 Mike's Pastry ★$ Every type of caloric Italian treat one could possibly crave—cream cakes, candy, cookies, breads, cannoli—along with that most un-Italian of baked goods, the oat-bran muffin, is sold at this perpetually busy bakery. Since this place is trying to cover all the bases, quality varies, and you should scout out the smaller *pasticcerie* for your favorite sweets. That said, the *biscotti di Prato* are very good and cinnamony here. Or try a "lobster tail," a particularly diet-devastating concoction of pastry with cheese, custard, *and* whipped cream. There are some tables, and **Freedom Trail** pilgrims find this to be a convenient spot to rest their weary feet and fuel up with a cup of coffee before continuing their trek through local history. ♦ Cafe ♦ M-Sa 9AM-9PM; Su 8AM-9PM. 300 Hanover St (between Wesley Pl and Prince St). 742.3050

11 Pomodoro ★★★$$$ Seating a maximum of 24 diners, this cozy restaurant is a joy. New chef Seth Trafforo prepares such classic dishes as chicken carbonara with wild mushrooms and prosciutto, and *seafood fra diavolo* (clams, mussels, and other shellfish in a spicy red sauce over linguine). Whimsical modern art and a full list of Italian wines complete the sensory experience. ♦ Italian ♦ Daily lunch and dinner. 319 Hanover St (between Lothrop Pl and Prince St). 367.4348

12 Caffè dello Sport ★$ No question about which sport this sunny cafe's name refers to: fluttering everywhere are pennants for Italian soccer teams. Take a window-side seat, and sip an intense espresso or foamy cappuccino while you join in the North End's favorite pastime: people watching. It gets ever more lively as the day progresses. ♦ Cafe ♦ Daily 7AM-midnight. 308 Hanover St (between Wesley Pl and Prince St). 523.5063 &

The Daily Catch

13 Daily Catch ★★$$ That's the tiny restaurant's official moniker, but the name **Calamari Cafe** and the portrait of a squid lovingly hand-painted on the front window tell the real story. Owners Paul and Maria Freddura have dedicated their culinary careers to promoting this cephalopod, which can be devoured here in many delicious ways. The menu's supporting cast includes Sicilian-style seafood options. The linguine with white or red clam sauce is another hit. Half-a-dozen or so tables flank the open kitchen, so enjoy the show as the young chefs deftly, flamboyantly toss your meal together (there's a lot of garlic in practically every dish). The drawback: There's no bathroom (but it doesn't take much resourcefulness to find neighboring facilities). There's always a line at this popular eatery, so come in good weather when you feel gregarious, or dine early. ♦ Italian ♦ Daily lunch and dinner. No credit cards accepted. 323 Hanover St (between Lothrop Pl and Prince St). 523.8567. Also at: 261 Northern Ave (between Trilling Way and D St Extension). 338.3093; 441 Harvard St (between Coolidge and Thorndike Sts), Brookline. 734.5696

FLORENTINE CAFE
BAR - BISTRO

14 Florentine Cafe ★$$$ The modern glassed-in room across from **St. Leonard's Church Peace Garden** (see below) is great for watching the scene along North End's main thoroughfare. It's also a dependable spot for good pasta: Top choices include crabmeat cannelloni, lobster ravioli, and Maine crab lasagna roll. Meat lovers might try the grilled prosciutto-wrapped black Angus filet mignon or the veal marinated in Marsala wine. The place takes on a particularly lively atmosphere in warm weather, when the floor-to-ceiling glass windows are opened to create a terrace cafe. ♦ Italian ♦ Daily lunch and dinner. 333 Hanover St (at Prince St). 227.1777

Just off North Square is Boston's most charmingly named intersection: the celestial meeting of Sun Court and Moon Street.

The Great Molasses Flood occurred on 15 January 1919 on Commercial Street below Copp's Hill Burying Ground. A four-story tank containing 2.5 million gallons of molasses burst, releasing a lavalike torrent that destroyed several buildings, killed 24 people, and injured 60. It took a week to clear the streets after the explosion, and a sticky-sweet aroma clung to the neighborhood for decades. Some North Enders claim they can still smell molasses from time to time.

15 St. Leonard's Church Peace Garden

With flowers and statuary that are spotlit at night, this place looks more like a garden center than a garden. It's a cheery spot, especially when decked out with lights at Christmastime. Planted at the close of the Vietnam War and maintained by Franciscan friars, the garden contains two shrubs that stood on the altar on **Boston Common** when Pope John Paul II celebrated mass in 1979. The adjacent church (pictured above), designed in 1891 by **William Holmes,** was the first Italian church erected in New England. ♦ Daily until 1PM in winter; until evening in summer. Hanover and Prince Sts. 523.2110

ROSTICCERIA & TRATTORIA

16 Artú ★★★$$

Don't let the unobtrusive door of this tiny, casual place fool you. Owner/chef Donato Frattarolli serves dishes that rival the best food anywhere, whether it's *quazzetto alla Donato* (shrimp, squid, mussels, clams, and sole in a stew) or *agnello arrosto* (roast leg of lamb with marinated eggplant and roasted peppers). Take-out orders are available. ♦ Italian ♦ Daily lunch and dinner. No credit cards accepted. 6 Prince St (between North Sq and Hanover St). 742.4336 &

17 North Square

Idiosyncratic interpretations of the civic "square" abound in Boston. This plaza is, in fact, a cobbled triangle. Nearly overwhelmed by the massive chain along its perimeter—a heavy-handed nod to a nautical past—the square is still winsome, made more so by its circular garden. A stone's throw from the waterfront and part of the first section of the North End to be settled, the square was frequented by a diverse community of artisans, merchants, seafarers, and traders. By late colonial times this had become a prestigious neighborhood. Boston's two most lavish mansions overlooked the square, then called **Clark Square.** The **Second Church of Boston,** seat of the powerful, preaching Mathers family, once stood where Moon Street enters the square. Nicknamed "Old North," the church was torn down by the British in 1776. Today, 17th-to 20th-century structures commune here.

Just around the corner is **4 Garden Court,** home for eight years to John F. "Honey Fitz" Fitzgerald, ward boss, congressman, Boston mayor, and one of the city's most famous citizens. His daughter Rose, President John F. Kennedy's mother, was born here in 1890, in what she described as "a modest flat in an eight-family dwelling." While in residence at **No. 4,** Honey Fitz began his political ascent; he was elected to Congress in 1894 and soon acquired the nickname the "Napoleon of the North End." After leaving Garden Court, Honey Fitz took his family to **No. 8 Unity Street,** also in this neighborhood. Throughout his career, Honey Fitz spoke so often of the "dear old North End" that North Enders were dubbed the "Dearos"; the name was also adopted by the Irish political and social organization Fitzgerald led.

Honey Fitz was born nearby on Ferry Street in 1863. (Both the Fitzgeralds and the Kennedys emigrated to Boston in the mid-1800s to escape the Irish potato famine. Honey Fitz's father became a grocer on North Street and on Hanover Street.) US senator Ted Kennedy has reminisced about how he and brothers John and Robert used to play a game to see who could cross Hanover Street first "in a hop, a skip, and a jump." ♦ At North St, Moon St, and Garden Ct

On North Square:

MAMMA MARIA

Mamma Maria ★★★$$$$ The dining room of this gracious turn-of-the-century town house is a model of understated elegance. But that's not why diners make the pilgrimage here; they come for new chef William Wallo's food, which is complex without being fussy. Recommended pasta dishes include *ravioli con tartufi* (handmade truffle-scented ravioli with grilled asparagus and portabello mushrooms) and *pappardelle con coniglio* (homemade pasta tossed with a traditional Tuscan sauce). For an entrée, consider the roasted game hens with risotto and wild mushrooms; the oven-baked pork chop with chestnut polenta; or the *carpaccio bistecca all Fiorentina* (paper-thin slices of beef tenderloin with Reggiano cheese and extra-virgin olive oil). There are also daily specials and a good selection of Italian and American wines. For a truly romantic evening, complete with captivating views of the Boston skyline, ask to be seated at table 99. ♦ Italian ♦ Daily dinner. Reservations recommended. No. 3 (at Prince St). 523.0077

Mariners' House Dedicated to the service of seamen, this respectable Federalist edifice was erected in 1838 and converted into a seamen's boardinghouse in the 1870s. It's a remnant of Boston's great seafaring days, now long gone, that fueled the city's rapid growth and many Bostonians' fabulous fortunes. From the cupola atop its roof, mariner residents reputedly kept watch on the sea, much nearer then than it is today (due to landfill). Bonafide seamen still board here. The building is closed to the public, but peer in the windows at the exceedingly nautical decor. ♦ No. 11 (at Garden Ct)

Sacred Heart Church Walt Whitman described this former bethel (a place of worship for seamen) as "a quaint ship-cabin-looking church." It opened in 1833, and for 38 years seamen flocked to hear the legendary Methodist preacher Father Edward Taylor, once a sailor himself. "I set my bethel in North Square," said Taylor, "because I learned to set my net where the fish ran." Whitman came to the services, calling Father Taylor the only "essentially perfect orator." Ralph Waldo Emerson anointed Taylor "the Shakespeare of the sailor and the poor" and often spoke from his close friend's pulpit. On one of his Boston visits, Charles Dickens made a special trip to hear the preacher, accompanied by Longfellow and Charles Sumner, abolitionist and US senator. In 1871 the bethel was sold, enlarged, and converted into a Catholic church, which it remains today. ♦ Daily. No. 12 (at Moon St). 523.1225

Paul Revere House Here is where America's most famous messenger hung his hat. A descendant of Huguenots named Revoire, Paul Revere was an exceptionally versatile gold- and silversmith, as well as a copper engraver and a maker of cannons, church bells, and false teeth—reputedly including a pair for George Washington.

Busloads of tourists stream in nonstop, but it doesn't take long to see the humble rooms in Revere's tiny, two-story wooden clapboard abode (pictured below). It's worth inching along with the crowd, because this house and the **Pierce-Hichborn** residence next door (see below) are remarkable rare survivors of colonial Boston.

Constructed in 1680, rebuilt in the mid–18th century, and renovated by **Joseph Chandler** in 1908, this National Historic Landmark was restored to what it looked like originally, before Paul added an extra story to accommodate his big family. Revere and his second wife, Rachel (who gave birth to 8 of his 16 children), owned the house from 1770 to 1800 and lived here for a decade until the war-ruined economy forced them to move in with relatives. From here Revere hurried off to his patriotic exploits, including participating in the Boston Tea Party. By the mid–19th century, the house slipped into decrepitude and

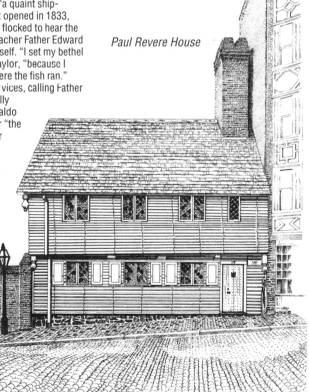

Paul Revere House

became a sordid tenement with shabby storefronts. The wrecking ball loomed at the start of this century, but a great-grandson of Revere's formed a preservation group that rescued the house.

From across North Square, look toward the medieval overhanging upper floor and leaded casements. These throwbacks to late 16th-century Elizabethan urban architecture are reminders that architectural styles were exported to the colonies from England and adapted with Yankee ingenuity long after they were out of fashion in Europe. Built after the devastating Boston fire of 1676, the fashionable town house violated the building code because it was made of wood, not brick. Today 90 percent of its frame and one door are genuine; its clapboard shell and interior are reproductions. See how artfully the house tucks into its tiny site in the colonial North End, where rabbit warren clusters of small houses are linked by a maze of alleyways. The dark, low-ceilinged, heavy-beamed rooms with their oversize fireplaces bear few traces of the Revere family, but recall colonial domestic arrangements. The pretty period gardens in back are equally interesting; study them with the help of the posted key and a pamphlet sold at the ticket kiosk. The multipurpose plants— with old-time names like Johnny-jump-up, bee-balm, Dutchman's-pipe, and lady's-mantle—remind visitors that gardens were once commonplace sources of pharmaceuticals, food, and domestic aids. ♦ Admission. Daily; closed Monday January-March, and major holidays. No. 19 (between Bakers Alley and Prince St). 523.1676

COURTESY OF PAUL REVERE MEMORIAL ASSOCIATION

Pierce-Hichborn House This stalwart structure to the left of Paul Revere's house was home to Paul's cousin, a boatbuilder by the name of Nathaniel Hichborn. A prized colonial urban relic, the house was built around 1710 by a glazier named Moses Pierce. Although built just 30 years later, this English Renaissance brick structure represents a huge stylistic leap from Revere's Tudor. Even the central stair is innovative— simple and straight instead of windy and cramped like that of the **Revere House.** The pleasing three-story residence reflects a pioneering effort to apply formal English architectural principles to early Boston's unruly fabric. When the house left Hichborn's family in 1864, it, too, fell on hard times,

becoming a tenement until it was restored in 1950. Four rooms are open to the public for guided tours given twice daily, the only times to see the interior. Enter at the **Revere House** gate. ♦ Admission. Tours daily at 12:30 and 2:30PM, but call beforehand to confirm; closed Monday January-March, and major holidays. No. 19 (at Bakers Alley). 523.1676

Around the corner from Pierce-Hichborn House:

Bakers Alley Walk down this alley to a pretty residential plaza ingeniously tucked in among the backsides of apartment buildings. The lucky residents have a number of handsome specimens of that scarce North End commodity: trees.

 Rachel Revere Park This tiny park is used as a playground for schoolchildren. It was dedicated to the patriot's wife by the Massachusetts Charitable Mechanics Association, a philanthropic group that was founded in 1795 with Revere as its first president. ♦ At North St

18 V. Cirace & Son Jeff and Lisa Cirace are the third generation and the second brother-sister act to run this almost 90-year-old Italian wine establishment. About half of the store's 1,500-plus wines are Italian, and there's an extensive collection of Cognacs, cordials, grappa, and other venerable vintages. This is not a self-service place, but the staff is friendly and helpful. The "V" in the name, by the way, is for Vincenza, the owners' grandmother. ♦ M-Sa. 173 North St (at Richmond St). 227.3193

19 McLauthlin Building The soft brownish-mauve facade of New England's first cast-iron building is adorned with lacy rows of arched windows crowned by fanlights. Built circa 1850, the structure was originally the home of the McLauthlin Elevator Company. Renovated in 1979 by **Moritz Bergmeyer,** it now houses condominum units. ♦ 120 Fulton St (between Richmond and Lewis Sts)

20 Lewis Wharf In the mid–19th century Boston's legendary clipper-ship trade centered on this wharf, originally named for Thomas Lewis, a canny merchant who acquired much of the city's waterfront property after the American Revolution. Ships carried tea to Europe and foodstuffs to California, where they were sold at exorbitant rates to Gold Rush prospectors (eggs went for $10 a dozen; flour for $44 a pound). The warehouse, attributed to architect **Richard Bond,** was built of Quincy granite between 1836 and 1840 and renovated in the late 1960s by **Carl Koch and Associates**, at which time the graceful gabled roof was replaced with an unwieldy mansard one. The building now houses residential and commercial units.

To the right stretches an attractive harborside park where members of the **Boston Croquet**

Club set up their wickets—a genteel sight that reminds the viewer how long gone the city's seafaring era really is. Local lore has it that Edgar Allan Poe's tale *The Fall of the House of Usher* was inspired by tragic events that took place on the wharf's site in the 18th century. Two lovers, a sailor and another man's wife, were trapped by the angry husband in their rendezvous, a hidden tunnel underneath the Usher house. When the structure was torn down in 1800, two skeletons locked in embrace were discovered behind a gate at the foot of the tunnel steps.

Set back at the Boston Harbor end of the wharf—where old, fallen-in wharf structures look ready for a harbor burial—is the popularly acclaimed **Boston Sailing Center** (227.4198), which offers a variety of sailing and racing lesson packages as well as captained harbor cruises aboard 23- to 30-foot sailboats. Boats also embark on day sails among the Boston Harbor Islands and on overnight trips to Provincetown, Martha's Vineyard, Newport, and Block Island. The sailing center also will arrange more extensive charters. ◆ Atlantic Ave (between Commercial Wharf E and Eastern Ave)

21 Piccolo Nido ★★★$$ Owner Pino Irano has developed an imaginative and tempting table of Northern and Southern Italian entrées at this trattoria. Try the *brodetto di pesce* (fish stew), semi-boneless roast duck served in Port wine with cherries, or the *crespelle al funghi di bosco* (wild mushroom-filled crepes with Madeira and thyme sauce). The in-depth wine list is not only laudable, it's applaudable. ◆ Italian ◆ M-Sa dinner. Reservations required. 257 North St (at Lewis St). 742.4272 ⅃

22 Giacomo's ★★$$ The open kitchen is close, but not too close, which means you're enveloped in tantalizing, spicy-sauce aromas, but you won't leave this cozy bistro drenched in the smell of garlic and smoke. The grill's the thing here—meaty swordfish and tuna steaks arrive succulent and smoky from the charcoal flame, and grilled chicken and sausage are a fine duo; or try linguine with *frutte di mare* (seafood), a house specialty, with "Giacomo" sauce—a feisty combination of white and red sauces. The unfinished brick walls and refinished wood floors—signs of unwanted gentrification throughout the North End—suit owner Jack Taglieri's unpretentious place. A handsome tin-stamped ceiling, oil-on-wood paintings of Rome and Venice, and black-and-white cafe curtains add warmth and character. ◆ Italian ◆ M-Sa dinner. 355 Hanover St (between Prince and Fleet Sts). 523.9026. Also at: 431 Columbus Ave (between Braddock Park and Holyoke St). 536.5723

23 St. Stephen's Church Located on the sunny side of Hanover Street's bend is **Charles Bulfinch**'s sole surviving church in Boston. In 1804 **Bulfinch** transformed a commonplace meeting house called the **New North** into an elaborate, harmonious architectural composition, for which the Congregational society in residence paid $26,570. Paul Revere cast the bell that was hung in the church's belfry in 1805.

Although **Bulfinch** was usually drawn to English architecture, Italian Renaissance campaniles also inspired him in this work —an architectural foreshadowing of the North End's future ethnic profile. The dramatic tower crowds to the front of the wide-hipped facade, a bold counterpoint to the subtle Federal architectural gestures inside. Notice how the windows and column styles metamorphose as they move toward the gracefully curving ceiling. Most of the woodwork is original, including the pine columns. The 1830 organ was restored by Charles Fisk of Gloucester, Massachusetts, a famous American organ conservator.

In 1862 the Roman Catholic Diocese of Boston bought the church to serve the North End's enormous influx of Irish immigrants and gave it its present name. In 1869 the entire building was moved back approximately 12 feet to accommodate the widening of Hanover Street, and in 1870 the structure was raised 6 feet so that a basement church could be installed. Rose Kennedy, the Kennedy family matriarch, was christened here. In 1964 Cardinal Richard Cushing launched a successful campaign to renovate and restore the church to **Bulfinch**'s design (**Chester F. Wright** carried out the restoration), respectfully returning the edifice—now on the National Register of Historic Places—to its original prominence. ◆ Daily. 401 Hanover St (at Clark St). 523.1230

The most popular of the North End's summer weekend *feste* are the "Big St. Anthony" in late August and the colorful Feast of the Madonna del Soccorso (nicknamed the "Fisherman's Feast") in mid-August. The *feste* have become increasingly commercial over time, and many North Enders avoid them because they draw hordes of outsiders and turn the neighborhood into a circus. But try to attend one anyway: They're the fullest expression of North End culture you'll ever encounter.

24 Ristorante Lucia ★$$ The fare—primarily dishes from Abruzzi—is good, but not exceptional. One pasta concoction reproduces the Italian flag with a white-cream, red-tomato, and green-pesto sauce. The walls are covered with takeoffs on Italian masterpieces. Upstairs is the opulent pink-marble barroom, whose ceiling is painted with replicas of scenes from the Sistine Chapel. Note the tasteful touch the indiscreet Michelangelo omitted: undergarments resembling diapers and swaddling clothes. ♦ Italian ♦ M-Th dinner; F-Su lunch and dinner. Reservations recommended. 415 Hanover St (at Harris St). 367.2353 &

25 Davide ★$$$ The interior of this restaurant is bordelloesque, right down to the overstuffed red-velvet banquettes and the overheated color scheme. The menu changes seasonally (uncommon in the North End). Try the duck served in a Port sauce flavored with figs, risotto with seafood, or panfried bass with lemon-caper butter. Valet parking is available. ♦ Italian ♦ M-F lunch and dinner; Sa dinner. Reservations required; jackets requested. 326 Commercial St (between Clark and North Sts). 227.5745

26 Bay State Lobster Company In business for more than 70 years, this is the East Coast's largest retail and wholesale seafood operation. The biggest draw here is lobster—you can buy the tasty crustaceans live on the spot to cook for tonight's dinner, or have a few shipped via UPS to anywhere in the continental US. Seafood of every kind—including shellfish prepared with all the trimmings, the company's own clam and fish chowders, and lobster pies—are also sold here and can be packed for traveling. As you might guess, it's often a madhouse. ♦ Daily. 379 Commercial St (between Battery and Hanover Sts). 523.7960

Enrico Caruso loved the North End. When the Italian tenor came to Boston, he often ate at a restaurant on Hanover Street called the Grotta Azzura (now closed). A famous anecdote tells how Caruso wasn't able to cash a check at a neighborhood bank because he had no acceptable identification. The tenor launched into "Celeste Aida," immediately delighting and convincing the skeptical bank manager.

Restaurants/Clubs: Red   **Hotels:** Blue
Shops/ 🌳 **Outdoors:** Green   **Sights/Culture:** Black

27 Paul Revere Mall (The Prado) Laid out in 1933 by Arthur Shurcliff, this tree-shaded park could have been plucked from Italy. It offers residents a comfortable cushion of space in their jam-packed quarter, and sightseeing pilgrims a pleasant passage from **St. Stephen's Church** to the **Old North Church** looming up ahead on Salem Street. The modest, slightly scruffy park has more personality than many of Boston's grander spaces. Though it isn't very old, it has a very lived-in look. The mall's brick walls and paving carve out a restful realm in which all generations of North Enders cheerfully converge. A serious game of checkers or cards often goes on among the elders while baby strollers are wheeled past, kids play, and dogs race about. The bronze equestrian statue of *Paul Revere* (designed by Cyrus E. Dallin in 1885 and erected in 1940) towers near the Hanover Street edge, giving the young park a historical stamp. Hardworking, pragmatic artisan that he was (not to mention unremarkable in physique), Paul Revere wouldn't recognize himself in this dashing figure. On some of the side walls, plaques commemorate North Enders' contributions to their city.

The mall ends at Unity Street; cross and enter the gate leading into the courtyard behind the **Old North Church.** On the way, look for the **Clough House** at 21 Unity Street. Built in 1715, it was the home of Ebenezer Clough, one of the Sons of Liberty, a Boston Tea Party "Indian," and a master mason who laid the bricks for the church. The courtyard itself occupies the former site of 19 Unity Street, which Benjamin Franklin bought for his two widowed sisters. ♦ Between Hanover and Unity Sts

At Paul Revere Mall:

Maurizio's ★★★$$ Bright, quiet, and understated, this restaurant serves some of the best Mediterranean cuisine in Boston. In addition to traditional pasta dishes like *penne al salmone e vodka* (with fresh and smoked salmon, sauteed shallots, and sun-dried tomatoes in a light vodka cream sauce) and *linguine al frutti di mare* (with shrimp, scallops, clams, mussels and calamari in a spicy tomato sauce), the menu offers meat selections like *filetto di vitello al forno* (pan-roasted veal tenderloin in a sun-dried tomato, brandy, and orange sauce) and daily fresh fish specials such as *bistecca di tonno al limone e rosmarino* (grilled tuna steak with lemon, rosemary, capers, and extra-virgin olive oil). All of the artwork on display is by local artists and is available for purchase. Owners Linda and Maurizio Loddo provide a thoroughly satisfying and tasteful dining experience. ♦ Italian ♦ Tu dinner; W-Su lunch and dinner. 364 Hanover St. 367.1123

28 Old North Church (Christ Church) Called the "Old North Church" by nearly everyone, this is the oldest church building in Boston (pictured below) and the second Anglican parish founded in the city. Architect **William Price,** a local draftsman and print dealer, emulated **Christopher Wren** quite nicely in this 1723 brick edifice, now a National Historic Landmark. Coping with a tiny site in cramped quarters, Price gave the church needed stature and eminence by boldly attaching a 197-foot-high, three-tiered steeple—one of New England's earliest.

What points to the sky today, however, is the 1955 replica of the original steeple, which was toppled by a gust of wind in 1804 and once again in 1954. The weather vane on top was made by colonial craftsman Deacon Shem Drowne. The 8 bells that ring from the belfry were cast in 1744 by Abel Rudhall of Gloucester, England, and range in weight from 620 to 1,545 pounds. Their inscription recalls long-extinguished aspirations: "We are the first ring of bells cast for the British Empire in North America, Anno 1744." The oldest and sweetest-sounding church bells in America, they have tolled the death of every US president since George Washington died in 1799. When he was 15, Paul Revere and 6 friends formed a guild to change ring the bells (a specific form of bell ringing). The tradition stuck, and the Old North Guild of Change Ringers still exists. Practice takes place on Saturday beginning at 11:30PM, with formal ringing after the 11AM Sunday service.

Years later, Revere starred in the celebrated drama that has enveloped this landmark building with enduring legend, though a lot of the facts are cloudy. On the night of 18 April 1775 Revere rode on horseback to warn the Minutemen at Lexington and Concord of the approaching British troops. And as Revere arranged before departing (or so the story goes), the church's sexton—Robert Newman—hung two signal lanterns in the belfry to alert the populace that the British were on the move. Although a number of other messengers, including William Dawes, rode out into the towns, Paul Revere has eclipsed them all in fame. Henry Wadsworth Longfellow can take the real credit for Revere's glory. Spellbound by the nearly forgotten tale, he wrote the inaccurate but entertaining poem "Paul Revere's Ride," published in *The Atlantic Monthly* in 1861. Every April, on the eve of Patriots' Day, descendants of Revere or Newman hang lanterns in the church belfry to commemorate that spring night. An unresolved controversy, however, concerns whether this is the real **Old North Church,** or whether the **Second Church of Boston** on North Square—nicknamed "Old North" and later burned down by the British—truly held the leading role in the events on the

eve of the American Revolution. If the other church was ever proven to be the real thing, it would require a major rerouting of the **Freedom Trail,** so no one is rushing to verify this theory.

No matter what the truth is, a sad and genuine chapter in this church's past was the divided loyalties of its Episcopalian congregation. Once the Revolution ignited, the church was closed until 1778 because of the tensions unleashed between Patriot and Tory parishioners.

The structure's white interior shimmers with light entering through pristine glass windowpanes. It's too bad there's rarely a chance to enjoy the unusual serenity and architectural clarity in solitude. The tall box pews—originally owned by parishioners, with brass plaques indicating which was whose—were designed to hold the warmth of hot bricks and coals during the winter. Look for the Revere family pew—No. 54. Inscriptions abound in the church and on the walls of the **Washington Memorial Garden** in back. Many offer interesting slants on colonial Boston. The clock ticking reassuringly at the rear of the gallery was made by a parishioner in 1726, and it's the oldest still running in an American public building. The brass chandeliers, also gifts, were first lighted on Christmas Day 1724. To the right of the apse, a 1790 bust of

Old North Church

MARJORIE VOGEL, RHODE ISLAND ORIGINALS

George Washington rests in a niche. When General Lafayette returned to Boston in 1824, he noticed this bust and said, "Yes, that is the man I knew, and more like him than any other portrait." Before leaving the church, look for the tablet on the left side of the vestibule, which identifies 12 bricks set into the wall. These were taken from a cell in Guildhall in Boston, England, where William Brewster and other Pilgrims were held after attempting to flee that country in 1607. In 1923, on the church's 200th anniversary, the mayor of Boston, England, sent the bricks as a gesture of friendship.

To the left as you exit is a curious museum and gift shop amalgam (open daily) housed in a former chapel built in 1917 to serve the North End's tiny community of Italian-speaking Protestants, now vanished. In front of the chapel's street entrance, notice the amusing, stout little columns resting on the pair of lions' backs. Inside the museum, look for the "Vinegar Bible," a gift of King George II in 1733 and so nicknamed for its famous typo: On one page heading, the "Parable of the Vinegar" appears instead of the "Parable of the Vineyard." Tea retrieved from the boots of a Boston Tea Party participant is also on display. There are lots of fun things to buy here, from spice gumdrops and maple sugar candy to copies of Longfellow's poem and Wedgwood china decorated with the church's image.

Behind the church on both sides are charming small gardens nestled among clusters of nearby residences. In early summer the courtyard of the **Washington Memorial Garden** is awash in the fragrance of roses. Among its many commemorative tablets, one intriguingly states, "Here on 13 Sept. 1757, John Childs, who had given public notice of his intention to fly from the steeple of Dr. Cutler's church, performed it to the satisfaction of a great number of spectators." Said Childs did indeed leap from on high, strapped to an umbrella-like contraption that carried him safely for several hundred feet.

Cross Salem Street and look back at the church. Ever since its completion, the steeple has towered over the swath of redbrick that makes up the North End's fabric. The church's colonial neighbors are gone now, but unlike the **State House,** it has not been overwhelmed by 20th-century urbanism. None of the newer buildings in the area exceed 5 stories, so you still get a vivid picture of the early 18th-century landscape. Historical talks are offered by staff ad hoc. ♦ Daily; Su services 9AM, 11AM (with choir), and 4PM. 193 Salem St (between Tileston and Charter Sts). 523.6676

29 Copp's Hill Burying Ground One of Boston's many wonderful outdoor pantheons, this cemetery not only offers the finest gravestones in Boston, but also some of the best views of the city's most elusive feature—the Waterfront. From this promontory you can see down to the boat-clogged Boston Harbor and over to Charlestown and its **Navy Yard,** where the venerable warship "Old Ironsides," the USS *Constitution,* berths. This cemetery was established in 1659 when **King's Chapel Burying Ground** got too crowded. Once an Indian burial ground and lookout point, "Corpse Hill" (as it is also known) has accommodated more than 10,000 burials. In colonial days black Bostonians settled at the base of the hill in what was called "New Guinea." A granite pillar marks the grave of Prince Hall, black antislavery activist, Revolutionary War soldier, and founder of the Negro Freemasonry Order.

Sexton Robert Newman, who flashed the signals from **Old North Church**—and was imprisoned by the British for doing so—is also buried here. And the Mathers—Increase, his son Cotton, and Cotton's son Samuel—that formidable dynasty of Puritan churchmen and educators, rest in a brick vault near the Charter Street gate. (Increase was awarded the first doctor of divinity degree conferred in America.) During the Revolution, British generals directed the shelling of Bunker Hill from here and their soldiers used the gravestones for target practice—as visitors can still discern. Look for Captain Malcolm's bullet-riddled marker. His patriotic epitaph particularly incensed the British soldiers: "a true son of Liberty/a friend to the Publick/an enemy to oppression/and one of the foremost/in opposing the Revenue Acts on America." Legend tells of two tombs that were stolen here: Interlopers ejected the remains of the graves' rightful owners, whose names were carved over with those of the thieves for future burial. ♦ Snowhill St (between Hull and Charter Sts)

30 Copp's Hill Terrace After scrutinizing the Puritan view of death, head downhill to this graceful plaza set into the sloping hill, beleaguered by neglect and vandals. It's still a wonderful architectural progression, most frequented by the youngest and oldest neighborhood residents. There are a few outdoor stone tables with chessboards laid in them. In the field below, by the harbor, male residents of the North End gather day and night to play their game of passion—boccie. ♦ Charter St (between Foster and Commercial Sts)

31 Hull Street Leading up the hill from the **Old North Church** and abutting the **Copp's Hill Burying Ground,** is this tree-lined, winding street—one of the North End's most pleasant roads. It was named after Boston's first mint-master, John Hull, who coined the city's famous "pine-tree shillings" and had an estate that encompassed this neighborhood. ♦ Between Salem and Snowhill Sts

On Hull Street:

No. 44 Located across from the Hull Street entrance to **Copp's Hill Burying Ground** is a circa-1800 house that is indisputably the narrowest in Boston, one window per floor at the street end, squeezing up for air between its stout companions. An amusing tale claims that this house was an act of revenge, built solely out of spite to block the light and view of another house behind. In truth, this is a lonely survivor of a breed of modest dwellings called "10 footers," sometimes depicted in old prints of colonial Boston-town. The picturesque dwelling is nine feet, six inches wide, to be precise. A floral wrought-iron fence leads to its charming entry.

32 Oasis Cafe ★$ If you aren't in the mood for marinara, hop off the Italian express at this casual, comfy little cafe, where the order of every day is American home-style cookery: meat loaf, barbecued pork, Cajun catfish, burgers, corn bread, and the like. The signature offering is the roast of the day, which can be accompanied by real mashed potatoes. There's a special daily fritter, too, either fruit or vegetable, and for dessert there's Key lime pie. Everything is homemade right down to the salad dressings. Be ready for whopping portions. You'll dine to the sounds of 1930s and 1940s jazz in a pink-and-black Art Deco setting. When you leave, find where Endicott Street intersects North Margin Street at odd, appealing **Alfred Wisniski Square.** Look down Endicott Street toward downtown from here for one of the North End's few unimpeded views. ◆ American/Takeout ◆ Tu-Sa lunch and dinner; Su brunch. 176 Endicott St (between Thacher St and Endicott Ct). 523.9274

33 Pizzeria Regina ★$$ Everybody but everybody knows Boston's most famous (though not necessarily best) pizza joint. This is brick-oven pizza of the thin-crust, oily variety. Customers from New York and Florida fly home with as many as eight pies. It's a little tricky finding the curved corner building, but any North Ender can point you in the right direction. ◆ Pizza/Takeout ◆ Daily lunch and dinner. No credit cards accepted. 11½ Thacher St (at N Margin St). 227.0765. Also at: Faneuil Hall Marketplace, Quincy Market. 742.1713

34 The Nostalgia Factory After seven years on Newbury Street, the owners of this eclectic gallery/antiques shop moved their huge inventory of old collectibles and ephemera to these more spacious North End digs. Anglophiles Rudy and Barbara Franchi scour fairs, flea markets, and Great Britain to come up with their ever-changing assortment of rare posters, old postcards and advertisements, political buttons, antique signs, soda-pop art, English royalty souvenirs, and memorabilia of all kinds. A browser's delight, the gallery chronicles changing societal attitudes and trends. Look for magazine ads from the 1920s through the 1950s, which extol products once considered safe and now known to be harmful, such as cigarettes, asbestos shingling, and lead paint. ◆ M-Sa. 51 N Margin St (between Cooper and Thacher Sts). 720.2211

N B S S

35 North Bennet Street School Founded in 1881 by Pauline Agassiz Shaw, this school was originally designed to help North End immigrants develop job skills. No longer a social service agency, it now offers classes in furniture making, carpentry, piano tuning, violin making and restoration, bookbinding, jewelry making, watch repair, and other fields. Its students are trained in traditional methods and graduates are respected throughout New England. ◆ 39 N Bennet St (at Salem St). 227.0155

36 Salem Street This intimate, bustling street was dominated in the 19th century by the millinery and garment businesses owned by Jewish immigrants who settled in this area. Now butcher shops, restaurants, and great produce markets, many with no signs and run by proprietors who serve *all* customers—North Enders or not—with the same brusqueness, are tucked into tiny shopfronts. Most of the people you see lugging parcels are returning from this street; here one gets a glimpse of daily North End goings-on. The south end of the street offers a great view of the trucks and cars creeping along on the elevated Central Artery. Enjoy your pedestrian freedom.

36 A. Parziale & Sons Bakery This is a businesslike shop, and its business is to make lots of great bread. The place is bursting with it. The Parziale family sells a thousand loaves a day of French bread alone. But why not stick to the Italian varieties and try a handsome loaf of *scali, bostone,* or fragrant, rich raisin bread? The *pizzelle* and anisette toasts are great, too. ◆ Daily. 80 Prince St (at Salem St). 523.6368

36 Bova Italian Bakery Suffer from insomnia? Why not discover what the North End is like at four in the morning with a trip to the Bova family's corner shop, which is open round-the-clock? For more than 70 years this clan has been baking all its bread and pastries right on the premises. There's nothing fresher. ◆ Daily 24 hours. 134 Salem St (between Noyes Pl and Prince St). 523.5601

37 Lo Conti's ★$ If you like your Italian fare fresh and light, and are not keen on the heavy trappings of typical bordello-style decor, try this small, bright restaurant with teal-laminate wooden tables and modernist leanings. Specialties include *gnocchi mascarponi* (potato dumplings tossed in a rich cheese sauce) and *calamari bianco* (fresh squid simmered with white wine). The service here is brisk and no-nonsense; the pricing and portioning quite generous. ◆ Italian ◆ Daily lunch and dinner. 116 Salem St (at Baldwin Pl). 720.3550 ⑤

L'Osteria

38 L'Osteria Ristorante ★★$$ This Northern Italian place serves delectable entrées made from the very freshest ingredients. House specialties include *chicken finiziare* (served with veal, shrimp, and assorted vegetables) and *veal bocconcini* (rolled and stuffed with tomato cream sauce). There is a large dining area downstairs that is ideal for business meetings or festive gatherings. ◆ Italian ◆ Daily lunch and dinner. Reservations recommended. 104 Salem St (at Cooper St). 723.7847 ⑤

39 Boston Public Library, North End Branch Come by when the library is open to inspect the remarkable 14-foot-long plaster model–diorama of the Doge's Palace in Venice. This clever creation was the consuming passion of Henrietta Macy, who taught kindergarten in this neighborhood before moving to Europe. After she died in Venice, her handiwork was presented to the library. Painted settings and dolls enacting 16th-century scenes were added by Louise Stimson of Concord, Massachusetts. Architect **Carl Koch**'s attention to Italian-American cultural heritage in this 1965 building has tempered and transformed the coldness of 1960s modernism into an extraordinary neighborhood addition. The library's atrium is cobbled like an Italian piazza, with plants and a small pool, and a bust of Dante on the wall. Umbrellalike concrete vaults supported by nine columns form a roof, raised to create a clerestory that illuminates the library interior. The brick exterior is punctuated by colored glass ceramics, adding festive notes to what is an otherwise drab streetscape. ◆ M-F. 25 Parmenter St (between Hanover and Salem Sts). 227.8135

40 Fratelli Pagliuca's ★$$ There's most definitely nothing fancy about the brothers'

Joe, Freddy, and Felix Pagliuca's popular place. A goodly number of locals eat here, Monday and Tuesday especially, as do businesspeople who know their way around. This is satisfying, stick-to-the-ribs Italian red-sauce cuisine served in a family atmosphere. Favorites include the chicken-escarole soup, chicken Marsala, and sweet roast peppers with provolone and sausage, which come in large portions for reasonable prices. Don't look for the four basic food groups here: pasta and meat, not veggies, get priority. ◆ Italian ◆ Daily lunch and dinner. Reservations recommended for parties of four or more on weekends. 14 Parmenter St (between Hanover and Salem Sts). 367.1504

41 Polcari's Coffee A fragrant North End fixture since 1932, congenial Ralph Polcari's shop sells more than a hundred spices from all over the world as well as a fine selection of coffees. Innumerable specialty items fill every inch of shelf and floor space: chamomile flowers, *ceci* (dried chickpeas), Arborio rice, flax seed, carob and vanilla beans, pine nuts, braided garlic, and bunches of fresh oregano. Polcari's wares are the stuff of alchemy in everyday cooking. ◆ M-Sa. 105 Salem St (at Parmenter St). 227.0786

Terramia

42 Terramia ★★★★$$$ Nestled along narrow Salem Street is one of Boston's smallest but very best restaurants. Owner and chef Mario Nocera has won the hearts and palates of sophisticated critics and diners alike. Don't look for veal parmagiana here. Nocera prepares authentic Italian cuisine. (Italians visiting the US have been known to fly in to Boston just to eat here.) Featured are dried salted cod, reconstituted with potato and onions in white truffle oil; roast quail risotto with porcini and shiitake mushrooms; and swordfish stuffed with pine nuts and raisins. It's all served in an elegant but spare setting, with views of the copper-laced Old World kitchen. ◆ Italian ◆ M-W, Su dinner; Th-Sa lunch and dinner. 98 Salem St (at Bartlett Pl). 523.3112

43 Dairy Fresh Candies If you like sweets, it's impossible to pass by without stopping; once you're inside, it's all over. Those who suffer from chocoholism will tremble at the sight of loose chocolates of every sort, including massive chunks of the plain-and-simple sinful stuff and gorgeous packaged European assortments. The entire confection spectrum is here, including hard candies, old-fashioned nougats, and teeth-breaking brittles. But the amiable Matara family's retail and wholesale business, in operation for more than 30 years, goes way beyond candy. Also sold are Italian cakes and cookies, dried fruits, nuts, exotic oils and extracts, vinegars, antipasti, pastas, cooking and baking supplies, and more—an extravaganza of delicacies. You can assemble a wonderful gift box here. "Thank you, stay sweet," says the hand-lettered sign by the door. ♦ M-Sa. 57 Salem St (between Cross and Parmenter Sts). 742.2639, 800/336.5536 &

Maria's Pastry Shop

44 Maria's Pastry Shop What's a *pasticceria* without a display of marzipan in fruit and animal shapes, lurid with food coloring? Here you'll find that popular almond-sugar confection, and plenty more. Butter, anise, and almond scent the air, and through the kitchen door you can see bakers taking cookies out of the oven. Try the *savoiardi napolitani* (citrus-layered cookies), or, at Halloween time, the intriguing *moscardini*

ossa di morta (cinnamon cookies that really do resemble bones). The *sfogliatelli* (clam-shaped pastries) are creamy, citrony, and not too sweet. ♦ M-Sa; Su until 1PM. 46 Cross St (between Hanover and Salem Sts). 523.1196

45 Purity Cheese Company Four people make all the marvelous ricotta and mozzarella sold fresh in this unobtrusive storefront. It's easy to miss unless you glance in and spot the giant, pungent wheels of parmesan and tubs of olives. Grating cheeses, pastas, oils, and big serving bowls are available, too. The business began in 1938, and the operation is as unfussy as ever. People come from all over for the high-caliber cheese choices. And it smells delicious inside. ♦ Tu-Sa. 55 Endicott St (between Cross and Morton Sts). 227.5060 &

45 Pat's Pushcart ★$$ The decor here is nothing to speak of (the place looks like a dive from the outside), but it's packed with North Enders and others wily enough to t rack it down. Entrées are basic, tasty, and inexpensive. ♦ Italian ♦ Tu-Sa dinner. 61 Endicott St (at Morton St). 523.9616

Bests

Patrick B. Moscaritolo
President & CEO, Greater Boston Convention & Visitors Bureau, Inc.

Boston is America's walking city. What better way to relive America's history than to walk the **Freedom Trail** and the **Black Heritage Trail**?

The **Water Shuttle** that runs to and from **Logan Airport** to **Rowes Wharf** in downtown Boston is the most elegant way to enter or leave Boston. A short eight-minute trip from the airport takes you across **Boston Harbor** with its beautiful waterfront sky-scrapers, condos, sailboats, fishing boats, and cruise ships as your backdrop. Best of all: On the harbor crossing you encounter no stoplights, tolls, or traffic!

The Reverend Robert W. Golledge
Retired Vicar, Old North Church

Boston is a major metropolitan center, but it has the character of a small town. We drive offensively but you should walk. Park your car and try our subway system, the first in America.

The best way to start is by walking the **Freedom Trail** that will take you by the principal 18th-century sites connected with the American Revolution.

The best of the trail takes you through the **North End**, where you experience Europe without a passport—especially Italy. The best sidewalk cafes are on **Hanover Street** for cappuccino and espresso. Pick up a cannoli for a shot of energy at **Modern Pastry**. The best sandwich is available at **Artú** on **Prince Street**. There are lots of restaurants but for a special dinner, the best is **Mamma Maria**'s, a few steps away from the **Paul Revere House**.

The best expression of church and country is experienced at **Old North Church**, where two lanterns

set in motion America's drive for independence. It's the oldest church building in Boston and your visit will be complete if you attend a service there.

The next best walk is around **Boston Common** (America's oldest public park) and the **Public Garden**. Take the children to see the *Make Way For Ducklings* sculptures at the corner of **Charles** and **Beacon Streets** in the Garden.

Finally, walk through the six glass towers of the **New England Holocaust Memorial** and you'll know this must never happen again.

David R. Godine
Publisher

First, everyone should read Walter Muir Whitehill's *Boston: A Topographical History*.

For entertainment, check out **Jordan Hall** at the **New England Conservatory of Music**; free faculty and student concerts are scheduled here.

Spend at least a day walking around **Cambridge** and visiting its many museums

Eat at least one dinner or lunch at **Locke-Ober**. Also consider tea at the **Ritz-Carlton Hotel**, very relaxing.

Finally, attend a Sunday morning service at **King's Chapel** or **Trinity Church** in **Copley Square**.

The Associated Daughters of Early American Witches, founded in 1987, is a society of women who are descended from someone accused, tried, or executed for witchraft prior to 31 December 1699 (the Salem Witch Trials took place in 1692).

Waterfront/ Fort Point Channel

Newcomers to Boston who have heard of its great maritime past are often surprised to discover that its waterfront area is quite elusive. Hills that once overlooked **Boston Harbor** were leveled long ago, and the shoreline, for centuries Boston's lifeline, has been sheared from the city's core by **Atlantic Avenue**, the **Central Artery**, and a shield of modern buildings. With a little perseverance, however, you can cross this divide to see where Boston began. An urban treasure, the Waterfront is vibrant with light and color and the constant motion of water and air. The neighborhood's heyday is recorded in the street and wharf names, and captured in grand old buildings that are getting a new lease on life. The harbor itself, until recently among the nation's most polluted, has undergone a massive cleanup. Sludge dumping has ceased, and a primary sewage treatment plant has been built, resulting in much-improved water quality. Eventually, the sprinkling of more than 30 harbor islands here, which comprise a National Park Area, will have the sparkling setting they deserve. From little **Gallops, Grape,** and **Bumpkin** to big **Peddocks** and **Thompson**, the **Boston Harbor Islands** will entice you with picturesque paths, beaches, and views of the city.

In colonial times young Boston looked to the Atlantic Ocean for commerce and prosperity. Throughout the 17th, 18th, and 19th centuries profit-minded Bostonians industriously tinkered with the shoreline, which originally reached to where **Faneuil Hall Marketplace** and Government Center are today, once the **Town Dock** area. Citizens built piers, shipyards, warehouses, and wharves extending ever farther into the sea, until the shoreline resembled a tentacled creature reaching hungrily for its nourishment: trade. The ocean brought profitable European and Chinese trade and established the city's legendary merchant princes.

One of Boston's most glorious moments was the clipper-ship era of the 1850s, when the harbor's horizon was alive with masts and sails. Toward the turn of

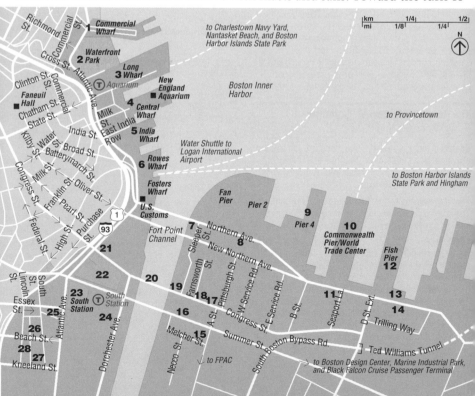

the century, as rails and roads replaced sea routes and manufacturing supplanted maritime trade, fishing, and shipbuilding, Boston's liaison with the sea began to suffer, languishing for decades until the late 1960s, when the city began to reclaim it. Since that time the Waterfront has been resurrected gradually, its connections to the heart of Boston reforged. The harbor activities that remain have shifted elsewhere, primarily to Charlestown and the **Black Falcon Cruise Passenger Terminal** in **Marine Industrial Park** and the **Fish Pier** in South Boston.

Boston is also reinterpreting the Waterfront's role as a place for leisure, luxurious residences and offices, pleasure boats, and waterside restaurants and hotels. Excursion and commuter boats depart from the numerous wharves for the Boston Harbor Islands, **Provincetown** on **Cape Cod**, **Cape Ann**, and **South Shore** communities. The **Water Shuttle** serves travelers between **Logan International Airport** just across the harbor and **Rowes Wharf** on the downtown waterfront. Harborwalk, the pedestrian route along the Waterfront, is lengthening; it ultimately will stretch from the Charlestown Navy Yard—where *Old Ironsides* was exhaustively restored for her 200th birthday in 1997—to Fort Point Channel, linking with walks along Boston's second waterfront, the **Charles River Basin**, to create a pathway of more than 20 miles. For now, however, you can take one great stroll that begins at **Waterfront Park** and **Commercial Wharf**, proceeds past the **New England Aquarium** and around sumptuous **Rowes Wharf**, crosses over the channel via the **Northern Avenue Bridge** up to the Fish Pier, from which it doubles back to **The Children's Museum, The Computer Museum,** and the **Boston Tea Party Ship and Museum** before carrying on to **South Station,** and concluding with a brief meander in the little **Leather District.**

Fort Point Channel and the Leather District aren't part of the historic Waterfront per se, but are natural companions because they, too, reveal facets of Boston's workaday life. Developed during the late 19th century, the Fort Point Channel neighborhood was the center for Boston's fishing, shipping, warehousing, and manufacturing industries; during the same era, the garment and raw leather goods industries thrived in the Leather District. In both atmosphere and architecture, these two neighborhoods, like the Waterfront, are acquiring new vitality as galleries, restaurants, and shops move into restored buildings, following the trail of artists and other urban pioneers. Walking the entire length of this far-flung neighborhood at one time is an ambitious undertaking, but definitely can be achieved if you're not with children. It's a great Boston experience.

Waterfront

1 Commercial Wharf When Atlantic Avenue sliced through the Waterfront in 1868, it split a rugged 1834 building of Quincy granite and Charlestown brick in two. Now the western half of the building, renovated by **Anderson Notter Associates** in 1971, is home to **Michael's Waterfront and Wine Library**, and the larger eastern half, renovated by **Halasz and Halasz** in 1969, houses offices and upscale apartments with enviable views. Original architect **Isaiah Rogers** also designed Boston's famed **Tremont Hotel**, long gone, the nation's first luxury overnight digs. If you walk to the wharf's end, you'll see ramshackle buildings, relics of days gone by. Now pleasure boats in the adjacent yacht marina crowd the pier. ♦ Atlantic Ave (between Richmond and Commercial Sts)

On Commercial Wharf:

Boston Sail Loft $ Strange as it seems in a seaside city, there aren't many restaurants in Boston where you can sit and look out at the water. This is one of the few. Longtime residents fondly recall its predecessor, a rundown, quiet hole-in-the-wall called **TheWharf**. But things change; even if this is now a hopping touristy spot on the Happy Hour trail, you get a nice view of Boston Harbor along with your oversize portions of decent seafood. ♦ American/Seafood ♦ Daily lunch and dinner. No tank tops allowed. 80 Atlantic Ave. 227.7280. Also at: One Memorial Dr (at Main St), Cambridge. 225.2222

Michael's Waterfront and Wine Library
★★$$$ Its windows crowded with wine bottles and books, this restaurant announces

up front the two features that keep it from being just another fern bar. The books, some of which are quite old, are donated by libraries and individuals, and patrons may borrow them. The sports-oriented bar, which offers a large selection of international wines by the glass, is frequented by a nonbookish crowd that occasionally includes rock musicians, entertainers, and TV people. As for the food, it's basic seafood and New England cuisine, including a great rack of lamb. There's valet parking. ♦ American ♦ M-F dinner; Sa-Su lunch and dinner. Reservations recommended. 85 Atlantic Ave. 367.6425

2 Waterfront Park This friendly park, designed by **Sasaki Associates** in 1976, opened a window to the sea and drew Bostonians back to where their city began. In fact, the park was built to complete the "walk to the sea" that starts at City Hall Plaza in Government Center, proceeds through **Faneuil Hall Marketplace,** then passes under the Central Artery to end by Boston Harbor. A handsome trellis promenade—its greenery gradually is growing in—crowns the park's center, with huge bollards and an anchor chain marking the seawall. The park offers views of the harbor and wharves, and a sociable scene: From morning until late at night, this versatile oasis hosts sea gazing, ledge sitting, suntanning, Frisbee throwing, dog walking, and romantic rendezvous. Watch planes take off across the harbor at **Logan International Airport** and the steady boat traffic. On a summer afternoon sit and read amid the grove of honey locust trees or in the **Rose Fitzgerald Kennedy Garden,** fragrant with her namesake blooms. **Quincy Market** is just a five-minute walk away; pick up some treats and picnic with the cool ocean breezes rustling by. ♦ Bounded by Boston Harbor and Atlantic Ave, and Long and Commercial Wharves

---

Early New Englanders, popular illustrations to the contrary, did not dress in black with steeple-crowned hats. They actually preferred bright colors for their clothing, furniture, and wall hangings.

Tradition holds that Elizabeth Foster, second wife of Issac Goose (or Vergoose), known as Mother Goose, is buried in Old Granary Burial Ground. But if she is, there is no gravestone (although there is one for Mary Goose, Issac's first wife). Elizabeth is said to have written stories for her 10 children and 10 stepchildren. Later, widowed, she lived with her eldest daughter and entertained her grandchildren with nursery rhymes. It is thought that her son-in-law, printer Thomas Fleet, published them as *Songs for the Nursery* or *Mother Goose's Melodies.*

3 Long Wharf Boston was already America's busiest port when farsighted Captain Oliver Noyes constructed this wharf—the city's oldest and now a National Historic Landmark—in 1710. It originally extended from what is now State Street far out into what was then Town Cove, creating a half-mile avenue to the farthest corners of the world. It was the **Logan Airport** of its day, where even the deepest-drawing ships could unload cargo on the pier lined with warehouses. The painter John Singleton Copley played here as a child, where his mother ran a tobacco shop. Landfill and road construction demolished most of the wharf by the 1950s, but the restoration of its remaining buildings and the arrival of the **Boston Marriott Long Wharf** hotel have made it a destination once more. Walk to the spacious granite plaza at the wharf's end for fresh air and lovely views. ♦ Atlantic Ave and State St

On Long Wharf:

Boston Marriott Long Wharf $$$$
It's certainly pleasant to stay here at the city's edge in rooms surveying the lively Waterfront, with **Waterfront Park** next door, the **New England Aquarium** one wharf over, and the North End *ristoranti* and **Faneuil Hall Marketplace** mere minutes away. Many of the 400 rooms have good views, and two luxury suites have outside decks. The **Concierge Level** offers premium services; on-site amenities include a business center, an indoor swimming pool, other exercise facilities, and a gameroom. This 1982 hotel, designed by **Cossutta and Associates,** has a couple of counts against it as a Waterfront neighbor, however: It rudely crowds what should have remained a generous link in the Harborwalk, and the architects' attempt to mimic Waterfront warehouses and the lines of a ship has resulted in an awkward, aggressively bulky building. The hotel's red-garbed porters are a striking sight. Be sure to see the 19th-century fresco depicting Boston Harbor that is mounted in the lobby upstairs. Relax by a window or (in warm weather) on the outside harborfront terrace **Waves Bar & Grill;** there is also the formal **Oceana** restaurant and a more casual cafe. ♦ 296 State St. 227.0800, 800/228.9290; fax 227.2867 ㊟

The Chart House ★★$$$ The **Gardner Building,** a simple and solid circa 1763 brick warehouse—the Waterfront's oldest, renovated in 1973 by **Anderson Notter Associates** —was recycled for this chain restaurant. Inside, rustic bricks and beams recall the building's former life. Steak, prime rib, and seafood are the ticket, with children's plates available. Lots of stories circulate about the building's history—some possibly true— claiming it was called "Hancock's Counting House" because John Hancock had an office here, and that tea was stored here prior to the Boston Tea Party. The free valet parking is a great boon in a neighborhood born long before the days of autos. ◆ Seafood/American ◆ Daily dinner. 60 Long Wharf. 227.1576

Custom House Block Before his writing career finally freed him from ordinary pursuits, Nathaniel Hawthorne spent two years (1838-40) recording cargoes in the cramped predecessor to this building, demolished in 1847. The "new" structure, designed by **Isaiah Rogers** and restored as a National Historic Landmark by **Anderson Notter Associates** in 1973, was never used for customs collection. Nonetheless, this building bears the signature eagle and a misleading sign on its granite facade. It now accommodates offices and apartments.

4 Central Wharf In the early 19th century Boston rebounded from the devasting economic effects of the American Revolution and became a booming seaport once again. The daring developer Uriah Cotting formed the Broad Street Association to modernize the dilapidated Waterfront. With architect **Charles Bulfinch** designing, the association created broad streets flanked by majestic four-story, brick-and-granite warehouses, and completed this pier and **India Wharf** in 1816. Only a fragment of the original wharf remains, with a handful of its structures stranded across the expressway. ◆ Atlantic Ave and Milk St

On Central Wharf:

New England Aquarium
The aquarium takes visitors on a trip around the world—from Boston Harbor to the Amazon River—with exhibits of fish and other aquatic creatures in recreated habitats. The complex boasts more than 70 exhibit tanks and is home to more than 18,000 fish, birds, and mammals. Among the major exhibits are the spectacular 4-story, 200,000-gallon **Giant Ocean Tank,** which offers multi-angle views of sharks, sea turtles, moray eels, and tropical fish; the **Ocean Tray,** home to African and

rockhopper penguins; the **Edge of the Sea** hands-on tidal pool; the floating pavilion *Discovery,* where sea lions appear in shows that combine entertainment and education; and the **Aquarium Medical Center,** where visitors can watch staff veterinarians and biologists examine and care for sick sea animals. There are also issue-oriented changing exhibits.

The boxy, concrete building (designed by **Cambridge Seven** in 1969) is somewhat like a sea creature grown too big for its shell. A model in its day, the aquarium is now in the midst of a three-phase expansion project that will triple its original size. The first phase was completed in January 1998 with the opening of an expanded **West Wing,** which has a new outdoor seal exhibit and a two-level gallery for special exhibits. Designed by **Schwartz/Silver Architects,** the wing has a multi-angled exterior meant to call to mind stony outcroppings or shards of ice; it is covered with stainless-steel panels that create a shimmering "fish scale" effect. The second phase of the project is the construction of a new auditorium/movie theater, due to be finished in late 1999. The final phase, a new **East Wing** housing new major exhibits, including a giant wave tank, is slated for completion in 2003. ◆ Admission. Daily. 973.5200 &

New England Aquarium Whale Watching
Because the aquarium considers the whales that live at **Stellwagen Bank,** a rich feeding ground 25 miles due east of Boston, to be yet another of its many exhibitions, it organizes trips to visit the massive mammals in the spring, summer, and early fall. During the five-to six-hour voyage (round-trip), aquarium naturalists tell whale tales and describe other marine life. Whales frequenting New England coastal waters include humpbacks, finbacks, and, occasionally, right whales. In 1987 two blue whales, the largest creatures ever to live on earth, were sighted off Cape Cod.

Be sure to dress warmly in layers—even in summer—and bring waterproof gear, rubber-

New England Aquarium

COURTESY OF SCHWARTZ/SILVER ARCHITECTS

soled shoes, and sunscreen. The boat offers a full-service galley. Children under 36 inches tall aren't permitted on board. ♦ Apr-Oct; call for schedule. Reservations by credit card; payment in cash only. 973.5200, recorded information 973.5277 ঙ

5 India Wharf Another success of the Broad Street Association's 19th-century scheme to revamp the Waterfront, this wharf (begun in 1805) was once a half-mile stretch of piers, stores, and warehouses designed by **Charles Bulfinch.** The last vestiges of the handsome structures were leveled to make room for the upstart **Harbor Towers.** ♦ Atlantic Ave and East India Row

On India Wharf:

Harbor Towers Whereas Boston's historic Waterfront buildings stretched like fingers into the harbor, waves lapping among them, these modern towers aren't so involved in the maritime scene. The standoffish pair (designed by **I.M. Pei** in 1971) is more intrigued by the sky. At their nascent stage, the 40-story interlopers brought dramatic new style and scale to this part of town. Originally somewhat alienating, the towers have acquired a kind of folk appeal, partly because newer buildings more brazen and far less clever have pushed their way in—such as **International Place** across the Central Artery. The towers are more exciting to live in than to look at; the residents enjoy stunning views. David von Schlegell's *India Wharf Project,* a stark 1972 sculpture composed of four folded planes, stands at the edge of the harborside terrace. The flat surfaces clad in stainless steel also ignore the harbor and reflect what's happening above instead.

Boston Harbor Sailing Club Sail in the harbor and among the islands that once witnessed stirring arrivals and departures of Boston's majestic clipper ships. In a city famous for its exclusive clubs, this is not a club per se, but rather a private enterprise founded in 1974 to offer sailing classes that are taught by experts. The one-week courses are very popular, attracting novices from all over. Properly certified visitors can rent boats from a fleet of 65, ranging in length from 26 to 39 feet. ♦ Daily May-Oct. 72 East India Row. 523.2619

6 Rowes Wharf Many Bostonians consider **Skidmore, Owings & Merrill**'s grand, redbrick complex—luxury condos, offices, shops, a 38-slip marina, and a hotel—the best addition to Boston in years. A resplendent six-story arch lures pedestrians from Atlantic Avenue to the water's edge. The 15-story development was built in 1987 on the 1760s' **Rowes** and **Fosters Wharves.** Many don't even realize it's new, because unlike **Harbor Towers,** the complex takes its inspiration from the past. The ornamental overkill borders on kitsch, but the building is generous, capable of grand gestures. **Rowes Wharf** has further privatized the Waterfront, yet gives back to Bostonians the heroic arch, an observatory, open space, a splendid **Harborwalk** extension leading past enormous yachts, and best of all, an entry to the city via the water shuttle that zips between **Logan International Airport** and the wharf. This speedy journey is worth taking just for the sake of enjoying the most picturesque approach to Boston and to see the flipside view through the monumental portal. It's not a cheap thrill, but do it once (see "Orientation" for more information). ♦ Atlantic Ave (between Northern Ave and East India Row)

On Rowes Wharf:

Boston Harbor Hotel $$$$ This 230-room hotel's public spaces are tranquil and attractively dressed in warm woods, pearly grays, and subdued burgundies, with companionable textures and tapestry patterns. Cove lighting adds a subtle glow and paintings by Massachusetts artists decorate the first two floors. Pay more for a room where you can gaze out at Boston Harbor instead of peering across the elevated expressway at the Financial District. Deluxe rooms all have separate sitting areas and all but a few rooms have king-size beds. All rooms are sound-proofed. Amenities include a posh health club and spa with a pristine three-lane lap pool (fees apply), 24-hour room service, rooms for nonsmokers and people with disabilities, and pet services from catnip to counseling. There's easy access to the airport **Water Shuttle** whose embarkation point is directly in front of the hotel. Indoor parking and marina slips are also available.

In the hotel's **Magellan Gallery** is a largely undiscovered treasure: a private collection of early maps and charts depicting New England and Boston. Owned by The Beacon Companies, developers of the **Rowes Wharf** complex, the display includes Virginian captain John Smith's 1614 map of the New England coast, the first ever produced, which later guided the Pilgrims to Plymouth. Another fascinating map (created in 1625 by Sir William Alexander) records The Council of New England's scheme to turn the region into an elite association of English estates, which was ultimately overturned by competition from the Massachusetts Bay Colony and support for the Puritan cause. There are also two restaurants (see below). The **Rowes Wharf Bar** is located in the hotel lobby, it makes up for its lack of views with blissful quiet and an excellent array of single-malt Scotch labels. ♦ No. 70. 439.7000, 800/323.7500; fax 330.9450 &

Within Boston Harbor Hotel:

Rowes Wharf Restaurant ★★★★$$$$
The views here are only exceeded by the excellent food and highly professional service. Chef Daniel Bruce—who came from New York's 21 and Le Cirque and has demonstrated his considerable talent in places like Venice and Paris—performs with equal distinction in Boston. The American menu, which changes daily, includes seafood and meat dishes with a hint of France. An added touch is a prix fixe menu with a wine matched to each dish. Recent offerings have included an appetizer of smoked salmon served with a crisp potato cake topped with crème fraîche and caviar, and an entrée rack of veal with wild mushrooms and roasted red potatoes. Desserts are creative as well as delicious. The overall atmosphere is one of sophistication and patrons leave feeling pampered and very satisfied. ♦ American ♦ M-F breakfast, lunch, and dinner; Sa breakfast and dinner; Su breakfast and lunch. 439.3995 &

Intrigue ★★★$$ This comfortable cafe, furnished with wing chairs and sofas, is less formal than its big sister. Also under the expert supervision of chef Daniel Bruce, it serves up American dishes in a room that overlooks the hotel's harborfront terrace. ♦ Cafe ♦ Daily breakfast, lunch, dinner, and snacks (until midnight). 439.7000 &

Fort Point Channel

Most Bostonians have yet to stumble upon this fascinating place, and those who love it hope that won't change too soon. This no-nonsense neighborhood exposes some of the city's practical inner workings. The slender channel is now all that divides the original **Shawmut Peninsula** from **South Boston,** once a far-off neck of land. In the 1870s the Boston Wharf Company cut the channel and erected warehouses on the South Boston side to store lumber, sugar, coal, imported fruit, wool, raw pelts, and ice. **Fish Pier** and **Commonwealth Pier** were both built on landfill, the second becoming the center of the Boston fishing industry. By the 1890s the area was the major transfer point for raw materials fueling most New England industries, and was bursting with wharves, machine shops, iron foundries, glassworks, wagon factories, soap producers, brickyards, and printing trades. Business boomed through the early 20th century, then slackened as the fishing and wool industries, shipping, and manufacturing declined.

The construction of the **Central Artery** isolated the area further and speeded its decline.

Artists rediscovered the neighborhood in the 1970s, creating a SoHo-like atmosphere that early on earned the district the affectionate nickname "NoSo," short for North of South Boston. Now more than 300 artists belong to the **Fort Point Arts Community (FPAC),** the largest community of visual artists in New England. Headquartered at 249 A Street, an artists' cooperative, **FPAC** sponsors several open-studio weekends annually.

The **World Trade Center** and the massive **Boston Design Center,** the latter New England's major showroom facility for the interior-design trade, have comfortably settled in now, too. What port activity remains in Boston is located along **Northern Avenue** and at **Fish Pier,** home of the **New England Fish Exchange.** Various megadevelopment proposals for long-vacant **Fan Pier** nearby ended with a decision to build a new **Federal Court House** on the site; it was slated to be completed at press time. Nevertheless, the area is still full of the old Waterfront district's industrial flavor and vitality. Look for the Boston Wharf Company's architecturally inventive warehouses on **Summer** and **Congress Streets.** Trucks and tractor-trailers rule the roads in this part of town. Back across the channel, skyscrapers spread like weeds; here, low-rise buildings and empty lots let light flood in. Unfamiliar vantage points show off the city's skyline. Down Summer Street on the way to South Boston is **Marine Industrial Park** and Boston's state-of-the-art **Black Falcon Cruise Passenger Terminal.**

7 The Barking Crab ★★$$ Take a hard right rudder after the Northern Avenue Bridge and you'll find this restaurant, the city's only urban clam shack. John Geoffrion and Bill Lombardi have extended the traditional clambake fare with all kinds of fried, boiled, steamed, and grilled seafood. Sit at tables under the giant heated tent, with a wonderful view juxtaposing lobster boats and the city skyline. ♦ Seafood ♦ Daily lunch and dinner. No credit cards accepted. 88 Sleeper St (at Northern Ave). 426.2722 &

8 Our Lady of the Good Voyage Chapel In addition to regular weekend Masses, an annual "Blessing of the Animals" service is held the first Sunday in October at this humble little chapel. ♦ Services: Sa 7PM; Su 11:30AM, 7 and 8PM. 65 Northern Ave (between New Northern Ave and Sleeper St). 542.3883

Charles Dickens was one of Boston's greatest admirers. Said Dickens: "Boston is what I would like the whole United States to be." On the other hand, Edgar Allen Poe was perhaps the city's greatest detractor. Poe said he was "heartily ashamed to have been born in Boston" and referred to his native city as "Frogpondium."

Short Trips to the Boston Harbor Islands

The 30 islands that dot the inner and outer harbors offer wonderful respite from city crowds and new perspectives on Boston's connection to the sea.

These "away from it all" islands, only a few miles from, and within sight of, Boston's downtown skyline, may have been used more enthusiastically 150 years ago as venues for summer excursions than they are today. Then, public steamers carried passengers to the islands for picnics or fancier meals at the flourishing summer resorts on several of the islands. Gambling and illegal Sunday boxing matches on other islands added to the allure. Today, Boston's harbor islands, a National Recreation Area, still are the settings for a wide range of activities.

Georges Island, the hub of the chain, is dominated by **Fort Warren,** massive 19th-century granite fortifications where Confederate soldiers were imprisoned during the Civil War. Restored and a national historic landmark, it is an explorer's delight with drawbridge, dungeons, and cavernous vaulted-ceilinged common rooms. Guided tours and programs are offered by state park staff (**Metropolitan District Commission,** 727.7676) six months of the year. The 30-acre island is the perfect place for a picnic overlooking the distant cityscape, and has rest rooms, an information booth, public food grills, and a first-aid station.

Sixteen-acre **Gallops Island** also has picnic grounds, a pier with a large gazebo, shady paths, meadows, and remnants of a World War II maritime radio school. **Lovell Island,** 62 acres large, offers a supervised swimming beach, a picnic area with hibachis and tables, campsites, and walking trails.

One of the harbor's biggest islands, 188-acre **Peddocks** also has picnic and camping areas and the remains of **Fort Andrews** occupying its **East Head.** Because the **West Head** is a protected salt marsh and wildlife sanctuary, access beyond recreational areas is restricted to organized tours or by permission of park staff. Tranquil **Bumpkin Island** offers trails to an old children's hospital ruins and stone farmhouse, and its rocky beach is popular for fishing. Wild rabbits and raspberry bushes proliferate. Some campsites are available. **Grape Island,** named for the vines that grew here in colonial times, feeds many birds with its wild bayberries, blackberries, and rose hips. Come here for birding, picnicking, camping, and meandering. Although rugged **Great Brewster Island** can only be reached by private boat, it offers 23 pristine acres and splendid views of **Boston Light,** the country's oldest lighthouse, which is located on nearby **Little Brewster.** The lighthouse on Little Brewster began blinking in 1716. Destroyed by a 1751 fire, rebuilt, destroyed by the

evacuating British in 1776 and rebuilt again, **Boston Light** is visible 27 miles out to sea. The last manned (by the Coast Guard) lighthouse in the country, the 89-foot-tall structure has been threatened with automation—forestalled for now with the help of Senator Edward Kennedy. The first lightkeeper, George Worthylake, drowned with his family when his boat capsized on the way back to Little Brewster in 1718. Benjamin Franklin wrote a poem about the tragedy. The names of the present and former keepers are etched on island rocks. The interior of the lighthouse is closed to the public.

Owned by the **Thompson Island Outward Bound Center** (328.3900), 157-acre **Thompson Island** is open on a limited basis for guided tours, hiking, picnicking, educational programs, and conferences—you must call ahead. The center provides boat transportation to the island.

No fresh water is available on Gallops, Lovell, Bumpkin, Grape, and Great Brewster Islands. Day-use permits are required for large groups; permits are also necessary for camping and for alcohol consumption on some islands. A number of the islands belong to the **Boston Harbor Islands State Park** and can be reached by ferries departing from **Long Wharf** or **Rowes Wharf** on the Waterfront. Privately operated, the ferries charge fees and most go to Georges Island, where free water taxis depart for five other islands. For more information or to obtain permits for Georges, Lovell, Gallops, Bumpkin, Grape, Great Brewster, and Peddocks Islands, call the **Metropolitan District Commission** (727.7676). Georges, Bumpkin, and Thompson Islands are wheelchair accessible.

Friends of the Boston Harbor Islands (740.4290), a nonprofit organization dedicated to preserving the islands' resources, sponsors year-round public education programs, history tours, and boat trips.

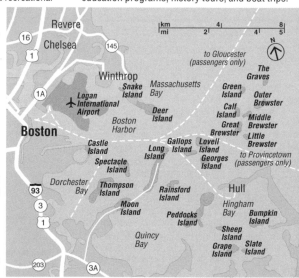

9 Anthony's Pier 4 ★$$$ There are better places to go in Boston for an expensive seafood dinner, but this place is worth a visit at least once to experience a big-time restaurant formula that keeps 'em coming, and coming, and coming. Owner Anthony Athanas, an Albanian immigrant, started out as a shoeshine boy, built a restaurant, and wound up ruling a fiefdom of five gigantic seafood houses. Enjoy towering popovers, raw oysters or clams, steamed lobster, or simply cooked seafood.

The colonial-nautical motif is milked for all it's worth, but Anthony needn't have gone to the trouble: big views of Boston Harbor steal the show. There are no quiet corners here, where as many as 3,000 meals a day are served. Take a good look at the "Wall of Respect"—make that "Walls"—crammed with photographs of Anthony and the Pope, Anthony and John F. Kennedy, Anthony and Frank Sinatra, Anthony and Liz Taylor, Anthony and Gregory Peck. Valet parking is available. ♦ Seafood/American ♦ M-Sa lunch and dinner; Su dinner. Reservations recommended; jacket required and tie requested for main dining room at dinner; no jeans, sneakers, or gym attire in evening. 140 Northern Ave (at B St). 423.6363

10 Commonwealth Pier/World Trade Center Excursion boats depart from this pier for Provincetown, the Harbor Islands, and other points. The monumental, beflagged business center accommodates all kinds of enormous functions. A pedestrian walkway connects the **Trade Center** with the hotel and conference center across the street. ♦ Northern Ave (between Seaport La and B St)

11 Seaport Hotel and Conference Center $$$$ In the heart of the Waterfront district overlooking Boston Harbor, this ultramodern hotel is tailor-made for the business person. Each of the 427 deluxe rooms features such extras as individual air-conditioning controls, a mini-bar, office supplies (Post-it notes and floppy disks), an in-room safe large enough to hold a laptop computer, color TV with on-demand movies and a separate channel for airport arrival and departure information, fluffy bathrobes, a hair dryer, and an iron and ironing board. Telephones are equipped with two lines, fax capability, speakerphone, and voice mail. In addition there is high-speed Internet access, in each room as well as in the hotel's 24-hour business center. Other amenities include concierge service, complimentary transportation to the Financial District, both ground and water shuttle service to the airport, and an executive sedan service (fees are charged for the latter services). On-site facilities include a restaurant (see below), a fitness center and spa, and an indoor heated lap pool. Note: This is a service-inclusive hotel—no tips are accepted. ♦ 1 Seaport La (between New Congress St and Northern Ave). 385.4000, 800/WTCHOTEL; fax 385.5090 &

Within the Seaport Hotel:

Aura ★★$$$$ The menu at this new hotel dining spot is American, but eclectic, with an emphasis on seafood. Entrées include pan-roasted lobster with steamed clams and cod fritters; grilled red snapper with citrus baby beets; applewood-roasted venison with black pepper and plum chutney; grilled aged sirloin with potato and roasted-garlic flan; and spring vegetable pot-au-feu with barley crisps and herbs. The dining room is accented with cherry wood screens, a mural depicting the spice trade between New England and the Far East, and specially commissioned pieces by local and national artists and craftspeople. There's also a bar with floor-to-ceiling windows overlooking the harbor. ♦ American/Seafood ♦ Daily breakfast, lunch, and dinner. Reservations recommended. 385.4000 &

12 Fish Pier Two long, arcaded rows housing fish-related businesses stretch more than 700 feet out onto the water, with the heroic **Exchange Conference Center at Fish Pier** (formerly the **New England Fish Exchange**) dominating the far end. The century-old building's arch is crowned with a wonderful carved relief of Neptune's head.

No longer the center of New England's—let alone America's—fish industry, Boston's catch keeps shrinking, with more and more fish brought in by trucks, not boats. But the venerable fish auction still starts up every morning around 6:30. It's well worth arriving by 6AM to watch the buyers haggle over the day's catch. ♦ Northern Ave and D St Extension

At Fish Pier:

No-Name ★★$$ Once upon a time this eatery had a name, but it sure doesn't need one now. The hungry hordes all know where to find this big-business restaurant that has been cooking up meals for fishers and pier workers since 1917: in the right-hand building of Fish Pier, just past the arcade's first curve. Hope for a table in the back overlooking the pier. Sitting elbow-to-elbow at boisterous communal tables, fill up on "chowdah" and big portions of impeccably fresh fried seafood, boiled lobster, broiled fish, fish o' the day, and delicious homemade pie. Expect to wait in line; they don't take reservations. ♦ Seafood ♦ Daily lunch and dinner. No credit cards accepted. No. 15½. 338.7539 &

Boston's first ferry service began in 1631, a year after the city was founded. Operating under a colonial charter, the boat carried passengers between Boston's waterfront peninsulas.

Restaurants/Clubs: Red   **Hotels:** Blue
Shops/Outdoors: Green   **Sights/Culture:** Black

13 Jimmy's Harborside Restaurant ★$$$
This Waterfront fixture has been around since 1924, starting out as a nine-stool joint serving Fish Pier workers and fishers. The seafood house's dated decor shows a refreshing lack of interest in fads. Notice the funky fish mosaics and neon on the facade. Showcased in walls of glass, the views are among the Waterfront's most colorful, with big boats docked close by. The reliably fresh seafood is at its best in simpler preparations, especially the chowder. The title "Home of the Chowder King" was earned in the 1960s when the late owner, Jimmy Doulos, was invited to bring his great fish chowder to Washington, DC. It pleased the palates of John F. Kennedy and members of Congress, and will undoubtedly please you. Jimmy's son is in charge now, but politicians and other celebs still crowd in with the tourists and regulars. While waiting for a table, have a drink at **Jimmy Jr**, the boat-shaped bar. Valet parking is available. ♦ Seafood/American ♦ M-Sa lunch and dinner; Su dinner. Reservations recommended; jackets requested; no jeans, sneakers, or T-shirts allowed at dinner. 242 Northern Ave (between Trilling Way and Fish Pier). 423.1000 &

JIMBO'S

14 Jimbo's Fish Shanty ★$ Geared toward the family trade, this casual joint is run by the Doulos family, which also owns **Jimmy's Harborside Restaurant** across the way. Children are delighted with the trains-and-hobos decor and the three train sets zipping by on overhead tracks. You won't find harbor views, but the low prices for chowder, basic seafood, pizzas, salads, burgers, and other no-frills American food make up for it. Children's plates are available. The restaurant's tiny newsletter-menu advises you to check out the **New England Aquarium** "for a close look at the seafood on the hoof." There's valet parking at **Jimmy's Harborside.** ♦ Seafood/American ♦ Daily lunch and dinner. 245 Northern Ave (between Trilling Way and D St Extension). 542.5600 &

14 Daily Catch ★$$ An offspring of the popular North End hole-in-the-wall, this larger place is just as redolent with garlic and serves the same great seafood, although the original has more personality. Try one of the many calamari dishes; the owners love to turn people on to their favorite seafood. ♦ Seafood ♦ Daily lunch and dinner. 261 Northern Ave (between Trilling Way and D St Extension). 338.3093. Also at: 323 Hanover St (between Lothrop Pl and Prince St). 523.8567

15 A Street Deli Express $ While the rest of the city's asleep, get a hearty breakfast with lots of good grease to jump-start your day. For lunch, the food—pizza, soup, and salads—is cheap, basic, and tasty. From here, walk up Melcher Street to see its gracefully curving warehouses. ♦ American ♦ M-F breakfast and lunch. 324 A St (at Melcher St). 338.7571 &

16 Marco Polo Cafe ★$ Frequented by employees of local architecture offices, this stylishly sparse cafeteria-style lunch spot serves great coffee and Mediterranean fare, ranging from minestrone to moussaka. Most everything's made on the premises, including from-scratch morning muffins. ♦ International/Takeout ♦ M-F breakfast and lunch. 274 Summer St (east of Fort Point Channel). 695.9039 &

17 Mobius The name refers to both the **Mobius Performing Group** of 17 artists and to the multimedia gallery and performance space on the fifth floor of a former leather-sole manufacturing building where other artists can also present their work. The founding group works in performance, installation, sound art, new music, film, video, dance, and intermedia. Works-in-progress are presented frequently. Performances change just about every weekend; call ahead for times and to alert the staff you're coming. ♦ Admission. 354 Congress St (between Pittsburgh and Farnsworth Sts). 542.7416 &

18 Boston Fire Museum This chunky little 1891 granite-and-brick firehouse is now owned by the Boston Sparks Association, which welcomes visitors. ♦ Free. Sa noon-4PM. 344 Congress St (at Farnsworth St). 482.1344 &

19 The Milk Bottle $
A landmark in its own right, this vintage 1930s highway lunchstand (pictured at right) was installed in front of **The Children's Museum** in 1977, having first been sawed in half and floated down the Charles River. Donated to the museum by the H.P. Hood Company, the 40-foot-tall wooden bottle would hold 50,000 gallons of milk and 860 gallons of cream if filled. Served from within are a variety of soups and salads, and, of course, ice cream. ♦ American ♦ Daily Apr-Oct; closed November-March. Congress St and Fort Point Channel. 426.7074 &

19 The Children's Museum Kids adore this lively participatory museum located in a former wool warehouse (see the plan on page 69). Whatever your age, a visit here will revive that urge to touch and get into things, even if you restrain yourself and just watch. In ongoing

THE CHILDREN'S MUSEUM

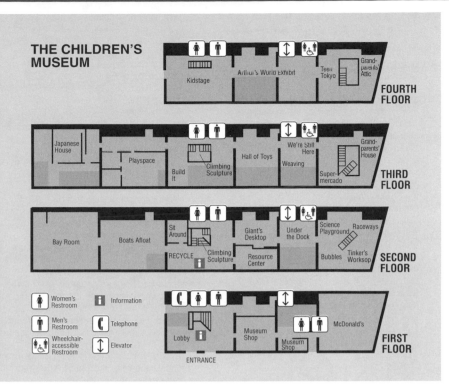

FOURTH FLOOR

Kidstage · Arthur's World Exhibit · Teen Tokyo · Grandparents' Attic

THIRD FLOOR

Japanese House · Playspace · Build It · Climbing Sculpture · Hall of Toys · Weaving · We're Still Here · Supermercado · Grandparents' House

SECOND FLOOR

Bay Room · Boats Afloat · Sit Around · RECYCLE · Climbing Sculpture · Giant's Desktop · Resource Center · Under the Dock · Science Playground · Bubbles · Raceways · Tinker's Workshop

FIRST FLOOR

Lobby · Museum Shop · Museum Shop · McDonald's

ENTRANCE

👩	Women's Restroom
👨	Men's Restroom
♿	Wheelchair-accessible Restroom
ℹ️	Information
📞	Telephone
↕	Elevator

exhibitions for toddlers to teens, kids may blow bubbles and spin tops in the **Science Playground;** scramble on the two-story **Climbing Sculpture;** learn personal health and well-being in "Mind Your Own Business"; visit "The Kid's Bridge," an exhibition that addresses Boston's multicultural heritage; and investigate what daily life is like in a Japanese silk merchant's reconstructed home from Kyoto, Boston's sister city. One of the museum's more popular exhibits is "Teen Tokyo," which is about the international culture of youth in Japan today; it includes a Japanese subway car, a karaoke booth, and an animation computer. The **Resource Center** offers educational materials and services to parents and teachers, such as RECYCLE, which sells in bulk dirt-cheap industrial raw materials discarded by local factories. **The Children's Museum Shop** is an unbeatable source for unusual gifts, toys, and books. ◆ Admission; reduced admission Friday 5-9PM. Tu-Su and school holidays. 300 Congress St (at Fort Point Channel). Recorded information 426.6500 ♿

19 The Computer Museum

A remarkable repository of technologies past and present, this is the only museum in the world devoted entirely to computers. Forget those graceless terms—nerd, hack, dweeb—computer "companions" are made here, the museum says. Whether you're computer-literate or -leery, more than 100 interactive exhibitions chronicle computers and their role in society. Walk through a spectacular 50-times-larger-than-life, two-story computer model that demonstrates how a personal computer functions, complete with a 25-foot-long keyboard, a 108-square-foot color monitor, and six-foot-tall floppy disks. David Macauley, writer and illustrator of *The Way Things Work* and other delightfully reassuring show-and-tell-style books, illustrated the "Walk-Through Computer" exhibit. Hands-on exhibitions let you "paint" pictures, compose melodies, create programs, simulate aircraft flight, design a house, even remodel your face.

Visit the amusing **Animation Theater,** and **Smart Machines Gallery** starring more than 25 robots. "People and Computers: Milestones of a Revolution" tracks the development of computers from the punch-card machines of the 1930s to today's microprocessors. "Tools and Toys: The Amazing Personal Computer" explores all the fascinating functions a PC can perform, including animation, video, and virtual reality. Ride the massive glass-enclosed elevator overlooking the Fort Point Channel. ◆ Admission; reduced admission Friday 5-9PM. Summer: daily. Winter: Tu-Su and Monday school holidays. 300 Congress St (at Fort Point Channel). 426.2800, computerized information 423.6758 ♿

20 Boston Tea Party Ship and Museum
The Boston Tea Party took place near here on Griffin's Wharf, long gone (its site is now landfill on Atlantic Avenue between Congress Street and Northern Avenue). On a cold December night in 1773, angry colonists dressed as Mohawk Indians boarded ships and heave-hoed 340 chests of costly British tea into the harbor to protest the tax imposed on their prized beverage. A cuppa was a costly commodity in those days. Moored alongside the Congress Street Bridge is the *Beaver II,* a Danish brig resembling one of the three original Tea Party ships and sailed here in 1973. For kids, it's an adventure to climb about the 110-foot-long working vessel, listen to costumed guides, and finally toss a bale of tea defiantly over the side (the fact that it's roped to the ship and hauled back up again doesn't lessen the thrill). On the adjacent pier, a small museum contains exhibitions, films, ship models, and memorabilia, with printed information available in seven languages. Tax-free tea is served at all times. ♦ Admission. Daily Mar-Nov; Su mid-Dec when a reenactment is held. Congress St Bridge. 338.1773

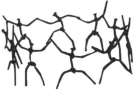

21 Artsmart This roomy, smart-looking shop features personal adornments and quirky home furnishings fashioned by some 120 local artisans. "It's comfortable, rather than pretentious—we make sure people can touch everything," says co-owner Dror Ashuah. Among the "unique objects" you may indeed want to fondle are their velvet hats, hand-painted picture frames, and faux-finished armoires. Duck next door to visit a sibling enterprise, the **Ashuah-Irving Gallery** (286 Congress St, 482.3343), a small, raw space whose selections are singularly astute. ♦ Call for hours. 272 Congress St (between Fort Point Channel and Atlantic Ave). 695.0151

22 Federal Reserve Bank of Boston
Whether you think this building (designed by **Hugh Stubbins & Associates** in 1977) resembles an old-fashioned washboard, goalposts, or a radiator, its shimmering aluminum-sheathed form is remarkably visible from many vantage points. The bank's art gallery on the ground floor is an alternative space where nonprofit New England–based artists and arts organizations mount six professional-level exhibitions annually.

A performance series is held in the adjacent auditorium September through December and March through June; call for program information. Free group tours of the bank's operational departments are offered with a month's notice. Public tours are held every Friday; and individual bank tours are offered by appointment only, generally on Friday. Visitors leave with souvenir packets of shredded money. ♦ Call for hours. 600 Atlantic Ave (between Summer and Congress Sts). Recorded gallery information 973.3453, tours 973.3451 ♿

23 South Station When construction on this station (designed by **Shepley, Rutan, and Coolidge**) at Dewey Square was completed in 1900, it was the world's largest railroad station, and it held that title for many years. By 1913, the station handled 38 million passengers a year, making it the busiest one in the country—even topping New York City's Grand Central Terminal. In peak year 1907, some 876 trains plied the rails on weekdays. The majestic five-story edifice, its shapely curved facade adorned with a nine-foot-wide clock surmounted by a proud eagle, proclaimed Boston's important place in the world. In its heyday, the station's comforts included a theater that screened newsreels and **Our Lady of the Railways Chapel.** But when airplanes, trucks, and autos eclipsed trains, the station slid into decrepitude. Eventually, most of it was demolished, except for the handsome headhouse, which nearly gave up the ghost in the 1960s.

Modern construction, respectful restoration, and intelligent planning have made the terminal (on the National Register of Historic Places) an exciting destination once more, with pushcart vendors, a food hall, coffee bar, newsstand, bank, and other services to lure pedestrians from nearby streets. Look for the old tin ceilings and beautiful carved details. More than 200 commuter trains and dozens of **Amtrak** runs come and go on the busiest travel days. With the *Red Line* subway on site, travelers are linked to the rest of Boston and the suburbs. With the addition of a commuter and long-distance bus terminal, even changing modes of transport has become convenient. ♦ Atlantic Ave and Summer St

24 US Postal Service-South Postal Annex
Boston's general mail facility looks like a 1920s ocean liner berthed alongside the channel. Always open, this is the mail processing hub for the Boston Division, with more than 1.2 million square feet of space and 12 miles of conveyors. Groups of 10 or more, minimum age 13 or eighth grade, can take a guided tour of the automated and mechanized facility and see how employees sort a daily average of nine million pieces of mail with the help of optical character readers, letter-sorting machines, bar-code sorters, and other sophisticated equipment. ♦ Free. Tours Tu-F Jan-Nov; call at least one week in advance to arrange a tour. 25 Dorchester Ave (just south of Summer St). 654.5081 ♿

Leather District

Like the Fort Point Channel area, this tiny appendage to the Financial District has a businesslike personality and lots of integrity. You can cover the entire seven-block neighborhood in one half-hour stroll. When Boston's Great Fire of 1872 swept clean more than 60 acres, it wiped out the city's commercial and wholesale centers, including the dense leather and garment district concentrated here. But slowly, businesses rose from the ashes and built sturdy new warehouses and factories, most along **Lincoln** and **South Streets,** some Romanesque in style and quite distinguished. Except for a few firms, the leather warehousing industry long ago departed for other countries. In the 1970s artists and urban pioneers began to move in, followed by art galleries, shops and services, and restaurants. The neighborhood's latest incarnation is still in the making.

25 The Essex Grill ★$$ On the first floor of the former **Hotel Essex,** now spiffed up as the **Plymouth Rock Building,** this big dining room looks across at trains idling in the **South Station** yards and fronts a major street, so diners can survey the urban scene. Nicely prepared seafood—including freshwater varieties—dominates the menu. On the same floor is the high-ceiling, airy **Essex Bar,** a throwback to another era with wonderfully fussy columns and drapes. ◆ Seafood ◆ M-F lunch and dinner. Reservations recommended for lunch. 695 Atlantic Ave (at Essex St). 439.3599 &

26 South Street Just a few years ago, this street was thriving as a venue for art galleries, and unique and intriguing shops. But what a difference a year can make. One of the reasons seems to be that because of popular and populous Boston's perpetual paucity of affordable housing, many of the buildings are being renovated for residential occupancy. Located within easy walking distance of Boston's business districts, South Street seems destined to become the new residential neighborhood. Art gallery tenants are understandably upset over this unexpected—and unwelcome—change. They will lose their leases and the street floors of many buildings, once rehabbed, will be leased commercially to restaurants and shops—and perhaps galleries—since it remains convenient to Chinatown, Downtown, the Waterfront, and other sections of Boston. ◆ Between Kneeland and Summer Sts

On South Street:

Initial Impressions Most Bostonians have yet to discover this captivating shop purveying inexpensive trinkets and toys. Yet many are familiar with its biggest seller: Clever rubber stamps of animals, buildings, cartoons, patterns, names, and hundreds of other designs all manufactured on the premises. Custom orders are taken, too.

There's also a line of eccentric doodads including lobster-claw–shaped harmonicas, plus all sorts of stationery, cards, and windup toys. ◆ M-Sa. No. 105A (between Beach and Tufts Sts). 426.6559

Les Zygomates ★$$ Located in the 1888 **Beebe Building,** this wine bar/bistro brings a touch of Paris to downtown Boston—surprisingly. The overall atmosphere is casual and very French, including the zinc-topped bar, where over 30 wines are served by the glass. The menu changes seasonally; among favorite items are chef Ian Just's tuna au poivre with Dijonaise sauce, sweetbreads, venison, and *terrain au foie gras.* There are also vegetarian offerings. Live jazz is featured on Sunday nights. ◆ French ◆ M-F lunch and dinner; Sa-Su dinner. Reservations recommended for dinner. No. 129 (between Beach and Tufts Sts). 542.5108

27 The Blue Diner/Art Zone ★$ These formerly separate restaurants have now combined, but have preserved their once individual characters in an unexpected meeting of space and place. The decor is pure diner: blue Formica-like tables, blue-and-white tiled floors, polished chrome, and Art Deco–style light fixtures. The menu is just as authentic with daily specials that include meat loaf, macaroni and cheese, turkey potpie, Louisiana bayou gumbo, as well as barbecued and Southern-styled dishes. There's an original working Seeburg sound system with a Wall-o-Matic selector: two plays per quarter let you listen to a parade of vintage 45s from the likes of Elvis, Aretha Franklin, Jerry Lee Lewis, and Louis Armstrong. Adjoining the diner is the darkened, cozy and kitschy **Art Zone,** with full-service bar and a half-dozen glass-topped tables that display the creations of local artists. ◆ American ◆ M-Th lunch and dinner; F-Su 11AM-7PM. 150 Kneeland St (at Utica St). 695.0087 &

28 F.C. Meichsner Company Founded in 1916, this family-owned and -operated business is the only East Coast establishment that can actually fix and repair all makes and models of binoculars and telescopes. Considered *the* source for binoculars, telescopes and accessories, barometers and ships' clocks, and replicas of old telescopes, it'll give you the best optics for your money. ◆ M-Sa. 182 Lincoln St (between Kneeland and Beach Sts). 426.7092

Financial District/Downtown

Boston's most on-the-go neighborhood is bounded by **Boston Common** and **Tremont Street** to the west, the **Central Artery** to the east, **Government Center** and **Faneuil Hall Marketplace** to the north, and **Chinatown** and the **Theater District** to the south. Celebrating the city's economic good health, the bumper crop of skyscrapers found here transforms the Boston skyline. The revitalized **Downtown Crossing** shopping area is cheerfully chaotic with pedestrians, pushcarts, and outdoor performers luring shoppers to the internationally famous **Filene's Basement** and dozens of other stores and boutiques.

History's imprint is here as well: Important **Freedom Trail** stops such as the **Old State House** and the **Old South Meeting House** impart a vision of a Revolution-era "Main Street." The **Custom House Tower, State Street Block,** and surviving wharf buildings designed by **Charles Bulfinch** speak of early wealth from the sea. Come during weekday work hours, when everything is open and in full swing. Walk along the profusion of twisty, tiny colonial lanes that have turned into busy arteries shadowed by architectural giants, creating windy, dark New York City–style canyons. Businesslike street names—**State, Court, Broad, Federal, School**—reflect the neighborhood's no-nonsense character. Numerous commercial palaces bear carved or fading traces of their original names, paying tribute to past lives.

From the city's earliest days, State Street was Boston's business artery—the most prestigious and spacious in town. Called **King Street** until the

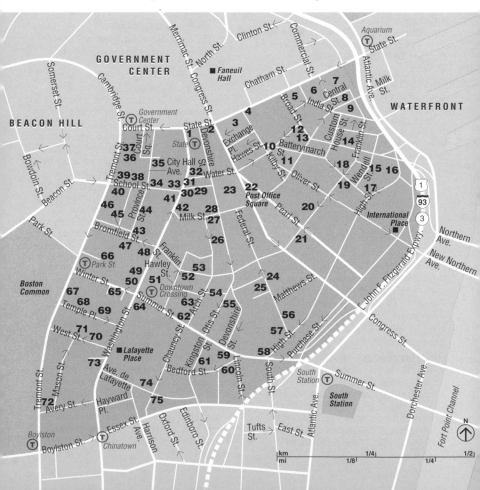

Revolution, State Street stretched 800 feet from the **Old State House** to **Long Wharf**, the noble pier that once served as the city's highway to the sea. The intersection of State Street and **Washington Street** was the epicenter of Boston's commercial and financial life.

An old Indian trail, Washington Street is now the major downtown commercial way, with great streetscapes down the **Ladder Block** side streets toward the **Common**. Always an important thoroughfare, in the 17th and 18th centuries it was the only road that ran the full length of Boston, linking the **Old State House** with the town gate at the neck of the Shawmut Peninsula. The street was renamed to honor George Washington's visit to the city in 1789. Today, it becomes seedy beyond **Temple Place** as it heads south toward the shrinking red-light district, the infamous **Combat Zone** (not a good place to be at night). Much of the existing Washington Street area was built after the Great Fire of 1872, which leveled 65 acres bounded by Washington, Broad, **Milk**, and **Summer Streets**, destroyed the heart of major New England industries, and left thousands without jobs. Many buildings still show scars and burns from the conflagration, which stopped just short of a number of Boston's historical treasures. Although the neighborhood was rapidly rebuilt, its residents had fled and commercialism took over. Boston's publishing and newspaper concerns flourished along **Newspaper Row** where Washington Street meets State and Court Streets, and insurance, banking, retail, garment, manufacturing, and other industries continue to call the area home. The famous **Omni Parker House** hotel and **Locke-Ober** restaurant also persevered in the face of change, and to this day remain pleasant, if somewhat stodgy, oases of gentility.

Economically, Boston was a Sleeping Beauty from 1895 until around 1965, when its building-boom prince arrived. Early skyscrapers are in short supply, but Boston does have its pleasing **Custom House Tower**, Art Deco **Batterymarch Building**, and lithe and lovely **Winthrop Building**. "If it ain't broke, don't fix it" is the Yankee credo, and Bostonians have a talent for recycling old structures. The city's fiscally conservative streak even influences new architecture. Unlike Chicago, where buildings shoot up to the sky unimpeded, Boston prefers a modest scale for its towers, so they politely accommodate older neighbors. Developers are subjected to stringent regulations and reviews. Some new buildings are dressed to the nines in decoration, but many are quite plain, even dowdy. It's as if the city is just getting used to its growing cosmopolitan stature and doesn't quite know how to dress the part.

---

1 Old State House This lovable 1713 brick building (pictured on page 74) has survived centuries of tumult and transformation, witnessing more than its share of dramatic moments in local and American history. A National Historic Landmark, the building has been remodeled and restored so often (**Goody, Clancy & Associates** performed the latest shoring-up in 1992) that its parts date from many eras. Situated at the head of State Street, the so-called "Temple of Liberty" originally commanded a clear view to the sea, and in the mid-18th century became the political and commercial center of the Massachusetts Bay Colony. Its first floor was a merchants' exchange, with the wheels of government turning on the floors above. Even the site occupied an important place in the town's history, for the earliest Boston market square was located here, as were the stocks, pillory, and whipping post used to mete out 17th-century Puritan justice. The building started life as a meeting place used by the British crown's provincial governor, as well as the seat of the government after the Revolution sent the British packing. The fantastical cavorting lion and unicorn on the elder edifice's gable, emblems of the hated crown, were frowned upon and removed (they have since been restored to their original home).

The ceremonial balcony at the east end overlooks the site—within a circle of cobblestones—where on 5 March 1770, frightened British soldiers fired on a large, angry mob of Bostonians, killing former slave Crispus Attucks and four others in the Boston Massacre. From this same balcony, the Declaration of Independence was first read to

Bostonians on 18 July 1776. Every year since, the Declaration has been read from the same spot on the Fourth of July. John Hancock was inaugurated here as the first governor under the new state constitution. And when George Washington visited Boston in 1789, he surveyed the great parade in his honor from here. But after the new **State House** was built on Beacon Hill, this monument became a jack-of-all-trades building, used and abused as a commercial center, newspaper office, and, for a decade, Boston's **City Hall.**

The outcast's cause was championed just in time in 1881, when a nonprofit organization called the Bostonian Society organized to restore the building and preserve the rich history it had witnessed. Ever since, the society has called it home and maintained a marvelous museum featuring changing and permanent exhibitions on the Revolutionary era, maritime history, and other important chapters in the city's life. The history of the building is chronicled, too. Paintings, portraits, figureheads, military and domestic artifacts, and other treasures tell the tale of this city. A vial of the original tea from the Boston Tea Party is on view, for instance, as is the coroner's report on Crispus Attucks. Look for John Hancock's family Bible and some of his clothing, and for Fitz Hugh Lane's painting *View of Boston Harbor.* A lovely spiral staircase leads to where inaugurations, daily government, and momentous meetings took place. For those

who want to dig deeper, the society's splendid library across the street on the third floor of the **Visitor Center** comprises more than 6,000 volumes and a thousand maps and architectural plans, plus rare manuscripts and broadsides.

The library also owns more than 10,000 Boston views in photographs, prints, watercolors, and drawings. Happily, the **Old State House** has flourished under the society's care. Unicorn and lion now prance with pride, copies elevated to the original animals' lofty perches. Another testament to the building's resilience: the presence of the **State Street** subway station that's tucked underneath. ♦ Admission. Daily. 206 Washington St (at State St). 720.3290

2 Visitor Center Located across the way from the **Old State House,** the center is operated by the Boston National Historic Park Service, which also runs the **Old South Meeting House, Faneuil Hall, Paul Revere House, Old North Church, Bunker Hill Monument, Charlestown Navy Yard,** and **Dorchester Heights.** In addition to offering information about these places, including a brief slide-show presentation, the center's staff of park rangers and volunteers answers questions about Boston and the entire National Park system. Find out about tours, many of which start from here. Pick up free **Freedom Trail** maps and pamphlets about all kinds of places, activities, and events. The center also sells books and souvenirs. And, equally important, well-kept rest rooms, water fountains, and telephones are available here, public conveniences hard to come by in Boston. There are also places to sit and rest weary bones. ♦ Daily. 15 State St (at Devonshire St). 242.5642 ♿

Old State House

MARJORIE VOGEL, RHODE ISLAND ORIGINALS

©MVOGEL

3 Exchange Place Opinions vary wildly about this blending of old and new. Actually, all that remains of the original 1891 **Stock Exchange Building** designed by **Peabody and Stearns** is a 60-foot segment of its worthy granite facade on the State Street side; the rest of the building is now engulfed by a glassy tower added in 1984 by the **WZMH Group.** From some vantage points, its dark reflective surfaces shimmer interestingly, but overall the newer building is, well, tacky. A handsome restored marble staircase is the atrium's incongruous centerpiece. This was the site of the historic **Bunch of Grapes Tavern,** located at the head of Long Wharf during the 19th century. A favorite watering hole for patriot leaders before the Revolution, the tavern reputedly served the best bowl of punch in Boston. ◆ 53 State St (between Kilby and Congress Sts)

4 75 State Street This unabashedly gilded and gaudy showpiece, erected in 1988 by **Graham Gund Associates,** is loved by some and hated by others. The lobby looks like an example of tender loving care gone too far, with its plethora of patterns, types of marble, and fancy fixtures—but the vast atrium lets in plenty of pure, unadulterated light. ◆ At Kilby St

5 Board of Trade Building This elaborate, urbane building designed in 1901 by **Winslow and Bradlee** has aged well. Its allegorical figures and vigorous stone carvings harken to seafaring days gone by, especially the galleons rushing forward into the viewer's space. ◆ 131 State St (between India and Broad Sts)

6 Custom House Tower This preposterous marriage of convenience between a Greek Revival temple dating from one century (**Ammi Young** was the architect in 1847) and a tower plunked on top during the next (**Peabody and Stearns** added it in 1915) originally appalled many Bostonians. After all, the proud **Custom House** was once the focal point of the thriving waterfront.

Situated at the base of State Street, the important colonial route that once led from the **Old State House** and neighboring financial establishments out onto the wharves, the original structure was mammoth, with each of its 32 Doric columns a single 42-ton shaft of Quincy granite. Before Atlantic Avenue was created, the building was so close to the waterfront that the bows of ships would bump the windows facing the harbor. As the 20th century progressed and skyscrapers sprouted in other cities, Boston was mired in an economic slump. The federal government forked over the funds for the addition of the 495-foot tower; built between 1912 and 1917, it was the city's first skyscraper and for decades was New England's tallest structure.

It took a while, but Bostonians eventually became very attached to their peculiar

Custom House Tower

landmark, now a familiar friend. No matter how many new structures crowd the skyline, the steadfast tower is the most memorable silhouette, its 22-foot-wide clock (repaired and refurbished in 1997) aglow at night. The lobby beneath the original building's rotunda—skylit until the tower leapt on top—deserves a look.

The city bought the entire edifice from the federal government in 1987, but later leased it to developers. Today it is a time-share property owned by the Marriott Corporation (see below). At press time plans were on the drawing board for a ground-floor museum on the premises to honor Boston's maritime trade history and the role the **Custom House** played in it. ◆ State St (between McKinley Sq and India St)

Within the Custom House Tower:

Marriott's Custom House $$$
Opened in 1997, this time-share complex offers accommodations to short-term guests (reservations are required). Overlooking Boston Harbor and just a short distance from **Faneuil Hall Marketplace,** the **New England Aquarium,** and the waterfront hotel and shopping complexes, the property has 82 units, all 1-bedroom suites with skyline and harbor views. Each has a wet bar, a microwave oven, two color TV sets, and a VCR. On-site amenities include concierge service, valet parking, and an exercise room, but there's no restaurant. ◆ 3 McKinley Sq (between Central and State Sts). 310.1600, 800/881.6824; fax 310.6301 ♿

7 State Street Block Gridley J.F. Bryant, one of the architects for the **Old City Hall** on School Street, not to mention **Boston City Hospital** in the South End and the **Charles Street Jail** on Cambridge Street, also built a number of large granite warehouses that once extended to the harbor. He designed this massive granite block in 1858. Look for the big granite globe squeezed under the arched cornice facing the **Custom House Tower.** The mansard roofs were added later. ♦ Bounded by John F. Fitzgerald Expwy and McKinley Sq, and Central and State Sts

Within State Street Block:

Dockside $ At one of Boston's most popular sports bars, fans have their choice of seven TVs and two big screens on which to watch the games. The drinks, rah-rah decor, camaraderie, and celebrity customers are the draw—not the cuisine. Expect bar-food basics like pizza, barbecue, and burgers. Many fans bring autograph books because sports stars have been known to drop by. One memorable night, Jack Nicholson tended bar. ♦ American ♦ Daily lunch and dinner. 183 State St. 723.7050

Harborside Inn of Boston $$ Victorian period furnishings characterize this small hotel housed in a renovated granite mercantile building. The 54 rooms and suites also offer queen-size beds, private baths, individual climate control, voice mail, and free local phone calls. Some rooms have convertible sofas. There's no on-site restaurant, but many are located nearby. ♦ 185 State St. 723.7500, 888/723.7565

Tatsukichi ★★$$
Its unremarkable looks are deceiving, since this is one of Boston's most authentic Japanese restaurants. Explore the enormous sushi selection, and try teriyaki, sukiyaki, *kushiage* (skewers threaded with meats and vegetables, then batter-fried), or *shabu shabu* (pot-cooked dinners for two). Twenty percent of the menu is raw fish, and many uncommon entrées will pique an adventurous eater's curiosity. If you'd like privacy for your party, request a tatami room. For lively entertainment, there's a karaoke lounge. ♦ Japanese ♦ M-F lunch and dinner; Sa-Su dinner. Reservations recommended. 189 State St. 720.2468

8 **Central Wharf Buildings** This humble but handsome row of eight brick buildings between India Street and the elevated expressway are all that remain of the 54 designed by **Charles Bulfinch,** which together extended nearly 1,300 feet to where the **New England Aquarium** now stands. All of the structures, built in 1817, originally opened onto the water to receive goods from the ships docked out front. On the opposite side of the Central Artery, Central Wharf ends at the harbor's edge. ♦ Milk St (between Atlantic Ave and India St)

9 **Flour and Grain Exchange Building** This commercial castle brings a surprising fillip of fantasy to the hard-nosed Financial District. The conical roof of the exchange's curvaceous corner is bedecked with pointy dormers that look like a crown. Architect **Henry Hobson Richardson**'s influence is palpable in this 1893 design by his successors, **Shepley, Rutan, and Coolidge,** who also built the impressive **Ames Building** on Court Street. Look for the extraordinary cartouche adorned with an eagle straddling a globe and cornucopias spilling fruit and coins. The exchange was built for the Chamber of Commerce and once housed a large trading hall on the third floor. Now architects hold court within. Don't bother to visit the lobby, as the original was renovated into oblivion. With its lanterns and scattering of trees, the building's triangular plaza is an oasis in this unexpectedly quiet corner of the city. ♦ 177 Milk St (at India St)

10 **Liberty Square** At this triangular intersection is another of Boston's quaintly misnamed "squares" squeezed into a busy block. This one commemorates the 14 August 1765 destruction of the British Stamp Tax office that was located here. (A year later, England repealed the Stamp Act.) The square was formally named in 1793 in a gala ceremony honoring the French Revolution, complete with extravagant feasting and 21-gun salute, and is dominated by Gyuri Hollosy's memorial to the Hungarian Revolution of 1956, dedicated in 1986. For those who love old urban pockets lingering in modern cities, this site is a treat. It's surrounded by businesslike 19th-century buildings that reveal curious and delightful details, if you take time to notice. The old street pattern's turns and angles provide interesting vistas. ♦ At Batterymarch, Kilby, and Water Sts

11 **Appleton Building** Coolidge and Shattuck designed this powerful, austere Classical

Revival edifice in 1924; **Irving Salsberg** renovated it in 1981. Named for Samuel Appleton, a Boston insurance magnate, the building's most expressive gesture is its generous curve to accommodate converging streets on Liberty Square, its best side. (The Milk Street facade is far less interesting.) All else is measured, pragmatic, restrained—just right for the industry it housed. But the more you study the structure, the more inventive it appears, especially its syncopated window patterns and entrance facade friezes depicting a violin maker, carpenter, glassblower, sculptor, draftsman, and other artisans. Peek into the elliptical lobby with its elegant gilded ceiling. ◆ 110 Milk St (at Oliver St)

12 Broad Street Indefatigable developer Uriah Cotting led his Broad Street Association in many ambitious 19th-century urban redevelopment schemes, of which this street was but one by-product. Laid out about 1805 according to **Charles Bulfinch**'s plans, it quickly became a handsome commercial avenue to the sea, bordered by many Federal-style Bulfinch buildings, such as that at **No. 104.** A scattering of these still stand among more recent but distinguished structures such as **No. 52** (which was completed in 1853). With its many low-rise buildings, this street is one of the neighborhood's most open, sunny spots. A historical note: In a store located on this very thoroughfare, Francis Cabot Lowell, one of Cotting's partners, developed a power loom that ultimately revolutionized American textile manufacture. ◆ Between John F. Fitzgerald Expwy and State St

12 Bakey's ★★$ This appealing upscale delicatessen with a full bar serves all sorts of sandwiches for lunch and supper, plus an extensive continental breakfast. The story behind the shop's amusing logo of a man asleep on an ironing board (see the illustration above) is that owner George Bakey once found his father in this pose, ensconced on the family ironing board. There are two very pleasant dining rooms—one called **The Snug**, named for the room women retired to when it wasn't considered proper for the sexes to mingle in bars. George has gone all-out in his establishment's decor: wooden bars and booths imported from England (be sure to notice **The Snug**'s cozy little square bar), antique lighting, Oriental rugs, fresh linen and flowers. Be forewarned—smoking isn't

allowed anywhere. ◆ American/Deli ◆ M-F lunch and dinner. 45 Broad St (at Water St). 426.1710 &

13 Sakura-bana ★★★$$ Sushi is the house specialty—as you might guess if you notice the poem by the entrance extolling "sushi rapture" —and you can even order "sushi heaven," a sampler of more than two dozen varieties of sushi and sashimi. If you order à la carte, you can be as daring or timid as you wish, staying with salmon, tuna, and mackerel, or exploring exotica like flying fish roe and sea urchin. The daily *bento* (lunch box) specials served with soup, salad, rice, and fruit are also very good choices. For dinner, try seafood *teppan yaki* (broiled with teriyaki sauce and served on a sizzling iron plate). Not only is this trim and tidy restaurant's cuisine outstanding, its prices are reasonable and portions generous. Lots of Financial District workers regularly queue up for lunch. The name, by the way, means "Cherry Blossom." ◆ Japanese ◆ M-Sa lunch and dinner; Su dinner (closed first Sunday of the month). Reservations recommended for dinner. 57 Broad St (at Milk St). 542.4311 &

14 Sultan's Kitchen ★$ Located in a remnant of **Charles Bulfinch**'s 19th-century Broad Street development, this self-service restaurant cooks up fresh and delicious renditions of Middle Eastern and Greek favorites for the lunch crowd: kabobs, grape leaves, Greek salad, *baba ganooj*, egg-lemon-chicken soup, falafel, and tabbouleh. Try the cool, crisp Sultan's Salad or rich *tarama* salad made with fish roe. If too many dishes tempt you, order one of the sampler plates. ◆ Middle Eastern/Takeout ◆ M-Sa lunch. 72 Broad St (at Custom House St). 338.7819, recorded menu 338.8509

15 Nara ★$$ Lawyers, brokers, bankers, and other professional types favor this cozy, private little place located along an alley. One might easily miss it altogether, so watch for the Japanese lanterns and red awnings. Sushi lovers find happiness in the extensive selection, and others can sample tempura, teriyaki, or *katsu* (deep-fried) entrées. This friendly, family-run restaurant is crowded by day, quieter by night, but always enjoyable. ◆ Japanese/Korean/Takeout ◆ M-F lunch and dinner; Sa dinner. Reservations recommended. 85 Wendell St (between Batterymarch and Broad Sts). 338.5935 &

16 Country Life ★$ Boston's most complete vegetarian dining experience allows you to sample plentiful all-you-can-eat lunch, brunch, and dinner buffets. Absolutely no dairy, meat, refined grains, or sugar sneak into any of the dishes. Substitutes include "milk" and "cheeses" made from nuts and soy. The inventive menu changes daily—with a new one printed each month—featuring soups like garbanzo dumpling, lentil, and Russian potato; entrées such as lasagna, enchiladas, and vegetable potpie; and an interesting choice of vegetables. Afterward, treat yourself to one of their desserts. Everything is self-serve, and the decor is neat but plain; the emphasis of this restaurant is entirely on hearty, healthy food. ♦ Vegetarian/Takeout ♦ M-Th lunch and dinner; F lunch; Su brunch and dinner. Reservations requested. No credit cards accepted. 200 High St (at John F. Fitzgerald Expwy). 951.2534, recorded menu 951.2462

17 Chadwick Leadworks Though one-upped by the bulky Neo-Classical **International Place,** a nearby high-rise, this forceful rustic structure still holds its own on the Financial District fringe. Built in 1887 by Joseph Houghton Chadwick, once described as "Lead King of Boston," it was designed by **William G. Preston,** who also created the former **New England Museum of Natural History** in Back Bay (now the upscale **Louis, Boston** clothing store). Handsome three-story arches with a graceful ripple of spandrels are topped by a row of little windows and a bold parapet. A gargoyle glares from one corner, and other grotesques and dragonlike lizards cling to the facade. At the back is the square shot tower, inside which molten lead was poured from the top, cooling into shot before reaching the bottom floor. ♦ 184 High St (at Batterymarch St)

18 Batterymarch Building Named for the street it adorns—once part of a marching route for military companies from **Boston Common** to now-leveled Fort Hill—this heroically optimistic Art Deco assemblage designed by **Henry Kellogg** in 1928 is wonderful to behold in the midst of a district becoming ever more crowded and shadowed by impersonal modern giants. The three slender towers linked by third-story arcades undergo a truly marvelous transformation as they push through the crowded block to the sky. Their dark-brown brick at ground level gradually lightens in color until it becomes a glowing buff at the top, as if bleached by sunlight (the one commodity always in short supply in congested downtowns). Under the handsome entrance arches, look for the charming reliefs of boats, trains, planes, stagecoaches, and clipper ships. Unlike the heavy-handed gilding of nearby **75 State Street,** this building's discreet touches of gold enhance rather than bedizen its fine form. The second floor of the building now serves as a downtown campus for **Northeastern University.** ♦ 60 Batterymarch St (between Franklin St and Batterymarch Arm)

19 Brandy Pete's ★★$$ During Prohibition thirsty Bostonians flocked here in droves after a flip of the venetian blinds signaled that a new shipment of booze had come in. When that period ended, owner Peter Sabia was persuaded by his customers to transform his speakeasy into a restaurant. Today Bostonians on the hunt for traditional "Beantown" fare come to the large brass- and mahogany-appointed pub where the menu features good, simple dishes, including scrod, chicken potpie, and an award-winning meat loaf. There's also alfresco dining for eight on the patio. Whether eating indoors or out, you'll find the best of the basics here. ♦ American ♦ M-F lunch and dinner. 267 Franklin St (between Batterymarch and Oliver Sts). 439.4165

20 Le Meridien $$$ Now under Forte Hotel management, this former **Old Federal Reserve Bank,** a Renaissance Revival palazzo designed by **R. Clipston Sturgis** in 1922, has been happily preserved—to the tune of $33 million—as part of this prestigious European hotel. The 326 guest rooms are contemporary in decor, while the lobby and public spaces feature restored original architectural details. Because a glass mansard roof was plunked on top of the old structure to add additional floors, many rooms feature sloping glass walls, offering great views. **Suite 915** is especially popular, as are the loft suites. There are 15 rooms specially equipped for people with disabilities, and 7 floors are reserved for nonsmokers. There's a posh health club called **Le Club Meridien** on the third floor, featuring a pool, whirlpool, sauna, and exercise equipment; and a full-service business center complete with foreign currency exchange. French chocolates and a daily weather forecast appear bedside in each of the rooms every night—a nice touch. Other amenities include a multilingual staff, valet parking, 24-hour concierge and room services, and express laundry and dry cleaning. Paid parking is offered in the adjacent 400-car garage.

The big plus for guests is the location in the heart of the Financial District; it's an easy walk from here to many popular attractions and the Theater District. Adjoining the hotel is **One Post Office Square,** a 41-story tower that was added in 1981 by **Jung/Brannen Associates** and **Pietro Belluschi,** and houses conference rooms and business offices. ♦ 250 Franklin St (between Oliver and Pearl Sts). 451.1900, 800/543.4300; fax 423.2844 &

Within Le Meridien:

Restaurants/Clubs: Red   Hotels: Blue
Shops/♥ Outdoors: Green   Sights/Culture: Black

Boston in Fact . . . and Fiction

With its long and distinguished literary tradition, it's
understandable Boston has become the subject of
and/or setting for many a volume. Here are some of
the best titles.

Nonfiction

AIA Guide to Boston by Susan and Michael
Southworth (Globe Pequot Press, 1991). The official
American Institute of Architects informative and
entertaining survey of over 500 notable landmarks.

Boston, A Topographical History by Walter Muir
Whitehill (Belnap Press of Harvard University Press,
1968). An urbane discourse on Boston's history
describing the changing face of the city, and the
society that changed with it, over 300 years.

The Boston Irish by Thomas H. O'Connor
(Northeastern University Press, 1995). The history of
the Irish immigration to Boston and how the Irish
helped mold the city into what it is today.

**In Common Ground: A Turbulent Decade in the
Lives of Three American Families** by J. Anthony
Lukas (Alfred A. Knopf, 1985). A vivid portrayal of the
era of court-ordered school busing in Boston.

Fiction

All Our Yesterdays by Robert B. Parker (Delacorte
Press, 1994). Filled with Boston settings and lore,
this sprawling saga of spans the 20th century and
reaches from Ireland's IRA to Boston's **Beacon Hill**
mansions. Parker, a Boston resident, is the author of
the acclaimed Spenser detective stories.

Anger by May Sarton (W.W. Norton & Company,
1982). A romantic, realistic novel about a successful
Boston banker and a mezzo-soprano.

April Morning by Howard Fast (Crown, 1961). An
admirable fictional historical re-creation of the events
on 19 April 1775 at **Lexington** and **Concord** as
observed by a 15-year-old boy, who signed the
muster roll of the Lexington militia.

Back Bay by William Martin (Warner Books, 1979). A
six-generation story of a driven clan, obsessively
pursuing a lost Paul Revere treasure, set in an older
Boston and in today's exclusive
Back Bay.

Boston Adventure by Jean
Stafford (Houghton Mifflin,
1944). This novel brings James
Carroll's best-seller Mortal Friends
(see below) up to the present
day, spanning three generations
in the tale of the Doyle brothers.
The central character is Boston
itself, with its turf wars.

Divine Inspiration by Jane
Langton (Penguin, 1993). One
of 10 locally set Homer Kelly
mysteries (others include
Memorial Hall Murder and God in
Concord), this story has a Back
Bay church as a backdrop.

The Friends of Eddie Coyle by George V. Higgins
(1972, reissued 1987; Viking/Penguin). This and
several other mysteries in the ongoing series—The
Patriot Game, Cogan's Trade, Impostors, Outlaws,
Penance for Jerry Kennedy—are set in Boston; the
focus is on small-time crooks and Irish politics.

The Godwulf Manuscript by Robert B. Parker (Dell
Publishing, 1973). This is the first in the 25-book
(and counting) series of detective novels featuring
literature-quoting tough guy private eye Spenser.
Parker is a native Bostonian and Boston and its
environs play a significant role in each book. The
latest in the series is Sudden Mischief (1998).

Johnny Tremain by Esther Forbes (Dell Publishing,
1987). This young person's classic is set in 18th-
century revolutionary Boston.

Joy Street by Francis Parkinson Keyes (Julian
Messner, Inc., 1950). This out-of-print novel, still on
library shelves, is set on Beacon Hill, and covers the
period from Christmas Eve 1936 to November 1946.

The Last Hurrah by Edwin O'Connor (Little, Brown
and Company, 1956). Considered one of the most
entertaining novels ever written about American
politics, and twice made into a film, it's the story of
Frank Skeffington, making his final race for mayor.
The character is based on the real-life Boston mayor
James M. Curley.

The Late George Apley by John P. Marquand (1937,
reissued 1967; Little, Brown and Company). A novel
told in the form of the memoir of the character
Horatio Willing, who satirizes himself as he recounts
the life of a conventional and somewhat pathetic
Bostonian. It was awarded the Pulitzer Prize.

Make Way for Ducklings by Robert McCloskey
(1941, reissued 1976; Penguin). This is the beloved
children's picture book about Mr. and Mrs. Mallard
and their eight ducklings, who settle in Boston's
Public Garden.

Mortal Friends by James Carroll (Dell Publishing,
1978). A masterful plot that follows Colman Brady
from the Irish rebellion through his flight to Boston
with his infant son, and evolving into intimate
connections with the Mafia, the Roman
Catholic Church, Washington's
powerful, and Boston's elite.

The Rise of Silas Lapham by
William Dean Howells (1885,
reissued 1991; Random House). A
self-reliant businessman who has
become wealthy moves to Boston,
and learns about pretention and social
and ethical standards on Beacon Hill.

The Scarlet Letter by Nathaniel
Hawthorne (1850, reissued 1992;
Alfred A. Knopf). Hester Prynne,
condemned to wear the scarlet
embroidered letter "A" as punishment
for adultery, refuses to reveal the name of
her child's father.

Julien ★★★$$$$ Named for Boston's first French restaurant, which opened on this same site in 1794, this restaurant draws a predominantly business clientele. Yet the restaurant's lofty refined splendor and creative French cuisine make it a good choice for a serious evening out. Chef Dominique Rizzo combines fresh native ingredients with French/Mediterranean touches in dishes such as black peppercorn–crusted yellowfin tuna steak with sweet red pearl onions, raisins, and snow peas; rack of New Zealand lamb with asparagus, artichokes, radishes, and olives in a garlic-and-thyme sauce; and grilled Atlantic salmon with marinated mushrooms, wrapped in a spinach leaf and topped with lemon zest. Desserts are equally inspired, and the wine list exceptional.

The vast dining room is located in the high-ceilinged hall that once served as the bank's boardroom; tables are all generously spaced and diners settle into Queen Anne wingback chairs, promoting privacy and conversation. The **Julien Bar,** resplendent with gilded coffered ceilings and wonderful carved details, provides background piano music. Look for the pair of N.C. Wyeth murals portraying Abraham Lincoln and George Washington. Complimentary valet parking is provided at dinnertime. ◆ French ◆ M-F lunch and dinner; Sa dinner. Reservations recommended; jacket required at restaurant; no blue jeans allowed at bar. 451.1900 ⟐

Cafe Fleuri ★★$$$ Situated beneath the six-story atrium in **One Post Office Square,** connected to the hotel, this airy and open cafe features brasserie-style cuisine. It is popular for business breakfasts and lunches, and the spectacular, belly-bludgeoning Sunday jazz brunch.

Attention all chocoholics: On Saturday afternoons (except in the summer) the cafe puts on a sumptuous all-you-can-eat Chocolate Bar buffet, a truly hedonistic, decadent display of cakes, pies, tortes, fondues, mousses, cookies, brownies, and the like. Valet parking is available. ◆ Cafe ◆ Daily breakfast, lunch, and dinner. Reservations recommended. 451.1900

21 Bell Atlantic Headquarters Building A 1947 design by **Cram & Ferguson,** this step-top Art Deco throwback occupies its place with pride. **Goody, Clancy & Associates** renovated the facade in 1992 in a spiffy homage; check

out the spiky beacons, echoed in the phone booths on either side. (Everything has been touched with a Deco wand, from the garden guardrails and trash receptacles, right down to the sidewalk pattern.) Off the main lobby, you can see a re-creation of inventor Alexander Graham Bell's garret. Dean Cornwell's frenzied and colorful Norman Rockwell-esque mural, which circles the lobby, is really something to see. Called *Telephone Men and Women at Work,* the 160-foot-long, action-packed painting depicts 197 lifesize figures in dramatic groupings. Painted in 1951, it lionizes not only Bell and other telephone pioneers, but also employees on the job and those risking life and limb in the face of disaster to keep those calls coming. Cornwell was an old hand at this sort of thing, having created murals honoring steelworkers, pioneers in medicine, various states' histories, and the like.

Bell's laboratory is a painstaking replica of his original studio at 109 Court Street in old Scollay Square, where he electrically transmitted the first speech sounds over a wire on 3 June 1875. (The following March, in a different lab, Bell succeeded in sending not just sounds but intelligible words, when he issued his famous line: "Mr. Watson, come here, I want you.") The studio was saved from demolition, dismantled, and eventually brought here in pieces and rebuilt. On display are models, telephone replicas, drawings, references, and historic artifacts, plus a wonderful diorama of the view of Scollay Square from Bell's window. Pamphlets about Cornwell's creation and Bell's garret are usually available. ◆ Free. M-F. 185 Franklin St (between Pearl and Congress Sts). 743.4747 ⟐

22 Post Office Square This popular public space tops a 1,400-car garage. One of the busiest and most visually exciting pockets in the city, it's surrounded by the Art Deco post office and telephone company headquarters, and affords wonderful views of the city's most eclectic architecture—a delightful hodgepodge of new and old. The square was landscaped by Craig Halvorson, and harbors 125 species of plants, including seven different species of vines climbing an elegant 143-foot-long trellised colonnade. **Harry Ellenzweig** designed the sparkling glass quarters of the **Milk Street Cafe** (see below); sculptor Howard Ben Tre the handsome green-glass fountains. ◆ Bounded by Pearl, Congress, and Franklin Sts

At Post Office Square:

Angell Memorial Plaza At the triangle's tip opposite the post office is a pocket park dedicated to George Thorndike Angell, founder of the Massachusetts Society for the Prevention of Cruelty to Animals and the American Humane Education Society. A sculpture of a small pond and its inhabitants is located in the middle of a brick circle inset with reliefs of birds, beasts, and bugs. Look for

Angell's wise words: "Our humane societies are now sowing the seeds of a harvest which will one of these days protect not only the birds of the air and beasts of the field but also human beings as well." Looming near the pond is the fountain designed by **Peabody and Stearns** as a watering place for horses in 1912.

23 John W. McCormack Post Office and Court House A commanding Art Deco building with plenty of ornament and vertical window ribbons, this post office (designed in 1931 by **Cram & Ferguson** with **James A. Wetmore**) has a nicely weathered gray facade. ♦ Congress and Milk Sts (main entrance at 90 Devonshire St, at Water St). 654.5676

24 BankBoston **Campbell, Aldrich & Nulty** designed this ungainly brown tower with a big belly in 1971. It quickly earned a famous nickname, "The Pregnant Building." ♦ 100 Federal St (between Matthews and Franklin Sts). 434.2200 ♿

25 Champlain Chocolates Hard to find outside their native Vermont, these treats are surpassingly tasty. Offerings range from truffles and Turkish delight to edible gift packs such as a chocolate heart stuffed with nonpareils. There's also a small ice-cream bar on the premises. Be sure to stroll the building lobby, too. The building is a **Kohn Pederson Fox** structure appended to the Deco-era **75 Federal Street**; the result is a handsome hybrid. Be sure to get a look at the elevators. ♦ M-F. 101 Federal St (at Sullivan Pl). 951.4666 ♿

26 Arch St. Deli $ For years known as **Hole in the Wall,** one of the district's tiniest tidbits of real estate, this diminutive deli manages to turn out a huge assortment of breakfast and lunch items to go. You'd be hard-pressed to think of a hot or cold sandwich that isn't served here (okay, so there's no peanut butter), not to mention the salads, soups and stews, egg combos, burgers, and snacks. Join the line at the outside counter, or step inside to watch how skillfully counter staff dart past each other in close quarters. It was a passerby's chance remark—"Look at that hole in the wall"—that gave the 12-by-4-foot deli its original apt appellation. With brown bag in hand, take a moment to examine Richard Haas's trompe l'oeil mural across the street, painted on the back of 31 Milk Street, which portrays a cutaway of the actual facade. Haas also painted the well-known mural on the **Boston Architectural Center** in Back Bay. ♦ Deli/Takeout ♦ M-F 5:30AM-4PM. 24 Arch St (between Franklin and Milk Sts). 423.4625 ♿

27 International Trust Company Building Max Bachman's allegorical figures *Commerce* and *Industry* adorn the Arch Street side, while *Security* and *Fidelity* are ensconced on Devonshire Street, adding a fanciful representation of business rectitude modern

buildings sorely lack. This edifice, built in 1893 by **William G. Preston,** enlarged in 1906, and now listed on the National Register of Historic Places, incorporated the remains of a building partly destroyed by Boston's terrible 1872 fire. ♦ 39-47 Milk St (between Devonshire and Arch Sts)

28 Milk Street Cafe ★$ Downtown shoppers and Financial District denizens love this crowded cafeteria, and many a politician stops in for kosher dairy, vegetarian home-style cooking that includes muffins and bagels, soups, pizzas, pastas, quiches, salads, and sweet treats. ♦ Cafe/Takeout ♦ M-F breakfast and lunch. 50 Milk St (at Devonshire St). 542.3663 ♿

29 Bob Smith Sporting Goods Specializing in gear for running, tennis, skiing, fishing, and, of late, in-line skating, this small shop is staffed by "professionals who play and understand the sport they sell." The service is indeed more than perfunctory—it's educational—and the selections are top-of-the-line. In 1643 this corner was the site of Governor Winthrop's home, conveniently located by Great Spring, for which it's named (that source ran dry in the mid-19th century). ♦ M-Sa. 9 Spring La (between Devonshire and Washington Sts). 426.4440 ♿

30 Fanny Farmer A Boston classic, this shop has been selling chocolates, fudge, and other candy, ice cream, and nuts on this site for more than 50 years. It is part of the huge national chain named for Fanny Merritt Farmer, Boston's legendary cookbook author. Among other innovations, Fanny introduced the level measurement system that revolutionized food preparation. The company also owns all rights to Fanny's immensely popular *The Boston Cooking School Cookbook,* which can be purchased here. ♦ Daily. 288 Washington St (between Milk St and Spring La). 542.7045. Also at: 3 Center Plaza, Tremont and Cambridge Sts. 723.6201

A bookshop once stood near the Old State House, where the first Bibles printed in America were sold and where Edgar Allan Poe's first volume of verse was published. No copies of Poe's work were sold here, a first blow among the many that darkened his view of life.

31 Winthrop Building Boston's first building with a steel skeleton instead of load-bearing masonry walls, this sliver slips gracefully into a tapering lot. Conceived in 1893 by one of Boston's more adventurous architects, **Clarence H. Blackall,** the gently curving building flows between Spring Lane and Water Street. Now on the National Register of Historic Places, its golden airiness and dressy decoration, especially on the lower levels, delight the eye. Blackall's Chicago training was a fantastic boon to Boston. He designed a number of majestic theaters and other public buildings. Among Boston's other early steel-frame office buildings are a charming pair nearby: **Cass Gilbert's Brazer Building** of 1896 and **Carl Fehmer's Worthington Building** of 1894, standing side by side at 27 and 33 State Street. ♦ 276-278 Washington St (between Spring La and Water St)

Within the Winthrop Building:

Caffé Paradiso $ Another spin-off of the favorite North End meeting place, this cafe sells quick Italian treats (there are counters, but no tables). In addition to steaming cappuccino, espresso, and Italian beverages, they offer savory calzones, pizzas, quiches, cannoli, and delicious desserts, including a popular hazelnut truffle torte. ♦ Italian/ Takeout ♦ Daily 7AM-midnight. No credit cards accepted. 3 Water St. 742.8689 ♿ Also at: 255 Hanover St (between Mechanic and Richmond Sts). 742.1768; 1 Eliot St (at Eliot Sq), Cambridge. 868.3240

Mrs. Fields Cookies Ultrarich, chewy, and chocolaty cookies bring a steady stream of sweet-toothed customers to this cookie cove, one of hundreds in the national chain. Choose from the rich repertoire of chocolate-chip varieties, or try oatmeal raisin or cinnamon sugar. The brownies and muffins are equally tempting. ♦ Daily. 264 Washington St (at Water St). 523.0390 ♿ Also at: Copley Place, 100 Huntington Ave (between Garrison and Dartmouth Sts). 536.6833; Marketplace Center, 200 State St (between Atlantic Ave and Commercial St). 951.0855

32 Merchants Wine & Spirits This former bank now houses liquid treasures. One of the city's finest wine and spirits shops, it carries unusual vintages as well as inexpensive drinkable specials. Rare Cognacs and superior Burgundies are a specialty; there's also a large California section. Tastings are held regularly in the old bank vault, its walls still lined with safety-deposit boxes. The cheese department sells superb cheeses from small New England farmsteads, plus imports. Pick up the informative, chatty house newsletter. ♦ M-Sa. 6 Water St (between Devonshire and Washington Sts). 523.7425

33 3 School Street This redbrick, gambrel-roofed building now on the National Register of Historic Places, was built circa 1711 for Thomas Crease, who opened Boston's first apothecary shop within. In 1828 Timothy Carter, a bookseller, took over, installed printing presses, and opened the **Old Corner Bookstore.** Thus began the building's long career as the locus of Boston's publishing industry and literary life.

Here Ticknor & Fields published works by Harriet Beecher Stowe, Charles Dickens, Alfred Lord Tennyson, Elizabeth Barrett Browning, Henry David Thoreau, Nathaniel Hawthorne, William Makepeace Thackery, Julia Ward Howe, and Ralph Waldo Emerson, helping to establish a native literature. Gregarious Jamie Fields in particular gained respect as counsel, friend, and guardian to writers, and was especially loved as an innovator who believed writers ought to be paid for their pains. Here, too, the *Atlantic Monthly* was founded and rose to cultural eminence. The *Boston Globe*'s downtown offices once occupied the building, whose preservation the newspaper ensured by opening its namesake, the **Globe Corner Bookstore,** in 1982. Sadly, the bookshop at this location closed in 1998, although branches remain in Back Bay and Cambridge. The building now houses a bank, shops, and the offices of Globe-Pequot Press. ♦ At Washington St

Brookstone®

34 Brookstone The brainchild of engineer Pierre de Beaumont, a frustrated hobbyist who sought unusual tools that weren't available, this specialty store stocks more than a thousand well-made, practical, and sometimes pricey tools and gifts. The inventory focuses on unusual, hard-to-find items, and includes shop and gardening tools, small electronics, housewares, personal care items, exercise and sports equipment, indoor and outdoor games, office supplies, and travel and automotive accessories. De Beaumont started simply with a mail-order catalog business, then launched the innovative retail system that resulted in more than 100 outlets nationwide. It works this way: Each store is like a giant 3D catalog, with information cards accompanying all displayed goods. Customers pick up and examine whatever interests them, fill out order forms and present them at the desk, then wait for purchases to be delivered by conveyor belt. Mail-order catalogs are available, too. ♦ Daily.

29 School St (between Washington St and City Hall Ave). 742.0055 & Also at: Copley Place, 100 Huntington Ave (between Garrison and Dartmouth Sts). 267.4308; Marketplace Center, 200 State St (between Atlantic Ave and Commercial St). 439.4460

35 Boston Public Library, Kirstein Business Branch This branch of the Boston Public Library, designed by **Putnam and Cox** in 1930, specializes in noncirculating business and financial references. It's located off the beaten trail on a pedestrian lane connecting School and Court Streets. An interesting feature of the building is its Georgian Revival facade, which replicates the central pavilion of daring **Charles Bulfinch**'s architecturally innovative (for America) and financially disastrous Tontine Crescent residential development, built on Franklin Street in 1794 and demolished in 1858. It was this speculative real-estate scheme's failure that cost Bulfinch his inheritance and turned him from an architect by choice into one by necessity. Several blocks away, part of Franklin Street still follows the footprints of the vanished Tontine's curve. ◆ M-F. 20 City Hall Ave (at Pi Alley). 523.0860

35 Pi Alley The printer's term "pi," meaning spilled or jumbled type, is probably the origin of this alley's name. As the story goes, type would spill from printers' pockets as they went to and from a popular colonial tavern located at the alley's end. A less common account claims the alley is actually Pie Alley, paying tribute to the tavern's popular pies. ◆ East of City Hall Ave

36 Hungry Traveler $ Across from the **BPL**'s **Kirstein Business Branch,** tucked into a quiet street behind **Old City Hall,** is an ideal cafeteria-style restaurant for an early-bird breakfast or a quick, cheap lunch. Five or six hot entrées are prepared daily, as are salads and soups. Hang back until you know what you want, because once the no-nonsense counter-help spots you, they'll demand your order. A lot of people come here— tourists and on-the-job Bostonians— and the staff likes to keep things moving. ◆ Cafeteria/ Takeout ◆ M-F breakfast (from 5:45AM) and lunch. No credit cards accepted. 29 Court Sq (between City Hall Ave and Court St). 742.5989 &

37 Rebecca's Cafe ★$ They're popping up all over Boston, offering made-from-scratch hot entrées, pastas, soups, salads, sandwiches, pastries, and dreamy desserts, and are winning more and more fans. ◆ Cafe/Takeout ◆ M-F breakfast, lunch, and dinner; Sa breakfast and lunch. No credit cards accepted. 18 Tremont St (between School and Court Sts). 227.0020 & Also at: 112 Newbury St (between Clarendon and Dartmouth Sts). 267.1122; Prudential Center, 800 Boylston St (between Exeter and Dalton Sts). 266.3355; 560 Harrison Ave (between Waltham and Randolph Sts). 482.1414

38 Old City Hall Replaced by modern **City Hall** at **Government Center,** this empress dowager is an exuberantly ornamental artifact of a more flamboyant era. The days when colorful Boston politicos like James Michael Curley held sway are long gone. Retired in 1969, the 1865 hall designed by **Gridley J.F. Bryant** and **Arthur Gilman** is no longer in the thick of things. For many visitors, it's a surprise to discover this French Second Empire edifice tucked away from the street. Still graced with ample arched windows and an imposing pavilion, the National Historic Landmark building now accommodates offices and a restaurant; the foyer contains a nice trompe l'oeil reminder of its former finery by muralist Josh Winer, and further embellishments are planned. The exterior was painstakingly renovated by **Anderson Notter Associates** in 1970.

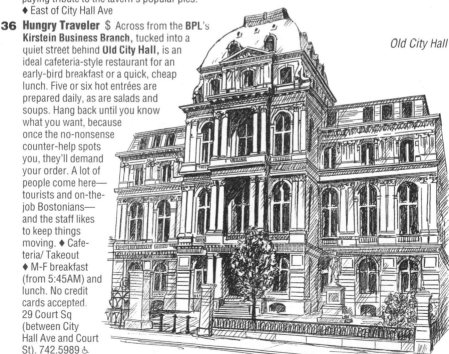

Old City Hall

On either side of the entrance stand Richard S. Greenough's 1855 statue of *Benjamin Franklin* and Thomas Ball's 1879 statue of *Josiah Quincy,* Boston's second mayor, who built **Quincy Market** and served as president of **Harvard College.** Franklin's likeness was the first portrait statue in Boston. Embedded in the sidewalk in front of the hall's cast-iron fence is Lilli Ann Killen Rosenberg's appealing 1983 mosaic, *City Carpet,* which commemorates the oldest public school in the US. Erected near this site in 1635, the **Boston Public Latin School** gave School Street its name and contributed influential alumni to American history books, including Franklin, John Hancock, **Charles Bulfinch,** Charles Francis Adams, and Ralph Waldo Emerson. The school is now located near the Fenway. Rosenberg also created the mosaic located on the wall side of the *Green Line*'s outbound platform in **Park Street Station,** offering a delightful pictorial account of Boston's first subway. ◆ 45 School St (between City Hall Ave and Tremont St)

Within Old City Hall:

mr

maison
robert

Maison Robert ★★★$$$$ The colorful political wheelings and dealings of **Old City Hall** belong to the past. But deals are still made here, love affairs launched, marriages proposed, and momentous occasions celebrated. For more than 20 years, this superb French restaurant has made a happy home in the old hall. Look for the vaulted brick ceilings and distinguished old doors—vestiges of the original interiors. Ann and Lucien Robert offer such fine classic dishes as lobster bisque; fresh foie gras sautéed with apples in a honey and apple-vinegar glaze; chicken breast stuffed with morel mushrooms; and grilled filet mignon. Dessert choices include chocolate–Grand Marnier cake with raspberry sauce, wondrous *tarte tatin* (apple tart), and crème brûlée. (Lucien has been honored by the French government with the *Chevalier du Mérite* award for his contributions to French culture.) Wine- and Champagne-tasting dinners (put your name on the mailing list) are held here. And on the first Friday of each month, there's "The French Table" prix-fixe dinner, beginning with an aperitif social hour. As many as 80 attend, native speakers and novices alike (reservations are required).

Upstairs is **Bonhomme Richard,** which is named for the flagship of the fledgling American navy during the Revolution. These beautiful formal dining rooms, featuring butternut woodwork, overlook the **King's**

Chapel Burying Ground and are used for formal affairs and catered functions. Downstairs is the less fancy but very inviting **Ben's Cafe.** Named for Ben Franklin, it serves somewhat lighter and less expensive dishes. When spring comes, cafe tables and umbrellas appear on the lovely outdoor terrace, and the garden blooms again, signaling the return of a delightful spot.

The Roberts's daughter Andrée skillfully discharges the duties of executive chef for all three restaurants, while chef Jacky Robert holds forth in the kitchen. For private parties of 10 to 12 people, ask about dining in **The Vault,** the original City Hall vault. Valet parking is offered Wednesday through Saturday. ◆ French ◆ M-F lunch (cafe); M-Sa dinner (cafe and upstairs); Su open for private parties. Reservations recommended; jacket and tie required upstairs. 227.3370 ♿

39 King's Chapel The original 1688 chapel stirred Bostonians' ire, since it was the city's first place of worship for Anglicanism, the official Church of England that had driven Puritans from their homeland. The plain wooden structure was built at the behest of Sir Edmund Andros, the royal governor who took the reins when the Massachusetts Bay Colony charter was revoked—just one early link in the long chain of events leading to the Revolution. To avoid interrupting services, the substantial 1754 Georgian chapel of Quincy granite standing today (a National Historic Landmark) was actually erected *around* the original building, which was then dismantled and heaved out the windows of its replacement. If the chapel seems squat, it's because the elaborate stone steeple architect **Peter Harrison** envisioned atop its square tower was never built; funds ran out. But in one splendid finishing touch, the facade was embellished with a portico supported by Ionic columns.

The Georgian interior has weathered the centuries well. Its raised pulpit is the oldest still in use in America on the same site. The pew dedicated to early royal governors' use later accommodated George Washington on his Boston visits, and other American worthies. Slaves sat in the rear gallery on the cemetery side, and condemned prisoners sat to the right of the entrance for a last sermon before being hanged on the **Common**. After the Revolution, once the British and Loyalists had evacuated Boston, the chapel was converted around 1789 into the first American Unitarian church. Some of the rich presents given to the earlier chapel by William and Mary of Britain are still in use, but most are now displayed at the **Boston Athenaeum**.

One of the church's other treasures is Paul Revere's largest bell, which he called "the sweetest bell we ever made." Come hear the resonant Charles Fisk organ, a replica of the church's 1756 original. There are free musical recitals every Tuesday at 12:15PM; every Wednesday there's an organ prelude before the worship service. On Thursday there are free poetry readings in "the King's English." No tours are offered, but guides are on hand to answer questions during summer months. ♦ Tu-Sa; May-Oct until 4PM, Nov-Apr until 2PM. 58 Tremont St (at School St). 227.2155 &

Adjacent to King's Chapel:

King's Chapel Burying Ground Boston's earliest town cemetery's first resident was Isaac Johnson, who owned the land and was buried here in his garden in 1630. So many Boston settlers so quickly followed suit that some wag noted, "Brother Johnson's garden is getting to be a poor place for vegetables." A pleasant neighbor today, the church next door was erected on land seized from the burying ground. Burials continued until 1796, although a gravedigger complained in 1739 that this and two other local graveyards "were so fulled with dead bodies that they were obliged oft times to bury them four deep."

As in other Boston cemeteries, grave markers were moved about to accommodate newcomers, an unsettling practice that caused Oliver Wendell Holmes to complain: "The upright stones have been shuffled about like chessmen and nothing short of the Day of Judgment will tell whose dust lies beneath . . . Shame! Shame! Shame!" The burying ground's inhabitants include governors John Winthrop and John Endicott. On the chapel side, look for the 1704 gravestone of Elizabeth Pain, who supposedly bore a minister's child and probably was Nathaniel Hawthorne's model for Hester Prynne in *The Scarlet Letter*. Also buried here is Sons of Liberty courier William Dawes, who rode through the night just as bravely as Paul Revere, but didn't have the posthumous good fortune to be lionized in a Longfellow poem. And for a sample of the Puritans' pessimistic stance on the snuffing of life's candle, look for Joseph Tapping's marker. Stone rubbings are not allowed. ♦ M-Sa &

40 Omni Parker House $$$ Boston's genteel dowager hotel proclaims itself "the choice of legends since 1854," and it's true: US presidents and celebrities of every stripe, from Joan Crawford to Hopalong Cassidy, have made themselves at home here. Now under the management of TRT Holdings, Inc., the oldest continuously operating hotel in America has been treated to a long-overdue multimillion dollar face-lift, which was due to be completed as this book went to press. This ambitious undertaking has already resulted in the restoration of the hotel's centerpiece lobby fashioned in original oak woodwork, crystal chandeliers, and carved gilt moldings.

The hotel represents the success story of Maine native Harvey D. Parker, who came to Boston with less than a dollar and became its leading hotelier. Rebuilt numerous times, the current structure dates to 1927 and attracts a mainly business-oriented clientele. There are 541 rooms on 14 floors including rooms for people with disabilities and floors for nonsmokers. The concierge in attendance in the lobby is supplemented by a computerized concierge system. Paid valet parking is available. Starting around 1855, the famous erudite Saturday Club met here on the last Saturday of every month, its circle including American literary and intellectual luminaries such as Nathaniel Hawthorne, John Whittier, Ralph Waldo Emerson, and Henry Wadsworth Longfellow; a spin-off group founded the *Atlantic Monthly* in 1859. During one long Boston visit, the high-spirited, sociable Charles Dickens stayed at the hotel and joined the club's congenial gatherings, often fixing gin punch for his pals. The sitting-room mirror before which Dickens practiced his famous Boston readings now hangs on the mezzanine. On a more somber note, just 10 days before assassinating Abraham Lincoln, actor John Wilkes Booth stayed here while visiting his brother Edwin, also an actor, who was performing nearby. John spent some time practicing at a nearby shooting gallery. During this century, this hotel was the site of Senator John F. Kennedy's announcement of his candidacy for the presidency.

Parker's Bar is known for its classic martini; live music is played here Wednesday through Saturday. By the way, the famous secret recipe for the soft "Parker House roll" was first created here (they bake more than a thousand of the fragrant rolls each day), as was the tasty, but very un-pielike, Boston cream pie. Both are available in the restaurants and to take out. ♦ 60 School St (at Tremont St). 227.8600, 800/843.6664; fax 742.5729

Within Omni Parker House:

Parker's Restaurant ★★$$$ With vaulted ceilings and high, wing-backed chairs, the restaurant is tranquil, roomy, and timeless. The good, reliable American cuisine—accompanied by those famous rolls—is undeservedly overlooked. A guitarist strums during the award-winning Sunday brunch, and piano music drifts in from the bar the rest of the week. Valet parking is available. ♦ American ♦ M-F breakfast and lunch; Th-Sa dinner. Reservations recommended; jacket required at dinner, requested at lunch. 227.8600 &

The Last Hurrah! Bar and Grill ★$$ This place looks dated, but that's the point—the walls are plastered with political memorabilia harking back to when **Old City Hall** down the street was in full swing. And speaking of swing, there's a swing brunch on Sunday. You can dine as well as drink here, but the food is nothing special. The bar is popular with the **State House** and **City Hall** sets. ♦ American ♦ M-Sa lunch and dinner; Su brunch and dinner. Reservations recommended. 227.8600

BORDERS®

BOOKS · MUSIC · CAFE

41 Borders: Books, Music, Cafe With an inventory of more than 200,000 book, music, and video titles, along with an extensive selection of periodicals, and newspapers from 55 US cities and 25 foreign countries, this national bookstore now occupies some 39,000 square feet of a former bank. Adding on to the Renaissance-styled structure (originally designed in 1926 by **Parker, Thomas & Rice**), architects **Kallmann and McKinnell** created a dynamic building. The firm's 1972 addition gracefully adapted to a tricky site and earned the building its place in one of Boston's most historic quarters. A corner of the building was cut away, creating an open urban area in front that offers breathing space from Washington Street crowds, as well as good views of its 18th-century neighbor, the **Old South Meeting House.** In true **Borders** tradition, the store hosts many free community events such as readings, musical performances, and book signings, all while glorifying the fine art of browsing. The staff is knowledgeable and helpful. On a mezzanine balcony overlooking the enormous light-filled and multiwindowed ground floor, there's an in-store **Cafe Expresso.** ♦ Daily. 10 School St (at Washington St). 557.7188

42 Old South Meeting House This is Boston's second-oldest church (the **Old North Church** in the North End predates it). Built in 1729 by **Joshua Blanchard,** the National Historic Landmark (pictured below) is a traditional New England brick meeting-house fronted by a solid square wooden tower that blossoms into a delicate spire. When nearby **Faneuil Hall**'s public meeting space grew too cramped, Bostonians congregated here for town meetings peppered with fiery debate to prepare for the coming Revolution and plan such events as the Boston Tea Party of 1773. That cold December night, which Boston loves to remember, more than 5,000 gathered within to rally against the hated tea tax. Three ships filled with tea to be taxed were anchored at Griffin's Wharf, and the royal governor refused Bostonians' demands that the tea be sent back to England. Samuel Adams gave the signal igniting the protest that turned Boston Harbor into a teapot. During the British occupation, Redcoats struck back at the patriots by using their revered meeting place for the riding school of General "Gentleman Johnny" Burgoyne's light cavalry, complete with an officers' bar. By the time the British had

Old South Meeting House

MÁRJORIE VOGEL, RHODE ISLAND ORIGINALS

evacuated, the church was in a sorry state. The congregation finally moved back in, then decamped in 1875 to the new **Old South Church** in Copley Square. Among the early congregation members were Phillis Wheatley, a freed slave and one of the first published African-American poets; Elizabeth Vergoose, aka "Mother Goose"; and patriots James Otis, Samuel Adams, and William Dawes.

After escaping destruction by the Great Fire of 1872, the edifice was nearly demolished in a plan to make room for commercial businesses. But Bostonians, including Julia Ward Howe and Ralph Waldo Emerson, contributed funds to purchase and restore the historic property, which has been maintained as a national monument and museum by the Old South Association ever since. Step inside and experience restful simplicity. Because the British stripped the interior in 1776, only the sounding board and corner stairway are original. The award-winning, permanent multimedia exhibition *In Prayer and Protest: Old South Meeting House Remembers,* includes audio programs that emanate from the walls, tapes with reenactments of the Boston Tea Party debates, a scale model of colonial Boston, profiles of famous churchgoers, and artifacts. The museum shop sells cards and theme souvenirs such as penny whistles, quill pens, and soldiers' dice made from musket balls. "Middays at the Meeting House," an excellent series of monthly concerts and Thursday lectures on American history and culture, runs October through April. Events are free with museum admission. In addition to hosting educational programs and performances, the church hosts public debates, forums, and announcements of candidacies for office. During July and August, re-creations of 18th-century Boston town meetings are staged every Saturday on the Plaza across the street, and bystanders are encouraged to participate. Outside on the corner is one of Boston's largest and prettiest flower stands. ♦ Admission. Daily. Tours for groups of 10 or more by reservation. 310 Washington St (at Milk St). 482.6439 &

43 Bromfield Street This short little street was once the location of Revolutionary hero Thomas Cushing's residence, where the Massachusetts delegates to the first Continental Congress assembled, among them Samuel and John Adams and Robert Treat Paine. Today it's one of Boston's more interesting, lively commercial streets, packed with small establishments specializing in cameras, antiques, collector's coins and stamps, jewelry, watches, and pens, not to mention pawnshops. Some great old buildings reside here, too, such as **Nos. 22** and **30** of 1848 and the **Wesleyan Association Building** at No. 36 of 1870, all made of granite.
♦ Between Washington and Tremont Sts

43 Skylight Jewelers Edward Spencer, an old-fashioned artisan with a gift for modern design, has been a Bromfield Street fixture for more than two decades. His studio display cases suggest his range and feature fluid settings for organic shapes (freshwater pearls are a specialty, as are moonstones—carved into mysterious moon faces). He's happy to accommodate your own design suggestions.
♦ M-Sa. 52 Province St (at Bromfield St). 426.0521 & (will assist)

44 Sherman's It's an unlikely spot for a department store, but once people find it, they come back often for last-minute gifts, travel items, and housewares. In addition to major appliances and office equipment, cameras, calculators, electronics, luggage, TVs, telephones, small appliances, cookware, and jewelry, miscellany for the manse are sold here. They also carry a number of items in overseas electrical currents, and arrange all shipping—including customs—to foreign destinations. ♦ M-Sa. 26 Province St (between Bromfield and School Sts). 482.9610

45 Province House Steps From Province Street, mount the weathered steps that once led to the gardens of a 17th-century house, the luxurious official residence of the royal governors of Massachusetts Bay. Renamed **Government House** after the Revolution, the mansion was inhabited until 1796. Here General Gage ordered the Redcoats to Lexington and Concord. Here, too, General Howe ordered his men to flee after George Washington and his troops managed to fortify Dorchester Heights, aiming big guns at the British. Years later, Nathaniel Hawthorne wrote about the by then decaying tavern and inn in *Twice-Told Tales.* Nary stick nor stone remains of the mansion except these steps.
♦ Province and Bosworth Sts

45 Cafe Marliave ★$$ Dressed up with bits of wrought iron and balconies, this restaurant has stood on its corner for so long—more than a century—that many Bostonians forget it exists. Then again, a cadre of loyalists keeps coming back. The Italian-American cooking is nothing to swoon over, but it's good and reasonably priced, with plenty of dishes to choose from. The same family has run the place since 1935. The cafe sits high above the street, at the top of the Province House Steps; dine on the second floor by the windows and become part of the streetscape. ♦ Italian-American ♦ Daily lunch and dinner. 10 Bosworth St (at Province St). 423.6340

BROMFIELD PEN SHOP

45 Bromfield Pen Shop Accustomed to inexpensive, use-and-abuse disposable pens? Wander into this little shop, gaze upon gleaming rows of new and antique pens, and reconsider your choice of writing instrument. Imagine what that handsome handful of a lovingly restored Bakelite pen might do for your prose! In addition to such standard brands as Parker and Sheaffer, Mont Blanc, Lamy, Pelikan, Yard-O-Led of England, S.T. Dupont, Waterman, Omas of Italy, delicate glass pens, and plenty of ink varieties are in stock. Engraving is free. The best store of its kind in New England, a plethora of local politicians, and medical, literary, legal, and media types (including author Jimmy Breslin) choose their pens here. They also sell the same never-fail inexpensive pen used by Boston traffic cops. The shop also stocks art supplies. ♦ M-Sa. 39 Bromfield St (between Province and Tremont Sts). 482.9053 &

45 J.J. Teaparty Quality Baseball Cards A city that's passionate about sports in general and baseball in particular is the perfect place for this business. The tiny storefront, often crowded with wheeling-and-dealing kids, is owned by Peter Leventhal, whose father runs the coin shop one door away.

Leventhal buys and sells mostly baseball cards, but also some for football, basketball, and hockey. He's got cards from the 1950s and 1960s, including past and future Hall of Famers. Unusual items crop up, like turn-of-the-century tobacco cards. Collectors can pick up the latest series by Score, Topps, Fleer, and others. ♦ M-F, Sa until 4PM. 43 Bromfield St (between Province and Tremont Sts). 482.5705 &

45 J.J. Teaparty Coin Numismatists take note: Owner Ed Leventhal has been buying and selling coins at Bromfield Street's premier coin shop since 1963. Both casual collectors and serious investors come by to drop some coins of their own for proof sets, mint sets, and bullion coins like the American Eagle and Canadian Maple Leaf. ♦ M-F, Sa until 2PM; closed Saturday July-August. No credit cards accepted. 51 Bromfield St (between Province and Tremont Sts). 482.2398

46 Tremont Temple The fanciful Venetian stone facade of this structure, made of 15 delicate shades of terra-cotta, incongruously

hides an office and church complex inside. It gets more and more curious with the added adornment of several elaborate balconies. The 1895 building, designed by **Clarence H. Blackall**, stands on the site of the famous **Tremont Theater,** where illustrious 19th-century thespians, performers, lecturers, and politicians—including Abe Lincoln—enthralled the public. ♦ 88 Tremont St (between Bosworth and School Sts). 523.7320

47 Bruegger's Bagel Bakery $ Ten varieties of excellent bagels—Boston's best—are baked throughout the day at this family business, and are never more than a few hours old. Bruegger's own factory also produces nine different cream cheeses to spread on top. If you want a more filling meal, try a sandwich-on-a-bagel accompanied by freshly made soup. Its decor is fast-food basic, but the restaurant is neat and clean, with plenty of seating. ♦ Bagels/Takeout ♦ Daily breakfast and lunch. No credit cards accepted. 32 Bromfield St (between Washington and Tremont Sts). 357.5577 & Also at: numerous locations throughout Boston and Cambridge

48 Jewelers Building Though stripped of its frilly original copper trim, this Beaux Arts–inspired early "skyscraper" designed by **Winslow and Bigelow** in 1898 still serves the function it was designed for: housing nearly 100 jewelry dealers, most of whom sell retail as well as wholesale. In the lobby, you can't miss a crude but informative bronze bas-relief depicting the history of diamond mining and cutting. ♦ M-Sa. 379 Washington St (between Winter and Bromfield Sts) &

49 Barnes & Noble Discount Bookstore This big general bookstore specializes in reduced-price best-sellers and discounted paperbacks and hardcovers, as well as publishers' overstocks. It also sells children's books, magazines, board games, cards, and local maps, and classical and jazz records, tapes, and CDs. ♦ Daily. 395 Washington St (between Winter and Bromfield Sts). 426.5502 & Also at: 660 Beacon St (between Raleigh St and Kenmore Sq). 267.8484; 603 Boylston St (between Clarendon and Dartmouth Sts). 236.1308

50 The Food Emporium $ Inside the otherwise undistinguished **Corner Mall** is a food court teaming with international cuisine. Among the 13 fast-food stands are giants such as **McDonald's** and **Sbarro**, and tiny local favorites like **Vouros Pastry,** featuring fresh Greek specialties: moussaka, gyros, and spinach pie. Other offerings range from Mexican to Japanese. This bustling arena is a standby for local office workers, and a great place to pick up a multicultural picnic to enjoy on **Boston Common.** ♦ International/Takeout ♦ M-Sa breakfast, lunch, and dinner until

6:30PM; Su lunch and dinner until 6PM.
425 Washington St (between Winter and
Bromfield Sts). 695.9080 &

51 Filene's One of 33 stores in New England
and New York, this full-service department
store sells formal, casual, and career fashions
(designer and major brand labels) and
accessories for men, women, children,
and the home. The **Gift Gallery** stocks fine
crystal, sterling, porcelain, and other specialty
merchandise. Founder William Filene opened
his first retail business in 1851. The present
building was designed by **Daniel Burnham
& Company** in 1912. It was the first—and
probably only—department store to have a
"zoo" on its roof, with a baby elephant flown
in from Bangkok, plus lions, monkeys, and
other wild animals; 60,000 children visited
the zoo before it was demolished by the same
hurricane that toppled **Old North Church**'s
steeple in 1954. The distinguished Chicago-
style building boasts a grand corner clock.
♦ Daily. 426 Washington St (at Summer St).
357.2100

Below Filene's:

FILENE'S BASEMENT

Filene's Basement Far surpassing the fame
of its parent store (the companies are now
separately owned), America's first off-price
store opened in 1908. There are now 40
replicas in nine states, but nothing equals the
original. The inventory includes designer-label
and bargain clothing and accessories for men,
women, and children, and housewares of all
kinds. Retail stock is regularly featured from
such prestigious stores as **Saks, Brooks
Brothers, Bergdorf Goodman,** and **Neiman
Marcus.**

Because of its automatic markdown policy,
Filene's Basement offers dedicated shoppers
a true treasure hunt. It works this way: The
price tag for each item also carries the date
of the day it first came on the selling floor.
Fourteen days from that date the item is
marked down 25 percent from its original
Basement price. Seven days after that, it is
marked down an additional 25 percent. After
another seven days, it is marked down another
25 percent, making that a total of 75 percent
off the original asking price. After another
seven days, you may still buy the item at
75 percent off, but you must take it to the
Customer Service desk and pay for it by
making out a check to one of the listed charity
organizations. Any items remaining on the
floor after that are donated directly to charities.
The markdown dates in effect on any given day
are posted at key locations on the **Basement**'s
two floors, and checking them is the first point
of business for practiced shoppers.

Many a quickie course has been offered on
how to come away flushed with success and
laden with low-cost treasures from the
legendary emporium. The simple formula:
perseverance, skill, and luck. Strike it lucky
and you might bring home a wedding dress,
winter coat, business suit, evening attire,
luggage, lingerie, goose-down comforter,
fine linen, or even a diamond ring for a
fraction of its original price.

Crowds gather on the legendary "Big Sale"
days, when doors open early. Try to flip
through a local Sunday paper, since many
sales begin Monday. If you watch, you'll see
how veterans work the room; you'll also see
neat piles and racks of clothing and goods
reduced to colorful, chaotic heaps, and
glassy-eyed, overstimulated novices escaping
to the upper levels in defeat. A women's
dressing room was added in 1991 after
complaints of sexism (the men's department
had been equipped with changing rooms for
years). However, true shopping mavens won't
stand for the lines that form and instead take
advantage of the liberal return policy (14 days,
with receipt) for home tryouts. Many also still
use the time-honored method of slipping stuff
on in an out-of-the-way aisle.

The **Basement** has two levels; it may be
entered from **Filene's** proper, or underground
from the **Downtown Crossing** subway station
(on the *Red* and *Orange Lines*). ♦ Daily.
542.2011 & (enter from Filene's, use the
elevator)

52 Lauriat's Books Part of a chain throughout
New England and New York, this store caters
to the general public, selling mass-market
hardcover and paperback books. ♦ Daily. 45
Franklin St (between Arch and Hawley Sts).
482.2850 & (rear entrance) Also at: Copley
Place, 100 Huntington Ave (between Garrison
and Dartmouth Sts). 262.8858

53 London Harness Company Rest assured
you'll find only the finest in very proper gifts
for travel, home, office, and personal use,
tastefully arrayed amid the shop's gleaming
old wooden fixtures. The oldest operating
retailer in the country, the shop has done
business in this general location since the
1700s. Benjamin Franklin was among the early
shoppers, and traveled with trunks purchased
here. Honor momentous occasions—
weddings, graduations—or get yourself
something indispensable that will last forever.
Fine leather goods are the focus here, although
there are other gift items as well. Perhaps you'd
like a wooden box with **Fenway Park** hand-
painted on it, or a chess set, or an umbrella that

will stand up to Boston's gusty winds. Clocks, luggage, wallets and accessories, leather frames and photo albums, jewelry boxes, briefcases, bookends, desk sets, old prints and maps, and more—you'll find all the appurtenances for a civilized existence. ♦ M-Sa. 60 Franklin St (between Arch and Hawley Sts). 542.9234 ♿ (through rear entrance)

54 Winthrop Lane This short-and-sweet brick lane would be unremarkable except for the florist and **Boston Coffee Exchange** shops at one end, and an imaginative work of public art called *Boston Bricks: A Celebration of Boston's Past and Present,* created by Kate Burke and Gregg Lefevre in 1985. The artists have inset dozens of bronze brick reliefs amid the lane's bricks from start to finish. Each relief tells a significant, interesting, or entertaining piece of Boston's story. Have fun trying to figure out what's what. Some images and references are quite familiar: the **Custom House Tower, Boston Common**'s cows, the **Boston Pops,** the city's ethnic groups, the Underground Railroad, the **Boston Marathon,** the **Red Sox,** whale watching, rowers on the Charles River, swans in the **Public Garden,** and an amusing representation of the notorious Boston driver. Others may keep you puzzling a while. Collectively, the clever bricks present a good likeness of the city. ♦ Between Devonshire and Arch Sts

55 One Winthrop Square Ralph Waldo Emerson's nephew, **William Ralph Emerson,** is responsible for several vigorously unconventional Boston structures, including the **House of Odd Windows** on Beacon Hill and the **Boston Art Club** in Back Bay. In this collaborative effort carried out with **Carl Fehmer** in 1873, William Emerson's influence dominates in the eccentric mixing of architectural motifs. Originally a dry-goods emporium and later headquarters for the *Boston Record-American* newspaper, the building has since been adapted to offices. Out front, where trucks once loaded up with newspapers, is an attractive park with Henry Hudson Kitson's bronze of *Robert Burns* briskly striding along, walking stick in hand and collie at his side. ♦ At Otis St

56 United Shoe Machinery Corporation Building Now renovated, placed on the National Register of Historic Places, and renamed "The Landmark," Boston's first Art Deco skyscraper—built in 1929 by **Peter, Thomas, and Rice**—forms a handsome ziggurat crowned by a pyramid of tiles. At street level, look for the fine cast-metal storefronts set into limestone. Rude buildings shove against this proud bulwark, which recalls the era when shoes were big business in Boston. ♦ 160 Federal St (between High and Matthews Sts)

57 Boston Airline Center This is a handy walk-in center—with no phone number—

where you can make on-the-spot reservations or pick up tickets for various airlines, including **American, Continental, Delta, Northwest, United, TWA,** and **USAir.** ♦ M-F. 155 Federal St (at High St) ♿

𝕾𝖈𝖍𝖗𝖔𝖊𝖉𝖊𝖗'𝖘

58 Schroeder's ★$$$ Despite its relative youth (it opened in 1977), this restaurant has the look of old money—with a client list and menu to match. All the standbys are here— from vichyssoise and escargots to lobster thermidor and chateaubriand—plus a quartet of signature schnitzels *à la maison.* Although the decor leans more toward a ladies' club than a gentlemen's, this dining spot clearly aspires to **Locke-Ober**'s (see page 91) prestige, and judging from the pleased looks on the well-fed, prosperous faces, it's succeeding quite well. ♦ Continental ♦ M lunch; Tu-Sa lunch and dinner. 8 High St (between Federal St and Milton Pl). 426.1234 ♿

59 Church Green Building This fine addition to the city's stock of 19th-century granite mercantile buildings is named for Church Green, the triangular intersection of Summer, Lincoln, and Bedford Streets, which in turn was named for the lovely church designed by **Charles Bulfinch** that once stood here (just another example of how history haunts many Boston place names). It was built circa 1873 by an unknown architect, although it is widely attributed to **Jonathan Preston.** Behind this structure rises red-roofed **99 Summer Street,** a 1987 interloper by **Goody, Clancy & Associates** that tries mightily to fit in. Across the way is **125 Summer Street,** a 1990 building by **Kohn Pederson Fox,** lurking behind an eclectic row of commercial facades now belonging to **No. 125.** A swath of old streetscape has been nicely preserved, but the huge modern tower bursting from its midst is a little disconcerting in contrast. ♦ 105-113 Summer St (at Bedford St)

60 Bedford Building Red granite, white Vermont marble, and terra-cotta blend well on the Ruskinian Gothic–style facade of this 1876 **Cummings & Sears** creation, renovated in 1983 by the **Bay Bedford Company** and placed on the National Register of Historic Places. The proud building lost its original clock, but its stained-glass timepiece (created by Cambridge artisan Lynn Hovey) is particularly striking at night. ♦ 89-103 Bedford St (between Lincoln and Columbia Sts)

61 Proctor Building On sunny days, it's bathed in light, and is the preferred perch for many pigeons. On any day, the small Spanish Renaissance–style building, built in 1897 by **Winslow and Bigelow,** is an orchestra of ornament crowned by a tiaralike cornice.

Shells, birds, flowers, garlands, cherubs, urns, and more parade across the curving cream-colored facade. ♦ 100-106 Bedford St (at Kingston St)

62 Dakota's ★★$$$ Hailing from Dallas, this clubby-looking dining spot does big business in Boston, attracting the briefcase crowd at lunchtime and the *Playbill* crowd in the evening. The menu's focus is on American grill with a Southwestern accent. Many dishes are good and colorfully presented: try the calamari, venison-sausage quesadillas, onion rings, gulf seafood chowder, tortilla soup, roast chicken, or lamb chops. Desserts are intensely rich, and the freshly made breads pleasantly fragrant. Sit in the elevated bar area and look over the fast-paced dining room, spiffed up with marble, ceiling fans, Roman shades, and club chairs.

The restaurant inhabits the second level of a 21-story office tower called **101 Arch Street,** which preserved under glass a section of the facade of **34 Summer Street** (an 1873 commercial palace) as a decorative piece in the lobby. And, if you're arriving by **T**, look for a vintage wooden escalator—more than 80 years old—on the outbound Chauncy Street side of the *Red Line*'s **Downtown Crossing** stop. The grooved slats are so slanted, it's a challenge to ascend. There's valet parking after 5:30PM on the Summer Street side. ♦ American ♦ M-F lunch and dinner; Sa dinner. Reservations recommended. 34 Summer St (between Arch and Hawley Sts). 737.1777 ♿

THE SOCIETY OF ARTS AND CRAFTS

63 The Society of Arts and Crafts A satellite of the nonprofit crafts organization headquartered at 175 Newbury Street in Back Bay (266.1810), this educational outreach gallery on the second level of **101 Arch Street** is the first step toward establishing **The Craft Museum of Boston** (which was still in the works at press time, with no opening date set). The 1,200-square-foot gallery showcases contemporary works-for-sale in a variety of media by society member artists, plus works on loan from museums and private collections, and rotating exhibitions of crafts by distinguished and emerging artists. In addition to bringing crafts to a part of town that can always use a little color and creativity,

the gallery is a great place to find exceptional, interesting objects like jewelry, glass, ceramics, and small furniture. ♦ M-F. 101 Arch St (at Bussey Pl). 345.0033 ♿ Also at: 175 Newbury St (between Dartmouth and Exeter Sts). 266.1810

64 Macy's Although the **Macy's** sign was raised in 1996, Bostonians will always think of this place as **Jordan Marsh.** The slogan, "A tradition since 1851," referred to the department store's beginning as a small, high-quality dry-goods establishment, founded in Boston by Eben Dyer Jordan and partner Benjamin L. Marsh. Interestingly, **Macy's** also was founded in 1851, and has grown to a chain of 85 full-service department stores nationwide, offering both trendy and fashionable goods. ♦ Daily. 450 Washington St (at Summer St). 357.3000 ♿

65 Locke-Ober ★★★$$$ The winds of change may howl through Boston, but this bastion of Brahmin traditions mutes them to a whisper. After trying his hand at numerous occupations, including taxidermy and barbering, Louis Ober, an Alsatian, opened **Ober's Restaurant Parisien** in 1870 in this tiny residential alley. In 1892 Frank Locke opened a wine bar next door. Ober's successors combined the two restaurants and their founders' names, an ingenious partnership that has flourished to this day. For nearly a hundred years, the **Men's Cafe** downstairs was reserved for men; escorted women were admitted only on New Year's Eve and on the night of the **Harvard-Yale** game. (Incidentally, if **Harvard** lost, the nude painting of *Yvonne* in the first-floor barroom was draped in black.) But one fateful day in 1974, modern times came knocking, and this hallowed enclave reluctantly began admitting women. Both sexes now enjoy its Victorian splendor, tried-and-true rich Yankee-European cuisine, and perfectly discreet—if not exactly friendly—black-tie, Old World service. You may share the dining room with members of the Kennedy family or those ubiquitous **Harvard** students who come from across the Charles River to toast their graduations. The famous downstairs is all dark-wood splendor, the hand-carved bar agleam with German silver, but the revamped and gilded upstairs is nice also. Private dining chambers are available for a fee. You'll see plenty of loyalists, mostly male, sitting in their customary places and dining on such delicious old favorites as oysters, lobster Savannah, steak tartare, filet mignon, Dover sole, roast-beef hash, rack of lamb, calf's liver, Indian pudding, and baked Alaska. Follow their example and keep to the time-tested selections and you won't be disappointed. After notifying the regular clientele in advance that more—gasp!—change was coming, healthful new dishes were introduced to the menu. The cafe's lock-shaped sign, by the way, was inspired by one that adorned Locke's original establishment. Women are discouraged from wearing slacks here—another barrier to breach? Valet parking is available after 6PM. ♦ Continental ♦ M-F lunch and dinner; Sa-Su dinner (hours vary in July and August). Reservations recommended; jacket and tie required. 3-4 Winter Pl (at Winter St). 542.1340

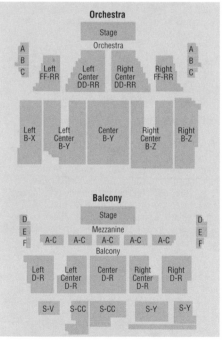

Orchestra

Stage

Orchestra

| A B C | Left FF-RR | Left Center DD-RR | Right Center DD-RR | Right FF-RR | A B C |

| Left B-X | Left Center B-Y | Center B-Y | Right Center B-Z | Right B-Z |

Balcony

Stage

Mezzanine

| D E F | A-C | A-C | A-C | A-C | A-C | D E F |

Balcony

| Left D-R | Left Center D-R | Center D-R | Right Center D-R | Right D-R |

| S-V | S-CC | S-CC | S-Y | S-Y |

66 Orpheum Theatre Originally called the **Music Hall,** this worldly theater (see chart above), built in 1852 by **Snell and Gregorson,** has seen a thing or two. It housed the fledgling **New England Conservatory** and witnessed the **Boston Symphony Orchestra**'s debut concert in 1881. The **Handel and Haydn Society** performed here for years. Tchaikovsky's first piano concerto had its world premiere, Ralph Waldo Emerson and Booker T. Washington lectured, and Oscar Wilde promoted a Gilbert

and Sullivan operetta here. Today the theater mostly books rock concerts. ♦ Box office: M-Sa. No credit cards accepted at box office. Hamilton Pl (southeast of Tremont St). Recorded information 482.0650; Ticketmaster 931.2000 ᵫ

67 Cathedral Church of St. Paul Most of Boston's old buildings mingle comfortably enough with their modern neighbors, but this dignified edifice looks uncomfortable sandwiched between two towering commercial structures—as if wondering what happened to the spacious rural town of its day (the 1820s). Once surrounded by handsome homes, the Episcopalian cathedral, on the National Register of Historic Places, is now situated in Boston's workaday district. The church is a simple temple of gray granite, Boston's first example of Greek Revival architecture. The massive sandstone Ionic columns supporting its porch add conviction to a stretch of street that can use it. Architect **Alexander Parris,** the avid practitioner of the Greek Revival style, also designed **Quincy Market.** If the temple's tympanum looks strangely blank, that's because the bas-relief figures intended for it were never carved—another example of a Boston building where ambitious aspirations exceeded funds. Visit the starkly impressive interior, which was revised somewhat by architect **Ralph Adams Cram** in the 1920s. ♦ M-F noon service. Free organ concerts Th 12:45-1:15PM. 138 Tremont St (between Temple Pl and Winter St). 482.5800 ᵫ (enter through the side entrance)

Within Cathedral Church of St. Paul:

Cowley and Cathedral Bookstore This full-service book shop, which is operated by the **Society of St. John the Evangelist** and the Episcopal Diocese, specializes in religious books, primarily with a liberal Christian focus. There are also children's books, ministry resources, icon reproductions, and gifts. ♦ M-Sa. Entrance also at 28 Temple Pl (between Washington and Tremont Sts). 423.4719

68 Santacross Distinctive Shoe Service In business since 1917, this shop will heal your footware woes. Walk-in repairs, shoe shines, and handbag repairs are done on the premises. And orthopedic shoes are a specialty here. ♦ M-Sa 11AM-4:30PM. 16 Temple Pl (between Washington and Tremont Sts). 426.6978 ᵫ

69 Stoddard's Open since 1800, the country's oldest cutlery shop sells plenty of other invaluable items, too: row upon row of nail nippers—who'd ever think so many kinds existed?— pocket knives, corkscrews, clocks, manicure sets, mirrors, magnifiers, binoculars, brushes, scissors, lobster shears, fishing rods and lures, and almost anything else that could possibly come in handy. A great source for practical presents, this place is also one of only a handful remaining where cutlery is sharpened by hand—the only way to give blades their proper edge. An expert grinder works upstairs, giving scissors and such a new lease on life. ♦ M-Sa. 50 Temple Pl (between Washington and Tremont Sts). 426.4187 & Also at: Copley Place, 100 Huntington Ave (between Garrison and Dartmouth Sts). 536.8688

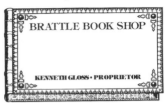

70 Brattle Book Shop Both foreign and domestic bibliophiles find their way to this humble-looking establishment. Not only is it one of America's few surviving urban-based bookshops of its kind, it's also the successor to the country's oldest operating antiquarian bookshop (founded in 1825). For a good part of this century, this literary establishment was run by the late George Gloss, a former fruit peddler, who once exchanged a bunch of grapes for a paperback Dickens novel. Gloss truly earned the nickname "the Pied Piper of book lovers": At one time, he drove a covered wagon through the city, tossing free books to passersby. His son Ken now runs the place, having worked here since age five.

The three-level shop holds every sort of used and rare book imaginable, with fine selections on Boston and New England, and a wealth of autographs and photo albums. The resilient store has risen from the ashes of two big fires and relocated numerous times. Many a treasure has passed through these portals, including a well-read copy of *The Great Gatsby*, given by F. Scott Fitzgerald to T.S. Eliot, which contained Fitzgerald's misspelled inscription and Eliot's annotations. Be sure to peruse the outdoor racks—under the watchful eyes of 18 influential authors (from Leo Tolstoy to Gish Jen) painted by South End artists Jeffrey Hull and Sarah Hutt. Valuable volumes are appraised here, often for free, and the helpful staff are expert book sleuths. ♦ M-Sa. 9 West St (between Washington and Tremont Sts). 542.0210, 800/447.9595 &

70 15 West Street This three-story town house, described as "Mrs. Peabody's caravansary" by Nathaniel Hawthorne, was home to the Peabody family from 1840 to 1854. In the rear parlor, Hawthorne married his beloved Sophia, the Peabody's youngest daughter, and Mary Peabody wed Horace Mann, the founder of American public

education. In the front parlor, headstrong and brilliant Elizabeth Peabody opened Boston's first bookstore selling foreign works. Elizabeth was a fervent abolitionist, an early advocate of kindergartens in America, and the model for the formidable Miss Birdseye in Henry James's novel *The Bostonians.* Here, with Ralph Waldo Emerson, Elizabeth published *The Dial,* the quarterly journal of the Transcendentalists. And each Wednesday local ladies came to hear journalist Margaret Fuller's "Conversations"—landmark lectures on the history of American feminism. These days, the town house is given over to the **West Street Grill.** ♦ Between Washington and Tremont Sts

Within 15 West Street:

West Street Grill ★★$$ Especially popular with the late-night crowd, this spot offers three levels of dining and drinking. The downstairs bar seats about 15, but there are always plenty of standees here and at the smaller upstairs bar. Among the favorite creations are goat cheese fondue; *calamari fritti* with ginger-spiced cilantro sauce; Old Bay crab cake sandwich; and pizza with portobello mushrooms, roasted garlic, artichoke hearts, and asiago cheese. The grill's customers are always satisfied and eager to return. ♦ American ♦ M-F lunch and dinner; Su dinner. 423.0300

71 Fajitas & 'Ritas ★$ Unabashedly fun, this ultraloose joint attracts a surprising number of buttoned-up types. Not content to scribble on the paper tablecloths (crayons are provided), the clientele have spread their doodles and graffiti across every surface; the whole place is a communal work of art in progress. When you fill out your own order forms for assorted fajitas and other Tex-Mex dishes, you can also check off a 'rita (that's margarita) or beer or wine, including sangria by the liter. ♦ Tex-Mex/Takeout ♦ M-Sa lunch and dinner. 25 West St (between Washington and Tremont Sts). 426.1222 &

The Old Corner Bookstore, site of the one-time home of Anne Hutchinson, subsequently housed several publishing firms, once of which was Ticknor & Fields. In order to lure fine American writers and to secure exclusive American publishing rights for English authors, Fields formulated the royalty system, which gave authors both the standard manuscript sum and 10 percent of retail sales.

Boston By Bike: Plum Paths for Pedal Pushers

Thanks to the many reckless drivers who dominate the city's streets, bicycling in Boston can be more akin to navigating the Indianapolis 500 than a pleasurable pastime. But there's hope on the horizon. In an effort to make the city—which is naturally conducive to two-wheelers due to its relative flatness and compact distances—more "bicycle-friendly," Boston's Transportation Department has begun implementation of an official city bicycle policy. The purpose is to encourage bicycling for both recreation and commuting to and from work by linking neighborhoods with bike trails, publicizing safety regulations, and instituting a repair and maintenance program for the city's existing bike paths.

Student-packed **Cambridge,** across the **Charles River,** has a head start on Boston in establishing bicycle-friendly streets. It is the only city in New England with designated bicycle lanes, and is a leader in providing bicycle paths and parking. Cambridge actively promotes bicycle-safety guidelines and enforces a law that makes it illegal to ride bicycles on sidewalks in designated business districts, including **Harvard** and **Central Square.** Cambridge puts out an excellent brochure on alternative forms of transportation in the city, including bicycling. To obtain a free copy of *How to Get Around Cambridge* call 349.4600.

Over the past two decades, lobbying groups have made significant progress in making Boston more welcoming to two-wheelers, primarily by promoting bike paths. The centerpiece is the **Dr. Paul Dudley White Charles River Bike Path,** a 14-mile loop that's increasingly bucolic the farther from downtown you get. This trail hugs both banks of the Charles from the **Museum of Science** all the way to **Watertown Square.** Shorter in-town stretches include the **Southwest Corridor Park Bike Path** (five miles in reclaimed **South End** parkland), the wooded **Riverway Bike Path** (from Boston's **Park Drive**

to Brookline's **Brookline Avenue**), and the scenic **Jamaicaway Bike Bath** (landscape architect Frederick Law Olmsted's former bridle path along the **Muddy River**).

The latest thoroughfare is the **Minuteman Bikeway**—an 11-mile swath linking the **Alewife Station** in **Cambridge** (the outermost *Red Line* subway stop) to the towns of **Arlington, Lexington,** and **Bedford.** Former congressman Joseph Kennedy, himself an avid biker, managed to eke out $1.2 million in federal funds to connect the **Minuteman Bikeway** with the **Dudley Bikepath.** As this book went to press the project was still in the works, with no completion date set.

Meanwhile, Boston's serious bikers—and they are legion—have grown adept at improvising patchwork itineraries. All subway lines except the *Green Line* (which is usually about as roomy as a sardine can) will accommodate bikes during nonpeak hours; call the **Massachusetts Bay Transportation Authority** (722.3200, 800/392.6100) for details.

To find out about other trails, including some to **Provincetown** on **Cape Cod,** contact the **Massachusetts Department of Environmental Management** (Division of Forests and Parks, Salstonstall Building, 100 Cambridge St, Boston, MA 02202, 727.3180). You can rent wheels at the **Community Bike Shop** (496 Tremont St, at E Berkeley St, 542.8623) or **Back Bay Bicycles & Boards** (333 Newbury St, between Hereford St and Massachusetts Ave, 247.2336). For general tips on bike trails, rules of the road, and rentals or repairs, call the **Bicycle Coalition of Massachusetts** (491.7433). **American Youth Hostels** (1020 Commonwealth Ave, between Babcock St and Winslow Rd, 731.6692) and the **Appalachian Mountain Club** (5 Joy St, between Beacon and Mount Vernon Sts, 523.0636) organize cycling trips.

72 The Boston Music Company Open for more than 100 years, this august music emporium purveys New England's largest selection of sheet music and books about music. One glance inside tells you this shop's an oldie but goodie. Its clientele encompasses music lovers and musicians, professional and amateur, who seek anything from choral pieces to the latest rock 'n' roll hit. This place is proud of its enormous collection of music-related gifts, like its cases of music boxes for $5,000 or so. A musical instrument department sells traditional and electronic instruments. Owned by Hammerstein Music

and Theatre Corp., which, in turn, is owned by the estate of the legendary Oscar Hammerstein, this subsidiary is the educational music publisher, whose titles are distributed throughout the world. ♦ M-Sa. 172 Tremont St (at Avery St). 426.5100

73 Opera House Sadly dilapidated, the stage of this theater has been dark since 1991. Though this building and the **Paramount Theatre** next door have been marked for preservation by the National Registry of Historic Places, so far the funds to restore the 1928 theater—designed by **Thomas Lamb**—and the 1932 Art Deco **Paramount** (take note of Arthur Bowditch's sign) to their former splendor have not come through. The house was first named the **B.F. Keith Memorial Theatre** to honor the show-biz wizard who coined the term "vaudeville." Keith introduced the concept of continuous performances of high-quality variety acts suitable for family viewing, to contrast with the lowlife entertainment offered at Scollay Square's notorious **Old Howard** theater. He owned a chain of 400 theaters, after which movie "picture palaces" were modeled. More recently, this one was called the **Savoy Theatre.** Later it was home to Sarah Caldwell's **Boston Opera Company.** The Spanish Baroque terra-cotta facade is best seen from Avenue de Lafayette across the way. The interior is closed to the public. ◆ 539 Washington St (between Avery St and Harlem Pl)

73 Joy Boston Adjacent to the old **Opera House** is this three-story dance club. Its severe black facade and urbane lighting contrast starkly with the faded opulence of its aged neighbor. The action is upstairs at **The Domain:** a dark dance club where a DJ spins R&B and high-energy "techno" tunes. Validated parking is available at the Lafayette Place shopping complex. ◆ Admission. Th-Su 10PM-2AM. 533 Washington St (between Avery St and Harlem Pl). 338.6999 &

swissôtel

74 Swissôtel Boston $$$ Having undergone an $11-million makeover, the 500 rooms and suites on this hotel's 16 floors are far more sumptuous and contemporary in decor than the severely impersonal exterior implies. In fact, this hotel is one of the best-kept secrets in Boston, as many don't anticipate finding such stellar accommodations in this part of town. Guest services include a concierge, parking, a multilingual staff, same-day laundry and valet services, an indoor swimming pool and exercise equipment, and a sun terrace. There are rooms for people with disabilities plus two floors for nonsmokers. Swiss chocolates appear not only in guest rooms, but in a bowl at the registration desk.

Divided into four atriums, each with its own lounge, the **Executive Level** (encompassing 135 rooms) offers 24-hour butler service. Other **Executive Level** perks include a complimentary continental breakfast, afternoon hors d'oeuvres, a fax machine, a private board room, and two-line phones in every room. The hotel was the anchor to the adjoining **Lafayette Place** shopping complex, which was built in the early 1980s and has since gone bust. At press time plans were being considered for its revival. ◆ 1 Ave de Lafayette (at Chauncy St). 451.2600, 800/621.9200; fax 451.0054

Within the Swissôtel Boston:

Caffe Suisse ★$$ The setting is a bit bland, except for some contemporary artwork by Swiss emigré artists. The bill of fare is a mix of American and continental, with a few Swiss specialties (*rösti* potatoes and spaetzle dumplings) thrown in for color. The ambience livens up a bit on Sunday for the jazz brunch buffet. ◆ International ◆ M-Sa breakfast and lunch; Su brunch. 451.2600 &

75 Baker's Plays The oldest American play publishing company was established under the name of the Herbert Sweet Company on Washington Street in 1845. Relocated after the great Boston fire of 1872, it was handed down through several generations, and survives today under the genial custodianship of manager Jack Welch and two resident cats "who let us think we run the place." Boston's small but impassioned theater community counts on finding the latest scripts, trade papers, and casting news here. ◆ M-F. 100 Chauncy St (at Ave de Lafayette). 482.1280

Bests

Arthur Dion
Director/Art Dealer, Gallery Naga

After luxuriating in the city's great art galleries (the **Institute of Contemporary Art,** the **Museum of Fine Arts,** the **Isabella Stewart Gardner,** and the **Albert and Vera List Visual Arts Center**), walk around **Newbury Street** and environs.

The King & I has the best Thai cuisine in town—classic pad thai, beautiful chicken basil.

Davio's, for haute Italian, irresistible homemade sausages, and supernal soups and sauces.

The holiday lights in the trees of **Boston Common** on a winter night during December.

The views driving along **Storrow Drive** or **Memorial Drive** along the **Charles River** day or night, to/from the **Museum of Science**; it's almost worth renting a car or bike.

Ice skating on the **Lagoon** in the **Public Garden** (I've never done it, but it looks great).

The **Charles River Esplanade** is just gorgeous, especially if it's the first Sunday in June and you've just finished the 10K From All Walks of Life, which raised millions of dollars for AIDS care and research.

The **Museum of Afro American History**—a gem.

The **Cyclorama** at the **Boston Center for the Arts** is a huge, odd, wonderful exhibition space.

The amazing flower beds in the **Public Garden.**

Spring and fall weekends the largest clusters of Boston's many thousands of artists' studios are open to all. (Check the paper or call a gallery for details.) **Fort Point Channel,** the **South End,** and **Vernon Street,** to name only the biggest, are all primers to the city's art world.

Chinatown/Theater District

This checkered neighborhood's story has had many acts, characters, triumphs, and tribulations over the years. Here, in a geographically awkward and angular fringe of the city, three principal dramatis personae converge— and sometimes collide: the **Theater District**, the **Combat Zone** (Boston's red-light district), and **Chinatown.**

Beginning in the 1920s, Boston was a favorite tryout city for Broadway-bound plays—a glittering, glamorous mecca when all the big stage names were in town. After movies outstripped theater in popularity and the suburbs eclipsed the city, great playhouses such as the **Wilbur** and the **Majestic** deteriorated. As roofs leaked, walls crumbled, and paint and plaster peeled, the shadow of the wrecking ball loomed. But Boston's 1980s boom, also known as the "Massachusetts Miracle," rescued a number of theaters. The **Wilbur** is now repaired, the **Shubert** refurbished, the **Majestic** resuscitated, and the **Colonial** forges on. Other houses cling to life or remain dark, awaiting a savior. Today, Boston's rialto is clustered around **Tremont** and **Stuart Streets.**

The Combat Zone, a sleazy "adult-entertainment" district concentrated on lower **Washington Street,** took root in the 1960s and flourished during the 1970s as home to many X-rated movie houses and dozens of seamy strip joints, peep shows, and porn shops. Developers and neighborhood associations have almost succeeded in strangling the Zone—nearly 30 establishments have been closed down since 1986, reducing the size of the area from seven blocks to one. Shady sorts still hang out here, so it's unsafe at night, but the Zone's days are numbered—or so residents hope.

Chinatown's official entry point is a massive ceremonial gateway on **Beach Street,** but pedestrians approach this quarter from every which way. Bounded by the **Central Artery** and Washington, **Kneeland,** and **Essex Streets,** this four-block-wide neighborhood is known for its restaurants and colorful storefronts. Cramped it may be, but Chinatown is always full of activity, and exudes a festive ambience with its subtitled signs and banners and pagoda-topped phone booths. Popular events are Chinese New Year and the August

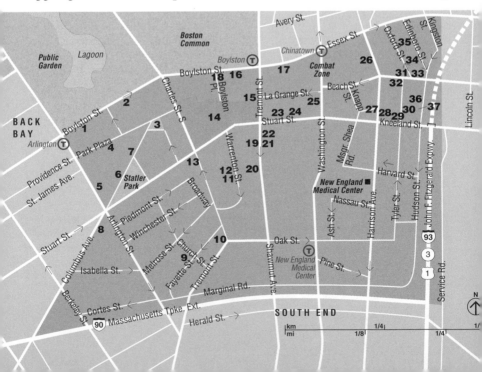

Moon Festival, when local martial-arts groups don dragon costumes and dance through the streets amid exploding firecrackers and crowds of celebrants. Jammed into these dense blocks are about 200 restaurants (many open as late as 4AM), bakeries, gift and curio shops, and markets selling live poultry, fresh fish, and vegetables. The remains of the textile and garment industry (Chinatown's economic mainstay before restaurants and grocery wholesalers took the lead) are located where **Harrison Avenue** intersects **Kneeland Street. Tyler Street** is the showiest thoroughfare, with some of the most flamboyant storefronts, while Beach Street harbors the workaday scene. A community at a crossroads, Chinatown is struggling to preserve its ethnic character. The first Chinese came to Boston soon after the Revolution. The subsequent China trade brought workers to the seaport, but a permanent community wasn't established until 1875. With the liberalization of immigration laws in the mid-1960s, Chinatown ballooned, but then lost half its land to highway expansion, downtown encroachment, and the **New England Medical Center.** Today, the population has swelled to more than 8,000, with Vietnamese, Laotians, and Cambodians enriching the ethnic composition.

Bursting at the seams, troubled by refuse-strewn streets, and demoralized by the decaying Combat Zone and a lack of affordable housing, not long ago Chinatown seemed destined to a grim future. In recent years, however, there have been signs of change. The Neighborhood Council now acts as liaison to the mayor's office and reviews all plans for development; in fact, nothing happens in Chinatown anymore without the council's involvement. A denouement to the neighborhood drama will be the urban megadevelopment called the **Midtown Cultural District,** scheduled for completion in the year 2000. The project will serve as a catalyst for restoring historic theaters, ensuring Chinatown's prosperity and **New England Medical Center's** growth, and boosting downtown nightlife in the two-square-mile mixed-use community of office towers, department stores, hotels, restaurants, clubs, and cultural space that encompasses **Park Square,** the Theater District, the Combat Zone, and Downtown Crossing (the intersection of Washington Street and Winter/Summer Streets). In the process, one unsavory neighborhood character—the troublemaking Zone—eventually will be eliminated.

In the midst of these changes, Chinatown and the Theater District will undoubtedly remain the places to go in Boston for great performances in the gorgeous old theaters, vibrant comedy club acts, authentic Chinese culture and cuisine, and innovative meals in sophisticated restaurants.

1 The Heritage on the Garden One of Boston's more accommodating architectural presences is this mixed-use complex of retail and commercial space and luxurious residential condos designed by **The Architects Collaborative** in 1988. A number of upscale shops and restaurants are located on the premises—albeit with confusingly varied street addresses—including **Sonia Rykiel Boutique** (280 Boylston St, 426.2033); **Villeroy & Boch** (288 Boylston St, 542.7442); **Escada** (308 Boylston St, 437.1200); and **Hermès** (22 Arlington St, 482.8707). ♦ 300 Boylston St (between Hadassah Way and Arlington St) ♿

Within The Heritage on the Garden:

Restaurants/Clubs: Red	**Hotels:** Blue
Shops/♥ Outdoors: Green	**Sights/Culture:** Black

Biba ★★★★$$$ Boston's wild about the adventurous inspiration of Boston-born and -trained chef Lydia Shire, who rose to eminence through stints at several renowned local restaurants. After a hiatus in California, she returned and opened this dining spot filled with joie de vivre. A daring chef, Shire experiments with international cooking styles, and diners may order  appetizers or vice versa, making for tailor-made meals. Marvelous flatbread arrives hot from the Indian tandoori oven in the corner. The menu changes daily, but surprises have included fried, boned quail with parsnip chips, calf's brains with crisp-fried capers, green-tea duck with ginger-and-scallion pancakes, maple- and rum-smoked salmon, wood-roasted chicken, and sour-cherry ice cream with chocolate cake and "something crunchy." Service is spotty, but always good-natured, and the place gets pretty noisy, so don't plan on sotto voce confidences. New York architect **Adam Tihany** designed the restaurant, a quirky ensemble of styles. The second-floor dining room features an expansive view of the **Public Garden** lagoon. But if upstairs is booked, you can mix and match a delightful eccentric repast from the bar menu downstairs. The sultry ground-floor bar, decorated with a Robert Jessup mural depicting well-fed people, is where many stylish singles find each other. There's valet parking daily except Sunday. ◆ Continental ◆ M-F, Su lunch and dinner; Sa dinner. Reservations recommended for dining room. 272 Boylston St. 426.7878 ᕐ

Le Pli

AT THE HERITAGE

Le Pli at the Heritage Six kinds of massage; facials; body wraps; manicures; any kind of pampering for your body, skin, or hair; and aerobics classes are available to the public—for a fee—at this ultrachic and expensive European-style spa/health club/salon. Only the workout facilities and the three-lane lap pool are limited to members or guests of member hotels. Plenty of special packages with the works are available, some including hotel accommodations and food. **Schwartz/Silver Architects** designed the pristine interior, collaborating with artist Stephen Knapp. The same owners operate the equally elite **Le Pli** spa in Cambridge (547.4081). ◆ 28 Arlington St. Spa 426.6999, salon 482.2424

FOUR SEASONS HOTEL
Boston
A FOUR SEASONS · REGENT HOTEL

2   Four Seasons Hotel $$$$ Half of the 288 rooms and the restaurants at this luxurious hostelry feature views of the lovely **Public Garden** across the way. Among the celebrities who have stayed in the posh Presidential Suite are Bruce Springsteen, Glenda Jackson, Christopher Plummer, Luciano Pavarotti, and John Williams. Maybe they like the friendly and solicitous staff or the hotel's concern for niceties. For those traveling with children, every crib is equipped with a teddy bear, and kids get bedtime milk and cookies and receive kits with

cameras or magic tricks. The concierge distributes duck and squirrel treats for feeding those voracious park denizens across the way, and the hotel will pack picnic baskets for guests on request. For joggers, a pair of running shoes is provided, along with maps outlining trails that start right outside the front door. The accommodations are on eight floors, and there are special rooms for people with disabilities, as well as rooms for nonsmokers. Additional amenities feature concierge services, around-the-clock room service, same-day laundry and 24-hour valet and pressing services, valet parking, and business services. The health spa has a lap pool, Jacuzzi, sauna, and on-call trainers. ◆ 200 Boylston St (between Charles St S and Hadassah Way). 338.4400, 800/332.3442 in the US, 800/268.6282 in Canada; fax 426.9207 ᕐ

Within the Four Seasons Hotel:

AUJOURD'HUI

Aujourd'hui ★★★$$$$ An ultrarefined setting for an elegant meal, this restaurant is the most pleasant when light lingers in the **Public Garden** beyond (be sure to reserve a window-side table). Executive Chef David Fritchey's acclaimed menu is complemented by a lengthy international wine list. His specialties range from Mediterranean and classic French cuisine to regional American favorites. Among the potential offerings are juniper-roasted venison chop with sweet potato and turnip cake and cider-glazed chard; Maine lobster with spicy Thai ginger sauce, crusty potato wonton, and snow peas; and red-pepper pasta with marinated vine ripened tomato, basil olive oil, and garlic. Reduced-calorie, sodium- and cholesterol-free dishes are also available. Local designers and shops are featured at lunchtime fashion shows every Tuesday (September through June). Theatergoers pressed for time may opt for the prix-fixe pretheater menu. For a cozy party, reserve one of two private dining rooms. Valet parking is available. ◆ Continental ◆ M-F breakfast, lunch, and dinner; Sa breakfast and dinner; Su brunch and dinner. Reservations recommended; jacket and tie requested at dinner. 451.1392 ᕐ

The Bristol ★★$$ Pick one of the discretely positioned clusters of chairs and sofas for lunch, afternoon tea, cocktails, before- and after-theater supper, and dessert (there's a lush Viennese dessert table from 9PM to midnight on Friday and Saturday evenings). A children's menu, a rarity in Boston, is offered here. Pianists provide classical music and soft jazz in the afternoon and evening. A fireplace warms the place during the cold winter months, and afternoon tea is served daily from 3 to 4:30PM. ◆ Continental ◆ Daily. Reservations recommended for lunch. 338.4400 ᕐ

ADESSO

Adesso Co-owners Rick Grossman and Françoise Theise are retail pioneers, dedicated to discovering and introducing Americans to up-to-the-moment furniture and lighting from France, Italy, West Germany, Holland, and Austria (and some from the US, too). Called "new classics" by the owners, these smashing, versatile pieces are often architect-designed and may be available only to the trade in other cities. They'll ship anywhere in the world, and you can buy directly from their newsletters and catalogs. ◆ M-Sa; Th until 8PM. 451.2212 ♿

3 The Great Emancipator Across the street from the **Boston Park Plaza Hotel** (see below) stands one statue Boston could do without. This 1879 hero-worshiping homage to Abraham Lincoln, copied from the Washington original and sponsored by legislator Moses Kimball, portrays the president anointing a kneeling former slave, with the inscription "A race set free/A country at peace/Lincoln rests from his labors." From today's vantage point, the work appears paternalistic. ◆ Park Plaza and Columbus Ave

4 Ben & Jerry's Ice Cream This franchise dishes up the populist entrepreneurs' delicious ice cream, shipped fresh from their Vermont factory. Chocolate Chip Cookie Dough, Coconut Milk Chocolate Almond, and Cappuccino Chocolate Chunk are among the perennial favorites. All flavors are available in sundaes, shakes, cones, and ice-cream cakes, as well as between brownies and cookies. Coffee and muffins baked on the premises are sold in the morning until they run out. ◆ Daily. No credit cards accepted. 20 Park Plaza (between Columbus Ave and Arlington St). 426.0890 ♿ Also at: 174 Newbury St (between Dartmouth and Exeter Sts), Back Bay. 536.5456

5 Boston Park Plaza Hotel $$$ Steps away from the theaters and one block from the **Public Garden,** this 1927 hotel, a member of Historic Hotels of America, has 972 rooms. Decor and room sizes vary considerably: Of special interest are the hotel's "double/double" rooms featuring two double beds and two baths. All rooms feature individual voice mail; other pluses include a weight room, privileges at the nearby elegant **Le Pli at the Heritage** spa (see page 98), 24-hour room service, floors for nonsmokers, and a pharmacy. You can check out and order breakfast via video. On the premises are airline-ticket offices, a travel agency, and a ticket agency for sports, theater, and concert events. Within or adjacent to the hotel are restaurants and lounges. **Swans Court** in the lobby, where Liberace began his career, serves tea and pastries and offers a full bar. The hotel has achieved international recognition for its landmark Environmental Action Program which focuses on waste reduction, reuse, and recycling. ◆ 64 Arlington St (between Columbus Ave and Park Plaza). 426.2000, 800/899.2076; fax 654.1999

6 Legal Sea Foods ★★$$$ "If it's not fresh, it's not Legal." The food lives up to the slogan at the Berkowitz family's fleet of seafood restaurants. This one's the flagship. Observe the long and patient lines—it's hard to believe the empire began as a lowly fish-and-chips joint. Now an endless menu offers all the fruits of the sea, always superior and flapping-fresh. First, choose your fish, then decide on a mode of preparation—broiled, grilled, fried, stuffed, sautéed, steamed, pan-blackened, Cajun-style, even in spicy Chinese recipes devised by visiting chefs from China's Shandong province. The fish chowder could double for wallpaper paste in consistency, but has hordes of fans—including US presidents—as do the smoked salmon and bluefish pâtés. And this is one place where it's always safe to eat raw clams and oysters—every batch is tested at an in-house laboratory. The extraordinary, extensive wine list lives up to the menu.

But be forewarned: This is not the spot for lingering conversation. There are no reservations, so you can cool your heels interminably while the loudspeaker incessantly barks out names. The dining rooms are both noisy and jammed, and the policy is to bring food to tables when it is ready, so you may get your meal well before or after your companions get theirs. Still, superb seafood is worth some concessions. When you require brain food yet can't endure a mob scene, the smaller cafe/take-out operation next door is the answer. The seating here is more snug, but the cafe offers almost the same menu plus full bar, and operates a little faster. And if the cafe is too full, get your dinner to go. ◆ Seafood ◆ Daily lunch and dinner. 35 Columbus Ave (between Arlington St and Park Plaza). Restaurant 426.4444, cafe/takeout 426.5566 ♿ Also at: Prudential Center, 800 Boylston St (between Exeter and Dalton Sts). 266.6800; Copley Place, 100 Huntington Ave (between Garrison and Dartmouth Sts). 266.7775; 5 Cambridge Center, Main St (between Kendall Sq and Fulkerson Sts), Cambridge. 864.3400

Child's Play

With its parks, waterfronts, and participatory museums, Boston is a city custom-designed for family sight-seeing. Just don't hard-sell the educational/historic sites. (It's usually the adults who romanticize such events as the midnight ride of Paul Revere and the Boston Tea Party).

1 **USS Constitution** Board "Old Ironsides," the oldest commissioned ship afloat. Doing so will make you feel like an authentic seafarer—and convince you that life at sea was anything but glamorous.

2 **The Computer Museum** Pilot a DC-10 into a volcano, draw on walls without getting in trouble, explore a virtual reality world, and step into the "Walk-Through Computer," a disco-like cave of flashing lights and rainbow-colored wiring.

3 **New England Aquarium** Watch creatures of the deep swim round and round in the giant, 187,000-gallon ocean tank.

4 **Freedom Trail** This is truly a fun way of tracing the role of Boston in the American Revolution. The 3-mile journey covers 16 sites—remember to wear your athletic shoes!

5 **The Children's Museum** "Touch" is the magic word here. The hands-on museum features exhibits such as the "Recycle Room" where leftover

materials get an artistic makeover. Don't miss the dancing skeleton bones, a climbing structure for older kids.

6 **The Milk Bottle** Refreshment awaits outside the **Children's Museum,** where a snack stand shaped like a giant milk bottle serves up sandwiches, salads, and ice cream.

7 **FAO Schwarz** No trip to Boston is complete without a visit to this fantasyland of toys, games, and stuffed animals of every creation. The entrance is guarded by a 12-foot-high bronze bear.

8 **Franklin Park Zoo** Spend a day in the **African Tropical Forest,** home to more than 150 animals—among them gorillas, leopards, pygmy hippos, and monkeys. Or watch the big cats in the **Lions of Serengeti** section.

9 **Public Garden** Take a ride on a **Swan Boat** or, in winter, a brief spin on ice skates. Be sure to see the knee-high brass statues of Mrs. Mallard and her brood, characters in the children's classic *Make Way for Ducklings.*

10 **John Hancock Tower Observatory** For a great view, zoom up 60 floors and focus on favorite attractions using "fun-scopes."

7 **Legal Sea Foods Cash Market** The gargantuan Berkowitz enterprise has yet another giant offshoot: this one-stop gourmet shop featuring a counter stocking at least a dozen kinds of fresh fish from the same supplier used by the restaurant. Pick up live lobster packed to travel, whatever fish you wish, the clan's own famous chowders, pâtés, cheeses, crackers, salads, soups, sauces, condiments, marinades, coffees and teas, chocolates, even the house cookbook. The liquor department carries 600 wines, cold beer, and a full liquor selection. All the bases are covered, but don't expect any bargains. ♦ M-Sa until 8PM. 15 Columbus Ave (between Arlington St and Park Plaza). 426.7777 ♿

8 **Park Plaza Castle** The imposing granite "Castle," as the eye-catching landmark is universally known around Boston, was built in 1897 by **William G. Preston** as an armory for the First Corps of Cadets, a private Massachusetts military organization founded in 1741 and commanded at one time by John Hancock. The Victorian fortress, now on the National Register of Historic Places, was a social center for prominent Bostonians in the late 1800s, and its luxurious, clubby interior was the site for billiards, imbibing fine wine, and the popular **Cadet Theatricals.** The corps now operates a private military museum in

Back Bay. The lofty hexagonal tower, turrets, crenellated walls, lancet windows, and drawbridge create the illusion of a strong structure that's ready for medieval-style combat. But much calmer events transpire at this exhibition and convention center now owned by the **Boston Park Plaza Hotel.** Bostonians flock to the annual "Crafts at the Castle" sale held in early December and sponsored by Family Services of Greater Boston. Next door is the **Grillfish Seafood Restaurant**—built in 1886 as **Carter's Ink Factory**—which boasts an impressive terra-cotta and brick facade. ♦ 130 Columbus Ave (at Arlington St). For events information, call Boston Park Plaza Hotel's sales office 426.2000 ♿

9 **Bay Village** For the flavor of 19th-century Boston, take a 15-minute stroll along this insular nook on Winchester, Church, Melrose, and Fayette Streets. Difficult to find by car and easy to miss on foot, the tight cluster of short streets bordered by diminutive brick houses was mostly laid out during the 1820s and 1830s. Many of the artisans, houseights, and carpenters who worked on fashionable Beacon Hill's prestigious residences concurrently built their own small homes here. The neighborhood's residents once encompassed other colorful professions: sailmakers, paperhangers, blacksmiths, harness- and rope-makers, painters, salt merchants, musical instrument makers, and cabinet- makers. Edgar Allan Poe was born in a lodging house in the vicinity in 1809; his parents were actors in a stock company playing nearby. Because it's so close to the Theater District, Bay Village gradually acquired a bohemian flavor and spillover nightlife. On Fayette Street, look for brief Bay Street with its single house, a concluding punctuation mark. ♦ Bounded by Charles St S, Broadway, Arlington, Tremont, and Piedmont Sts, and Marginal Rd

10 Beacon Hill Skate This is where you can rent or purchase roller blades, skates, skateboards, and safety equipment to whiz along the esplanade that borders the Charles River, or, in winter, ice skates to skim over the **Public Garden** lagoon while it's vacated by ducks and **Swan Boats** for the season. (Skates are available lagoonside, too, through this shop.) ♦ Daily. 135 Charles St S (at Tremont St). 482.7400

11 Charles Playhouse The Theater District's oldest playhouse—built by **Asher Benjamin** in 1843, renovated by **Cambridge Seven** in 1966, and listed on the National Register of Historic Places—began life as a church and today is a rental facility for private productions, all managed separately. The show playing on **Stage I** changes sporadically, but on **Stage II**, *Shear Madness* has played for over 15 years, and is likely to go on as long as new visitors come to town. It has already made the *Guinness Book of World Records* for longest-running nonmusical play. The audience-participation comedy whodunit, set in a Boston beauty salon on Back Bay's Newbury Street, often stars good local professional actors. The solution to the murder mystery changes nightly, and new improvisations, local color, and topical humor are added continually. ♦ Box office daily; shows Tu-Su. No credit cards accepted at box office. 74-78 Warrenton St (between Charles St S and Stuart St). Stage I 426.6912, Stage II 426.5225, Charge-Tix 542.8511

12 Nick's Entertainment Center A fixture on Boston's entertainment scene that has survived by changing with the times, this happening spot once had a cabaret/dinner theater, a comedy club, and a sports bar.

Now, it is home to **Nick's Comedy Stop**, a club featuring local and national comics. ♦ Cover. Shows W, Th, Su 8:30PM; F-Sa 8:15, 10:15PM. 100 Warrenton St (between Charles St S and Stuart St). 482.0930

13 57 Park Plaza/Radisson Hotel Boston $$ This former Howard Johnson hostelry boasts 350 refurbished rooms. Conveniently located, the 24-story hotel features 2 restaurants and a bar, an indoor heated pool, a sauna, a sundeck, room service, and indoor parking with direct access to the hotel. Rooms designed for those with disabilities and nonsmoking floors are available. ♦ 200 Stuart St (at Charles St S). 482.1800, 800/468.3557; fax 451.2750 &

14 Massachusetts State Transportation Building The architectural firm of **Goody, Clancy & Associates** designed this enormous (it occupies an entire city block) state transportation office complex (pictured below), with the participation of local business, cultural, and neighborhood groups, to relate to the surrounding low-rise brick structures. The redbrick exterior, with asymmetrical cantilevers, is fairly self-effacing. The real excitement awaits within, where an atrium— with trendily exposed endoskeletal support beams—vaults above a pedestrian mall with shops and restaurants to draw that vitality inward. Noontime music concerts entertain the milling lunchtime throngs, and a small art gallery operated by the Artists Foundation adds an avant-garde frisson. ♦ Gallery Tu-Sa afternoons. Stuart St (between Tremont St and Charles St S)

Within the Massachusetts State Transportation Building:

Brew Moon $$ The eye-catching Art Deco decor makes this spot a standout among Boston's numerous brew pubs. In addition to a few regular draught beers, the special offerings—Munich Gold lager, Dunkel Bock, and seasonal specials—are popular. The Lunar Sampler, five four-ounce samples of the hand-crafted beers, is a terrific buy. The food is just as varied: beer-battered flounder; spiced-

Massachusetts State Transportation Building

bronzed swordfish; and herb-crusted sirloin top the menu along with some tasty pasta dishes. Live acoustic music in the bar/lounge follows no set schedule. ♦ American ♦ Daily lunch and dinner. 115 Stuart St. 742.5225 ♿ Also at: 50 Church St (between Palmer and Brattle Sts), Cambridge. 499.BREW

15 Emerson Majestic Theatre Originally famous for its musicals and opera performances, this extravagantly ornate Beaux Arts–style theater, designed by **John Galen Howard** in 1903, was bought in the 1950s by a movie-theater chain that slapped tacky fake materials on top of marble and Neo-Classical friezes. **Emerson College** rescued the theater in 1983, spent several million dollars on renovations, and has made it "majestic" once more.

Today, the 859-seat multipurpose performance center serves as a stage for nonprofit groups, including **Dance Umbrella, Boston Lyric Opera,** the **New England Conservatory,** and **Emerson Stage.** Patrons favor the theater for its sense of excitement and inclusion with performers; entertainers like the space for its rococo high style and fine acoustics. This was the first theater in Boston to incorporate electricity into the building's design. ♦ Box office daily. 219 Tremont St (between Stuart and Boylston Sts). 824.8000 ♿

16 Colonial Theatre Built in 1900, the most gloriously grand theater in Boston is also one of the most handsome in the country. The play may disappoint, but the arena, never. Actually, this is a very uncolonial-style structure, a 10-story office building with a theater tucked in. It does, however, brim with classical ornament, ebulliently gilded and mirrored. H.B. Pennell's interiors feature glittering chandeliers, lofty arched ceilings, sumptuous frescoes and friezes, allegorical figures—all the ruffles and flourishes imaginable. Yet the 1,658-seat theater is also intimate and comfortable, with excellent sight lines and acoustics. **Clarence H. Blackall**'s other local credits include the nearby **Wilbur Theater** and **Metropolitan Theater** (now the **Wang Center**), as well as the **Winthrop Building** downtown. Thankfully, Blackall and Pennell's masterpiece has been spared the ups, downs, and indignities of many ravaged Boston theaters, and has been lovingly preserved.

The theater continues to book major productions, often musicals, many on their way to Broadway. In the theater's 90-odd years in business, Flo Ziegfeld, Irving Berlin, Rodgers and Hammerstein, Bob Fosse, and Tommy Tune have launched shows here. Ethel Barrymore, Frederic March, Helen Hayes, Katharine Hepburn, Henry Fonda, Fred Astaire, Eddie Cantor, W.C. Fields, the Marx Brothers, Will Rogers, Danny Kaye, and Barbra Streisand have all trod the boards. Half-price tickets are offered for persons with disabilities and one companion. ♦ Box office open daily. 106 Boylston St (between Tremont St and Boylston Pl). 426.9366 ♿

16 Boylston Street The slice of this thoroughfare facing **Boston Common** was once known as "Piano Row" for its concentration of piano-making and music-publishing establishments—enterprises in which music-loving Boston led the nation during the 19th and early 20th centuries. The businesses occupied (or, in some cases, still occupy) several handsome buildings that are physical expressions of the city's traditional high esteem for music: The Wurlitzer Company (now at 96-98 Boylston) resided at **No. 100** with its elegant, elaborate storefront designed by **Clarence H. Blackall;** the building is also home to the distinguished **Colonial Theatre.** The Steinway Piano Company is located at Beaux Arts–style **No. 162,** designed by **Winslow and Bigelow** in 1896. While you're on this stretch, look for the **Little Building, No. 80,** a 1916 commercial edifice designed by Blackall's firm with a Gothic-influenced terra-cotta facade, now part of **Emerson College.** Then cross Tremont Street to see **No. 48,** the eye-catching Ruskinian Gothic **Young Men's Christian Union** of 1875, by **Nathaniel J. Bradlee,** listed on the National Register of Historic Places.

A few steps farther is the **Boylston Building,** an 1887 edifice, also on the National Register of Historic Places, and the work of **Carl Fehmer,** architect of numerous important Boston office buildings and homes, including the grandiose **Oliver Ames Mansion** in Back Bay. It's now home to the **China Trade Center,** an office/arcade complex organized by the Bay Group and the Chinese Economic Development Group. **The Boston Architectural Team** carved out an appealing atrium, decorated with a mosaic walkway and wall plaque by Lilli Ann and Marvin Rosenberg, elucidating the Chinese lunar zodiac. Several food shops are on the premises, and at noon a group of actors called the **Winter Company** performs on a small stage in the atrium's well. ♦ Between Washington St and Charles St S

17 Jack's Joke Shop "Yes, We Have Warts!" a shop notice reads. Pick out your latest

disguise at Harold Bengin's wholesale/retail emporium for tricksters. Or make an unforgettable impression with a unique gift from an inventory topping 3,000 different items, including backward-running clocks, instant worms, garlic gum, sneeze powder, or the gross but ever-popular severed heads, fake wounds, and—dare we say it—even worse. Open since 1922 (it's the oldest shop of its type in the US), this is definitely one of the city's more colorful institutions. Halloween is the shop's biggest selling season, naturally, but kids and adults stream in throughout the year for jokes, tricks, magic, novelties, complete costumes, masks, wigs, beards, flags of all countries, and other oddities galore. Bengin and his staff clearly get a kick out of this business. ♦ M-Sa. No credit cards accepted. 38 Boylston St (between Washington and Tremont Sts). 426.9640 ♿

18 Walker's Horseback riding outfitters since 1932, this stuffed-to-the-rafters store doesn't play favorites, carrying a selection of both English (black velvet helmets and modern Lycra jodhpurs) and Western (cowboy shirts and pointy boots) gear. It's got to be the only place in town that carries scorpion-motif belt buckles. ♦ Daily. 122 Boylston St (between Tremont St and Boylston Pl). 423.9050 ♿

18 Boylston Place Located off Boylston Street along Piano Row, this pedestrian cul-de-sac reputedly was where football was born in 1860, when a student of **Mr. Dixwell's Private School** organized the first game. The rubber sphere used for a ball is in the Society for the Preservation of New England Antiquities' collections. Enter via a fanciful arch replete with theatrical and local allusions, and pass through a phalanx of night spots popular among the young and impecunious, such as **Alley Cat** (No. 1, 351.2510), **Avenue C** (No. 25, 423.3832), and **The Big Easy** (see below). At the end, a pedestrian passage leads through the **Transportation Building** to Stuart Street, a handy shortcut.

On Boylston Place:

The Big Easy One of the city's most popular dance and party spots is this two-story, Cajun-theme playhouse with a spacious dance floor. A DJ spins a satisfying mix of Top 40 and rock 'n' roll floor-burners what tends to be an upscale crowd, generally ranging in age from mid-20s to mid-40s. There's valet parking on weekends. ♦ Cover. W-Su. Jacket and tie requested. No one under 21 is admitted. No. 1. 351.7000 ♿

Sweetwater Cafe $ When you want to be casual and anonymous, try this laid-back, cheap eats place for big portions of Tex-Mex and bar food—nachos, tostadas, burritos, barbecue beef, and super-hot Buffalo wings. There's a bar on the second level, but the downstairs is quieter, with booths. Two juke-boxes—one stocked with old 45s—crank out tunes. You can eat outdoors in nice weather. ♦ Tex/Mex ♦ Tu-Sa dinner until 2AM. No. 3. 351.2515

The Tavern Club This exclusive club, which barred women until the late 1980s, has resided since 1887 in three quaint brick row houses built in the early- to mid-19th century. For generations the club has been famed for its private performances of outrageous plays starring club members. ♦ Daily. Nos. 4-6. 338.9682

19 Shubert Theatre In 1910 **Hill, James & Whitaker** designed this refined 1,680-seat theater with a graceful marquee; today it's listed on the National Register of Historic Places. It's part of the famous chain, but has a fine reputation in its own right among both actors and audiences. The illustrious Sir Laurence Olivier, John Barrymore, and Sir John Gielgud performed on this stage, as did Sarah Bernhardt, Mae West, Humphrey Bogart, Ingrid Bergman, Cary Grant, and Helen Hayes. Recent productions have included the Broadway hit *Bring In Da Noise, Bring In Da Funk*. Discounted tickets are offered for persons with disabilities and one companion. ♦ Box office open daily. 265 Tremont St (between Charles St S and Stuart St). 482.9393 ♿

TREMONT
H·O·U·S·E

20 The Tremont House $$ Named after Boston's first grand hotel, long gone, and filling the shoes of the former **Bradford Hotel**, where 1950s big bands played, this 15-floor independent hostelry boasts a $9 million renovation to all 320 rooms, including accommodations for people with disabilities and for nonsmokers. Given its location in the theater district, it quite naturally caters to the theater crowd (both performers and spectators): Casts often stay here, and special packages, including tickets, are available. Amenities include a new concierge level, room service, and valet parking. Its **Broadway** restaurant is open daily for breakfast, lunch, and dinner. The hotel was built in 1926 as the national headquarters for the Benevolent and Protective Order of Elks, which explains why the public spaces are so grand. Look for the brass **Elks Club** doorknobs. ♦ 275 Tremont St (between Charles St S and Stuart St). 426.1400, 800/331.9998; fax 338.7881 &

Within The Tremont House:

NYC Jukebox/Eight Tracks Here are two clubs under one roof. At **Jukebox** patrons can shake, rattle, and roll to 1960s through 1980s tunes; Sunday is Brazilian night. A younger crowd flocks to **Eight Tracks** to watch Top 40 videos and dance to club classics. There's a full bar, but no food. ♦ Cover. F-Su. No one under 21 admitted. No T-shirts, tank tops, or sweats permitted. 542.1123 &

20 The Roxy If you want to kick loose, this may be just the place. A gorgeous setting for any kind of dancing, it attracts a younger crowd on Friday nights for international rock and "techno" (you *must* have high energy for this!). On Saturday nights, the flavor changes to Top 40 and club classics. You can take a break and watch the action from any of seven bars or the stunning balcony. ♦ Cover. F-Sa from 11PM. No jeans, T-shirts, or sneakers allowed. 279 Tremont St (between Charles St S and Stuart St). 338.7699 &

21 The Wang Center for the Performing Arts It's worth the ticket price to whatever performance you can catch here just to see the inside of this former motion-picture cathedral. Predating New York City's Radio City Music Hall, this mammoth entertainment palace, designed by **Blackall, Clapp and Whittemore,** was considered the "wonder theater of the world" when it opened in the Roaring Twenties, built to pack in huge crowds four times daily for variety revues and first-run movies. An architectural extravaganza, the 7-story, 3,800-seat theater (see seating chart below) boasts a succession of dramatic lobbies—concluding with the 5-story **Grand Lobby**—bedecked with Italian marble columns, stained glass, bronze detailing, gold leaf, crystal chandeliers, and florid ceiling murals. In the theater's early days, billiards, Ping-Pong, card parties, and other games in four ornate lobbies occupied the crowds until the next show got started.

First called the **Metropolitan Theater** and later the **Music Hall,** it was expanded by **Jung/Brannen Associates** in 1982, renamed for benefactor An Wang in 1983, and renovated by **Notter, Finegold & Alexander** in 1990 to accommodate a variety of performing arts, including opera, ballet, and Broadway musicals. Later, additional painstaking restoration work brought back more of the

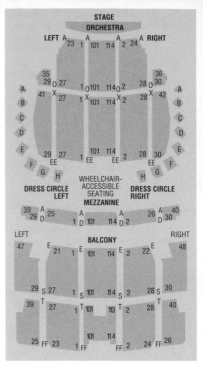

auditorium's former splendor and updated its facilities and theater technology. On the National Register of Historic Places, it now has one of the largest stages of any theater in the world. For plays, try to get down-front center seats in the orchestra, where the sight and sound are best.

The center's Young at Arts educational outreach program involves Boston children in the visual and performing arts through workshops, performances held in the theater's lobbies, and an annual art contest. Reduced-rate tickets are available, and many events are free; call to inquire. The theater also brings back a hint of its past history with a classic film series shown on one of the world's largest screens.

The **Boston Ballet** makes its home here, and famous visiting companies such as the **Alvin Ailey American Dance Theater** and the **Bolshoi Ballet Academy** perform frequently. ♦ 268 Tremont St (between Oak and Stuart Sts). General information 482.9393, Ticketmaster 931.2000 &

22 Wilbur Theatre This distinguished Colonial Revival theater has witnessed its share of dramatic debuts, including the pre-Broadway production of Tennessee Williams's *A Streetcar Named Desire* starring Marlon Brando and Jessica Tandy. Another of Boston's **Clarence H. Blackall** treasures, built in 1914 and now on the National Register of Historic Places, this stage endured dark days and decay; its nadir was a brief stint as a cabaret that flopped. But the lights are on again: The proud theater has rebounded and is in full swing.

The 1,200-seat fan-shaped house was renovated to accommodate Broadway and Off Broadway–style productions. Among the shows staged here in recent years were *The Gin Game* and *Sunset Boulevard.* Look up at the facade and note the three theatrical masks—grinning, grimacing, and agape— above the upper windows. Half-price tickets are offered for people with disabilities and one companion. ♦ Box office open daily. 246 Tremont St (between Oak and Stuart Sts). 423.4008 &

22 Hub Ticket Agency Located in a trailer parked on a corner, this agency sells sports and theater tickets, including those for out-of-town events in New York City, Providence, Rhode Island, and Worcester, Massachusetts. The friendly staff is often willing to drop tickets off at box offices for pickup before shows. Many local performances are sold out well in advance, so call first. The day of the game or performance is a good time to check on last-minute availability. For those who plan ahead, order by mail; the zip code is 02116. ♦ M-F; Sa until noon. 240 Tremont St (at Stuart St). 426.8340

23 Montien ★★$$ A solid favorite with theatergoers, businesspeople, and staff from the nearby medical complex, all the classic Thai favorites are served here, as are such unusual specials as *kat-thong-tong* (a crisp pastry shell filled with ground chicken, onions, corn, and coriander with a sweet dipping sauce). The tamarind duck and fried squid are superb. The hot-and-spicy set will find their pleasure, as will palates preferring subtler sensations. Service is efficient and prompt, so you'll make that curtain. ♦ Thai/Takeout ♦ M-Sa lunch and dinner; Su dinner. Reservations recommended for large parties. 63 Stuart St (between Washington and Tremont Sts). 338.5600 &

24 Jacob Wirth ★$$ Amid the whirl of Boston's dining fads and fashions, this venerable establishment—built in 1845 by **Greenleaf C. Sanborn** and now on the National Register of Historic Places (see the illustration at left)—plods along unwaveringly on its own steady course. It has been offering up the same hearty traditional German fare— bratwurst, knockwurst, sauerbraten, and sauerkraut, accompanied by heady, specially brewed dark beer in the same bowfront row house since its doors opened in 1868. All the furniture and fixtures—globe lighting, brass rails, dark paneling—are original. Even the wait staff's attire looks vintage. It's easy to step into the past here; in fact, that's the reason to come. The cavernous beer hall is a great place to bring a crowd and sample the long list of lagers. Those in your party with big appetites might attempt the German boiled dinner: pigs' feet, pork roast, ribs, and cabbage. Sing along with piano music on Friday. Patrons are offered two free hours of parking at the adjacent lot. ♦ German ♦ Daily lunch and dinner. 37 Stuart St (between Washington and Tremont Sts). 338.8586 &

25 Hayden Building Modest-sized and overlooked, this 1875 office building isn't one of **Henry Hobson Richardson**'s finer works but does display his characteristically vigorous Romanesque Revival approach. Unfortunately, the building, which is on the National Register of Historic Places, patiently awaits better days at the head of La Grange Street, once a thriving mercantile stretch with hatters, tailors, shoemakers, and such. From the 1960s onward, La Grange was caught in the midst of the Combat Zone and its once-reputable appearance has been shamefully besmirched. ♦ 681 Washington St (at La Grange St)

26 North End Fabrics Not only are the largest selection of fake "fun furs" around offered here—great for a come-as-you-were-half-a-million-years-ago party—but there's just about everything else in the way of fabrics you could possibly want: wool challis, velvets and velveteen, Thai silk, drapery and upholstery materials, bridal and theatrical fabrics, handkerchief linen, imported lace, odd bolts and remnants, notions, buttons—you name it. Professional dressmakers, designers, and home sewers all frequent this shop, around now for more than 30 years. ♦ M-Sa. 31 Harrison Ave (between Beach and Essex Sts). 542.2763

Chinatown—originally composed of tents—was born when Chinese workers were imported from the West to break a shoe-industry strike in the 1870s.

Sights for Sore Eyes

Boston looks great at ground level, and also when seen from above; it's attractive close up or from a more distant perspective. Whether you see them while on foot, boat, or bike, or while you are dining, the views in and of Boston are among the great pleasures of the city.

To see Boston at its best, go beyond its borders to the **Cambridge** side of the **Charles River.** From **Harvard Bridge** on **Memorial Drive,** look toward the **Royal Sonesta Hotel;** you'll be rewarded with a stunning view of **Back Bay, Beacon Hill,** and the gleaming gold-domed **State House,** with **Downtown** and the **Financial District**'s skyline behind. Late afternoon offers the best lighting effects.

For far-reaching views from high above Boston, travel more than 50 stories to the observatories in the **John Hancock Tower** (200 Clarendon St, between Stuart St and St. James Ave, 247.1977)or the **Prudential Tower** (800 Boylston St, between Exeter and Dalton Sts, 236.3318), both located in the heart of Back Bay.

Downtown, there's a heart-stopping view from the **Custom House Tower,** now **Marriott's Custom House** (3 McKinley Sq, between Central and State Sts, 310.1600), and from the **Bay Tower Room** (60 State St, at Congress St, 723.1666), where there's dining and dancing. In Cambridge stop in at the **Spinnaker Italia,** the region's only revolving restaurant, high atop the **Hyatt Regency Cambridge** (575 Memorial Dr, at Amesbury St, 492.1234, 800/233.1234).

If you're up to the climb to the top of the **Bunker Hill Monument** in **Charlestown,** you'll be rewarded with a fine view of Boston in the distance. If you find your way to **Castle Island** in **South Boston,** walk by the harbor to view the traffic in **Boston Harbor**'s main shipping lane, planes landing at **Logan International Airport,** and the harbor islands. Even Boston's subway system offers a view—between the **Charles/MGH** and **Kendall** stops on the **MBTA** *Red Line,* the subway car rises aboveground to cross the Charles River and offers terrific views.

John Hancock Tower

27 Dong Khanh ★$ Come to this clean and bright establishment for Vietnamese-style fast-food, including more than a dozen great noodle-soup dishes. The *bi cuon* (meat rolls) are tasty, as are the fish in spicy soup and assorted barbecue meats with vermicelli. Be daring and try a durian juice drink, made from the Asian fruit that looks like a hedgehog and smells like rotting garbage, but has plenty of fans for its flavor. ◆ Vietnamese ◆ Daily breakfast, lunch, and dinner. No credit cards accepted. 83 Harrison Ave (at Knapp St). 426.9410

28 Siam Square ★$ This Thai interloper at Chinatown's edge offers its own distinctive tastes. Lemongrass infuses a dish of steamed mussels; a pepper-garlic sauce spices frogs' legs; the *squid pik pow* is at once spicy and sweet; and Thai seasonings lend a signature kick to *chow foon* (fat noodles). ◆ Thai ◆ Daily lunch and dinner. 86 Harrison Ave (between Kneeland and Beach Sts). 338.7704

29 Carl's Pagoda ★★$$ Yes, there is a Carl, and many diners rely on his judgment when it comes to ordering. Carl is like a potentate ruling his personal fiefdom. But even if he's not there, a great meal can be made of tomato soup, Cantonese-style lobster, clams in black-bean sauce, and superbly prepared steamed

fish. A tiny place indeed, but it's one of only a few Chinatown establishments with table-cloths. ◆ Chinese/Takeout ◆ Daily dinner. Reservations recommended on weekends. No credit cards accepted. 23 Tyler St (between Kneeland and Beach Sts). 357.9837

30 Golden Palace ★★$ Many Chinatown restaurants are so innocuous looking that they're easy to miss, but not this one—it has the fanciest facade around. The main attraction is excellent dim sum—perhaps Boston's best—served daily until 3PM. There's no menu; when the carts roll up, simply select whatever tidbits strike your fancy in the sea of little plates loaded with dumplings, fried and steamed pastries, and noodle dishes. Try *har gao* (shrimp dumplings), spareribs in black-bean sauce, steamed *bao* (meat-filled buns), *shu mai* (pork dumplings), or more adventurous items like tripe and curried squid. This sprawling place—aglitz with reds, golds, pinks, and painted and carved dragons—is a noisy neighborhood favorite. People come to eat, not unwind, so the service is hurried and the atmosphere minimal. But the dim sum are piping hot, and the regular menu offers loads of superior dishes, including abalone and squab treatments. ♦ Chinese/Takeout ♦ Daily breakfast, lunch, and dinner. Reservations recommended for 10 or more. 14-20 Tyler St (between Kneeland and Beach Sts). 423.4565

31 Chau Chow Seafood ★★$ Definitely a Chinatown gem, this very busy, very basic place does great things with all sorts of seafood. There's crab with ginger and scallions, steamed sea bass and flounder, fried noodles with seafood and vegetables, salted jumbo shrimp in the shell, baby clams in black-bean sauce, and *chow foon,* to name a few. Pork, beef, chicken, and duck dishes abound, and all are delicious and excellently prepared. Sample stir-fried watercress, Swatowese dumplings (stuffed with pork and shrimp), or soup with sliced fish and Chinese parsley. Beer is served. There's always a long line for dinner. ♦ Chinese/Takeout ♦ Daily breakfast, lunch, and dinner. No credit cards accepted. 52 Beach St (between Oxford St and Harrison Ave). 426.6266

32 C.W.H. Company Step inside this small neighborhood grocery store for plenty of local flavor. Stock up on everything from herbs and candies to freshwater and vacuum-packed dried fish. Also available are large selections of tea, rice, noodles, and frozen items including Peking raviolis. ♦ Daily. No credit cards accepted. 55 Beach St (at Tyler St). 426.3619

32 Grand Chau Chow Seafood ★★$ For the price, you can't do better. The seafood is out of this world, but the bill isn't. Try the delicate steamed striped bass with ginger, the spicy, fried salted squid, or a plate of sizzling noodles with seafood. Presentation and service here are outstanding. ♦ Chinese ♦ Daily lunch and dinner. Reservations recommended. 45 Beach St (between Tyler St and Harrison Ave). 292.5166

33 Imperial Seafood Restaurant ★$ Right at the gateway to Chinatown, this noisy, cavernous restaurant is a good choice for its second-floor dim-sum parlor, where a fleet of carts laden with arrays of little treats—pork dumplings, shrimp balls, bean curd, stuffed meat buns, braised chickens' feet, and so forth—whiz past the packed tables. Just point to your selection and it's whisked onto your table. Always mobbed, the tearoom attracts a fascinatingly mixed clientele. There's usually a short wait. Downstairs, order traditional Cantonese dishes from the regular menu.

♦ Chinese/Takeout ♦ M-Th, Su breakfast, lunch, and dinner until 2AM; F-Sa breakfast, lunch, and dinner until 4AM. Reservations recommended for large parties at dinner. No credit cards accepted. 70-72 Beach St (between Kingston and Oxford Sts). 426.8439

34 Dynasty ★$$ This big-league kind of restaurant has lots of mirrors and golden columns and offers good Cantonese dishes: panfried spiced shrimp, chicken with cashews, clams in black-bean sauce, and steamed sea bass and gray sole, to name a few. Even better, it stays open nearly around-the-clock. Dim sum is served on the second floor 8AM-3PM. ♦ Cantonese ♦ Daily breakfast, lunch, and dinner until 4AM. 33 Edinboro St (between Kingston and Essex Sts). 350.7777

35 Moon Villa $ By no means the romantic place its name implies, this hangout for hungry night owls serves family-style Cantonese dishes while the rest of the city snoozes. For dim sum, however, you have to come Saturday or Sunday during the day. The waiters tend to be brusque. ♦ Chinese/ Takeout ♦ Daily lunch and dinner until 4AM. 15-19 Edinboro St (between Kingston and Essex Sts). 423.2061

36 Ho Yuen Ting ★$ People flock to this no-frills restaurant not for ambience or decor, but for such delectable seafood specials as lobster with ginger, salted-and-spiced squid, shrimp with spicy sauce, or stir-fried sole and vegetables served in a crunchy edible bowl made of batter-fried shredded potatoes. Also recommended are the pork-and-watercress soup and fish-stomach soup with mushrooms or sweet corn. This is a good place to explore the unknown. The restaurant is located below street level, so be on the lookout or you'll pass right by. ♦ Chinese/Takeout ♦ Daily lunch and dinner. No credit cards accepted. 13A Hudson St (between Kneeland and Beach Sts). 426.2316

37 New Shanghai ★★$$ You won't be hungry one hour after finishing a meal here, nor will you crave more elegant decor. Chef C.K. Sau prepares an extraordinary Peking duck; another favorite is scallops with black pepper. Top off the meal with a dessert of fried banana fritters. It's all served in the sleekest of settings. ♦ Chinese ♦ Daily breakfast, lunch, and dinner. 21 Hudson St (between Kneeland and Beach Sts). 338.6688

Back Bay

Boston's sumptuous centerpiece of illustrious institutions and architecture is also the best place in the city for extravagant shopping sprees and leisurely promenades. Back Bay attracts a stylish international crowd that's as fun to look at as any of **Newbury Street**'s artful windows. It is also a comfortable, compact neighborhood of gracious streets bordered by harmonious four- and five-story Victorian town houses. Its residents are well-to-do families, established professionals, footloose young people, and transient students for whom the **Public Garden** is an outdoor living room and the **Charles River Esplanade** a grassy waterside backyard.

In the 19th century Boston's wealthy old guard and brash new moneymakers together planted this garden of beautiful homes and public buildings, creating a cosmopolitan, Parisianlike quarter wrapped in an aura of privilege and prosperity. The lingering mystique has even tricked some Bostonians into believing Back Bay is one of the city's oldest neighborhoods, when it's really one of the youngest. What began as Boston's marshy wasteland was transformed in the late 1800s into its most desirable neighborhood by a spectacular feat of urban design.

In the 1850s Boston boasted a booming population and exuberant commercial growth. Railroads and manufacturing supplanted the sea as the city's primary source of capital. The nouveaux riches were hungry for spectacular domiciles, but the almost waterbound city was already overcrowded on its little peninsula. The problem: Where to get land? In 1814 a mile-and-a-half-long dam had been built from the base of **Beacon Hill** to what is now

Kenmore Square to harness the Charles River's tidal flow and power a chain of mills. The scheme failed, and the acres of water trapped by the dam became a stagnant, stinking, unhealthy tidal flat called Back Bay that Bostonians longed to eradicate. This became the unlikely site that developers clamored to fill with daring urban design schemes. To do so, land had to be reclaimed from the sea by a fantastically ambitious landfill program. Inspired by the Parisian boulevard system Baron Haussmann had built for Emperor Louis Napoleon, architect **Arthur Gilman** proposed Back Bay's orderly layout. Starting at the Charles River, the principal east-west streets are **Beacon Street, Marlborough Street, Commonwealth Avenue, Newbury Street,** and **Boylston Street,** all intersected by eight streets named alphabetically after English peers (from **Arlington Street** to **Hereford Street**). Sixteen-foot-wide public alleys interlace these blocks and provide access to the rear of buildings, originally designed for service and deliveries. Gilman's rational grid remains a startling departure from Old Boston's labyrinthine tangles.

In 1857 the gigantic landfill wave began its sweep across the marshland block by block, from Arlington Street at the **Public Garden's** western edge toward **Fenway.** As soon as a lot was ready, another architectural beauty debuted. By the time the wave subsided in 1890, 450 acres and more than 1,500 new buildings had been added to the 783-acre peninsula. Gone was the loathsome eyesore; in its place was a charming neighborhood of the same name. Completed in just 60 years, Back Bay is an extraordinary repository of Victorian architectural styles, perhaps the most outstanding in America. As an urban design scheme, it was surpassed in its era only by Pierre-Charles L'Enfant's plan for Washington, DC.

The newborn Back Bay instantly became Boston's darling, a magnificent symbol of civic pride and the city's coming of age. No Puritan simplicity or provincialism here. Affluent Boston had learned how to stage a good show, from **Copley Square's** lofty cultural monuments to Commonwealth Avenue's architectural revue of fancy brickwork, stained glass, cut granite, ornate ironwork, gargoyles, and other European conceits. In Back Bay's golden hours, the city's leading financiers, authors, industrialists, artists, architects, and legendary Brahmins lived here. But as the city's economy soured late in the 19th century, the ostentatious single-family dwellings were gradually converted to more modest uses. Though Back Bay's shining moments as a residential district faded after the Great Depression, the neighborhood has resiliently adapted to 20th-century incursions of shops, offices, and apartments. Beginning in the 1980s with the emergence of condominium conversion, it has become regentrified.

1 John Hancock Tower When towering new edifices invade historic neighborhoods, they often try to gain public acceptance with lame gestures—by aping local architectural modes or bribing with street-level shops, skimpy parks, or outdoor art. Making no such insincere overtures, in 1976 **I.M. Pei & Partners** designed a cool, aloof, and inscrutable tower with its own singular style. And that's why more and more Bostonians have grown fond of this skyscraper—New England's tallest—as the years pass. A 62-story glass rhomboid, it has a shimmering surface that serves as a full-length mirror for **Trinity Church** while reflecting the constant shifts of New England weather. The tower's crisp form is mesmerizing from all angles, whether you glimpse the broad faces or razor-blade edges standing two-dimensional against the sky.

The now-popular tower had a rocky start: Its construction caused serious structural damage to architectural landmark **Trinity Church** across the street, and inadequate glass was used in its sheathing so that when the tower was first erected the windowpanes randomly popped out due to wind torquing, raining onto the square below. Sidewalks had to be cordoned off to protect pedestrians. All 13 acres of the 10,344 glass panels were replaced; today the panes are continuously monitored for visible signs of potential breakage. Making matters worse, a later engineering inspection revealed that the building was in danger of toppling, which required reinforcing its steel frame and installing a moving weight on the 58th floor to counter wind stress. Once Bostonians could walk by the tower without flinching, however, they began to notice what a dazzling addition it is to the Boston skyline.

For stunning views that will put all of Back Bay and Boston in perspective, visit the **John Hancock Observatory** on the 60th floor. Binoculars are already zeroed-in on some of the city's most famous sights. The taped narrative by the late architectural historian Walter Muir Whitehill is wonderful not only for his vast knowledge, but for his "proper" Bostonian accent. There's also a little sound-and-light show about Boston in 1775—with a topographical model of the city when all the hills were in place and Back Bay was its watery old self. ♦ Admission. Daily until 11PM. 200 Clarendon St (between Stuart St and St. James Ave). 247.1977

2 **Copley Square** Once called "Art Square" for the galleries, art schools, and clubs clustered around it, the plaza's modern name honors John Singleton Copley, Boston's great colonial painter. Originally an unsightly patch created by the disruption of Back Bay's grid by two rail lines, the square blossomed after the **Museum of Fine Arts** opened its doors there. (The museum stood at the site of today's **Copley Plaza Hotel** until the institution moved to its current address in the Fenway and its old residence was demolished.) **Trinity Church** and the **Boston Public Library** were spectacular additions, and the presence of numerous ecclesiastical and academic institutions nearby enhanced the square's reputation (in Bostonians' minds least) as the "Acropolis of the New World." The plaza's latest look, created in 1989 by **Dean Abbot,** is pleasant, but fails to satisfy Bostonians' century-old dreams of a magnificent public space. ♦ Bounded by Clarendon and Dartmouth Sts, and St. James Ave and Boylston St

After graduating from Harvard College in 1859, Henry Hobson Richardson, a Louisiana native, went to study architecture at the Ecole des Beaux Arts in Paris. Returning to the United States seven years later, Richardson created works that were at once robust and monumental. He began his practice in New York, then moved to Boston upon winning the Trinity Church commission.

Commonwealth Avenue, with its double street and long parklike mall between—a span of 240 feet—is slightly wider than Paris's Champs-Elysees.

Within Copley Square:

Boston Athletic Association Boston Marathon Monument Unveiled just in time for viewing by the 38,500 official participants of the 100th running of the **Boston Marathon** in 1996, the medallion-shaped granite monument, which lies flush to the ground near the northwest corner of Copley Square, is just a short distance from the finish line of the 26.2 mile annual event. The eight varieties of marble and the eight crests in the monument honor the eight cities and towns through which the marathon route runs. Measuring 15 feet in diameter with a sculpted center, the medallion consists of two concentric rings that contain the names of all male and female champions of the open, masters, and wheelchair divisions since the inaugural **BAA Marathon;** the outer ring has room for the names of future champions. Designed by landscape architect Mark Flannery, it is encircled by a laurel wreath, the symbol of victory.

The Tortoise and the Hare A more whimsical tribute to the 100th running of the Boston Marathon is this sculpture by Nancy Schon, who also sculpted the *Mrs. Mallard and Her Brood of Eight Ducklings* in the **Public Garden.** Unveiled near the fountain in Copley Square in 1995, the fabled tortoise and hare honor the runners worldwide who have participated in the city's marathon. They particularly appeal to children, who enjoy sitting on the figures.

Trinity Church Approach Copley Square from any direction, and your eyes will be drawn to this grandiose French-Romanesque–inspired edifice. A National Historic Landmark, it is one of the great buildings in America. The century and more that has passed since this church first graced the city has taken nothing from its power to fascinate. Like a wise and tolerant elder, it offers a model of urbane dignity and grandeur that has never been equaled in Boston. The church is nicely complemented by the handsome, old **Boston Public Library** across the way.

Henry Hobson Richardson was at the summit of his career when he designed this ecclesiastic edifice in 1877. In the 1860s its leaders decided to move the parish from Summer Street (downtown) to the Copley Square site. In retrospect their decision seems prescient; one of Boston's great conflagrations destroyed the Summer Street building in November 1872. In March of that year, six architects had been invited to submit designs for the new structure. Thirty-four years old at the time and a New York City resident, Richardson had already contributed one admired piece to the emerging Back Bay fabric, the **New Brattle Square Church** (now the **First Baptist Church**), then under construction on Clarendon Street.

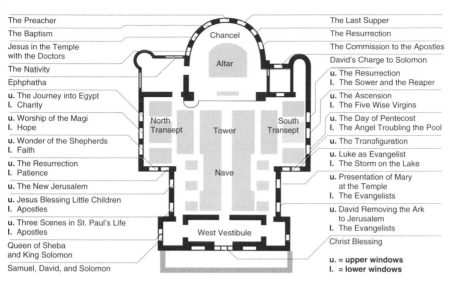

The Preacher
The Baptism
Jesus in the Temple with the Doctors
The Nativity
Ephphatha
u. The Journey into Egypt
l. Charity
u. Worship of the Magi
l. Hope
u. Wonder of the Shepherds
l. Faith
u. The Resurrection
l. Patience
u. The New Jerusalem
u. Jesus Blessing Little Children
l. Apostles
u. Three Scenes in St. Paul's Life
l. Apostles
Queen of Sheba and King Solomon
Samuel, David, and Solomon

Chancel
Altar
North Transept
Tower
South Transept
Nave
West Vestibule

The Last Supper
The Resurrection
The Commission to the Apostles
David's Charge to Solomon
u. The Resurrection
l. The Sower and the Reaper
u. The Ascension
l. The Five Wise Virgins
u. The Day of Pentecost
l. The Angel Troubling the Pool
u. The Transfiguration
u. Luke as Evangelist
l. The Storm on the Lake
u. Presentation of Mary at the Temple
l. The Evangelists
u. David Removing the Ark to Jerusalem
l. The Evangelists
Christ Blessing

u. = upper windows
l. = lower windows

The cruciform church's fluid massing is an inimitable Richardson tour de force, especially the leaping exterior colonnade. To contend with the awkward triangular site, he designed the great square tower as the central element. Assisting Richardson with the tower was apprentice **Stanford White**—later of **McKim, Mead & White**, the **Boston Public Library** architects. The church's ageless vitality comes from the tension between Richardson's powerful vision of the whole and his spirited treatment of its parts. Elegant bands of red sandstone hold the coarse granite's brute force in check. Inside and out, the church is richly polychromatic in wood, paint, glass, and stone—another Richardson signature. With the aid of six assistants, most notably young Augustus Saint-Gaudens, John La Farge decorated the majestic interiors. Look for his 12 oil paintings in the arches beneath the vaulted ceilings below the tower, 103 feet above the nave. La Farge orchestrated production of the stained-glass windows (see the diagram above), among them glowing creations of his own—look for the lancet windows on the west wall—and some jointly executed by Edward Burne-Jones and William Morris and Company. The interior resembles a gigantic tapestry woven in intricate patterns of gold and rich colors. The most wonderful time of the year to visit is Christmas, when the church is filled with candlelight and carols during special services. Free half-hour organ recitals are offered at noon on Friday from September through June. Located in the vestibule is a gift desk with books, cards with pictures of the church, and recordings by the choir.

Outside, Saint-Gaudens added a fine flourish: On the church's northeast corner stands his dramatic depiction of *Phillips Brooks*, the

Copley Square Trinity's first rector, the Episcopal Bishop of Massachusetts, and author of *O Little Town of Bethlehem*. A somber, shrouded Christ stands behind the orating preacher. It was daring Brooks who convinced his congregation to move to the new frontier of Back Bay. Saint-Gaudens died before his design was sculpted; assistants completed the statue in 1910, and it was set into a marble canopy designed by **McKim, Mead & White.** The cloistered colonnade to your left overlooks a pretty enclosed garden with a much humbler statue of *St. Francis of Assisi.* ♦ Sunday services at 8AM, 9AM and 11AM with choir music, and 6PM. Tours available following the 11AM service and by arrangement. Reception desk at 206 Clarendon St (at St. James Ave). 536.0944 &

3   The Fairmont Copley Plaza Hotel $$$$
The empress dowager of Boston's hotels embodies the mature, full-flowered Back Bay. It not only draws business and international guests, but also lovers of grand epochs gone by. Designed in 1912 by **Clarence Blackall** and **Henry Hardenbergh** (the latter was the architect of the Plaza Hotel in New York and the Willard Hotel in Washington, DC), this Italian Renaissance Revival structure has endured well.

The six-story building's exterior includes both French and Venetian Renaissance elements; terra-cotta accents decorate the limestone facade. The European interior is nothing short of grand: The 5,000-square-foot lobby contains period antiques and numerous flamboyant architectural touches. Towering over the lobby is a gilded ceiling festooned with trompe l'oeil paintings of the sky. The **Grand Ballroom** and the **Oval Room** are equally opulent.

The 379 guest rooms and 61 suites are decorated in a luxurious classic English style and contain such amenities as marble bathrooms, mini-bars, fax machines, hair dryers, clock radios, voice mail, modem jacks, and irons and ironing boards. Rooms for nonsmokers and people with disabilities are available. The hotel also features two restaurants (see below), a fitness center, a business center, laundry and dry cleaning service, a beauty salon, a barber shop, child care, a concierge, and 24-hour room service. Pets are allowed. ♦ 138 St. James Ave (between Trinity Pl and Dartmouth St). 267.5300, 800/527.4727; fax 247.6681 &

Within The Fairmont Copley Plaza Hotel:

Oak Room ★★★$$$ Steaks, chops, seafood, and exactly one chicken dish are what you will find at this upscale-but-staid hotel dining room with a high ceiling and lots of windows. The menu offers all the traditional favorites. Appetizers include raw clams and oysters, clams casino, oysters Rockefeller, shrimp and lobster cocktail, crab cakes, steak tartare, and lobster bisque. Among the entrées are chateaubriand; grilled aged steaks, lamb, veal, and pork chops with a choice of sauces (bearnaise, mint jelly, chutney, red wine demi-glace); seafood including shrimp, scallops, lobster, halibut, haddock, salmon, and swordfish; and roast chicken. For dessert there's—what else?—Boston cream pie. A piano and jazz trio plays during dinner. ♦ American ♦ Daily dinner. Reservations recommended; jacket required. 267.5300 &

Copley's Grand Cafe ★$$$ A fine view of Copley Square accompanies your meal at this breakfast and lunch spot, which is decorated with pink table linen and lots of woodwork. Among the appetizers on the eclectic lunch menu are clam chowder, matzoh-ball soup, a bruschetta sampler (wild mushroom, tomato and basil, lobster with avocado salsa), and panfried polenta with sun-dried tomato, goat cheese, basil, garlic, and tomato sauce. Entrées include linguini with mussels, clams, and shrimp in a tomato and white-wine broth;

panfried salmon wrapped in Savoy cabbage topped with a rosemary butter sauce; chicken potpie; Boston scrod; and Yankee pot roast. Burgers, sandwiches, salads, and quiche are also available. The adjacent lounge, a men's club–style retreat with leather couches and lots of dark wood, offers a late-afternoon lunch menu (burgers, salads, and sand-wiches) and is open until 1AM for drinks. ♦ American ♦ Daily breakfast and lunch. Reservations recommended. 424.0196 &

4 Boston Public Library Boston boasts the oldest municipally supported library system in the world (founded in 1852) and the second-largest library system in the US, serving more than two million people each year. The city's first library was located in a former school-house on Mason Street, but, in keeping with its self-image as the "Athens of America," Boston demanded a splendid main library building that would set an example for the nation. A "Palace for the People" was what the library's trustees had in mind, and that's precisely what architect **Charles Follen McKim**'s firm **(McKim, Mead & White)** achieved. In its every detail this coolly serene Italian Renaissance Revival edifice, which was built in 1895 and is on the National Register of Historic Places, enshrines and celebrates learning. The library's decoration and design brought together the most magnificent crew of architects, artisans, painters, and sculptors ever assembled in the US until that time. Materials alone reflect the nothing-but-the-best attitude of its creators; for instance, a palette of more than 25 different types of marble and stone was used. Years of neglect had diminished much of the building's beauty, but a massive $65-million restoration project that will continue until the end of the century has returned much of the library to its original glory. Flanking the Dartmouth Street entrance are Bela Pratt's huge 1911 bronzes of two seated women personifying *Art* and *Science,* their pedestals carved with the names of artists and scientists. Prickly wrought-iron lanterns bloom by the doorways, looking startlingly Halloweenish. Note the library

Boston Public Library

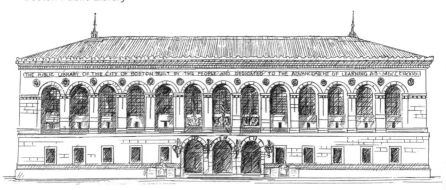

parapets carved with the names of important people in the history of human culture. There are 519 names in all; the carvers mistakenly repeated four. When one local newspaper reported that **McKim, Mead & White** had amused themselves by working the firm's name into the first letters in three of the panels, enough taxpayers were incensed that the architects had to erase their clever acrostic.

Pass through the bronze portals and enter the main entrance hall. Everywhere you turn there are more inscriptions, dedications, and names of the forgotten great and zealous benefactors. Brass intarsia of the zodiac signs decorate the marble floor, while intricate mosaics adorn the ceilings. A grand staircase of tawny Sienna marble leads past a noble pair of lions to the second-floor gallery, which features enormous contemplative Arcadian allegories by Puvis de Chavanne (artist of the poetic murals in the Hôtel de Ville in Paris).

Adjacent to the gallery is **Bates Hall,** a cavernous reading room (218 feet long) with a barrel-vaulted ceiling 50 feet high. To the right is the former **Delivery Room,** where Bostonians once waited for their requested books to arrive, transported from the stacks by a tiny train hidden from view.

In the library's remotest reaches on the third floor resides one of Boston's forgotten treasures: the **Sargent Gallery.** Few people ever find their way up the gloomy stairs to this poorly lit place, yet John Singer Sargent considered this gallery the artistic apex of his career. He devoted 30 years to planning the historical murals—their theme is Judaism and Christianity—and designing the entire hall where they were placed. The gallery wasn't quite complete when he died in 1916. The somber murals are tragically faded (they are scheduled for restoration), but nonetheless deserve attention. Also on the third floor is the **Wiggin Gallery,** which mounts frequent exhibitions of local artists, and the **Cheverus Room,** housing library treasures such as the *Joan of Arc Collection.*The most satisfying way to end any trip to "the BPL" (the library's nickname) is to visit its peaceful central courtyard with reading material in hand. (Nonresidents will have to bring their own books.) Follow the example of the locals and pull a chair between the sturdy stone columns of the cloister, modeled after the one in the Palazzo della Cancelleria in Rome. The landscaping is simple—just a few trees, a reflecting pool and fountain, and some plants. Even on a rainy day this is a pleasant, restful place to read. ♦ Free. M-Th 9AM-9PM; F-Sa 9AM-5PM; Su 1-5PM Oct-May. One-hour art and architecture tours M 2:30PM; Tu-W 6:30PM; Th, Sa 11AM. Dartmouth St (between Blagden and Boylston Sts). 536.5400 &

Within the Boston Public Library:

Boston Public Library Addition When the **Boston Public Library** outgrew **McKim, Mead & White**'s palatial structure, this annex was added in 1972. In materials and monumentality, **Philip Johnson**'s addition echoes the original structure, yet has a colder, starker feel. The interior connection between the new and old buildings is circuitous—you reach the old from the new by turning left just beyond the entry turnstiles and following a corridor past Louise Stimson's appealing dioramas to an innocuous door that leads back to the original building. Nevertheless, Bostonians use the "new" building like mad; here the stacks are open, so there's immediate access to the books. Exhibitions are held regularly in the lofty central space. In the basement is a comfortable theater, where a free film series offers weekly screenings, and regular readings are held.

The **Access Center** on the concourse level serves people with disabilities, offering special equipment and materials. There are large rest rooms in the basement here (a plus in a city with a dearth of public bathrooms), as well as telephones. ♦ Free. Daily; closed Sunday June-September. 666 Boylston St (between Dartmouth and Exeter Sts). 536.5400 &

5 House of Siam ★★$ Though tucked in an inconvenient block across Huntington Avenue from the **Westin Hotel,** this little pink haven is worth seeking out for an inexpensive respite from Back Bay's pervasive costliness. The duck and other standard dishes are excellent; try chicken or beef typhoon sautéed with bamboo shoots, minced hot chili peppers, garlic, and basil. ♦ Thai/Takeout ♦ M-Sa lunch and dinner; Su dinner. 21 Huntington Ave (between Blagden and Exeter Sts). 267.1755 &

6 Copley Place The largest private development in Boston's history, this complex covers 9.5 acres of land and air rights above the Massachusetts Turnpike. With 3.7 million square feet of space, it is the size of 2,500 average American homes, 822 football fields, or more than two **John Hancock Towers.** It includes two hotels—the **Westin** (see below) and the **Boston Marriott** (see below)—more than 100 upscale shops and restaurants, an 11-screen cinema, four office buildings, 1,400 parking places, and 104 residences. In the central atrium, 1,000 gallons of water per minute cascade over Dimitri Hadzi's 60-foot-high water sculpture made of more than 80 tons of travertine and granite.

Needless to say, the genesis of this giant created a furor that hasn't entirely abated. Plunked down at one corner of Copley Square, the behemoth has become a formidable barrier to the neighboring South End. But as bland, anonymous, and prefab-looking as the exterior is, inside, it's marble, marble everywhere, and hardly a bench to sit on. Shoppers are meant to come with laden pockets—among its tenants are **Nieman Marcus** and **Tiffany & Co.**—and to be ready to empty them in shops identical to those in many other cities, with a few exceptions. By and large, visitors should stick to Newbury Street unless the weather is bad, because although prices are exorbitant there, too, it's much more genuinely Boston. ♦ Daily. 100 Huntington Ave (between Garrison and Dartmouth Sts). 375.4400 &

Within Copley Place:

Westin Hotel, Copley Place $$$ One of Boston's many major chain hotels, this hostelry has 804 rooms and suites on 36 floors, with good views to be had above the 11th floor and 2 specialty suites on the 36th floor. There are floors designed for people with disabilities and others reserved for nonsmokers. Other amenities include 24-hour room service, a bilingual concierge, valet parking, a health club with an indoor pool, a car-rental desk, many stores, and five restaurants (including **Turner Fisheries,** see below). Small pets are allowed. ♦ 10 Huntington Ave (at Dartmouth St). 262.9600, 800/228.3000; fax 424.7483

Within the Westin Hotel, Copley Place:

Turner Fisheries ★$$$ This softly lit, spacious restaurant is also *quiet.* You can enjoy conversation along with absolutely fresh, simply prepared seafood. The clam chowder has been elevated to the citywide annual Chowderfest's Hall of Fame. For a quick, light meal, take a seat at the oyster bar—or sit in the lounge and order the smoked-bluefish appetizer. There's live music nightly. ♦ Seafood ♦ Daily lunch and dinner. Reservations recommended. 424.7425 &

Trinity Church's resplendent interior illustrates architect Henry Hobson Richardson's penchant for the Romanesque style; he often enlisted celebrated artists and sculptors to collaborate on the decoration of his houses, churches, schools, libraries, hospitals, bridges, and railroad stations. The stamp of such craftsmen can be seen in many of his works.

Restaurants/Clubs: Red   Hotels: Blue
Shops/♥ Outdoors: Green   Sights/Culture: Black

Artful Hand Gallery Representing only US artists, the crafts featured here are contemporary, sophisticated, and eclectic, and available at a wide range of prices. On a $12 budget, you could take home handmade earrings, beeswax candles, a glazed ceramic mug, or a wooden letter opener. The prohibitively expensive glass sculptures by Orient and Flume are exquisite, as is the ceramic jewelry. ♦ Daily. First floor. 262.9601

Pavo Real Custom-designed, hand-knit sweaters from Peru and Boliva are a highlight here. For men and women, the richly colored garments are made with luxurious alpaca wool and pima cotton. Also available are jewelry, hats, gloves, scarves, wallets, and pocketbooks—some quite whimsical in design—that make wonderful gifts. ♦ Daily. 437.6699

Boston Marriott Copley Place $$$ This massive 38-story hotel complex rode into town in the early 1980s with the **Copley Place** megadevelopment (so there are movies and plenty of shops right next door). The highest-up of the 1,139 rooms and suites offer pleasing views; all the guest rooms are furnished in Queen Anne style, with cable TV, and individual climate control. There are units designed for people with disabilities, and four floors are reserved for nonsmokers. The "executive rooms" cost more and include such extras as breakfast, a private lounge, and special concierge service. The hotel also boasts a four-story atrium with a gushing waterfall, along with three restaurants: **Bello Mondo** (Northern Italian), **Gourmeli's** (American), and **Champions Sports Bar** (burgers and sandwiches). Other features include 24-hour room service, valet parking, valet service, a travel agency, an indoor swimming pool, fitness facilities, barber and beauty shops, meeting facilities and business services, an exhibit hall, and Boston's largest ballroom. The building is connected to **Prudential Center** and the **Hynes Convention Center** by an enclosed footbridge. Though a tunnel insulates guests from noise and pollution, the hotel is directly above the Massachusetts Turnpike. ♦ 110 Huntington Ave (between Garrison and Stuart Sts). 236.5800, 800/228.9290; fax 424.9378 &

7 **Copley Square Hotel** $$ One of Boston's oldest, this modest-size 1891 hotel is a Back Bay bargain and attracts an international clientele. It's nothing fancy, but has a pleasantly low-key, informal European style. All 143 rooms and suites, which vary greatly in size, feature coffeemakers, individual climate control, closet floor safes, and windows you can open. The nearby **Westin Hotel**'s health facilities are available to guests for a small fee. Dining options include **Cafe Budapest** (see below); the **Original Sports Saloon,** where the baby-back ribs are as

famous as the athletes who occasionally drop in; and an inexpensive coffee shop. Other perks include rooms for nonsmokers and inexpensive adjacent parking; airport limo service is available for a fee. ♦ 47 Huntington Ave (at Exeter St). 536.9000, 800/225.7062; fax 267.3547 &

Within the Copley Square Hotel:

Cafe Budapest ★★$$$ Propose marriage, celebrate an anniversary, or toast true love in this intimate, Old European spot with alcoves for two. For almost 25 years this has been the most romantic restaurant in Boston—but be *sure* to request the tiny blue or pink dining room. Contrary to common opinion, lovers usually have perfectly good appetites—possibly even needing extra fuel—and the Central European cooking is certainly rich, hearty comfort food, albeit elegant. Perennial favorites are the iced tart-cherry soup, *Wiener schnitzel à la Holstein* (sautéed veal topped with a fried egg and anchovies), veal *gulyas* (goulash), and sauerbraten. The homemade pastries include extraordinary strudels, of course, and Hungarian wines are served. A pianist and violinist perform Tuesday through Saturday. ♦ Hungarian ♦ Daily lunch and dinner. Reservations recommended; jacket and tie required. 266.1979 &

8 Boylston Street This once-unkempt road bordering Boston's rail yards has been revamped, and today is a fashionable stretch with new shops and restaurants scattered among imposing historic, cultural, and religious institutions. ♦ Between Arlington St and Massachusetts Ave

8 Gyuhama ★★$$ One of Boston's best sushi bars is also the only place in town serving lobster sashimi. It's a spectacular presentation that's not for the fainthearted—the lobster pieces may still be twitching when served! Less daring choices include delectable sukiyaki. The basement dining room is intimate, though a trifle seedy. There are always many Japanese diners, a strong testament to the fastidiously fresh and imaginatively prepared food. In fact, there are so many regulars that it can sometimes have a cliquey air. Dine early or be prepared for a wait. ♦ Japanese ♦ Daily lunch and dinner. 827 Boylston St (between Fairfield and Gloucester Sts), Basement level. 437.0188

9 J.C. Hillary's ★$$ A little nondescript, but well established and nicer looking than the other Back Bay restaurants of its ilk, this place offers respectable seafood, pasta, and burgers at reasonable prices. There's also a bar. Another plus: Valet parking is available in the evenings. ♦ American/Takeout ♦ Daily lunch and dinner. Reservations recommended on weekends. 793 Boylston St (at Fairfield St). 536.6300

9 The Famous Atlantic Fish Company ★$$ With a long menu and better prices than many seafood houses in Boston, this is a reliable choice for a casual meal. Fried-clam lovers will be particularly content. At lunchtime, meals are guaranteed to arrive within 12 minutes after ordering or they're on the house, so there's always a crowd of time-is-money professionals. ♦ Seafood ♦ Daily lunch and dinner. 777 Boylston St (between Exeter and Fairfield Sts). 267.4000 &

10 Back Bay Brewing Company ★$$ Offering a classic brewpub atmosphere, this place offers a wide range of microbrews along with an eclectic menu put together by chef Ed Doyle (formerly of **The Boston Harbor Hotel**). Popular entrées include cedarwood-roasted cod, jerk-spiced chicken sandwich, and grilled Black Angus steak. There's also a good selection of wine and vintage ports. ♦ American ♦ M-Sa lunch and dinner; Su brunch and dinner. 755 Boylston St (between Exeter and Fairfield Sts). 424.8300

11 The Lenox Hotel $$ When this historic hotel opened in 1900 it stood alone in the midst of railroad tracks. That year the *Boston Sunday Post* said the edifice would "scrape the sky and dally with the gods." In its heyday, Enrico Caruso stayed here. Later, like its city, the hostelry fell on hard times. Having undergone a multimillion-dollar renovation, today it has all the luxury of a newcomer and all the charm of a European-style pensione. The 214 classically decorated rooms line spacious corridors and feature high ceilings, hand-carved gilt moldings, separate sitting areas, and walk-in closets. The corner rooms with working fireplaces are definite favorites. Some floors are reserved for nonsmokers. Long popular with travelers on a budget, in recent times the establishment has raised its rates—but a genuine personal touch is still present. Amenities include an exercise room, valet service, valet parking, and baby-sitting. Pets are welcome. The **Samuel Adams Brew House** serves hearty, casual pub fare downstairs; more formal entrées are offered in the **Upstairs Grill**. ♦ 710 Boylston St (at Exeter St). 536.5300, 800/225.7676; fax 266.7905 &

THE STEAKHOUSE

12 Morton's of Chicago ★★$$$$ This restaurant's stock of tender, prime-grade dry-aged beef is flown in fresh daily from Chicago. One of a chain of 19 restaurants, the place has a fabulous way with steak, especially the 24-ounce porterhouse, its hallmark. Come famished enough to eat a side of beef, a flock of chickens, or a school of fish—even the baked potatoes are behemoths. There are some "smaller" cuts of meat, but most people will still consider them huge. A favorite of businessfolk, it's just the place for a power meal. The steakhouse is set in what Bostonians have derisively dubbed "The Darth Vader Building"—the architectural equivalent of a bad haircut, the structure sticks out in all the wrong places. There's valet parking.
♦ Steakhouse/American ♦ M-F lunch and dinner; Sa-Su dinner. Reservations recommended. 1 Exeter Plaza, Boylston and Exeter Sts. 266.5858 ₺

13 New Old South Church The **Old South Church** moved here from its 18th-century meeting house on Washington Street—better known as the **Old South Meeting House** on the **Freedom Trail.** The Northern Italian Gothic structure—executed by **Cummings & Sears** in 1874-75 and now a National Historic Landmark—is pleasingly picturesque, with its multicolored ornamentation, tall campanile, and copper-topped Venetian lantern (see the illustration below). On the entry portico's right wall, look for the tombstone remnant, set in concrete, that records the death of John Alden, congregation member and eldest son of John and Priscilla Alden of the Plymouth Colony. With a subway station entrance and newsstand located near its porte cochere, the church is always witness to lively comings and goings. Only the sanctuary and chapel are open

New Old South Church

to the public. The church periodically hosts other musical programs. ♦ M-F; Su until 2PM. 645 Boylston St (between Dartmouth and Exeter Sts). 536.1970

13 Copley Square News Max has run this newsstand next to the **New Old South Church** for more than 65 years. He carries periodicals in English, Spanish, French, Italian, and German. ♦ M-Sa 3AM-6:30PM. Boylston St (between Dartmouth and Exeter Sts). 262.1477 (a pay phone; Max or a helper will answer)

14 Bromer Booksellers A stop for the serious browser and buyer only, and *not* for casual page-thumbers, this impeccable second-floor gallery displays rare books of all periods. Earnest collectors themselves, Anne and David Bromer sell literary first editions, private press and illustrated books, books in finely crafted bindings, and rare children's books. The Bromers are internationally recognized as major dealers in miniature books (less than three inches in both dimensions) on all subjects; they may have on hand a minuscule *New Testament* written in shorthand and published in 1665, or *Mite,* a late-1800s English compendium of funny nonsense. ♦ M-F. 607 Boylston St (at Dartmouth St). 247.2818

15 Angelo's ★★$$$ The original **Angelo's** in the nearby town of Stoneham is famous for its pasta dishes, and that tradition is carried on at this new Back Bay branch. Fresh, handmade pasta is well cooked and topped with exemplary sauces, including a spicy *amatriciana* with smokey pancetta, tomatoes and hot peppers aplenty, and a classic tomato, basil, and mozzarella. The long menu also includes Italian favorites and seasonal specialties. Among the appetizers to try are grilled New Zealand langoustines, and prosciutto with fresh mozzarella, marinated mushrooms, and roasted artichokes. Out-of-the-ordinary entrées include grilled sausage glazed with honey and served with roasted apples over soft polenta, and pan-roasted pheasant. For dessert choose from *torta della nonna* (a thin layer of custard over pastry), Black Forest cake, and lemon sorbet in a hollowed-out lemon. Though the wine list is predictable, the prices are good if you stick to the Italian selections. ♦ Italian ♦ M-Sa lunch and dinner. 575 Boylston St (between Clarendon and Dartmouth Sts). 536.4045

15 Small Planet Bar and Grill ★$ Almost any palate will be pleased by the wide range of dishes—from stir-fry to vegetable lasagna, paella to pizza—offered at this neighborhood bistro. Owner Frank Bell has kept his prices as appealing as his array of entrées. After dinner, walk across Copley Square to the **Hancock Tower,** and ride up to the observatory to see illuminated Boston compete with the stars.
♦ International ♦ Daily lunch and dinner. 565 Boylston St (between Clarendon and Dartmouth Sts). 536.4477 ₺

16 500 Boylston Street Called "a sort of box covered with architectural clothes" by architect/*Boston Globe* architectural critic **Robert Campbell**, this 1988 building designed by **John Burgee** and **Philip Johnson** is an overblown, outscaled complex that houses fancy shops and offices. Its famous architects must have lost interest during the project—the building is unimaginative kitsch that turns a cold shoulder to its perennially inviting neighbor, **Trinity Church**. The bowling-ball spheres and urns along the parapets look ready to topple. Johnson was the architect of the **Boston Public Library Addition**, and **Johnson** and **Burgee** designed **International Place** near **South Station** in the Financial District, another graceless building that dismays many Bostonians. Local citizens tried to halt the construction of this building—to no avail. ♦ At Clarendon St

Within 500 Boylston Street:

Skipjack's ★$$ This Art Deco and neon restaurant with an underwater motif looks like what it is: an upstart rival to Boston's venerable seafood establishments. The favorite seafood emporium of many younger Bostonians, it purveys 33 different types of fish and shellfish—including many Pacific varieties like Hawaiian mahimahi—all available not just broiled or fried, but prepared in more adventurous ways, including the restaurant's signature coating of lemon, soy, and spice. This brash contender draws long lines and gets very hectic; if you feel daunted when you arrive, you can opt for a take-out dinner. Or phone in an order; they'll deliver to Boston, Cambridge, and Brookline. Live jazz accompanies the Sunday brunch. Valet parking is available in the evenings. ♦ Seafood/Takeout ♦ M-Sa lunch and dinner; Su brunch and dinner. Second entrance at 199 Clarendon St (between St. James Ave and Boylston St). Restaurant 536.3500, takeout 536.4949 ⅋ Also at: 2 Brookline Place, Route 9 (between Brookline Ave and Harvard St), Brookline. 232.8887

17 Hard Rock Cafe ★$ The crowds of tourists and teens piling up under a fake rock facade inscribed "Massachusetts Institute of Rock" should clue you in: Here's Boston's rendition of the famous chain of restaurants where rock 'n' roll is family fare. There's no live music here, as anyone in the know knows—just eardrum-pummeling recordings of old hits and a menu of surprisingly good bar food starring burgers and barbecue. The

rock 'n' roll theme plays itself out all over. The bar is shaped like a Fender Stratocaster guitar; stained-glass windows honor Elvis Presley, Jerry Lee Lewis, and Chuck Berry; and one wall is covered with bricks taken from the demolished Cavern Club in Liverpool, England, where the Beatles got their start. Like all of its siblings, the cafe overflows with memorabilia: Roy Orbison's autographed Gibson, John Lennon's original scribblings for *Imagine,* an Elvis necklace, and a cavalcade of objects belonging to other stars. But really, why come here unless you like to din with your dinner, want to personally experience a legendary marketing coup, or have a young friend who's hot on the idea? ♦ American ♦ Daily lunch and dinner. 131 Clarendon St (at Stuart St). 424.7625 ⅋

18 The Lyric Stage The oldest resident professional theater company in Boston now performs in spacious quarters within the **YWCA** and mounts such neglected classics as George Bernard Shaw's works. Led by artistic director Ron Ritchell, the company is one of the area's few non–university-sponsored theaters to warrant critical attention. ♦ 140 Clarendon St (between Columbus Ave and Stuart St). 437.7172 ⅋

Club Café

19 Club Cafe ★★$$ Attracting a predominantly (though not exclusively) gay clientele, this sophisticated spot is ideal for a light meal. Chef Julia Brant's menu ranges from pizza to cold duck salad with jicama and endive. Also on the premises is **Moonshine Room,** an intimate setting for occasional (and often stellar) musical performances. ♦ International ♦ Cafe: daily lunch and dinner. Moonshine Room: Th-Sa 9PM-2AM. 209 Columbus Ave (at Berkeley St). 536.0966 ⅋

When the land-filled Back Bay was laid out, its main open space was named Art Square, since it fronted the original building of the Museum of Fine Arts. In 1883 the square was renamed for Boston artist John Singleton Copley.

Fanny Merrit Farmer introduced modern measurements, such as the teaspoon, to American cooking. Her cooking school, founded in 1902, occupied 40 Hereford Street (now the site of condominiums) for years. Farmer's *Boston Cooking-School Cookbook* was a smash hit, and her books are still a staple in kitchens all across America.

Boston on Screen

Renowned as the setting for the TV classic "Cheers," Boston is also a thriving film production venue. Here are flicks featuring the city and environs.

Amistad (1997) tells of a 1839 mutiny aboard a slave ship and the Africans who were put on trial for the murder of the ship's crew. Set in New England, it was partially filmed in Boston and **Quincy**, Massachusetts, and in **Providence** and **Newport**, Rhode Island. Anthony Hopkins, Morgan Freeman, Matthew McConaughey, and Djimon Hounsou star in this Steven Spielberg epic.

Blown Away (1993) offers high action when an explosion jolts downtown Boston. An ex–bomb squad expert is brought back to work on the case. Starring Jeff Bridges, Tommy Lee Jones, and Lloyd Bridges, it was filmed in Boston and **Gloucester.**

The Bostonians (1984) is based on the novel by Henry James, set in 1876 Boston, where the social cause of female emancipation wrecks a relationship. Starring Vanessa Redgrave, Christopher Reeve, and Jessica Tandy, it captures settings in Boston and other Massachusetts locations.

Boston Strangler (1968) is a semifactual account of the sex maniac who terrified Boston in the 1960s. Tony Curtis, Henry Fonda, and George Kennedy star.

The Brink's Job (1978) re-creates Tony Pino's heist of $2.7 million from a Brink's truck. The comedy stars Peter Falk, Peter Boyle, and Paul Sorvino.

Celtic Pride (1996) stars Dan Aykroyd and Damon Wayans in a comedy about two **Boston Celtics** fans who consider kidnapping the opponent's star player to assure another Boston championship.

Charly (1968), based on the novel *Flowers for Algernon* by David Keyes, is about a mentally retarded young man who is made a genius by a new experimental surgery. Unfortunately the effect wears off. The film stars Cliff Robertson and Claire Bloom.

Coma (1978), based on the novel by Robin Cook, stars Genevieve Bujold, Richard Widmark, and Michael Douglas. A doctor in a Boston hospital discovers that patients suffer irreparable brain damage when surgery takes place in a particular operating room.

The Crucible (1996) features Daniel Day-Lewis, Winona Ryder, Paul Scofield, Joan Allen, and Jeffrey Jones in Arthur Miller's original play (he also wrote the screenplay) about the 1692 Salem Witch Trials.

The Firm (1993) traces the career of a **Harvard Law School** graduate who joins a small, yet corrupt, Memphis law firm. The movie features Tom Cruise, Gene Hackman, and Jeanne Tripplehorn.

The Friends of Eddie Coyle (1973), based on a novel by George V. Higgins, is about an aging hoodlum who becomes a police informer and is then hunted down by his former associates. It stars Robert Mitchum, Peter Boyle, and Richard Jordan.

Glory (1989), filmed at **Old Sturbridge Village, Boston Common,** the **South End,** and **Ipswich,** is a rich historical spectacle chronicling the first black volunteer infantry unit in the Civil War. Stars Denzel Washington, Matthew Broderick, and Jane Alexander.

Good Will Hunting (1997) tells the story of a mathematically gifted **MIT** janitor (Matt Damon), his best friend (Ben Affleck) from the old neighborhood, a washed-up shrink (Robin Williams) who is trying to help him achieve his dream, and his new love (Minnie Driver). There are plenty of recognizable Boston and Cambridge sites. The film won two Academy Awards: for Best Supporting Actor and for Best Screenplay.

Hocus Pocus (1992) stars Bette Midler, Sarah Jessica Parker, and Kathy Najimy as 17th-century **Salem** witches conjured up by pranksters.

Housesitter (1991), a comedy filmed in Boston, **Concord,** and **Cohasset,** follows Steve Martin and Goldie Hawn as they seek to establish a relationship.

Little Women (1994) is the classic Louisa May Alcott novel about four sisters. Starring Winona Ryder and Susan Sarandon, it was filmed in **Deerfield.**

Love Story (1970) stars Ryan O'Neal and Ali McGraw who discover "love is never having to say you're sorry." The setting is **Harvard University.**

Malice (1992) features Alec Baldwin, Nicole Kidman, and Bill Pullman in a drama about a doctor being sued for malpractice.

Mrs. Winterbourne (1996), with Ricki Lake, Shirley MacLaine, and Brendan Fraser, is a romantic comedy about a woman who pretends to be the widow of a wealthy Bostonian.

Now, Voyager (1942) is a classic variation on Cinderella. Claude Rains plays a psychiatrist who enables a repressed **Back Bay** resident (Bette Davis) to become an attractive, vibrant woman.

The Paper Chase (1973) captures the scholarly environment of **Harvard Law School** with stars John Houseman, Timothy Bottoms, and Lindsay Wagner.

Sabrina (1995) is the remake of the great romantic comedy in which two brothers fall in love with the same woman. Shot on **Martha's Vineyard**, the film stars Harrison Ford and Julia Ormond.

Starting Over (1979), a comedy starring Burt Reynolds as a recently divorced Bostonian.

The Thomas Crown Affair (1967) is a visual travelogue of Boston. Steve McQueen and Faye Dunaway star in this story of a multimillionaire who decides to plot and execute the perfect crime.

The Verdict (1982) stars Paul Newman as an attorney who takes on the system against impossible odds. It features James Mason and Jack Warden.

The Witches of Eastwick (1986) is about three New England women (Susan Sarandon, Cher, and Michelle Pfeiffer) and their liberation by Jack Nicholson. It was filmed in Cohasset, **Marblehead,** and Ipswich.

With Honors (1993), a comedy-drama about university life on the **Harvard** campus, stars Joe Pesci and Brendan Fraser.

20 Grill 23 & Bar ★★$$$$ A sea of white linen, mahogany paneling, banker's lamps, and burnished brass give this place a formal demeanor—the ideal setting for a festive but seemly occasion. During the week you'll see many more wheeling-and-dealing Boston professionals than tourists here. Famous for its sure touch with red meat, especially the perfectly aged and charbroiled 18-ounce New York sirloin, the restaurant turns out splendid seafood and poultry, too. The old-fashioned American practice of topping off hearty fare with equally hearty sweets is enthusiastically followed here; the dessert list features good old apple pie and New York cheesecake. Be sure to come famished, but be forewarned: With few rugs on its wooden floors and an open kitchen, the cavernous dining room gets very noisy.

The restaurant is located in the renovated **Salada Tea Building,** which was designed by **Densmore, LeClear, and Robbins** in 1929. On your way out, be sure to look for the fantastic bronze doors at the Stuart Street entrance. Cast from Englishman Henry Wilson's design, they depict exotic scenes from the tea trade and won a silver medal at the 1927 Paris Salon. Elephants and solemn human figures protrude dramatically in bas-relief from the bronze doors and their carved stone setting. ♦ American ♦ Daily dinner. Reservations recommended; jacket and tie required. 161 Berkeley St (at Stuart St). 542.2255 &

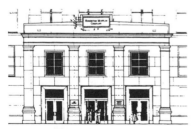

21 Houghton Mifflin Building Posh digs for Boston's venerable publisher (and several other tenants), this 22-story high-rise designed by **Robert A.M. Stern** (the entrance is pictured above) turns inward for luxury, unlike its ostentatious neighbor, **500 Boylston Street.** The outside is all clean, tasteful lines; the interior is creamy marble with a five-story skylighted "winter garden," complete with splashing fountains, tables and chairs, and a cafe on a mezzanine off the foyer—a secret indoor retreat in the heart of Back Bay. ♦ 222 Berkeley St (between St. James Ave and Boylston St)

Within the Houghton Mifflin Building:

Cottonwood Cafe ★★$$ Haute Tex-Mex is the most appropriate rubric for this bountiful, robust fare, served in an evocative, pared-down setting that always seems to suggest the desert at sunset, even at high noon. Indulge in the delicious Rocky Mountain lamb (mesquite-grilled, with raspberry chipotle sauce on one half of the enormous platter, cilantro pesto on the other) in the cafe, which is more like a bar with some tables, or in the restaurant proper, where a booth is your best choice. Lunch is not served in the cafe, but otherwise the menu is the same in both rooms, and both are informal. The service is attentive but unintrusive, and the fresh-fruit margaritas here are just heavenly. ♦ Tex-Mex ♦ Restaurant: daily lunch and dinner. Cafe: daily afternoon snacks and dinner. Reservations recommended. 247.2225 & Also at: 1815 Massachusetts Ave (between Roseland St and Porter Sq), Cambridge. 661.7440

City Sports A popular local outfitter, this rapidly growing chain has chosen to decorate its flagship store with raw beams and exposed ducts, and somehow the stripped-away aesthetic is effective. The high-energy music pumping through doesn't hurt. ♦ Daily. 267.3900 &

22 FAO Schwarz A 6,000-pound, 12-foot-tall bronze bear, the largest teddy in the world, has served as this toy store's official greeter since 1991 and is now on the list of Historic Boston Landmarks. The fun continues inside, as visitors pass under a 22-foot-high animated clock tower that dances, talks, pops, chugs, and sings. Nearly as huge as the New York City flagship, the store stocks toys of every description and price (including ultra-expensive). And there are few places that offer better customer service (personal shopping and same-day delivery are available). ♦ M-Sa 10AM-9PM; Su 11AM-9PM. 440 Boylston St (at Berkeley St). 262.5900

23 Berkeley Building Stand on the opposite side of the street to get a full view of this striking Beaux Arts–inspired office building, designed in 1905 by **Codman & Despredelle.** Look for its spectacular cornice and colorful banners waving above. Clad in enameled terra-cotta, the steel frame supports five-story towers of glass edged in sea-foam green. There's only one elegant embellishment of gilt (over the front door)—the facade is dressy enough. Parisian architect **Desiré Despredelle** taught design classes across the street, where the **Massachusetts Institute of Technology School of Architecture** was once located. ♦ 420 Boylston St (at Berkeley St)

24 The Rattlesnake Bar & Grill ★★$
Oblivious to its high-rent neighbors, Gordon
Wilcox's down-home joint claims to serve
"food of the Americas." But just about
anything goes at this whimsical joint—the
menu offers duck confit as well as quesadillas
and state-of-the-art Sauza Gold margaritas.
Out back, there's an "Urban Canyon" patio
with an Aztec-motif mural painted by David
Omar White's class at the **Museum of Fine
Arts.** Brace yourself for bustle and din as TV
sets blare sports and young singles try to
corral one another. ◆ Pan-American ◆ Daily
lunch and dinner. 384 Boylston St (between
Arlington and Berkeley Sts). 859.8555 &

**24 Women's Educational and Industrial
Union (WEIU)** Floating above this local
institution's decorative entry (the building was
designed by **Parker, Thomas & Rice** in 1906,
and restored in 1973 by **Shepley, Bulfinch,
Richardson & Abbott**) is a gilded swan: It was
chosen as a logo because the union was
launched in 1877, the same year the **Swan
Boats** settled in the **Public Garden**'s lagoon.
A small group of women established the
association to further employment and
educational opportunities for women and to
help the elderly, disabled, and poor. In 1891
Julia Ward Howe became the first president of
the union's Traveler's Information Exchange,
which began as a secret underground organization for women travelers, unaccompanied
by men, to share information. Today men
participate in all of the organization's
programs. In 1926 Amelia Earhart found a
job as a social worker through a career
services program here. Her application
carried the note "Has a sky pilot's
license???"

The genteel retail shop run by this
private social service organization
offers an avant-garde mix of antiques
and crafts and is a favorite with
Bostonians, particularly at holiday
time. Staffed by friendly volunteers,
the store is filled with handmade
articles of all kinds, books and
toys for children, knitting and
craft supplies, stationery and
wrapping paper, and household
treasures. There's also a pastry
counter. Be sure to visit the
antiques consignment
shop on the upper level,
where great finds
often surface.
There's a flower
stand outside.
◆ M-Sa. 356 Boylston
St (between Arlington
and Berkeley Sts).
536.5651 &

SHREVE, CRUMP & LOW

25 Shreve, Crump & Low Since 1800,
innumerable brides have registered at this
renowned institution, and countless
marriages have been launched with jewelry,
sterling, crystal, and china purchased from
the city's jeweler of choice. You can also pick
up a baby-sized silver cup here, or order
personalized stationery. The antiques
department displays 18th- and 19th-century
English and American furniture and prints;
China-trade furniture and porcelain; and
English, Irish, and American silver. The
service here is expert and assiduous. ◆ M-Sa.
330 Boylston St (at Arlington St). 267.9100

**26 Arlington Street Church, Unitarian
Universalist** This church's most striking
feature is its shapely tower (pictured below),
inspired by St. Martin's-in-the-Fields in
London. The first building erected in Back Bay
(completed in 1861), the simple brownstone
structure by **Arthur Gilman** is quite conservative in style—as if unsure of its leadership role
in storming the mudflats. The outspoken
minister William Ellery Channing served here
for years; his statue just across the way in the
Public Garden keeps watch still. A staunch
abolitionist, Channing invited Harriet
Beecher Stowe and William Lloyd Garrison
to address his congregation. During the
Vietnam War, the church was active in
the peace movement. Attendance sky-
rocketed with the arrival of Reverend
Kim Crawford Harvie—a woman—who
still ministers here. Inside, look for the
Tiffany windows. ◆ Su services at
11AM. Sanctuary tours May-Sept;
call for details. 351 Boylston St (at
Arlington St). 536.7050 &

26 The Parish Cafe ★$ Named
for a fictional boîte in Gabriel García
Márquez's *Love in the Time of
Cholera,* this intentionally funky
cafe features sandwiches that pay
homage to the great chefs of Boston:
Lydia Shire, Chris Schlesinger, et al.
It's owned by Gordon Wilcox, who
also owns **The Rattlesnake Bar
& Grill** across the street.
◆ American/ Takeout ◆ Daily
lunch and dinner. 361
Boylston St (between
Arlington and Berkeley
Sts). 247.4777 &

*Arlington Street Church,
Unitarian Universalist*

27 Harbridge House In 1893 Boston's grande dame and arts patron Mrs. J. Montgomery Sears combined **12 Arlington Street,** a formidable five-story French and Italian–style mansion built by **Arthur Gilman** in 1860, with **1 Commonwealth Avenue,** creating a small palace to house her famous art collection and music room. Pianist Ignace Paderewski and violinist Fritz Kreisler visited Mrs. Sears here, as did John Singer Sargent, who executed a portrait of his patron and her daughter at home. Today the building houses condominiums. Gilman also designed **Arlington Street Church** down the block. ♦ 12 Arlington St (at Commonwealth Ave)

28 The Gibson House Facades can only reveal so much; here's your best chance to peer into family life during Back Bay's early years. Three generations of Gibsons lived in decorous luxury in this Victorian residence, one of the neighborhood's oldest. It was built in 1860 for Catherine Hammond Gibson and bequeathed nearly a century later to the Victorian Society in America by her grandson Charles to be made into a museum enshrining his family's life and times. Not much to look at on the outside, the interior is a wonderful six-story repository of perfectly preserved Victoriana. The Gibsons' ghosts would be quite content to wander through their beloved dim rooms (sunshine was considered common then), still crowded with the ornaments, overstuffed furniture, fixtures, keepsakes, and curios they amassed and passed down to one another. The tour includes the kitchen, laundry, and other service areas, giving visitors a full portrait of daily life at the Gibson home. ♦ Admission. Tours W-Su afternoons May-Oct; Sa-Su afternoons Nov-Apr. Groups of 12 or more by appointment only. 137 Beacon St (between Arlington and Berkeley Sts). 267.6338

29 Goethe Institute, German Cultural Center New England's branch of the Munich-based institute inhabits a 1901 Italian Renaissance Revival building designed by **Ogden Codman.** It was constructed to house Boston financier Eben Howard Gay's formidable Chippendale and Adams furniture collection, parts of which are now in the **Museum of Fine Arts** (Gay donated the collection displayed in the museum's **Chippendale Wing**). The institute library's collection of more than 6,000 volumes and 40 periodicals and newspapers is open to the public, though only cardholders may check out materials. The institute also offers language programs and film series,

exhibitions, and other cultural events. ♦ Offices and library M-F. 170 Beacon St (between Berkeley and Clarendon Sts). 262.6050

30 Marlborough Street This peaceful, shady, residential street in the midst of urbane Back Bay is humbler than Commonwealth Avenue, and more picturesque with its brick sidewalks, gaslights, and tidy little black iron fenced front gardens. Some houses are still single-family town houses, but the majority have been converted into condominiums over the last 20 years. ♦ Between Arlington St and Massachusetts Ave

30 The French Library in Boston Ever since the dashing young Marquis de Lafayette won Bostonians' hearts during the Revolutionary War, the city has had a special fondness for all things French. Since its founding in 1946, Boston's center for French language and culture (pictured above) has grown quite a bit. Today it holds more than 45,000 books and hundreds of Cds, cassettes, records, and periodicals (only members may borrow materials). A special treat is its collection of *bandes dessinées* (comic books for mature readers); they provide readers with a good workout in idiomatic and colloquial French. The library offers language lessons, lectures, exhibitions, concerts, children's activities, and many other events. Every 14th of July, this block of Marlborough Street is closed off for the library's annual Bastille Day celebration, an evening of dining, music, and dancing that Bostonians enjoy with French flair—as if Lafayette had never left. The library has a cozy reading room and a theater where French films are regularly screened. Whether to ponder Sartre, flip through a travel guide, get a quick phrase translation, or ask anything at all about *La Belle France,* this is the place to come. ♦ Tu-Th until 8PM; F-Sa. 53 Marlborough St (at Berkeley St). 266.4351

31 First and Second Church In 1968, the **First Church** burned down, but the conflagration spared some remnants of the 1867 structure (designed by **William R. Ware** and **Henry Van Brunt**) that architect **Paul**

Rudolph ingeniously incorporated into this 1971 hybrid. **Rudolph** is best known for **Yale University**'s **School of Art and Architecture** in New Haven, Connecticut. Even using coarse striated concrete—the brutal material that is his trademark—**Rudolph** creates poignant connections with the ruined fragments, particularly the square stone tower and rose window. ♦ M-F (call first). 66 Marlborough St (at Berkeley St). 267.6730 ♿

32 First Lutheran Church Entering from Berkeley Street, enjoy a quiet moment in the small landscaped courtyard nestled against this modest brick church, designed by **Pietro Belluschi** in 1959. ♦ 299 Berkeley St (at Marlborough St). 536.8851

33 Commonwealth Avenue and Mall This expansive, ruler-straight street served as Bostonians' first major clue that the new Back Bay wouldn't resemble the city's maze-like older districts. Modeled after the grand Parisian boulevards, "Comm Ave"—its undignified, unpunctuated nickname—was the first street of its kind in America, setting a chic French example for the rest of Back Bay to follow. The boulevard is 240 feet wide, with a 100-foot-wide central mall that Winston Churchill deemed one of the world's most beautiful. The avenue is shaded with elm trees and dotted with statues memorializing both the famous and forgotten. In spring, when the magnolias are in bloom, it's a pleasant place indeed. This Victorian promenade was once the place for the fashionable to stroll and be seen. Today a more casual collection of Bostonians ambles along, including plenty of dogwalkers and young mothers wheeling infants. The avenue boasts block after block of handsome buildings that were once aristocratic town houses but now house luxury condos, apartments, and distinguished firms and clubs. Unfortunately, a number of the buildings have had suburbanite roof decks and unsympathetic stories tacked on, ruining many a graceful roofline. The boulevard's northern, sunny side was the most desirable residential stretch in Back Bay, and many grandly residential showplaces remain. "Comm Ave" starts to run out of charm as it nears Massachusetts Avenue, so linger longest closer to the **Public Garden.** ♦ Between Arlington St and Massachusetts Ave

---

The Boston Public Library is the repository of John Adams's presidential papers. It's the only public library in the country that also serves as a presidential library.

The largest teddy bear in the world sits in front of FAO Schwarz on Boylston Street. The bronze bear is 12 feet high, weighs around 6,000 pounds, and cost about $500,000.

33 Baylies Mansion In the early 1900s, textile industrialist Walter C. Baylies moved to Boston, married into a wealthy family, and promptly metamorphosed into a full-fledged Brahmin. He tore down an 1861 house to build this showy Italianate mansion (designed by **Thomas and Rice** in 1912), adding a fabulous Louis XIV ballroom for his daughter's debut. A site for glittering society events, the room did its stint of civic service, too: During World War I bandages were rolled here. Since 1941 this has been the home of the **Boston Center for Adult Education.** Many of the mansion's original ornaments and interior finishes remain untouched. ♦ 5 Commonwealth Ave (between Arlington and Berkeley Sts)

34 First Baptist Church Henry Hobson **Richardson** was just starting to flex his creative muscles when he won the commission for this 1871 pudding stone church (originally called **New Brattle Square Church**) in a competition. Its marvelous campanile springs into the air to create one of Back Bay's most striking silhouettes. The belfry's frieze was modeled in Paris by Frédéric-Auguste Bartholdi, sculptor of the Statue of Liberty (Bartholdi had a way with drapery), and its scenes depict the sacraments of baptism, communion, marriage, and last rites. Some of the sculpted faces supposedly belong to famous Bostonians, including Hawthorne, Emerson, and Longfellow.

Protruding proudly from the corners, the angels' trumpets won the figures the irreverent nickname, "The Holy Bean Blowers." Come at sunset to admire their profiles etched crisply against a darkening sky. Unfortunately, the original congregation disbanded and funds ran out, so Richardson's lofty plans for the church interior never came to be. The church, still home to a Baptist congregation, is fairly unremarkable inside, with lots of dark wood. ♦ M-F; service Su 11AM. 110 Commonwealth Ave (at Clarendon St). 267.3148

35 The Vendôme You'd think the marsh-bottomed Back Bay would sag under the weight of this magnificent monster, a hybrid of **William G. Preston**'s 1871 corner building and **J.F. Ober**'s main building, both renovated in 1975 by **Stahl Bennett.** For 100 years, this was Boston's most fashionable hotel, the only place where Sarah Bernhardt would deign to lay her weary head. General Ulysses S. Grant, President Grover Cleveland, John Singer Sargent, Oscar Wilde, Mark Twain, and countless other worthies stayed here as well.

During its heyday, the hotel boasted previously unheard-of luxuries: It was the first public building in the city to have electric lighting, powered in 1882 by a plant Thomas Edison had designed. Every room featured a private bathroom and fireplace, as well as

steam heat. Inevitably, the hotel's glory days passed, and it became a rundown white elephant. In the 1970s the interior decor was obliterated during renovation, and a terrible fire destroyed portions of the roof and building in 1972. (A black granite memorial to the nine firefighters who lost their lives in that blaze is located on the **Commonwealth Avenue Mall** between Clarendon and Dartmouth Streets.) Now functioning as a condominium complex, **The Vendôme** has accepted its comedown as gracefully as possible. To the left at Dartmouth Street is Preston's original structure, forced to play a supporting role to **Ober**'s enormous addition on the right. The duo's conjoining marble facades ripple with opulent ornamentation.
♦ 160 Commonwealth Ave (at Dartmouth St)

Within The Vendôme:

Spasso ★★$$ Painted the color of butter, with lively prints and graffiti and a sunken outside patio on Commonwealth Avenue, this trattoria is jolly and appealing (fitting for a place whose name means "fun"). Beyond such pasta dishes as *scallops aromatica* (fettuccine covered with scallops, pine nuts, black olives, and garlic) and pizzas topped with wild mushrooms and pine nuts, there are several substantial *secondi* (entrées), and an array of *dolci* (desserts), too. As the menu advises, "Mangia! Mangia!" Valet parking is available. ♦ Italian ♦ Daily lunch and dinner. 536.8656 &

36 William Lloyd Garrison Statue In Olin L. Warner's posthumous (1885) rendition, Boston's famed abolitionist looks as though he had been intently reading when the artist interrupted and asked him to pose. The statue suggests a man taut with energy, feigning relaxation, stretching back in his armchair with his books and papers hastily stuffed underneath. His profile is truly memorable. The fiery inscription here reads, "I am in earnest—I will not equivocate. I will not excuse. I will not retreat a single inch, and I will be heard!"—expressing all of Garrison's unquenchable conviction and taken from the inaugural manifesto of *The Liberator,* a journal he both founded and edited.
♦ Commonwealth Mall (between Dartmouth and Exeter Sts)

37 Ames-Webster House This mansion was built by **Peabody and Stearns** in 1872 for railroad tycoon and US congressman Frederick L. Ames. Its massive pavilion and porte cochere were added 10 years later by **John Sturgis,** and the whole was renovated in 1969 by the architectural firm **CBT/Childs Bertman Tseckares.** The exterior is impressive enough, with wrought-iron gates, a two-story conservatory, a monumental tower, and a commanding chimney. But inside is the extraordinary grand hall bedecked with elaborately carved oak woodwork. The theatrical staircase ascends toward the skylit stained-glass dome, past murals by French painter Benjamin Constant. There's a compact jewel of a ballroom—decorated in celery green and gilt, and delicately proportioned, particularly its "heavens," the balcony where musicians played. Now housing private offices, the building, unfortunately, is no longer accessible to the public. ♦ 306 Dartmouth St (at Commonwealth Ave)

38 Admiral Samuel Eliot Morison Statue In Penelope Jencks' statue, the sailor and historian is seated on a rock by the sea, binoculars in hand, dressed in oilskins with a jaunty yachting cap on his head. Notice the coppery lichen on his stony perch, and the sand crabs on the beach below. Smaller rocks are inscribed with such quotes from Morison's books as "Dream dreams then write them/Aye, but live them first." Just across the street is the exclusive **St. Botolph Club** (199 Commonwealth Ave) to which Morison belonged. ♦ Commonwealth Mall (between Exeter and Fairfield Sts)

39 Algonquin Club It would be hard to find a haughtier facade in the city than this one by **McKim, Mead & White,** with its overblown frieze and projecting pair of falcons. The Italian Renaissance Revival palace, which was built in 1887 for the private club that's still based here, certainly catches the eye with its self-confident, flamboyant architectural maneuvers. ♦ 217 Commonwealth Ave (between Exeter and Fairfield Sts)

39 1st Corps of Cadets Museum Military history buffs won't want to miss this place. Established in 1726, the First Corps of Cadets is one of America's oldest military organizations, and it has members who have served in most US wars and conflicts. The corps originally acted as bodyguards to the royal governors of the Province of Massachusetts Bay; John Hancock served as a colonel in 1774. The museum has extensive displays of armaments dating back to King George II, many of which were brought back from action by corps members. Also featured are flags, uniforms, drums, and paintings. ♦ Free. Two-hour tours by appointment only. 227 Commonwealth Ave (between Exeter and Fairfield Sts). 267.1726

40 Nickerson House Architects **McKim, Mead & White**'s last Back Bay residence offers one monumental gesture in the sweep of its bulging granite bowfront. The 1895 building is a model of chilly restraint, but enjoyed a brief fling as the site of two of Boston's most lavish debutante balls, held by Mrs. Pickman, wife of the house's second owner, for her daughters. It's still a private residence. ♦ 303 Commonwealth Ave (between Gloucester and Hereford Sts)

41 Burrage Mansion Not all Bostonians were willing to surrender their highfalutin aspirations to fit Back Bay's decorous mold. Certainly not Albert Burrage; his theatrical 1899 limestone mansion simultaneously pays homage to the Vanderbilts' Fifth Avenue mansions and Chenonceaux, the French château on the Loire. A multitude of strange carved figures peer down from and crawl across the highly ornamented facade. Burrage once cultivated orchids in the splendid glass-domed greenhouse at the rear. The mansion is now a rather luxurious retirement home. Peek inside to see how enthusiastically the interior, with its sculpted marble staircase and abundant embellishments, competes with the exterior. ♦ 314 Commonwealth Ave (at Hereford St)

42 Oliver Ames Mansion The original owner was head of the Ames Shovel Manufacturing Company, president of the **Union Pacific Railroad,** a philanthropist, owner of the Booth Theatre in New York, and a Massachusetts governor. Clearly, a lion like Ames would command Back Bay's biggest mansion. **Henry Hobson Richardson** prepared a sketch for the house, but it was rejected and **Carl Fehmer** took over in 1882. Note the frieze panels portraying the activities that occurred in the rooms behind. Now an office building, the mansion served as the longtime headquarters of the National Casket Company. ♦ 355 Commonwealth Ave (at Massachusetts Ave)

43 Church Court Condominium In 1978 an up-and-coming young architect named **Graham Gund** caused a furor when he purchased the burnt-out shell of **Mount Vernon Church** for commercial development, but this elegant amalgam—with a clerestory topped by sculptor Gene Cauthon's ethereal bronze angel—set a brave standard for creative reuse. ♦ 490 Beacon St (at Massachusetts Ave)

44 Berklee Performance Center Associated with the highly regarded **Berklee College of Music,** this center (see the seating chart below) hosts popular performances of all types of contemporary music, especially jazz and folk. ♦ Admission. Box office M-Sa. No credit cards accepted. 136 Massachusetts Ave (between Belvidere and Boylston Sts). 266.1400, recorded concert information 266.7455

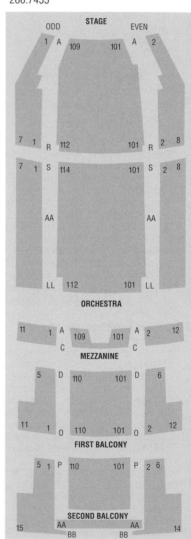

Sheraton Boston
HOTEL & TOWERS

45 Sheraton Boston Hotel & Towers $$$
Here's where the sports teams stay, with one staffer solely dedicated to their needs and wants. The 1,143-room property abuts the **Hynes Convention Center,** which conventioneers can enter without ever going outdoors. Be sure to reserve a room on an upper floor for splendid views of the Charles River. For those who want absolute luxury, four floors offer exclusive perks including private butler service and a VIP lounge. The hotel features a seafood restaurant (see below), an indoor/outdoor pool, a health club with Jacuzzi, and a beauty salon/barbershop. There's also a complete business center. Small pets are welcome. ♦ 39 Dalton St (at Belvidere St). 236.2000, 800/325.3535; fax 236.6061 &

Within the Sheraton Boston Hotel & Towers:

The Mass Bay Company ★$$ Come to this casual dining spot when you can't tolerate the lines or prices at Boston's higher-profile seafood houses. Specialties include award-winning clam chowder, salmon and trout smoked on the premises, and fish grilled over mesquite charcoal. ♦ Seafood ♦ Daily breakfast, lunch, and dinner. Reservations recommended for dinner. 236.2000 &

46 Back Bay Hilton $$$ A stone's throw from the **Hynes Convention Center,** this rather nondescript 25-story hotel caters assiduously to the business traveler. All 385 rooms are soundproofed, with small bathrooms, and decorated in soothing pastels. Many have balconies and bay windows you can open. Amenities include a steakhouse restaurant (see below), a year-round swimming pool, a fitness room, 24-hour room service, a parking garage, meeting and banquet rooms, and nonsmokers' floors. In addition to a lounge, there's an upscale nightclub with musical entertainment nightly. ♦ 40 Dalton St (at Belvidere St). 236.1100, 800/874.0663; fax 236.1506 &

Within Back Bay Hilton:

Boodle's of Boston ★★$$$ A sillier name for such an earnest grill room would be hard to find. The English decor is a little

ponderous, but perfectly appropriate to the main business at hand: expertly grilling massive cuts of meat over hardwoods, including sassafras and hickory. Seafood and vegetables take many a pleasant turn on the grill here, too, and there are oyster dishes galore. You can dress up the entrées by choosing from 20 butters, sauces, and condiments. ♦ Steakhouse/American ♦ Daily breakfast, lunch, and dinner. Reservations recommended for dinner. 266.3537 &

47 Christian Science International Headquarters It's easy to overlook the little acorn from which this gigantic oak grew. **Franklin J. Welch**'s original 1894 Romanesque **Christian Science Mother Church,** which founder Mary Baker Eddy called "our prayer in stone," is now dwarfed by a behemoth extension. The 1906 addition designed by **Charles E. Brigham** (with **Solon S. Beman, Brigham Coveney and Bisbee**) soars to a height of 224 feet. This Renaissance basilica bears the weight of its towering dome like giant Atlas holding the world upon his shoulders. Designed to seat 3,000, it boasts one of the world's largest working pipe organs, a 13,595-pipe Aeolian Skinner manufactured locally. Located on what was the outer edge of respectability, the old and new sections of the church clung together in the midst of tenements and crowded residential blocks until 1973, when **I.M. Pei**'s master plan carved a great swath of 22 acres out of the neighborhood, populating its core with monumental church administration buildings.

Strategically flanking the church like Secret Service agents are the 28-story **Church Administration Building,** the fan-shaped **Sunday School,** and the low-slung **Colonnade Building.** They surround a vast public space dominated by a 670-foot-long, 100-foot-wide reflecting pool rimmed with red granite, a pleasant feature with a hidden agenda: to cool water from the air-conditioning system. The circular fountain at one end is dull when shut off, but, gushing on hot days, it becomes a hectic playground and contributes a badly needed note of spontaneity to this austere, over-planned setting. With rows of manicured trees, flowerbeds, and water, the plaza is a popular lunchtime spot. But in the winter the wind can whip through here fiercely, treating the office tower as a sail.

To one side of the church is the **Christian Science Publishing Society** building, home of the well-regarded *Christian Science Monitor,* founded in 1908. Inside, look up at the two extraordinary glass globe lanterns suspended from the lobby ceiling; one lights up to tell the time, the other the date. Follow signs to the fabulous *Mapparium,* a vividly colored stained-glass globe 30 feet in diameter, traversed by a glass bridge. Since glass doesn't absorb sound, you can stand at one end and send whispered messages echoing eerily across the way to a partner. Made of more than 600 kiln-fired glass panels, the *Mapparium* is illuminated from behind by 300 lights. Designed by the building's architect, **Chester Lindsay Churchill,** the globe was completed in 1932 and has not been altered since. It's outdated, but all the more interesting for its pre-World War II record of political boundaries. Ten-minute guided tours of the *Mapparium,* and guided tours of the original church and the extension are offered. Concerts on the 18-bell chime keyboard in the original church tower are given daily. ♦ Free. Mother Church: daily. Concerts: M-Tu noon; W 7PM; Th-Sa noon; Su 9:30AM, 6:30PM. Mapparium: M-Sa; closed Sunday and holidays. Mother Church: 175 Huntington Ave (between Massachusetts Ave and Belvidere St). Mapparium (within the Christian Science Publishing Society Building): 1 Norway St (at Massachusetts Ave). General information 450.2000

48 Horticultural Hall Founded in 1829, the Massachusetts Horticultural Society sponsors the nation's oldest annual spring flower show. It is a spectacular event, but has bloomed too large for this exhibition hall (designed in 1901 by **Wheelwright and Haven** and now on the National Register of Historic Places), the society's headquarters. Unfortunately, the show was uprooted to the impersonal (and remote) **Bayside Expo Center** in Dorchester. The Horticultural Society launched America's school-gardening movement, which now brings gardening studies into many Boston public schools and spreads the love of growing things via its traveling Plantmobile exhibits. In addition to operating the world's largest independent horticultural library, the society runs a shop selling seeds, books, and prints. You can even call for free advice. The society's decorative building—which it now shares with other organizations, including *Boston* magazine—makes a striking couple with **Symphony Hall** across the street. ♦ Free. M-F; Sa until 2PM. 300 Massachusetts Ave (at Huntington Ave). 536.9280 &

49 Newbury Street With what are said to be the third-highest retail rents in the US—tying with New York City's Fifth Avenue and coming

in behind Beverly Hills's Rodeo Drive and Palm Beach's Worth Avenue—this thoroughfare aspires to commercial heights. It's increasingly fashionable the closer you are to the Arlington Street end, where you can feel underdressed just strolling along. In addition to boutiques and galleries offering art, literature, antiques, and costly geegaws galore, there are dozens of hair "designers," tanning and facial salons, and modeling studios along this stretch. There's also a thriving cafe society. ♦ Between Arlington St and Massachusetts Ave

49 360 Newbury Street An early 1900s warehouse designed by **Arthur Bowditch** was metamorphosed into a dramatic iconoclast by architect **Frank O. Gehry** with the assistance of **Schwartz/Silver Architects** in 1989. The building towers over the Massachusetts Avenue end of Newbury Street. Viewed from the Massachusetts Turnpike and from many Back Bay angles, the structure is a challenging, alert, eye-catching presence—critically lauded though not universally beloved. Its brash projecting struts, canopy, and cornice make it appear scaffolded and still in process, as if the building hasn't quite decided what it wants to be yet. Step into the bank-breaking splendor of the lobby on the Newbury Street side, and also check the wall next door for Morgan Bulkeley's surrealist mural *Tramount,* depicting—in odd little vignettes—the history of the city. ♦ At Massachusetts Ave

Within 360 Newbury Street:

Tower Records/Video Calling itself "the largest record store in the known world," this enormous multilevel emporium is one of a chain of almost 100 stores in the US, England, and Japan, and sells LPs, 45s, CDs and cassettes (including single recordings), and videos. It covers all the music bases, but this isn't the place to come for unconventional, hard-to-find recordings. You can purchase tickets to most concerts in person at the **Ticketmaster** counter. A lot of late-night socializing goes on here. ♦ Daily until midnight. 247.5900 &

50 The Capital Grille ★★$$$$ Top-grade steak—dry-aged in plain view on the premises—is this upscale restaurant's primary raison d'être. Some straightforward seafood is also served. The decor is modeled after an old-fashioned men's club: lots of dark paneling (lifted from a 16th-century Welsh castle), marble floors, and a long brass bar with private wine lockers. It attracts a prosperous crowd whose business image requires a certain show of conspicuous consumption. There's valet parking. ♦ American ♦ Daily dinner. Reservations recommended. 359 Newbury St (between Hereford St and Massachusetts Ave). 262.8900 &

50 Johnson Paint Company Look for the famous sign with bright multicolored stripes and real gold leaf. The Johnson family's business has occupied this former carriage house—where horses owned by wealthy Back Bay residents once slept—for more than 50 years. In addition to selling good old-fashioned paint products—they've carried the same lines of paint since 1936—the store is a fixture in the fine arts community, stocking what the staff refers to as "fancy painting stuff"—brushes imported from five countries, easels, tables, pads, powdered pigments, and art books. If you have a tricky wall color to match, this is a good place to come. Renowned citywide, the color mixer here has worked for more than 30 years and is better than a computer at matching samples. Classes on faux painting, glazing, gilding, and other techniques are also held here. You can even buy a T-shirt with the store's gaily colored emblem. ♦ M-F; Sa until 1PM. 355 Newbury St (between Hereford St and Massachusetts Ave). 536.4244 &

51 Avenue Victor Hugo Bookshop Just a glance in the window reveals what a treasure trove this used book-store is. Row upon row of nine-foot-tall bookshelves are crammed with used books in 250 subject areas, ranging in price from 25¢ paperback romances to $200 limited editions. Put yourself in a nostalgic mood browsing through the used periodicals dating from 1854 to the present. Also look for new fiction, comic books, a great card and postcard selection, old maps, and vintage sheet music, too. Prowling the premises is Feet, the store's lordly cat. "All used bookstores should have one," says owner Vincent McCaffrey. ♦ Daily. 339 Newbury St (between Hereford St and Massachusetts Ave). 266.7746 &

Trident Booksellers

52 Trident Booksellers & Cafe ★$
"Boston's alternative bookstore" sells some fiction, but is particularly strong in Jungian psychology, acupuncture, poetry, Eastern religions, and Buddhist, women's, and metaphysical works. Crystals, incense, scented oils, tarot cards, and bonsai trees are also on sale. The cafe is a popular neighborhood meeting place for a broad spectrum of

Bostonians, who come for its no-fuss, down-to-earth menu of tasty homemade soups, salads, sandwiches, bagels, croissants, and rib-sticking desserts like carrot cake, plus a variety of coffees and juices. ♦ Cafe ♦ Daily 9AM-midnight. 338 Newbury St (between Hereford St and Massachusetts Ave). 267.8688

52 Newbury Comics This oddball store started as a comic-book outpost, then branched into anything music-related. They still sell comics, including some aimed at adult readers, but the eccentric inventory now encompasses independent label and import music on CDs and cassettes, music and comic T-shirts, music videos, music books, portable "music makers" and accessories, posters, biker-style jewelry, and bizarre novelties. College students flock here for hard-to-find recordings. ♦ Daily. 332 Newbury St (between Hereford St and Massachusetts Ave). 236.4930 &

53 Sonsie ★★$$$ Complete with bar and brick oven, this fashionable bistro offers bustling sidewalk tables or more quiet, elegant dining at inside booths. Not to be outdone in originality, chef Bill Poirer prepares a range of dishes that will satisfy any number of palates. Among the stunning pizza variations are a tasty delight with spicy shrimp, peppers, ricotta, and leeks, and another topped with lime chicken, salsa, guacamole, and monterey jack cheese. Entrées include sake-steamed salmon fillet with cucumber nori rolls and toasted sesame, and white lasagna with chicken, eggplant, and sweet marjoram. Vegetarian choices include whole roasted onion soup, wild mushroom tamale, *orecchiette* with broccoli and extra virgin olive oil, and a vegetable mixed grill. Many of the dishes are low fat, little or no dairy products are used, and special dietary preferences are accommodated. There's outdoor dining in season. ♦ International ♦ Daily breakfast, lunch, dinner. 327 Newbury St (at Hereford St). 351.2500

54 Boston Architectural Center (BAC) This bulky concrete block of a building is a 1967 exemplar of "Brutalism" by **Ashley, Myer & Associates,** the architectural firm that is now called **Arrowstreet.** The structure has turned out to be an unexpectedly amiable addition to Back Bay, but don't let the contemporary look fool you: It houses an architecture school founded in 1889. The school began as a free atelier run by the Boston Architectural Club, where deserving youth were given drawing lessons. Today it is the only architecture school in the US that requires students to work full-time as fledgling architects while taking classes at night from an all-volunteer faculty. The inviting, glass-sheathed ground floor is a public space for student work and art and architectural exhibitions.

On the building's exterior west wall, New York artist Richard Haas painted one of his best murals in 1977. It has since become a Back Bay landmark. This six-story trompe l'oeil is a cross-sectional view of a French Neo-Classical palace in the Beaux Arts style. Look for the mural's teasers: the shadow of a man against a corridor wall, a foot disappearing through a closing door, and a man appearing in a doorway on his way to the top of the rotunda. ♦ Gallery M-Th until 10:30PM; F-Su. 320 Newbury St (at Hereford St). 536.3170 ㅎ

55 Institute of Contemporary Art (ICA) and Engine and Hose House Number 33
A police station and firehouse shared this building (designed by city architect **Arthur H. Vinal**) in the 19th century. The police eventually relocated next door (**Arrowstreet** performed the renovation in 1975) and the museum moved in after **Graham Gund Associates** handsomely restored the police station in 1975. Inside the Romanesque-style shell are multilevel galleries and a 140-seat theater for mixed-media exhibitions, films, and performances in the visual arts. Established in 1936, the museum has no permanent collection and is famous for its eclectic, sometimes uneven, but always interesting shows of work by known and unknown artists. One-of-a-kind in Boston, the institute aims to be a research and development laboratory for new ideas. A fire station continues to occupy half of the building; as you head over to the museum entrance, you'll see firefighters on the job, taking a break from time to time to watch the colorful crowd on the trendy art trail. The ornate turret tower on the Hereford Street side is still used for drying fire hoses. ♦ Admission; free Thursday from 5PM to closing. W, F-Su noon-5PM; Th noon-9PM. Docent tours Sa and Su 1PM. 955 Boylston St (at Hereford St). 266.5152 ㅎ

55 Division Sixteen ★$ Located in a former police station, this sleek Art Deco restaurant is a popular spot with students and youngish singles. At night there's inevitably a wait, and the horrendous din and clatter will drown out any conversation unless you insist on a booth in the back. But there is a reason to come here: monster portions of reasonably priced, decently prepared casual food, such as sandwiches, salads, omelettes, burgers, nachos, and the like. The shoestring fries are made from scratch. On a weeknight, particularly a rainy one, this place goes well with an evening at one of the movie theaters nearby. ♦ American ♦ Daily lunch and dinner. 955 Boylston St (at Hereford St). 353.0870 ㅎ

56 John B. Hynes Veterans Memorial Convention Center Commonly called "the Hynes," this facility (pictured below) is ordinarily not open to the public. Cross to the opposite side of Boylston Street to study the impressive facade and ground-floor loggia, then peek inside at the magnificent main rotunda. A much admired structure, rebuilt in 1988 by **Kallmann McKinnell & Wood Architects** (who also designed Boston's unusual **City Hall**), the center is so conciliatory toward its surroundings that it's easy to forget it can handle a convention of 22,000. Bankers, dentists, lumberers, and

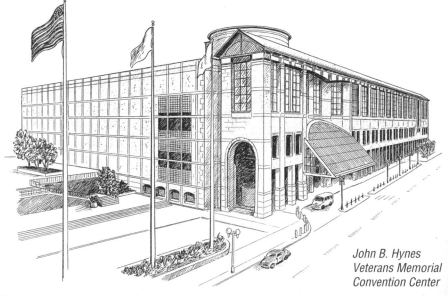

John B. Hynes Veterans Memorial Convention Center

teachers—even the Association of Old Crows—have passed through its handsome portals. The center is connected to **Copley Place** through the **Prudential Center** by an enclosed glass walkway. ♦ 900 Boylston St (between Exeter and Dalton Sts). 954.2000, recorded information 424.8585 &

sky w**∕lk**

57 Prudential Center Former home of the insurance giant, "The Pru," which dates from the early 1960s, is a many-times winner of the most unattractive building in Boston award. But the controversial complex, unloved by many and the worse for wear, was given new life, at least inside, in 1993. The sprawling 27-acre complex—housing six million square feet of offices, apartments, hotels, and stores in a network of elevated blocky buildings and windy plazas—was plopped down here in the early 1960s by **Charles Luckman and Associates** and **Hoyle, Doran, and Berry** to cover the unsightly **Boston & Albany** rail yards. At the time, the structure introduced a new scale to Back Bay, and stirred high hopes for a rejuvenated modern Boston. It's worth a visit to grasp the radical 1960s concept of American urban renewal. Once the city's tallest skyscraper, the inelegant 52-story **Prudential Tower** has been outraced to the heavens by its rival, the sleek **John Hancock Tower.** Still, Bostonians have grown used to the homely smaller tower. Take an elevator up to the **Skywalk,** the observation deck on the 50th floor, and see what's happening for miles around. There also are interesting exhibits on Boston history and contemporary life. At Christmastime, an enormous tree, a gift to Boston from Nova Scotia, is illuminated on the south plaza in front of the tower, facing Huntington Ave. ♦ Admission to Skywalk. Daily 10AM-10PM. 800 Boylston St (between Exeter and Dalton Sts). 236.3318 &

Within Prudential Center:

Top of the Hub ★★★$$$$ Known for its memorable view, this restaurant boasts a memorable menu as well. Floor-to-ceiling windows flank two sides of the restaurant and bar, affording diners dramatic 52nd-story views of Back Bay, the Charles River, and Boston Harbor. Attractive "sails" on the ceiling not only decorate but act as sound absorbers, allowing comfortable conversation even when the restaurant is full. Among the recommended dishes are Maine crabmeat spring roll with melon, baby green oak-leaf salad, aged Black Angus sirloin, medaillons of venison, and seared yellowfin tuna with Asian spices. Executive chef Dean A. Moore also offers a *menu degustation,* a six-course meal that changes with the season. The wine list is

augmented by a selection of dessert wines, Cognacs, and vintage ports. Live music is featured nightly. There's no smoking in the restaurant. ♦ American ♦ M-Sa lunch and dinner; Su brunch and dinner. Reservations recommended. 536.1775 &

58 The Cactus Club ★$ The American Southwestern motif is so out of hand here, it must be parody (intense aqua everywhere, O'Keeffe-esque skulls, a buffalo over the bar). But as the big, high-ceilinged rooms fill up, the design assault recedes. Beneath this garishly cheerful disguise lurks a fern bar. The nouvelle Southwestern cuisine highlights ribs, grilled fish and meat, pasta, barbecue, and the like, with such welcome accents as fresh coriander and chipotle peppers. If you have a penchant for swimming in fishbowl-size glasses, you'll like the drinks. This has become a popular hangout for a youngish crowd. The restaurant inhabits the handsome **Tennis and Racquet Club** building (constructed in 1904), and has a splendid gate in its lobby that prevents access to upstairs offices after hours. ♦ Southwestern ♦ Daily lunch and dinner. 939 Boylston St (at Hereford St). 236.0200 &

STEVE'S
GREEK & AMERICAN CUISINE

59 Steve's Greek & American Cuisine ★$ Lots of locals, students, and conventioneers from the nearby **Hynes** come to this cheerful restaurant whose owner, Steve Kourtidis, says, "It's our pleasure to serve the people." On one side is the take-out operation, on the other the simple and pleasant plant-entwined dining room overlooking Newbury Street. The menu features Greek and Middle Eastern favorites—moussaka, grape leaves, baklava, shish kebabs—as well as burgers and omelettes. Don't come here if cigarette smoke bothers you. ♦ Greek/ American/Takeout ♦ Daily breakfast, lunch, and dinner. 62 Hereford St (at Newbury St). 267.1817

60 John Fleuvog If you want your feet to make a particularly eccentric or up-to-the-minute fashion statement, buy your footwear here. English-made in plenty of colors, with crests and bows and buckles and tapestry, the quality leather shoes are all ready for action of some sort. ♦ Daily. 302 Newbury St (between Gloucester and Hereford Sts). 266.1079

Boston proper is 48.6 square miles; the Greater Boston area covers some 2,100 square miles. Boston has 790 miles of streets, 43 miles of waterfront, 349 bridges, 8 historic or preservation districts, and 8 major medical research centers.

61 L'Espalier ★★★$$$$ This refined and sophisticated establishment started Boston's restaurant revolution in 1978, yanking the city out of its doldrums into a new era of posh cuisine. Frank McClelland, acclaimed successor to the original owner, leans a bit more toward contemporary American cuisine and uses native products. But dinner here is as rarefied and highfalutin an event as ever. Set in a stately 1873 town house, the stunning dining rooms allow guests to imagine that they're feasting back in Back Bay's heyday. The prix-fixe menu might include sautéed yellowfin tuna steaks, squab and fig salad, grilled partridge, or duck breast coupled with foie gras. Every dish is tenderly treated and gorgeously presented in modest—sometimes overly so—portions. The service is exceedingly proper. Valet parking is available. ♦ American ♦ M-Sa dinner. Reservations required weekends; jacket and tie required. 30 Gloucester St (between Newbury St and Commonwealth Ave). 262.3023

CASA ROMERO

61 Casa Romero ★$$$ The prices are steep, though there's compensation in the picturesque dining rooms brightened with hand-painted tiles and Mexican handicrafts. A number of dishes are outstanding: avocado soup, chicken with *mole poblano* (a rich garlic, onion, chili peppers, and chocolate sauce), and *puerco adobado* (pork with smoked chilies) are a sampling. Enter at the public alley that runs between Gloucester and Hereford Streets. ♦ Mexican ♦ M-F lunch and dinner; Sa-Su dinner. Reservations recommended. 30 Gloucester St (between Newbury St and Commonwealth Ave). 536.4341

62 Culture Shock Wunderkind Patrick Petty is probably the most radical clothing designer working on Newbury Street, and his shop is decidedly the most daring. These are street styles with pedigrees: Vivienne Westwood, Moschino, BCBG. The clientele varies from Roxbury kids to suburban matrons, all equally energized by Petty's custom music mix. ♦ Daily. 286 Newbury St (between Gloucester and Hereford Sts). 859.7508

62 Cafe Jaffa ★$ An inviting storefront with broad picture windows and bare brick walls, this modest cafe has been an instant hit with its authentic—and affordable—Middle Eastern fare. Order hummus, falafel, *shawarma* (ground roasted lamb or chicken), and other traditional dishes. ♦ Middle Eastern/Takeout ♦ Daily lunch and dinner. 48 Gloucester St (between Boylston and Newbury Sts). 536.0230 &

63 Miyako ★★$$ The former site of several trendy restaurants that lacked staying power has turned out to be the perfect setting for this elegant Japanese restaurant. It's a choice duplex on a corner, with a roomy patio. Inside the decor is minimalist: gray walls with the odd extravagant floral display. All the better to focus on exquisitely delicate tastes. A sushi bar is tucked into the sub–street level, and the airy second floor features traditional tatami seating. ♦ Japanese ♦ Daily lunch and dinner. 279A Newbury St (at Gloucester St). 236.0222

64 Industry Billing itself—tongue-in-cheek—as "the ultimate factory store," this shop produces its own line of avant-garde products and accessories. Local artisans and craftspeople supply an assortment of pieces, from vases and jewelry to lighting fixtures and pillows, all cutting edge and fun. ♦ Daily. 276 Newbury St (at Gloucester St). 437.0319. Also at: Omni Parker House, 60 School St (at Tremont St). 227.0005

65 Tapeo ★★★$$$ Tapas—especially garlic shrimp, salmon balls with caper sauce, and beef tenderloin with pimento on toast—and sangria on the patio are reasons enough to stop by this popular spot. But a good and affordable wine list, along with main dishes like *pescado a la sal* (fish baked in coarse salt), *lomo de buey a las frutas* (beef tenderloin with dried figs, apricots, and prunes in a cream brandy sauce), and, of course, paella are other good reasons. There's a cozy brick dining room on the ground floor; the second-floor dining room has rustic Spanish decor and a fireplace. There's a $10-per-person food minimum. Valet parking is available. ♦ Spanish ♦ M-F dinner; Sa-Su lunch and dinner. Reservations recommended. 266 Newbury St (between Fairfield and Gloucester Sts). 267.4799

66 Newbury Guest House $$ Located in three adjoining 1880s town houses, this place offers pleasant accommodations in the heart of Boston. The interior boasts polished hardwood floors and several distinctive touches, including original Tiffany glass windows. Guests have use of the bay-windowed lobby lounge. All 35 rooms feature modern bath, cable TV, and telephone (no charge for local calls). Rates include continental breakfast, which is served in the large dining room. For added convenience, reduced-rate parking is provided behind the house. ♦ 261 Newbury St (between Fairfield and Gloucester Sts). 437.7666

67 Frontier Owner Mimi Packman has a knack for rounding up resonant retro artifacts, often adapting them to brave new uses. Old upholstery fabrics become charming dresses and jackets, vintage tablecloths, and comfy pillows. The stock is always evolving, but the white picket fence out front is a reliable sign of what you'll find inside. ♦ Tu-Sa. 252 Newbury St (between Fairfield and Gloucester Sts). 421.9858

68 Ciao bella ★★$$ Convivial singles like to lunch at the bar, looking out at Newbury Street. In the evening the dressy dining room draws a chic clientele. Choose from the appealing selection of appetizers, like *involtini di melanzani* (stuffed eggplant), then turn to pasta or a simple meat dish like the *cotoletta di vitello* (veal cutlet). Dine alfresco on the patio in nice weather. There's valet parking. ♦ Italian ♦ Daily lunch and dinner. Reservations recommended F-Su. 240A Newbury St (at Fairfield St). 536.2626

69 Eastern Accent Table- and desktop items, most imported from Japan, are displayed against a vivid chartreuse backdrop. Lovely glass pens, surrealist cutlery, cast-iron and concrete clocks, artful bowls and teapots, clever jewelry, and textured writing papers reflect the store's motto, "living with design," and the Japanese precept that the functional should be well made. Pieces are crafted of such straightforward materials as stainless steel, celluloid, Bakelite, natural porcelains, silk, and anodized aluminum. ♦ M-Sa. 237 Newbury St (between Exeter and Fairfield Sts). 266.9707

70 Vose Galleries of Boston Now under the direction of the fifth generation of Voses, this gallery, established in 1841, is the oldest continuously run art gallery in America. More than 30,000 paintings have passed through here since 1896. The family specializes in 18th-, 19th-, and early 20th-century American painting, and they've sold works to nearly every major American museum. They frequently show paintings by artists of the Hudson River School and the Boston School, as well as Luminists and American Impressionists (including Childe Hassam and John Henry Twachtman). At the turn of the century a Vose again returned from France with a full-length male nude by Géricault. High-minded Seth Vose decided to cut off the improper lower portion and sold the torso to the wife of the **Museum of Fine Arts'** president. Fifty years later Vose's descendants came upon the unseemly portion in their basement and gave it to the **MFA,** where it was joined to the previously donated upper portion, thus making the poor man whole again. ♦ M-Sa. 238 Newbury St (between Exeter and Fairfield Sts). 536.6176

71 Emporio Armani Obviously no longer a fashion backwater, Boston has earned a third outpost of the infamous designer's coterie of stores. (The others are **Giorgio Armani** at 22 Newbury Street and **Armani A/X** at **Copley Place**.) This one claims 24,500 square feet in the rehabbed **United Business Services** office building. ♦ Daily. 210-212 Newbury St (between Exeter and Fairfield Sts). 262.7300 ₺

71 Armani Express ★★★$$$$ This elegant restaurant is, as you might expect from the shrewd Giorgio, purely upscale Italian. The *ambiente* is impeccable: soft-toned woods, cream-and-yellow walls, pastel linens. Goose prosciutto and tuna carpaccio are but two of the sumptuous antipasti featured here. Other popular dishes include *ravioli d'arigosta al marsala* (filled with lobster and ricotta cheese and sautéed in a Marsala, fresh tomato, and basil sauce), *agnolotti d'anatra al pomodori secchi* (homemade ravioli with confit of duck meat, sautéed with sun-dried tomatoes, white wine, and parmesan cheese), and *linguine alle cozze e vongole* (with clams and black mussels in a garlic, olive oil, red chili, white wine, and fresh tomato sauce). For dessert, try the *sacripantina*—a sweet, crispy tart filled with frangipane cream and strawberries. There's a bustling cafe under the same name downstairs. ♦ Italian ♦ Daily lunch and dinner. Reservations required; jacket and tie required.

214 Newbury St (between Exeter and Fairfield Sts). 437.0909 ♿

72 Exeter Street Theatre Building This Victorian gem of granite and brownstone, the 1884 work of **H.W. Hartwell** and **W.C. Richardson,** was built as a temple for the Working Union of Progressive Spiritualists. It had a long run as a repertory movie theater, and then was converted to impressive retail space (see below). A greenhouse extension was appended to its street level during a 1975 renovation by **CBT/Childs Bertman Tseckares Casendinon;** this addition is now the site of **Friday's** (266.9040), a popular branch of the chain of casual eateries/singles bars. ♦ 26 Exeter St (at Newbury St)

Within the Exeter Street Theatre Building:

Waterstone's Booksellers One of the most civilized enclaves on Newbury Street, this British shop offers three roomy floors filled with well-stocked bookshelves to satisfy myriad interests; there's even a reading area on the third floor so you can skim before buying. The store's highly regarded authors' reading series—several events a week—attracts stellar talents, and the free quarterly newsletter, *Voices,* is at once witty and pithy. ♦ Daily. 859.7300. Also at: Faneuil Hall Marketplace, Quincy Market. 589.0930

73 Stephanie's on Newbury ★★$$$ A favorite of local foodies, this cafe/food shop/bakery is a light-filled space with green marble-topped tables, a bar, and a conversation area next to full-length windowed doors that in warm weather open onto a large sidewalk seating area. In the rear are another two dining rooms, both decorated in pleasant earth tones and offering a rustic European ambience. Specialties include chicken potpie, meat loaf, duck with mushroom risotto, and smoked salmon. A hardwood grill is used for pizza and other dishes. ♦ Cafe ♦ Daily breakfast, lunch, and dinner. Reservations recommended for dinner. 190 Newbury St (between Dartmouth and Exeter Sts). 236.0990

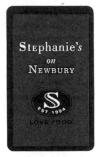

74 Nielsen Gallery Nina Nielsen has run this gallery for more than three decades, and exhibits contemporary works by Joan Snyder, Jake Berthot, Harvey Quaytman, Jane Smaldone, and Porfirio DiDonna. Not a trend-chaser, Nielsen looks for artists—many young, awaiting their first break—whose work expresses highly personal, often spiritual, viewpoints. She also shows work by such famous 20th-century artists as Jackson Pollock and David Smith. Nielsen likes what she likes and has many clients who feel the same way. She doesn't shy away from making one of her biggest interests—the continuum of spiritual substance in art—apparent. Says Nielsen about purchasing art: "Buy for love after talking to knowledgeable people." ♦ Tu-Sa. 179 Newbury St (between Dartmouth and Exeter Sts). 266.4835 ♿ (with advance notice)

MARCOZ

74 Marcoz Something splendid always graces the show windows here. The two handsomely preserved floors of a Victorian town house make a divine setting for furniture and decorative items from the 18th to the early 20th centuries. The hard-to-find accent pieces are imported from England or France, or purchased from New England estates. Knowledgeable and friendly, Mr. Marcoz will tell you all about whatever strikes your fancy, be it the 17th-century Madonna and Child processional figures, a 19th-century French *boule de petarque* (boccie-style ball), exquisite engravings, ivorine and sterling-silver napkin rings, a desktop inkwell, a pocket watch, or other singular finds. ♦ M-Sa. 177 Newbury St (between Dartmouth and Exeter Sts). 262.0780

74 The Society of Arts and Crafts Stop in here for a special handmade, one-of-a-kind something or other. The oldest nonprofit craft association in America, operating since 1897, the society promotes established and up-and-coming artisans by putting their wares before the public. All work is selected by jury; merchandise includes jewelry, ceramics, glass, quilts, woven items, wood and leather pieces, collages, clothing, accessories, and furniture (always especially noteworthy). Themed exhibitions are held on the second floor. ♦ Daily. 175 Newbury St (between Dartmouth and Exeter Sts). 266.1810. Also at: 101 Arch St (at Bussey Pl). 345.0033

74 Pucker Gallery More than 25 years in the business, this gallery displays local and international contemporary artists' graphics, paintings, sculptures, and porcelains. It also carries modern masters such as Chagall, Picasso, and Hundertwasser. Israeli art is a gallery specialty; works by Samuel Bak and David Sharir and others are shown. ♦ M-Sa. 171 Newbury St (between Dartmouth and Exeter Sts). 267.9473

75 La Ruche The perfect source for whimsical house gifts, this shop owned by Maria Church and Apple Bartlett (the daughter of legendary designer Sister Parrish), is best known for trompe l'oeil and painted furniture and lampshades, as well as Italian and French faience. They also carry flora- and fauna-shaped mugs, teapots, and jars; lovely French ribbon; garden ornaments; unusual glasses; linens; lamps; tapestry pillows; and other decorative wares. Potpourri scents the air. ♦ M-Sa. 168 Newbury St (between Dartmouth and Exeter Sts). 536.6366

76 Kitchen Arts At this wonderful resource for cooks, both expert and far-from, you can pick up any kitchen tool your culinary sleight-of-hand requires. The emphasis here is on performance, not pretty-to-look-at gifts. These wares are ready to go to work immediately—slicing, dicing, decorating, coring, chopping, cracking, grinding, and so on. Kitchen cutlery and knife sharpening are subspecialties. ♦ Daily. 161 Newbury St (between Dartmouth and Exeter Sts). 266.8701

76 Du Barry $$ Don't expect French cooking worthy of accolades here. Nonetheless, the quiet, old-fashioned restaurant, family-owned and -operated since 1936, is a Back Bay landmark. Locals are loyal to this place, and it attracts its share of both students and celebrities. The owners are French, and their son is responsible for the classical and provincial cuisine. Dining out back on the terrace is pleasant during the warm-weather months. Be sure to peruse Josh Winer's amusing Second Empire–style faux-facade mural along the side of the 19th-century building, which features a roster of nobs local and far-fetched (everyone from Paul Revere to Babe Ruth puts in an appearance). When you give up guessing who's who, check the bronze plaque key that's attached to the fence near the adjacent parking lot entrance. ♦ French ♦ M-Sa lunch and dinner; Su dinner; closed Sunday July–mid-September. Reservations recommended for parties of four or more. 159 Newbury St (between Dartmouth and Exeter Sts). 262.2445 &

77 The Copley Society of Boston The oldest art association in America, this nonprofit society was founded in 1879 to promote access to art, particularly new European trends, and to exhibit the work of its members and other artists of the day. Members John Singer Sargent and James McNeill Whistler showed their work in galleries run by the society. In 1905 the organization mounted Claude Monet's first American exhibition, a controversial event, and in 1913 Marcel Duchamp's *Nude Descending a Staircase* was shown here, creating an enormous furor. Today the society has more than 800 committee-selected members from around the world, though most are New Englanders. It operates two floors of galleries, with individual artists renting space upstairs and an ongoing members' show downstairs. The society has become somewhat mired in tradition, although recently it has focused more attention on contemporary work. Though the shows are

uneven in quality, works by noted and rising artists are often on view, so the galleries here are worth investigating. ♦ Tu-Su. 158 Newbury St (between Dartmouth and Exeter Sts). 536.5049

77 Boston Art Club This artful 1881 assemblage is the work of Ralph Waldo Emerson's clever nephew, **William Ralph Emerson,** also creator of the fascinating **House of Odd Windows** on Beacon Hill. Emerson let loose his entire artillery of architectural forms and ornament on the Queen Anne–style facade: From every angle, there's something peculiar or interesting to see. An alternative high school now occupies the building. ♦ 270 Dartmouth St (at Newbury St)

78 Papa Razzi ★★$$ This inviting, busy Italian trattoria, complete with a wood-burning pizza oven, has a menu that leans toward rustic Northern Italian dishes with California overtones. Chef Tim Conway's hearty fare includes an array of splendid crispy-crust pizzas, polenta with grilled Italian sausages, and bountiful antipasti and pastas. ♦ Italian ♦ Daily lunch and dinner. 271 Dartmouth St (between Boylston and Newbury Sts). 536.9200

79 GBS Geoffrey B. Small is one determined designer. Having launched his business from his mother's suburban attic with some strategic—and costly—full-page ads in *Vogue*, he made the leap to Newbury Street. He turns out "bespoke" clothing for men and women: custom-made with the help of several computer-aided fittings. For true individualists, it's the only way to go. ♦ By appointment only. 129 Newbury St (between Clarendon and Dartmouth Sts). 536.6393 &

79 Autrefois Antiques The name means "yesteryear" in French, and 18th- and 19th-century France is captured here in fine imported hardwood furnishings such as armoires, tables, chairs, chandeliers, and mirrors. Other epochs and places of origin also slip in, with the biggest shipments of new merchandise arriving in the spring and fall. The expert owners, Charles and Maria Rowe, will do on-site restoration and adapt old furnishings for modern needs. Updating lighting is their specialty. ♦ M-Sa. 125 Newbury St (between Clarendon and Dartmouth Sts). 424.8823 & Also at: 130 Harvard St (between Harvard Ave and Auburn St), Brookline. 566.0113

SERENELLA

80 Serenella Women come to this small, friendly boutique to invest in luxurious, classic, timeless clothes that will serve them well for years. The emphasis is on European designer daytime wear, with some accessories and shoes. Owner Ines Capelli does all the buying, and is always on the lookout for styles that are just right for her regular customers. ♦ M-Sa. 134 Newbury St (between Clarendon and Dartmouth Sts). 262.5568 &

riccarDi

80 Riccardi The latest exemplars of European fashion rendezvous here. All of the clothing, for men and women, is made in Italy, but designs and influences come from throughout Europe. Even the store's facade looks Italian. Designers include Ann Demeulemeester (Belgium), Comme des Garçons (Japan), and Dolce e Gabbana and Romeo Gigli (Italy). The shoes and accessories are multinational, too. An entire department is devoted to sporting wear. The staff is always up-to-date and informative on fashions. This is one of Boston's most worldly shops; they even accept JCB, the Japanese credit card. ♦ M-Sa. 128 Newbury St (between Clarendon and Dartmouth Sts). 266.3158

81 Bargain Box Many a discarded treasure is discovered at this high-quality thrift shop. It's run by the Junior League of Boston, Inc., a nonprofit women's organization dedicated to promoting community volunteerism. ♦ M-Sa. 117 Newbury St (between Clarendon and Dartmouth Sts). 536.8580

81 Cuoio For women only, this store showcases fashionable boots and shoes (the name means "leather" in Italian), many imported from Italy, and such accessories as jewelry, hats, and fabulous hair ornaments. Many of these smart styles aren't available elsewhere in the city. ♦ Daily. 115 Newbury St (between Clarendon and Dartmouth Sts). 859.0636 & Also at: Faneuil Hall Marketplace, South Market. 742.4486

82 Rebecca's Cafe ★$ Everything is made fresh daily at this gourmet take-out place. Lines form all day long for homemade muffins and scones, fresh salads, hot entrée specials, and the spectacular desserts and pastries that this cafe's progenitor in Beacon Hill made famous. The chocolate-mousse cake and the fresh-fruit tarts are pure pleasure. There are a few tables at the back. ♦ Cafe/Takeout ♦ Daily breakfast, lunch, and dinner. No credit cards accepted. 112 Newbury St (between Clarendon and Dartmouth Sts). 267.1122

83 David L. O'Neal Antiquarian Booksellers, Inc. Specializing in antiquarian books for more than 25 years, this shop focuses on fine and rare books from the 15th century to the present, including first editions in literature, many with superior bindings or leatherbound in sets. A large number of the works sold here have remarkable printing, typography, and illustrations. Original, historical, and decorative American and European prints from the 16th to the 19th century are also available. First-edition Jane Austen works; Nathaniel Bowditch's wonderful navigation book; James Fenimore Cooper's rare, anonymous first novel; Cotton Mather's *Psalter;* and Shelley's *Prometheus Unbound* represent a mere sampling of what many come to covet. An illustrated catalog of current offerings is available. ♦ M-Sa; appointments are encouraged. 234 Clarendon St (between Newbury St and Commonwealth Ave). 266.5790 &

83 ökw Irene Kerzner and Henry Wong (the "o" in **ökw,** pronounced *oh*-koo, is the initial of a departed partner) are the designers of choice for prominent businesswomen and socialites too distinctive to buy off the rack. Their creations are compellingly playful yet impeccably crafted of opulent fabrics. ♦ By appointment. 234 Clarendon St (between Newbury St and Commonwealth Ave). 266.4114 &

84 Trinity Church Rectory The massive arched entry bellows the name of the 1879 rectory's masterful architect, **Henry Hobson Richardson,** who designed its parent **Trinity Church** at Copley Square. The building is now on the National Register of Historic Places; look at its surface, vigorously alive with twisting flowers and ornament. A third story was, unfortunately, added by **HHR**'s successor firm after his death. ♦ 233 Clarendon St (between Newbury St and Commonwealth Ave)

85 New England Historic Genealogical Society Many an aspirant to the lofty branches of some illustrious Yankee family tree has zeroed in on this private, nonprofit research library, the oldest of its kind in the nation and the first in the world. The mission: to plumb the past, to root out those roots.

Housed in a former bank and founded in 1845, the society now holds 200,000 volumes and more than a million manuscripts dating as far back as the 17th century. The organization's dedication to the study and preservation of family history has resulted in records and histories for all US states and Canadian provinces, plus Europe. There's no better place to try to entangle one's heritage with that of the Adamses, the Cabots, the Randolphs, and other American Olympians. There are more than 13,000 members with access to the archives. Visitors pay a half- or full-day research fee. ♦ Tu; W-Th until 9PM; F-Sa. 101 Newbury St (between Berkeley and Clarendon Sts). 536.5740

85 John Lewis, Inc. Wave upon wave of silver strands swinging in the window lure passersby into this serene 1876 brownstone, where veteran Newbury Street proprietors John and Louise Lewis design jewelry. Working with solid precious metals and natural stones, the couple turns out a glittering array of imaginative designs. Some are simple marriages of rich materials and careful artisanship. Others are more intricate, such as the Lewis's line of Victorian-inspired jewelry embellished with cherubim, scrolls, flowers, and bows. ♦ Tu-Sa. 97 Newbury St (between Berkeley and Clarendon Sts). 266.6665 &

85 Kakas This over-a-century-old furrier ("five generations of recognized integrity") gained some unwelcome notoriety when it was learned that erstwhile manager Charles Stuart used its safe to store the gun with which he shot his wife. It's still considered the source of the finest—and costliest—fur coats in the city. ♦ M-F. 93 Newbury St (between Berkeley and Clarendon Sts). 536.1858 &

85 Haley & Steele It's fun to rifle—gingerly, of course—through the flat files crowded with prints of all kinds. The gallery focuses on 18th- and 19th-century prints in scores of categories, including botanical, sporting, architectural, military, New England maritime, birds, historical, and genre. You're sure to find a print here that will add the proper accent to your decor. The custom-frame shop specializes in painting conservation and French line matting, and has served local artists since 1899. ♦ M-Sa. 91 Newbury St (between Berkeley and Clarendon Sts). 536.6339 &

86 Martini Carl The Ventola family's boutique stocks sophisticated European apparel for men and women ranging from very casual to very dressy, with all the requisite accessories. The designer and private labels emphasize rich fabrics and leathers, superb tailoring, and enduring styles. ♦ M-Sa. 77 Newbury St (between Berkeley and Clarendon Sts). 247.0441 &

87 Church of the Covenant R.M. Upjohn designed this 1867 Gothic Revival treasure house, which is on the National Registry of Historic Places. The steeple, which Oliver Wendell Holmes said "to my eyes seems absolutely perfect," to many resembles the famed spire at England's Salisbury Cathedral. Within the church is the largest collection of work in the world by stained-glass master Tiffany, including 43 windows, some 30 feet high, and clerestories. Especially noteworthy is the sanctuary lantern with seven angels, originally wired for electricity by Thomas Edison. It was designed by Tiffany's firm for the Tiffany Chapel exhibited at the World's Columbian Exposition of 1893 in Chicago, then installed here. Also look for the Welte-Tripp pipe organ, a five-keyboard, manual, 4,500-pipe instrument, completed in 1929 as the last installation of that renowned German firm, and unique in Boston as a surviving example of and a testament to the firm's orchestral pipe building and voicing.

The Presbyterian church has a long history of giving generously to the community; the well-known **Women's Lunch Place** is resident in the basement. The church also founded the **Back Bay Chorale** and the **Boston Pro Arte Chamber Orchestra,** which perform regularly here and at **Harvard University.** ♦ M-Th 10AM-1PM, subject to staff availability. 67 Newbury St (at Berkeley St). 266.7480 &

Built on filled land (as was all of Back Bay), Trinity Church was constructed on a foundation of four massive granite pyramids with 35-foot square bases. Below these is a subterranean safety net of 4,502 wooden pilings. Carefully monitored since its construction in 1877, the foundation held firm until the early 1970s when the adjacent John Hancock Tower was begun. The Hancock construction damaged Trinity, a National Historic Landmark, actually twisting the church and cracking parts of its foundation, walls, some precious stained glass, and a La Farge mural. Trinity sued John Hancock for $4 million in 1975, and when the case was finally settled in 1987, the church received $11.6 million—the damage award plus 12 years of interest.

Romantic Retreats

For a city that's briskly businesslike, Boston has hidden charms that deserve slower savoring. While everyone else goes about their appointed rounds, you and your loved one can meander at a private pace, enjoying your own sweet *folie à deux.*

Many of Boston's better hotels offer specially priced weekend packages, with amenities ranging from Champagne and roses to spa privileges and limo service. The sexiest—simply because it's French—is **Le Meridien** (250 Franklin St, between Oliver and Pearl Sts, 451.1900, 800/543.4300), with stunning modern decor superimposed on a venerable old bank building. In its ornate but cozy bar, brass torchères cast a golden glow, and two splendid N.C. Wyeth murals lend a timeless air; the restaurant, **Julien,** offers outstanding French fare, luxurious service, and a degree of intimacy not matched elsewhere, thanks to comfy, encompassing armchairs. The area tends to shut down at night (all the better for focusing on each other), but by day it is convenient to **Beacon Hill,** the **North End, Fort Point Channel,** and the **Leather District.**

Traditionalism has its piquancy, too, and if that's more your style, try the **Ritz-Carlton Hotel** (15 Arlington St, between Newbury St and Commonwealth Ave, 536.5700, 800/241.3333), a bastion for Boston's old guard. Ask for a room overlooking the **Public Garden,** and with any luck you'll get a Childe Hassam–like landscape suffused with slanting light. The bar is a cosseting world unto itself, but the elegant dining room, alas, lacks culinary verve. Instead, head outside to explore. The **Library Grill** at the **Hampshire House** (84 Beacon St, at Brimmer St, 227.9600), which also overlooks the **Public Garden,** is a romantic choice in a 19th-century Beacon Hill town house. Another good choice for a romantic dinner for two is the **Top of the Hub** restaurant on the 52nd floor of the **Prudential Tower** (Boylston St, between Exeter and Dalton Sts, 536.1775), which offers splendid views over **Back Bay** and the **Charles River.** After a night at the **Ritz,** browse the **Newbury Street** shops and galleries or take in a concert at the **Isabella Stewart Gardner Museum** (280 The Fenway, at Palace Rd, 566.1401), always an indulgence for the senses.

Cambridge attracts couples intent on reliving—or prolonging—their youth. **The Charles Hotel** (1 Bennett St, between Eliot St and University Rd, 864.1200, 800/882.1818) draws on the bustle of **Harvard Square,** while keeping just enough distance. It's calm, pampering, and pretty, with patchwork quilts on the pine beds and a premier jazz club, the **Regattabar.** Street performers in Harvard Square range from balladeers to an oldies-by-request player piano, and the many cafes and bookstores (for love sonnets, search out **The Grolier Poetry Book Shop,** 6 Plympton St, between Bow St and Massachusetts Ave, 547.4648) are perfect for peaceful sojourns.

And don't forget, one of the area's most romantic pleasures is also one of its simplest—a stroll along the bank of the **Charles River,** hand in hand.

Within the Church of the Covenant:

Gallery NAGA Director Arthur Dion mounts interesting exhibitions of contemporary painting, sculpture, photography, and prints by the known and unknown. He likes to bridge the division between fine art and craft, and shows furniture and glass. Exhibits have included the work of Henry Schwartz, James Gemmill, and Irene Valincius, and furniture designers such as Tom Loesser and Judy McKie. The gallery occupies a generous swatch—1,400 square feet—in the church, whose progressive congregation has given art a boost by making a long-term space commitment to the gallery. ♦ Tu-Sa mid-July–Labor Day by appointment only. 267.9060

"The Pledge of Allegiance" was written by Francis Bellamy, who lived at 142 Berkeley Street (now known as "The Pledge of Allegiance House").

88 Louis, Boston Until the **New England Museum of Natural History** moved to its current site straddling the Charles River and changed its name to the **Boston Museum of Science,** it was jammed into this French Academic structure, designed in 1863 by **William G. Preston.** The museum was one of Back Bay's pioneers. When it vacated, part of the moving-day chaos included lowering a stuffed moose from an upper-story window, a scene captured in a photograph that the museum now prizes. **Bonwit Teller** then resided here for decades until this astronomically priced clothier took over in 1987 and gave the building a much-needed restoration.

Three floors are dedicated to men's apparel and one to women's—everything of exceptional quality. Also on the premises is the **Mario Russo** women's hair salon (424.6676). The building's splendid isolation makes it appear even more magnificent than it is. Inside, its spaciousness makes for enjoyable browsing. ♦ M-Sa. 234 Berkeley St (between Boylston and Newbury Sts). 262.6100 &

Within Louis, Boston:

Cafe Louis ★★$$ The clothier's cafe deserves a special visit. High-ceilinged and furnished with lacquered bamboo chairs and tapestry banquettes, this pleasant nook echoes the store's sunny palette, but in a warm butterscotch. It's possible to enter at the cafe's main entrance off the parking lot, but more fun to stroll through the store, past $1,000 sweaters and $200 scarves. The menu marries Italian and French flavors. Indulge in seductive pastries, smoked fish, or French toast ordered by the slice in the morning; antipasto for two or a sandwich handsomely composed and garnished for lunch; or a splendid slice of cake with tea in late afternoon. You can eat outdoors at tables on the cement landing, though the view of the parking lot and the **New England Life Building** across the way isn't exactly breathtaking. A small gourmet shop offers prepared and packaged treats of all kinds to go. The cafe's major flaw: It closes much too early. ♦ Cafe/Takeout ♦ M-Sa breakfast, lunch, and afternoon tea (dessert and takeout until 6PM). 266.4680 ⑤

89 **Alan Bilzerian** The dramatic clothes in this store's striking display windows need few props; they speak for themselves. A native of Worcester, Massachusetts, Bilzerian started out with a college student clientele more than two decades ago, then began selling to rock stars. Now his is the local name in fashion best known outside of Boston. In fact, New Yorkers with the fashion world at their feet still make special trips, and lots of celebrities drop in when in town—Cher and Mick Jagger among them. Featured are art-to-wear fashions, accessories, and shoes for men and women: the work of such European and Japanese designers as Yohji Yamamoto, Michele Klien, Issey Miyake, Katharine Hamnett, Rifat Ozbek, Jean Paul Gaultier, Azzedine Alaia, and Romeo Gigli, to name a few. Complementing the other collections are Bilzerian designs for men and designs for women by his wife, Bê. Of course, outlandishly stylish wear commands outlandishly high prices. ♦ Daily. 34 Newbury St (between Arlington and Berkeley Sts). 536.1001 ⑤ (The staff will carry wheelchairs up the stairs; once inside, there's an elevator to the second-floor women's department.)

90 **Milano's Italian Kitchen** ★$ Wood-fired oven specialties enjoy ever-widening popularity in Boston, and they are as good here as anywhere. Panini, pasta, salads, and the antipasto are also worth a try. Start with the polenta cup (a polenta shell filled with a ragout of vegetables covered with pesto sauce, and served with broccoli, peppers, and sun-dried tomatoes in a marinara sauce), or the popular *antipasti Milano* (genoa salami, prosciutto, mozzarella, and marinated mixed

vegetables drizzled with extra-virgin olive oil). Jugs of Chianti are placed on every table, and patrons are on the honor system to keep track of how many glasses they drink. ♦ Italian ♦ Daily lunch and dinner. 47 Newbury St (at Berkeley St). 267.6150

91 **Caffe Romano's Bakery & Sandwich Shop** ★★$ The Back Bay needs all the unpretentious, reliable spots it can get, and this small (40-seater), cafeteria-style eatery is one such place. It has won a dedicated clientele with its fragrant fresh muffins, bagels, Danish pastries, and croissants in the morning—the busiest time—and homemade soups, quiches, sandwiches, and tantalizing desserts later on. You can also get cappuccino and espresso. ♦ Cafe/Takeout ♦ Daily breakfast and lunch until 5PM. No credit cards accepted. 33 Newbury St (between Arlington and Berkeley Sts). 266.0770

91 **29 Newbury** ★★★$$ This perennially trendy bistro, a favorite with modeling, music, and media types, serves inventive cuisine that's considerably priced. Certain dishes sing, such as the wild mushroom ravioli in Madeira cream sauce, and even the burgers are prepared exactly as they should be. The semi-subterranean dining room also doubles as an art gallery, and deep-set booths ensure privacy. More sociable types crowd around the bar or, in good weather, spill onto the sidewalk patio. Sunday brunch earns raves. ♦ American ♦ M-Sa lunch and dinner; Su brunch and dinner. Reservations recommended. 29 Newbury St (between Arlington and Berkeley Sts). 536.0290

91 **Emmanuel Church** Its uninspired rural Gothic Revival architecture (an 1862 effort by **Alexander R. Estey**, enlarged by **Frederick R. Allen** in 1899 and pictured above) doesn't do justice to this Episcopal church's lively,

creative spirit. Dedicated since the 1970s to "a special ministry through art," the church organizes a variety of music and cultural events. A professionally performed Bach cantata accompanies the liturgy every Sunday from September through May. Jazz celebrations are held periodically. ♦ Su 10AM service. 15 Newbury St (between Arlington and Berkeley Sts). 536.3355 ♿ (A portable ramp is available with advance notice.)

Within Emmanuel Church:

Leslie Lindsey Memorial Chapel This 1924 Gothic chapel was commissioned by Mr. and Mrs. William Lindsey as a memorial to their daughter, Leslie, who with her new husband was bound for a European honeymoon on the ill-fated *Lusitania*. Some time after the boat sank, Leslie's body supposedly washed ashore in Ireland, still wearing her father's wedding gift of diamonds and rubies; they were sold to help pay for her memorial. The chapel is sometimes called the "Lady Chapel" for its marble carvings of female saints. It was designed by **Allen & Collens** already nationally renowned at the time for the Riverside Church in New York City.

92 **Charles Sumner** Great imported and American women's designer apparel by Donna Karan, Valentino, Louis Ferraud, Missoni, Akris, and others, plus shoes, handbags, makeup, hosiery, jewelry, gloves, and hats are all carried at this head-to-toe boutique. The enthusiastic salespeople try hard to work with customers and make them feel at home. ♦ M-Sa. 16 Newbury St (between Arlington and Berkeley Sts). 536.6225 ♿

92 **Alpha Gallery** The best free shows in town are often on display here. A family affair, the gallery is owned by Alan Fink, managed by his daughter Joanna, and often shows work by his wife Barbara Swan and son Aaron Fink—both of whom merit the attention. The gallery specializes in 20th-century and contemporary American and European painting, sculpture, and prints. The work of such distinguished artists as American painters Milton Avery, Bernard Chaet, and Fairfield Porter, and Europeans Mimmo Paladino and Georg Baselitz has been exhibited here. Other shows have featured Massachusetts realist Scott Prior and such gifted young artists as T. Wiley Carr. Over its 30-year history the gallery has mounted major exhibitions of work by John Marin, Max Beckman, and Stuart Davis as well as Picasso's complete *Vollard Suite*. ♦ Tu-Sa. 14 Newbury St (between Arlington and Berkeley Sts). 536.4465

For all of Back Bay's French influences, its street names are strictly British.

92 **Barbara Krakow Gallery** Don't pass by this fifth-floor gallery. (It's the one with the eye-catching marble bench carved with enigmatic messages by Jenny Holzer on the sidewalk out front.) After selling art for more than 30 years, it is perhaps Boston's most important art gallery, and it uses its prestige to benefit numerous worthy causes. Many of the most significant contemporary artists are shown here, among them Holzer, Agnes Martin, Cameron Shaw, Jim Dine, Donald Judd, and Michael Mazur. Despite the superstars on the walls, this is a very hospitable, unpretentious place, combining sure taste with a willingness to take risks—showing work created by high-school kids, fo example. ♦ Tu-Sa. 10 Newbury St (between Arlington and Berkeley Sts). 262.4490 ♿

Café de Paris

93 **Café de Paris** ★$ This is some kind of a fast-food joint, with velvet banquettes, burled paneling, and Art Deco sconces. The food is a cut above, too, ranging from croissants and omelettes to true Parisian pastries. Grab a booth or place an order to go and cross over to the **Public Garden** for breakfast in the park. ♦ French/Takeout ♦ Daily 7:30AM-9PM (7PM in winter). 19 Arlington St (at Newbury St). 247.7121

94 **Domain** It's fun to prowl through this mecca of home embellishments, a fantasy habitat for a menagerie of antique, traditional, and designer pieces, none commonplace or conventional. The aim here is to mass-market one-of-a-kind-looking furnishings. A multitude of quirky accessories crowd in among the beds, tables, and sofas. Textures, colors, patterns, and styles veer crazily in all directions. ♦ Daily (call for summer evening hours). 7 Newbury St (between Arlington and Berkeley Sts). 266.5252 ♿

94 **Ritz-Carlton Hotel** $$$$ The nationwide hotel chain's reputation for luxury, elegance, and superlative service is exquisitely exemplified at this, the oldest **Ritz-Carlton** in the country. Built in 1927 by **Strickland and Blodget,** and subtly expanded by **Skidmore, Owings & Merrill** in 1981, the hotel provides all the little niceties proper Bostonians love so well. The elevator attendants, for example, wear white gloves. The understated edifice perfectly expresses the fastidious courtesies and traditions of its inhabitant. There's nothing flashy or eye-catching about this building, except for its parade of vivid blue awnings, but it has become a timeless, steadfast fixture.

The 278 rooms and suites are simply and traditionally appointed in European style and offer safes, locking closets, and windows that open. The 41 suites have wood-burning fireplaces. Request a room with a view of the **Public Garden.** The hotel boasts a venerable dining room, a cafe, a lounge, and a bar (see below). There's also a small health club, and guests may use (at no charge) the fancy spa at **The Heritage** a block away. Other amenities include 24-hour room service, valet parking, same-day laundry service, a multilingual staff, baby-sitting, a concierge, a barber shop, and a shoe-shine stand. Rooms for nonsmokers and people with disabilities are available. Pets are allowed if they're leashed. ♦ 15 Arlington St (between Newbury St and Commonwealth Ave). 536.5700, 800/241.3333; fax 536.1335 &

Within the Ritz-Carlton Hotel:

The Dining Room ★★$$$$ New hub restaurants open every day—but there will never be another dining room like this. It's the hotel's showpiece, with cobalt-blue Venetian crystal chandeliers and matching table crystal, a gold-filigreed ceiling, regal drapery, and huge picture windows overlooking the **Public Garden.** There's no better place for wedding proposals, anniversaries, and other momentous occasions. Piano music and an occasional harpist add to the spell. Such timeless classics as rack of lamb and chateaubriand for two commune with a few more stylish offerings on the menu. But the chef introduces innovations very carefully; the old-guard patrons would rise up in arms if Boston cream pie and other old-time favorites were seriously challenged. Entrées low in sodium, cholesterol, and calories are available, as is a children's menu. Fashion shows are held here every Saturday, and chamber music accompanies the fabulous Sunday brunch. ♦ French ♦ M-Sa lunch and dinner; Su brunch and dinner. Reservations required; jacket and tie required. 536.5700 &

The Ritz Cafe ★★$$$ With its views of Newbury Street, quiet vanilla decor, and cordial service, this cafe offers respite during a hectic day. When you've had it with the world, come for a restorative touch of civility. Since you can't see the **Public Garden** from here, it has been reproduced in a mural. On weekday mornings, many of Boston's business heavy-hitters breakfast here. At night the cafe caters to the after-theater crowd. Children may order from a special menu. ♦ American ♦ Daily breakfast, lunch, and dinner. Reservations recommended at lunch; jacket and tie required evenings; no denim allowed. 536.5700 &

The Ritz Lounge ★★★$$ Perch in a high-backed chair in this soothing second-floor drawing room as a harpist plays and you sip your way through afternoon tea and its accompanying dainty delights (see "Boston Tea Parties" on page 40). This is also a lovely spot for evening drinks. ♦ Lounge ♦ Daily. Jacket suggested; no denim or running shoes allowed. 536.5700 &

The Ritz Bar ★★★$$ On a snowy evening, the gorgeous view of the **Public Garden** from this cozy street-level bar is right out of a storybook. Inside, there's no entertainment, just plenty of welcome serenity and a crackling fire burning in the hearth. A selection of soups, club sandwiches, pasta dishes, and salads is served at lunch. The bar is famous for its perfect martinis; ask for the special martini menu, which featured 16 varieties at last count, including the "James Bond." Boston mystery writer Robert B. Parker's fictional sleuth Spenser has quaffed many a beer here. ♦ American ♦ M-Sa lunch. Bar: M-Sa 11:30AM-1AM; Su noon-midnight. Jacket requested. 536.5700 &

Bests

Patrick Carrier
President, The Globe Corner Bookstores

Boston's **Freedom Trail** remains the best way to soak up Boston's history and appreciate how uniquely pedestrian-friendly the city is. The ubiquitous trolley tours, while offering good entertainment, should not serve as a substitute for actually visiting important Revolutionary-era sites like the **Old State House,** the **Old South Meeting House, Paul Revere's House,** and the **Old North Church.**

While walking the **Freedom Trail,** plan on lunch at **Maison Robert**'s outdoor terrace cafe on **School Street** (one of the best outdoor dining experiences in the city and an excellent value) or an early dinner at **Pomodoro,** a trattoria in the **North End** near the **Old North Church.**

Strolling the length of **Newbury Street** on a nice spring, summer, or fall day is one of the great window-shopping and people-gazing experiences in the city. Lunch or dinner at **Ciao bella** offers excellent Italian cuisine along with one of the best perches to view the promenaders on Newbury Street.

The street scene on any weekend evening in **Harvard Square** remains a unique American experience—great, free street music and entertainment; cutting edge, "non-mall" retailing (although that's changing); and food choices for all palates and budgets.

Slightly off-the-beaten track for geography lovers is the *Mapparium* at the **Christian Science Publishing Society**—a magnificent 30-foot in diameter stained-glass globe which visitors walk through on a glass bridge.

For book lovers, two often overlooked sites: the **Library** of **The Boston Athenaeum,** which is one of the oldest private libraries in the country and of interest both architecturally and bibliographically; and the **Brattle Book Shop,** one of the oldest used and antiquarian bookstores in the country.

In 1913, the nation's first credit union was opened by Boston's Women's Educational and Industrial Union.

Kenmore Square/Fenway

This section of Boston befuddles even Bostonians, who regularly scramble references to **Fenway Park** (the famous baseball stadium), **The Fenway** (a parkway), the **Fens** (part of the park system designed by Frederick Law Olmsted), and Fenway, the district containing all three. Kenmore Square is also a section of Fenway; it encompasses **Longwood Medical Area**, a dense complex of world-renowned medical and educational establishments that includes **Harvard Medical School**. A student mecca, Kenmore Square is practically a city unto itself. Unlike Beacon Hill or Back Bay, the Fenway lacks a cohesive personality, and its indeterminate boundaries are a constant source of confusion to visitors and residents alike. But it's worth navigating the helter-skelter neighborhood to explore its attractions: the **Museum of Fine Arts**, **Isabella Stewart Gardner Museum**, **Symphony Hall**, Olmsted's famous **Emerald Necklace**, and, of course, **Fenway Park**, home of the **Red Sox**.

Fenway was the last Boston neighborhood built on landfill, and only emerged after the noxious **Back Bay Fens** was imaginatively rehabilitated by Olmsted. Like the original Back Bay, whose stagnant tidal flats metamorphosed into the

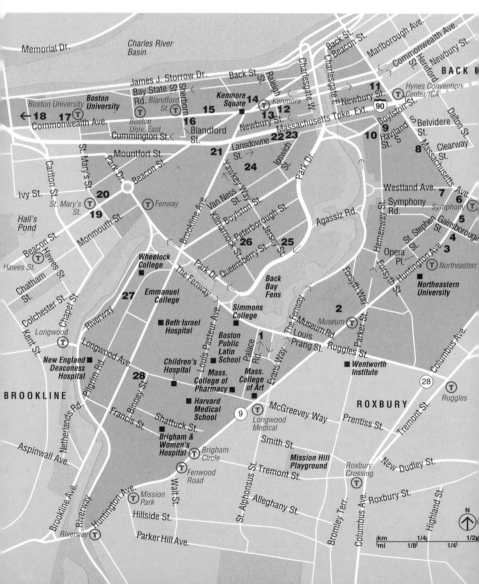

city's most fashionable neighborhood, the Back Bay Fens was considered an unusable part of town, a stinking, swampy mess that collected sewage and runoff from the **Muddy River** and **Stony Brook** before draining into the **Charles River**. The problem worsened after Back Bay was filled in and the Fens' unsanitary state became a concern for the city. A group of commissioners assembled to address its drainage problems and to simultaneously develop a park system for Boston, an idea that gained momentum in the 1870s. Co-creator of New York City's Central Park and founder of the landscape-architecture profession in America, Olmsted was called in as consultant and ultimately hired in 1878 to fix the Fens and create the Boston Park System. His ingenious solution involved installing a tidal gate and holding basin, and using mud dredged from the refreshed Fens to create surrounding parkland. Developers quickly recognized the neighborhood's new appeal, and it was "Westward-ho!" once again for overcrowded Boston.

The transformed Fens became the first link in Olmsted's **Emerald Necklace**, the most important feature in the Boston Park Department's plan for a city-scaled network of green space, and the first of its kind in the nation. Instead of a New York–style central park (inappropriate given Boston's topography), Boston wanted a system of open spaces throughout the city, offering breathing room to residents. Olmsted envisioned interconnected parks, recreation grounds, boulevards, and parkways that would not only beautify the environment and enhance public health and sanitation, but also direct urban expansion, population density, and the local economy. Boston and Olmsted were ideally matched: City officials appreciated not only his talents and civic-mindedness, but also his interest in solving practical problems through landscape design.

Olmsted's plan succeeded, as numerous cultural, medical, educational, and social institutions began relocating to the Fenway area. Boston's devastating downtown fire of 1872 and advances in public transportation also encouraged many to move. During the 1890s and early 1900s the **Massachusetts Historical Society, Symphony Hall, New England Conservatory of Music, Simmons College, Museum of Fine Arts**, and **Harvard Medical School** were built. Another neighborhood pioneer was **Fenway Court**, the fashionable residence where Isabella Stewart Gardner installed the magnificent personal museum of art that now bears her name. Since then, other institutions have followed the same trail; **Northeastern University** and **Boston University** now dominate the district. Fenway's resident educational and medical institutions have played the largest role in shaping its contemporary character. Today, the Kenmore Square/Fenway area claims a huge concentration of college students and young adults. It has the lowest median age of all Boston neighborhoods and a transient feel. Originally an extension of prestigious Back Bay, with fine hotels, offices, and shops, Kenmore Square is now largely geared toward its student population, with plenty of fast-food joints and cheap-eats delis, good ethnic restaurants, clubs, music shops, and the like.

---

1 Isabella Stewart Gardner Museum
On New Year's Day 1903 Isabella Stewart Gardner held a glorious gala-to-end-all-galas to unveil her private art collection in its opulent new **Fenway Court** home (pictured on page 148). No one could pass up this event, including those who typically snubbed flamboyant Isabella. Fifty **Boston Symphony** musicians played a Bach chorale, and when the crowd caught sight of the now-famous flower-filled palace **Courtyard**, a collective gasp was followed by awed silence. Admirers and detractors alike were wowed by Gardner's resplendent array of paintings, sculpture, tapestries, and objets d'art, all displayed in such a dazzling setting. An admiring Henry Adams wrote: "As long as such a work can be done, I will not despair of our age . . . You are a creator and stand alone." Gardner herself described her home, after 20 years of

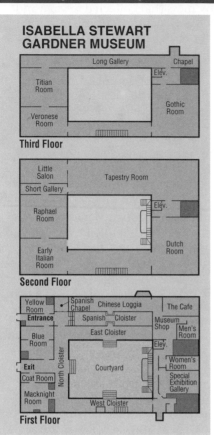

ISABELLA STEWART GARDNER MUSEUM

Third Floor

Long Gallery — Chapel — Elev. — Titian Room — Gothic Room — Veronese Room

Second Floor

Little Salon — Tapestry Room — Short Gallery — Elev. — Raphael Room — Early Italian Room — Dutch Room

First Floor

Yellow Room — Spanish Chapel — Chinese Loggia — The Cafe — Entrance — Spanish Cloister — Museum Shop — Men's Room — Blue Room — East Cloister — Elev. — North Cloister — Courtyard — Women's Room — Exit — Coat Room — Special Exhibition Gallery — Macknight Room — West Cloister

residence, as "very nice, very comfortable, and rather jolly."

In keeping with Gardner's wishes, after her death in 1924 the mansion became a museum (see floor plan above). Her will, however, stipulates very demanding terms for the museum's operation: Everything has to remain *exactly* as it was upon her death, or else everything will be sold and the proceeds given to **Harvard University.** This accounts for the hodgepodge manner in which the works of art are displayed here—Gardner's preferences have been preserved into perpetuity. Until recently the museum director lived rent-free in Gardner's own lush apartment; the most liberal reinterpretation of her will to date was to transform these fourth-floor living quarters into office space, a controversial move. More recently, a tiny new gallery (17 by 22 feet) was reclaimed from storage space and deemed a "reasonable deviation" from the will. Museum curators have also initiated an artists-in-residence program to perpetuate Gardner's own predilections as a patron of the arts.

For countless Bostonians and visitors, Gardner's museum has no equal, and many return again and again for another heady dose of her compelling creation. The museum's appeal is in the total impression it creates. In a

series of singular stage-set galleries—the **Veronese Room, Gothic Room, Dutch Room, Titian Room**—works by Botticelli, Manet, Raphael, Rembrandt, Rubens, Matisse, Sargent, Titian, La Farge, and Whistler line the walls. Nearly 2,000 objects are on display, spanning more than 30 centuries, with emphasis on Italian Renaissance and 17th-century Dutch masters. Objects from different periods and cultures are liberally intermixed in the eclectic manner favored by the mistress of the mansion.

With its soft natural light, cloudy pink walls, picturesque balconies, quiet fountain, and fragrant fresh flowers and plantings supplied by the museum's own greenhouse, the four-story skylighted interior **Courtyard** is one of Boston's most serene and beloved places. It features authentic architectural and decorative elements collected by Gardner throughout Europe and Egypt. Of note, too, is the **Tapestry Room,** where classical music concerts are held on Saturday and Sunday from September through April. Also worth perusing is the **Blue Room,** which has a display of Gardner's correspondence with her distinguished friends—including John Singer Sargent, who twice painted her portrait, and the illustrious art historian Bernard Berenson, who advised her on what works to buy.

Despite the instructions so carefully outlined in Gardner's will, terrible empty spaces were created on the walls of her museum on 18 March 1990. Thirteen uninsured paintings and artifacts valued at $200 million were stolen by two thieves disguised as policemen in what the *Boston Herald* dubbed "the Heist of the Century." The most famous of the stolen works, *The Concert* by Jan Vermeer, cost Gardner $6,000 at an 1892 auction in Paris; it is now priceless. Also stolen were two Rembrandts—*The Storm on the Sea of Galilee* (his only known seascape) and *A Lady and Gentleman in Black.* The stolen paintings have not been recovered. In gentler times, Gardner often acted as her own security guard. Today the museum has a state-of-the-art security system and the entire collection is insured. (Also see "The House That Mrs. Jack Built" on page 148.) ♦ Admission; members and children under 12 free; reduced admission for senior citizens and students; additional fee for concerts. Tu-Su. Public guided tour Friday at 2:30PM. 280 The Fenway (at Palace Rd). 566.1401, recorded concert information 734.1359 ♿ (limited because of narrow spaces; museum provides wheelchairs that fit everywhere)

Within the Isabella Stewart Gardner Museum:

The Cafe at the Gardner ★★$$
Excellent lunches—quiches, salads, sandwiches, and desserts—are served at this cafe. One popular menu item is the smoked salmon club sandwich. Weather permitting,

dine on the outdoor terrace overlooking the museum gardens. ◆ Cafe ◆ Tu-Su lunch. 566.1088 &

2 Museum of Fine Arts (MFA) The first exhibitions under the auspices of this institution were displayed upstairs at the **Boston Athenaeum** on Beacon Hill; the works were moved in 1876 to the museum's ornate Gothic Revival Copley Square quarters, since demolished. In 1909 the museum made the trek out to the newly fashionable Fenway area, joining a number of pioneering public institutions seeking more spacious sites than Boston proper could offer. Here the museum has remained, housed in an imposing, if dull, Classical Revival edifice designed by **Guy Lowell** in 1909. The original structure, with a majestic colonnade on the Fenway side and a temple portico on the Huntington Avenue side, is now flanked by two big wings, the newest designed in 1981 by **I.M. Pei & Partners.** Standing in the front courtyard is a statue of a mounted Indian gazing skyward, appealing for aid against the white man's invasion. Cyrus Edwin Dallin's *Appeal to the Great White Spirit* won a gold medal at the 1909 Paris Salon and attracted many admirers when it was erected here in 1913, but today looks somewhat odd in this ordered setting.

The museum's somber starkness ends abruptly indoors, where an embarrassment of riches begins, much of it acquired through the generosity of wealthy Victorian Bostonians committed to creating a cosmopolitan cultural repository. It is one of the country's greatest museums and deserves repeated exploration (see floor plan on page 144). Begin with a dose of familiar sights and historic names and faces in the American collections. More than 60 works by John Singleton Copley, including his portrait of Paul Revere and his famous silver *Liberty Bowl,* and paintings by local boy Winslow Homer, Gilbert Stuart, Edward Hopper, John Singer Sargent, Fitz Hugh Lane, Mary Cassatt, James McNeill Whistler, and Thomas Eakins are permanently on exhibit here. Holdings range from native New England folk art and portraiture to works by the Hudson River School, American Impressionists, Realists, Ash Can School, and New York's Abstract Expressionists. The **Department of American Decorative Arts and Sculpture** is particularly noteworthy for its pre–Civil War New England items, and includes furniture, silver, pewter, glass, ceramics, sculpture, and folk art. The collection progresses from the rustic functional creations of early colonial times to the elegant pieces popular in the increasingly prosperous colonies. The **Department of Twentieth-Century Art** is a Johnny-come-lately, emphasized only since the 1970s, but includes works by Jackson Pollock, David Smith, Robert Motherwell, Helen Frankenthaler, Morris Louis, Joan Miró, and Georgia O'Keeffe.

The museum owns superb works from all major periods of European painting from the 11th to the 20th centuries, with a particularly rich representation of 19th-century French works. Victorian Bostonians loved French painting, eagerly exhibiting the Impressionists who were still awaiting acceptance in their own country. On display in the **Evans Wing** galleries are many of the museum's 38 Monets—considered the largest collection outside of France—and more than 150 Millets, including his best-known painting, *The Sower,* as well as works by Corot, Délacroix, Courbet, Renoir, Pissarro, Manet, Gauguin, and Cézanne. Other celebrated artists shown in this wing are van Gogh, van der Weyden, Il Rosso, El Greco, Rubens, Canaletto, Turner, and Picasso.

Museum of Fine Arts

MARJORIE VOGEL, RHODE ISLAND ORIGINALS

MUSEUM OF FINE ARTS

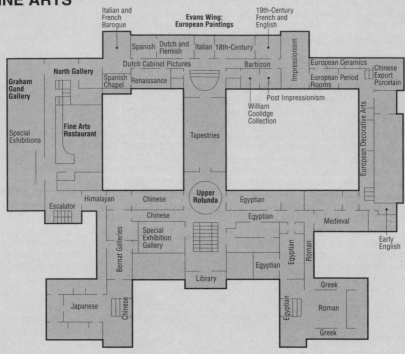

Second Floor

Graham Gund Gallery

Special Exhibitions

North Gallery

Fine Arts Restaurant

Escalator

Italian and French Baroque

Spanish — Dutch and Flemish — Italian — 18th-Century

Dutch Cabinet Pictures

Spanish Chapel — Renaissance

Evans Wing: European Paintings

Barbizon

19th-Century French and English

Impressionism

European Ceramics

European Period Rooms

Chinese Export Porcelain

William Coolidge Collection

Post Impressionism

European Decorative Arts

Tapestries

Upper Rotunda

Himalayan — Chinese

Chinese

Special Exhibition Gallery

Bernat Galleries

Egyptian — Egyptian

Egyptian — Egyptian

Egyptian

Medieval

Early English

Roman

Library

Greek

Roman

Greek

Japanese — Chinese

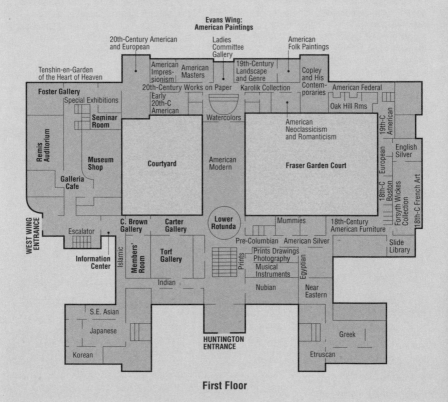

First Floor

Evans Wing: American Paintings

Tenshin-en-Garden of the Heart of Heaven

Foster Gallery

Special Exhibitions

Seminar Room

Remis Auditorium

Museum Shop

Galleria Cafe

Escalator

WEST WING ENTRANCE

Information Center

20th-Century American and European

American Impressionism — American Masters

20th-Century Works on Paper

Early 20th-C American

Ladies Committee Gallery

19th-Century Landscape and Genre

Karolik Collection

Watercolors

American Folk Paintings

Copley and His Contemporaries

American Federal

Oak Hill Rms

19th-C American

American Neoclassicism and Romanticism

English Silver

European

18th-C Boston

Forsyth Wickes Collection

18th-C French Art

Courtyard

American Modern

Fraser Garden Court

C. Brown Gallery — Carter Gallery

Members' Room

Torf Gallery

Islamic

Indian

Lower Rotunda

Mummies

Pre-Columbian — American Silver

Prints Drawings Photography

Prints

Musical Instruments

18th-Century American Furniture

Egyptian

Slide Library

S.E. Asian

Japanese

Korean

Nubian

HUNTINGTON ENTRANCE

Near Eastern

Greek

Etruscan

The **MFA**'s extraordinary assembly of Asiatic art—the largest under any one museum roof worldwide—features one of the greatest Japanese collections in existence, and important objects from China, India, and Southeast Asia. (Before you leave the grounds, be sure to visit **Tenshin-en-Garden of the Heart of Heaven,** a contemplative Japanese garden designed by garden master Kinsaku Nakane, located on the museum's north side.) The Egyptian and ancient Near Eastern art galleries are a favorite with kids—they love the mummies—and are also treasure troves of jewelry, sculpture, and other objects from throughout Asia's western regions. The array of Old Kingdom sculpture is equaled only by the Cairo Museum; the **MFA** cosponsored excavations in Egypt for 40 years with **Harvard University.** And it is apt that the "Athens of America" boasts a superb representation of ancient Greek, Roman, and Etruscan objects, including bronzes, sculpture dating from the sixth to the fourth centuries BC, and vases painted with fascinating figures and vignettes by some of the greatest early Greek artists.

Another highlight is the **Department of European Decorative Arts,** which features a collection of antique musical instruments that includes lutes, clavichords, harps, and zithers, replicas of which are often played in special concert programs. The **Department of Textiles** displays an international collection of tapestries, batiks, embroidery, silk weavings, costume materials, and other textiles. The Boston area was the capital of the textile industry in the late 19th century, and this was the first museum in America to elevate textiles to the status of art. Its collection ranks among the world's greatest. Spanning the 15th century to today, the **Department of Prints and Drawings** has particularly outstanding 15th-century Italian engravings and 19th-century lithography, many works by Dürer, Rembrandt, Goya, the Tiepolos, and the German Expressionists, Picasso's complete *Vollard Suite,* the **M. and M. Karolik Collection of American Drawings and Watercolors from 1800 to 1875,** a growing collection of original photographs, and more.

Special exhibitions are mounted in the modern light-filled **West Wing,** where you'll find the **Fine Arts Restaurant, Galleria Cafe,** and **Cafeteria** (see below) as well as a wonderful **Museum Shop.** Many Bostonians make special trips just to visit the latter for its great selection of books, prints, children's games, cards and stationery, reproductions of silver, jewelry, glass, textiles, and other decorative items aplenty. Excellent film, concert, and lecture series are held in the **West Wing**'s **Remis Auditorium.** Also in the neighborhood are the **School of the Museum of Fine Arts** (230 The Fenway, at Museum Rd, 267.6100) and **Massachusetts College of Art**

(621 Huntington Ave, at Longwood Ave, 232.1555), both of which maintain galleries. Paid parking is available on Museum Road.
♦ Admission; voluntary donation W 4-9:45PM (Graham Gund Gallery closed during this time); reduced admission when only West Wing is open; members and children under 17 free; reduced admission for students and senior citizens. M-Tu, Th-Su 10AM-4:45PM (West Wing open Th-F until 9:45PM); W 10AM-9:45PM. Free guided tours; free introductory walk in Spanish the first Saturday of every month. 465 Huntington Ave (between Forsyth Way and Museum Rd). 267.9300, daily schedules 267.2973, TTY/TDD 267.9703, concerts, lectures, film information 267.9300, ext 300 & (parking for people with disabilities near West Wing entrance)

Within the Museum of Fine Arts:

Fine Arts Restaurant ★★$$ The food is surprisingly good, with special themed menus playing off high-profile exhibitions. For example, French entrées were served in conjunction with "Monet in the 20th Century." This has become a popular destination for lunch, even with those who don't plan to look at any art. ♦ American ♦ M-Tu, Sa-Su lunch; W-F lunch and dinner. Second floor. 266.3663 &

Galleria Cafe ★$ Refuel for another foray through the galleries with a light meal, fruit, cheese, or dessert, accompanied by a cappuccino or a glass of wine, at this informal, open cafe. ♦ Cafe ♦ M-Tu, Sa-Su breakfast and lunch (until 4PM); W-F breakfast, lunch, and dinner. West Wing, First floor. 267.9300 &

Cafeteria $ If you're on a budget, this is the best option for a quick meal, and there's rarely a wait. ♦ American ♦ Tu, Sa-Su breakfast and lunch; W-F breakfast, lunch, and dinner. Lower level. 267.9300 &

3 Greater Boston YMCA $ The first of the nationwide association's outposts, it was founded in 1851. Stays are limited to 10 days, and guests must be at least 18 years old with a picture ID and luggage. There are 49 single and double rooms with shared baths and a suite with a private bath. Children can stay with a parent. Breakfast is free, as is use of the gym, indoor track, pool, and sauna. A cafeteria-style restaurant and laundry facilities are also on the premises. Smoking is allowed only in the guest rooms. A modest key deposit is required. Reserve two weeks in advance; walk-ins are accepted daily after 12:30PM.
♦ 316 Huntington Ave (between Gainsborough and Forsyth Sts). 536.7800 &

4 Jordan Hall at the New England Conservatory of Music (NEC) Like **Symphony Hall,** only smaller and more intimate, this venue is an acoustically superior concert space, ideal for chamber music. Designed in 1903 by **Wheelwright and Haven,**

the hall was funded by Eben Jordan, founder of the **Jordan Marsh** department stores. An extensive $8.2 million restoration project in 1995 carefully preserved its exceptional acoustics. The **NEC** was established in 1867 as the first music college in the country and is internationally renowned for its undergraduate and graduate music programs. Some 450 faculty and student concerts take place here annually, most free and held during the school term. In addition, a number of musical groups perform here, including the **Juilliard Quartet, Tokyo String Quartet, Boston Symphony Chamber Players, Cantata Singers,** and the **Boston Chamber Music Society**. ♦ Box office M-Sa; tickets may be purchased by mail or telephone. 30 Gainsborough St (at St. Botolph St). Box office 536.2414; concert information 262.1120 &

5 Boston University Theatre The acclaimed **Huntington Theatre Company (HTC),** the professional company-in-residence, puts on five plays annually at this charming 1925 Greek Revival theater, which seats 850. The focus here is both classic and contemporary, ranging from Shakespeare and musicals to new plays. Discounts are offered for senior citizens, students, and groups; subscriptions are also available. ♦ 264 Huntington Ave (between Gainsborough St and Massachusetts Ave). Ticket information 266.0800 &

6 Symphony Hall Deep-pocketed Brahmin philanthropist and amateur musician Henry Lee Higginson, who founded the **Boston Symphony Orchestra (BSO)** in 1881, wanted his creation's new home to be among the world's most magnificent, so he commissioned **McKim, Mead & White** as architects. The building, completed in 1900, is on the National Register of Historic Places. The hall's enduring fame stems not from its restrained Italian Renaissance style, however distinguished, but rather from its internationally acclaimed acoustics, which have earned it the nickname the "Stradivarius" among concert halls. It is one of only a handful of near acoustically-perfect halls in the world—and the only one in the Western Hemisphere.

This was the first concert hall to be built according to an acoustical engineering formula, the work of Wallace Sabine, an assistant professor of physics at **Massachusetts Institute of Technology** who probed the scientific basis of acoustics. The 2,625-seat auditorium (see seating chart on page 147) is basically a shoebox-shaped shell built to resonate glorious sound to astound the ears. The best seats are in the second balcony center, from where it is possible to hear the proverbial pin drop on the stage.

In 1998, Seiji Ozawa celebrated his 25th anniversary as director of the **BSO,** one of the world's preeminent orchestras. It is in residence here from October through April; in July and August it performs at Tanglewood, an open-air facility in western Massachusetts. The hall is also home to the beloved **Boston Pops,** which performs here from May through

Symphony Hall

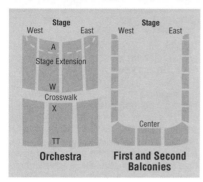

Stage		Stage	
West	East	West	East

Orchestra — A, Stage Extension, W, Crosswalk, X, TT

First and Second Balconies — Center

Orchestra　　**First and Second Balconies**

June. Formerly conducted by Arthur Fiedler and then by Oscar-winning composer John Williams, the **"Pops"** is now under the baton of Keith Lockhart. For **Boston Pops** concerts, the seats are removed from the main floor of the hall and replaced by tables and chairs, and food and drink are served. The **Handel & Haydn Society,** America's oldest continuously active performing arts organization, performs here, too, as do many other local, national, and international musical ensembles and musicians. The hall also boasts a magnificent 5,000-pipe organ. No one should miss the chance to experience a concert here, a delight music-loving Boston has always cherished. ◆ Box office M-Sa. To reserve and charge seats for **BSO** or **Pops** performances, call Symphony-Charge at 266.1200. Two hundred same-day, one-per-customer discounted seats for **BSO** performances are available for Tuesday and Thursday evenings and Friday afternoons. The line forms near the box office Tuesday and Thursday at 5PM, and at 9AM on Friday. 301 Massachusetts Ave (at Huntington Ave). 266.1492 ♿

7 Thai Cuisine ★$$ Before or after a concert at **Symphony Hall** or a foreign film at the **MFA,** dine on good Thai dishes—fiery or delicate—in this little 30-seater behind the hall. The owner has opened several other Thai restaurants in Greater Boston, all highly regarded. Go the spicy route with *kang liang* (peppered shrimp soup) or *gai pud gra prao* (chicken, onion, and chilies), or try more subtle dishes such as *tom you koong* (soup with shrimp, lemongrass, lime, and chilies), steamed whole fish, the Thai seafood combination, or the selection of curry dishes. The service is sometimes rushed. ◆ Thai/ Takeout ◆ M-Sa lunch and dinner; Su dinner. 14A Westland Ave (between St. Stephen and Hemenway Sts). 262.1485 ♿

8 Bangkok Cuisine ★$ A favorite with students and people who work nearby, Boston's oldest Thai restaurant is still turning out great beef and chicken *satay* (marinated, skewered, and grilled or broiled), *duck choo chee* (curry), *pad thai* (thin noodles served with shrimp, egg, bean sprouts, and peanut

sauce), whole fried bass with chili sauce, and Thai bouillabaisse, which features assorted tender seafood served in a puffed pouch. The long, narrow dining room empties and fills quickly, but service is sometimes desultory, so allow extra time if you have a concert or movie ahead. ◆ Thai/Takeout ◆ M-Sa lunch and dinner; Su dinner. 177A Massachusetts Ave (between Westland Ave and Haviland St). 262.5377 ♿

9 Boston International American Youth Hostel (AYH) $ There's no cheaper lodging available in the city, and it's near the **Museum of Fine Arts.** Offering 150 beds in the winter and 220 in the summer, the hostel accommodates men and women of all ages in six-bunk, dormitory-style rooms, separated by sex. Every floor has showers and bathrooms, and the building houses laundry facilities plus two kitchens with utensils. Sleeping bags are not allowed; you can rent a sleep sheet for a modest fee and deposit. The hostel fills up quickly from May until fall. The fee is lower if you're a member, and you can join on the spot—only members can get bunks in summer. Bikes and packs can be stored securely on the premises. No alcohol is allowed, there is no smoking except in one public room, and there's a four-night limit per 30-day period. Reservations can be made by phone with a credit card; 25 percent of the beds are reserved for walk-ins. ◆ 12 Hemenway St (between Haviland and Boylston Sts). 536.9455

9 Counterpoint Cafe ★$ Inexpensive fare served in a stylish setting is what you'll find here. Try the omelettes, fresh muffins, and steamed hot chocolate for breakfast; smoked turkey and avocado on homemade mini-baguette, Green Goddess salad (topped with prosciutto, swiss cheese, and sliced turkey), or tasty daily specials for lunch. This is an ideal spot for a light preconcert bite. ◆ Cafe ◆ M-F breakfast and lunch until 6PM; Sa-Su breakfast and lunch until 2PM. 1124 Boylston St (at Hemenway St). 424.1789

Socialite and art collector Isabella Stewart Gardner delighted in shocking staid Boston—among other affronts, she wore diamonds mounted on wires like antennae in her hair and walked her two pet lions on Beacon Street. Soirees at her Fenway palazzo featured her favorite refreshments: Champagne and doughnuts.

Writer John Updike, a die-hard Red Sox fan, calls Fenway Park "a lyric little bandbox of a park. Everything is painted green and seems in curiously sharp focus, like the inside of an old-fashioned peeping-type Easter egg."

The House That Mrs. Jack Built

The larger-than-life Isabella Stewart Gardner (1840-1924) was a charismatic, spirited, and independent New Yorker who married into Victorian Boston's high society but never bowed to its conventions. (Her husband, John, was known as Jack to close friends, hence her nickname, "Mrs. Jack.") Though she became a prominent private art collector and flamboyant socialite, many proper Bostonians forever dismissed her as a brash outsider. But Isabella didn't give a hoot. A passionate woman, she loved the spotlight, so much so that she built a showcase mansion that is now a museum (see page 141) to enshrine her collections and to throw gala parties.

Gardner delighted in upstaging her critics and creating a stir with outrageous behavior, but with a regal awareness of her lofty social stature. Among her many pleasures were art, literature, and music, and she surrounded herself with the most fashionable talents of her time. However, most of her tremendous energy went toward acquiring fabulous art objects.

When their posh Back Bay mansion on **Beacon Street** became too small for Isabella's treasures, the Gardners started planning for a museum. After John's death in 1898, she built **Fenway Court,** a 15th-century Venetian-style palazzo that proudly towered alone in the unfashionable Fenway. While "Mrs. Jack's Palace" was under construction, Gardner was always on the scene, and often got into the action, at one point climbing on scaffolds to daub the paint to her liking on the courtyard walls. She was accompanied by a trumpeter who summoned workers when she wanted to confer with them: one note for the architect, another for the plumber, and so on. Anyone ignoring the summons was fired.

Gardner held court among her collections, blurring the distinction between residence and museum in an extraordinary, idiosyncratic way. Signs of her presence remain—a table is set for tea as if she were in the next room. Prevented by gender from the prestige and power for which she was suited by temperament, Gardner found in the museum the stage, cultural forum, artistic medium, and professional avocation denied her by her times. Look for the plaque she first affixed over the door in 1900, giving her home its official name. Then find the seal designed for her achievement—carved in marble and set into the museum facade's brick wall, it bears her motto, *"C'est mon plaisir"* (it is my pleasure), and a phoenix, a symbol of immortality. Henry James thought she resembled "a figure on a wondrous cinquecento tapestry." John Singer Sargent's portrait of Gardner started a scandal when it was first unveiled in 1888 at the private, then all-male **St. Botolph Club,** to which her husband belonged. Isabella had posed bare-armed in a clingy décolleté gown, which so shocked proper Bostonians that her husband became infuriated, threatened to horsewhip any gossipers, and forbade the picture to be publicly displayed. But today you can see it through untitillated 20th-century eyes at Isabella's museum, where it finally found its niche in 1924.

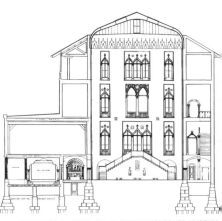

COURTESY OF THE ISABELLA STEWART GARDNER MUSEUM

9 Looney Tunes This music emporium is a good source for both serious and dilettante collectors of used and out-of-print jazz, classical, and rock records, some rare. The shop also sells movie and Broadway soundtracks, comedy, country, blues, and opera LPs and 45s, plus "cutouts" (discontinued recordings), CDs, cassettes, and videos. They carry a few new items, too, and also buy and trade. ♦ Daily. 1106 Boylston St (between Massachusetts Ave and Hemenway St). 247.2238 & Also at: 1001 Massachusetts Ave (between Dana and Ellery Sts), Cambridge. 876.5624

10 The Massachusetts Historical Society The first historical society founded in the New World (in 1791) is housed in an 1899 National Historic Landmark designed by **Edmund March Wheelwright.** It largely operates as a research center for the study of American history and in that role is surpassed only by the Library of Congress. The focal point is the library, which contains some 3,200 collections of manuscripts and several hundred thousand books, pamphlets, broadsides, maps, early newspapers, and journals, including the papers of Governor John Winthrop and the Adams family, Paul Revere's accounts of his famous ride, two copies of the Declaration of Independence (one written in John Adams's hand, the other in Thomas Jefferson's), and a staggering quantity of other such treasures.

The society's rare-books collection includes most of the important early books printed in America or about the US's discovery and settlement. Government, politics, women's history, slavery, the China trade, railroads, science, and technology—the breadth of topics addressed is immense. The society also owns prints, engravings, furniture, antique clocks, personal belongings, and several hundred works of art. The first map produced in British North America, an 18th-century Indian archer weather vane by Deacon Shem Drowne (maker of **Faneuil Hall**'s grasshopper weather vane), a list of Americans killed in the Battle of Concord, and Jefferson's architectural plans for Monticello are among the items preserved here. But there's a catch: To use the library, you must fill out a form in advance, demonstrating that you are a "serious" person with a "worthy" pursuit. ♦ Free. M-F. Free guided tours are given if requested in advance. 1154 Boylston St (between Hemenway St and The Fenway). 536.1608 &

11 The Other Side Cosmic Cafe ★$

The "other side" refers to the extension of Newbury Street (west of Massachusetts Avenue) that most people don't even know exists, and "cosmic" alludes, one presumes, to its other-worldly aspirations. In any case, this "Seattle-style coffeehouse/cafe," with its classical/industrial decor (cast-iron railings, red-velvet drapes) and standard fare (soups, salads, and sandwiches), is just the ticket for the young throngs who tip the balance of trade on the "downscale" end of Newbury Street. It's handy, too, for the concert-bound. ♦ Coffeehouse/Cafe ♦ Daily breakfast, lunch, and dinner. 407 Newbury St (at Massachusetts Ave). 536.9477 &

11 Oceanic Chinese Restaurant ★$

It would take hundreds of visits to exhaust this versatile restaurant's enormous menu. In addition to unadventurous old favorites like spareribs and spring rolls, unusual specialty seafood items are served here, including shark's fin and shredded duck soup, whole fried sole, abalone with tender vegetables, clams with black-bean sauce, and various fish and shellfish dishes flavored with ginger and scallions. Treats that don't hail from the sea include crisp roasted duck, spicy Szechuan dishes, and sizzling hot pots. The restaurant is a trifle fancier than the average Chinatown spot, but it replicates that neighborhood's estimable authentic cuisine—not surprising, since that's where the owners and staff started out. ♦ Chinese/Takeout ♦ Daily lunch and dinner. 91 Massachusetts Ave (between Newbury St and Commonwealth Ave). 353.0791 &

THE ELIOT HOTEL

11 The Eliot Hotel $$ Located on the edge of Back Bay, this all-suite hotel built in 1925 (and extensively renovated in 1993) is a convenient place to stay. It's minutes from **Symphony Hall** and the **Museum of Fine Arts,** and a five-minute walk from **Fenway Park** and the **Public Garden.** There used to be a pack of historic hotels along Commonwealth Avenue—the Vendome, the Tuilerie, and the Somerset, to name a few—but this hostelry is the sole survivor. There are 90 rooms on 9 floors; all are swathed with traditional English-style chintz fabrics and further decorated with authentic botanical prints and antique furnishings. Lovely French doors separate the living rooms from the bedrooms. Amenities include Italian marble baths, two TV sets with a free movie channel, and pantries with coffeemakers, microwave ovens, and stocked mini-bars. The privately owned hotel attracts international visitors, conventioneers, and visiting professors mostly, and is one of the city's best buys. The overall ambience is quiet and luxurious, with the old-fashioned intimacy of a European hotel. There's also an excellent new restaurant on the premises (see below). Nonsmoking rooms and paid parking are available. ♦ 370 Commonwealth Ave (at Massachusetts Ave). 267.1607, 800/44ELIOT; fax 536.9114

Within The Eliot Hotel:

Clio ★★★★$$$$ This new French-American eatery has been winning raves since it opened in June 1997. Owned by restaurateur Ken Oringer (of River Cafe and Al Forno fame), the plush Parisian-style supper club serves excellent food at high prices. Among the highlights of the appetizer selection are the puree of sweet potato soup; the bone-marrow custard with corn, mushrooms, and fresh black truffles; and the smoked salmon terrine with fennel salad and marinated clams. Notable entrées include garlic-rubbed organic chicken with a cassolette of spring vegetables, smoked bacon, and potato gnocchi; filet mignon of veal with melted veal cheeks, fava beans, and morel mushrooms; and butter-basted Maine lobster with baby spring turnips, purple kohlrabi, and vidalia onion puree. ♦ French ♦ M-Sa dinner; Su brunch and dinner. Reservations required. 536.7200

Restaurants/Clubs: Red   **Hotels:** Blue

Shops/🌱 **Outdoors:** Green   **Sights/Culture:** Black

12 Nuggets This was the first store in the area to sell new, used, rare, and out-of-print records, CDs, tapes, and 12-inch dance singles, along with related posters, T-shirts, and magazines. Aficionados can find jazz, reggae, blues, and more. ♦ M-Sa until 1AM; Su. 486 Commonwealth Ave (between Charlesgate W and Kenmore St). 536.0679. Also at: 1354A Beacon St (at Harvard St), Brookline. 277.8917

13 Cornwall's ★$ Hearty food, games and magazines up for grabs, and, above all, a great assortment of esoteric brews on tap explain the appeal of this tiny shoebox of a pub, which has fortified **BU** students for a decade. ♦ British/International ♦ Daily lunch and dinner until 2AM. 510 Commonwealth Ave (between Kenmore St and Brookline Ave). 262.3749

13 Rathskeller (The Rat) One of the very few places in town serving up both good music and good food, **The Rat**'s not much to look at (to say the least), but it was Boston's first New Wave club. Many local groups got a boost here, and this was the first Boston club to headline the Cars, Police, Talking Heads, and Go Gos. The club still books high-quality local and touring rock bands, up to four a night. On weekends you can listen for free to bands playing on the balcony. There are four bars serving cheap drinks, plus pinball, videos, and a great jukebox. A number of musicians—and locals—have enjoyed chef Paul DelTrecco's American menu of ribs, chicken, crisp french fries and onion rings, salads, coleslaw, corn bread, and sweet-potato pie. Some struggling performers have even done stints in the kitchen. There's outdoor patio seating in season. ♦ Cover. Daily lunch and dinner; performances begin at 9:30PM. Patrons must be 21 or older, unless a special all-ages show is scheduled. No credit cards accepted. 528 Commonwealth Ave (between Kenmore St and Brookline Ave). 536.2750

14 Barnes & Noble at Boston University
You won't have any trouble locating this store—blinking away on top is Kenmore Square's famous landmark, the **Citgo Sign** (see below). This is one of the largest bookstores in New England, with three floors of books to browse among. In addition to textbooks, there's a great selection of current and backlist hardcover and paperback books: best-sellers, cookbooks, children's books, classics, hobbies, gardening, law, women, history, politics—the works. The store sponsors frequent events, including author signings and children's story readings. In addition to books, this six-story department store offers specialty shops selling clothing and accessories, chocolates, stationery, housewares, office supplies, flowers, electronics and cameras, and more. There's even a travel agent. If you're in the square with time to spare before a **Red Sox** game, this is

the place to dawdle. ♦ Daily. 660 Beacon St (between Raleigh St and Kenmore Sq). 267.8484 ♿ Also at: 395 Washington St (between Winter and Bromfield Sts). 426.5502; 603 Boylston St (between Clarendon and Dartmouth Sts). 236.1308

At Barnes & Noble at Boston University:

Cafe Charles ★$ There are plenty of places to grab a quick bite in Kenmore Square, but few are as serene as this pretty cafe. Soups, sandwiches on French bread, muffins, cappuccino, and desserts (including an excellent hazelnut torte) are served. Bring a book and relax at a table, or watch the nonstop activity on the streets below from the windowside marble counter. The cafe overlooks the last mile marker for the **Boston Marathon.** A good place for conversation, it attracts university students and faculty members—as well as neighborhood residents—but most Bostonians haven't discovered it yet. ♦ Cafe/Takeout ♦ Daily breakfast, lunch, and dinner. Second floor. 267.8484

Citgo Sign The 60-square-foot, double-sided electric sign, with its 2 miles of blinking red, white, and blue neon tubing, dates from 1965. An immediate Pop Art hit, the sign inspired one filmmaker to create a short film called *Go, Go Citgo,* in which the sign did its off-and-on routine to music by the Monkees and Indian sitarist Ravi Shankar. The sign was turned off during the energy crisis of the 1970s and came close to being torn down in 1982. It was saved by its fans, led by Arthur Krim, a Cambridge resident, college professor, and member of the Society for Commercial Archaeology (which works to preserve urban and roadside Americana such as neon signs, diners, and gas stations). Eventually, the Oklahoma-based Citgo corporation agreed to keep Kenmore Square's illuminated heartbeat plugged in and maintained.

15 Howard Johnson Kenmore $$ Just beyond Kenmore Square on **Boston University**'s campus, this bustling stopover is convenient to **Fenway Park,** western Boston, and Back Bay. Lots of tour groups stay here. An older but well-kept hotel, it has 180 rooms on seven floors—including an executive section offering such extras as larger rooms, VCRs, and complimentary coffee and newspapers. Also on site are a restaurant, lounge, and indoor swimming pool. Rooms for nonsmokers and free parking are available. ♦ 575 Commonwealth Ave (between Kenmore Sq and Sherborn St). 267.3100, 800/654.2000; fax 864.0242

Photographic Resource Center

16 Photographic Resource Center (PRC)
One of the few centers for photography in the country, this nonprofit arts organization

leases space from **Boston University** and houses three galleries and a non-lending photography library. The 1985 building's intelligent, award-winning design (by **Leers, Weinzapfel Associates/Alex Krieger Architects**) evokes the mechanical process of photography and its manipulation of light—particularly in the architects' use of industrial materials and glass. The exhibitions emphasize new and experimental photography from the US and abroad, and frequently feature works by students and members. Check local papers or call to find out about the center's regular lectures/slide presentations; Chuck Close, Mary Ellen Mark, John Baldessari, and William Wegman have all spoken here. The organization publishes a monthly newsletter and offers educational programs. ♦ Admission. Tu-Su; Th until 8PM. Call in advance to arrange a tour. 602 Commonwealth Ave (at Blandford St). 353.0700 &

17 Mugar Memorial Library of Boston University Few outside the university community know about this library's marvelous and massive **Department of Special Collections,** dedicated to scholarly research but also open to the public. Preserved and exhibited here are rare books, manuscripts, and papers pertaining to hundreds of interesting people, famous and not, from the 15th century onward (the 20th-century archives are especially strong).

Of particular note are the large collections of Theodore Roosevelt's and Robert Frost's papers and memorabilia, and the archives of **BU** alumnus Dr. Martin Luther King Jr., some of which are displayed in the third-floor **King Exhibit Room.** The papers of numerous journalists, politicians, mystery writers, film and stage actors, musicians, and others are housed here. Browse awhile and you'll find material by and about Frederick Douglass, Bette Davis, Florence Nightingale, Albert Einstein, Tennessee Williams, Irwin Shaw, Arthur Fiedler, Eric Ambler, Rex Harrison, Fred Astaire, and Abraham Lincoln. ♦ Library: daily. Special Collections: M-F. Tours by reservation. 771 Commonwealth Ave (between Granby St and University Rd). 353.3696 &

18 Paradise Rock Club This club and adjacent **M-80** (see below) are west of Kenmore Square, but shouldn't be overlooked because they are two of Boston's best places to dance and to see national and international groups in concert. New Wave and rock are the mainstays; but jazz, folk, blues, and country are also frequently booked. The Buzzcocks, Rickie Lee Jones, U2, Tower of Power, the Scorpions, and Nick Lowe have all appeared here. Get tickets in advance, since few if any are available for performances by popular groups on the day of the shows. On Saturday nights when there's not a show patrons dance to DJ-mixed music. There's a full bar, and minimum age requirements vary by shows. Take the *B Green Line* to the **Pleasant Street** stop. ♦ Admission. Box office M-Sa. Doors open at 8PM for shows; sometimes two are scheduled per night. Cash only at the door; credit cards accepted at box office and bar. 969 Commonwealth Ave (between Gaffney and Babcock Sts). Recorded information 562.8804; Ticketmaster 931.2000

18 M-80 DJs spin dance music at this European-style club. Many international exchange students seek it out, and it is jam-packed some nights. There's a full bar, but no food is served. ♦ Cover. W, F-Sa 11PM-2AM. Patrons must be 21 or older. No jeans or sneakers allowed. 967 Commonwealth Ave (between Gaffney and Babcock Sts). 562.8801

19 Savoy French Bakery One owner of this savory spot (just over the border in Brookline) was trained by a French baker, so the goods are classic French. Go out of your way to sample the fantastic apple-and-almond, apricot, chocolate, plain, and other croissant varieties baked here. Equally delicious are the decorative fresh-fruit tartlets, mini-cakes such as hazelnut frangipane, the assortment of cookies (try the traditional French *palmier,* nicknamed "elephant's ear") and the breads, including baguettes, *batards,* and *petit pain* (rolls). Truffles are also a taste treat. ♦ Daily. No credit cards accepted. 1003 Beacon St (at St. Mary's St), Brookline. 734.0214

20 Sol Azteca ★★$$ Dinner begins with some of the best salsa and chips to be had in Boston, and progresses to marvelous Mexican fare like *chiles rellenos* (chili peppers stuffed with cheese), *enchiladas verdes* (in a green sauce), *camarones al cilantro* (shrimp seasoned with cilantro), and *puerco en adobo* (pork tenderloin with spicy red peppers). With the meal, enjoy excellent sangria or Mexican beer; afterward, try coffee flavored with cinnamon and the great coffee-flavored flan. The rustic dining rooms are festively decorated with hand-painted tile tables and handicrafts. ♦ Mexican ♦ Daily dinner. Reservations recommended M-Th, Su. 914A Beacon St (between Park Dr and St. Mary's St). 262.0909 &

21 Boston Beer Works ★$$ Yet another on-site brewery complete with gleaming tanks, this one is unusually well situated, a stone's throw from the ballpark. The menu is surprisingly ambitious, with such interesting entries as onion-and-ale soup, barbecued Cajun andouille sausage, shark shish kebabs, and "beer-basted" burgers. There's brunch each Sunday—except when the **Red Sox** are at home in nearby **Fenway Park.** ♦ American ♦ M-Sa lunch and dinner; Su brunch and dinner. 61 Brookline Ave (between Overland and Beacon Sts). 536.2337 &

22 Avalon This mammoth dance club holds up to 1,500 people for a rotating roster of music. Thursday there's international music, Friday Top 40 hits are featured, Saturday look for high-energy dance tunes, and Sunday is gay/lesbian night. There's a full bar, but no food is served. Expect to wait, but barring late arrival, everyone gets in eventually. ♦ Cover. Th-Su until 2AM. Patrons must be 21 or older. No sneakers, jeans, or athletic wear allowed. Credit cards accepted at bar only. 15 Lansdowne St (between Ipswich St and Brookline Ave). 262.2424 &

22 Axis Music changes nightly and includes progressive, punk, funk, heavy metal, hard rock, live bands, alternative dance tunes, and DJ spins. Creative dress is encouraged; "When in doubt, wear black" is the club's advice. On Sunday, this smaller club (800 capacity) connects with its next-door neighbor for gay/lesbian night—enter through **Avalon.** ♦ Cover. Tu-Su until 2AM. Call for information on age minimums and shows. 13 Lansdowne St (between Ipswich St and Brookline Ave). 262.2437 &

22 Karma Club The former **Venus de Milo** now strives for an exotic ambience, with lots of carvings of Sivas, Buddhas, and god-desses. Wednesday is gay night, Thursday is jazz night, Friday and Saturday feature international music. ♦ Cover. W-Sa until 2AM. Patrons must be 21 or older. No jeans or sneakers permitted. 9 Lansdowne St (between Ipswich St and Brookline Ave). 421.9595 &

22 Bill's Bar This small (250 maximum capacity) 1950s-homage bar features hot music and cold beer, and changes personas nightly for a 21-plus crowd. A local band plays on Tuesday; Friday is DJ night with no cover; Saturday features pop tunes; and on Sunday

evening the music is strictly funk. ♦ Cover. Daily; call ahead for hours. 5½ Lansdowne St (between Ipswich St and Brookline Ave). 421.9678 &

23 Jake Ivory's Audience participation is prized at this spot—there are dueling pianos and sing-alongs after many **Red Sox** games. "If you don't have a good time here, it's your own fault," says the *Boston Globe.* ♦ Cover. W-Sa until 2AM. 1 Lansdowne St (at Ipswich St). 247.1222 &

23 Jillian's Billiard Club Get behind the eight ball at one of 50 tourna-ment-quality billiard, pocket billiard, and snooker tables. You'll find darts, shuffleboard, a batting cage, Ping-Pong tables, video games, virtual sports, and wide-screen TVs, too. Cafe fare, beer, and wine are served, and on the first floor the **Atlas Bar and Grill** offers innovative American fare. ♦ Fee. M-Sa 11AM-2AM; Su noon-2AM. Only those 18 and over are admitted after 8PM. No hats, tank tops, sweats, or cutoffs allowed. 145 Ipswich St (at Lansdowne St). 437.0300

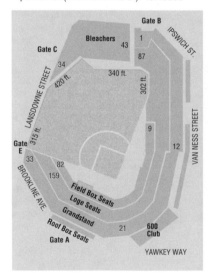

24 Fenway Park Fans are thrillingly close to the players at the country's smallest major-league baseball stadium—it has a 34,000-person capacity (see the seating chart above). Which is why, legendary though it may be, this ballpark's days are numbered. Owners have set the year 2001 as a target date to move to a new ballpark, though no definite site or plans had been settled upon at press time. Legends including Carl Yastrzemski, Ted Williams, Dwight Evans, and Roger Clemens have all dominated the famous diamond. Babe Ruth made his debut as a **Red Sox** pitcher here 11 July 1914. He was later traded.

Built in 1912 and rebuilt in 1934, the park is a classic, with plenty of quirks that enhance its battered charm. One odd characteristic is the legendary "green monster" wall that looms 37 feet high in the outfield. Thanks to the wall, players who hit a high fly ball here score one of the shortest home runs in any major league ballpark. But if the hit isn't high enough to clear the wall, a line drive that might have been a homer in any other park could wind up a mere double here. The park still has real green grass, and its idiosyncratic shape is the result of an awkward site, since the surrounding lots weren't for sale when the ballpark was embedded in the city. Even if baseball leaves you unmoved, come for the show—just sitting among Boston's demanding, impassioned, extremely vocal fans is fun. (For those who prefer to avoid overly raucous spectators, there's an alcohol-free reserved zone; tickets are available on a first-come, first-served basis.)

The ballpark opens 1.5 hours before game time. Ask about special youth, senior citizen, and family discounts available for designated dates. Souvenirs are sold on all sides of the park—look for the amazing **Souvenir Store** (19 Yawkey Way, 421.8686) across from the box office. Before and after the games, crowds flock to the **Cask 'n Flagon** sports bar (62 Brookline Ave, at Lansdowne St, 536.4840) and other neighborhood watering holes. ♦ Box office: M-F. 4 Yawkey Way (between Van Ness St and Brookline Ave). Tickets 267.1700, recorded information 267.8661 ♿

25 **Buteco Restaurant** ★$ Don't be put off by the shabby facade; good food lurks inside. With Latin music pulsing in the background (a band plays on Monday), a diverse, youngish clientele packs the tiny dining room. Plates get piled with such spicy Brazilian dishes as mandioca (fried cassava root with carrot dipping sauce), hearts of palm salad, black-bean soup, picadinho a carioca (beef stew with garlic), vatapá a Baiana (sole baked in coconut milk and served on shrimp with peanut paste), and churrasco (mixed grill). On weekends order feijoada, the Brazilian national dish—a hearty stew with black beans, pork sausage, beef, collard greens, and orange. ♦ Brazilian ♦ M-F lunch and dinner; Sa-Su dinner. Reservations recommended Saturday and Sunday. 130 Jersey St (between Park Dr and Queensberry St). 247.9508 ♿

26 **Thorntons Fenway Grill** ★★$ Though there are many grilled dishes on the menu, this place is known for its generous sandwiches and super salads. Come to the sprawling corner restaurant for a summer supper and some beer or wine before or after a **Red Sox** game. ♦ American ♦ M-Sa breakfast, lunch, and dinner; Su brunch and dinner. 100 Peterborough St (at Kilmarnock St). 421.0104 ♿

26 **Wheatstone Baking Company** Through picture windows, watch as bakers whip up the croissants, muffins, sticky buns, coffee cakes, and breads available for sale at the counter. Breakfast treats don't come any fresher. This is primarily a wholesale bakery, but there are four little cafe tables. ♦ Daily. 96 Peterborough St (between Jersey and Kilmarnock Sts). 247.3566 ♿

26 **Sorento's** ★★$$ The decor is pretty dramatic for a neighborhood pizza place: Everything is black and white, including the harlequin tile floor. This is no ordinary pizza, either, not with toppings like imported prosciutto, fried eggplant, and fontina cheese. Try the chicken àla Abruzzi (pâté sautéed with basil and spinach and served over cappellini). It's just one of a full array of luscious pasta dishes that share star billing here. ♦ Italian/ Takeout ♦ Daily lunch and dinner. 86 Peterborough St (between Jersey and Kilmarnock Sts). 424.7070 ♿

27 **Wheelock Family Theatre** Boston's only Actor's Equity theater company serving younger audiences staunchly upholds a nontraditional casting policy and mounts ambitious, polished productions in February, April, and October. It seats 650. ♦ Box office: M-F noon-5:30PM; Sa-Su noon-2PM. 180 Riverway (between Longwood and Brookline Aves). 734.4760 ♿

28 **The Inn at Children's Boston** $$ Smack dab in the middle of the **Longwood Medical Area** (the name refers to **Children's Hospital**, across the street) this 152-room economical hotel attracts many guests connected with the hospitals in the neighborhood. The **Museum of Fine Arts** and **Isabella Stewart Gardner Museum** are also nearby, and it's less than 15 minutes to Back Bay via the Green Line. Rooms for nonsmokers and for people with disabilities are available; and there is a restaurant as well as room service. The hotel is connected to a galleria of fast-food shops, a health club, and other services. ♦ 342 Longwood Ave (at Binney St). 731.4700, 800/528.1234; fax 731.4870 ♿

Having outgrown its building in the Back Bay, the Museum of Fine Arts moved to new quarters in the Fenway in 1909. The collection was moved by means of two horse-drawn carriages, making several trips. No guards were considered necessary, and nothing of value was broken or damaged in the move.

For all its substantial contributions to American history, education, and culture, Boston is a geographically small city. If Los Angeles, for instance, were overlaid on Boston, it would stretch from Plymouth to the New Hampshire border.

South End

This part of Boston is often overlooked by sightseers, who tend to favor neighboring **Back Bay** with its **Copley Place** and **Prudential Center** developments. But it does attract urban explorers who like to stray from the beaten tourist track and make their own discoveries. Enticements include block after block of undulating Victorian bowfront town houses, intimate residential parks, vibrant street life, out-of-the-ordinary shops, and restaurants of excellent quality.

The South End is one of Boston's most diverse neighborhoods—racially, economically, ethnically, and religiously. After a brief flowering as a genteel enclave, the neighborhood became home to Boston's immigrant populations. Today it still exudes port-of-entry flavor: Various blocks are predominantly Lebanese, Irish, Yankee, Chinese, West Indian, African-American, Greek, or Hispanic. The neighborhood also has a bohemian side, attracting visual artists, architects, writers, performers, designers, craftspeople, and musicians. Many of Boston's gay residents live here, too. And over the past 25 years young middle-class professionals have moved in, gentrifying patches of this crazy quilt.

Like Back Bay, the entire South End rests on landfill. The neighborhood was originally marshland bordering **Washington Street**, which was once a narrow neck that linked the peninsula to the mainland. By the mid–19th century upwardly mobile Bostonians wanted fashionable new quarters, and from 1850 to 1875 the South End emerged as speculators filled in blocks of land and auctioned them off. While Back Bay is French-inspired and cosmopolitan in style, the South End follows more traditional English patterns. To attract buyers, developers created London-style residential squares such as **Worcester**, **Rutland**, and **Union Park**, oases loosely linked by common architecture. **Boston City Hospital** was also constructed in the

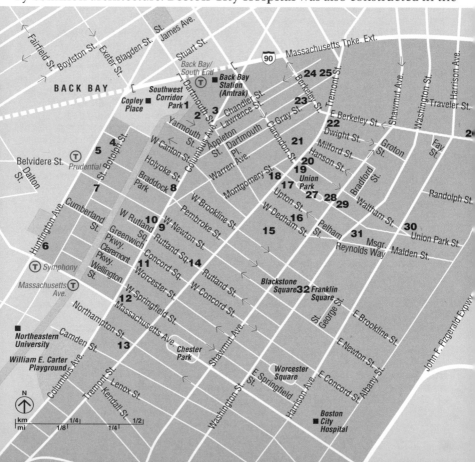

South End during this period of development. Founded in the 1860s, it is now the oldest institution on **Hospital Row**, a dense cluster of university and municipal medical buildings located near Roxbury.

Many of the structures built during the South End's genesis still stand. Within this scant square mile is the largest Victorian row-house district extant in the US, with more than 3,000 original buildings intact. Boston made the neighborhood a city landmark district in 1983, and it is listed on the National Register of Historic Places.

The South End rose and fell from grace in less than a decade, eclipsed by glamorous Back Bay and the allure of streetcar suburbs. By 1900 prosperous Bostonians had abandoned their handsome row houses, which were then divided into multiple units and lodging rooms to accommodate waves of immigrants and working-class families. Industries and businesses sprang up. The South End also became the largest lodging-house district in the country, gaining a reputation for dens of vices and unsavory pursuits. Finally declared a federal urban renewal area in 1965, the South End was torn apart, setting the stage for development and gentrification.

Today the neighborhood endures, changeable and fascinating as ever. While suffering all the trials and tribulations that gentrification can bring—the demolition of historic buildings, the construction of unpopular developments, tensions between old-time residents and newcomers—many buildings and blocks here are being recycled and renewed. Residents and community groups take active roles in healing old wounds—the **Southwest Corridor Park** is but one attractive result.

Explore **Columbus Avenue** and **Tremont Street** for the greatest concentration of good shops and restaurants. Take a walk through tiny Rutland Square or tranquil Union Park, both hugged by carefully restored residences. Stroll along **Chandler, Lawrence**, and **Appleton Streets**, lined with appealing, smaller-scale brick houses. From block to block, the architecture changes from down-in-the-dumps to resplendently restored. And with each block you'll sense the presence of the neighborhood's different populations—the African-American community to the south, for example, and the Middle Eastern and Armenian enclaves along **Shawmut Avenue** to the east.

A cautionary note: The South End's changeable nature means that shops and restaurants come and go quickly, and those that stay sometimes keep erratic hours. The best approach is to call ahead when possible, be prepared for occasional disappointments, and be alert to interesting new finds.

---

1 Southwest Corridor Park Where an ugly gash once slashed the South End, a ribbon of attractive parkland now curls. In the early 1970s more than 100 acres of housing in the South End and adjoining Roxbury and Jamaica Plain were demolished to make way for a highway project. Community protests killed that plan, but the blight remained, a sore spot awaiting healing. In 1977, 52 acres of this area were reclaimed for parkland to reknit divided neighborhoods. More than a decade in the making, the park—landscaped by Roy B. Mann—has become a valued part of the city. Twenty-three architectural and engineering firms worked with more than 15 community groups to chart the course of the new green trail. The result: 4.7 miles of walkways and bike paths graced with young trees and plantings and dotted with tot lots, street-hockey rinks, and basketball and tennis courts. The lauded fingerlike park is as narrow as 60 feet in spots and as wide as a quarter mile in others, and continues all the way to **Franklin Park**, the **Arnold Arboretum**, and **Forest Hills Cemetery**. An adjunct project, the 13-acre, community-run **Southwest Corridor Farms**, provides plots of land and training to urban gardeners.

Starting behind **Copley Place**, stroll as far southwest as your fancy takes you, and see how intensely used the well-loved park has become by all ages, races, and economic groups. Along the way, note the words of 18 local writers chiseled on walls near **T** stops.

The park is just one piece of the enormous and controversial $750-million-plus Southwest

Back Bay/South End Station   COURTESY OF KALLMANN MCKINNELL & WOOD ARCHITECTS

Corridor Project still underway. The project also involved relocating and depressing Boston's old elevated **MBTA** *Orange Line* and constructing nine new rapid transit stations, including two in the South End. The **Back Bay/South End Station** is a well-crafted structure designed by **Kallmann McKinnell & Wood Architects.** It extends a full block from Dartmouth Street, across from the park's northeastern end, to Clarendon Street. In its heroic navelike concourse, which is vaulted by massive wooden arches and illuminated by clerestory windows, the station recalls the sense of grandeur of Victorian railway stations.

The **Massachusetts Avenue Station,** by **Ellenzweig, Moore and Associates,** is a sleek, sinuous brick, glass, and aluminum structure located where the park intersects Massachusetts Avenue. Another aspect of the Southwest Corridor Project is the creation of development parcels that are intended to revitalize neglected Boston neighborhoods by providing employment and development opportunities for those communities. A city police department and a shopping mall have been constructed as a result of this effort. ♦ Dartmouth St (between Columbus Ave and Stuart St)

2 Tent City The construction of affluent **Copley Place** across the way was the catalyst that brought African-American community activists to this site to protest the South End's gentrification. This forced Boston to alter plans to put a parking lot here and to build affordable housing instead. The result—designed by **Goody, Clancy & Associates** in 1988—is a gentle addition to the neighborhood. One-quarter of the units in the cheerful patterned-brick complex of apartments and row houses are market-rate, one-quarter are for low-income residents, and one-half are for moderate-income residents. The biggest surprise is the name, which preserves the political moment when activists set up tents

here in protest. It was among the earliest in the wave of tent cities that spread across the country as the homelessness crisis worsened ♦ Dartmouth St (between Columbus Ave and Stuart St)

3 The Claddagh ★$ This Irish pub offers just the sort of filling, unfussy food you'd expect to find in a neighborhood bar. You're best off with burgers, chicken, stews, and other straightforward items. The walls are adorned with Irish family crests. ♦ Irish-American/Takeout ♦ Daily lunch and dinner. 335 Columbus Ave (between Clarendon and Dartmouth Sts). 262.9874

4 Copley Inn $$ Set in a European-style brick town house, this hotel has 21 contemporary studio units, each with a sitting area, fully equipped kitchenette, double bed, private bath, cable TV, and telephone with voice mail. The inn is located on the corner of an attractive Victorian-era residential street that is convenient to Back Bay's Copley Square. There are no public rooms, no meal service, and no elevator. Children under 12 stay free. ♦ 19 Garrison St (at St. Botolph St). 236.0300, 800/232.0306; fax 536.0816

5 The Colonnade Hotel $$$ Named for the columns that cross its concrete Bauhaus facade, this modern hotel has gracious public rooms and 285 guest rooms with traditional decor, city views, and marble bathrooms. Located on the premises is the **Brasserie Jo** restaurant, serving Alsacian French cuisine. Other amenities include a lounge, a fitness room, an outdoor rooftop pool, indoor parking, a multilingual staff, 24-hour room service, same-day valet service (for an additional fee), and foreign currency exchange. ♦ 120 Huntington Ave (between W Newton and Garrison Sts). 424.7000, 800/962.3030; fax 424.1717 &

The MidTown Hotel

6 The MidTown Hotel $ A well-kept secret, this two-story, 159-room hotel is older and far less fashionable than the numerous luxury hotels located nearby, but also much less expensive. It's frequented by families, tour groups, and businesspeople. The rooms are spacious, and there's free parking, an outdoor pool with a lifeguard (in season), and a multilingual staff. Children under 18 stay free with parents. Winter packages are available on request. The restaurant **Tables of Content** is located on the premises. ♦ 220 Huntington Ave (between Massachusetts Ave and Cumberland St). 262.1000, 800/343.1177; fax 262.8739 &

7 St. Botolph Street Stroll down this pleasant stretch of street, which New York City's Ash Can School painter George Benjamin Luks portrayed in *Noontime, St. Botolph* (on view in the **Museum of Fine Arts**). Look for the **Musician's Mutual Relief Society Building** at **No. 56,** an 1886 commercial hall designed by **Cabot and Chandler** that was renovated and suitably ornamented for the society's use in 1913 (it now houses apartments). Separated by stone lyres beneath the cornice are composers' names. At the Cumberland Street intersection is an attractive schoolhouse dating from 1891, converted to condominiums in 1980 by **Graham Gund Associates.** ♦ Between Gainsborough and Harcourt Sts

On St. Botolph Street:

HARVEY'S

Harvey's ★$$$ Formerly the **St. Botolph Street Restaurant,** this neighborly new two-story eatery in a rehabbed 19th-century town house is becoming popular with the local crowd. The American menu includes very good burgers, bratwurst, and roast chicken. There is a lively bar area and the place is jumping on weekends, when the restaurant is open until 2AM. ♦ American ♦ Daily lunch

and dinner. No. 99 (at W Newton St). 266.3030

8 Charlie's Sandwich Shoppe ★★$ Family-run for more than 50 years, this unpretentious luncheonette is a melting pot, attracting all types of folks in search of a hearty breakfast or lunch. Owner Christi Manjourides stays up all night baking pies and muffins, while sons Chris and Arthur wait tables by day. Relax among the awards, accolades, and smiling photos taken at the eatery since opening day in 1927. Start your day with a platter of cranberry pancakes or a Cajun omelette with spicy sausage. Lunch specials include cheeseburgers, Greek salad, turkey hash, frankfurters and beans, fried clams, hot pastrami on a bulky roll, sweet-potato pie, and more. It's pleasant to linger here—that is, if you can ignore the lines of people waiting impatiently for a table. Duke Ellington and other famous African-American musicians were welcomed here in the 1940s, a period when people of color were barred from most Boston restaurants. ♦ American ♦ M-Sa breakfast and lunch. No credit cards accepted. 429 Columbus Ave (between Braddock Park and Holyoke St). 536.7669

9 La Bettola ★★$$$ Small-but-ambitious, bustling-yet-chic, this Italian eatery is representative of the South End's offbeat and urbane persona. Though the restaurant's culinary base is Italian, chef Rene Michelena's dishes reflect Asian influences. The menu changes every eight weeks but might include such dishes as sirloin of lamb, served with gingered caponata (vegetable relish) and braised-lamb tortellini flavored with tumeric, paprika, and cumin. The handmade pasta dishes feature unusual ingredients—potato canneloni with turnip puree, portobello mushrooms, summer truffles, and fava beans, for example, and truffle-and-corn gnocchi with yellow peppers. Desserts include plum pie and bread pudding with bittersweet chocolate and Grappa-soaked cherries. ♦ Italian ♦ Daily dinner. Reservations recommended. 480A Columbus Ave (between Rutland Sq and W Newton St). 236.5252

On the eve of the Civil War, and following the Irish migrations beginning with the Great Hunger of 1846, Boston's population was one-third Irish.

The Emerald Necklace

Ponds and parks strung together by parkways form Boston's prized **Emerald Necklace,** which, when charted on a map, looks like it's dangling from Boston Harbor like a chain around a slender neck. Executed by the Boston Park Commission in 1895, landscape architect Frederick Law Olmsted's design encompasses more than 2,000 acres of open land, it's main artery the 5-mile-long "necklace."

The largest continuous green space through an urban center in the country, the **Emerald Necklace** crosses a number of communities and is adorned with five major parks—**Back Bay Fens, Muddy River Improvement, Jamaica Park, Arnold Arboretum,** and **Franklin Park**—all connected by parkways. Olmsted's necklace was further embellished by the joining of **Boston Common** and the **Public Garden.** The **Charles River Esplanade** is often considered an additional jewel on the chain, although it wasn't built until 1931, long after Olmsted's death. The necklace has missing links (which the city promises to eventually fix), the most important of which is the never-realized **Columbia Road** extension by which Olmsted intended to connect **Franklin Park** with **Marine Park** in **South Boston.** At press time such improvements were on hold until the year 2000 at the earliest.

The only way to see the entire **Emerald Necklace** at one time is to drive its length along the parkways, but the twisting route will offer only fleeting glimpses of greenery and water, not at all the restful communion with nature Olmsted had in mind. Instead, pick a fair-weather day and jog, bicycle, walk, or ride a horse through a segment of the park system.

The **Emerald Necklace** starts at **Boston Common (1),** proceeds through the **Public Garden (2),** then continues along **Commonwealth Avenue Mall (3)** to **Charlesgate (4),** the original connection forged between the **Mall** and the **Back Bay Fens (5),** where the Muddy River entered the **Charles River Estuary. Charlesgate's** open wetlands were largely destroyed when elevated overpasses to **Storrow Drive** were built during the 1960s, but it still provides a tenuous link between the **Mall** and the **Fens.**

Olmsted's first contribution to Boston's park system, the **Back Bay Fens** (named after the marshlands of eastern England) originally embodied the designer's love of idyllic English rural landscapes. Dredging, draining, and landscaping rescued the area from its reeking muddy past and made way for tranquil salt-marsh meadows. The damming of the **Charles River** in 1910 changed the water from salt to fresh, however, and destroyed Olmsted's original scheme. Years of neglect have also taken their toll. Yet the park is still a pleasant spot

to wander among willows, dogwoods, lindens, and hawthorns. The **Victory Gardens** planted during World War II and the spectacular **Rose Garden** behind the **Museum of Fine Arts,** as well as an athletic field, have settled in to stay. And the pudding stone bridge where **Boylston Street** crosses the river is a poetic charmer, designed in 1880 by Olmsted's friend **Henry Hobson Richardson.** A cautionary note: Don't walk in the **Fens** after dark and never stray into the stands of debris-laden tall reeds.

The **Muddy River Improvement (6)** is the next ornament in the chain, although its connection to the **Fens** via the **Riverway** was obliterated by construction of the former **Sears Roebuck** building. Make your way around the building to reach this meandering riverside park with graceful bridges, placid ponds, lush plantings, and bridle, walking, and running paths. The **Improvement**—unpoetically named for the spruce-up job it accomplished—widens at a section now called **Olmsted Park,** where **Leverett, Willow,** and **Wards Ponds** are located. Just south of these is **Jamaica Park (7),** its centerpiece the largest freshwater pond in Boston. Fringed by a tree-shaded promenade lit by gas lanterns, **Jamaica Pond** is popular for sailing, rowing, walking, jogging, and fishing. **Edmund March Wheelwright** designed the decorative 1913 boathouse and gazebo.

From Jamaica Pond, **Arborway** leads to the world-renowned **Arnold Arboretum (8)** (details on page 199), which belongs to the Boston park system but is administered by **Harvard University.** Charles Sprague Sargent, a landscape gardener and the arboretum's first director, collaborated with Olmsted in 1878 in designing this living museum of trees.

Linked to the arboretum by the **Arborway,** the **Emerald Necklace's** massive pendant is **Franklin Park (9),** named for Benjamin Franklin. One of Olmsted's three greatest parks, its design expresses his precept that the natural world offers the ideal antidote to the dehumanizing quality of urban living. Within this 500-acre tract straddling **Dorchester, Jamaica Plain,** and **Roxbury,** Olmsted preserved and enhanced existing natural features. **Franklin Park** is a great green swath of rolling hills and broad fields and meadows, with hickory, hemlock, locust, oak, and tulip trees, as well as a myriad of other plants, enormous boulders, and park ornaments fashioned from Roxbury pudding stone. But because the park is four miles from the heart of Boston and tricky to reach, it never achieved the popularity it deserved, and languished from the 1940s until the present. And like the **Fens,** changes have been made that spoil the integrity of Olmsted's original plan. It's still a gem, though, a sanctuary from the city where one can walk, jog, picnic, bird-watch, play golf or baseball, visit the zoo, and generally let loose a little. The 18-hole, par-70 golf course is the country's second-oldest municipal course. Although it will take time for **Franklin Park** to shake its unfair poor reputation, it is actually one of the city's safer parks. Nonetheless, don't linger after dark or stray into the overgrown areas.

The **Necklace** breaks after **Franklin Park,** but it should have led via **Columbia Road** through **Upham's Corner** and on to **Marine Park (10).** (A lack of funds kept Columbia Road from becoming the spacious green boulevard Olmsted intended.) Eclipsed long ago by suburban beaches, **Marine Park** no longer draws crowds, but the sea breezes and harbor views are worth an outing, and this is where you can look at the shiny bellies of the big jets as they descend to **Logan International Airport.** It's best to drive here; there's always plenty of parking.

Now missing from the **Emerald Necklace, Charlesbank** was a pioneering neighborhood park (designed by Olmsted in the 1890s) that once bordered the Charles River near **Massachusetts General Hospital.** The park was intended to alleviate the overcrowding suffered by residents of the **West End,** a neighborhood largely wiped out by urban renewal in the 1960s. **Charlesbank** featured the city's first playgrounds and America's first sandboxes, called "sand courts." Today **Charlesbank** is mostly buried under a tangle of roadways.

Boston's park rangers direct all kinds of activities throughout the Boston park system: historical tours, educational programs, nature walks through the **Arnold Arboretum,** bird watching along the Muddy River, fishing on Jamaica Pond, an architectural exploration of **Commonwealth Avenue,** and more. Some events require reservations; all are free. For information, call the **Boston Parks and Recreation Department** (635.4505) or the **Boston Park Rangers** (635.7383 or 635.7488).

Additional recreational and educational programs are planned for kids during the summer, including golf clinics at **Franklin Park,** "Sox Talk" with **Red Sox** players, and sailing on Boston Harbor and Jamaica Pond. Call the **Parks and Recreation Activities Eventline** (635.3445) for daily updates. Boston parks are officially closed from 11:30PM to 6AM.

10 Union United Methodist Church
Designed by **Alexander R. Estey,** the architect of **Emmanuel Church** in Back Bay, this 1877 Gothic Revival creation has the gracious proportions and picturesqueness of a rural parish church. Its demure size makes it all the more friendly and inviting. ♦ Daily. 485 Columbus Ave (at W Rutland Sq). 536.0872

11 Jae's Cafe and Grill ★$ The healthful Korean fare served in this crowded, bustling storefront has attracted the trendies; there's almost always a line. A full array of sushi and sashimi awaits, along with soups, satays (skewered meat or poultry with various sauces), and "rice specials" such as *yuk hai bi bim bab* (shredded raw beef marinated in seasoned sesame oil). There's valet parking. ♦ Korean ♦ Daily lunch and dinner. 520 Columbus Ave (between Worcester St and Concord Sq). 421.9405. Also at: 156 Cambridge St (at Hancock St). 367.3500; 1281 Cambridge St (between Prospect and Hampshire Sts), Cambridge. 497.8380

12 Harriet Tubman House Named for the "Moses of the South," a runaway slave and Underground Railroad organizer, this iconoclastic complex greets the street with a sense of spirit and purposefulness. It's home to United South End Settlements, a social service organization responsible for vital community programs. The architect, **Don Stull Associates,** deserves applause for doing a lot with a small budget. Incidentally, the house stands on the site of one of Boston's famous jazz clubs, **The Hi Hat,** which burned down. ♦ Daily. 566 Columbus Ave (at W Springfield St). 536.8610 ♿

13 Piano Craft Guild When new in 1853, the Chickering piano factory (pictured above) was reputedly the second-largest building in the country, dwarfed only by the US Capitol Building. The surprisingly graceful industrial structure is enlivened by a sprightly octagonal tower. It was renovated in 1972 by **Anderson Notter Associates** with **Bruner Cott Associates** and now houses artists' studios and living spaces. The project was one of the first and largest mill conversions in the state, an early example of the creative lengths local artists have gone to obtain affordable housing. The

two-story gallery shows works by residents. ♦ Call for hours. 791 Tremont St (at Northampton St). 437.9365

14 Rutland Square Bracketed by two rows of three-story bowfronts, this shady, slim, elliptical park is one of the South End's most intimate oases. A number of facades break from the neighborhood pattern of warm redbrick, and instead are prettily painted and detailed in light colors. Only one block long, the square is a lovely sliver of green. ♦ Between Tremont St and Columbus Ave

15 Villa Victoria Built in 1976 by **John Sharratt Associates,** this housing complex is a local success story. The South End's Puerto Rican community not only participated in every stage of its development, but also collaborated with the architect so that residents' cultural values and traditions would be expressed with dignity. While the complex is by no means beautiful, given limited funds, it has developed its own strong identity. ♦ Bounded by Shawmut Ave and Tremont St, and W Brookline and W Dedham Sts

16 Buteco II ★$ This easygoing hole-in-the-wall (its name is Portuguese slang for "joint") serves authentic Brazilian dishes like *mandioca frita* (fried cassava root with carrot sauce), *moqueca de peixe* (fish in spicy coconut sauce), and—Saturday and Sunday only— the popular *feijoada* (black-bean stew with sausage, dried beef, pork, rice, collard greens, and orange). Some traditional Spanish dishes are offered, too. The lively restaurant attracts an appreciative South American clientele. ♦ Brazilian/Spanish ♦ M-Sa lunch and dinner; Su dinner. Reservations recommended for groups of five or more. 57 W Dedham St (between Shawmut Ave and Tremont St). 247.9249 ♿

17 Geoffrey's Café and Bar ★★$ The 1950s decor and American comfort food make this a popular neighborhood spot. The big, juicy burgers are excellent, and there are sandwiches and salads for those looking for lighter fare. Though the service can be slow and the wait for a table long on weekends, it is a fine place to stop for breakfast, lunch, or coffee while exploring the South End. ♦ American ♦ M-F breakfast, lunch, and dinner; Sa-Su brunch and dinner. No reservations. 578 Tremont St (between Upton St and Union Park). 266.1122

18 Garden of Eden ★★$ All the fixings for a proper tea are prettily presented at this cafe, decorated with dried flowers and garden statuary. They carry top-notch teas, coffees, and jams, and such stellar baked goods as hearty whole-wheat loaves, rosemary focaccia, fruit tarts, and a full range of authentic French pastries. In addition, superb pastas, soups, and salads are available to eat on site or to take home. Try the garlic-parsley basil pasta tossed with sundried tomato–basil sauce and fresh pine nuts, or the *haricots verts* (thin string beans) tossed in a traditional French mustard-vinaigrette dressing. The most popular summer soup is the creamless cream of asparagus soup, thickened with puree of white rice. Sandwiches are topped with endive, watercress, romaine, or radicchio, and the meats arrive by truck once a week from New York City. It's the perfect place to grab a meal-on-the-run or to linger and stock a larder. ◆ Continental ◆ Daily breakfast and lunch. 577 Tremont St (between Dartmouth St and Union Park). 247.8377

TRUC

19 Truc ★★★$$$ "*Truc*" is French slang for "that little thing," but this small (only 42 seats), busy spot has attracted a rather large following among the chic set. Diners sit either in the greenhouse or in the long room with marble floors and tin ceilings. The menu, like the name, is French. Among the appetizers are seared foie gras served with fluffy mashed potatoes, and pork rillettes with toast points and fig jam. Entrées include halibut served over flageolet beans and tomato salsa; duck breast with caramelized onions served with celery puree and duck confit; and the more traditional coq au vin. Desserts include chocolate gateau, *quatre-quarts au citron* (a lemon pound cake with lemon curd), and crème brûlée. ◆ French ◆ Daily lunch and dinner. No reservations. 560 Tremont St (between Union Park and Waltham St). 338.8070

20 Addis Red Sea Ethiopian Restaurant ★★$ Adventurous diners sit around a *mesob* (woven table) and use bits of *injera* (crepelike bread) to scoop up morsels of chicken, lamb, beef, or vegetables. There are two basic preparations to choose from: *watt* (spicy) dishes are infused with *berbere* (cayenne pepper) sauce; the *alicha* (yellow pepper) choices tend to be a bit milder. Wash your dinner down with Ethiopian beer or wine. ◆ Ethiopian ◆ M-F dinner; Sa-Su lunch and dinner. 544 Tremont St (between Waltham and Hanson Sts). 426.8727

BOSTON CENTER FOR THE ARTS

21 Boston Center for the Arts (BCA) Since 1970, the city has subsidized art and cultural events at this three-acre complex. In addition to studios for some 60 artists chosen by their peers, there is office and performance space for various theater and dance groups.

One of the complex's many converted buildings is the **Cyclorama,** a beautiful, shallow, steel-trussed dome built by **Cummings & Sears** in 1884. Its original raison d'être was to house a novel tourist attraction: a 400-by-50-foot circular mural of the *Battle of Gettysburg* by Paul Philippoteaux, which is today exhibited in Gettysburg. Subsequently, the building served as a skating rink; a track for bicycle races; a gymnasium and workout ring for boxers, where Boston's famous prizefighter John L. Sullivan fought; Alfred Champion's garage, where he invented the spark plug; and a flower market from 1923 to 1968. The **Cyclorama** currently houses three theaters and is the site of annual and antiques shows, flea markets, and other large-scale events. The theaters (the **BCA Theater, The Black Box,** and the **Leland Center**) have hosted more than 30 different Greater Boston performing arts groups, which have presented both new and classical works here. The attractive kiosk out front was originally a cupola atop a Roxbury building designed by **Gridley J.F. Bryant**—architect of the **Old City Hall,** the original **Boston City Hospital** building, and other Boston landmarks. ◆ 539 Tremont St (between Clarendon and Berkeley Sts). 426.5000, recorded information 426.7700 &

Within the Boston Center for the Arts:

Mills Gallery Run by the **BCA,** this nonprofit gallery mounts far-ranging group shows by regional contemporary artists working in various media. Some performance pieces and installations are also shown. ◆ Th-Sa. 549 Tremont St. 426.8835 & (staff will assist)

Boston Ballet Center Corps of ballerinas leapt for joy when work was completed in 1991 on this splendid and spacious dance center—the largest in New England—designed by **Graham Gund.** The foyer itself is like a stage set, with a grand pair of bifurcating staircases. The largest of the studios duplicates the dimensions of the **Wang Center** stage, so that *The Nutcracker*—the most popular rendition in the world—can be rehearsed under authentic conditions. ◆ Tours can be arranged through the volunteer office. 19 Clarendon St (at Warren Ave). 695.6950 &

Hamersley's Bistro ★★★★$$$ Ambitious in cuisine, modest in decor, Gordon and Fiona Hamersley's restaurant is one of the most appealing in Boston. In the exposed kitchen Gordon and his crew don baseball caps and deftly turn out favorites inspired by French country cooking—golden roasted chicken, sirloin with mashed potatoes, bouillabaisse, cassoulet—as well as more adventurous flights of fancy like roasted salmon with oysters, bacon, and hollandaise sauce, or a marvelous grilled mushroom-and-garlic sandwich on country bread. Sunday is a day of rest for Gordon, with a slightly more casual and lower-priced evening menu. The cozy dining rooms are filled with an interesting assortment of neighborhood people, suburban visitors, and artists, actors, musicians, architects, and other creative folk. Valet parking is available. ♦ French ♦ Daily dinner. Reservations recommended. 553 Tremont St. 423.2700 ₷

22 **Olde Dutch Cottage Candy** This labyrinthine shop is notable for its kitschy atmosphere and eclectic merchandise—an odd mix of antiques, bric-a-brac, and handmade chocolate. ♦ Daily noon-5PM. 518 Tremont St (at Dwight St). 338.0233

23 **Berkeley Residence Club** $ Run by the **YWCA,** this 200-room residence for women combines features of a hotel, dormitory, and old-fashioned rooming house. The clientele is an interesting mix: tourists, students, and working and professional women, some of them long-term residents. The rooms are tiny—just the basics—with some doubles available. Each well-kept bathroom is shared by 13 to 16 women. There's a library, sitting room, laundry room, TV room, and pretty outdoor courtyard. The dining room serves two full meals a day (extra charge), with takeout available. Conveniently located, the residence is affordable and secure. Inquire about the rules, which aren't excessive and protect residents. The second floor has a less restrictive policy on gentlemen callers. There are nightly and weekly rates; short-term guests also pay a nominal fee for temporary membership. ♦ 40 Berkeley St (at Appleton St). 482.8850 ₷

CHANDLER INN
HOTEL

24 **Chandler Inn Hotel** $ Although a bit drab, this place is clean, safe, and a steal. The 56 rooms boast all the basic amenities, including air-conditioning, and there's a bar (but no restaurant) on the premises. Although it has a large gay clientele, it is genial to all, especially the budget-conscious traveler. ♦ 26 Chandler St (at Berkeley St). 482.3450, 800/842.3450

25 **Icarus** ★★$$$ The mood is muted and relaxed; the decor and cuisine, eclectic. Beneath a ceiling edged with neon, a statue of winged *Icarus* surveys the two-tiered dining room, where a diverse clientele enjoys chef/co-owner Chris Douglass's seasonal inspirations. The menu might include polenta with wild mushrooms and thyme, lobster in ginger-cream sauce on homemade noodles, grilled tuna with wasabi and sushi, pork loin with mango and jalapeño salsa, caramel-apple

tart, and cherry–chocolate-chunk ice cream with icebox cookies. The lengthy wine list is superb. Valet parking is available Wednesday through Sunday. ♦ International ♦ M-Sa dinner; Su brunch; closed Sunday in summer. Reservations recommended F-Su. 3 Appleton St (between Tremont and Berkeley Sts). 426.1790

25 **Appetito** ★★$$ Northern Italian cuisine is chef Richard Ansara's pride and joy. His spring menu features *rigatoni con pollo* (with grilled chicken and sun-dried cranberries in a spinach-brandy-cream sauce), *filetto di manzo* (beef tenderloin in a mushroom, Marsala, and plum-tomato sauce), and *gabbiano pizza* (brick-oven pizza with shrimp, fresh garlic, tomato, and mozzarella). The enticing cuisine is complemented by a daring color scheme of rich purple (bar and tables), deep red (columns), and rich amber (walls). ♦ Northern Italian ♦ Daily dinner. 1 Appleton St (at Tremont St). 338.6777 ₷

26 **Medieval Manor** $$$$ What to say about this inexplicably popular and long-running themed theater/restaurant? Well, simply this: An evening here involves a three-hour, gargantuan, eat-with-your-fingers, fixed-price feast of sorts, and bawdy musical comedy starring singing wenches, oafs, strolling minstrels, and a sexist "Lord of the Manor." More than enough said. The whole thing's participatory, which means you can get into the action if you so choose—joined by many others from the typically vocal audience. Students pack the place. Though the feast is heavy on roast meat and chicken, vegetarians can join the orgy, too, with 48 hours' advance notice. Parties of 4 to 8 are recommended, and no party of more than 10 is accepted if all male, all female, or all Harvard. There are more numbers-related rules; call to inquire. The best—possibly only—way to get here is by car: Take the John F. Fitzgerald Expressway south to the Albany Street exit; then turn right onto East Berkeley Street. ♦ American ♦ Admission. Call for show times. Reservations required. 246 E Berkeley St (between Albany St and Harrison Ave). 423.4900

27 **Union Park** Designed in the 1850s, the first square to be finished in the South End remains one of its most special places. Enclosed by an iron fence, the elliptical park is lush and shady and accented with fountains and flowers. It's bordered by big brick town houses dating from the neighborhood's brief shining moment before Back Bay became *the* place to lay out one's welcome mat. The handsome houses and perfect park commune harmoniously in their own little world. Regrettably, gauche modern hands have tacked on unsightly extra stories to the houses here and there, marring an otherwise splendid composition. ♦ Between Shawmut Ave and Tremont St

28 On the Park ★★$$ A sunny, friendly spot with windows all around, this cafe is a few strides away from the South End's prettiest swatch of green space, **Union Park.** It serves homemade breads and satisfying rustic dishes with roots that run the gamut from Southeast Asian to Latin American. Sunday brunch with Bellinis (Champagne and peach nectar) is a neighborhood event. The ever-changing art on the walls comes from local artists and Newbury Street galleries. Regulars and word-of-mouth keep the cafe's 34 seats filled. ♦ International ♦ M-F dinner; Sa breakfast, lunch, and dinner; Su brunch and dinner. Reservations required for groups of six or more. 1 Union Park St (at Union Park). 426.0862

29 To Go Bakery Here's the place to pick up marvelous breads, muffins, pastries, and desserts (try the ultrarich chocolate crater cake or the chocolate chubby cookies). As the name suggests, take-out orders are the main focus here, although the bakery does have a couple of tables and sells some lunch items, coffee, and sodas. Cakes can be made to order. ♦ Daily. No credit cards accepted. 312 Shawmut Ave (at Union Park St). 482.1015 &

ars libri, ltd.

30 Ars Libri Hidden away on the third floor of a nondescript converted factory building now occupied by architects, designers, and dancers is a quiet shop renowned internationally for its large and comprehensive inventory of rare and out-of-print books and periodicals about the fine arts (including architecture and photography). A visitor might encounter such treasures as: all of Francisco de Goya's *Los Caprichos;* drawings by Albrecht Dürer; a complete set of *Pan,* the stunning journal of the German *Jugendstil;* and an extremely rare edition of *La Prose du Transsibérien,* an extended poem illustrated by Sonia Delaunay. The owners buy and sell out-of-print and rare scholarly works, exhibition catalogs, print portfolios, and books with original graphics dating from the 16th century onward. Chances are you'll be pretty much alone here, since most business is conducted via subject-oriented catalogs sent to universities, libraries, museums, and individuals. **Machado Silvetti** designed this collector's sanctuary. ♦ M-Sa. No credit cards accepted. 560 Harrison Ave (between Waltham and Randolph Sts). 357.5212 &

30 Bromfield Gallery Boston's oldest artist-owned cooperative gallery exhibits contemporary art in a variety of media, realist to abstract, by member artists as well as emerging and established visiting artists. Exhibits change once a month and are solo or group shows. ♦ W-Sa noon-5PM. 560 Harrison Ave (between Waltham and Randolph Sts). 451.3605

31 Cathedral of the Holy Cross An unexpected sight along a sadly run-down stretch of Washington Street is this heroic Gothic Revival structure, completed in 1875 by **Patrick C. Keely.** New England's biggest church, and the largest Catholic church in the country when it was built, the cathedral recalls an era when Irish Roman Catholic immigrants were a dominant presence in the South End. The Roxbury pudding-stone cathedral seats 3,500 and accommodates 7,000, when you include standing room. It's still the principal church of the Archdiocese of Boston but is now used mainly for special occasions, such as when the Pope came to call in 1979. The front vestibule's arch contains bricks rescued from a Somerville (then called Charlestown) convent burned during anti-Catholic rioting in 1834. As is true of so many Boston ecclesiastical edifices, the intention was to surmount the two towers with spires, but that never happened. ♦ Daily. Washington and Union Park Sts. 542.5682

32 Blackstone and Franklin Squares Divided by Washington Street, both squares were built in the 1860s but originated in an 1801 plan to which **Charles Bulfinch,** then chairman of Boston's Board of Selectmen, was a major contributor. Although they have lost something to time, the squares' original grandeur remains palpable. Look for the brownstone houses overlooking the square on West Newton Street. These exemplars of old-world architectural elegance will transport you into the neighborhood's genteel past. At 11 East Newton Street stands the **Franklin Square House** apartments for the elderly. Built in 1868, the lumbering French Second Empire building—equipped with two steam-powered elevators—was originally the **St. James Hotel,** once considered the South End's poshest lodging place. At the height of the hotel's brief eminence, President Ulysses S. Grant stayed here. ♦ Bounded by St. George St and Shawmut Ave, and Newton and Brookline Sts

During the American Revolution, when churches associated with Tory sentiments were regarded as enemy outposts by many colonists, Trinity Church—predecessor to the Trinity Church that now stands in Copley Square—was the only Anglican church that remained open in Boston. Christ Church (today's Old North Church) closed in 1775, and the ministers of King's Chapel and Trinity fled north to Halifax, Nova Scotia, during the British evacuation of 1776. But Trinity's assistant minister, Samuel Parker, kept the parish doors open, wisely agreeing to delete prayers for the British king from the church's liturgy. He also endorsed the patriot cause.

Charles River Basin

Paths, playgrounds, lagoons, and lawns lace the Charles River Basin and its esplanade. Together, they form a lovely urban water park and the most spectacular section of the **Charles River Reservation**. Of all Boston's landmarks, this waterway is the most visually striking, especially the views of the downtown and **Back Bay** skylines and **Beacon Hill** from the Cambridge side. In this majestic, romantic setting, Bostonians congregate for promenades, outdoor concerts, picnics, jogging, bicycling, games, sailing, sculling, canoeing, and feeding the hungry ducks made famous in Robert McCloskey's 1941 children's book *Make Way for Ducklings*. In winter the riverside is still and quiet, and the Cambridge shoreline seems far away. But in fall, spring, and summer the 2-mile length of the esplanade from Beacon Hill to **Boston University** brims with activity, and the river sparkles with white sails. As the days heat up, free evening concerts draw enormous crowds to the **Hatch Shell**, where the pièce de résistance is the traditional Fourth of July **Boston Pops** concert, which attracts hundreds of thousands.

The lazy brown-green Charles casually zigs and zags, coiling left and right, even appearing at times to change its mind and turn back, before traversing an 80-mile course from **Hopkinton** to **Boston Harbor**—a distance of less than 30 miles as the crow flies. In general, the sluggish Charles is not an impressive river, shrinking to a mere stream in some places. But the Charles River Basin is the splendid lakelike section nine miles long that progresses from **Watertown**, past **Harvard University** and the **Massachusetts Institute of Technology (MIT),** and on to the Atlantic Ocean. Here the Charles has been sculpted into a splendid urban waterway.

The river got its name 15 years before the Puritans arrived, when explorer Captain John Smith sent early maps of New England home to 15-year-old Charles Stuart, the future King Charles I, and asked him to give its prominent features good English names. The river has always been a vital economic asset. Throughout the 18th and 19th centuries, industries fueled by the Charles included gristmills, sawmills, spinning and weaving companies, and manufacturers of paper products, leather, and chocolate. But intense industrialization polluted the river, and its estuary shrank from incessant landfilling. At low tide, the Charles was a malodorous eyesore bordering wealthy Back Bay, which is why that neighborhood appears physically to turn its back to the river.

In the early 1900s a long crusade to make the lower Charles healthy and attractive gained momentum. Prominent Boston and Cambridge residents, including landscape architect Charles Eliot (a colleague of Frederick Law Olmsted and founder of the Trustees of Reservations, a nonprofit conservation group) and philanthropists James J. Storrow and Henry Lee Higginson (founder of the **Boston Symphony Orchestra**) led the drive to build the **Charles River Dam** in 1908. This created the freshwater basin, with an embankment extending from **Charlesgate West** (where the **Back Bay Fens** meets the river) to the old **West End**. In the early 1930s Arthur A. Shurcliff, landscape architect of Colonial Williamsburg, greatly embellished the embankment, designing the picturesque esplanade and its lagoons with funding provided by Storrow's widow, Helen Osborn Storrow. In 1951 Boston's **Museum of Science** took up residence astride the **Charles River Dam** on the Boston-Cambridge boundary. In the early 1950s, **Storrow Drive**, the frenetic autoway, was built on the original embankment and, ironically, named for James Storrow, the avid supporter of the park it shouldered aside; Storrow Drive's counterpart on the Cambridge side of the river is **Memorial Drive.**

The Charles River has been steadily rebounding from severe abuse and pollution since the late 1970s. But while above **Watertown** the river is rated Class B (okay for swimming and fishing), below Watertown it is not swimmable. To see the river in its most protected natural state, visit the Massachusetts Audubon Society's **Broadmoor Wildlife Sanctuary**, a 600-acre tract along the Charles in **South Natick** and **Sherborn** (280 Eliot St, between South and Lake Sts, South Natick, 508/655.2296), about 18 miles from downtown Boston.

1 The Publick Theatre Inc.  Boston's oldest resident professional theater company has been staging performances under the stars for more than 20 years, in cooperation with the Metropolitan District Commission (MDC). Recent productions have included *A Little Night Music, Macbeth,* and *Richard III.* The company's season runs from late May to early September, with subscriptions and special discounts for families available. Purchase tickets at the on-site outdoor box office after 7PM on performance nights, or charge by phone; tickets are also available at **BosTix** outlets (see "Tickets" on page 10). The theater seats 200, and free parking and picnic facilities are nearby.
♦ Shows W-Su 8PM, weather permitting, late May–early September. Soldiers Field Rd and Everett St. 782.5425 &

2 Doubletree Guest Suites Hotel Boston/ Cambridge $$$ The site is inauspicious, right by the Cambridge/Allston exit on the Massachusetts Turnpike, but the 310 units on 16 floors are all two-room suites, most with good views (request one facing the river). Each suite has two TV sets, a wet bar and refrigerator, a living room with a fold-out sofa bed, and a bedroom with a king-size bed. Some bi-level suites are available on upper floors, and suites for people with disabilities and for nonsmokers are also available. There's an indoor pool, sauna, whirlpool, and exercise room, and reasonably priced on-premises parking. Complimentary van service is provided to downtown Boston and Cambridge. Ask about the hotel's special weekend rates.
♦ 400 Soldiers Field Rd (at Cambridge St). 783.0090, 800/424.2900; fax 783.0897 &

Within the Doubletree Guest Suites Hotel Boston/Cambridge:

Scullers Jazz Club If you're seeking jazz and light fare (pâté, smoked salmon, and the like) then this comfortable listening room will fit the bill. Local and national jazz and cabaret acts are booked here, with an emphasis on vocalists, and the crowd generally ranges in age from 25 to 75. ♦ Cover. Tu-Sa; two shows nightly. Reservations recommended. 562.4111 &

Scullers Grille ★$$ Seafood, including a great bouillabaisse, is featured here. Another highlight is the marvelous river view. ♦ Seafood ♦ M-Sa breakfast, lunch, and dinner; Su breakfast and dinner. Reservations recommended. 783.0090 &

3 Howard Johnson Cambridge $$ Most of the rooms (202 in all) in this modern high-rise have lovely views. Most folks prefer to overlook the river, although the Cambridge skyline is nice, too. The property also offers an indoor pool, free parking, and the **Bisuteki Japanese Steakhouse** and two other restaurants. It's about a 15-minute walk along the Charles (best by day) to Harvard Square. Rooms for nonsmokers are available, and pets are welcome. ♦ 777 Memorial Dr (at Pleasant St), Cambridge. 492.7777, 800/654.2000 &

4 Hyatt Regency Cambridge $$$$ A glitzy, glassy ziggurat-shaped structure nicknamed the "Pyramid on the Charles," the hotel has 469 rooms, some with outdoor terraces overlooking the river and Boston. The atrium rises 14 stories, with balconies, trees, fountains, and glass-cage elevators that offer a view of it all. The skylit health spa has an indoor pool, sauna, whirlpool, exercise room, and sundeck, plus a retractable ceiling and walls. There's also an outdoor basketball court. The hotel has adult's and children's bicycles for rent, so you can take a leisurely riverside journey. The place is popular with families (there's a special rate for a second room when traveling with children) and locals seeking a little weekend luxury as well as the usual business and convention crowds. Choose between valet or self-parking; a free van shuttles guests hourly to Harvard Square, Kendall Square, **Faneuil Hall Marketplace, Boston Common,** and **Copley Place.** Accommodations for people with disabilities and for nonsmokers are available. ♦ 575 Memorial Dr (at Amesbury St), Cambridge. 492.1234, 800/233.1234; fax 491.6906 &

Restaurants/Clubs: Red	Hotels: Blue
Shops/♥ Outdoors: Green	Sights/Culture: Black

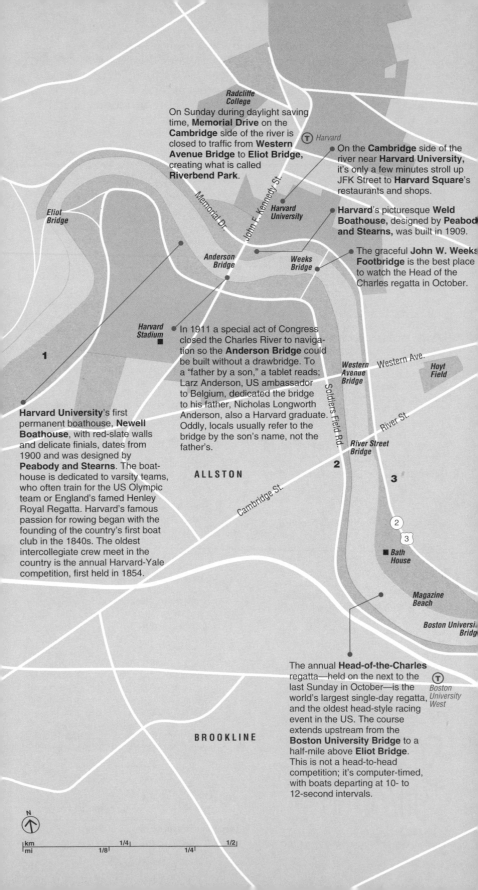

_Radcliffe
College_

On Sunday during daylight saving
time, **Memorial Drive** on the
Cambridge side of the river is
closed to traffic from **Western
Avenue Bridge** to **Eliot Bridge**,
creating what is called
Riverbend Park.

(T) _Harvard_

On the **Cambridge** side of the
river near **Harvard University**,
it's only a few minutes stroll up
JFK Street to **Harvard Square**'s
restaurants and shops.

_Harvard
University_

Harvard's picturesque **Weld
Boathouse**, designed by **Peabody
and Stearns,** was built in 1909.

_Eliot
Bridge_

_Anderson
Bridge_

_Weeks
Bridge_

The graceful **John W. Weeks
Footbridge** is the best place
to watch the Head of the
Charles regatta in October.

_Harvard
Stadium_ ■

In 1911 a special act of Congress
closed the Charles River to navigation so the **Anderson Bridge** could
be built without a drawbridge. To
a "father by a son," a tablet reads;
Larz Anderson, US ambassador
to Belgium, dedicated the bridge
to his father, Nicholas Longworth
Anderson, also a Harvard graduate.
Oddly, locals usually refer to the
bridge by the son's name, not the
father's.

1

_Western
Avenue
Bridge_

Western Ave.

_Hoyt
Field_

Soldiers Field Rd.

River St.

_River
Street
Bridge_

ALLSTON

2

3

Cambridge St.

②
③

Harvard University's first
permanent boathouse, **Newell
Boathouse**, with red-slate walls
and delicate finials, dates from
1900 and was designed by
Peabody and Stearns. The boathouse is dedicated to varsity teams,
who often train for the US Olympic
team or England's famed Henley
Royal Regatta. Harvard's famous
passion for rowing began with the
founding of the country's first boat
club in the 1840s. The oldest
intercollegiate crew meet in the
country is the annual Harvard-Yale
competition, first held in 1854.

■ _Bath
House_

_Magazine
Beach_

_Boston Universit
Bridg_

The annual **Head-of-the-Charles**
regatta—held on the next to the
last Sunday in October—is the
world's largest single-day regatta,
and the oldest head-style racing
event in the US. The course
extends upstream from the
Boston University Bridge to a
half-mile above **Eliot Bridge**.
This is not a head-to-head
competition; it's computer-timed,
with boats departing at 10- to
12-second intervals.

(T)
_Boston
University
West_

BROOKLINE

N
↑

| km | | 1/4 | | 1/2 |
| mi | 1/8 | | 1/4 | |

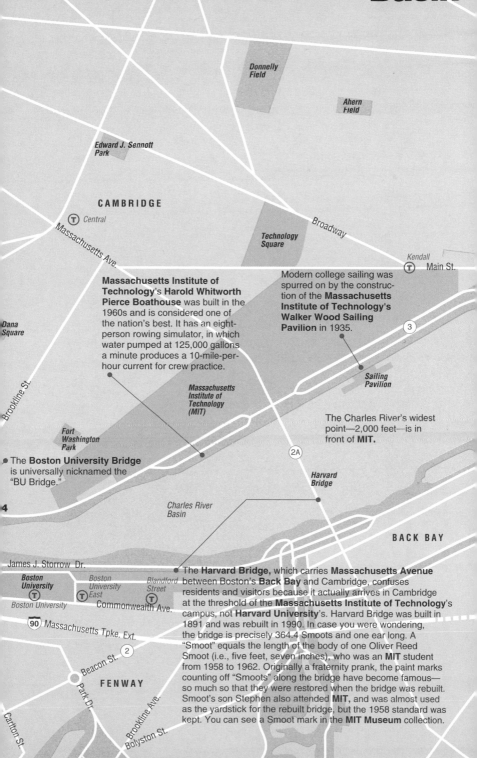

Charles River Basin

Donnelly Field

Ahern Field

Edward J. Sennott Park

CAMBRIDGE

(T) Central

Broadway

Massachusetts Ave.

Technology Square

Kendall
(T) Main St.

Dana Square

Massachusetts Institute of Technology's Harold Whitworth Pierce Boathouse was built in the 1960s and is considered one of the nation's best. It has an eight-person rowing simulator, in which water pumped at 125,000 gallons a minute produces a 10-mile-per-hour current for crew practice.

Modern college sailing was spurred on by the construction of the **Massachusetts Institute of Technology's Walker Wood Sailing Pavilion** in 1935.

3

Brookline St.

Massachusetts Institute of Technology (MIT)

Sailing Pavilion

Fort Washington Park

The Charles River's widest point—2,000 feet—is in front of **MIT.**

2A

• The **Boston University Bridge** is universally nicknamed the "BU Bridge."

Harvard Bridge

Charles River Basin

4

BACK BAY

James J. Storrow Dr.

Boston University
(T)
Boston University

Boston University
(T) East

Blandford Street

Commonwealth Ave.

(90) Massachusetts Tpke. Ext.

(2)

Beacon St.

Park Dr.

FENWAY

Brookline Ave.

Boylston St.

Carlton St.

• The **Harvard Bridge,** which carries **Massachusetts Avenue** between Boston's **Back Bay** and Cambridge, confuses residents and visitors because it actually arrives in Cambridge at the threshold of the **Massachusetts Institute of Technology's** campus, not **Harvard University's.** Harvard Bridge was built in 1891 and was rebuilt in 1990. In case you were wondering, the bridge is precisely 364.4 Smoots and one ear long. A "Smoot" equals the length of the body of one Oliver Reed Smoot (i.e., five feet, seven inches), who was an **MIT** student from 1958 to 1962. Originally a fraternity prank, the paint marks counting off "Smoots" along the bridge have become famous—so much so that they were restored when the bridge was rebuilt. Smoot's son Stephen also attended **MIT,** and was almost used as the yardstick for the rebuilt bridge, but the 1958 standard was kept. You can see a Smoot mark in the **MIT Museum** collection.

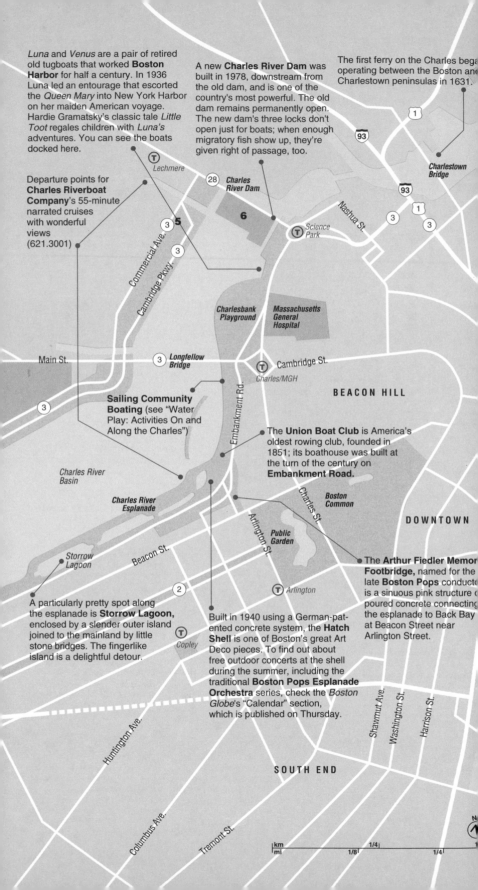

Luna and *Venus* are a pair of retired old tugboats that worked **Boston Harbor** for half a century. In 1936 Luna led an entourage that escorted the *Queen Mary* into New York Harbor on her maiden American voyage. Hardie Gramatsky's classic tale *Little Toot* regales children with *Luna's* adventures. You can see the boats docked here.

Departure points for **Charles Riverboat Company**'s 55-minute narrated cruises with wonderful views (621.3001)

A new **Charles River Dam** was built in 1978, downstream from the old dam, and is one of the country's most powerful. The old dam remains permanently open. The new dam's three locks don't open just for boats; when enough migratory fish show up, they're given right of passage, too.

The first ferry on the Charles began operating between the Boston and Charlestown peninsulas in 1631.

Lechmere

Charles River Dam

Science Park

5

6

Charlestown Bridge

Nashua St.

Charlesbank Playground

Massachusetts General Hospital

Main St.

Longfellow Bridge

Cambridge St.

Charles/MGH

BEACON HILL

Sailing Community Boating (see "Water Play: Activities On and Along the Charles")

The **Union Boat Club** is America's oldest rowing club, founded in 1851; its boathouse was built at the turn of the century on **Embankment Road.**

Charles River Basin

Charles River Esplanade

Charles St.

Boston Common

DOWNTOWN

Storrow Lagoon

Beacon St.

Public Garden

Arlington St.

Arlington

The **Arthur Fiedler Memorial Footbridge,** named for the late **Boston Pops** conductor, is a sinuous pink structure of poured concrete connecting the esplanade to Back Bay at Beacon Street near Arlington Street.

A particularly pretty spot along the esplanade is **Storrow Lagoon,** enclosed by a slender outer island joined to the mainland by little stone bridges. The fingerlike island is a delightful detour.

Built in 1940 using a German-patented concrete system, the **Hatch Shell** is one of Boston's great Art Deco pieces. To find out about free outdoor concerts at the shell during the summer, including the traditional **Boston Pops Esplanade Orchestra** series, check the *Boston Globe*'s "Calendar" section, which is published on Thursday.

Copley

Huntington Ave.

Shawmut Ave.

Washington St.

Harrison St.

SOUTH END

Columbus Ave.

Tremont St.

km
mi
1/8   1/4
1/4

Water Play: Activities On and Along the Charles

The Charles River is one of Boston's favorite places to enjoy outdoor sports and activities. Many people run, skate, and bicycle along the banks of the river, while numerous canoes, sailboats, and rowing shells ply its waters.

Sailing

Sailing vessels bearing passengers and freight, and later tugboats, tankers, and barges once navigated the river, but today recreational craft rule: canoes, rowboats, sailboats, and powerboats. The river is dotted with numerous boathouses and yacht clubs, many dating from the turn of the century, that offer rentals of various conveyances and classes and sponsor competitions.

Sailing Community Boating (21 Embankment Rd, between James J. Storrow Dr and Charles St, 523.1038; TTY 523.7406) is a nonprofit organization that offers sailing tours and instruction for everyone at the lowest possible prices. Located behind the **Hatch Memorial Shell,** its fleet includes more than 150 sailboats, plus Windsurfers. It is America's oldest and largest public sailing program, and offers many different options: monthlong and summer memberships, two- and seven-day visitor packages, and discounted programs for senior citizens and youths.

Canoeing and Rowing

More than 60 of the Charles River's 80 miles can be explored by canoe, although a few portages are required. The **Charles River Watershed Association** (527.2799), a private, nonprofit conservation group founded in 1965, recommends the *Charles River Canoe Guide;* on the last Sunday in April, it sponsors a set of popular races called the Run of the Charles.

The Massachusetts Audubon Society's **Broadmoor Wildlife Sanctuary** (280 Eliot St, between South and Lake Sts, South Natick, 508/655.2296) is a very popular destination for canoers. Many say the waterway is at its prettiest there.

Rowing and the Charles have had a long, romantic liaison. A single figure sculling gracefully over the river's surface is a common early morning sight in the pleasant-weather months. So, too, are "eights," crew boats with exhorting coxswains, which skim past and then disappear beneath the next bridge. Each year rowers from around the world and from a variety of American colleges compete in the **Head-of-the-Charles** regatta on the next-to-last Sunday in October. (Call 864.8415 for more information.)

Rent canoes, kayaks, and rowing shells at the **Charles River Canoe and Kayak Center** at the **Metropolitan District Commission (MDC)** building (2401 Commonwealth Ave, between Islington Rd and I-95, Newton, 965.5110). The center offers canoeing, kayaking, and rowing classes for all levels. Better

still, begin your journey farther up the river and rent your canoe at **Tropicland Marine and Tackle** (100 Bridge St, between Doggett Cir and Veterans of Foreign Wars Pkwy, Dedham, 329.3777).

For group or private rowing instruction, contact **Community Rowing Inc.** (1400 Soldiers Field Rd, between Telford St and Western Ave, 782.9091). Open to the public from April through October, it charges very reasonable monthly fees. **Community Rowing** also organizes adaptive rowers' groups for people with disabilities.

Running, Roller Skating, In-Line Skating, and Skateboarding

The favorite places to run and bicycle in Boston are the paths on both sides of the Charles. Roller and in-line skating, and skateboarding are popular here, too. Skates and boards can be rented from the **Beacon Hill Skate Shop** (135 Charles St S, between Melrose and Stuart Sts, 482.7400). For more information on bicycling, see "Boston By Bike: Plum Paths for Pedal Pushers" on page 94.

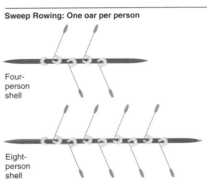

Sweep Rowing: One oar per person

Four-person shell

Eight-person shell

Sculling: Two oars per person

One-person shell

Two-person shell

Four-person shell

Within the Hyatt Regency Cambridge:

Spinnaker Italia ★$$ Boston's one and only revolving rooftop lounge and restaurant lets patrons gaze upon the city's twinkling night skyline, stretching from the Financial District and Beacon Hill to Back Bay and the **Prudential Center.** Although the cuisine is not as spectacular as the views, the Northern Italian menu includes tasty pastas, gourmet pizzas, and *petti di pollo* (roasted chicken breasts sautéed with artichoke). ♦ Italian ♦ M-Sa dinner; Su brunch and dinner. Reservations recommended; no jeans, sneakers, or T-shirts allowed. Free two-hour parking. 492.1234 ♿

5 Royal Sonesta Hotel Boston/Cambridge $$$ Ask for a room facing the river and look across at the gold dome of the **State House** gleaming above Beacon Hill. The hotel, which boasts an excellent modern art collection with pieces by Frank Stella, Andy Warhol, and Robert Rauschenberg, has 400 rooms furnished in contemporary style on 10 floors. On-site facilities include an indoor pool under a retractable roof, a fitness center, and two restaurants (see below). A courtesy van provides transportation to Harvard and Kendall Squares and Boston. The hotel provides guests with free ice cream, bicycles, and cameras during the summer, and vouchers for a free narrated river tour are available from early June to mid-September. There are rooms for nonsmokers and for people with disabilities. ♦ 5 Cambridge Pkwy (at Commercial Ave), Cambridge. 491.3600, 800/766.3782; fax 661.5956

Within the Royal Sonesta:

Davio's Ristorante ★★$$$ A favorite with Bostonians, this restaurant features Northern Italian cuisine and splendid views of the Charles River. The kitchen makes its own pasta and sausages, and lavishes attention on soups, seafood, venison, and veal. Some outstanding entrées include butternut squash fettuccini with red pepper, goat cheese, and toasted breadcrumbs, and grilled rosemary chicken with mushrooms, artichokes, lemon, and Pinot Grigio. A good wine list completes the dining experience. ♦ Italian ♦ M-F breakfast, lunch, and dinner; Sa-Su lunch and dinner. Reservations recommended. 491.3600. Also at: 269 Newbury St (between Fairfield and Gloucester Sts). 262.4810

Gallery Cafe $$ It's easy to relax at this casual eatery, where tasty seafood dishes are served. The room is bright and comfortable and there's riverfront dining in season. ♦ Continental ♦ M-F breakfast, lunch, and dinner; Sa-Su lunch and dinner. 491.3600

6 Museum of Science One of Boston's most familiar sights is this museum's funky 1950s silhouette above the Charles. Streams of families and fleets of school and tour buses arrive all day long. If you're with kids, you can be sure they'll have a great time. If not, you might wish the crowds would thin and the decibels lower, but you'll still squeeze past many interesting exhibits (see floor plan on page 171).

In the beginning, the museum was the **Boston Society of Natural History,** founded in 1830, then the **New England Museum of Natural History,** residing in an imposing French Academic edifice in Back Bay. In 1951 the museum moved to modern quarters on this site straddling the Charles River Dam and changed its name to reflect the forward-looking attitude that has made it so innovative. Under former director Bradford Washburn, a world-renowned explorer, mountaineer, and mapmaker, the pioneering museum embraced modern science and the high demands of today's sophisticated visitors, becoming a flexible, participatory place.

The **Exhibit Hall**'s 400-plus exhibits date from 1830 to this minute, covering astronomy, astrophysics, natural history, and much more. All-time favorites are the Plexiglas *Transparent Woman* with light-up organs, the chicken hatchery with its active eggs, the world's largest Van de Graaff generator spitting 15-foot lightning bolts, a space capsule replica, and the 20-foot-high model of tyrannosaurus rex. Walk on the moon or fly over Boston at the **Special Effects Stage,** or see how an ocean wave is made. Other popular features of the museum complex are the **Charles Hayden Planetarium** and **Mugar Omni Theater** (see below).

The museum sponsors exceptional educational programs for families, schools, and communities. Special events include the *Inventor's Weekend Exhibition,* when students' inventions—such as an automatic baseball-card stacker—are exhibited along with the creations of adults.

There are three cafeteria-style restaurants, but the one to try is the **Skyline Room Cafeteria**

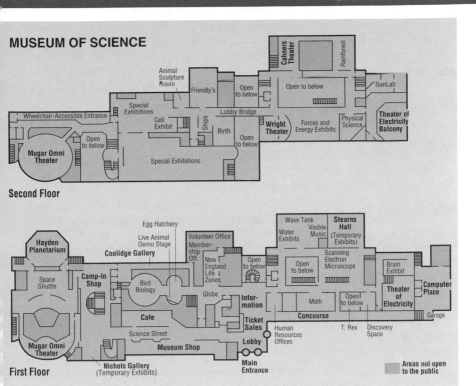

MUSEUM OF SCIENCE

Second Floor

- Animal Sculpture Room
- Cahners Theater
- Rainforest
- Friendly's
- Open to below
- Open to below
- SunLab
- Special Exhibitions
- Lobby Bridge
- Theater of Electricity Balcony
- Wheelchair-Accessible Entrance
- Cell Exhibit
- Ships
- Birth
- Wright Theater
- Forces and Energy Exhibits
- Physical Science
- Mugar Omni Theater
- Open to below
- Open to below
- Special Exhibitions

First Floor

- Hayden Planetarium
- Egg Hatchery
- Live Animal Demo Stage
- Coolidge Gallery
- Volunteer Office
- Membership Off.
- Wave Tank
- Water Exhibits
- Visible Music
- Stearns Hall (Temporary Exhibits)
- Space Shuttle
- Camp-In Shop
- Bird Biology
- New England Life Zones
- Open to below
- Open to below
- Scanning Electron Microscope
- Brain Exhibit
- Computer Place
- Cafe
- Globe
- Information
- Math
- Open to below
- Theater of Electricity
- Garage
- Mugar Omni Theater
- Science Street
- Museum Shop
- Ticket Sales
- Concourse
- Human Resources Offices
- T. Rex
- Discovery Space
- Nichols Gallery (Temporary Exhibits)
- Lobby
- Main Entrance
- Areas not open to the public

for its captivating views—perhaps the city's best—of Boston on one side of the Charles, Cambridge on the other, and boats passing through the dam below and cruising upriver. Also be sure to explore the unparalleled **Museum Shop**, which has a fantastic inventory of science-related projects, gadgets, toys, jewelry, books, and T-shirts. Parking is available for a fee. ◆ Admission; discounts for senior citizens and children 3 to 14; children under three free. Separate admission fees for the **Charles Hayden Planetarium** and **Mugar Omni Theater**; combination discount tickets available. Daily; F until 9PM. Monsignor O'Brien Hwy (between Charles St and Commercial Ave). 723.2500, TDD 227.3235 &

Within the Museum of Science:

Charles Hayden Planetarium A $2-million Zeiss planetarium projector and state-of-the-art multi-image system create enthralling programs on what's happening in the heavens: everything from the seasonal skies over Boston to phenomena like black holes and supernova. There are also special laser shows. Not recommended for children under four. ◆ Admission; discounts for senior citizens and children 4 to 14. M-Th; F 9AM-9PM; Sa-Su. Call for show times. 723.2500 &

Mugar Omni Theater In Massachusetts' only OMNIMAX theater, a tilted dome 76 feet in diameter and four stories high wraps around the audience, and state-of-the-art film

technology makes them feel as though they're surrounded by the images on the screen. The regularly changing films project viewers into locales such as the tropical rain forest or Antarctica, inside the human body, on a rocket to outer space, or on a roller-coasterlike tour of Boston. Not recommended for children under four. ◆ Admission; discounts for senior citizens and children 4 to 14. Daily. Call for show times. Reservations recommended. 723.2500 &

Bests

Jeffrey Twiss
Director of Public Relations, Boston Celtics

Fenway Park—unique pro-baseball stadium.

Museum of Science—terrific displays.

Mugar Omni Theater—great feature films.

New England Aquarium—always a treat for any age.

John F. Kennedy Library and Museum—something everyone must see.

Public Garden (summer)—**Swan Boats** and people watching!

Faneuil Hall Marketplace—great stores and food!

The Children's Museum—great hands-on stuff.

Top of **Prudential Tower**—outstanding views of Boston.

Filene's Basement—great bargains on clothes!

Legal Sea Foods restaurant—the *best* in seafood!!

Cambridge

Across the **Charles River** is Boston's intellectual, self-assured neighbor, Cambridge Both Boston and Cambridge are crowded with numerous college campuses, but it's Cambridge that exudes a true Ivy-League ambience. Many identify Cambridge with **Harvard University**, the nation's first college, which is as old as the city itself; others associate it with the prestigious **Massachusetts Institute of Technology (MIT)**, which moved here from Boston in 1916. The two giant institutions have a total of more than 28,000 students, hailing from nearly 100 nations. Since World War II, **MIT** and **Harvard**, with government and industry support, have made Cambridge a world-renowned research center that focuses on military and aerospace industries, artificial intelligence, and genetic engineering. These partnerships have spurred the growth of related industries in Cambridge and other Massachusetts cities, creating the state's high-tech economy.

In 1630 **Newtowne** village was founded by the Massachusetts Bay Colony, led by Governor John Winthrop. Eight years later the settlement was nostalgically renamed Cambridge, after the English university where many Puritans had been educated. That same year, the college founded here two years earlier by the colony's Great and General Court was named **Harvard College** to memorialize John Harvard, a young Charlestown minister who bequeathed his 400-volume library and half his estate to the fledgling school. And in 1639 the New World's first printing press was established in Cambridge, publishing the first American document, *Oath of a Free Man*. No other settlement in the colony was permitted a press until 1674, so Cambridge became the earliest publishing center of the hemisphere, ensuring its prominence as a place of ideas.

Today Cambridge is still a place of ideas. The engine of academia drives this 6.25-square-mile city of over 95,000 "Cantabrigians" (as Cambridge residents are known), half of whom are affiliated in some way with the local universities. But that is by no means the whole story. Cambridge has traditionally been a place for progressive politics and lawmaking, where generations of residents have embraced such causes as the abolition of slavery, women's rights, the antinuclear movement, environmentalism, opposition to the Vietnam War and US foreign policy in Central America, and many other concerns. So strong is its reputation as a bastion of liberalism that some people of a more conservative political bent dismiss Cambridge as an uppity enclave of eggheads and bleeding hearts.

But the city is known for cultural diversity as well, for it is full of people from somewhere else. The cafes, bookstores, shops, and restaurants here reflect a multicultural mix—a mélange of Yankee gentry, blue-collar workers, conservatives, liberals, immigrant newcomers, and long-established ethnic groups. They live in **Brattle Street** mansions, crowded triple-deckers, chic condos, and subsidized housing. In 1846 Cambridge officially became a city when **Old Cambridge** joined with the industrial riverside communities of **East Cambridge** and **Cambridgeport**. Today the city consists of several distinctive but loosely defined neighborhoods: **Kendall Square**, East Cambridge, **Inman Square**, **Central Square**, Cambridgeport, **Riverside**, **Mid-Cambridge**, **North Cambridge**, **West Cambridge**, and the famous **Harvard Square**. **Massachusetts Avenue**, which connects Boston with Cambridge via the **Harvard Bridge** across the Charles River, runs the entire length of Cambridge through **MIT**'s campus to Harvard Square and northward.

It would take several days to fully comb Cambridge, so most visitors head directly to Harvard Square (commonly referred to as "the Square"), the city's centerpiece and the heart of Old Cambridge. Overdevelopment and the invasion of franchises have eroded some of its quirky charm, but you can still sit in cafes and browse in bookstores, pretending to read while overhearing amazing conversations among an extraordinarily eclectic group. On a warm afternoon sit at the **au bon pain** outdoor cafe and watch all of Cambridge stroll by. In summer the nighttime street life bustles, especially near **Brattle Square** (a tiny square-within-the-Square) where outdoor entertainers hold forth every few yards. Harvard Square boasts a galaxy of bookstores catering to every interest, and many stay open very late. Among the commercial landmarks are the **Harvard Coop, Out of Town News, WordsWorth**, and **Charles Square**, a hotel-and-shopping complex. Student-oriented "cheap eats" as well as fine dining opportunities abound; as do vintage and avant-garde clothing boutiques and housewares and furnishings stores. Experience the overwhelming aura of **Harvard Yard**, then walk up Brattle Street (formerly **Tory Row**) and visit lovely **Radcliffe Yard**. You'll see plenty of historic edifices and some interesting modern architecture. The square offers good theater, movies, and music in a variety of settings, plus **Harvard**'s great museums. Along with **MIT** and other local colleges and institutions, **Harvard** hosts a long menu of lectures, exhibitions, symposia, and cultural and sports events throughout the academic year.

To get to Cambridge from Boston, take the **MBTA** *Red Line*: The **Kendall Station** is closest to **MIT** and is also near East Cambridge. (The **Lechmere Station** on the *Green Line* is even more convenient to East Cambridge.) The **Central Station** is a five-minute walk from Inman Square; the **Harvard Station** brings you right to the heart of the Square and is convenient to parts of North Cambridge; the **Porter Station** is nearest to North Cambridge. In addition, *Bus #1* runs along Massachusetts Avenue from Harvard Square in Cambridge across the Charles River to Boston's Back Bay, continuing on Massachusetts Avenue to **Roxbury**.

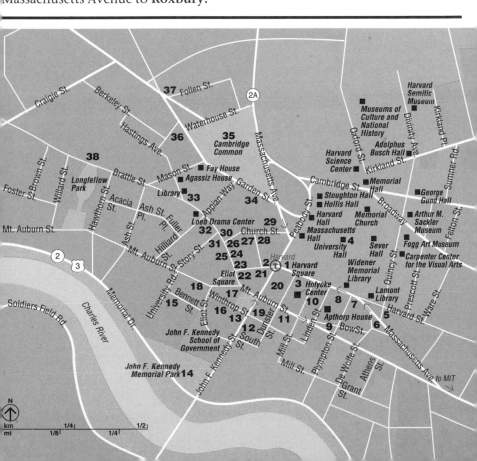

1 Harvard Square Not really a square at all, it's officially located where Massachusetts Avenue turns and widens into a big triangle, on which the 1928 landmark kiosk, **Out of Town News,** is located. On one side of this triangle is **Harvard University;** on the other two lies commerce. But to students and Cantabrigians, "the Square" always refers to the much larger area radiating from this central point, with most shops, restaurants, clubs, and services concentrated on Brattle, JFK, and Mount Auburn Streets, as well as on many small side streets like Church, Plympton, Dunster, and that whimsical pair, Bow and Arrow Streets. All around the Square, sidewalks are crowded with college students, professors, canvassers, protesters, businesspeople, and entertainers—in fact, you can safely assume you're heading beyond the Harvard Square area when the foot traffic around you starts to dwindle. ♦ Massachusetts Ave, Brattle St, and John F. Kennedy St

On Harvard Square:

Cambridge Visitor Information Booth
Located near the subway station entrance is a kiosk that distributes bus and train schedules, maps, brochures, and a wealth of other material on Cambridge and its universities. Some of the publications, including a seasonal calendar and a guide to the myriad area bookstores, are free and some are sold for modest fees. Especially noteworthy are the free booklets that describe great self-guided walking tours of Old Cambridge. Many of the volunteers who staff this information booth speak languages other than English and are well equipped to respond to questions from visitors and locals alike. To request information in advance of your visit, write **Cambridge Visitor Information Booth,** Cambridge, MA 02138. ♦ Daily. 497.1630 ໒

Out of Town Newspapers Busy from opening to closing, this National Historic Landmark newsstand—always called **Out of Town News**—sells newspapers from every major American city and many large cities worldwide, plus a huge array of magazines, maps, comic books, and **Harvard** T-shirts. Many a rendezvous is kept at this ornate kiosk. If your craving for newspapers and mags isn't sated here, try **Nini's Corner** (547.3558) across the way, next to the **Harvard Coop,** where there are lots of souvenirs and postcards, too. Also on this traffic island is sculptor Dimitri Hadzi's 21-foot-tall *Omphalos* (Greek for navel), signifying the center of the universe. Generations of **Harvard** students and Cantabrigians have considered the Square precisely that. ♦ Daily. No credit cards accepted. 354.7777 ໒ (use the rear entrance)

> Harvard College was the only college in North America until 1693.

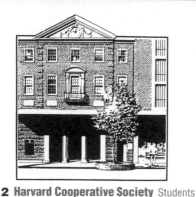

2 Harvard Cooperative Society Students angered at local merchants' price gouging founded the society in 1882. Their enterprise sold goods to faculty and students, and gradually blossomed into a the largest college cooperative in the US, today universally known as **The Coop** (pronounced like the chicken abode). The store (see the illustration above) is owned by its members: **Harvard** and **MIT** students, faculty, employees, and alumni.

In 1996 the booksellers **Barnes & Noble** took over management of **The Coop,** and major renovation to the building created a new look inside, but the institution essentially remains the same. Some departments were expanded (books, music), some closed (housewares, sports equipment, fashions, electronics, luggage), and some remain as they've always been (New England's best selection of posters, prints, and frames; basic clothing; stationery products; basic furnishings for apartments and dormitory rooms; and, of course, anything and everything imaginable emblazoned with Harvard colors and the *Veritas* seal). Sidewalk sales are often set up on Palmer Street, between the original building facing the Square and its annex. Happily, you can also find rest rooms here, the only public ones in the Square. ♦ M-Sa. 1400 Massachusetts Ave (at JFK St). 499.2000 ໒ Also at: Numerous locations throughout Cambridge

3 au bon pain ★$ The mass-produced croissants are surprisingly tasty; they also sell muffins, sandwiches, and soups. The real reason to come here is to relax outside on the large terrace in nice weather and watch the incessant tide of humanity flow to and from the Square. Students of human nature won't find a better vantage point or more varied collection of people in Greater Boston. Singers, jugglers, and promoters of various causes often hold forth alongside the cafe. A local chess master regularly plays against the clock for a small sum at one of the cafe's chess tables, attracting aficionados. ♦ Cafe ♦ Daily 6AM-midnight. No credit cards accepted. 1360 Massachusetts Ave (at Dunster St). 497.9797

4 Harvard University The first and foremost of the famed "Ivy League" schools was originally founded to train young men for the ministry. The university's seal (pictured above) was adopted in 1643; *Veritas* is Latin for "truth." **Harvard College** gradually moved from Puritanism to intellectual independence, and became a private institution in 1865. In the mid–19th century the college became the undergraduate core of a burgeoning modern university, with satellite professional schools.

Today there are 11 **Harvard** graduate schools: **Arts and Sciences, Business Administration, Dental Health, Design, Divinity, Education,** the **Extension School, Government, Law, Medicine,** and **Public Health.** With 400-odd buildings on 380 acres of land in the Cambridge/Boston area, the university and its Cambridge surrounds are so entwined that it's hard to tell where town ends and gown begins. The current endowment of $11.2 billion (give or take many millions) represents the largest of any university in the world. **Harvard** "houses," where students live after their freshman year, dot the Square toward the river and include lovely Georgian-style brick residences with courtyards. Most memorable are the **River Houses,** best seen from the Charles.

Within Harvard University:

Harvard University Information Center/Holyoke Center Located on the ground floor of **Holyoke Center,** in the arcade, the center distributes maps, pamphlets, self-guided walking tours, and other materials (some free, some sold) on the university and area events. Tickets for university events are sold here, too. Get a free copy of the *Harvard University Gazette,* which lists activities open to the public. Students also offer free one-hour tours (departing from the **Information Center**) that give visitors a good general introduction to the university.

Also in **Holyoke Center,** at street level, is a branch of **BosTix** (482.BTIX), which sells tickets to Harvard events as well as performances by some 150 area arts groups. It's open daily. ♦ Information Center: M-Sa. Campus tours: M-F 10AM and 2PM; Sa 2PM during the academic year; daily in summer. 1350 Massachusetts Ave (between Holyoke and Dunster Sts). 495.1573 ⅃

 Harvard Yard Verdant and dappled with sun and shade, its great trees sentinels to the education of generations, this expanse—now on the National Register of Historic Places—exudes an aura of privilege and prestige, the very essence of the institution. Anyone is welcome to relax on its grassy lawns, although when late spring arrives the air becomes thick with lawn fertilizer and noisy with machinery as the university starts sprucing up for another commencement. Summer mornings are particularly tranquil here; early fall heralds the return of the students and faculty with their brisk, purposeful traffic to and from classes.

The university's oldest buildings date from the early 18th century; its newest were built yesterday. From **Holyoke Center,** cross Massachusetts Avenue and enter the gate, where you'll find the **Benjamin Wadsworth House,** an attractive yellow clapboard house, built in 1726, where **Harvard** presidents resided until 1849. It briefly served as General George Washington's headquarters when he took command of the Continental Army in Cambridge in 1775. Walk through the western side of the yard (considered the "Old Yard"); to the left is Early Georgian **Massachusetts Hall,** the oldest university building, dating from 1720, where the president's offices are now located. Patriot regiments were once housed here and in several other buildings nearby. Opposite is **Harvard Hall** (built in 1766); between the two halls is **Johnston Gate** (erected in 1889), the main entrance, which was designed by **McKim, Mead & White.** Standing at attention by the gate is a bit of frippery, a tiny guardhouse designed by **Graham Gund.** Next on the left is **Hollis Hall** (completed in 1763), where John Quincy Adams, Ralph Waldo Emerson, and Henry David Thoreau roomed. Beyond is **Holden Chapel** (built in 1742), a High Georgian gem, complete with a family coat of arms. Once called "a solitary English daisy in a field of Yankee dandelions," it has been tarnished through constant alterations. Next is **Stoughton Hall,** designed in 1805 by Harvard graduate **Charles Bulfinch.**

Opposite **Johnston Gate** on the right stands **University Hall,** designed by **Bulfinch** in 1815. It was this building that created the illusion of an academic enclave, instead of merely clusters of buildings facing outward. In front stands Daniel Chester French's 1884 statue of John Harvard (French also sculpted the statue in the Lincoln Memorial in Washington, DC). This statue is famous for the three lies set forth in its plaque stating "John Harvard, founder 1638." It is the image of an 1880s **Harvard** student, not of Harvard himself; Harvard was a benefactor, not a founder; and the college was founded in 1636. Nevertheless, the false John is nearly always surrounded by tourists and visitors. Although the light here is poor for photos, you'll probably have to swing wide of clusters of people posing.

Behind **University Hall,** in the "New Yard," is **Memorial Church** (constructed in 1932), with its soaring needle-sharp spire. By school regulations, the church's wonderful **University Choir** only performs during religious services here. Installed in the church is a glorious organ, a creation of the late C.B. Fisk of Gloucester and one of the greatest American instruments built according to Baroque principles. Many important international organists have vied to play it. Looming opposite is the massive **Widener Memorial Library** (see below), which is across the grassy **Tercentenary Theatre,** where the university's commencements are held with all the traditional ruffles and flourishes—even a Latin oration. As you head in that direction you'll pass Romanesque Revival **Sever Hall** on your left, designed by **Henry Hobson Richardson** in 1880, a National Historic Landmark and one of his greatest buildings. Study its brilliantly animated and decorative brickwork.

Alongside **Widener Library** are **Pusey Library,** where the university's archives and map and theater collections are stored, and **Houghton Library,** home to its rare books and manuscripts, including memorabilia and furnishings from Emily Dickinson's Amherst home, and the single book remaining from John Harvard's library. **Pusey** often exhibits selections from its theater collection on the first floor, and **Houghton** offers public displays of some of its many treasures, with an emphasis on fine bookmaking. Near **Lamont Library,** which is tucked in the corner, is a Henry Moore sculpture called *Four-Piece Reclining Figure.* ♦ Bounded by Quincy and Peabody Sts, Massachusetts Ave, Broadway, and Cambridge St

Within Harvard Yard:

Harry Elkins Widener Memorial Library
A more triumphal and imposing entrance than this would be hard to find, with its massive Corinthian colonnade and grand exterior staircase. Chilly gray and austere, this library (built in 1915) is the patriarch in **Harvard**'s family of nearly 100 department libraries campuswide. It was named for Harry Elkins Widener, who went down with the *Titanic;* a plaque inside the entrance tells the story.

The largest university library in the world, it has 7.5 million volumes on more than five miles of bookshelves; the collection of books found here is only surpassed by the Library of Congress and the New York City Public Library. (The entire **Harvard** library system contains more than 12 million volumes, plus manuscripts, microforms, maps, photographs, slides, and other materials.) The building is open to the public, but access to its stacks is limited to cardholders with **Harvard**

affiliation and those with special permission. In the resplendent **Harry Elkins Widener Memorial Room,** bibliophile and collector Harry's books are on display, including a *Gutenberg Bible,* one of only 20 complete copies remaining, and a First Folio of Shakespeare's plays dated 1623, the first collected edition. Look for the dioramas depicting Cambridge in 1667, 1775, and 1936; and the John Singer Sargent murals in the main stair hall. ♦ Daily when school is in session; M-F during school vacations. 495.4166 &

Harvard Science Center
The largest building on **Harvard**'s campus—built by **Sert, Jackson and Associates** in 1973—looks like a giant Polaroid Land camera, with a complex and multiterraced exterior. Science buffs take note: On the center's lower level you'll find **Harvard**'s *Collection of Historical Scientific Instruments,* a repository for scientific apparatus used for **Harvard** teaching and research in astronomy, surveying, physics, geology, electricity, navigation, and other subjects since 1765, with additional devices donated to the university dating back to 1450. On view are telescopes, sundials, clocks, vacuum pumps, microscopes, early computing devices, and more. There are occasional exhibitions of private collections as well. Outside, the *Tanner Fountain,* designed by sculptor Peter Walker, is a jet-misted cluster of rocks that's always alluring to children. ♦ Free. Tu-F; closed June through August. Oxford and Kirkland Sts. 495.2779 &

Museums of Culture and Natural History
Sharing one roof are four separate **Harvard University** museums dedicated to the study of archaeology, botany, comparative zoology, and minerals. The most famous exhibition is the **Botanical Museum**'s *Blaschka Glass Flowers* collection, handblown by Leopold and Rudolph Blaschka in Dresden, Germany, from 1887 to 1936 using a process that was lost with their deaths. More than 840 plant species are represented, with a few irrevocably lost when shattered by sonic booms. Another odd **Botanical Museum** exhibit is Rosalba Towne's 19th-century series of paintings depicting every plant and flower mentioned in the works of Shakespeare. Particularly wondrous is the **Mineralogical and Geological Museum**'s collection of gemstones, minerals, ores, and meteorites. Look for the giant Mexican crystals.

The **Peabody Museum of Archaeology and Ethnology** is the oldest museum of its kind in this hemisphere, with treasures from prehistoric and historic cultures from all over the world. Founded in 1866 by George Peabody, the museum owns many items brought back from **Harvard**-sponsored expeditions. The **Peabody**'s largest collections focus on North, Central, and South American Indian cultures.

The **Hall of the North American Indian,** for example, boasts some 500 artifacts, including magnificent towering totem poles, peace pipes, a Plains Indian ceremonial outfit, warriors' long bows, and a number of items brought back by the Lewis and Clark expedition. The exceptionally comprehensive collection includes objects from 10 different Indian cultures over 5 centuries.

Tracing the evolution of animals and man, the **Museum of Comparative Zoology** delights kids with such treasures as whale skeletons; a 180-million-year-old *Paleosaurus;* the 25,000-year-old **Harvard** mastodon; the giant sea serpent *Kronosaurus;* George Washington's pheasants; the world's oldest egg, 225 million years old; and the largest known fossilized turtle shell. The museum also displays a skeleton of the *Coelacanth,* a fish thought to have been extinct for 70 million years until fishermen began to catch some live in 1938. Visit the museums' gift shop, a largely undiscovered treasure trove. The **Peabody** has a separate gift shop, also excellent. ♦ Admission (one fee for all four museums); free Sa 9-11AM; children under 5 free; reduced fee for senior citizens, students, and children 5 to 15. Daily. 24 Oxford St (between Kirkland and Hammond Sts). 495.3045, recorded information 495.1910 ♿ (inquire at admission desk)

Harvard Semitic Museum Founded in 1889, the museum participated in the first US archaeological expedition to the Near East that year, and the first scientific excavations in the Holy Land, from 1907 to 1912. The museum closed during World War II and reopened in 1982. It now presents special exhibitions drawn from its archaeological and photographic collections, which include 28,000 photographs of 19th-century life in the Near East. ♦ Admission. M-F; Su 1-4PM. 6 Divinity Ave (north of Kirkland St). 495.3123

Adolphus Busch Hall Named for the famous beer baron, this noble hall was formerly the **Busch-Reisinger Museum.** It is now occupied by **Harvard**'s **Center for European Studies.** Designed by a German architect and completed in 1917, the Medieval-style edifice was built to house the university's Germanic collections. Full of carved heroes, solemn inscriptions, and other lavish details, it was enormously expensive to build. Originally created to laud German culture, the hall and its purpose have been influenced by the world wars and changes in international opinion toward Germany. Much of the former museum's 20th-century German art was collected during the rise of Hitler, when the works were declared degenerate, banned by the Nazis, and shipped to the US.

The **Busch-Reisinger**'s Renaissance, Baroque, and modern holdings have been moved to the newer **Werner Otto Hall,** the creation of architects **Gwathmey and Siegel,** located behind the **Fogg Art Museum** (see page 178). It is not open to the public. Still displayed in **Busch Hall** are medieval statuary, stained glass, metal, and other works not needing a climate-controlled environment. Overlooking the wonderful courtyard garden are carved stone heads depicting characters in Wagner's *Ring of the Nibelungen.* Evening concerts are given on the famous Flentrop organ as part of the **Fogg** music series; a small fee is charged. Across Kirkland Street from the hall is a Gothic Swedenborgian church, a little jewel. ♦ Courtyard M-F 11AM-3PM; collection 1-5PM second Sunday every month. 29 Kirkland St (at Divinity Ave). Concert information 495.9400

Memorial Hall Just north of Harvard Yard looms this Ruskinian Gothic giant (pictured above). With its square tower, pyramidal multicolored slate roofs, gargoyles, and colorful ornamentation, the cathedral-like structure has pomp and circumstance to spare. Designed in 1878 by two Harvardians, **Henry Van Brunt** and **William R. Ware,** the hall was built as a monument to university alumni who died in the Civil War—on the Yankee side, of course. Their names are inscribed in the transept inside. Some of the stained-glass windows were produced in the studios of Louis Comfort Tiffany and John La Farge. Innumerable momentous events— depending on one's perspective—have occurred here, from college registration and examinations to major lectures and concerts. Fine as the building was, until a major renovation was completed in 1996 it had been a drab-looking structure. But a rebirth into a student commons and freshman dining hall, coordinated by oft-time controversial Philadelphia architect **Robert Venturi,** has restored its original glory. Busts and portraits retrieved from storage, new chandeliers copied from lost gas-lamp originals, stained-glass windows, and a painted azure ceiling can now be seen in the building's **Annenberg Hall. Loker Commons,** in the basement of **Memorial Hall,** is a food and schmooze court, and open to the public. ♦ Cambridge St (between Quincy St and Massachusetts Ave) ♿

Within Memorial Hall:

Sanders Theatre Celebrated painter Frank Stella and many other illustrious figures have lectured in the richly carved wooden theater, which seats 1,160. Such national performers as the **Beaux Arts Trio** and local music groups, including the **Pro Arte Chamber Orchestra of Boston, Cantata Singers, Cecilia Society,** and the **Cambridge Society for Early Music** have also appeared here. Festive Christmas Revels is an annual event. ♦ Admission for most events. General information 496.2222, recorded information 495.4595 & (use the Kirkland St entrance)

George Gund Hall Home of the **Harvard Graduate School of Design,** this modern concrete building—completed in 1972 by **John Andrews**—is notable for the striking nighttime silhouette created by its stepped-glass roof, beneath which design students toil at their drawing boards late into the night. Within this hall is the **Frances Loeb Library,** which has architecture and urban design collections (not open to the public). The first-floor gallery hosts changing architecture exhibits. ♦ Gallery: daily 9AM-11PM. 48 Quincy St (at Cambridge St). 495.4731 &

ARTHUR M. SACKLER MUSEUM

Fourth Floor Galleries
5 Ancient Chinese Jades, Bronzes, & Ceramics
6 Chinese Buddhist Stone Sculpture
7 Chinese Sculpture
8 Indian & Southeast Asian Art
9 Ancient Roman Art
10 Ancient Greek Art
11 Egyptian & Ancient Near Eastern Gallery

Fourth Floor

Second Floor Galleries
1 Islamic & Later Indian Art
2-4 Asian Painting, Ceramics, Prints, & Textiles

Second Floor Fine Arts Dept.

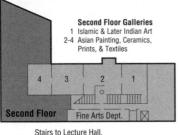

Stairs to Lecture Hall, Restrooms, & Phone

Special Exhibition Gallery
Shop
Ramp
Entrance
BROADWAY

First Floor

Photographic Services
Elevator

Arthur M. Sackler Museum Across Broadway from the **Fogg Art Museum** is this relative newcomer to **Harvard.** Except for its brick stripes, interesting window arrange-

ments, and touches of bright lime paint, the chunky Postmodern building is quite ordinary looking. It was designed in 1986 by British architect **James Stirling,** who aptly called **Harvard**'s campus "an architectural zoo." Exhibited here (see floor plan above) are Asian and Islamic art, including the world's finest collections of ancient Chinese jades, cave reliefs, and Chun-ware ceramics, and an exceptional selection of Japanese woodblock prints. Special exhibitions are also mounted here, and the **Harvard University Art Museum Shop** is on the first floor. The very odd portal and pillar arrangement on the upper facade facing Broadway marks where a skyway was to connect this museum with the **Fogg,** but the plan was quashed by community opposition. ♦ Admission (includes Fogg Art Museum); free Sa 10AM-noon; free for those under 18; reduced fee for senior citizens and students. Tu-Su. Free tours Sa at 1PM. 485 Broadway (at Quincy St). 495.9400 &

Fogg Art Museum Founded in 1891, **Harvard**'s oldest art museum houses a comprehensive collection representing most major artistic periods in the history of Western art from the Middle Ages to the present. In this 1927 **Coolidge, Shepley, Bulfinch, and Abbot** design, art galleries on two levels surround an Italian Renaissance courtyard modeled after a 16th-century canon's house. The French Impressionist, British, and Italian holdings are especially strong; look for works by Whistler, Rossetti, Géricault, Fra Angelico, Rubens, Ingres, Beardsley, and Pollock, as well as Monet, Renoir, and Picasso, in the **Wertheim Collection** on the second floor.

Also on the second floor is **Harvard**'s first permanent gallery of decorative arts, which rotates treasures from the university's vast collection of furniture, clocks, chests, Wedgwood, silver vessels, and other household goods bequeathed by alumni and others over the past 300 years. Probably the most famous item is the *President's Chair,* a knobby, uncomfortable-looking triangular-seated chair made in England or Wales in the 16th century and brought to **Harvard** by Reverend Edward Holyoke, college president from 1737 to 1769. Since Holyoke (who is shown seated in the chair in a portrait by John Singleton Copley), the *President's Chair* has supported every **Harvard** president during commencement. During the academic year, the museum holds wonderful concerts in its courtyard, with music by everyone from Renaissance Italian composers to Gershwin. ♦ Admission (includes Sackler Museum); free Sa 10AM-noon; free for children under 18; reduced fee for senior citizens and students. Daily; free tours at 11AM. 32 Quincy St (between Massachusetts Ave and Broadway). 495.9400 &

Carpenter Center for the Visual Arts

Coolly surveying **Harvard Yard** across the way, this sculptural edifice is the only structure designed by **Le Corbusier** in North America. It was built in 1963 and is now on the National Register of Historic Places. The iconoclastic concrete-and-glass form carries on an interesting dialogue with the sedate **Fogg Art Museum** next door and other conservative architectural neighbors. The building, which contains **Harvard's Department of Visual and Environmental Studies**, hosts lectures and the wonderful *Harvard Film Archive* series, and has two public galleries that offer a rotating program of contemporary art exhibits. The center also houses a film archive, photography collection, and studios. ♦ Daily. 24 Quincy St (between Massachusetts Ave and Broadway). 495.3251, recorded information on film showings 495.4700 &

Apthorp House

This 1760 structure, now surrounded by newer buildings, was built for the first rector of **Christ Church,** East Apthorp. Its extravagance so shocked Puritans that they dubbed the house "The Bishop's Palace," sparking a controversy so fierce that Apthorp quickly returned to England. The building now houses Harvard undergraduates; it is not open to the public. ♦ 10 Linden St (between Bow St and Massachusetts Ave)

5 The Inn at Harvard $$$ Graham Gund's 1992 design earned a "Worst New Architecture" award from *Boston* magazine, which observed that it "looks like a plywood prop from Universal Studios and feels like an upscale hospital inside." Drop in and decide for yourself. There are 113 basic rooms plus a **Presidential Suite.** The four-story atrium—furnished with couches, tables, and shelves of up-to-date books—functions as a living room and salon. It also serves as the hotel's only dining room, with meals and bar service available. Unfortunately it works well as neither. ♦ 1201 Massachusetts Ave (at Quincy St). 491.2222, 800/458.5886; fax 491.6520 &

6 Cafe Pamplona ★$ This is the most European of Cambridge cafes, a place where patrons linger comfortably for hours drinking espresso and writing, reading, or engaging in conversation from the mundane to the supremely esoteric. The tiny cafe is on the lower level of a snug red house, with an outdoor terrace where people hang about past midnight in the summer. The eclectic clientele leans toward the highbrow. In addition to teas and coffees of all kinds (try the "mokka" drink), gazpacho, sandwiches, and specials are served, as are flan, parfaits, chocolate mousse, and delightful little pastries. ♦ Spanish ♦ M-Sa 11AM-1AM; Su 2PM-1AM. No credit cards accepted. 12 Bow St (between Arrow St and Massachusetts Ave). No phone

7 Bartley's Burger Cottage ★$ A fixture in the Square since 1960, the Bartleys (and their son, Bill) have ushered several generations of ravenous college students through their undergraduate years. According to the owners, their roasted, marinated chicken is "a degree above the rest," but the real draw is the big juicy burger—available in 30 standard variations, plus a dozen or so topical guises, such as The Madonna ("a naked burger stripped of its roll"). The place is chockablock with tiny tables and decorated with odd remnants of popular culture—e.g., a vintage ad with Ronald Reagan hawking cigarettes. For its many fans, it's the next best thing to home. ♦ American ♦ M-Sa lunch and dinner. 1246 Massachusetts Ave (between Bow and Plympton Sts). 354.6559 &

7 Harvard Book Store Open since 1932, this Cambridge institution and family business is a general-interest bookstore that emphasizes scholarly works and customer service. The shop, which puts out a monthly newsletter, is particularly strong in philosophy, literary theory and criticism, psychology, African-American and women's studies, classics, and books from university presses. People flock in for the great remainders selection and the basement inventory of used paperbacks, hardcovers, and texts. ♦ Daily. 1256 Massachusetts Ave (at Plympton St). 661.1515 & (street level only)

7 The Grolier Poetry Book Shop, Inc.
This all-poetry bookshop was founded in 1927 as a rare-books store, then converted to its specialty in 1974 by poetry-loving owner Louisa Solano. She has 15,000 poetry titles today, including books and cassettes, first editions, small-press publications, and little magazines. Solano cosponsors a poetry-reading series, hosts autograph parties about once a week from September through May, and keeps a mailing list and bulletin board going as well as a gallery of photographs of poets who are patrons. The shop is also a meeting place; lots of visiting poets use it as an information center and sounding board. ♦ M-Sa noon-6:30PM. 6 Plympton St (between Bow St and Massachusetts Ave). 547.4648, 800/234.7636

8 Briggs & Briggs Established in 1890, this distinguished shop is known for its stock of classical and popular sheet music and books. It also sells musical instrument accessories, stereo equipment, and a variety of classical, jazz, blues, folk, and world music on CDs and tapes. ♦ M-Sa. 1270 Massachusetts Ave (between Plympton and Linden Sts). 547.2007 & (they offer assistance)

9 Harvard Lampoon Castle Cambridge's most whimsical building—designed by **Wheelwright and Haven** in 1909—is home to the offices of the *Harvard Lampoon,* an undergraduate humor magazine that inspired the *National Lampoon* (although there's no formal affiliation). "Poonies" have long been famous for their pranks, from stealing the **Massachusetts State House**'s *Sacred Cod* in 1933, to hiring an actress in 1990 to hold a press conference and pretend she was Marla Maples, Donald Trump's girlfriend (now ex-wife). Pick out the eyes, nose, mouth, and hat on the entrance tower. Atop is a statue of an ibis, frequently absconded by *Harvard Crimson* staffers. William Randolph Hearst, a former *Lampoon* business manager, donated the land. ♦ Mount Auburn St (between Plympton and Bow Sts)

Within Harvard Lampoon Castle:

Starr Book Shop This academic bookstore purveys antiquarian sets and scholarly works in literature, philosophy, classics, history, biography, and general subject areas. They carry current reviewers' copies, too. Graduate and undergraduate students frequent the shop, which is owned and operated by Peter Starr. ♦ Daily. 29 Plympton St (at Bow St). 547.6864

10 The Hasty Pudding Building This rather ramshackle little theater is home to the undergraduate **Hasty Pudding Theatricals,** a dramatic society established in 1795 and renowned for its annual Hasty Pudding Awards to the Man and Woman of the Year. The celebrity recipients—Cher, Kevin Costner, and Jodie Foster are past winners—are honored with parades through Cambridge in February, accompanied by male club members in female attire. The guest is then treated to an irreverent performance and comedic roast, and presented with a ceremonial pudding pot. In February and March the theater is also used by the **American Repertory Theatre** (see the **Loeb Drama Center** on page 188) for its "New Stages" series; in the spring and fall it's home to the **Cambridge Theatre Company,** a venture stirred up in the mid-1990s from the ashes of the **Poets' Theatre** of the 1950s. ♦ 12 Holyoke St (between Mount Auburn St and Massachusetts Ave). Box office 496.8400

Within The Hasty Pudding Building:

Up Stairs at the Pudding ★★★$$$$
The main dining room on the top floor, with dark green walls decorated with posters of past Hasty Pudding performances, is a setting for a convivial repast away from the Square's commotion. This atmospheric restaurant offers continental fare with Northern Italian and Mediterranean influences. Favorite dishes include roast sweet red pepper soup, grilled steak Florentine, glazed veal chop, Mediterranean bouillabaisse with an orange and tomato broth, and chicken paillard with sweet basil pesto. Many entrées are accompanied by a generous array of vegetables. The à la carte Sunday brunch is deliciously out of the ordinary. In season, there's seating on the rooftop terrace, which features topiary trees and an herb garden. The **Club Bar** on the second floor is dramatic, with dark red walls, a black-and-white tiled floor, and a wooden bar, above which is mounted a family of crocodiles shot by Teddy Roosevelt. This is definitely not a student stomping ground, except perhaps when Mom and Dad come to town. ♦ Northern Italian/European ♦ M-F lunch and dinner; Sa lunch; Su brunch and dinner. Reservations recommended. 864.1933

10 Sandrine's ★★$$$ Dinner here is truly evocative of Alsace, with dishes like roasted loin of venison, duck confit with lentil salad, and Alsatian rhubarb tart; lunch sandwiches have a distinctly Californian influence. The french fries that accompany the sandwiches are excellent. The menu also includes nightly specials and a variety of *Flammekueche,* a savory Alsatian tarte. In keeping with the menu, the decor melds country French and Californian elements, and the mood is always casual and low-key. ♦ French/Alsatian ♦ M, Su dinner; Tu-Sa lunch and dinner. Reservations recommended. 8 Holyoke St (between Mount Auburn St and Massachusetts Ave). 497.5300 &

Lobster Logistics

Indulging in your first lobster? Anxious to develop the knack of cracking this tasty crustacean? There's hardly a better place to learn than in Boston, where the critters are often caught and served the same day. Getting the meat out of a lobster takes practice, patience, and a little perseverance. This guide covers the basics, but it's best to take an experienced lobster-cracking friend along for encouragement and coaching. And, despite how funny you may look, wear a bib—you're going to get more than a little messy.

4 Bend back the flippers and break them off of the tailpiece.

1 Twist off the claws.

2 Crack each claw with a nutcracker.

3 Separate the tailpiece from the body by arching the back until it cracks.

5 Insert a fork where the flippers broke off and push the meat out.

6 Unhinge the back from the body. This contains the tomalley (or liver), which some folks are known to consume.

7 Open the remaining part of the body by cracking it sideways (the meat in this section is particularly good.)

8 The small claws are good eating—just suck the meat out as illustrated here.

11 Schoenhof's Foreign Books, Inc.
Writer John Updike, **Harvard** economist John Kenneth Galbraith, and chef Julia Child have all shopped here. And soon after arriving in the United States, many of Boston's foreign residents and students immediately head to the understated shop in the basement of **Harvard**'s Spee Club (a student organization). The reason: It's the best foreign bookstore in the country, with more than 35,000 titles—original works, not translations—representing 200 languages (other than English). Founded in 1856 by Carl Schoenhof to serve Boston's German community, this store's mission today is to bring together people and books of all nationalities. The sales staff are fluent in several languages and work together to choose books, with an emphasis on history, philosophy, literature, and literary criticism. The biggest selections are in French, Spanish,

German, Italian, and Russian. There's a great department of reference works, records, and tapes for language learning, and there are children's books, too. The wholesale/retail store runs a worldwide mail-order service and is tenacious in tracking down even the most esoteric special orders—a French book on termites or a $5,000 German edition on Freud, for example. ♦ M-W; Th until 8PM; F-Sa. 76A Mount Auburn St (between Mill and Dunster Sts). 547.8855

12 Iruña ★★$$ Despite Harvard Square's international population, most of its restaurants have an Americanized style. Not this little cafe tucked down a short alley. The relaxed and simple European ambience and good food offered here for over a quarter-century have earned it a devout clientele. The Spanish specialties are moderately priced and good: Try the gazpacho, garlic soup, paella, stuffed chicken breast, or potato omelette, and wash your choices down with red or white sangria. Daily specials feature whatever's fresh. In warm weather, there's a small outdoor patio for dining, but it's actually more pleasant inside, especially if you dine early. ♦ Spanish ♦ M-Sa lunch and dinner. Reservations recommended for Friday and Saturday dinner. No credit cards accepted. 56 John F. Kennedy St (between South and Winthrop Sts). 868.5633

13 Bombay Club ★$$ Decked out in authentic Indian artifacts, carvings of goddesses and temples, and paintings of Indian landscapes, this dining room overlooks a small park just off Harvard Square. Try *sheemi kabob* (deep-fried ground lamb patties) or *boti* (barbecued lamb chop). ♦ Indian ♦ Daily. Reservations recommended. 57 John F. Kennedy Sts (between Eliot and Winthrop Sts). 661.8100 ♿

14 John F. Kennedy Memorial Park Often nearly empty of people and very well maintained, this big, grassy park is wonderful for lounging. There's an interesting variety of trees, many still quite young, since the park was only completed in 1990. It's behind the **John F. Kennedy School of Government** and **The Charles Hotel** (see below), with the river just across the street. Look for the fountain inscribed with JFK quotes. ♦ John F. Kennedy St and Memorial Dr ♿

15 The Charles Hotel $$$ Harvard University guests, entertainment-industry folk, and business travelers who like to be near the late-night liveliness of the Square stay here, many on a long-term basis. The hotel is also popular with writers, and sponsors readings. Part of the **Charles Square** complex, which features shops, condominiums, a health club, and restaurants, the 299-room, 10-story hotel offers many rooms overlooking the **John F. Kennedy Memorial Park** and the Charles River, with Shaker-style furniture, telephones and TVs in all bathrooms, and a patchwork down quilt on every bed. The King Charles mini suites have four-poster beds. Eighteenth-century quilts, New England antiques, and works by local artists enliven the hotel's main entry and halls. The new **Tini Bar** off the lobby provides guests with a quiet place to relax, have a drink, and converse; there are also two restaurants and a popular jazz club (see below) on the premises. A concierge, a multilingual staff, complimentary overnight shoe shines, 24-hour room service, valet parking, and special rooms for people with disabilities and for nonsmokers are just some of the amenities available. Guests have complimentary access to the exercise equipment and pool at the neighboring **Wellbridge Health and Fitness Center** (441.0800). The hotel and **Charles Square** jointly sponsor free jazz concerts in the courtyard on Wednesday from 6 to 8PM (depending on the weather) from late June through September. ♦ 1 Bennett St (between Eliot St and University Rd). 864.1200, 800/323.7500; fax 864.5715 ♿

Within The Charles Hotel:

RiALTO

Rialto ★★★$$$$ This formal dining room features subdued lighting in a living room–like setting of moss green banquettes, crisp white tablecloths, and black blinds that add a touch of drama. As prepared by chef Jody Adams (winner of the 1997 James Beard Award for Best Chef in the East), the seasonal menu is shaded with hints of French, Italian, and Spanish cuisine. Start off with *Provençale* fisherman's soup with rouille, gruyère, and basil oil, or a plate of chicken and duck liver and country pâtés garnished with porcini mushrooms, currants, Jerusalem artichokes, and pickled red onions. Entrées include seared scallops on a shredded potato cake with cider sauce and hazelnuts; seared peppered venison with semolina gnocchi layered with gorgonzola *dolce*, toasted walnuts, grilled portabello mushrooms, and Cabernet sauce; and sole poached in white wine with chanterelle mushrooms and mussels. Desserts are every bit as appealing: Try the hot chocolate cream and malted vanilla ice cream, or Breton butter cake with warm spiced pears, currants, and whipped crème fraîche. ♦ American ♦ Daily dinner. Reservations required. 661.5050 ♿

Henrietta's Table ★★$$ The motto is "fresh and honest," and that's exactly what diners get from the open kitchen in this place. Menu highlights include Yankee pot roast, apple wood–smoked Maine salmon, chicken potpie, stuffed cabbage, and rotisserie roasted Vermont pheasant with lingonberry sauce. An extensive list of regional ales and beers and wines is also available. There is outdoor dining in season. ♦ American ♦ M-Sa breakfast, lunch, and dinner; Su brunch and dinner. Reservations recommended for groups of six or more. 661.5005

The Regattabar Here's a comfortable spot to listen and dance to local and nationally acclaimed jazz acts. The George Shearing

Duo, the Milt Jackson Quartet, Gary Burton, Herbie Hancock, Ahmad Jamal, Pat Metheny, Herbie Mann, and the Four Freshmen have all performed in this popular venue. Tickets for Friday and Saturday sell out fast, so plan a week in advance. Jazzophiles drive up regularly from New York City to hear good music for reasonable prices. Hotel guests are admitted free to all shows Tuesday through Thursday and to any 11PM show; sign up with the concierge. All customers may purchase one-and-a-half tickets and stay for both shows on one night. ♦ Cover. Tu-Sa evenings. No jeans, tank tops, or sneakers allowed. 876.7777 ♿

15 The Shops at Charles Square Among the establishments at this stark modern shopping complex are a branch of the **Giannino Restaurant and Bar** (576.0605); **Le Pli Salon** (547.4081), an elegant spa; and some national chain stores such as **Talbot's** (576.2278). Originally viewed by locals as an unwelcome upscale intruder, this complex has proved to be a congenial addition to the neighborhood—thanks in part to such public events as courtyard concerts, but mainly because the design is low-key and browser-friendly. The **Charles Square Parking Garage** is open 24 hours convenient for late-night revelers. ♦ Daily. Bennett St (between Eliot St and University Rd). 491.5282 ♿

16 House of Blues ★$ The brainchild of "Blues Brother" Dan Ackroyd, the late John Belushi's wife Judy, and other celebrity investors, this is one of a chain of eatery/nightclubs that pays homage to blues music and Southern cooking. The local headquarters for blues lovers, the place re-creates the ambience of the Southern Delta with its juke-joint decor. There are nightly performances of blues and blues-inspired music, and the kitchen turns out Southern dishes with a Southwestern twist: everything from barbecue to chicken to pizza. ♦ Southern ♦ Cover. Restaurant: daily lunch and dinner; Su gospel brunch. Club: daily until 2AM. 96 Winthrop St (between John F. Kennedy and Eliot Sts). 491.2100 ♿

17 Grendel's Den ★$ The food is nothing to flip over, but it's plentiful and cheap (many an impecunious student has subsisted on the refillable salad bar). There's a restaurant on the first floor, with high ceilings and wood paneling, a popular spot that still hints of its former grandeur as a university club. The actual den is downstairs, getting its name

from the underground location. ♦ International ♦ Daily lunch and dinner. 89 Winthrop St (between John F. Kennedy and Eliot Sts). 491.1160 ♿ (staff will assist)

HARVARD SQUARE
HOTEL

18 Harvard Square Hotel $$ In the heart of the Square, this low-key, friendly motel has 73 simple, basic rooms on 4 floors. Lots of visiting parents and professors at the nearby **John F. Kennedy School of Government** stay here. There is a small restaurant, but no room service. ♦ 110 Mount Auburn St (between Eliot St and University Rd). 864.5200; fax 864.2409 ♿

19 Casa Mexico ★★$$ This small basement shrine to fine Mexican cuisine is a secret treasure. Atmosphere it has in spades, plus some hard-to-find dishes like chicken *mole poblano* (with a rich garlic, onion, chili peppers, and chocolate sauce). After more than a quarter-century in business, the tiny restaurant still does everything just right. ♦ Mexican ♦ Daily lunch and dinner. 75 Winthrop St (at John F. Kennedy St). 491.4552

20 Starbucks ★$ Ensconced in **The Garage,** a complex of youth-oriented stores and restaurants, this former **Coffee Connection** is the Square's premier rendezvous for potent fresh-roasted coffee and equally full-bodied conversation. The abundant pastries and desserts are good, but the coffee's the thing here, all different kinds served all different ways. You'll likely see at least one frazzled student nursing giant cups. The setting offers exposed brick walls, and tables set by arched windows for people watching. You can also enter from Dunster Street, up a short flight of stairs and to the left. The retail operation sells 30-plus different award-winning coffees, excellent teas, and every kind of brewing paraphernalia imaginable. You can order by mail, too. ♦ Cafe ♦ Daily. 36 John F. Kennedy St (between Mount Auburn St and Massachusetts Ave). 492.4881 ♿ Also at: Numerous locations throughout Cambridge and Boston

---

Harvard College was the only college in North America until 1693.

Thomas Brattle—the early Harvard College treasurer for whom Brattle Street was named—ensured himself a spirited send-off by bequeathing "a half crown bill to each of the students of Harvard College that shall come to my funeral."

20 John Harvard's Brew House ★★$ What makes this spot so appealing are the six brews created on the premises and out-of-the-ordinary pub fare, which may include grilled sausages with fresh spaetzle and buttermilk fried chicken with spiced corn bread. Look for a series of Hogarthian panels conceived by muralists Josh Winer and John Devaney that depicts a semispurious (but hilarious) biography of John Harvard, the infamous brewmaster. ♦ American ♦ Daily lunch and dinner. 33 Dunster St (between Mount Auburn St and Massachusetts Ave). 868.3585 ⅁

20 La Flamme A classic eight-seater, this old-fashioned barber shop (women welcome) has shorn such distinguished heads as Henry Kissinger's. Prices are still holding steady at a reasonable $10 a clip. ♦ M-Sa. 21 Dunster St (between Mount Auburn St and Massachusetts Ave). 354.8377 ⅁

20 Herrell's Ice Cream Steve Herrell is generally credited with starting the whole gourmet ice-cream boom at his out-of-the-way Somerville shop back in 1972. He made his fame selling his first name (Steve's Ice Cream), and then started up again with a chain of stores bearing his last name. His hand-cranked ice cream, dense and intense and in luscious flavors like moccacino and chocolate pudding, is still among the best in the business. The "back room" here—a former bank vault painted to resemble an underwater grotto—is the coolest place in Cambridge on a hot summer evening. ♦ Daily noon-midnight. 15 Dunster St (between Mount Auburn St and Massachusetts Ave). 497.2179.

The first American poet was Anne Bradstreet, who lived at what is now 1348 Massachusetts Avenue, the heart of today's Harvard Square. Her work was printed in England in 1650.

---

21 Urban Outfitters All the chic-looking students and the rest of the under-30 crowd shop here for the latest in men's and women's attire, fashion accessories, housewares, and a whole slew of trendy novelties. You'll find lots of popular name brands and the store's own label. A bargain basement sells vintage clothing, too. You can enter the store from Brattle Street, making this a convenient cut-through. ♦ Daily. 11 JFK St (between Mount Auburn and Brattle Sts). 864.0070. Also at: 361 Newbury St (at Massachusetts Ave), Boston. 236.0088

22 Brattle Street Called **Tory Row** in the 1770s because its residents were loyal to King George, this glorious avenue still retains its share of magnificent homes (they were once country estates whose spacious grounds spilled right to the river's edge). In the summer of 1775 the patriots under George Washington appropriated the homes. Today the thoroughfare is far more densely inhabited, but its sumptuous properties secure its reputation as one of the country's poshest streets. **Henry Hobson Richardson** designed the **Stoughton House** at **No. 90** in 1882; it's still a private residence. **No. 159** is the **Hooper-Lee-Nichols House,** parts of which date back to the 1600s; it's now the headquarters of the **Cambridge Historical Society.** The building is open to the public on some afternoons and the society offers tours (497.1630) of Tory Row and the Old Burial Ground. John Bartlett, the Harvard Square bookseller who compiled the famous *Bartlett's Familiar Quotations,* lived at **No. 165;** the house was erected for him in 1873. It is still a private home. ♦ Between Harvard Sq and Fresh Pond Pkwy

22 WordsWorth The Square's busiest bookshop discounts all but textbooks, publishes a newsletter, and sponsors an excellent reading series at the **Brattle Theatre** (readings are free, but tickets must be obtained in advance). This is a full-service general bookstore with a fully computerized inventory system, developed by the owner and adopted by other bookstores, tracking 60,000 to 100,000 titles in 95 subject areas. There's also a selection of greeting cards, calendars, and wrapping papers. Across the street is **WordsWorth Abridged** (5 Brattle St, between John F. Kennedy and Palmer Sts, 354.5277) selling gifts, jewelry, an extensive collection of stationery, and greeting cards. For kids there's **Curious George Goes to Wordsworth,** located on Harvard Square (John F. Kennedy and Brattle Sts, 498.0062). ♦ Daily. 30 Brattle St (at Brattle Sq). 354.5201

23 Motto/MDF Side by side are two small shops with different wares, but the same distinctive esthetic. Both are owned and operated by Jude Silver, whose own art background has influenced her preference for modern, functional, and sophisticated creations. **Motto** sells abstract avant-garde jewelry of striking materials, textures, compositions, and tones. They can suggest European élan, classical coolness, industrial efficiency, or Southwestern warmth. **MDF (Modern Design Furnishings)** offers personal and home and office accessories, lamps, small furniture, and men's jewelry—all fabricated from nontraditional materials. Brides-to-be can register at this store, and both stores will gladly take special orders, pack, and ship all over the country. ◆ Daily. 17-19 Brattle St (between Palmer and Church Sts). Motto 868.8448, MDF 491.2789 ♿

23 Bertucci's ★$ One of many in a chain that serves myriad delicious pizzas along with pasta and Italian entrées, this popular addition to Harvard Square is usually packed with students and other locals. The family-friendly menu, casual atmosphere, and reasonable prices make it a good bet for dinner out with the kids. ◆ Italian ◆ Daily. 21 Brattle St (between Palmer and Church Sts). 864.4748. Also at numerous other locations in Boston and Cambridge

24 Jasmine/Sola Moderately expensive women's clothing and accessories are featured here, as are women's shoes (which range widely in price), including some hard-to-find brands. The couture ranges from casual to dressy, with an emphasis on unusual rich fabrics and striking styles. The jewelry is always fun, much of it produced by independent and emerging jewelry makers. Also here is **Sola Men**, a modest selection of great-looking men's clothing and shoes, often European in style. ◆ Daily. 37 Brattle St (between Palmer and Church Sts). 354.6043 ♿

24 Billings and Stover Apothecaries If you're old enough to remember when ice cream was served at the drugstore soda fountain and not at a national chain store, this place will be a pleasant trip down memory lane. Ice cream, malteds, sundaes, and frappes (local lingo for milk shakes) are served at the counter, while the usual drugstore merchandise fills the shelves. ◆ M-Sa; Su noon-6PM. 41A Brattle St (between Palmer and Church Sts). 547.0502

BRATTLE THEATRE

25 The Brattle Theatre This more-than-a-century-old independent movie house extraordinaire has struggled to preserve its identity in the midst of increasingly commercial Harvard Square and in an era of movie-chain monopolies. Renovated from top to bottom, but retaining its rare rear-screen projection system, this is one of the country's oldest remaining repertory movie houses. If it doesn't look much like a movie house, that's because it opened as **Brattle Hall** in 1890, founded by the Cambridge Social Union as a place for literary, musical, and dramatic entertainments. From 1948 to 1952 the **Brattle Theatre Company** put on nationally acclaimed performances from Shakespeare to Chekhov with many notable stars, including Jessica Tandy and Hume Cronyn. The theater made a policy of hiring actors blacklisted during the US government's political witch hunts of the era, including Zero Mostel. Subsequent financial difficulties inspired **Harvard** grads Bryant Haliday and Cyrus Harvey Jr. (who brought the first films of Fellini, Antonioni, Bergman, and Olmi to America) to convert it to an art cinema in 1953.

A local Humphrey Bogart cult was born here in the 1950s, when owners Harvey and Haliday screened neglected "Bogie" movies during **Harvard** exam time, drawing college students and other fans in droves. As the revived Bogie mystique spread across the country, a weeklong Bogart series became an annual tradition.

The movie house has shared its quarters with a variety of retail businesses since the 1960s. Today a faithful following comes for classic Hollywood and foreign movies, independently made films, new art films, staged readings, and concerts. Operated since 1986 by the Running Arts company, the theater offers genre double features nearly every night. The general roster: Monday, film noir; Tuesday, author readings sponsored by nearby **WordsWorth** bookstore, independent films, or other art-related activities; Wednesday, Friday, and Saturday, selections based on a theme such as a particular director, style, or content; and Thursday, international films. Innumerable Cambridge-area movie lovers are drawn by the attractive lineup and two-shows-for-one-price admission. A free two-month calendar of events is available in front of the theater. ◆ Daily. 40 Brattle St (between Brattle Sq and Story St). 876.6837 ♿

Within The Brattle Theatre:

Algiers Cafe ★★$ Head upstairs to the domed hideaway to sip minted coffee and feast on *baba ganooj* or tabbouleh. This cafe made out like a bandit in **The Brattle Theatre** rehab: once a grungy (if atmospheric) underground cafe, now it's airy and gorgeous, with balletic little tables and prize rugs on the walls. Best of all, you're still left in peace to converse or cogitate. ◆ Middle Eastern ◆ Daily. 492.1557 ♿

Restaurants/Clubs: **Red**   Hotels: Blue

Shops/ 🌱 Outdoors: **Green**   Sights/Culture: **Black**

Casablanca ★★$$ Long the last word in student romance, this Bogie classic's namesake has graduated from mostly bar to full-scale restaurant—keeping its oversize rattan chairs-for-two and David Omar White's beloved movie-homage murals (even though it meant moving whole walls). The menu offers dishes from Spain, Portugal, Turkey, and Provence. Specialties include braised beef short ribs with star anise, Turkish lamb and vegetable kabobs, and garlic chicken soup with almonds and bread. ◆ Mediterranean ◆ Daily lunch and dinner. 876.0999 &

26 Sage's Market When you're tired of eating at restaurants, or it's a beautiful day and you have nothing to do but lounge on the lawn at **Harvard Yard,** this gourmet-food market is the perfect place to pick up the makings of a picnic. Breads are baked fresh daily on the premises. The deli counter slices cold cuts from Angus beef and the finest poultry, and offers barbecue chicken, pasta salads, and every other kind of prepared food or salad you can think of. For dessert, you can choose from numerous brands of imported cookies. But the fruits look so fresh and inviting, you may forgo the forbidden sweets for nature's own. Or do it the French way: Pick up a bottle of wine and a chunk of brie, and thou will be all set. ◆ Daily. 60 Church St (at Brattle St). 876.2211

27 Cybersmith $ The real attraction here is not the food, but the upstairs computer terminals that allow patrons to check their e-mail or "surf" the Internet. Nerds and novices can chow down on such casual fare as salads, sandwiches, and pastries. Several computer classes are offered on a regular basis. ◆ Cafe ◆ Daily lunch and dinner. 42 Church St (between Palmer and Brattle Sts). 492.5857 &

28 The Globe Corner Bookstore An outpost of the Boston original, this shop specializes in books, maps, and guides for New England and world travel, and also carries travel-oriented novelties, games, and accessories. ◆ Daily. 28 Church St (at Palmer St.) 497.6277. Also at: 500 Boylston St (between Berkeley and Clarendon Sts), Boston. 859.8008

28 Club Passim ★$ One of America's oldest and best-known coffeehouses, a below–street-level venue that began featuring folk music around 1971, today is a nonprofit club. Latin for "here and there," the name is pronounced *Pass*-im, although just about everybody says Pass-*eem*. This is the only remaining commercial coffeehouse presenting live music in Boston and Cambridge. The original owners Bob and Rae Donlins have always been true-blue friends to local folk and bluegrass performers; among those they helped boost to fame are Jackson Browne, Tracy Chapman, Suzanne Vega, and Tom Waits.

The stalwart club has weathered well, and continues to showcase contemporary (and some traditional) acoustic music. It's small (50-person capacity), unpretentious, and has no liquor license. There's a light menu of soups, sandwiches, quiches, desserts, coffees, teas, and cider during the day when it is a combination cafe/gift shop. No smoking is permitted (except during the day, in one section). Performances on weekend nights feature a headliner with an opening act, the latter usually new local talent. Seating is first-come, first-served, and the admission prices are low. ◆ Coffeehouse/Cafe ◆ Cover for performances. Restaurant: Tu-Sa lunch. Gift shop: Tu-Sa afternoon. Call for show times. 47 Palmer St (between Brattle and Church Sts). 492.7679

29 First Parish Church and Old Burying Ground This wooden Gothic Revival church, the 1833 creation of **Isaiah Rogers,** was partly funded by **Harvard** in return for pews for students' use. Numerous Revolutionary War veterans—including two African-American slaves, Cato Stedman and Neptune Frost, who fought alongside their masters— and **Harvard**'s first eight presidents are buried in the adjacent cemetery. ◆ 3 Church St (between Massachusetts Ave and Brattle St)

Within the First Parish Church:

Nameless Coffeehouse The country's oldest free, volunteer-run coffeehouse is a neighborly venue where local folk musicians play. Tracy Chapman sang here during her days as a Harvard Square street performer. ◆ Weekend entertainment, call for schedule. 864.1630

30 Cambridge Artists' Cooperative This casual and funky shop, which represents some 180 artists (most regional), covers three floors with handmade arts and crafts. The unusual, fun, and interesting selection of eclectic wares features jewelry, pottery, clothing, and glassware. There is usually at least one artist at work in the store. ◆ Daily.

59A Church St (between Massachusetts Ave and Brattle St). 868.4434

HARNETTS ®

30 Harnett's Homeopathy & Body Care
Here's the place to stock up on vitamins, herbs, and a wide variety of aromatherapy treatments. Also on hand are books and products concerning holistic medicine, yoga, and meditation. ♦ Daily. 47 Brattle St (at Church St). 491.4747 Ꮹ

30 Colonial Drug This 50-year-old establishment produces more than 900 essences, using natural ingredients according to centuries-old formulations. Also look for a complete line of cosmetics, skin and hair products, Kent brushes, and other high-quality personal care items. ♦ M-Sa. No credit cards accepted. 49 Brattle St (between Church St and Farwell Pl). 864.2222

31 Brattle House This 1727 frame house, on the National Register of Historic Places, belonged to William Brattle, a Tory who fled in 1774 and for whom the street is named. Margaret Fuller, the feminist editor of *The Dial*, lived here from 1840 to 1842. The house is now headquarters for the **Cambridge Center for Adult Education** (547.6789), which sponsors a heady array of courses as well as a well-attended holiday season crafts fair. ♦ 42 Brattle St (between Brattle Sq and Story St)

31 Charrette Catering to design professionals, this shop has a sleek inventory of top makers' and the store's own lines of great-looking fine art and office supplies, portfolios, framing and modeling supplies, drafting instruments, furniture, and desktop-publishing software. The shop is a magnet for the local architecture and design community and students from the **Harvard University Graduate School of Design.** (There's a small outlet at the school for emergencies.) This branch stocks more than 6,000 products, with 41,000 available at the warehouse. If you need something the store doesn't have, check out the thick catalog; your purchase can sometimes be sent from the warehouse that same day. Also on the premises is a spin-off enterprise called **Charrette Reprographics,** which specializes in the latest technologies for design

professionals' presentations. ♦ Daily. 44 Brattle St (between Brattle Sq and Story St). 495.0200 Ꮹ (weekdays only). Also at: 777 Boylston St (between Exeter and Fairfield Sts), Boston. 859.0989. Charrette Reprographics also at: 1033 Massachusetts Ave (at Ellery St). 495.0235; 184 South St (between Kneeland and Beach Sts), Boston. 292.8820

31 Design Research Building/Crate & Barrel Benjamin Thompson built this architectural equivalent of a giant glass showcase in 1969 for **Design Research,** the store he founded to introduce Americans to international modern design products for the home. The store was taken over by **Crate & Barrel** in the mid-1970s. Under the national houseware store chain's auspices, Thompson has seen his notion spread all over the country and made more affordable, though less imaginative. He certainly knows how to put together an interesting display, as a later project, **Faneuil Hall Marketplace,** attests. ♦ M-W, F 10AM-7PM; Th 10AM-9PM; Sa 10AM-6PM; Su noon-6PM. 48 Brattle St (at Story St). 876.6300

32 Clothware Mix and match carefully selected, uncommon women's garments made from natural fibers, especially cottons and silks, at this small, well-known shop. The designer lines, including the private label of one of the original owners, focus on graceful, classic, and fun-to-wear styles. The lingerie selection here is especially tempting. Some accessories, including leggings, tights, scarves, hats, socks, jewelry, wallets, and handbags, are carried as well. The shop has regular sales, but this is not a place for a bargain-hunting excursion. ♦ Daily. 52 Brattle St (at Story St). 661.6441

32 Hi-Rise Pie Co. ★$$ "Under a spreading chestnut tree/The village smithy stands/The smith a mighty man is he/With large and sinewy hands—." The smithy in Henry Wadsworth Longfellow's famous poem *The Village Blacksmith* lived in this old yellow house dating from 1811, the **Dexter Pratt House.** (A stone nearby marks the former site of the famous chestnut tree.) There's been a bakery on the premises for more than 45 years, although it has changed hands a couple of times. The newest owner, baker Rene Becker, makes wonderful breads and creates very tempting sandwiches. Enjoy lunch or just a snack. The house belongs to the **Cambridge Center for Adult Education,** which offers courses, lectures, seminars, films, and cultural activities. ♦ Bakery/Cafe/Takeout ♦ Bakery: daily. Cafe: M-Sa breakfast, lunch (until 5PM), and tea; Su brunch. 56 Brattle St (between Story and Hilliard Sts). 492.3003 Ꮹ

33 Radcliffe Yard Radcliffe College was founded for women in 1879, named for **Harvard**'s first female benefactor, Ann Radcliffe. It was **Harvard**'s sister school until 1975, when the two colleges were united, their administrations merged, and equal admission standards adopted for men and women. **Radcliffe** remains an independent corporation with its own president, but students share housing, classes, facilities, and degrees.

Stroll through **Radcliffe's** pretty campus green and note the college's first building, **Fay House,** an 1806 Federal mansion. Other noteworthy **Radcliffe Yard** buildings include the stately **Agassiz House,** where the **Harvard Gilbert and Sullivan Players** put on operettas, and the **Arthur and Elizabeth Schlesinger Library,** which has the country's most extensive collection of books, photographs, oral histories, and other materials related to women's history—including manuscripts and papers belonging to a number of famous women and organizations. ♦ Brattle St (between Appian Way and Mason St)

Within Radcliffe Yard:

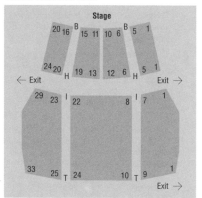

Loeb Drama Center Harvard University's theater—built in 1959 by **Hugh Stubbins**—is home to the prestigious **American Repertory Theatre (ART),** a nonprofit professional company affiliated with the university that presents new American plays, neglected works from the past, and unconventional interpretations of classics. The **ART** has premiered works by Jules Feiffer, Carlos Fuentes, Philip Glass, Marsha Norman, Milan Kundera, Larry Gelbart, and David Mamet. The student **Harvard-Radcliffe Dramatic Club** is also based here.

The center's main theater (see the seating chart above) seats 556 people and boasts the first fully flexible stage in the country, which can easily be converted into different configurations. Free student performances are held in the experimental theater; information is available at the box office. ♦ Daily. 64 Brattle St (at Hilliard St). 547.8300 ♿ (infrared hearing amplifiers available on request)

34 Christ Church America's first trained architect, **Peter Harrison,** designed this church as well as **King's Chapel** in Boston. Cambridge's oldest church, the former Tory place of worship later served as barracks for Connecticut troops, who melted down the organ pipes for bullets during the Revolution. Theodore Roosevelt taught Sunday school here while at **Harvard.** Like the Boston chapel, the church's interior is simple. ♦ Garden St (between Massachusetts Ave and Appian Way)

35 Cambridge Common The site of General Washington's main camp from 1775 to 1776 is now basically a scruffy traffic island. ♦ Bounded by Massachusetts Ave, Garden St, and Waterhouse St

On Cambridge Common:

Dawes Island Look for the bronze horseshoes embedded in the sidewalk here, marking William Dawes's ride through town on the way to warn the populace in Lexington with the famous cry "The British are coming!" The shoes were given to the city of Cambridge by Dawes's descendants as a US Bicentennial gift. ♦ Garden St and Massachusetts Ave

36 Sheraton Commander Hotel $$ Near **Cambridge Common** and a short walk to the Square, this gracious old reliable often welcomes prominent political figures. The 175 understated but pleasant rooms include 8 "executive king" suites, each with a sitting area, small dining area, canopy bed, and whirlpool bath. Hotel amenities include a fitness room, multilingual staff, a concierge, a business center, and complimentary valet parking. Rooms for people with disabilities and for nonsmokers are available. **The Cafe at 16 Garden Street** serves continental fare. ♦ 16 Garden St (between Mason and Berkeley Sts). 547.4800, 800/325.3535; fax 868.8322 ♿

37 Longy School of Music Founded in 1915 and housed in the 1889 **Edwin Abbot Mansion** (listed in the National Register of Historic Places), this is a very active—and esteemed—music school. It hosts a wide array of notable concerts of every era and style in intimate **Pickman Hall.** ♦ 1 Follen St (at Concord Ave). 876.0956 ♿

38 Henry Wadsworth Longfellow House During the Siege of Boston from 1775 to 1776, George Washington moved his headquarters from **Wadsworth House** near **Harvard Yard** to this stately Georgian residence (pictured above), built in 1759 by a wealthy Tory, John Vassall, who fled just before the Revolution. Longfellow rented a room here in 1837, then was given the house by his wealthy new father-in-law upon marrying heiress Frances Appleton in 1843. (She died here tragically years later, burned in a fire in the library.) Longfellow wrote many of his famous poems in this mansion, including *Hiawatha* and *Evangeline.* He lived here for 45 years, with prominent literary friends often gathered round. The house has been restored to the poet's period, with thousands of books from his library, plus many of his possessions. Vestiges of the spreading chestnut tree that inspired him were made into a carved armchair, presented to the poet on his 72nd birthday by Cambridge schoolchildren and now on display. The home stayed in the Longfellow family until 1973, and is now operated by the National Park Service as a National Historic Site. Visitors can see the house during half-hour tours, which are given throughout the day. Special events are held here regularly, including children's programs, a celebration of the poet's birthday in February, and poetry readings and concerts held on the east lawn in the summer. A bookstore offers most of the Longfellow books in print, plus books on his life, the literary profession, poetry, and more. Incidentally, the first of Longfellow's poems to win national acclaim was *Song of Hiawatha,* published in Boston on 10 November 1855. ♦ Admission; free for those under 16 and over 62. Daily mid-March–Oct. Guided tours only; reserve in advance for groups. 105 Brattle St (between Mason and Craigie Sts). 876.4491 ♿ (staff will assist)

39 Harvard College Observatory Built after the appearance of "the Great Comet" in 1843 sparked interest in astronomy, the observatory now opens its doors to the public once a month. "Observatory Nights" feature an hour-long lecture/film program geared toward teens and adults; afterwards, if the sky is clear, visitors have the chance to look through some nifty telescopes. For the "Sky Report," a recorded update of astronomical information, call 491.1497. The domed pavilion is the only surviving element of the original building, designed by **Isaiah Rogers** in 1851. ♦ Free. Open to the public the third Thursday of every month; doors open at 7:30PM, lecture at 8PM. 60 Garden St (between Bond St and Garden Terr). 495.9059

40 Mount Auburn Cemetery This serene spot is worth seeking out for a sunny afternoon stroll, a picnic, and some fine bird-watching. Now one of its illustrious residents, Henry Wadsworth Longfellow once called **Mount Auburn** the "city of the dead." When it was founded in 1831, the cemetery introduced a new concept of interment to the US. Before, burial grounds were rustic graveyards where the dead were buried in an erratic fashion. Grave markers were frequently moved about along with bodies, with the dead's remains even shuttled from one burial ground to another. (Boston's cemeteries offer plenty of evidence of these casual practices.) But with

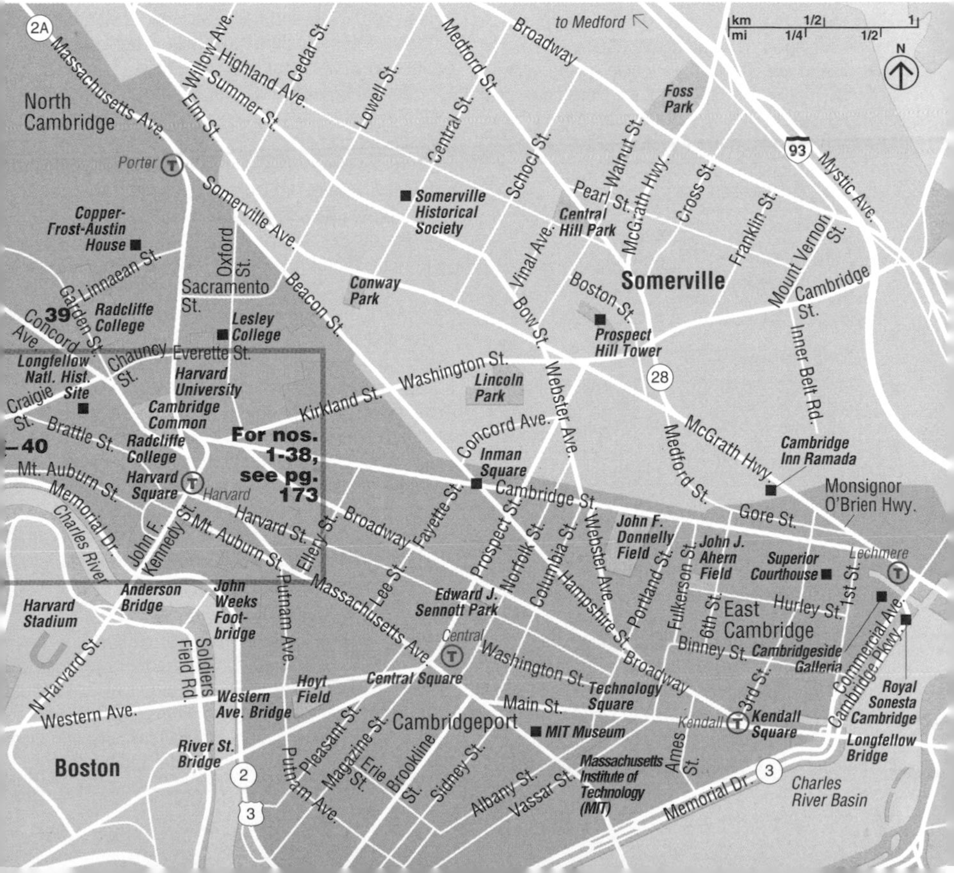

the creation of this cemetery, the idea of commemorating an individual with a permanent, unencroachable burial place was instituted. A ritual of memory took root in America, with personal gravesites becoming a new status symbol. Oliver Wendell Holmes, Isabella Stewart Gardner, Mary Baker Eddy, and Winslow Homer are among the more than 70,000 people buried here. The first garden cemetery in America, it has 170 verdant acres planted with unusual native and rare foreign trees (more than 3,000 in all) and flowering shrubs. To take a self-guided tour, stop by the office and pick up maps and audio tapes; a horticultural tour and a tour of the cemetery's notable memorials are available. The **Friends of Mount Auburn** sponsors special walks, talks, and other activities. ◆ 580 Mount Auburn St (between Coolidge Ave and Cottage St). 547.7105 &

Kendall Square

Visitors who arrive at Kendall Square via the **MBTA** *Red Line* are in for a treat. Located in the station is a kinetic musical sculpture by artist/inventor Paul Matisse (grandson of Henri) consisting of three pieces titled *Pythagoras, Kepler,* and *Galileo. Pythagoras* has wall handles on either side of the subway tracks that when cranked set large teak hammers into motion, which strike 16 tuned tubular chimes and produce melodious bell-like music. *Kepler* features a handle that, after being pulled a number of times, causes a triple-headed steel hammer to strike an aluminum ring, producing a low F-sharp note. *Galileo*'s mechanism makes rumbling, windlike music. When operated in unison by passersby, the pieces produce a pleasing concert that soothes impatient **T**-riders. The sculpture is part of the **MBTA**'s "Arts on the Line" program, which has commissioned works for 23 Boston-area subway stations.

The **Kendall** stop is the closest **T** station to **Massachusetts Institute of Technology (MIT)**, which dominates this section of Cambridge. **MIT** was founded in 1861 on the Boston side of the river by William Barton Rogers, a natural scientist. **MIT**'s first president, Rogers envisioned a pragmatic institution fitted to the needs of an increasingly industrialized and mechanized America. The modest technological school, then called **Boston Tech,** moved to its current site in 1916, quite comfortable with its industrial surroundings. **MIT** has never aspired to **Harvard**'s

picturesque Olympian aura, but rather has focused on scientific principles as the basis for advanced research and industrial applications. Appropriately, the school's motto is "Mens et Manus" (Mind and Hand). The institute grew rapidly and played a significant role in scientific research with the onset of World War II. In hastily assembled laboratories, **Harvard** and **MIT** scientists developed the machinery of modern warfare. One of **MIT**'s most significant research contributions was the development of radar. In peacetime the same labs have produced instrumentation and guidance devices for NASA and nuclear submarines.

The institute has an international identity, and graduates have founded local, national, and multi-national high-tech and biotechnology companies. Today, it has schools of **Engineering, Sciences, Architecture and Planning, Management, Humanities, Health Sciences and Technology,** and **Social Science.**

For general information on **MIT** or to join one of the free student-guided campus tours, lasting just more than an hour and offered weekdays, stop by the **Information Center** (Rogers Bldg, 77 Massachusetts Ave, between Memorial Dr and Vassar St, 253.4795), open Monday through Friday 9AM to 5PM. Arrange tours in advance by calling 253.1875.

Or fashion your own campus tour, ambling across the 150-acre campus weighted with monumental architecture. Despite the institute's well-deserved image as the temple of high-tech, it gives the arts elbow room, too, and has several excellent museums as well as some superb modern architecture and public art. Take a chance on getting lost for a bit in the domed Neo-Classical **Rogers Building** with its factorylike maze of hallways. The **MIT Museum** (265 Massachusetts Ave, at Front St, 253.4444) houses photos, paintings, holograms, scientific instruments, and technological artifacts. The museum shop (253.4462) offers gadgets, technological wizardry, games, puzzles, books, and posters. **The Albert and Vera List Visual Arts Center** (Weisner Bldg, 20 Ames St, between Amherst and Main Sts, First floor, 253.4680) has three galleries that display challenging art and design in diverse media. If you're an old/young salt or trekking about with kids, visit the display of ships' models and plans representing vessels from all over the world in the **Hart Nautical Galleries** (Rogers Bldg, First floor, 253.5942). Science buffs will enjoy a walk through **Strobe Alley** (Rogers Bldg, Fourth floor) a demonstration of high-speed stroboscopic equipment and photographs by the late Harold E. "Doc" Edgerton, class of 1927. Admission is free to all but the **MIT Museum.** Call for days and hours; many o the galleries close during the summer.

MIT's **East Campus,** on the east side of **Massachusetts Avenue,** has an impersonal, businesslike look, thanks in part to the new office and research buildings that have sprouted around Kendal Square since the early 1980s. In the last few years, **Main Street** at Kendall Square has gotten a sprucing up, with the arrival of a major hotel and numerous afes and restaurants. But **MIT** has, fortunately, reserved a network of big green spaces, where fine outdoor art can be found. In **Killian Court** behind the **Rogers Building** is Henry Moore's *Three-Piece Reclining Figure,* erected in 1976. (Another Moore work, *Reclining Figure,* is located off Ames Street between **Whitaker College** and **I.M. Pei's Weisner Building, Center for Arts & Media Technology,** pictured at right) Michael Heizer's sculpture *Guennette* stands opposite.

The **Great Dome, MIT's** architectural focal point, looms over **Killian Court.** From this grassy expanse, the view to the river and Boston beyond is magnificent. At **McDermott Court,** look for **I.M. Pei's Green Building, Center for Earth Sciences,** constructed in 1964. In front is the giant black-steel sculpture *La Grande Voile* ("The Big Sail"), designed by Alexander Calder. Nearby is a 1975 black-steel sculpture by Louise Nevelson called *Transparent Horizon.* At the end of Main Street near the **Longfellow Bridge** is a small outdoor plaza adorned with a controversial creation called *Galaxy* by sculptor Joe Davis. The focal point is a meteoritelike stainless-steel globe encrusted with strange topographic textures and patterns, clouds of steam billowing from below. The mysterious globe is ringed by 12 smaller ones that cast unusual illuminations at night. Picasso's *Figure découpée,* completed in 1963, stands in front of the **Hermann Building** at the far east end of campus. A five-mile system of underground passages, the "infinite corridor," connects the **East Campus** buildings.

Not surprisingly, this area has several bookstores that cater to the university crowd. The **MIT Press Bookstore** (292 Main St, between Hayward and Dock Sts, 253.5249) sells scholarly books and journals on engineering, computer science, architecture, philosophy, linguistics, economics, and more. The **MIT Coop** (3 Cambridge Center, Main St, between Kendall Sq and Fulkerson St, 499.3200) is the scion of the **Harvard Coop;** both are now managed by the book giant Barnes & Noble. **Quantum Books** (4 Cambridge Center, Broadway, between Kendall Sq and Fulkerson St, 494.5042) is a technical bookstore with one of the largest collections of computer books and periodicals in the world.

Also in the neighborhood is a branch of the acclaimed **Legal Sea Foods** (★★★$$$; 5 Cambridge Center, Main St, between Kendall Sq and Fulkerson St, 864.3400). All kinds of fresh fish are served just about any way you could imagine in this crowded and noisy place.

For a variety of other dining options, visit the **One Kendall Square** development (Hampshire St and Broadway), a handsomely renovated factory complex. It's home to **The Blue Room** (★★★★ $$$; 494.9034), a jazzy modernist boîte featuring good cooking, and the **Cambridge Brewing Company** ($$; 494.1994), a comfortable pub/restaurant that serves up the company's own beers and ales. Adjacent to the parking garage of **One Kendall Square** is the **Kendall Square Cinema**

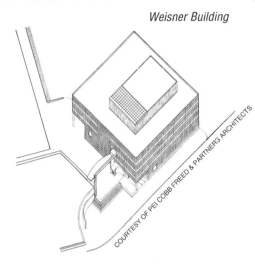

Weisner Building

COURTESY OF PEI COBB FREED & PARTNERS ARCHITECTS

(494.9800), an arts movie house with six high-tech theaters showing first-run films, and several upmarket eateries.

Nearby is the area's newest hostelry, **The University Park Hotel at MIT** ($$; 5 Sidney St, at Massachusetts Ave, 577.0200, 800.222.8733). Part of the 27-acre mixed-use **University Park at MIT** complex, it features 183 rooms and 27 suites with 2-line telephones, dataports, and work stations. Also on the premises is an exercise facility and **Sidney's Grill,** serving American regional cuisine. Other pluses include valet and self-service parking and 24-hour room service. The **Cambridge Center Marriott** ($$; 2 Cambridge Center, Broadway, between Kendall Sq and Fulkerson St, 494.6600, 800/228.9290; fax 494.0036) is another lodging option. It offers 431 rooms, 12 suites, a pool, a 24-hour health club, an Italian restaurant, and a sports bar.

MIT's West Campus, west of Massachusetts Avenue, has a more residential and relaxed atmosphere. Look for **Kresge Auditorium** (48 Massachusetts Ave, between Amherst and Vassar Sts) designed in 1955 by **Eero Saarinen,** unmistakable with its curving roof, one-eighth of a sphere resting on three abutments and floating free of the auditorium structure beneath. Also designed by **Saarinen,** the exquisite interfaith **MIT Chapel** is illuminated by a skylight that focuses light on the altar and is surrounded by a small moat that casts reflections upward on the interior walls. Harry Bertoia designed the sculpture behind the altar. Sought after as a site for weddings, the cylindrical structure is topped by Theodore Roszak's aluminum bell tower and bell.

The first printing of a book in English in the colonies took place in Cambridge in 1640. The *Bay Psalm Book* was printed by the Puritans to replace the disliked English version of the psalms.

Nearby is **Baker House** (362 Memorial Dr, between Danforth and Endicott Sts; pictured at left), a 1949 dormitory designed by **Alvar Aalto,** whose serpentine form cleverly maximizes views of the Charles, and the **Miracle of Science Bar & Grill** (★$$; 321 Massachusetts Ave, at State St, 828.2866), a newfangled eatery and drinkery modeled (loosely) on a chem lab.

East Cambridge

This multicultural community—predominantly Italian and Portuguese—was once a prosperous Yankee enclave. In the 19th century, factories turning out glass, furniture, soap, boxes, woven hose, and other goods flourished here along the Charles, and "Quality Row," a line of fine town houses (now 83-95 Third St), sprang up. Then, slowly, the riverside industries declined. After suffering through decades as a forgotten backwater, East Cambridge recently underwent major urban renewal and development. Look for the magnificently restored **Bulfinch Superior Courthouse Building,** original site of the Middlesex County court system, now occupied by the **Cambridge Multicultural Arts Center** (41 Second St, at Otis St, 577.1400), which has two spacious galleries and a theater.

A relatively new addition to the neighborhood (built in 1990) is the **Cambridgeside Galleria** on First Street, where you'll find **Filene's** (621.3800) and **Sears** (252.3500) along with **J. Crew, Ann Taylor, Banana Republic,** and other shops, restaurants, and services. A shuttle bus runs every 15 minutes Monday through Saturday between **One Kendall Square** and the **Cambridgeside Galleria.**

Nearby is pleasant **Lechmere Canal Park** with its lagoon and 50-foot geyser. It's the pickup point for picturesque cruises on the Charles River basin with the **Charles River Boat Co.** (261.3001). Bostonians and Cantabrigians alike flock to **Salamander** (★★★★$$$$; Athenaeum and First Sts, 225.2121), popular for its innovative menu of Southeast Asian dishes, many prepared in a wood-burning oven.

A new hotel in the area is the **Cambridge Inn Ramada** ($$; 250 Monsignor O'Brien Hwy, just west of Sciarappa St, 441.9200, 800.272.6232). Each of the 112 rooms and suites has a microwave oven, refrigerator, coffeemaker, mini-bar, cable TV, dataports, and telephones with voice mail. There are smoking and nonsmoking floors, and a restaurant, the **Commons Room.**

> The building of bridges—particularly the West Boston Bridge of 1793 and the Craigie Bridge of 1809—turned Cambridge into a more viable city by opening direct routes to Boston.

Central Square/Riverside

Central Square is a sprawling area located straight down Massachusetts Avenue from **Harvard Square** toward Boston. This section of Cambridge, which has been most resistant to gentrification, is now becoming more attractive thanks to an influx of city and federal funds. From a visitor's point of view, it's noteworthy for the concentration of international restaurants and interesting clubs.

Close to Harvard Square, and relatively upscale, **Cafe Sushi** (★★$$$; 1105 Massachusetts Ave, between Trowbridge and Remington Sts, 492.0434) offers a spectrum of sushi and sashimi, and a wide choice of other dishes. **Dolphin Seafood** (★★$$; 1105 Massachusetts Ave, between Trowbridge and Remington Sts, 661.2937) is a friendly little family place serving good and reasonably priced seafood. In Central Square proper, the **Middle East Cafe** ($$; 472 Massachusetts Ave, at Brookline St, 492.9181, 354.8238), a combination restaurant/ nightclub, books some interesting eclectic acts and serves traditional Middle Eastern fare. **Mary Chung** (★★$$; 464 Massachusetts Ave, between Sidney and Brookline Sts, 864.1991) is a modest-looking place with superb Mandarin and Szechuan specialties. Central Square also has lots of noteworthy Indian restaurants, the best of which is **India Pavilion** (★$$; 17 Central Sq, 547.7463).

For some of the best ice cream, stop by **Toscanini's** (899 Main St, between Bishop Richard Allen Dr and Columbia St, 491.5877). For superb regional American cuisine, visit **Salts** (★★$$; 798 Main St, between Windsor St and Massachusetts Ave, 876.8444). For home-style Italian cuisine, try **La Groceria** (★$$; 853 Main St, between Bishop Richard Allen Dr and Columbia St, 876.4162). A little out of the way, but worth the effort, **Green Street Grill** (★★★$$$; 280 Green St, between Pearl and Magazine Sts, 876.1655) shares space with old-time **Charlie's Tap** and serves flamboyant dishes with Caribbean influences in a funky setting.

Evening entertainment in Central Square centers on music of all kinds, with clubs ranging from neighbor-hood-casual to somewhat chic. Coffeehouses to sample: **Phoenix Coffeehouse** (675 Massachusetts Ave, between Prospect and Temple Sts, 547.2255), **Carberry's Bakery & Coffee House** (74-76 Prospect St, between Bishop Richard Allen Dr and Harvard St, 576.3530), and **Liberty Cafe** (479B Massachusetts Ave, between Main and Douglass Sts, 492.9900). If you're looking to sip a pint in an authentic Irish pub, visit **The Field** (20 Prospect St, between Massachusetts Ave and Bishop Richard Allen Dr, 354.7345) or **Phoenix Landing** (512 Massachusetts Ave, between Brookline and Pearl Sts, 576.6260). The tiniest and rowdiest of the area's Irish pubs is **The Plough and Stars** (912 Massachusetts Ave, at Hancock St, 492.9653), which features live Irish blues, country, and bluegrass music. You can hear local bands and dance the night away at the slightly seedy but fun **Cantab Lounge** (738 Massachusetts

Ave, between Central Sq and Pleasant St, 354.2685); **T.T. The Bear's Place** (10 Brookline St, between Green St and Massachusetts Ave, 492.BEAR), a homey rock 'n' roll club, also showcases local talent. More cutting-edge is **Manray** (21 Brookline St, at Green St, 864.0400), an art-bar featuring progressive underground New Wave and rock, with live music and dancing Wednesday through Saturday nights.

Inman Square

A 20-minute walk east on **Cambridge Street** from **Harvard Square** (or the same distance north on **Prospect Street** from **Central Square**), Inman Square is a quieter residential district with a surprising array of great restaurants, both ethnic and American. The square is slowly being gentrified, shedding much of its character as a family neighborhood with a variety of ethnic populations. It's definitely worth making a dinnertime journey here.

Although renovated beyond recognition, the **S&S Restaurant Deli** (★$$; 1334 Cambridge St, between Prospect and Hampshire Sts, 354.0777) is an Inman Square old-timer, serving both traditional and gourmet deli/diner fare. The nationally known and very popular **East Coast Grill** (★★★$$$$; 1271 Cambridge St, between Prospect and Oakland Sts, 491.6568) will more than satisfy cravings for barbecue and great grilled fare. **Cafe China** (★★$$; 1245 Cambridge St, at Prospect St, 868.4300) serves gourmet Chinese dishes. For southern Cajun cooking, try **Magnolia's** (★★$$$; 1193 Cambridge St, between Tremont and Prospect Sts, 576.1971). Come with a ravenous group to family-run **Casa Portugal** (★$$; 1200 Cambridge St, between Tremont and Prospect Sts, 491.8880) to enjoy heaping helpings of excellent Portuguese cuisine. **Daddy O's Bohemian Cafe** (★★$$$; 134 Hampshire St, between Elm and Norfolk Sts, 354.8371) proffers 1950s comfort food, along with contemporary cuisine.

For after-dinner entertainment, go to **Ryles** (212 Hampshire St, at Inman St, 876.9330), a casual and comfortable jazz club that books top local and national acts, or **The Druid Restaurant** (1357 Cambridge St, between Oak and Springfield Sts, 497.0965) for Irish music. For dessert, visit **Rosie's** (243 Hampshire St, between Cambridge and Dickenson Sts, 491.9488) for "chocolate orgasms" and other shockingly delicious treats.

North Cambridge/ Porter Square

Cambridge's neighborhoods offer an almost mind-boggling selection of international eateries. Head northward on **Massachusetts Avenue** toward Porter Square for still more ethnic restaurants. **Chez Henri** (★★$$$$; 1 Shepard St, at Massachusetts Ave, 354.8980) offers bistro-style French food with a Cuban flair. The magnificently decorated **Changsho** (★★$$; 1712 Massachusetts Ave, at Martin St, 547.6565) offers a wide array of Chinese dishes. The **Cottonwood Cafe** (★★$$$; 661.7440) and its

downscaled sidekick, **Snakebites Cantina** ($$; 354.6555), serve neo–Tex-Mex fare (both at 1815 Massachusetts Ave, at Roseland St); **Snakebites** also has live music.**Christopher's** ($$; 1920 Massachusetts Ave, at Porter Rd, 876.9180) is popular with locals for its pubby atmosphere. **Finnegan's Wake** ($$; 2067 Massachusetts Ave, between Hadley and Russell Sts, 576.2240) offers Irish food, including a Guinness beef stew. And **Ristorante Marino** (★★$$$; 2465 Massachusetts Ave, at Gold Star Rd, 868.5454) features cooking from the Abruzzi region of Italy, and uses all natural, organic products from local farms.

This stretch of Massachusetts Avenue also offers interesting shopping, including international clothing boutiques, shops purveying natural foods and products, and antiques. At **Porter Exchange** (1815 Massachusetts Ave, at Roseland St) there's a collection of Japanese shops and small countertop sushi cafes. Stop in at **Sasuga Japanese Bookstore** (7 Upland Rd, at Massachusetts Ave, 497.5460), the only one of its kind in New England. **Pepperweed** (1684 Massachusetts Ave, between Hudson and Martin Sts, 547.7561) sells contemporary attire from American, Japanese, and European designers. **Joie de Vivre** (1792 Massachusetts Ave, between Lancaster and Arlington Sts, 864.8188) is a delightful shop selling unusual and artful trinkets and gifts. Keep on going until you reach **Kate's Mystery Books** (2211 Massachusetts Ave, between Chester and Day Sts, 491.2660), an eccentric "Murder-Mystery Central" for all of New England.

For elegant digs, try **A Cambridge House B&B** ($$$; 2218 Massachusetts Ave, between Rindge Ave and Haskell St, 491.6300, 800/232.9989; fax 868.2848; (pictured above). Built in 1892 and listed on the National Register of Historic Places, it has 16 rooms (12 with private baths), all of which are handsomely restored and decorated. An elaborate breakfast is included. **The Mary Prentiss Inn** ($$$; 6 Prentiss St, between Frost St and Massachusetts Ave, 661.2929; fax 661.5989), set in an 1843 Greek Revival–style estate built by a prominent Cambridge housewright, is family-owned and -operated. A large, airy, high-ceilinged foyer with Victorian and Federal-era details leads to the parlor lounge with fireplace. Breakfast is served in the dining room, or on the sunny garden deck. Twenty rooms, which vary in size, decor, and price, are spread over three floors; six additional sleeping-loft duplexes are in a new attached wing. All rooms have baths, telephones, cable TV, and air-conditioning; a number have four-poster beds.

Other Neighborhoods

Boston's outer neighborhoods are close-knit communities with distinctive personalities. And that makes sense, because most of them developed independently before being absorbed by Boston. Over the years, annexation has increased the city's size even more than landfilling. Boston was an overcrowded seaport in 1850, but by 1900 the metropolis had flung itself across a 10-mile radius engulfing 31 cities and towns. Public transportation—horsecars, followed by electric trolleys—made it possible for people to live in "streetcar suburbs" within easy traveling distance to their workplaces. Immigrant families and the expanding middle-class began moving beyond Old Boston, rapidly swelling the commuter ranks. As a result these Boston neighborhoods and nearby suburbs are largely residential, with a smattering of important historical, recreational, and cultural attractions.

Charlestown

The **North End** and this neighborhood stare at one another across the mouth of the **Charles River**. Now a small satellite that's rather tricky to get to—reached by crossing the **Charlestown Bridge** by car or on foot, departing by boat from **Long Wharf** in the summer, or riding an **MBTA** bus—Charlestown was settled one year before Boston, in 1629. Most of the harborside town was burned by the British during the Battle of Bunker Hill in 1775, then rapidly rebuilt as a flourishing port where wealthy captains and ship owners lived in grand mansions on the hillsides.

The opening of the **Charlestown Navy Yard** brought jobs and prosperity from the 1800s to the early 1900s, attracting waves of European immigrants while well-to-do families moved out. Charlestown was annexed to Boston in 1874. Maritime activities began shrinking and the Great Depression increased the neighborhood's economic woes. Charlestown deteriorated faster as the **Navy Yard** dwindled and was shut down by the federal government in 1974.

But the neighborhood has been rebounding steadily, with the beautifully sited **Navy Yard** transformed into residential, office, retail, and medical-research space. Many have recognized the charm of Charlestown's narrow colonial streets bordered by neat little residences. A predominantly white, Irish-American enclave since the turn of the century, Charlestown is still a family-oriented neighborhood entrenched in tradition. Young professionals have been moving in, however, and it appears that gentrification will further open up this insular spot.

One of Charlestown's main tourist attractions is the USS *Constitution*, (pictured on page 196), the oldest commissioned ship afloat in the world. Ordinarily visible from **Copp's Hill** in the **North End,** the ship is still in active duty and is maintained by the US Navy. Launched in Boston on 21 October 1797, the ship served in Thomas Jefferson's campaign against the Barbary pirates, and won 42 battles in the War of 1812, never losing once. Nicknamed "Old Ironsides" for its combat-proven wooden hull (not for any iron plating), the ship is permanently moored at Constitution Wharf in the **Charlestown Navy Yard.** It makes one tour of the harbor—called the "turnaround"—every Fourth of July to remain a

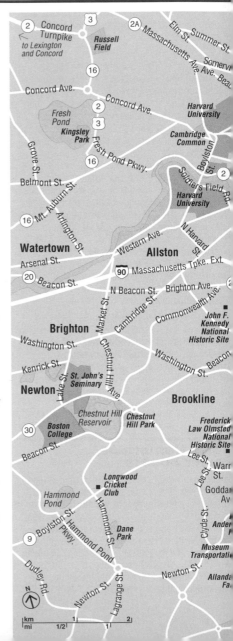

commissioned warship and to have a different side of the ship face the weathering effects of the ocean.

The *Constitution* received an extensive overhaul and restoration for its 200th anniversary in 1997. It's open for daily free tours led by Navy personnel dressed in uniforms from the era of the War of 1812 (call 242.5670 for information). The **Constitution Museum** (Constitution Wharf, 426.1812) screens a film revealing more about the ship and its history than the tours ever could. Originally a pumphouse, the museum also displays original documents and other artifacts from the historic vessel; it is open daily, and there is an admission charge. Before leaving the museum area, visit **Shipyard Park** just to the east.

Also of note in Charlestown is the enormous **Charlestown Navy Yard,** which was founded in 1800 to build warships and evolved over 170 years to meet the Navy's changing requirements. Now a National Historic Park under the direction of the **National Park Service** (242.5601), the navy yard is a physical record of American shipbuilding history. Among its 19th-century structures are the **Ropewalk** (see illustration on page 197)—the last in existence—designed by **Alexander Parris** in 1836 and nearly a quarter-mile long, where all rope for the navy was made for 135 years; **Dry Dock Number 1,** tied with a Virginia dry dock as the first in the US, and called **Constitution Dock** because "Old Ironsides" was the first ship to dock here; the ornate **Telephone Exchange Building,** completed in 1852; and the **Commandant's House,** an 1809 Georgian mansion. Visitors can also board the USS *Cassin Young,* a World War II destroyer of the kind once built here.

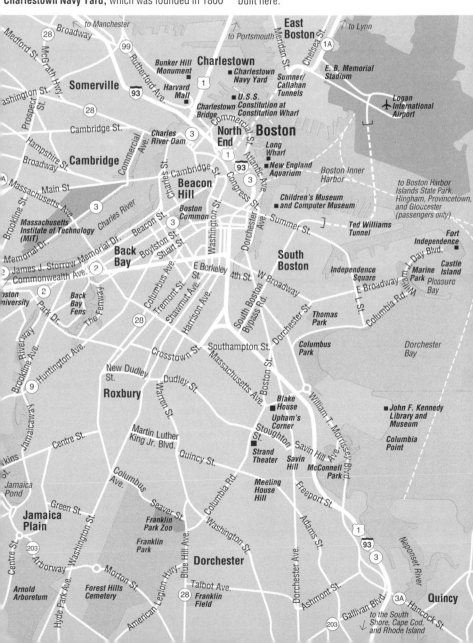

USS Contitution

MARJORIE VOGEL, RHODE ISLAND ORIGINALS

Every American schoolchild learns how the Battle of Bunker Hill was really fought on **Breed's Hill,** where **Solomon Willard**'s **Bunker Hill Monument** (242.5641), visible from many Boston locations, now points to the sky. The hill rises from the midst of formal **Monument Square** and its handsomely preserved 1840s town houses. Climb the grassy slope to the monument, part of the **Boston National Historic Park.** The Marquis de Lafayette laid the cornerstone in 1825, visiting the US for the first time since his days as a dashing youthful hero. The monument was finally completed in 1843, and Daniel Webster orated at the dedication. The 220-foot-tall obelisk of Quincy granite rises from the area where, on 17 June 1775, Colonel William Prescott reportedly ordered his citizen's militia not to fire "until you see the whites of their eyes." The Redcoats ultimately seized the hill, but suffered more than 1,300 casualties, a devastating cost that boosted the colonists' morale. Climb the 295 steps to the monument observatory for fine views; back at the bottom, notice the dioramas portraying the battle. The monument is open daily; there's no admission charge. Boston Park Rangers offer free talks in the summer. Adjacent to the **Navy Yard** is the "Whites of Their Eyes" exhibit (55 Constitution Rd, between Warren and Chelsea Sts, 241.7576), a 14-screen multimedia show that re-creates the Battle of Bunker Hill. It's open daily April through November.

Leave Monument Square and descend serene **Monument Avenue** to **Main Street.** If you visit the **Bunker Hill Monument** late in the afternoon and then dawdle, you can plan on enjoying a wonderful dinner at **Olives** (★★★$$$$; 10 City Sq, at Park and Main Sts, 242.1999). Olivia and Todd English's bistro-style restaurant is friendly, noisy, and known for such creatively rustic dishes as savory tarts, bouillabaisse, spit-roasted chicken, and butternut-squash *raviolini;* many of the specialties are cooked in a wood-burning brick oven. Reservations are accepted only for six or more, so get your name on the list very early—at least by 5:30PM. That likely means an early dinner, but it's the only way to ensure seating. (Note: They're closed on Sundays.) Or while away some time at the circa-1780 **Warren Tavern** (2 Pleasant St, at Main St, 241.8142) nearby, which offers drinks and plenty of atmosphere. Named for the Revolutionary War hero General Joseph Warren, who died in the Battle of Bunker Hill, the tavern reputedly was the first edifice rebuilt in Charlestown following the massive destruction of the area during that battle.

Continue sight-seeing on Main Street up **Town Hill** to **Harvard Mall.** The young minister John Harvard and his family lived near this site, which is now on the National Register of Historic Places. When Harvard died at 31, he bequeathed half of his fortune and all of his library to the college in Cambridge that adopted his name in thanks. At the mall's edge is **Harvard Square**—not to be confused with the square in Cambridge—and its modest mid–19th-century dwellings. Before leaving Charlestown, visit the **Charles River Dam Visitors' Information Center** (250 Warren St, west of Constitution Rd, 727.0059) on the river, for a multimedia presentation explaining the Charles River Dam's operations: flood control, fish ladders, and boat locks. You can take guided tours of the dam, which has one of the mightiest pumping stations in the country.

South Boston is famed, among other things, for its "L Street Brownies." This group of people "of a certain age" have for years taken a much publicized swim off Columbus Park's Carson Beach on New Year's Day, plunging into the frigid waters dressed only in bathing suits and caps. They get an annual picture in Boston newspapers for their daring.

South Boston

Expanded by landfill since the 18th century, South Boston is now a peninsula of approximately four square miles, with broad beaches and parks. Founded in 1630 as part of Dorchester, it was largely undeveloped until annexed to Boston in 1804. The first bridge to the main part of the city was built the next year and with it came the real-estate speculators. Soon Yankee gentry built handsome wooden houses along **East Broadway** and around **Thomas Park** on **Telegraph Hill**. The building of bridges to Boston, railways, and the growth of industry at century's end brought great numbers of Irish-Americans to South Boston, where they established the tight-knit neighborhood known as "Southie" today. Lithuanians, Poles, and Italians also settled here. The wealthy merchants moved out as immigrants moved in and Back Bay became the latest magnet for fashion seekers.

Like Charlestown and East Boston, South Boston is now a white enclave with a family focus and few minority residents. More than half the neighborhood population is of Irish ancestry, and a major local event is the annual St. Patrick's Day parade and festivities.

Drive to South Boston for great views of the harbor and islands from **Day Boulevard** and **Castle Island** at **Marine Park**. On Castle Island (actually no longer an island, since it is linked to the mainland by pedestrian and vehicular causeways), visit star-shaped **Fort Independence** (727.5290), which is open afternoons from Memorial Day to Labor Day (free tours are offered). The fort is less than 200 years old (1801), but the site it occupies—strategically located at the entrance to Boston Harbor—has been continuously fortified since 1634. Near the fort is a statue of Donald McKay, who designed Boston clipper ships, including the famous *Flying Cloud*. Castle Island, with its wide-open harbor views, is also a great place for a picnic. Then walk along **Pleasure Bay**, designed by Frederick Law Olmsted.

From **Dorchester Heights**, patriots commanded a clear view of the redcoats during the Siege of Boston in 1776. Here George Washington and his men set up cannons, heroically hauled through the wilderness for three months by Boston bookseller-turned-general Henry Knox. The guns were trained on the British, powerful persuasion that convinced them to flee for good. Located in **Thomas Park** (between G and Old Harbor Sts, 242.5642), Dorchester Heights is now a National Historic Site, with a recently restored monument. The park is open daily.

For a hearty meal or a quick pint, stop at **Amrhein's** (★$$; 80 W Broadway, at A St, 268.6189), a popular Irish bar near the *Broadway* T station. More than a century old and family-owned and -run, it boasts the oldest beer-pump system in Boston and the oldest hand-carved, mirror-backed wooden bar in the country. People come from all over for great meat-and-potatoes meals, fabulous onion rings, and of course, beer.

Dorchester

If it weren't part of Boston, racially, ethnically, and economically diverse Dorchester would be an important Massachusetts city in its own right. Originally, it was even larger and included South Boston and Hyde Park. Dorchester is an area of intimate neighborhoods, like the close-knit **Polish Triangle,** and **Dudley,** home to Hispanic and Cape Verdean families. **Dorchester Avenue,** nicknamed "Dot Ave," is the community's spine, with lots of ethnic and family-owned businesses: Irish pubs and bakeries next to Southeast Asian markets alongside West Indian grocers selling curries and spices.

In 1630 the Puritans landed at Mattapannock, today called **Columbia Point,** and, fearing Indian attacks, established homesteads near a fort atop **Savin Hill.** The area now known as **Upham's Corner** was once called **Burying Place Corner** because of the cemetery founded there in 1633, the **Dorchester North Burying Ground** (open occasionally; call 635.4505 for information). Nearby is Boston's oldest standing house, the 1648 **Blake House** (735 Columbia Rd, between Dorchester Ave and E Cottage St, 265.7802); it's open from 2 to 4PM on the second and fourth Saturday of each month (except August). Both the burying ground and house are on the National Register of Historic Places. Atop **Meeting**

Rope Walk,
Charlestown
Navy Yard

COURTESY OF THE BOSTONIAN SOCIETY

Massachusetts Archives

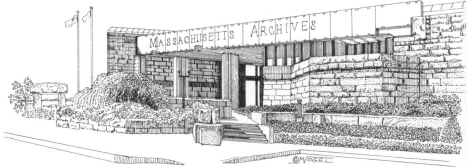

MARJORIE VOGEL, RHODE ISLAND ORIGINALS

House Hill is the **Mather School** (1 Parish St, at Winter St, 635.8757), the oldest elementary school in the nation, founded in 1639 as a one-room schoolhouse. It is occasionally open to the public; call for information.

Dorchester was an agricultural community well into the 1800s. Gradually, rich Bostonians built country estates and summer residences on its southern hilltops. In the early 1800s, commercial villages grew up along the **Neponset River** and the waterfront. With the electric tram's inauguration in 1857, Dorchester became a suburb of Boston, annexed in 1869. Lovely Victorians are sprinkled throughout this neighborhood, but the best-known architectural style in Dorchester is the distinctive three-family house called the "triple decker," which became the rage in the early 1900s. But after World War II the suburban ideal of single-family homes and shopping malls emerged, and Dorchester suffered from flight and neglect. Though still not a safe place to wander at night, attempts are being made to upgrade its image. One sign of the neighborhood's vitality is the rejuvenation of the 1918 **Strand Theater** (543 Columbia Rd, between Hancock St and Cushing Ave, 282.8000), a former movie palace restored as a grand venue for the performing arts and community events.

Dorchester is also home to one of Boston's two daily newspapers, *The Boston Globe* (135 William T. Morrissey Blvd, between Old Colony Terr and Columbia Rd, 929.2653). Free hourlong tours that explain how a major metropolitan daily gets printed every day, as *The Globe* has been for more than 120 years, are scheduled Tuesday and Thursday; reservations are required.

The **John F. Kennedy Library and Museum** (929.4500), a 1979 design of **I.M. Pei & Partners,** couldn't find a home in Cambridge and landed out on Columbia Point—inconvenient for tourists but a dramatic site with glorious unobstructed views of the ocean. The stark, magnificent building is the official repository of JFK's presidential papers, classified and declassified, as well as all of his speeches on film and video and many personal belongings. The library also houses Robert F. Kennedy's senatorial papers. The museum displays seven exhibitions on JFK and two on RFK, with tapes and videos. Interestingly, in addition, the library possesses 95 percent of Ernest Hemingway's works. The library and museum are open daily except Thanksgiving, Christmas, and New Year's Day. There's an admission charge, with discounts for senior citizens and children under 16; children under 6 are admitted free. During the summer months, a water shuttle operates between the downtown Boston waterfront and the library.

Next to the library is the **Massachusetts Archives** (220 William T. Morrissey Blvd, south of Mount Vernon St, 727.9268; see the illustration above), within which is the **Commonwealth Museum,** with exhibits on the history of the state. Reserve in advance to view the archive documents, including the 1620 *Mayflower Compact* signed by the pilgrims aboard the *Mayflower* upon their arrival in the New World. The archives and museum are closed Sunday and holidays; admission is free.

The first chocolate manufacturer in the New World was Walter Baker of Dorchester. Baker's Chocolate is still in existence today.

There is some dispute over the origin of the name of the Boston neighborhood called Jamaica Plain. The *Dictionary of Place Names* suggests that the name originated with an Indian tribe called the Jamaco or Jameco (Algonquin for "beaver"). A booklet issued by the City of Boston for the US Bicentennial, however, indicates that the name is related to the Jamaican rum trade, through which many prominent local families made their fortunes. And an apocryphal local legend tells of an English woman whose husband told her he was heading for Jamaica—on her way to track him down, she found him, quite by chance, in the Boston neighborhood.

Jamaica Plain

Originally part of neighboring **Roxbury,** Jamaica Plain ("JP" to Bostonians) was once fertile farmland. In the late 1800s it became a summer resort for wealthy Back Bay and Deacon Hill residents, who drove their carriages along the tree-shaded **Jamaicaway** to pass the season at splendid estates surrounding **Jamaica Pond** ("The Pond"). On the other side of town, thousands of factory workers labored in JP's 17 breweries, all of which eventually closed. (Boston Beer Company, maker of the award-winning Samuel Adams Lager Beer, took up the torch of tradition in 1984.) In the 1830s, railroads began bringing well-to-do commuters who built Greek Revival, Italianate, and mansard residences; in the 1870s, streetcars brought the growing middle class. Today JP is one of Boston's most integrated neighborhoods, its three square miles filled mostly with families.

Centre Street developed early as JP's main artery and retains its small-town character. Along its bumpy, narrow length are good, cheap ethnic restaurants, bodegas, Irish pubs, mom-and-pop stores, and a slowly growing number of upscale establishments. Boston has few vegetarian restaurants, and one of its very good ones is the macrobiotic **Five Seasons** (★★★$$; 669A Centre St, between Burroughs and Myrtle Sts, 524.9016), offering simply prepared, innovative international dishes. Another popular Centre Street spot is the spacious and spare **Today's Bread** (★★$$; 701 Centre St, between Thomas and Burroughs Sts, 522.6458), with its big windows on the street, wonderful croissants, muffins, desserts, quiches, salads, and sandwiches.

One of Boston's best Irish bars and a local institution is **Doyle's Cafe** (★$$; 3484 Washington St, between Williams and Gartland Sts, 524.2345), known for its clock logo. In a cavernous vintage setting full of memorabilia, try fine Irish coffee and Bloody Marys, abundant brunches, delicious basic food, and a variety of beers on tap.

Some of the loveliest sections of Frederick Law Olmsted's **Emerald Necklace** are in or border Jamaica Plain. The **Arnold Arboretum of Harvard University** (125 Arborway, between Morton and Centre Sts, 524.1718), is the country's oldest arboretum (created in 1895) and has more than 15,000 species of woody plants, trees, shrubs, and vines from throughout the world. Rare specimens from China, Tibet, Borneo, Japan, and the Americas abound. The arboretum is the site of Lilac Sunday, a favorite annual event held in May. Azaleas, magnolias, and fruit trees also bloom in profusion here. Along the **Chinese Path** are some rarer, older Asian specimens—among them the Dove Tree from China, a magical sight in spring when its creamy white bracts flutter like wings. Olmsted interlaced the park's 265 acres with walks and drives, affording visitors a pleasant progression through meticulously sited plantings. The arboretum is open daily; guided walking tours can be arranged for a fee.

Nearby is the 70-acre **Franklin Park Zoo** (1 Franklin Park Rd, at Blue Hill Ave, 442.2002). Its prime attraction is the domed **African Tropical Forest Pavilion** (see map below), the largest in North America, with sculpted cliffs and caves, waterfalls, wooden footbridges, and lush African vegetation. The three-acre environmental exhibit is home to gorillas, leopards, forest buffalo, bongo antelopes, dwarf crocodiles, three-inch–long scorpions, and exotic birds. There are 75 species and 250 specimens in all, with no cages and almost imperceptible barriers between the residents and onlookers. Exhibits provide information on the crisis caused by human destruction of African and South American rain forests. The zoo's **Hooves and Horns** section stars zebras and camels, including Boomer the dromedary.

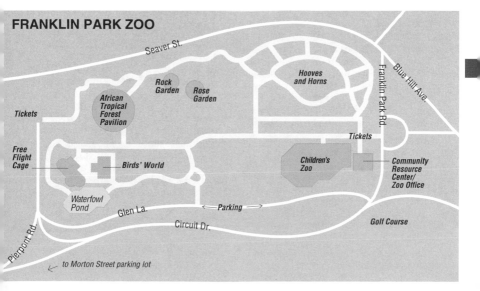

FRANKLIN PARK ZOO

Seaver St.

Blue Hill Ave.

Franklin Park Rd.

Tickets

Rock Garden

Rose Garden

African Tropical Forest Pavilion

Hooves and Horns

Tickets

Free Flight Cage

Birds' World

Children's Zoo

Community Resource Center/ Zoo Office

Waterfowl Pond

Glen La.

← Parking →

Circuit Dr.

Golf Course

Pierpont Rd.

← to Morton Street parking lot

Birds' World features more than 50 species of birds in a Chinese-pagoda birdhouse and free-flight cage, which dates from the zoo's 1913 opening. In the **Lions of Serengeti** section, visitors can observe lions in a natural setting. The zoo also features a **Children's Zoo** with a petting barn, where kids learn about New England farm animals. The zoo is open daily; there's an admission charge (children 3 and under free).

Jamaica Plain is also the site of the city's last working farm: **Allandale Farm** (259 Allandale St, west of Centre St, 524.1531), open from May through Christmas Eve. As spring turns to summer, and summer turns to fall, visitors can buy plants, fruits, vegetables, cider pressed on the premises, and Christmas trees and wreaths. The farm has been operating on the old **Brandegee Estate** for more than 125 years.

Brookline

Actually, Brookline isn't part of Boston—although not for lack of Boston's trying. When the cramped city began annexing towns to solve its land crunch, independent-minded Brookline refused to be swallowed. Today it remains a suburban town with a somewhat high cost of living and an increasingly diverse population. **Coolidge Corner,** where Harvard and Beacon Streets meet, is a mini–Harvard Square with both old-fashioned and new-fashioned establishments. The **Coolidge Corner Theatre** (290 Harvard St, 734.2500) was saved from the development scourge by movie lovers, and offers interesting, vintage and contemporary films. A few blocks from the theater is the house where John F. Kennedy was born in 1917. The Kennedys lived here until 1921. Now called the **John F. Kennedy National Historic Site** (83 Beals St, between Harvard and Stedman Sts, 566.7937), it's open daily. There's an admission charge (except for senior citizens and children under 12).

An undiscovered gem in Brookline is the **Frederick Law Olmsted National Historic Site** (99 Warren St, between Lee and Walnut Sts, 566.1689), the rambling home and office named "Fairsted" by its owner, who was America's first landscape architect and founder of the profession in this country. Olmsted's successor firm practiced here until 1980, and the site is now open to the public Friday through Sunday, by appointment on other days. On display here are valuable plans, photographs, and other documentation of the firm's work. The archives are open by appointment. There's no admission charge.

Stop for lunch at one of the town's excellent delis, including the **B & D Deli** (★$; 1653 Beacon St, between University and Winthrop Rds, 232.3727) and kosher **Rubin's** (★★$$; 500 Harvard St, at Kenwood St, 731.8787) on the Allston border. Enjoy casual comfort food at the **Tam O'shanter** (★$$; 299 Harvard St, between Green and Babcock Sts, 277.0982), nicknamed "The Tam," which doubles as a club with a regular schedule of live music.

Also in Brookline is the **Museum of Transportation** (Carriage House, Larz Anderson Park, 15 Newton St, east of Goddard Ave, 522.6140), which explores the cultural and sociological impact of the automobile on American society. There are also special exhibitions on other transportation-related topics such as aviation. The annual Classic Lawn Series, featuring vintage cars, takes place on Sunday from mid-May through September. The museum is open Wednesday through Sunday; there's an admission charge.

Parking in Brookline, by the way, is limited to two hours during the day and is notoriously impossible overnight, when all visitors' cars on the street between 2AM and 6AM are subject to ticketing.

Allston-Brighton

Polyglot Allston-Brighton is Boston's most integrated district, where Irish, Italians, Greeks, and Russians are joined by growing numbers of Asians, African-Americans, and Hispanics. Most Bostonians associate this neighborhood with students from the local universities, large numbers of whom live here. An agricultural community founded in 1635, the neighborhood later was the locale for huge stockyards, slaughterhouses, and meat-packing operations serving the region, then became industrialized. Since World War II there has been dramatic change led by the construction of the Massachusetts Turnpike, which further split Allston from Brighton, already divided by railroad tracks. Allston-Brighton has developed in a haphazard way that makes it confusing to navigate, but it has many pleasant streets with nice old homes, apartment buildings, and a cozy feel. The neighborhoods have ethnic restaurants and markets, pubs, interesting shops, and antiques stores. A popular hangout is **Harper's Ferry** (156 Brighton Ave, between Harvard and Park Vale Aves, 254.9743), an established blues club. **The Sunset Grill and Tap** (130 Brighton Ave, between Linden St and Harvard Ave, 254.1331) is known for its international array of beers.

Somerville

Once primarily a working-class suburb, Somerville has become an increasingly popular place to live among students and yuppies crowded—or priced—out of Cambridge. In keeping with this trend, the town has developed a steadily growing restaurant/club scene. Try **Dali** (★★★★$$$$; 415 Washington St, at Beacon St, 661.3254), an authentic and lively Spanish restaurant with irresistible tapas—great for satisfying multiple urges or for groups that are into sharing. **Redbones** (★★★★$$$; 55 Chester St, between Elm and Herbert Sts, 628.2200) stands out for its authentic Southern barbecue. The **Elephant Walk** (★★★★$$$$; 70 Union Sq, Somerville Ave and Washington St, 623.9939) is a Cambodian-French venue guaranteed to intrigue the most jaded palate. After dinner, catch some rock at **Johnny D's Uptown** (17 Holland St, between Davis Sq and Winter St, 776.2004) or, for music of a more improvisational nature, stroll into the **Willow Jazz Club** (699 Broadway, between Boston Ave and Bristol Rd, 623.9874).

Going for the Laurels: The Boston Marathon

Those who know Boston would unequivacably agree it's a walker's city. However, each year in mid-April it becomes a runner's town, thanks to its remarkable marathon. Known formally as the **Boston Athletic Association (BAA) Marathon,** but simply as "Boston" to the running world, the annual event celebrated its 100th running in 1996. The 36,748 starters in the centennial race (of whom 35,810 finished) made it the largest single running event in history—about 10,000 qualified runners per year is the usual number of participants in a marathon.

The Boston Marathon is the oldest in North America and one of the most prestigious races in the world; 10,000 runners in the 100th marathon came from outside the US. But the annual event is more than a race: For spectators as well as runners, it is one of Boston's best-loved traditions, with a mystique all its own.

The first Boston Marathon was run on 19 April 1896, after Tom Burke dug a line in the dirt with his heel at Metcalf's Mill in **Ashland,** about 25 miles southwest of Boston, and shouted "Go" to 15 men shod in heavy boots to protect their feet from the rutted roads. John McDermott of New York won the race in less than three hours, losing 10 pounds in the process.

Since that very first race, the Boston Marathon has been run on Patriot's Day, a holiday commemo-rating the beginning battles of the American Revolution. (Today, Patriots' Day is celebrated and the Boston Marathon is run on the third Monday in April.) The starting point of the race, however, was changed in the early years of this century, when the standard length of a marathon was changed from 25 miles to 26.2 miles.

There's an amusing story as to how the standard marathon course came to be lengthened. At the **Olympic Games** held in London in 1908, illness in the Royal Family was going to prevent several of its members from attending the much-touted marathon. So Olympic officials brought the starting line to them, at Windsor Castle. This extended the course one mile and 385 yards, and the new distance stuck. The Boston course was adjusted by moving the starting line to the town of **Hopkinton,** where it remains today.

Another innovation was introduced in the 1996 marathon, when computer chips were tied to the runners' shoelaces. The chips calculate how long it actually takes each athlete to run the 26.2-mile course—a time that was difficult to gauge in the past, since many thousands of runners are still backed up at the starting line long after the race starts at noon. While each runner's official time actually begins when the starting gun is fired, runners may use their computer-chip calculated time to qualify for following year's race (qualifying standards were introduced by the **BAA** in the 1970s).

What sets the Boston course apart is that at about 20 miles into the race, at the point at which a runner's body begins to undergo traumatic chemical changes—known as "hitting the wall"—runners unfortunately also hit the hills of **Newton.** These hills are actually not very high—the third and final one, the infamous **Heartbreak Hill,** rises only 90 feet from sea level—but their location makes Boston's one of the most challenging marathon courses in the world. The course record for men, set in 1994 by Cosmas Ndeti of Kenya, is 2:07:15; the women's record time, set in 1994 by Uta Pippig of Germany, is 2:21:45.

Women have run officially in the Boston Marathon since 1972, though not in the Olympic Marathon until 1984. Shortly thereafter, in 1975, Boston became the world's first major marathon to allow wheelchair racers to compete.

The winner in each division is crowned with a coveted wreath of laurel leaves made of branches cut from groves in Marathon, Greece. But most spectators and runners agree that in the Boston Marathon, just to finish is to win. For information, contact the **BAA** (131 Clarendon St, at Stanhope St, 236.1652).

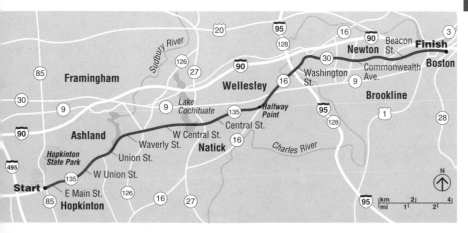

Day Trips

Boston is a wonderful place to explore, yet when you've had your fill of city life, it's easy to leave town for some stimulating day—or weekend—trips. In just an hour or two, public transportation or a car can take you to the rocky beaches of **Cape Ann** or the dunes of **Cape Cod**; it's just a bit farther to the green hills of the **Berkshires**; the beckoning mountains, lakes, and fall colors of New Hampshire and Vermont; or Maine's coastal villages and idyllic islands. And if Boston begins to seem too large an urban center, in only an hour you can escape to the small-city pleasures of **Providence, Rhode Island.** Just a bit farther south is **Newport**, Rhode Island, site of the elaborate "summer cottages" of the Vanderbilts and Astors and still a popular yachting center.

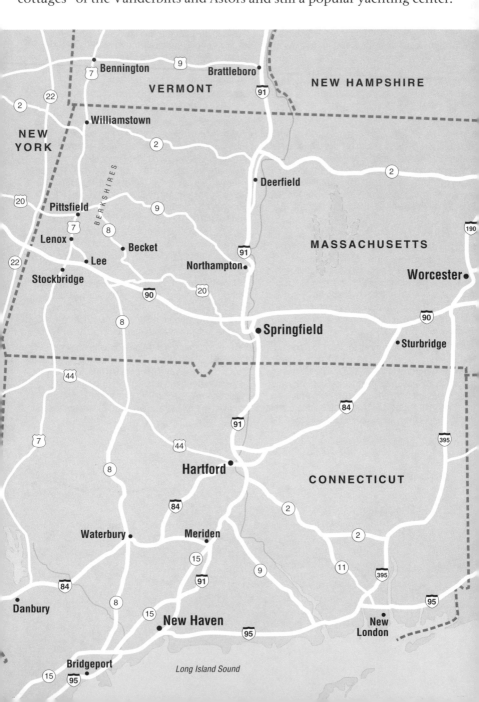

A great source for guidebooks on travel throughout New England is **The Globe Corner Bookstore** (500 Boylston St, between Berkeley and Clarendon Sts, 859.8008; 28 Church St, at Palmer St, Cambridge, 497.6277). Also, get a wealth of free information on what to see and do in Massachusetts by calling or writing the **Massachusetts Office of Travel and Tourism** (100 Cambridge St, 13th floor, Boston, MA 02202, 727.3201, 800/447.6277).

The following are destination ideas rather than itineraries; arm yourself with information on hours and prices before you go—or just head out with a good map or two and a spirit of exploration. And keep in mind that the off-season can have its charms as well. Cape Cod and the islands in winter, for example, have their own compelling moods.

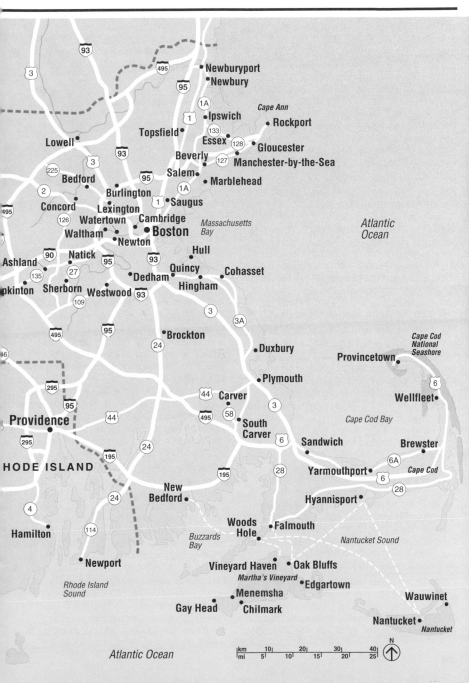

The North Shore

Head north of Boston for the best clams in the world. While on the quest, there's plenty to see. The infamous **Saugus Strip** along **Highway 1,** for instance, is an eyesore to some and beloved by others for its garish roadside signs and attendant establishments, vintage kitsch inspired by America's love affair with the auto. This stretch of Highway 1 is home base for several of America's biggest, gaudiest restaurants. A giant cactus sign and herd of life-size cattle heralds the **Hilltop Steak House,** affectionately called "The Hilltop" (★$$$; Hwy 1, southbound, 781/233.7700), home of slabs of red meat, potatoes, and overeating. A Polynesian theme reigns at **Kowloon** ($$$; Hwy 1, northbound, 781/233.9719), located across from "The Hilltop," and for Chinese food in a Disneylike ambience, there's gargantuan **Weylu's** ($$$; Hwy 1, northbound, 781/233.1632). As you ride along, keep an eye out for a miniature golf course with a towering tyrannosaurus rex; a ship-shaped restaurant; the **Prince Restaurant** ($$; Hwy 1 and Lynn Fells Pkwy, 781/233.9950), which is a pizza place shaped like the Leaning Tower of Pisa; and other quirky sights.

For a different historical slant, take the Main Street exit off Highway 1 to the **Saugus Iron Works National Historic Site** (244 Central St, 781/233.0050), a reconstruction of the first integrated iron works in North America (created in 1646). The site includes a furnace, a forge, seven water-powered wheels, and a rolling and slitting mill. It's open daily; free admission. A well-kept Saugus secret is the **Breakheart Reservation** (177 Forest St, 781/233.0834), a park with 600 acres of oak-, hemlock-, and pine-covered hills, 2 freshwater lakes, 10 miles of trails, and lots of birds.

Take **Route 1A** north from Boston to **Route 129** to **Marblehead,** a picture-postcard New England seaside town with early New World flavor and historical attractions, splendid views of the ocean, plus boutiques and good seafood restaurants. It's a perfect place for a leisurely day of walking and poking around. The **Old Town** predates the American Revolution and boasts Federal-style sea captains' homes and neat cottages. For more information, contact the **Marblehead Chamber of Commerce** (62 Pleasant St, 781/631.2868). **Salem,** "The Witch City," is a short drive west from Marblehead on **Route 114** to Route 1A. The notorious witchcraft trials of 1692, one of the Massachusetts Bay Colony's most troubled chapters, caused 19 people to be hanged before the hysterical Puritan populace regained reason. Pick up self-guided walking tour maps (and any other tourist information you may need) from the **Salem Chamber of Commerce** (32 Derby St, 978/744.0004).

Don't miss the **Salem Maritime National Historic Site** (174 Derby St, 978/740.1660), where American maritime history is enshrined in the **Custom House, Derby House/Wharf, Bonded Warehouse, West India Goods Store,** and lighthouse. The site is open daily except Thanksgiving, Christmas, and New Year's Day. There's no charge for admission, but they do charge a nominal fee for guided tours. Also visit **The House of the Seven Gables** (54 Turner St, 978/744.0991), the inspiration for Nathaniel Hawthorne's novel. It's open daily; there's an admission charge. The **Peabody Essex Museum** (East India Sq, Liberty and Essex Sts, 978/745.9500, 800/745.4045) is also noteworthy for its period houses and collections covering three centuries of maritime history, ethnology, natural history, and Asian trade. It's open daily June through October, closed Monday the rest of the year. There's an admission fee. Less critical to see, but beloved by kids, is the **Salem Witch Museum** (19½ Washington Sq N, 978/744.1692). The museum is open daily; there is an admission charge. If you don't want to direct your own steps, take the **Salem Trolley Tour**, run by **Hawthorne Tours** (978/744.5469); it departs from the **Visitor Center.**

Continue north on Route 1A to **Beverly** for an afternoon of vaudeville-esque entertainment. *Marco the Magi's Production of Le Grand David and His Own Spectacular Magic Company* plays at the 750-seat **Cabot Street Theatre** (286 Cabot St, 978/927.3677) on Sunday and at the more intimate 450-seat **Larcom Theatre** (13 Wallis St, 978/922.6313) for on Saturday shows. Or catch a Broadway musical (often with Broadway stars) or a big-name concert at the **North Shore Music Theatre** (162 Dunham Rd, 978/922.8500).

En route northeast from Beverly to **Gloucester** is **Manchester-by-the-Sea,** the first North Shore summer resort, which catered to "Proper Bostonians" in the 1840s. The pretty-as-a-picture **Singing Beach** is a favorite of Boston day-trippers. To avoid the parking hassle, rise early and take a morning beach train on the **Rockport Line Commuter Rail** from **North Station** (978/722.3200). When you've had enough sunning, swimming, and clambering over rocks, it's a short, pleasant walk into town for a bite to eat before the train ride back.

To drive **Cape Ann**'s rugged shore, continue northeast on **Route 127** to **Gloucester**. The largest town on the North Shore, Gloucester was settled as a fishing colony in 1623 and is still an important fishing port. On its seafront promenade is the memorable *Gloucester Fisherman* statue, dedicated to those "who go down to the sea in ships." Unveiled in 1923 as part of Gloucester's tricentennial observances, the statue depicts a man in oilskins at a ship's wheel, eyes on the horizon. The local fishing fleet is blessed annually, with attendant colorful festivities in late June. Whale watching excursions leave from here.

Visit the **Cape Ann Historical Association** (27 Pleasant St, 978/283.0455) to see the stunning collection of 19th-century American painter Fitz Hugh Lane's luminous views of **Gloucester Harbor** and islands. The museum is open Thursday through Saturday; there's an admission charge. Across town is **Rocky Neck**, the oldest artists' colony in the US. Perched on rocks overlooking the harbor is "Beauport," the **Sleeper-McCann House** (75 Eastern Point Blvd, 978/283.0800). Beauport was built in the early 1900s by architect/interior designer **Henry Davis Sleeper,** who greatly influenced contemporary tastes and style-setters, including Isabella Stewart Gardner. The second owner of the mansion, Charles McCann, lived there with his wife, Helena Woolworth, of the five-and-dime empire. Within are 18th- and 19th-century decorative arts and furnishings. It's open Monday through Friday from 15 May to 15 September; daily 15 September to 15 October. There's an admission charge.

Then move on to the **Hammond Castle Museum** (80 Hesperus Ave, 978/283.2080, 800/283.1643). The medieval-style castle was the humble home of inventor Dr. John Hays Hammond Jr., whose brainstorms included shaving cream, the car starter, electrified toy trains, the forerunner of stereophonic sound, and the precursor to remote control—more than 437 patented inventions. Hammond's resplendent digs contain medieval furnishings, paintings, and sculpture. Monthly organ concerts are played on the 8,600-pipe organ, the largest in a private American home. Call in advance for schedule of tours; there is an admission charge.

For dinner, fresh lobster is the way to go. Two Gloucester restaurants that are especially good are **Bistro** (★★$$; 2 Main St, 978/281.8055) and **White Rainbow** (★★$$$; 65 Main St, 978/281.0017). Afterward, spend an illuminating evening at the **Gloucester Stage Company** (267 E Main St, 978/281.4099), housed in a rehabbed fish factory. The plays of patron/resident playwright Israel Horovitz often deal with the local way of life.

A short drive up Cape Ann from Gloucester is tiny **Rockport**, a fishing-community-turned-artists' colony that can be happily meandered through in a day. (It's a dry town, by the way.) Parking can be difficult in the center of town unless you arrive as early as the birds, so take the commuter train from **North Station** (722.3200) in Boston if you can—it's a very pretty ride. Rockport's light is particularly beautiful at day's end and in early spring and late fall. The **Toad Hall Book Store** (51 Main St, 978/546.7323) is wonderful for old-time friendliness and service and has a large selection of books on local geography, history, and lore. The more touristy restaurants and shops are densely clustered on **Bearskin Neck** (closed to cars); for more interesting galleries and restaurants, walk along **Main Street** (where, incidentally, the movie *Mermaids* was

filmed). Just beyond town is a windswept haven and public park, the 68-acre **Halibut Point State Park and Reservation** (Rte 127, 978/546.2997). The acclaimed **Rockport Chamber Music Festival** (978/546.7391) is held each June, with performances on Thursday through Sunday evenings.

Inland on **Route 133** from Gloucester is **Essex,** with a staggering concentration of antiques shops in a single-mile stretch. Stop for sustenance at supercasual, rambling **Woodman's** (★★$$; Main St, 978/768.6451), a North Shore favorite, where Lawrence Woodman first dipped clams in batter and deep-fried them in 1916. Come early or late to avoid huge family crowds, but if you can't, the steamers, lobsters, fried clams, scallops, chowder, etc., are worth a wait. Nearby is the town of **Ipswich,** also prized for its clams and more so for having more 17th-century houses than any other town in America (more than 40 of them were built before 1725). On **Ipswich Bay,** the **Crane Memorial Reservation** includes four miles of shoreline and an excellent sandy stretch at **Crane's Beach.** In the old Crane residence, the **Great House** (290 Argilla Rd, 978/356.4351), there are weekend concerts and art lectures during the summer, complemented by gorgeous Italianate gardens with sea views. The house is also open to the public on Wednesdays and Thursdays in summer; there's an admission charge.

Near the northeastern tip of Massachusetts, via Route 1A, is **Newburyport,** once a shipbuilding center and the birthplace of the US Coast Guard. Stroll along the waterfront park and promenade, and through the restored commercial district, an enclave of three-story, brick-and-granite buildings. Many folks think the town has gone overboard gussying itself up for tourists, but it's a nice place to while away a few hours if you're in the mood for shopping, eating, or strolling.

A Massachusetts treasure is the **Parker River National and State Wildlife Refuge** on **Plum Island** (978/465.5753), which offers unsullied beauty, refreshing sea air, and glimpses of wildlife. From Newburyport, head south on Route 1A to **Newbury** and watch carefully for signs to Plum Island and the wildlife refuge. Headquartered at the old Coast Guard lighthouse at the island's northern end, the 4,662-acre refuge has six miles of sandy beaches, hiking trails, observation towers for spotting more than 300 bird species, saltwater and freshwater marshes, sand dunes, surf fishing, nature-study hikes, cross-country skiing, beach plum and cranberry picking, waterfowl hunting, and clamming. Come early on summer weekends because the refuge closes when its quota of 240 cars is reached, which often happens before 9AM. It reopens at 3PM, so if you're shut out early, spend the day in Newburyport and try again later. In late summer and autumn the marshland takes on rich, soft coloring and the sunsets are breathtaking. The island really empties out after the summer.

Northwest of Boston is **Lowell,** America's first successful planned industrial complex and now a National and State Historical Park. Located at the confluence of the **Concord** and **Merrimack Rivers,**

Lowell was transformed from a sleepy agricultural village into an industrial powerhouse in 1822 by Boston merchant Francis Cabot Lowell and fellow investors. Lowell's Boston Manufacturing Company had already successfully developed a textile mass-production system driven by water-powered looms in **Waltham.** Though Lowell (the town) first played a pioneering role in the American industrial revolution, it gradually became a squalid environment where women mill workers and immigrants were exploited. Now revitalized by high-tech industries, its fascinating past has been preserved. Today you can tour the mill complexes, operating gatehouses, workers' housing, and a five-and-a-half-mile canal system. Guided interpretive mill and canal tours are offered numerous times daily during the summer; reservations are required. **The Lowell Heritage State Park** waterpower exhibit (25 Shattuck St, 978/970.5000) is open daily; there's an admission charge. Self-guided city tour maps are available at the **Visitors' Center** (246 Market St, 978/970.5000), including one that points out sites related to native son Jack Kerouac. The town is also the birthplace of James Abbott McNeill Whistler. **The Whistler House Museum of Art** (243 Worthen St, 978/452.7641) displays 19th- and 20th-century American art, including works by Whistler. The museum is open Wednesday through Sunday from March through December; there's an admission charge.

In 1997, Lowell became the new home of **The Sports Museum of New England** (25 Shattuck St, 978/452.6775), which encapsulates "great moments in New England sports history." Holdings include more than a thousand hours of film and video highlights, action-packed displays, and interactive exhibits. There's also a museum store. The museum is open Tuesday through Sunday; there's an admission charge.

Bostonians and visitors alike often travel beyond Massachusetts's northern border for fall foliage splendor, hiking, cross-country and downhill skiing, rock climbing, canoeing, shopping at factory outlet stores, and natural beauty and tranquillity. For more information, contact the **New Hampshire Office of Travel and Tourism** (603/271.2666), **Vermont Travel and Tourism** (802/828.3239), or the **Maine Office of Tourism** (207/287.5710, 800/533.9595 out of state).

The state drink of Massachusetts is cranberry juice, in testament to the state's number one agricultural product. Over 400 growers work more than 12,000 acres, mostly located in southeastern Massachusetts. One town alone, Carver, produces half the nation's crop.

In 1903 the Boston Red Sox, then called the Boston Pilgrims, won their first pennant, and then went on to win the first ever baseball World Series against the Philadelphia Pirates.

Near Northwest

A few miles northwest of **Cambridge** on **Route 2A** are **Lexington** and **Concord,** historic towns where the first military encounters of the American Revolution took place. Concord grapes were first cultivated here, as were the ideas of Louisa May Alcott, Ralph Waldo Emerson, Nathaniel Hawthorne, and Henry David Thoreau. The most notable among the many historic sites is the **Lexington Battle Green** or **Common.** Here the first skirmish of the Revolutionary War broke out on 19 April 1775 between the Concord-bound British troops and Colonial Minutemen, alerted earlier by messengers on horseback of the Redcoats' approach. (A reenactment of the Battle of Lexington is staged annually.) The second battle of the day was fought in neighboring Concord, where the citizen militia attacked and drove the British soldiers from North Bridge. Daniel Chester French's famous *Minuteman* statue (pictured above) now stands guard over the bridge. The **Lexington Historical Society** (781/862.1703) offers tours of the green. For additional details, contact the **Lexington Visitors' Center** (1875 Massachusetts Ave, 781/862.1450).

Minute Man National Historical Park, encompassing 750 acres in Concord, Lexington, and **Lincoln,** commemorates the start of the colonies' War for Independence. The park is a narrow strip running on either side of **Battle Road** (a section of Route 2A). It begins beyond **Lexington Center** at the **Battle Road Visitor Center** (Airport Rd, 781/862.7753) and ends in Concord at the the **North Bridge Visitor Center** (Liberty St, 781/369.6993). Though interpretive films and information relate the historical facts, you'll need a bit of imagination to conjure scenes of strife in this bucolic setting. For sophisticated Provençal sustenance after your revolutionary-era explorations, stop in at **Aigo Bistro** (★★$$$$; 84 Thoreau St, Concord, 781/371.1333), the latest venture of Moncef Meddeb, whose greatest hits include **L'Espalier** (see page 130).

Concord's most precious asset—although it's sometimes not treated that way—is **Walden Pond Reservation** (Rte 126, 978/369.3254), open daily from 5AM to dusk. The quiet pond is 62 glimmering acres nestled in 333 woody ones. The transcendentalist and free-thinking Thoreau lived and wrote in a 10-by-15-foot hand-hewn cabin alongside the pond from 1845 to 1847. Visitors to the reservation will find woods and pathways descending to smooth water, where sandbars slope to hundred-foot depths. Bostonians delight in this gentle place, so it gets

overcrowded and overworked as summer
progresses, but slowly recovers during fall and
winter—the best time for waterside contemplation.

Architecture enthusiasts inevitably make the trek
to **Gropius House** in nearby Lincoln (68 Baker
Bridge Rd, 781/227.3956). Follow **Route 2** west
to **Route 126** and watch for **Baker Bridge Road.**
German architect **Walter Gropius** built the house in
1938, the year after he came to the United States.
His iconoclastic modern residence introduced the
Bauhaus principles of function and simplicity to
this country. The house's industrial quality is derived
from its commercial components, a revolutionary
architectural approach at the time. **Gropius's**
residence includes furniture designed by him,
Marcel Breuer, and others. The house is part of
the historic homes collection of the **Society for the
Preservation of New England Antiquities (SPNEA),**
which offers excellent guided tours. It's open to the
public Wednesday through Sunday; there's an
admission charge.

Nearby, and also located in Lincoln, is the
DeCordova Museum and Sculpture Park
(Sandy Pond Rd, 781/259.8355). The castlelike
museum shows work by mostly New England
contemporary artists in its galleries and 35-acre
sculpture park. July and August feature outdoor
concerts. This is a gorgeous spot for a picnic and a
stroll. The museum is open Tuesday through
Sunday; there's an admission charge.

On the way back toward Boston (via Route 2 or
Highway 20), stop in **Waltham** to take in a show at
the **Rose Art Museum** (781/736.3434) at **Brandeis
University.** It's open Tuesday through Sunday;
admission is free. You also might want to check
what's on stage at the college's **Spingold Theatre**
(781/736.3400). The best restaurant in this area—
it's up there in the Boston pantheon—is the **Tuscan
Grill** (★★★★$$$$; 361 Moody St, Waltham,
781/891.5486).

The Berkshires

"The Berkshires" refers to the westernmost part of
Massachusetts, a verdant region dappled with rivers,
lakes, and gentle hills. It's a romantic and serene area
with twin legacies: culture and leisure.

Nestled within mountains, the Berkshires offers
hiking, camping, biking, fishing, canoeing, fall
foliage, skiing—and welcoming country inns to
retire to after the day's activities. From March to
early April you can see tree-tapping, watch sap
reduce into real maple syrup, and savor the precious
end product. The region is also home to several
noted arts organizations. For information, call or
write the **Berkshire Visitor's Bureau** (The Berkshire
Common, Pittsfield, MA 01201, 413/443.9186,
800/237.5747).

It's possible to take the **Massachusetts Turnpike
(Interstate 90)** west from Boston all the way to
New York State; the more northerly and scenic
Route 2 also traverses the state. A popular

destination on the way to the Berkshires (about an
hour west of Boston) is **Old Sturbridge Village**
(508/347.3362), perfect for a family outing.
(Take Exit 9 off the Mass Pike to Highway 20.)
Encompassing more than 200 acres, the museum
is a re-creation of an early 19th-century New
England agricultural community, and features
some participatory activities. There's a working
farm, tended in the manner of the era, and gardens
of culinary and medicinal herbs. Demonstrations
explain the crafts of 19th-century blacksmiths,
shoemakers, potters, and coopers, while exhibits
display period clocks, folk art and portraiture, and
firearms and militia accoutrements. The village is
open daily; there is an admission charge.

The Berkshires town of **Becket,** north of **I-90** about
three hours from Boston, is the summer home of
Jacob's Pillow (413/243.0745), the oldest dance
festival in the country, which features performances
by some of the world's most exciting companies.
Picnic under the trees before a performance. Stay
and/or dine nearby at the **Federal House** ($$$; 102
Main St, Lee, 413/243.1824).

Nearby **Lenox** is the site of **Tanglewood** (Rte 183,
413/637.5165, 617/266.1492 in Boston), the well-
known summer home of another acclaimed arts
organization, the **Boston Symphony Orchestra.** The
lush 200-acre estate is a popular destination for a day
trip from Boston. Many listeners forgo seats in favor
of a picnic on the grass while taking in the symphony.
The world-renowned Tanglewood Music Festival is
held here annually from July through August, and
other events include the Popular Artists Series
(throughout the summer) and the Labor Day
Weekend Jazz Festival.

Not far from Lenox is **Stockbridge,** a perfectly cast
New England town known for its **Norman Rockwell
Museum** (Rte 183, 413/298.4100). It's open daily;
there's an admission charge. The town's landmark
Red Lion Inn ($$$; Main St, 413/298.5545) has been
in operation since 1773. The well-preserved inn
offers rural charm year-round with a lobby fireplace,
music from the grand piano, and a front porch lined
with rocking chairs.

Just west of Stockbridge is **Chesterwood**
(4 Williamsville Rd, 413/298.3579), the former studio
and summer residence of the prolific sculptor Daniel
Chester French, who created Abraham Lincoln's
famous image in the Washington, DC, memorial and
the *Minuteman* statue in Concord, not to mention
many works around Boston. Casts, models, tools,
drawings, books, and French's personal belongings
are displayed here. There's a garden and nature trail,
too. It's open daily from 1 May through 31 October;
there's an admission charge.

North from here on **Highway 7** is **Williamstown,**
home of **Williams College** and the **Sterling and
Francine Clark Art Institute** (225 South St,
413/458.9545). The institute houses a wonderful
collection of 15th- to 19th-century paintings,
drawings, prints, and antique silver. It's open daily;
there's an admission charge. The **Williamstown**

Theatre Festival (1000 Main St, 413/597.3400) is like a summer camp for well-known stars of stage and screen. There are performances all summer long, but tickets to this popular series must be purchased in advance.

A detour on Highway 20 (west of Rte 7), leads to **Hancock Shaker Village** (413/443.0188), a restoration of the Shaker community founded in 1790. Twenty buildings have been restored, including a remarkable round stone barn. Shakers lived here until 1960. The village is open daily April through November; there is an admission charge.

The South Shore

Head for gentle surf on the South Shore, the coastal stretch that lies between Boston and Massachusetts's much more well-known beach area, **Cape Cod.**

Motor south on **Interstate 93** to **Route 3A,** the winding shore road to **Hingham** with its graceful town center. This is the site of the **Old Ship Meetinghouse** (Main St, 781/749.1679), the oldest wooden church in continuous use in America, built in 1681 and with pulpit, pews, and galleries dating from 1755. Then visit a rare pastoral setting of human design: **World's End Reservation** (Martin's La, 781/749.8956), a 250-acre part of a harborside estate designed by Frederick Law Olmsted and one of the Massachusetts Trustees of Reservations' beautiful park holdings. Here you'll forget about Boston's proximity until you reach the park's edge on the water, where you'll find unusual urban views. **Boston Light,** the oldest operating lighthouse in America, is easily viewed from **Nantasket Beach** on Nantasket Avenue in **Hull,** a teeny town at the end of a peninsula stretching north of Hingham into Boston Harbor. Nantasket Beach is a two-mile stretch of sand with a bathhouse, a playground, a promenade, a 1928 carousel, and the tiny **Hull Lifesaving Museum** (1117 Nantasket Ave, 781/925.5433). The museum is open daily; there is an admission charge. The beach is also accessible by **Bay State Cruises'** ferry (781/723.7800) from Long Wharf on Boston's waterfront. Continue south on Route 3A to **Duxbury** and **Duxbury Beach,** one of the finest barrier beaches on the eastern shore and a paradise for birders and walkers year-round.

Take **Route 3** south to Exit 4 and **Plymouth,** former home of the pilgrims and now the site of **Plimoth Plantation** (137 Warren Ave/Rte 3A, 508/746.1622), a "living museum" that re-creates 17th-century Plymouth. The plantation is open daily April through November; there is an admission charge. The famed rock, as well as a replica of the *Mayflower* are located at the center of town. Also in Plymouth is **Cranberry World** (255 Water St, 508/747.2350), with two outdoor working bogs, which are quite a sight.

Cambridge is second only to Wales, in Britain, in the number of bookstores per capita in the world. The books sold in Cambridge range from manuscripts written in the 1200s to today's comic books.

Cape Cod, Martha's Vineyard, and Nantucket

Shaped like a large fishhook curving 75 miles into the Atlantic and gleaming with hundreds of freshwater ponds and lakes, Cape Cod was once a prosperous fishing and whaling center. Today, this peninsula, bounded by the **Atlantic Ocean** on the east and north, **Buzzards Bay** on the west, and **Nantucket Sound** on the south, is lined with resort communities offering beaches, clam shacks, summer theater, and the like.

Much of the Cape has been intensely developed, causing erosion to whittle away some lovely land, but fortunately residents are forcing the pace to slow. One of the state's great treasures is the **Cape Cod National Seashore,** a protected 30-mile-long system of pristine beaches, woodlands, and marshes, culminating in the magnificent **Provincetown** sand dunes. For additional information, call the national seashore headquarters (99 Marconi Site Rd, Wellfleet, 508/349.3785). For more on Cape Cod, including campsites, contact the **Cape Cod Chamber of Commerce** (Mid-Cape Hwy, Hyannis, MA 02601, 508/362.3225). Also see *ACCESS Cape Cod, Martha's Vineyard & Nantucket.*

From Boston, take Route 3 south and cross the **Sagamore Bridge** over the imposing **Cape Cod Canal** onto the Cape and **Highway 6.** (Warning: Traffic on summer weekends can be brutal.) A traffic-free alternative is to take the ferry from **Commonwealth Pier** on Boston's waterfront (**Bay State Cruises,** 457.1428) to Provincetown at the tip of Cape Cod. It's possible to make a round-trip excursion in one day, but the ferry ride is five hours long so it's better to stay at least one night.

Sightseeing on Cape Cod can be adapted to fit your preference: For up-to-the-minute action, follow **Route 28** along the Cape's southern coast; for a quick trip to Provincetown, take Highway 6, which bisects the Cape; and for a sense of history, follow old **Route 6A** along the north coast.

Also called Old King's Highway Historic District, Route 6A is protected from modern development by strict laws. The road travels through several quaint towns, including **Sandwich, Yarmouthport,** and **Brewster,** that are home to a number of museums and historic houses. Farther along the Cape, past where Route 6A and Highway 6 merge, is **Wellfleet** and the Massachusetts Audubon Society's **Wellfleet Bay Wildlife Sanctuary** (Hwy 6, 508/349.2615), one of Cape Cod's loveliest spots.

Pilgrim Monument & Provincetown Museum

New Bedford Whaling Museum

But perhaps the most interesting place to visit—the timing depends on your tastes—is **Provincetown** at the tip of the Cape, where the Pilgrims first landed. An artists' and Portuguese fishing community that welcomes everyone, Provincetown's population swells from 3,800 year-round residents in the off-season to 25,000 people in summer. It's a gay haven, with a sensuous atmosphere and active tourist life from Memorial Day weekend until summer's end, but it has a quiet side also. No matter what time of year, it feels comfortable and safe here; return in winter when "P-town" has shrunk and you'll feel as if you have the town and an ocean to yourself. Endowed with the loveliest National Seashore stretch, the town's outskirts are wonderful for bicycling and jogging. For a sweeping view of the tiny town and its ocean setting, climb to the top of the **Pilgrim Monument** (High Pole Hill Rd, 508/487.1310, 800/247.1620). The tallest granite structure in the US, the tower hovers high on the village skyline. Visit the funky, fascinating **Heritage Museum** (356 Commercial St, 508/487.7098), which traces the history of Provincetown. It's open daily from mid-June through October; there's an admission charge. **Commercial Street** is the Main Street of P-town, where the greatest concentration of restaurants, shops, and lodgings converge, and is the best place for strolling and people watching. The easiest way to find good accommodations and cuisine, including special off-season listings, is to call or write the very helpful **Provincetown Chamber of Commerce** office in advance (PO Box 1017, Provincetown, MA 02657, 508/487.3424). The office is located at 307 Commercial Street, on MacMillan Wharf.

Martha's Vineyard, an island south of Cape Cod, is another well-loved vacation spot; ferry reservations for cars are often sold out for summer weekends by Christmas. The "Vineyard" has wonderful beaches, sunsets, sailing, walking, picnicking, and bicycling. Its population balloons from 12,000 to 100,000 in the summer. Down-island—on the eastern side—are **Vineyard Haven, Oak Bluffs,** and **Edgartown.** The latter is the most popular with tourists and has a wide array of architectural styles from saltbox to Greek Revival. Up-island—on the western side—are **West Tisbury, Chilmark,** and **Gay Head,** which is known for its varicolored clay cliffs. Like Cape Cod and Nantucket, the Vineyard is just as wonderful—or more so—out of season.

To get to Martha's Vineyard, you and your car can ride the ferry from **Woods Hole** at the southwest corner of Cape Cod (**Steamship Authority,** 508/477.8600). Seasonal, passengers-only ferries leave for the Vineyard from **Hyannis** (508/775.7185) and Falmouth (508/548.4800). Passenger ferries (**Cape Island Express Lines,** 508/997.1688) also operate year-round from **New Bedford** on the Massachusetts coast, about two hours south of Boston. New Bedford is a historic and still-important seaport, where you'll find the excellent **New Bedford Whaling Museum** (pictured at left) (8 Johnny Cake Hill, 508/997.0046) and discount shopping, too. The museum is open daily; there is an admission charge. You can also fly into **Martha's Vineyard Airport** (508/693.7022); flights leave from **Logan International Airport** and **Hyannis.**

For information on Vineyard events, places, and accommodations, call or write the **Martha's Vineyard Chamber of Commerce** (PO Box 1698, Vineyard Haven, MA 02568, 508/693.0085). The office is located on Beach Road. Eat fresh and delicious seafood at the elegant, expensive **L'Etoile** in Edgartown (★★★★$$$$; 27 S Summer St, 508/627.5187); en route to Gay Head at the **Beach Plum Inn** in Menemsha (★★$$$; off North Rd, 508/645.9454); or at the **Oyster Bar** in Oak Bluffs (★★$$$; 162 Circuit Ave, 508/693.3300). In Oak Bluffs, wander among the **Carpenter Gothic Cottages,** a Methodist revival campground of Victorian Gothic cottages from the late 1800s, oddly ornate with filigree trim.

Located 30 miles south of Cape Cod, Nantucket is a historic whaling island known as the "Gray Lady of the Sea" for its gently weathering clapboards, and for the clothes worn by its early Quaker settlers. Nowadays, the island is a summer playground for the unflashy, monied crowd. When it's sweltering in Boston, the sea breezes keep Nantucket cool and its serene weathered beauty is restorative, with gray-shingled houses and rose-covered cottages, moors of heather, cranberry bogs, and gnarled pines. There's absolutely no need for a car here—you can walk, bicycle, or ride a moped from one end of the island to the other. Arrive via ferry from either Hyannis or Woods Hole. You can also fly to **Nantucket Memorial Airport** (508/325.5300) from **Logan International Airport** and **Hyannis.** For tourist information, call or write the **Nantucket Island Chamber of Commerce** (Main St, Nantucket, MA 02554, 508/228.1700).

The town of **Nantucket** is the exceedingly picturesque and quaint center of activity, and is packed with interesting shops and restaurants. The deli-style **Espresso Cafe** ($$; 40 Main St, 508/228.6930) is easy on the budget; **21 Federal** (★★★★$$$$; 21 Federal St, 508/228.2121) and the **Boarding House** (★★★$$$$; 12 Federal St, 508/228.9622) aren't, but they're worth every penny. For the ultimate in laid-back (if top-dollar) charm, plan a stay at the **Wauwinet** ($$$$; 120

21
FEDERAL

Wauwinet Rd, Wauwinet, 508/228.0145, 800/426.8718), a historic inn surrounded by beaches at the very edge of civilization. But as long as you reserve well ahead, you'll fare well at any of the island's reasonably priced bed-and-breakfasts. All of the island's beaches are dazzling and easily accessible.

Providence and Newport, Rhode Island

Beyond the commonwealth's southern border, yet within a one- to two-hour ride, are Providence and Newport, Rhode Island. Providence is the capital of the "Ocean State" and its industrial and commercial center, as well as a major port. The city was founded by Roger Williams, who was banished from Boston by the often intolerant Puritans. A city guide and map of landmarks is available at the **Greater Providence Convention and Visitor's Bureau** (30 Exchange Terr, Providence, RI 02903, 401/274.1636).

To drive to Providence from Boston, take **Interstate 93** south to **I-95** and head south. Or take the train from Boston's **South Station** (800/872.7245).

The skyline of Rhode Island's capital city features the tall, pointed spires of historic churches, plus the capitol building's white marble dome. Among the sights to see are the **State House** (82 Smith St, 401/277.2357), open Monday through Friday; **Waterplace Park,** an urban park built on the site of an old salt marsh: and the scenic half-mile riverwalk. The **Museum of Art** (224 Benefit St, 401/454.6500) offers a fine collection of works from ancient Greece, Rome, and Egypt through 20th-century Europe and America. It's open Tuesday through Sunday; there's an admission charge.

Providence's **College Hill** neighborhood is home to **Brown University** (Prospect St, 401/863.1000) and the **Rhode Island School of Design** (2 College St, 401/454.6100), both of which host plays, lectures, and cultural exhibits that are open to the public. Interspersed among the college buildings are a splendid colonial homes, columned mansions, and gardens, some of which are open to the public.

Try to have dinner at one of George Germon and Johanne Killeen's renowned restaurants: **Al Forno** ★★★★$$$$ or **Lucky's** ★★★$$$$ (both at 577 S Main St, 401/273.9760). **Al Forno** offers rustic Italian-style decor and food, the latter mainly grilled over hardwood or roasted in a brick oven; **Lucky's** tends toward French provincial in decor, but the cuisine is similar to that served at **Al Forno**. For an evening out, the **Trinity Repertory Company** (201 Washington St, 401/351.4242) is nationally renowned.

South of Providence is Newport, which still echoes its origins as a colonial seaport. The town has always been associated with opulence and the sea: yachts, the navy, competitive sailing, and seaside palaces of the rich. Annual celebrations include the star-studded Newport Jazz Festival, the country's oldest. The **Cliff Walk** is Newport's other most popular attraction, a three-and-a-half-mile shoreline path and a National Historic Walking Trail, with the Atlantic Ocean on one side and the famous summer mansions on the other.

Be sure to take a tour of one or more of these elaborate Victorian mansions. **The Breakers** (Ochre Point Ave) is the most splendid of the very magnificent lot. Built in 1895 for Cornelius Vanderbilt, it resembles a Northern Italian Renaissance palace. **Bellevue Avenue** is the site of a magnificent line of "cottages" from the Gilded Age, including **Marble House,** completed in 1892 for William K. Vanderbilt and still boasting its original furnishings; **Château-sur-Mer,** built in 1852 and one of the finest examples of ornate Victorian architecture in the US; and **Rosecliff,** the 1902 palace designed by **Stanford White,** that was featured in the film *The Great Gatsby*.

For more information about mansions and other attractions, contact the **Newport County Convention & Visitors Bureau** (23 America's Cup Ave, Newport, RI 02403, 401/845.9123, 800/326.6030).

Bests

Michael and Susan Southworth
Urban Designers, Planners, and Authors of the *AIA Guide to Boston*

The ornamental wrought- and cast-iron fences, balconies, and door and window grilles of **Back Bay, Beacon Hill,** and the **South End.**

Friday afternoon at **Symphony Hall,** the "Stradivarius" of concert halls.

Exploring the Underground Railroad stops and the many other significant black history sites in Boston.

Candlelight concerts at the **Isabella Stewart Gardner Museum.**

The first day the **Swan Boats** paddle the pond in the **Public Garden** each spring (mid-April).

A Sunday afternoon walk through the **Back Bay Fens** with its tall rushes, winding waterway, and stone bridge (by **Henry Hobson Richardson**), followed by visits to the **Museum of Fine Arts** and the **Isabella**

Stewart Gardner Museum.

The **Robert Gould Shaw Memorial,** by Augustus Saint-Gaudens, honoring the first regiment of freed blacks to serve in the Civil War.

The Italian Renaissance Revival interiors of **McKim, Mead & White**'s **Boston Public Library.**

Chiles rellenos at **Casa Romero,** an intimate Mexican restaurant that transcends tacos and smashed beans.

The **Peabody Essex Museum** in **Salem,** with its collection of important museum houses, furniture, and artifacts of the China trade.

Trinity Church by **Henry Hobson Richardson,** the best example of Romanesque Revival architecture in the country.

Saturday morning shopping at the Italian street markets in the **North End.**

The **Nichols House** and **Gibson House,** museums that transport us to domestic life in 19th-century Boston.

History

1614 Captain John Smith explores the Boston/**Massachusetts Bay** area and calls it "a paradise"; thereafter the region becomes known as New England.

1620 The Pilgrims arrive on the *Mayflower*, marking the establishment of **Plymouth Colony**, the first permanent English settlement in New England.

1624 William Blackstone settles on **Shawmut Peninsula** (Boston) with 200 books and a Brahma bull.

1630 A group of Puritans led by John Winthrop, sailing from England in a fleet of 11 ships, found Boston.

1632 Boston becomes the capital of the **Massachusetts Bay Colony.**

1635 **Boston Latin School** is established on 13 February, becoming America's first school; it remains open to this day.

1636 **Harvard College** is established to educate young men for the ministry.

1638 The first printing press in the English colonies is established at **Cambridge** by Stephen Day; four years later he publishes *Bay Psalm Book.*

1639 The New World's first post office is established in the Boston home of Richard Fairbank.

1644 Gallows are erected on **Boston Common.**

1660 Boston's population reaches 3,000.

1684 The Massachusetts Bay Colony charter is annulled by the British court.

1685 The Dominion of New England is created by Britain's King James II and includes all New England colonies plus New York, New Jersey, and Pennsylvania. Rebellions by colonists and the overthrow of James II end this union.

1688 **King's Chapel,** the first Anglican church in the country, is established in Boston.

1689 On 18 April, a rebellion overthrows British royal governor of New England, Sir Edmund Andros.

1691 A new Massachusetts charter abolishes church membership as a prerequisite for voting.

1692 "Witches" are tried in great numbers in **Salem;** the hysteria spreads until 20 women and men are executed.

1693 The first postal service is established between Boston and New York.

1704 The first successful newspaper in the colonies, the *Boston News-Letter,* is printed.

1712 The cornerstone is laid for the **Old State House,** the seat from which English governors ruled Boston prior to the Revolution.

1716 **Boston Light** is built on **Little Brewster Island** in **Boston Harbor;** it was destroyed by the British in 1776, and rebuilt in 1783. Today it's the oldest lighthouse in the US, and the only manned lighthouse on the east coast.

1719 Thomas Fleet publishes *Tales of Mother Goose.*

1729 Construction of the **Old South Meeting House** is begun.

1742 **Faneuil Hall,** the "Cradle of Liberty," is built.

1765 The Stamp Act is passed by Britain's Parliament; levying taxes on American colonists for the first time, it is repealed one year later.

1767 The Townshend Acts are passed by Parliament, placing new import duties on glass, lead, paint, paper, and tea used by American colonists.

1770 The Townshend Acts are repealed by King George, except for taxes on tea. The Boston Massacre occurs on 5 March, when five colonists are shot and killed by British soldiers outside the **Old State House.**

1773 The Tea Act is passed by Britain, giving the East India Company the rights to undersell American tea merchants. On 16 December the Sons of Liberty, disguised as Indians, dump 342 chests of tea shipped from England into Boston Harbor.

1774 On 31 March, Britain passes the Boston Port Bill which closes the harbor in retaliation for the Boston Tea Party. Britain places limits on the powers of the Massachusetts legislature and prohibits town meetings without the consent of the governor. On 5 September, the First Continental Congress meets in Philadelphia with delegates from all colonies and calls for a boycott on all British goods.

1775 The American Revolution begins. On 18 April, Paul Revere and William Dawes ride to warn the Minutemen that the British are marching. On 19 April, the first engagements of the American Revolution take place in the Battles of **Lexington** and **Concord,** where the "shot heard round the world" was fired. On 17 June, the Battle of **Bunker Hill** takes place in **Charlestown:** The British win but suffer heavy casualties. George Washington takes command of the Continental Army at Cambridge. In retaliation, Britain prohibits all trade with American colonies.

1776 British troops retreat from Boston. The *Declaration of Independence* is read for the first time in Boston from the balcony at the **Old State House.**

1781 The Massachusetts Medical Society is founded.

1784 The *Empress of China* makes her maiden voyage from Boston to the Orient; many local fortunes are built on the clipper ship trade out of Boston.

1792 The first *Farmer's Almanac* is published in Boston by Robert B. Thomas.

History

1793 Eli Whitney introduces the cotton gin in Boston.

1796 John Adams of Massachusetts is elected the second president of the US.

1797 The frigate USS *Constitution* (which became known as "Old Ironsides") is launched at **Boston Naval Shipyard.**

1798 The **Massachusetts State House** on **Beacon Hill,** designed by **Charles Bulfinch,** is completed.

1810 The **Handel & Haydn Society,** America's first musical and choral group, is formed.

1811 **Massachusetts General Hospital** is established.

1822 A city charter is granted to Boston.

1824 Massachusetts resident John Quincy Adams is elected sixth president of the US.

1825 The first city census is taken; Boston's population is 58,277.

1826 **Quincy Market** opens.

1829 On 16 October, the **Tremont House** (today the **Omni Parker House**) opens as the first hotel in the US.

1831 William Lloyd Garrison publishes the first issue of the *Liberator,* a newspaper dedicated to emancipation.

1832 The New England Anti-Slavery Society is formed in Boston.

1833 The first US steam railway is built, running between Boston and **Newton.**

1835 Horace Mann creates the nation's first normal schools for the training of teachers.

1839 Charles Goodyear invents vulcanized rubber.

1840 The *Unicorn,* the first transatlantic steamship of the **Cunard Line,** arrives in Boston. The first large influx of Irish come to Boston as a result of the potato famine.

1843 The 221-foot **Bunker Hill Monument** is dedicated on 17 July by US Secretary of State Daniel Webster, former state senator of Massachusetts.

1845 The sewing machine is invented in Boston by Elias Howe.

1846 Anesthesia is used for the first time at **Massachusetts General Hospital.**

1848 The **Boston Public Library,** the first free municipal library in the US, opens.

1851 The **YMCA** is organized in Boston; 15 years later the **YWCA** is formed.

1857 The first issue of the *Atlantic Monthly* magazine is published in Boston.

1859 The **Public Garden** is ratified as a garden forever public.

1862 Massachusetts sends the first all African-American regiment to the Civil War.

1872 The Great Fire of Boston destroys all of what is today Boston's **Financial District.**

1874 The **State House** dome is gilded.

1875 The **Cathedral of the Holy Cross** opens in Boston's **South End** as the largest Roman Catholic church in North America, seating 7,000.

1876 Alexander Graham Bell successfully demonstrates the first telephone in Boston, starting a new era in communications.

1877 **Trinity Church,** the masterpiece of architect **Henry Hobson Richardson,** opens on **Copley Square** on the newly filled land of **Back Bay.** A fleet of swan boats is launched on the **Public Garden** lagoon.

1880 The **Museum of Fine Arts** is founded.

1881 The **Boston Symphony Orchestra** is founded.

1884 The Boston **Cyclorama** is built to house the gigantic circular painting *The Battle of Gettysburg.*

1892 The **First Church of Christ Scientist,** the mother church for the Christian Scientist religion founded by Mary Baker Eddy, opens.

1894 The **Boston & Maine Railroad** opens **North Station.**

1897 The first subway in the US opens in Boston, running beneath **Tremont Street** from **Park Street** to **Boylston Street**. On 19 April the first **Boston Marathon** is run from **Hopkinton** to Boston.

1900 **Symphony Hall** opens as the new home for the **Boston Symphony Orchestra.**

1903 The first **World Series** baseball game is played in Boston between the **Boston Pilgrims** (later the **Boston Red Sox**) and the **Pittsburgh Pirates.**

1909 The **Museum of Fine Arts** moves to its present home.

1912 **Fenway Park** opens as the home of the **Boston Red Sox,** who win the pennant and the **World Series** in their new stadium.

1915 A 495-foot tower is added to the **Custom House,** making it Boston's first skyscraper and the tallest building in New England. Albert Champion invents the first spark plug.

1927 Sacco and Vanzetti are executed in the electric chair in the state prison in Boston's Charlestown district despite protests of their innocence; they were officially exonerated 50 years later.

1928 The world's first computer is developed at **Massachusetts Institute of Technology.**

1929 Arthur Fiedler organizes the first **Esplanade Concerts,** to become the **Boston Pops** in 1930.

1942 A fire in the **Coconut Grove** nightclub kills 491 people.

1946 Boston native John F. Kennedy is elected to the US House of Representatives from Boston's First Congressional District.

1947 Edward H. Land invents the Polaroid camera in Cambridge.

1950 On 17 January the infamous Brink's armored car robbery takes place.

1954 The steeple of the **Old North Church** is destroyed during a storm; its weather vane is sent on a national tour to raise money to help rebuild the historic landmark.

1955 The **Beacon Hill Historical District** is created.

1957 The **Boston Celtics** win the first of 16 **National Basketball Association** championships. The *Mayflower II* sails from Plymouth, England, to Plymouth, Massachusetts, on a voyage replicating that of the original *Mayflower*'s 1620 voyage.

1959 John F. Kennedy declares himself a candidate for president of the United States in Boston.

1962 The demolition of **Scollay Square** marks the beginning of the **Government Center** redevelopment project. Edward Kennedy begins his first term as US senator.

1966 Edward Brooke becomes the first African-American elected to the US Senate since Reconstruction.

1969 **Boston City Hall** is dedicated, with honors from the **American Institute of Architects**. The birthplace of John F. Kennedy in **Brookline** is declared a National Historic Site.

1972 Women are allowed to run in the **Boston Marathon.**

1976 The restored **Faneuil Hall Marketplace** opens, 150 years to the day after the original inauguration of the market buildings. Boston originates the "First Night" concept for the public celebration of New Year's Eve.

1980 A yearlong jubilee celebrates the 350th anniversary of Boston's settlement.

1990 Boston's population reaches 574,283, the first increase after four decades of decline. The **Women's Heritage Trail** is established.

1993 Thomas M. Merino is elected mayor, the first man not of Irish descent to hold the job in 63 years.

1994 **Salem** observes the 300th anniversary of the infamous witch trials.

1995 The beloved **Boston Garden**—home of the **Boston Celtics** and the **Boston Bruins**—closes its doors for the last time; its seats are sold to fans and collectors worldwide.

1996 The 100th running of the **Boston Marathon** takes place. Major additions and ongoing improvements to the **Freedom Trail** begin.

1997 Boston celebrates the 200th anniversary of the launching of the *USS Constitution.*

1998 The 200th anniversary of the **State House** is celebrated.

MARJORIE VOGEL, RHODE ISLAND ORIGINALS

Trinity Church

Index

A

Aalto, Alvar 192
Abbot, Dean 110
Accommodations 9
Acorn Street 20
Addis Red Sea Ethiopian Restaurant
 ★★$ 161
Adesso 99
Admiral Samuel Eliot Morison Statue
 123
Adolphus Busch Hall 177
African Meeting House 22
African Tropical Forest Pavilion 199
Aigo Bistro 206
Airlines 5
Airport 5
Airport services 5
Alan Bilzerian 137
The Albert and Vera List Visual Arts
 Center 190
Alex Krieger Architects 151
Al Forno ★★★★$$$$ 210
Algiers Cafe ★★$ 185
Algonquin Club 123
Allandale Farm 200
Allen & Collens 138
Allen, Frederick R. 137
Allston-Brighton 200
Alpha Gallery 138
Ames Building 31
Ames-Webster House 123
Amrhein's 197
Anderson Notter Associates 61, 62,
 63, 83, 160
Andrews, John 178
Angell Memorial Plaza 80
Angelo's ★★$$$ 116
Anthony's Pier 4 ★$$$ 67
A. Parziale & Sons Bakery 57
Appalachian Mountain Club 19
Appetito ★★$$ 162
Appleton Building 76
Appleton-Parker Houses 16
Apthorp House 179
The Architects Collaborative 41, 42,
 97
Arch St. Deli $ 81
Arlington Street Church, Unitarian
 Universalist 120
Armani Express ★★★$$$$ 131
Arnold Arboretum of Harvard
 University 199
Arrowstreet 127, 128
Ars Libri 163
Art Alfresco 48
Artful Hand Gallery 114
Arthur M. Sackler Museum 178
Artsmart 70
Artú ★★★$$ 50
Ashley, Myer & Associates 127
au bon pain ★$ 174
Aujourd'hui ★★★$$$$ 98
Aura ★★$$$$ 67

Autrefois Antiques 133
Avalon 152
Avenue Victor Hugo Bookshop 127
Axis 152
AYH (Boston International American
 Youth Hostel) 147

B

BAC (Boston Architectural Center) 127
Back Bay 108 (chapter and map)
Back Bay Brewing Company ★$$ 115
Back Bay Hilton $$$ 125
Baker House 192
Bakers Alley 52
Baker's Plays 95
Bakey's ★★$ 77
B & D Deli 200
Bangkok Cuisine ★$ 147
BankBoston 81
Banner, Peter 18
Barbara Krakow Gallery 138
Bargain Box 134
The Barking Crab ★★$$ 65
Barnes & Noble at Boston University
 150
Barnes & Noble Discount Bookstore 88
Bartley's Burger Cottage ★$ 179
Batterymarch Building 78
Battle Road Visitor Center 206
Bay Bedford Company 90
Baylies Mansion 122
Bay State Lobster Company 54
Bay Tower Room ★★$$$ 32
Bay Village 100
BCA (Boston Center for the Arts) 161
Beach Plum Inn 209
Beacon Hill 12 (chapter and map)
The Beacon Hill Garden Club 20
Beacon Hill Skate 101
Beacon Hill Thrift Shop 27
Beacon Street Mall 15
Bearskin Neck 205
Becket 207
Bedford Building 90
Bell Atlantic Headquarters Building 80
Bell in Hand Tavern $ 39
Belluschi, Pietro 78, 122
Ben & Jerry's Ice Cream 99
Benjamin, Asher 15, 22, 25, 42, 101
Benjamin Thompson & Associates 33
Bennett, Stahl 122
Bergmeyer, Moritz 52
Berkeley Building 119
Berkeley Residence Club $ 162
Berklee Performance Center 124
The Berkshires 207
Berkshire Visitor's Bureau 207
Bertucci's (Cambridge) ★$ 185
Bertucci's (Faneuil Hall) ★★$ 38
Beverly 204
Biba ★★★$$$ 97
Bicycles 6
The Big Easy 103

Bigelow, Henry Forbes 19
Billings and Stover Apothecaries 185
Bill's Bar 152
Bistro 205
Blackall, Clapp and Whittemore 104
Blackall, Clarence H. 82, 88, 102, 104,
 111
Black Goose ★★$$ 19
Black Heritage Trail 15
The Black Rose ★$ 37
Blackstone Block 38
Blackstone's of Beacon Hill 26
Blackstone Square 163
Blake House 197
Blanchard, Joshua 86
The Blue Diner/Art Zone ★$ 71
The Blue Room ★★★$$$$ 191
Boarding House ★★★$$$$ 209
Board of Trade Building 75
Boats 6
Bob Smith Sporting Goods 81
Bombay Club ★$$ 182
Bond, Richard 52
Boodle's of Boston ★★$$$ 125
Borders: Books, Music, Cafe 86
BOS (Logan International Airport) 5
BosTix 33
Boston 2 (map)
Boston Airline Center 90
Boston and Environs *See inside front
 cover* (map)
Boston & Maine Fish Company 35
Boston Antique Coop I & II 24
Boston Architectural Center (BAC) 127
The Boston Architectural Team 102
Boston Art Club 133
The Boston Athenaeum 19
Boston Athletic Association Boston
 Marathon Monument 110
Boston Ballet Center 161
Boston Beer Works ★$$ 152
Boston By Bike: Plum Paths for Pedal
 Pushers 94
Boston Center for the Arts (BCA) 161
Boston Chipyard 35
Boston City Hall 31
Boston Common 13
Boston Common Ranger Station 14
Boston English High School 21
Boston Fire Museum 68
Boston Harbor 66 (map)
Boston Harbor Hotel $$$$ 64
Boston Harbor Sailing Club 64
Boston in Fact...and Fiction 79
Boston International American Youth
 Hostel (AYH) $ 147
Boston Light 208
Boston Marathon Route 201 (map)
Boston Marriott Copley Place $$$ 114
Boston Marriott Long Wharf $$$$ 62
The Boston Music Company 94
Boston National Historic Park 196
Boston on Screen 118

Boston Park Plaza Hotel $$$ 99
Boston Public Library (Back Bay) 112
Boston Public Library Addition (Back Bay) 113
Boston Public Library, Kirstein Business Branch 83
Boston Public Library, North End Branch 58
Boston Sailing Center 53
Boston Sail Loft $ 61
Boston Subway Lines See inside back cover (map)
Boston's Tea Parties 40
Boston Tea Party Ship and Museum 70
Boston University Theatre 146
Botanical Museum 176
Bova Italian Bakery 57
Bowditch, Arthur 126
Boylston Building 102
Boylston Place 103
Boylston Street 102, 115
500 Boylston Street 117
Bradlee, Nathaniel J. 102
Brandegee Estate 200
Brandeis University 207
Brandy Pete's ★★$$ 78
Brattle Book Shop 93
Brattle House 187
Brattle Street 184
The Brattle Theatre 185
Breakheart Reservation 204
Breed's Hill 196
Brew Moon $$ 101
Briggs & Briggs 180
Brigham, Charles E. 125
Brimstone Corner 18
The Bristol ★★$$ 98
Broad Street 77
Bromer Booksellers 116
Bromfield Gallery 163
Bromfield Pen Shop 88
Bromfield Street 87
Brookline 200
Brookstone 82
Bruegger's Bagel Bakery $ 88
Bruner Cott Associates 160
Bryant, Gridley J.F. 75, 83, 161
Bulfinch, Charles 12, 15, 16, 18, 20, 21, 33, 42, 43, 45, 53, 63, 64, 72, 76, 77, 83, 84, 90, 163, 175
Bulfinch Superior Courthouse Building 192
Bull & Finch ★$ 28
Burgee, John 117
Burrage Mansion 124
Buses 7
Buteco Restaurant ★$ 153
Buteco II ★$ 160

C

Cabot and Chandler 157
Cabot, Edward Clark 19
Cabot Street Theatre 204

The Cactus Club ★$ 129
The Cafe at the Gardner ★★$$ 142
Cafe Budapest ★★$$$ 115
Cafe Charles ★$ 150
Cafe China 193
Café de Paris ★$ 138
Cafe Fleuri ★★$$$ 80
Cafe Jaffa ★$ 130
Cafe Louis ★★$$ 137
Cafe Marliave ★$$ 87
Cafe Pamplona ★$ 179
Cafe Sushi 192
Cafeteria (Museum of Fine Arts) $ 145
Caffè Bella Vita ★$ 27
Caffè dello Sport ★$ 49
Caffé Graffiti ★$ 47
Caffé Paradiso $ 82
Caffé Paradiso Espresso Bar ★$ 46
Caffe Romano's Bakery & Sandwich Shop ★★$ 137
Caffe Suisse ★$$ 95
Caffé Vittoria ★$ 47
Cambridge 172 (chapter), 173 (map), 189 (map)
Cambridge Artists' Cooperative 186
Cambridge Brewing Company 191
Cambridge Center Marriott 191
Cambridge Common 188
A Cambridge House B&B 193
Cambridge Multicultural Arts Center 192
Cambridge Seven 63, 101
Cambridgeside Galleria 192
Cambridge Visitor Information Booth 174
Campbell, Aldrich & Nulty 81
Campbell, Robert 117
Cantab Lounge 192
Cape Ann 204
Cape Ann Historical Association 204
Cape Cod 208
Cape Cod National Seashore 208
The Capital Grille ★★$$$$ 126
Carberry's Bakery & Coffee House 192
Carl Koch and Associates 52
Carl's Pagoda ★★$$ 106
Carpenter Center for the Visual Arts 179
Carpenter Gothic Cottages 209
Carrier, Patrick 139 (bests)
Cars, rental 6
Casablanca ★★$$ 186
Casa Mexico ★★$$ 183
Casa Portugal 193
Casa Romero ★$$$ 130
Cathedral Church of St. Paul 92
Cathedral of the Holy Cross 163
CBT/Childs Bertman Tseckares 123
CBT/Childs Bertman Tseckares Casendinon 132
Cedar Lane Way 27
Center for Arts & Media Technology, Weisner Building 191

Center for Earth Sciences, Green Building 191
Central Burying Ground 15
Central Square/Riverside 192
Central Wharf 63
Central Wharf Buildings 76
Chadwick Leadworks 78
Champlain Chocolates 81
Chandler Inn Hotel $ 162
Chandler, Joseph 51
Changsho 193
Chapman, Sturgis, and Andrews 16
Charles Hayden Planetarium 171
The Charles Hotel $$$ 182
Charles Luckman and Associates 129
Charles Playhouse 101
Charles River Basin 164 (chapter), 166 (map)
Charles River Boat Co. 192
Charles River Dam Visitors' Information Center 196
Charles Street Meeting House 25
Charles Street Supply 26
Charles Sumner 138
Charlestown 194
Charlestown Navy Yard 194
Charlie's Sandwich Shoppe ★★$ 157
Charlie's Tap 192
Charrette 187
The Chart House ★★$$$ 62
Chau Chow Seafood ★★$ 107
Chesterwood 207
13, 15 and 17 Chestnut Street 20
29A Chestnut Street 20
Chez Henri ★★★$$$$ 193
The Children's Museum 68
Child's Play 100
Chinatown/Theater District 96 (chapter and map)
Chocolate Dipper 37
Christ Church 188
Christ Church (Old North Church) 55
Christian Science International Headquarters 125
Christopher's 193
Church Court Condominium 124
Church Green Building 90
Churchill, Chester Lindsay 126
The Church of the Advent 26
Church of the Covenant 135
Ciao bella ★★$$ 131
Citgo Sign 150
City Sports 119
The Claddagh ★$ 156
Clarke's $$ 38
Cliff Walk 210
Climate 9
Clio ★★★★$$$$ 149
Clothware 187
Club Cafe ★★$$ 117
Club Passim ★$ 186
Codman & Despredelle 119
Codman, Ogden 27, 121

Index

Colonial Drug **187**
Colonial Theatre **102**
The Colonnade Hotel $$$ **156**
The Comedy Connection **34**
Commandant's House **195**
Commercial Wharf **61**
Commonwealth Avenue and Mall **122**
Commonwealth Brewing Company ★$ **41**
Commonwealth Museum **198**
Commonwealth Pier/World Trade Center **67**
The Computer Museum **69**
Concord **206**
Constitution Museum **195**
Coolidge and Shattuck **76**
Coolidge, Cornelius **16**
Coolidge Corner **200**
Coolidge Corner Theatre **200**
Coolidge, Shepley, Bulfinch, and Abbott **43, 178**
The Coop **174**
Copley Inn $$ **156**
Copley Place **113**
Copley's Grand Cafe ★$$$ **112**
The Copley Society of Boston **133**
Copley Square **110**
Copley Square Hotel $$ **114**
Copley Square News **116**
Copp's Hill Burying Ground **56**
Copp's Hill Terrace **56**
Cornwall's ★$ **150**
Cossutta and Associates **62**
Cottonwood Cafe (Back Bay) ★★$$ **119**
Cottonwood Cafe (Cambridge) **193**
Counterpoint Cafe ★$ **147**
Country Life ★$ **77**
Cowley and Cathedral Bookstore **92**
Cram & Ferguson **80, 81**
Cram, Ralph Adams **92**
Cranberry World **208**
Crane Memorial Reservation **205**
Crate & Barrel/Design Research Building **187**
Culture Shock **130**
Cummings & Sears **90, 116, 161**
Cunard Building **37**
Cuoio **134**
Custom House Block **63**
Custom House Tower **75**
C.W.H. Company **107**
Cybersmith $ **186**

D

Daddy O's Bohemian Cafe **193**
Daily Catch (Fort Point Channel) ★$$ **68**
Daily Catch (North End) ★★$$ **49**
Dairy Fresh Candies **58**
Dakota's ★★$$$ **91**
Dali ★★★★$$$$ **200**
Daniel Burnham & Company **89**

Danish Country Antique Furniture **24**
Davide ★$$$ **54**
David L. O'Neal Antiquarian Booksellers, Inc. **134**
Davio's Ristorante ★★$$$ **170**
Dawes Island **188**
Day Trips **202** (chapter and map)
DeCordova Museum and Sculpture Park **207**
De Luca's Market **27**
Densmore, LeClear, and Robbins **119**
Design Research Building/Crate & Barrel **187**
Despredelle, Desiré **119**
The Dining Room ★★$$$$ **139**
Dion, Arthur **95** (bests)
Division Sixteen ★$ **128**
Dockside $ **76**
Dock Square **32**
Dolphin Seafood **192**
Domain **138**
Dong Khanh ★$ **106**
Don Stull Associates **31, 160**
Dorchester **197**
Dorchester Heights **197**
Dorchester North Burying Ground **197**
Doubleday Book Shop **37**
Doubletree Guest Suites Hotel Boston/Cambridge $$$ **165**
Downtown **72** (chapter and map)
Doyle's Cafe **199**
Drinking **9**
Driving **6, 7**
The Druid Restaurant **193**
Du Barry $$ **133**
Ducklings **29**
Durgin-Park ★★$$ **35**
Duxbury **208**
Dynasty ★$$ **107**

E

East Cambridge **192**
East Coast Grill ★★★$$$$ **193**
Eastern Accent **131**
Ebenezer Hancock House **40**
Eight Tracks/NYC Jukebox **104**
Elephant Walk ★★★★$$$$ **200**
The Eliot & Pickett Houses $ **19**
The Eliot Hotel $$ **149**
Ellenzweig, Harry **80**
Ellenzweig, Moore and Associates **156**
The Emerald Necklace **158, 159** (map)
Emergencies **10**
Emerson Majestic Theatre **102**
Emerson, William Ralph **90, 133**
Emmanuel Church **137**
Emporio Armani **131**
Engine and Hose House Number 33 **128**
Espresso Cafe **209**
Essex **205**
The Essex Grill ★$$ **71**
Estey, Alexander R. **137, 160**
Eugene Galleries **25**

Exchange Place **75**
Exeter Street Theatre Building **132**

F

The Fairmont Copley Plaza Hotel $$$$ **111**
Fajitas & 'Ritas ★$ **93**
The Famous Atlantic Fish Company ★$$ **115**
Faneuil Hall **30** (chapter and map), **32**
Faneuil Hall Marketplace/Quincy Market **33**
1 Faneuil Hall Square **33**
Fanny Farmer **81**
FAO Schwarz **119**
F.C. Meichsner Company **71**
Federal House **207**
Federal Reserve Bank of Boston **70**
Fehmer, Carl **82, 90, 102, 124**
Fenway **140** (chapter and map)
Fenway Park **152**
Ferry *See inside back cover* (map)
The Field **192**
57 Park Plaza/Radisson Hotel Boston $$ **101**
Figs ★★$$ **26**
Filene's **89**
Filene's Basement **89**
The Fill-A-Buster $ **19**
Financial District/Downtown **72** (chapter and map)
Fine Arts Restaurant ★★$$ **145**
Finnegan's Wake **193**
First and Second Church **121**
First Baptist Church **122**
1st Corps of Cadets Museum **124**
First Lutheran Church **122**
First Parish Church and Old Burying Ground **186**
Fish Pier **67**
Five Seasons ★★★$$ **199**
Flagstaff Hill **15**
FleetCenter **41**
Florentine Cafe ★$$$ **49**
Flour and Grain Exchange Building **76**
Fogg Art Museum **178**
The Food Emporium $ **88**
Footbridge **28**
Fort Independence **197**
Fort Point Channel **60** (chapter and map), **65**
Four Seasons Hotel $$$$ **98**
Frances Loeb Library **178**
Franklin Park Zoo **199** (map)
Franklin Square **163**
Fratelli Pagliuca's ★$$ **58**
Frederick Law Olmsted National Historic Site **200**
The Freedom Trail **14** (map)
French Bouquet **27**
The French Library in Boston **121**

Frog Pond **15**
Frontier **131**

G

Galleria Cafe ★$ **145**
Gallery Cafe $$ **170**
Gallery NAGA **136**
Garden of Eden ★★$ **160**
GBS **133**
Gehry, Frank O. **126**
Geoclassics **37**
Geoffrey's Café and Bar ★★$ **160**
George Gravert Antiques **24**
George Gund Hall **178**
George Parkman House **16**
Getting around Boston **6**
Getting to and from Logan
   International Airport **6**
Getting to Boston **5**
Giacomo's ★★$$ **53**
The Gibson House **121**
Gilbert, Cass **82**
Gilman, Arthur **83, 109, 120, 121**
The Globe Corner Bookstore **186**
Gloucester **204**
Gloucester Fisherman **204**
Gloucester Stage Company **205**
Godine, David R. **59** (bests)
Goethe Institute, German Cultural
   Center **121**
Going for the Laurels: The Boston
   Marathon **201**
Golden Palace ★★$ **106**
Golledge, The Reverend Robert W. **59**
   (bests)
Goody, Clancy & Associates **73, 80,**
   90, 101, 156
Gordon, Ed **43** (bests)
Government Center/Faneuil Hall **30**
   (chapter and map)
Graham Gund Associates **33, 75, 128,**
   157
Granary Burying Ground **18**
Grand Chau Chow Seafood ★★$
   107
Great Dome **191**
The Great Emancipator **99**
Greater Boston YMCA $ **145**
Great House **205**
Green Building, Center for Earth
   Sciences **191**
Green Dragon Tavern ★$ **40**
Green Street Grill ★★★$$$ **192**
Grendel's Den ★$ **183**
Grill 23 & Bar ★★$$$$ **119**
The Grolier Poetry Book Shop, Inc.
   179
Gropius House **207**
Gropius, Walter **42, 207**
Gund, Graham **124, 161, 175, 179**
Gwathmey and Siegel **177**
Gyuhama ★★$$ **115**

H

Halasz and Halasz **61**
Haley & Steele **135**
Halibut Point State Park and
   Reservation **205**
Hamersley's Bistro ★★★★$$$ **161**
Hammond Castle Museum **205**
The Hampshire House **27**
Hancock Shaker Village **208**
Hanover Street **45**
Harborside Inn of Boston $$ **76**
Harbor Towers **64**
Harbridge House **121**
Hardenbergh, Henry **111**
Hard Rock Cafe ★$ **117**
Harnett's Homeopathy & Body Care
   187
Harper's Ferry **200**
Harriet Tubman House **160**
Harrison Gray Otis House **15, 21, 42**
Harrison, Peter **84, 188**
Harry Elkins Widener Memorial
   Library **176**
Hart Nautical Galleries **190**
Hartwell, H.W. **132**
Harvard Book Store **179**
Harvard College Observatory **189**
Harvard Cooperative Society **174**
Harvard Lampoon Castle **180**
Harvard Mall **196**
Harvard Science Center **176**
Harvard Semitic Museum **177**
Harvard Square **173** (map), **174**
Harvard Square Hotel $$ **183**
Harvard University **175**
Harvard University Information
   Center/Holyoke Center **175**
Harvard Yard **175**
Harvey's ★$$$ **157**
The Hasty Pudding Building **180**
Hayden Building **105**
The Haymarket **40**
Helen's Leather **24**
Henrietta's Table ★★$$ **182**
Henry Wadsworth Longfellow House
   188
Heritage Museum **209**
The Heritage on the Garden **97**
Herrell's Ice Cream **184**
Hill, James & Whitaker **103**
Hilltop Steak House ★$$$ **204**
Hilton's Tent City **41**
Hingham **208**
Hi-Rise Pie Co. ★$$ **187**
History **211**
Holiday Inn–Government Center $$ **42**
Holmes, William **50**
Holyoke Center/Harvard University
   Information Center **175**
Horticultural Hall **126**
Hotels, rating **5**
Houghton Mifflin Building **119**

Houlihan's $$ **32**
Hours **9**
House of Blues ★$ **183**
House of Odd Windows **21**
House of Siam ★★$ **113**
The House of the Seven Gables **204**
The House That Mrs. Jack Built **148**
Howard, John Galen **102**
Howard Johnson Cambridge $$ **165**
Howard Johnson Kenmore $$ **150**
Hoyle, Doran, and Berry **129**
Ho Yuen Ting ★$ **107**
Hub Ticket Agency **105**
Hugh Stubbins & Associates **70**
Hull **208**
Hull Lifesaving Museum **208**
Hull Street **56**
The Hungry i ★★$$$$ **25**
Hungry Traveler $ **83**
Hyatt Regency Cambridge $$$$ **165**

I

ICA (Institute of Contemporary Art)
   128
Icarus ★★$$$ **162**
Il Fornaio $ **46**
I.M. Pei & Partners **109, 143, 198**
Imperial Seafood Restaurant ★$
   107
India Pavilion **192**
India Wharf **64**
Industry **130**
Information, essential **9**
Initial Impressions **71**
Inman Square **193**
The Inn at Children's Boston $$ **153**
The Inn at Harvard $$$ **179**
Institute of Contemporary Art (ICA)
   128
International Trust Company Building
   81
Intrigue ★★★$$ **65**
Ipswich **205**
Iruña ★★$$ **181**
Isabella Stewart Gardner Museum **141**

J

Jack's Joke Shop **102**
Jacob's Pillow **207**
Jacob Wirth ★$$ **105**
Jae's Cafe and Grill ★$ **160**
Jake Ivory's **152**
Jamaica Plain **199**
James Billings Antiques & Interiors **25**
Jasmine/Sola **185**
J.C. Hillary's ★$$ **115**
Jewelers Building **88**
Jillian's Billiard Club **152**
Jimbo's Fish Shanty ★$ **68**
Jimmy's Harborside Restaurant ★$$$
   68
J.J. Teaparty Coin **88**

J.J. Teaparty Quality Baseball Cards **88**
John B. Hynes Veterans Memorial Convention Center **128**
John Callender House **20**
John F. Kennedy Federal Office Building **42**
John F. Kennedy Library and Museum **198**
John F. Kennedy Memorial Park **182**
John F. Kennedy National Historic Site **200**
John Fleuvog **129**
John Hancock Observatory **110**
John Hancock Tower **109**
John Harvard's Brew House ★★$ **184**
The John Jeffries House $ **24**
John Lewis, Inc. **135**
Johnny D's Uptown **200**
John Sharratt Associates **25, 160**
Johnson Paint Company **127**
Johnson, Philip **113, 117**
John W. McCormack Post Office and Court House **81**
Jordan Hall at the New England Conservatory of Music (NEC) **145**
Joy Boston **95**
Julien ★★★$$$$ **80**
Jung/Brannen Associates **78, 104**

K

Kakas **135**
Kallmann and McKinnell **86**
Kallmann, Gerhard **31**
Kallmann McKinnell & Wood Architects **31, 128, 156**
Karma Club **152**
Kate's Mystery Books **193**
Keely, Patrick C. **163**
Kellogg, Henry **78**
Kendall Square **190**
Kendall Square Cinema **191**
Kenmore Square/Fenway **140** (chapter and map)
The King & I ★$$ **24**
King's Chapel **84**
King's Chapel Burying Ground **85**
Kitchen Arts **133**
Koch, Carl **58**
Kohn Pederson Fox **81, 90**
Kresge Auditorium **191**

L

La Bettola ★★$$$ **157**
La Flamme **184**
La Groceria **192**
Lamb, Thomas **94**
La Piccola Venezia ★★$ **46**
Larcom Theatre **204**
La Ruche **132**
The Last Hurrah! Bar and Grill ★$$ **86**
Lauriat's Books **89**
Leather District **71**
Lechmere Canal Park **192**

Le Corbusier **179**
Leers, Weinzapfel Associates **151**
Legal Sea Foods (Cambridge) ★★★$$$ **191**
Legal Sea Foods Cash Market **100**
Legal Sea Foods (Chinatown/Theater District) ★★$$$ **99**
Le Meridien $$$ **78**
The Lenox Hotel $$ **115**
Le Pli at the Heritage **98**
Leslie Lindsey Memorial Chapel **138**
L'Espalier ★★★$$$$ **130**
Les Zygomates ★$$ **71**
L'Etoile ★★★★$$$$ **209**
Lewis Hayden House **22**
Lewis Wharf **52**
Lexington **206**
Lexington Battle Green **206**
Liberty Cafe **192**
Liberty Square **76**
Library Grill ★★★$$$ **27**
Limousines **6**
Little, Brown and Company **16**
Lobster Logistics **181**
Locke-Ober ★★★$$$ **91**
Lo Conti's ★$ **58**
Lodge's Pushcart **19**
Loeb Drama Center **188**
Logan Airport Hilton and Towers **5**
Logan International Airport (BOS) **5**
London Harness Company **89**
Long Wharf **62**
Longy School of Music **188**
Looney Tunes **148**
L'Osteria Ristorante ★★$$ **58**
Louis, Boston **136**
Louisburg Square **21**
Lowell **205**
Lowell, Guy **143**
The Lowell Heritage State Park **206**
Luce, Clarence **26**
Lucky's ★★★$$$$ **210**
Lyman Paine House **19**
The Lyric Stage **117**

M

Macy's **91**
Magnolia's **193**
Main Events **11**
Maison Robert ★★★$$$$ **84**
Mamma Maria ★★★$$$$ **50**
Manchester-by-the-Sea **204**
Manray **193**
Map key **5**
Marblehead **204**
Marco Polo Cafe ★$ **68**
Marcoz **132**
Maria's Pastry Shop **59**
Marika's **24**
Marine Park **197**
Mariners' House **51**
Marketplace Cafe ★$$ **35**
Marketplace Center **37**

The Marketplace Grill and Oar Bar ★★★$$ **35**
Marlborough Street **121**
Marriott's Custom House $$$ **75**
Marshall House ★★$$ **39**
Martha's Vineyard **208, 209**
Martha's Vineyard Airport **209**
Martini Carl **135**
Mary Chung **192**
The Mary Prentiss Inn **193**
Massachusetts Archives **198**
Massachusetts Avenue Station **156**
Massachusetts General Hospital **43**
The Massachusetts Historical Society **148**
Massachusetts Institute of Technology (MIT) **190**
Massachusetts State Transportation Building **101**
The Mass Bay Company ★$$ **125**
Mather School **198**
Maurizio's ★★★$$ **54**
McKim, Charles Follen **15, 112**
McKim, Mead & White **15, 111, 112, 113, 123, 124, 146, 175**
McKinnell, Michael **31**
McLauthlin Building **52**
MDF/Motto **185**
Meacham, George **28**
Medieval Manor $$$$ **162**
Meeting House Hill **197**
M-80 **151**
Memorial Hall **177**
Merchants Wine & Spirits **82**
101 Merrimac Street **41**
MFA (Museum of Fine Arts) **143**
Michael's Waterfront and Wine Library ★★$$$ **61**
Middle East Cafe **192**
Middleton-Glapion House **21**
The MidTown Hotel $ **157**
Mike's Pastry ★$ **49**
Milano's Italian Kitchen ★$ **137**
The Milk Bottle $ **68**
Milk Street Cafe ★$ **81**
Mills Gallery **161**
Mineralogical and Geological Museum **176**
Minute Man National Historical Park **206**
Miracle of Science Bar & Grill **192**
Mrs. Fields Cookies **82**
MIT Chapel **191**
MIT Coop **191**
MIT (Massachusetts Institute of Technology) **190**
MIT Museum **190**
MIT Press Bookstore **191**
Miyako ★★$$ **130**
Mobius **68**
Modern Pastry **46**
Money **9**
Montien ★★$$ **105**

Monument Square **196**
Moon Villa $ **107**
Morton's of Chicago ★★$$$$ **116**
Moscaritolo, Patrick B. **59** (bests)
Motto/MDF **185**
Mount Auburn Cemetery **189**
32 Mount Vernon Street **20**
Mugar Memorial Library of Boston University **151**
Mugar Omni Theater **171**
Museum of Afro American History **22**
Museum of Comparative Zoology **177**
Museum of Fine Arts (MFA) **143**
Museum of Science **170**
Museum of Transportation **200**
Museums of Culture and Natural History **176**
Myrtle Street **22**

N

Nameless Coffeehouse **186**
Nantucket **208, 209**
Nantucket Memorial Airport **209**
Nara ★$$ **77**
Near Northwest **206**
New Bedford **209**
New Bedford Whaling Museum **209**
Newbury Comics **127**
Newbury Guest House $$ **131**
Newburyport **205**
Newbury Street **126**
360 Newbury Street **126**
New England Aquarium **63**
New England Aquarium Whale Watching **63**
New England Conservatory of Music (NEC), Jordan Hall **145**
New England Historic Genealogical Society **134**
New England Holocaust Memorial **39**
New Old South Church **116**
Newport, Rhode Island **210**
A New Revolution On the Freedom Trail **23**
New Shanghai ★★★$$ **107**
Nichols House Museum **20**
Nickerson House **124**
Nick's Entertainment Center **101**
Nielsen Gallery **132**
No-Name ★★$$ **67**
Norman Rockwell Museum **207**
North Bennet Street School **57**
North Bridge Visitor Center **206**
North Cambridge/Porter Square **193**
North End **44** (chapter and map)
North End Fabrics **105**
The North Shore **204**
North Shore Music Theatre **204**
North Square **50**
North Station **41**
The Nostalgia Factory **57**
Notter, Finegold & Alexander **104**

Nuggets **150**
No. 44 **57**
NYC Jukebox/Eight Tracks **104**

O

Oak Room ★★★$$$ **112**
Oasis Cafe ★$ **57**
Ober, J.F. **122**
Oceanic Chinese Restaurant ★$ **149**
ökw **134**
Old City Hall **83**
Olde Dutch Cottage Candy **162**
Old North Church (Christ Church) **55**
Old Ship Meetinghouse **208**
Old South Meeting House **86**
Old State House **73**
Old Sturbridge Village **207**
Old West Church **42**
Oliver Ames Mansion **124**
Olives ★★★★$$$$ **196**
Omni Parker House $$$ **85**
One Winthrop Square **90**
On the Park ★★$$ **163**
Opera House **94**
Orientation **4**
Orpheum Theatre **92**
Other Neighborhoods **194** (chapter and map)
The Other Side Cosmic Cafe ★$ **149**
Our Lady of the Good Voyage Chapel **65**
Out of Town Newspapers **174**
Oyster Bar **209**
The Oyster Bar at Durgin-Park ★★$ **35**

P

Palladio **19**
Papa Razzi ★★$$ **133**
Paradise Rock Club **151**
Paramount Steak House ★$ **26**
Parker River National and State Wildlife Refuge **205**
Parker's Restaurant ★★$$$ **86**
Parker, Thomas & Rice **86, 120**
Parking **7**
Parkman Plaza **15**
Park Plaza Castle **100**
Park Street **18**
Park Street Church **18**
Park Street Station **14**
Park, Susan **43** (bests)
Parris, Alexander **16, 33, 43, 92, 195**
Pat's Pushcart ★$$ **59**
Paul Revere House **51**
Paul Revere Mall (The Prado) **54**
Pavo Real **114**
Peabody and Stearns **37, 38, 75, 81, 123**
Peabody Essex Museum **204**
Peabody Museum of Archaeology and Ethnology **176**
Pei, I.M. **30, 64, 125, 191**
Pepperweed **193**

Period Furniture Hardware Company **24**
Personal safety **9**
Peter, Thomas, and Rice **90**
Phoenix Coffeehouse **192**
Phoenix Landing **192**
Photographic Resource Center (PRC) **150**
Pi Alley **83**
Piano Craft Guild **160**
Piccolo Nido ★★★$$ **53**
Pierce-Hichborn House **52**
Pie-Shaped House **21**
Pilgrim Monument **209**
Pinckney Street **21**
9 ½ Pinckney Street **21**
20 Pinckney Street **21**
62 Pinckney Street **21**
Pizzeria Regina ★$$ **57**
Plants and Trees (Public Garden) **28**
Pleasure Bay **197**
Plimoth Plantation **208**
The Plough and Stars **192**
Plum Island **205**
Plymouth **208**
Polcari's Coffee **58**
Pomodoro ★★★$$$ **49**
Porter Exchange **193**
Porter Square **193**
Post Office Square **80**
The Prado (Paul Revere Mall) **54**
PRC (Photographic Resource Center) **150**
Preston, Jonathan **90**
Preston, William G. **28, 78, 81, 100, 122, 136**
Price, William **55**
Prince Restaurant **204**
Proctor Building **90**
Providence, Rhode Island **210**
Province House Steps **87**
Provincetown **209**
Prudential Center **129**
Publications **9**
Public Garden **28**
The Publick Theatre Inc. **165**
Pucker Gallery **132**
Purity Cheese Company **59**
Purple Windowpanes **16**
Putnam and Cox **83**

Q

Quantum Books **191**
Quincy Market/Faneuil Hall Marketplace **33**

R

Rachel Revere Park **52**
Radcliffe Yard **187**
Radio stations **9**
Rathskeller (The Rat) **150**
The Rattlesnake Bar & Grill ★★$ **120**
Rebecca's ★★★$$ **27**

Index

Rebecca's Cafe (Back Bay) ★$ 134
Rebecca's Cafe (Financial
District/Downtown) ★$ 83
Redbones ★★★★$$$ 200
Red Lion Inn 207
Regal Bostonian Hotel $$$ 38
The Regattabar 182
Rental cars 6
Restaurants 9
Restaurants, rating 5
Rialto ★★★$$$$ 182
Riccardi 134
Richardson, Henry Hobson 31, 76,
105, 110, 122, 124, 134, 158, 176,
184
Richardson, W.C. 132
Ristorante Lucia ★$$ 54
Ristorante Marino 193
Ristorante Saraceno ★$$ 47
Ristorante Toscano ★★★$$ 27
The Ritz Bar ★★★$$ 139
The Ritz Cafe ★★$$$ 139
Ritz-Carlton Hotel $$$$ 138
The Ritz Lounge ★★★$$ 139
Riverside 192
Robert Gould Shaw Memorial 15
Rockport 205
Rockport Chamber Music Festival
205
Rocky Neck 205
Rogers Building 190
Rogers, Isaiah 61, 63, 186, 189
Rollins Place 22
Romantic Retreats 136
Ropewalk 195
Rose Art Museum 207
Rosie's 193
Rowes Wharf 64
Rowes Wharf Restaurant
★★★★$$$$ 65
The Roxy 104
Royal Sonesta Hotel
Boston/Cambridge $$$ 170
Rubin's 200
Rudolph, Paul 122
Rutland Square 160

S

Saarinen, Eero 29, 191
Sacred Heart Church 51
Safety, personal 9
Sage's Market 186
St. Botolph Street 157
St. Leonard's Church Peace Garden
50
St. Stephen's Church 53
Saitowitz, Stanley 39
Sakura-bana ★★★$$ 77
Salamander ★★★★$$$$ 192
Salem 204
Salem Maritime National Historic Site
204
Salem Street 57

Salem Witch Museum 204
Salsberg, Irving 77
Salts 192
The Salty Dog Seafood Bar and Grille
★★$$ 35
Salumeria Italiana 47
Salumeria Toscana 47
Samuel Glaser Associates 42
Sanborn, Greenleaf C. 105
Sanders Theatre 178
Sandrine's ★★$$$ 180
S&S Restaurant Deli 193
Santacross Distinctive Shoe Service 92
Sasaki Associates 62
Sasuga Japanese Bookstore 193
Saugus Iron Works National Historic
Site 204
Savoy French Bakery 151
Schoenhof's Foreign Books, Inc. 181
3 School Street 82
Schroeder's ★$$$ 90
Schwartz/Silver Architects 63, 98, 126
Scullers Grille ★$$ 165
Scullers Jazz Club 165
Seaport Hotel and Conference Center
$$$$ 67
Sears Crescent Building 31
Sears, David 16, 31
Seasons ★★★★$$$$ 38
Serenella 134
Sert, Jackson and Associates 176
The Sevens ★★$ 25
Shepley, Bulfinch, Richardson &
Abbott 120
Shepley, Rutan, and Coolidge 31, 70,
76
Sheraton Boston Hotel & Towers $$$
125
Sheraton Commander Hotel $$ 188
Sherman's 87
Shipyard Park 195
Shopping 9
The Shops at Charles Square 183
Short Trips to the Boston Harbor
Islands 66
Shreve, Crump & Low 120
Shubert Theatre 103
Siam Square ★$ 106
Sights for Sore Eyes 106
Silvetti, Machado 163
Singing Beach 204
Skidmore, Owings & Merrill 64, 138
Skipjack's ★$$ 117
Skylight Jewelers 87
Sleeper, Henry Davis 205
Sleeper-McCann House 205
Small Planet Bar and Grill ★$ 116
Smoking 10
Snakebites Cantina 193
Snell and Gregorson 92
Society for the Preservation of New
England Antiquities (SPNEA) 42, 207
The Society of Arts and Crafts (Back

Bay) 132
The Society of Arts and Crafts
(Financial District/Downtown) 91
Sol Azteca ★★$$ 151
Solon S. Beman, Brigham Coveney
and Bisbee 125
Somerset Club 16
Somerville 200
Sonsie ★★$$$ 127
Sorento's ★★$$ 153
South Boston 197
South End 154 (chapter and map)
The South Shore 208
South Station 70
South Street 71
Southwest Corridor Park 155
Southworth, Susan and Michael 210
(bests)
Spasso ★★$$ 123
Spingold Theatre 207
Spinnaker Italia ★$$ 170
SPNEA (Society for the Preservation
of New England Antiquities) 42,
207
The Sports Museum of New England
206
Starbucks (Beacon Hill) ★$ 25
Starbucks (Cambridge) ★$ 183
Starr Book Shop 180
The State House 16
75 State Street 75
State Street Block 75
Statues of Mayor Curley 38
Statues (Public Garden) 29
Stephanie's on Newbury ★★$$$ 132
Sterling and Francine Clark Art
Institute 207
Stern, Robert A.M. 119
Steve's Greek & American Cuisine ★$
129
Stirling, James 178
Stockbridge 207
Stoddard's 92
Strand Theater 198
A Street Deli Express $ 68
Street plan 10
Strickland and Blodget 138
Stubbins, Hugh 188
Sturgis and Brigham 26
Sturgis, John 123
Sturgis, R. Clipston 78
Subways 6, 7
Sultan's Kitchen ★$ 77
Sunflower Castle 26
The Sunset Grill and Tap 200
Swan Boats and Lagoon 28
Sweetwater Cafe $ 103
Swissôtel Boston $$$ 95
Symphony Hall 146

T

Tam O'shanter 200
Tanglewood 207

Tapeo ★★$$$ 130
Tatsukichi ★★$$ 76
The Tavern Club 103
Taxes 10
Taxis 6, 7
Telephone 10
Telephone Exchange Building 195
Telephone numbers, essential 10
Tent City 156
Terramia ★★★★$$$ 58
Thai Cuisine ★$$ 147
Theater District 96 (chapter and map)
Thomas and Rice 122
Thomas Park 197
Thompson, Benjamin 33, 187
Thompson, Jane 33
Thorntons Fenway Grill ★★$ 153
Tickets 10
Tihany, Adam 98
Time zone 10
Tipping 10
Toad Hall Book Store 205
Today's Bread 199
To Go Bakery 163
Top of the Hub ★★★$$$$ 129
The Tortoise and the Hare 110
Tours 8
Tower Records/Video 126
Trains 8, *also see inside back cover* (map)
Transportation 5
Transportation, local 6
Trattoria a Scalinatella ★★★$$$ 46
The Tremont House $$ 103
Tremont Temple 88
Trident Booksellers & Cafe ★$ 127
Trinity Church 110, 213
Trinity Church Rectory 134
Trinity Repertory Company 210
Trio's 46
Truc ★★★$$$ 161
T.T. The Bear's Place 193
Turner Fisheries ★$$$ 114
Tuscan Grill ★★★★$$$$ 207
29 Newbury ★★★$$ 137
21 Federal ★★★★$$$$ 209
Twiss, Jeffrey 171 (bests)

U

The Union Club 18
Union Oyster House ★★$$$ 39
Union Park 162
Union United Methodist Church 160
United Shoe Machinery Corporation Building 90
Upham's Corner 197
Upjohn, R.M. 135
Up Stairs at the Pudding ★★★$$$$ 180
Urban Outfitters 184
US Postal Service-South Postal Annex 70

V

Vadopazzo ★★$$$ 46
Van Brunt, Henry 121, 177
V. Cirace & Son 52
The Vendôme 122
Venice Ristorante ★$ 22
Venturi, Robert 177
Villa-Francesca ★$$ 46
Villa Victoria 160
Vinal, Arthur H. 128
Visitor Center 74
Visitor Information Center 14
Visitors' information 10
Vose Galleries of Boston 131

W

Walden Pond Reservation 206
Walker's 103
Walking 8
Waltham 207
The Wang Center for the Performing Arts 104
Ware, William R. 121, 177
Warren Tavern 196
Waterfront 61
Waterfront/Fort Point Channel 60 (chapter and map)
Waterfront Park 62
Water Play: Activities On and Along the Charles 169
Waterstone's Booksellers (Back Bay) 132
Waterstone's Booksellers (Government Center/Faneuil Hall) 35
Wauwinet 209
Weisner Building, Center for Arts & Media Technology 191
WFIU (Women's Educational and Industrial Union) 120
Welch, Franklin J. 125
Wellfleet Bay Wildlife Sanctuary 208
Westin Hotel, Copley Place $$$ 114
15 West Street 93
West Street Grill ★★$$ 93
Wetmore, James A. 81
Weylu's 204
Wheatstone Baking Company 153
Wheelock Family Theatre 153
Wheelwright and Haven 14, 126, 145, 180
Wheelwright, Edmund March 148, 158
Whippoorwill 37
The Whistler House Museum of Art 206
Whitaker College 191
White Rainbow 205
White, Stanford 111, 210
Wilbur Theatre 104
Willard, Solomon 19, 196
William C. Nell House 22

William Hickling Prescott House 15
William Lloyd Garrison Statue 123
Williams College 207
Williamstown 207
Williamstown Theatre Festival 207
Willow Jazz Club 200
Winslow and Bradlee 75
Winslow and Bigelow 88, 90, 102
Winthrop Building 82
Winthrop Lane 90
Women's Educational and Industrial Union (WEIU) 120
The Women's Heritage Trail 36
Woodman's 205
WordsWorth 184
World's End Reservation 208
World Trade Center/Commonwealth Pier 67
Wren, Christopher 18, 55
Wright, Chester F. 53
WZMH Group 37, 75

Y

Young, Ammi 75

Z

Zuma's Tex-Mex Cafe ★$$ 37

Restaurants

Only restaurants with star ratings are listed below. All restaurants are listed alphabetically in the main (preceding) index. Always call in advance to ensure a restaurant has not closed, changed its hours, or booked its tables for a private party. The restaurant price ratings are based on the average cost of an entrée for one person, excluding tax and tip.

★★★★ An Extraordinary Experience
★★★ Excellent
★★ Very Good
★ Good

$$$$ Big Bucks ($20 and up)
$$$ Expensive ($15-$20)
$$ Reasonable ($10-$15)
$ The Price Is Right (less than $10)

★★★★

Al Forno $$$$ 210
Biba $$$ 97
The Blue Room $$$$ 191
Clio $$$$ 149
Dali $$$$ 200
East Coast Grill $$$$ 193
Elephant Walk $$$$ 200
Hamersley's Bistro $$$ 161
L'Etoile $$$$ 209
Olives $$$$ 196
Redbones $$$ 200
Rowes Wharf Restaurant $$$$ 65

Index

Salamander $$$$ 192
Seasons $$$$ 38
Terramia $$$ 58
Tuscan Grill $$$$ 207
21 Federal $$$$ 209

★★★

Armani Express $$$$ 131
Artú $$ 50
Aujourd'hui $$$$ 98
Boarding House $$$$ 209
Chez Henri $$$$ 193
Five Seasons $$ 199
Green Street Grill $$$ 192
Intrigue $$ 65
Julien $$$$ 80
L'Espalier $$$$ 130
Library Grill $$$ 27
Locke-Ober $$$ 91
Lucky's $$$$ 210
Maison Robert $$$$ 84
Mamma Maria $$$$ 50
The Marketplace Grill and Oar Bar $$
  35
Maurizio's $$ 54
New Shanghai $$ 107
Oak Room $$$ 112
Piccolo Nido $$ 53
Pomodoro $$$ 49
Rebecca's $$ 27
Rialto $$$$ 182
Ristorante Toscano $$ 27
The Ritz Bar $$ 139
The Ritz Lounge $$ 139
Sakura-bana $$ 77
Tapeo $$$ 130
Top of the Hub $$$$ 129
Trattoria a Scalinatella $$$ 46
Truc $$$ 161
29 Newbury $$ 137
Up Stairs at the Pudding $$$$ 180

★★

Addis Red Sea Ethiopian Restaurant $
  161
Algiers Cafe $ 185
Angelo's $$$ 116
Appetito $$ 162
Aura $$$$ 67
Bakey's $ 77
The Barking Crab $$ 65
Bay Tower Room $$$ 32
Bertucci's (Faneuil Hall) $ 38
Black Goose $$ 19
Boodle's of Boston $$$ 125
Brandy Pete's $$ 78
The Bristol $$ 98
The Cafe at the Gardner $$ 142
Cafe Budapest $$$ 115
Cafe Fleuri $$$ 80
Cafe Louis $$ 137
Caffe Romano's Bakery & Sandwich
  Shop $ 137

The Capital Grille $$$$ 126
Carl's Pagoda $$ 106
Casablanca $$ 186
Casa Mexico $$ 183
Charlie's Sandwich Shoppe $ 157
The Chart House $$$ 62
Chau Chow Seafood $ 107
Ciao bella $$ 131
Club Cafe $$ 117
Cottonwood Cafe (Back Bay) $$
  119
Daily Catch (North End) $$ 49
Dakota's $$$ 91
Davio's Ristorante $$$ 170
The Dining Room $$$$ 139
Durgin-Park $$ 35
Figs $$ 26
Fine Arts Restaurant $$ 145
Garden of Eden $ 160
Geoffrey's Café and Bar $ 160
Giacomo's $$ 53
Golden Palace $ 106
Grand Chau Chow Seafood $ 107
Grill 23 & Bar $$$$ 119
Gyuhama $$ 115
Henrietta's Table $$ 182
House of Siam $ 113
The Hungry i $$$$ 25
Icarus $$$ 162
Iruña $$ 181
John Harvard's Brew House $ 184
La Bettola $$$ 157
La Piccola Venezia $ 46
Legal Sea Foods (Chinatown/Theater
  District) $$$ 99
L'Osteria Ristorante $$ 58
Marshall House $$ 39
Michael's Waterfront and Wine
  Library $$$ 61
Miyako $$ 130
Montien $$ 105
Morton's of Chicago $$$$ 116
No-Name $$ 67
On the Park $$ 163
The Oyster Bar at Durgin-Park $ 35
Papa Razzi $$ 133
Parker's Restaurant $$$ 86
The Rattlesnake Bar & Grill $ 120
The Ritz Cafe $$$ 139
The Salty Dog Seafood Bar and Grille
  $$ 35
Sandrine's $$$ 180
The Sevens $ 25
Sol Azteca $$ 151
Sonsie $$$ 127
Sorento's $$ 153
Spasso $$ 98
Stephanie's on Newbury $$$ 132
Tatsukichi $$ 76
Thorntons Fenway Grill $ 153
Union Oyster House $$$ 39
Vadopazzo $$$ 46
West Street Grill $$ 93

★

Anthony's Pier 4 $$$ 67
au bon pain $ 174
Back Bay Brewing Company $$ 115
Bangkok Cuisine $ 147
Bartley's Burger Cottage $ 179
Bertucci's (Cambridge) $ 185
The Black Rose $ 37
The Blue Diner/Art Zone $ 71
Bombay Club $$ 182
Boston Beer Works $$ 152
Bull & Finch $ 28
Buteco Restaurant $ 153
Buteco II $ 160
The Cactus Club $ 129
Cafe Charles $ 150
Café de Paris $ 138
Cafe Jaffa $ 130
Cafe Marliave $$ 87
Cafe Pamplona $ 179
Caffè Bella Vita $ 27
Caffè dello Sport $ 49
Caffé Graffiti $ 47
Caffé Paradiso Espresso Bar $ 46
Caffe Suisse $$ 95
Caffé Vittoria $ 47
Casa Romero $$$ 130
The Claddagh $ 156
Club Passim $ 186
Commonwealth Brewing Company $
  41
Copley's Grand Cafe $$$ 112
Cornwall's $ 150
Counterpoint Cafe $ 147
Country Life $ 77
Daily Catch (Fort Point Channel) $$ 68
Davide $$$ 54
Division Sixteen $ 128
Dong Khanh $ 106
Dynasty $$ 107
The Essex Grill $$ 71
Fajitas & 'Ritas $ 93
The Famous Atlantic Fish Company $$
  115
Florentine Cafe $$$ 49
Fratelli Pagliuca's $$ 58
Galleria Cafe $ 145
Green Dragon Tavern $ 40
Grendel's Den $ 183
Hard Rock Cafe $ 117
Harvey's $$$ 157
Hilltop Steak House $$$ 204
Hi-Rise Pie Co. $$ 187
House of Blues $ 183
Ho Yuen Ting $ 188
Imperial Seafood Restaurant $ 107
Jacob Wirth $$ 105
Jae's Cafe and Grill $ 160
J.C. Hillary's $$ 115
Jimbo's Fish Shanty $ 68
Jimmy's Harborside Restaurant $$$ 68
The King & I $$ 24

The Last Hurrah! Bar and Grill $$ 86
Les Zygomates $$ 71
Lo Conti's $ 58
Marco Polo Cafe $ 68
Marketplace Cafe $$ 35
The Mass Bay Company $$ 125
Mike's Pastry $ 49
Milano's Italian Kitchen $ 137
Milk Street Cafe $ 81
Nara $$ 77
Oasis Cafe $ 57
Oceanic Chinese Restaurant $ 149
The Other Side Cosmic Cafe $ 149
Paramount Steak House $ 26
Pat's Pushcart $$ 59
Pizzeria Regina $$ 57
Rebecca's Cafe (Back Bay) $ 134
Rebecca's Cafe (Financial
  District/Downtown) $ 83
Ristorante Lucia $$ 54
Ristorante Saraceno $$ 47
Schroeder's $$$ 90
Scullers Grille $$ 165
Siam Square $ 106
Skipjack's $$ 117
Small Planet Bar and Grill $ 116
Spinnaker Italia $$ 170
Starbucks (Beacon Hill) $ 25
Starbucks (Cambridge) $ 183
Steve's Greek & American Cuisine $
  129
Sultan's Kitchen $ 77
Thai Cuisine $$ 147
Trident Booksellers & Cafe $ 127
Turner Fisheries $$$ 114
Venice Ristorante $ 22
Villa-Francesca $$ 46
Zuma's Tex-Mex Cafe $$ 37

Hotels

The hotels listed below are grouped according to their price ratings; they are also listed in the main index. The hotel price ratings reflect the base price of a standard room for two people for one night during the peak season.

$$$$ Big Bucks ($250 and up)
$$$ Expensive ($175-$250)
$$ Reasonable ($100-$175)
$ The Price Is Right
  (less than $100)

$$$$

Boston Harbor Hotel 64
Boston Marriott Long Wharf 62
The Fairmont Copley Plaza Hotel 111
Four Seasons Hotel 98
Hyatt Regency Cambridge 165
Ritz-Carlton Hotel 138
Seaport Hotel and Conference Center
  67

$$$

Back Bay Hilton 125
Boston Marriott Copley Place 114
Boston Park Plaza Hotel 99
The Charles Hotel 182
The Colonnade Hotel 156
Doubletree Guest Suites Hotel
  Boston/Cambridge 165
The Inn at Harvard 179
Le Meridien 78
Marriott's Custom House 75
Omni Parker House 85
Regal Bostonian Hotel 38
Royal Sonesta Hotel
  Boston/Cambridge 170
Sheraton Boston Hotel & Towers 125
Swissôtel Boston 95
Westin Hotel, Copley Place 114

$$

Copley Inn 156
Copley Square Hotel 114
The Eliot Hotel 149
57 Park Plaza/Radisson Hotel Boston
  101
Harborside Inn of Boston 76
Harvard Square Hotel 183
Holiday Inn–Government Center 42
Howard Johnson Cambridge 165
Howard Johnson Kenmore 150
The Inn at Children's Boston 153
The Lenox Hotel 115
Newbury Guest House 131
Sheraton Commander Hotel 188
The Tremont House 103

$

Berkeley Residence Club 162
Boston International American Youth
  Hostel (AYH) 147
Chandler Inn Hotel 162
The Eliot & Pickett Houses 19
Greater Boston YMCA 145
The John Jeffries House 24
The MidTown Hotel 157

Features

Art Alfresco 48
Boston By Bike: Plum Paths for Pedal
  Pushers 94
Boston in Fact…and Fiction 79
Boston on Screen 118
Boston's Tea Parties 40
Child's Play 100
The Emerald Necklace 158
Going for the Laurels: The Boston
  Marathon 201
The House That Mrs. Jack Built 148
Lobster Logistics 181
Main Events 11
A New Revolution On the Freedom
  Trail 23
Romantic Retreats 136
Short Trips to the Boston Har.
  Islands 66
Sights for Sore Eyes 106
Water Play: Activities On and Along
  the Charles 169
The Women's Heritage Trail 36

Bests

Carrier, Patrick (President, The Globe
  Corner Bookstores) 139
Dion, Arthur (Director/Art Dealer,
  Gallery Naga) 95
Godine, David R. (Publisher) 59
Golledge, The Reverend Robert W.
  (Retired Vicar, Old North Church) 59
Gordon, Ed (Executive Director,
  Gibson House Museum/President,
  Victorian Society in America, New
  England Chapter) 43
Moscaritolo, Patrick B. (President &
  CEO, Greater Boston Convention &
  Visitors Bureau, Inc.) 59
Park, Susan (President, Boston
  Harborfest) 43
Southworth, Susan and Michael
  (Urban Designers, Planners, and
  Authors of the AIA Guide to Boston)
  210
Twiss, Jeffrey (Director of Public
  Relations, Boston Celtics) 171

Maps

Back Bay 108
Beacon Hill 12
Boston 2
Boston and Environs See inside
  front cover
Boston Harbor 66
Boston Marathon Route 201
Boston Subway Lines, Commuter
  Rail, and Commuter Ferry See
  inside back cover
Cambridge 173, 189
Charles River Basin 166
Chinatown 96
Day Trips 202
Downtown 72
The Emerald Necklace 159
Faneuil Hall 30
Fenway 140
Financial District 72
Fort Point Channel 60
Franklin Park Zoo 199
The Freedom Trail 14
Harvard Square 173
Government Center 30
Kenmore Square 140
Map key 5
North End 44
Other Neighborhoods 194
South End 154
Theater District 96
Waterfront 60

...rcher

Writer and Researcher (Previous Edition)
H. Constance Hill

ACCESS®PRESS

Editorial Director
Lois Spritzer

Managing Editor
Laura L. Brengelman

Senior Editors
Mary Callahan
Beth Schlau

Associate Editor
Beatrice Aranow

Map Coordinator
Jonathan Goodnough

Editorial Assistant
Susan Cutter Snyder

Senior Art Director
Robin Arzt

Design Supervisor
Joy O'Meara

Designer
Alex Lindquist

Map Designers
Patricia Keelin
Mark Stein Studios

*Associate Director of
 Production*
Dianne Pinkowitz

*Director, Electronic
 Publishing*
John R. Day

Special Thanks
**Larry Meehan, Greater
  Boston Convention and
  Visitors Bureau
Aimee O'Brien, Greater
  Boston Convention and
  Visitors Bureau
Maura Smith, Cambridge
  Office for Tourism**

View of Boston across the Charles River

MARJORIE VOGEL, RHODE ISLAND ORIGINALS